Through the Maelstrom

MODERN WAR STUDIES

Theodore A. Wilson
General Editor

Raymond Callahan
J. Garry Clifford
Jacob W. Kipp
Jay Luvaas
Allan R. Millett
Carol Reardon
Dennis Showalter
David R. Stone
Series Editors

Through the Maelstrom

A Red Army Soldier's War on the Eastern Front, 1942–1945

Boris Gorbachevsky

Translated and Edited by Stuart Britton
Foreword by David M. Glantz

University Press of Kansas

© 2008 by the University Press of Kansas
All rights reserved

Published by the University Press of Kansas (Lawrence, Kansas 66045),
which was organized by the Kansas Board of Regents and is operated and
funded by Emporia State University, Fort Hays State University, Kansas State
University, Pittsburg State University, the University of Kansas, and Wichita
State University

ISBN-13: 978-0-7006-1605-3

British Library Cataloguing-in-Publication Data is available.

Printed in the United States of America

I dedicate this book to my fallen comrades, who now lie beneath the soil in the environs of Rzhev, where as a soldier I began my combat journey. I also dedicate this book to my dear, kind mother, who kept and treasured all my letters from the front until the end of her life.

Contents

A photograph section follows page 201.

Foreword

This extraordinary memoir describes the wartime experiences of Boris Gorbachevsky, a rank-and-file Soviet soldier who served for almost three harrowing years as a frontline infantryman in four Red Army rifle divisions during the Soviet-German War (1941–1945). Unlike millions of his less fortunate comrades, Gorbachevsky survived and is now able to share his experiences with others who are interested in military history, in general, and, in particular, the Soviet Union's self-proclaimed Great Patriotic (Fatherland) War, the most terrible of the twentieth century's many wars.

Virtually all memoirs published to date about the experiences of former Red Army soldiers who served the Soviet Union during World War II focus routinely on the service of veterans who participated in the army's most famous and dramatic battles, especially its well-known and magnificently proclaimed victories at Moscow, Stalingrad, Kursk, and Berlin. This memoir, however, stands in sharp and healthy contrast to these accounts. Instead of memorializing the greatest of the Red Army's many famous victories, it represents a veritable final testament to the countless millions of Soviet soldiers who fought and often perished in cruel anonymity, their exploits and achievements falling victim to the pens of wartime and postwar censors who strove to protect the combat reputation of the Red Army and many of its most senior commanders. These "forgotten" soldiers, who fought in countless partially successful or outright failed operations during the war that became "forgotten" because Soviet historians ignored or concealed them, were the real victors in the war.

Gorbachevsky did not serve in a vaunted "Siberian" division at Moscow, the renowned 62nd or 64th Armies at Stalingrad, the armies and divisions that emerged victorious at Kursk, or the armies that conducted the triumphal march on Berlin. Instead, he spent most of his wartime service fighting in the 31st Army, one of the Red Army's more ignored armies, subordinate to the less famous Kalinin, Western, and 3rd Belorussian Fronts, and fought in many "forgotten" or half-forgotten battles and operations that, nevertheless, mercilessly sapped the Wehrmacht's strength and will to fight.

Gorbachevsky's record of wartime service is as revealing and extensive as the battles he fought in have been obscured. Between May 1942 and January 1943, he participated in the vicious struggle for the city of Rzhev, first as a rifleman in the 30th Army's 215th Rifle Division, then as a junior lieutenant and company commander in the 31st Army's 220nd Rifle Division. Reluctantly assuming the position of his regiment's Komsomol organizer and assistant to the regiment's deputy commander for political affairs in January 1943, Gorbachevsky took part in the pursuit of the retreating German forces after the liberation of Rzhev, in the Red Army's major offensive in the Smolensk region from August through September 1943, and in the frustrating battles on the approaches to Orsha from October 1943 through February 1944. Notably, during this period he participated in virtually every stage of the Red Army's prolonged, fitfully successful but almost totally forgotten offensive. From July 1944 until the end of the war, during the fighting in Poland and East Prussia, Gorbachevsky served as an assistant to the division's chief of the political department with the 31st Army's 352nd and 331st Rifle Divisions, giving him an inside view of the problems and privileges of divisional command in the Red Army.

Eschewing the mixture of fantasy and sensationalism so rampant in many other soldierly memoirs, as indicated by careful examination of recently released Russian wartime archival materials, Gorbachevsky describes with accuracy and a tailor's keen eye for preserving detail both the tactical fighting in which he took part and the personalities and command styles of his superior commanders in the divisions and army in which he served. And he does this with refreshing candor regarding the real conditions that Red Army soldiers endured.

In short, this memoir is far more accurate, comprehensive, and even more linguistically appealing than Guy Sajer's best-seller memoir, *The Forgotten Soldier*, hitherto the finest of the many memoirs written by soldiers who fought on Germany's Eastern Front. In itself, the book's imposing length and rich details merely reflect the duration and immense complexity of the war. While its contents are marked by attention to detail, accuracy, and remarkable candor, thanks to the yeoman work and skillful efforts of the book's translator and editor, Stuart Britton, this memoir is also a superb literary work recalling the grand style and eloquence of traditional grand Russian literary works—in the spirit of the legendary Leo Tolstoy. The memoir's narrative and, in particular, the many conversations it contains ring true and contain uniquely candid exposés of the host of problems and challenges the Red Army and its soldiers confronted during wartime, such as the undo influence of political officers (commissars), the "bloody-mindedness" of many senior Red Army commanders, the ever-present problem of desertions from the ranks, and the often brutal nature of Soviet military discipline, including Joseph Stalin's infamous Order

227—the "not a step back" order—and ubiquitous employment of penal companies and battalions.

Together with Isaak Kobylyanskiy's appealing and noteworthy memoir, *From
Stalingrad to Pillau*, which the University Press of Kansas published in early
2008, this memoir propels the press's formidable Modern War Studies series to
new commanding heights.

David M. Glantz

Carlisle, PA

15 February 2008

Editor's Note

It was an exceptional privilege to translate Boris Gorbachevsky's memoirs about his service in the Red Army on the Eastern Front of World War II. Gorbachevsky offers a rare perspective of someone who began his combat service in the summer of 1942, at a time when Stalin, the Stavka (Soviet high command), and Soviet military commanders were still learning how best to contend with their enemy; still struggling to coordinate their forces; still launching unwise, costly attacks; and, in the south, still reeling from the German army's main summer drive toward Stalingrad and the Caucasus. Previous memoirs of the Red Army in World War II that have been translated into English have come primarily from those who began service in 1943 or even 1944, by which time the fortunes of war were turning irrevocably in the Red Army's favor. Consequently, they largely describe the lengthy pursuit of a defeated, albeit still dangerous, foe.

Gorbachevsky began his service just outside Rzhev in the summer of 1942, in an area that had witnessed prolonged, heavy fighting as the Red Army's Kalinin Front and Central Front struggled to encircle the German Army Group Center and to capture the city of Rzhev. Gorbachevsky's baptism of fire occurred with the 30th Army in August 1942, in yet another major Soviet assault to capture Rzhev. Costly assaults had been launched in the previous winter and spring, as Stalin drove his commanders to try to surround Army Group Center and liberate the city of Rzhev. Now, in the summer of 1942, he pushed his commanders to make one more effort to capture Rzhev, a city that lay tantalizingly close to his forces—whether out of personal ambition or as part of a careful strategy to pin the defending German forces in place, leaving them unable to transfer and reinforce the German summer offensive in the south.

Gorbachevsky's baptism of fire came in the form of his personal participation as a rifleman in one of the Red Army's notorious human-wave assaults. German veterans have given us many accounts of what it was like to face such an attack, but we have virtually nothing in the English language from a Russian veteran describing what it was like to be *part* of such an assault. Gorbachevsky's account is gripping and moving, putting a human face and giving human voice to the heretofore faceless human-wave attackers.

Wounded but fortunate to have survived this ordeal, Gorbachevsky gives us an inside look into many aspects of the Red Army's activities, practices, and daily operations, ranging from his experience as a cadet training in one of the Soviet Union's numerous combat specialist schools, to the treatment he received from the Red Army's combat medical services, to the role and function of the commissar in the Red Army, to a unique description of a female sniper team that operated in his division. He takes us on a prisoner "snatch" mission on a cold winter's night and describes the destruction of a rifle battalion in a sudden German counterattack. But he goes further than that, to give us an account of the starving citizens in the blockaded city of Leningrad and of the mood back home in Moscow as the war dragged on. As a platoon leader and company commander, Gorbachevsky had to grapple personally with the problem of desertion from the ranks of the Red Army, and he devotes a special chapter to it. With a professional writer's skilled eye, Gorbachevsky captures both the dramatic moments in battles and campaigns and the mundane daily grind of life in the trenches, and he offers a fascinating and informative account of his service, which eventually led him to the hills of the Czech Sudeten in 1945.

Gorbachevsky's military service took him through what the noted historian David Glantz has termed the "forgotten battles" of the Eastern Front—operations and battles ignored in Soviet war communiqués, then later neglected by historians, both Russian and Western, in favor of the more decisive, dramatic, and mobile operations between the Dnepr and Volga Rivers farther south. Thus, Gorbachevsky's memoir casts important light on these lesser-known campaigns and battles, which nevertheless involved heavy fighting and generated enormous casualties; they deserve closer attention.

Gorbachevsky makes extensive use of recreated dialogue to lend a sense of immediacy to his narrative, placing the reader in the middle of conversations around a campfire, at a division headquarters, and in the midst of battle. It is important for the reader to remember that the dialogue in the book is not a literal transcript. Rather, Gorbachevsky has reproduced the dialogue based upon his memory of the personalities of the speakers, fragments of remembered speech, and the situational details. While human memory is imperfect, as the book reveals, Gorbachevsky has been planning this book and writing chapters of it, if only in his own mind, ever since 1942. The language rings true though it is not an exact reproduction.

Throughout the book I have placed brief, bracketed explanations of Russian terms and the author's references to people and Russian history that may be unfamiliar to the average reader. Here and there, I have also created endnotes—prefaced by "Editor's Note:"—to distinguish them from the author's own endnotes. For the most part, these endnotes identify the particular German units that Gorbachevsky faced during his three long years of war, so the interested reader can obtain further information about the situation described by Gorbachevsky from German accounts.

I want to thank Artem Drabkin of Moscow, who is the director of the *Ia pomnyu* [I remember . . .] Russian website that contains a large and growing volume of information and memoir material related to the Red Army and its veterans. It was he who put me in touch with Mr. Gorbachevsky and gave me permission to translate his memoir into English. Boris Gorbachevsky's memoir was published first in Russia under the title *Rzhevskaia miasorubka: Vremia otvagi. Zadacha—Vyzhit'* (The Rzhev Meat Grinder: A Time of Courage. The Task—Survive) by Moscow's Iauza and Eksmo publishing houses in 2006. While this English version draws heavily on the published Russian version, it is not a direct translation. The author has restored some material to his memoir that was edited out of the Russian version because the Russian reader is already so familiar with it; he and I felt that certain details might be educational to the Western reader, who might be less informed about the Red Army. In addition, Gorbachevsky has written two new chapters for this book, which take his service through to the end of the war and the initial postwar occupation period.

A note on the translation: this memoir was a challenge to translate! The author recreated extensive dialogue among the Red Army soldiers and between the soldiers and their commanders. Naturally, the speech contained a lot of slang terms from the 1940s, as well as vintage colloquialisms, some of which have fallen out of current use in Russian. A few expressions defied ready translation into English. Gorbachevsky also sprinkled the memoir with song lyrics, poetry, and smatterings of Ukrainian and Polish. I could not have managed to translate some of this material without the assistance of Isaak Kobylyanskiy, who is himself a Red Army veteran living in Rochester, New York, and the author of his own wartime memoir, *From Stalingrad to Pillau: A Red Army Artillery Officer Remembers the Great Patriotic War* (Lawrence: University Press of Kansas, 2008). Mr. Kobylyanskiy is not only fluent in Ukrainian and knowledgeable of Polish but also as a veteran recalled many of the soldiers' slang terms and popular expressions. I must also recognize the assistance of Svetlana Nizhevskaia of Krasnodar, Russia, who assisted me in the project that produced Nikolai Litvin's memoir, *800 Days on the Eastern Front: A Russian Soldier Remembers World War II* (Lawrence: University Press of Kansas, 2007). Ms. Nizhevskaia stood by to offer her assistance whenever Mr. Kobylyanskiy was not available. I extend my deepest gratitude to them both. Of course, any errors in the translation are my own responsibility.

Preface

Why did I take up the writing of my memoirs of what we called the Great Patriotic War after sixty years have passed? The French writer and aviator Antoine de Saint-Exupéry once wrote, "For those who have fought in war, war never ends." How true! But this isn't the primary reason that prompted me now, in my later years, to undertake such an important social and literary task.

So what has been the most important thing? It is my desire to preserve for history a portion of living memory about times past and to talk about my comrades-in-arms who gave their lives for their motherland. That, if you will, is the primary motivation that convinced me to pick up my pen after all these years.

In recent years, I have been reflecting ever more frequently over three facts. They constantly trouble my soul, and I strive to understand them.

The first fact: no matter how sad it is to do, we must recognize that comprehension of the most important event of the twentieth century—the Great Victory over fascism—is probably disappearing from the popular consciousness. This victory, I will remind you, saved entire nations from slavery and physical destruction. My book is an opportunity to direct society's attention to its present carelessness, quite similar to the human thoughtlessness of the 1930s when the possibility to stop the madman Adolf Hitler and his generals was let slip.

The second fact: my generation suffered a tragic fate, mown down like grass by the war. Out of every 100 young Soviet soldiers who went off to fight in that war, only 3 returned. I repeatedly ask myself, "Why did the cost of victory turn out to be so unimaginably high?" Yet I cannot find a simple answer to this question. When you think about this war, you understand that it was a complete catastrophe with lasting repercussions. This insight didn't come immediately. But now we understand that if more people had survived, they could have greatly enriched the state. Perhaps new leaders would have appeared, which would have led our country down a new, different path.

The third fact: over the course of two years of war, an entirely new Red Army was raised to replace the regular Red Army that fell in battle in 1941.

This new army, under the command of new military leaders who in those first two years of war had passed through more than one "academy" of warfare over the bones of their fallen soldiers, turned into a mighty force that defeated the strongest and most dangerous enemy in the entire history of humankind.

My book is an opportunity to examine these extraordinary events.

We, the surviving veterans of that war, are often called the "disappearing generation." Alas, no one escapes the passage of time. Let another five or ten years pass, and only a very few of us will remain. True, the press sometimes informs us about rare exceptions. For example, in France, two veterans of World War I are still alive at the time of this writing, and in England, there is yet another such lucky fellow.

Having finished my work, I reread Remarque's classic book, *All Quiet on the Western Front*, which has been called "the book of a lost generation." We, the frontline soldiers of World War II, in contrast to Remarque's heroes, didn't return from the war as "a lost generation" but as proud victors! And we have preserved in our hearts our individual pride for our entire lives, against the wishes of the totalitarian power that ruled at that time.

I do not take the widespread view that all frontline soldiers returned from the war as complete fatalists, or with a faith in God, or as alcoholics, or as psychopaths. Of course, there were such people. Postwar life for many of us turned out to be hard, particularly for the invalids, of whom there were more than two and a half million after the war. Our country was not ready to create normal conditions of life for all of them. I have no intention of hushing up or simplifying our difficult past. But nevertheless, the majority of the war's participants returned to start their studies, to finish school, or to complete professional training or graduate study, and they managed to find a place for themselves in society.

My book describes real events and real people. True, I cannot claim strict, documentary truthfulness: my memory has not preserved everything. I have had to reconstruct some incidents and pieces of dialogue to the best of my ability. I have changed some names, though the individuals were real. I have strived to be objective in my judgments, but possibly here and there I have not been able to avoid subjective appraisals, especially with respect to the characters of some people.

I have laid down events in chronological order. It seemed to me that this would allow the reader to imagine and understand a man in the difficult circumstances of war, when he often had to confront death face to face.

Acknowledgments

This book first appeared in Russia thanks to the assistance and support of the Russian Internet site "Ia pomniu . . ." [I remember] and its director, Artem Drabkin. My deepest thanks to him for this!

Thanks also to my comrades and assistants in the preparation of this manuscript: to Maia Lakovskaia for her proofreading; to the graphics designer, Eugene Goldin; and to Tatiana Sirota, who carried out the computer typesetting and composition.

I am happy that the University Press of Kansas has taken note of my memoirs, first published in Moscow in 2007, and decided to familiarize the American reader with my work. I am grateful to the reviewers—the preeminent American military historian of the Red Army, Colonel (ret.) David Glantz; and professor Ken Slepyan—for their careful reading of the manuscript, helpful comments, and their positive reviews. I was also fortunate to have Stuart Britton, a thoroughly professional, intelligent man and an expert on military matters, as the translator for my manuscript.

The U.S. publication is fundamentally different from the earlier Russian publication. First, I submitted a manuscript with the title *The Harvested Generation* to the U.S. Library of Congress back in 1995 and obtained the copyright for its publication; the title has since changed to *Through the Maelstrom*. Second, the text of the book has, where necessary, been adjusted and clarified. Third, the English-language publication of my memoirs has been substantially expanded by restoring material cut by the Russian editors and by adding chapters on the end of the war in Czechoslovakia and on our first ninety days of occupation in postwar, conquered Germany. This new material is based on historical fact and my own still-vivid memories.

I have been given the opportunity to express my great gratitude to the American people for their enormous moral and material support to the Red Army in World War II, and I state this with a sincere heart. Without this support, it is difficult to imagine how events might have been different on the Eastern Front.

Through the Maelstrom

Part One

My Initial Military Education

January–May 1942

1

Students and Commanders
January–March 1942

How I Became a Soldier

At the end of 1941 my family was living in the city of Kyshtym in Cheliabinsk Oblast. I was working as a lathe operator's apprentice at the Red Metalworks factory. That November the Kyshtym City Party Committee summoned me from the factory and sent me to an outlying village in the oblast to work as its agent for a month. To my objection that I was a city fellow who wouldn't be able to distinguish wheat from rye, the city Party secretary burst out laughing and said, "I hope you will now learn!"

So, suddenly and for the first time in my life, I found myself in a rural village. The village was called Babkino. There were no radios, no telephones, no newspapers, not even any electricity in the village. They used kerosene lamps and candles instead. There was one hand water-pump for two streets, and women with buckets dangling from yokes came to it from far around. It is true that water supply and canalization had long been in the planning stage, but they were not implemented until 1960.

When I arrived, wheat that had not been reaped was lying beneath the snow. The village had two broken-down tractors; in order to start the tractors' engines the tractor driver had to spend half a day cranking them by hand, but, no matter how hard he tried, he didn't always succeed in starting them. There were virtually no men of military age in the village; they had all been called up for the army. Sensing the covetous glances of the women, I would get flustered and feel uncomfortable. The weather turned cold, and the livestock lived in the huts together with the home owners. The closest medical office, with only a *fel'dsher* [a medical assistant] on staff, was in the district center of Shumikho, 12 kilometers away. In the village shop, it seemed there were more mice than products to buy. The residents of Babkino had one pride and joy—every hut had a steam bathhouse. I can vouch for this: it was a real miracle.

By the time of my arrival, wives and mothers had already buried loved ones, and the tears of widows and mothers had already spilled onto the earth. For every funeral, the village chairman would write out an order for 10 kilograms of meat from the village storehouses for the funeral repast, and the villagers would buy vodka on credit—in the village shop, vodka was always present, and the mice, thank God, took no interest in this potion. The villagers would drown their sorrow and grief in vodka for several days. Of course, no one would go to work during these days. This annoyed me, but considering the circumstances, I remained quiet and continued to count the days until I would be able to escape this village. I felt quite awkward at these funeral meals: I was alone, young—and not at the front. I couldn't exactly explain to the residents that I had an exemption because our factory produced items for the military.

I soon had another reason to feel awkward. While in Babkino, I was staying in the hut of an elderly man who spent much of his time in a town several kilometers away. He was married to a much younger woman, named Serafima, who was perhaps in her late forties. She fed me well; for breakfast, I would normally get hot porridge, tea, milk, and honey. One day when the man of the house was away, I was enjoying a steam bath in their *bania* when his wife startled me with her sudden presence. She was wearing some sort of robe. She offered to wash my back, and then she disrobed. It was the first time I'd seen a nude woman. I was enormously embarrassed, but I could not tear my gaze away from her large breasts. I followed my instincts—blushing beet-red, I covered my private parts with both hands and bolted naked from the bath out into the frigid weather and snow. I covered the 20 meters to the hut in a flash, and then headed to the stove to warm myself. A couple of minutes later, Serafima entered the hut and hurled my clothes onto the floor. We didn't speak for the rest of the day, and I avoided her occasional glance. The cost of my spurning became clear the next morning: at the breakfast table, I found only a small, hard lump of bread and a glass of water at my place. I quickly contacted a representative of the district administration and obtained different accommodations.

Nevertheless, this month in the village, my contact with the people of Babkino, changed my fate. Having returned to Kyshtym, I immediately dropped by the *voenkomat* [military registration and enlistment center]. I wanted to enroll in the Cheliabinsk Armor Specialist School, but the medics recognized that I was color-blind, so they sent me instead to the Tiumen Combat Infantry School. Everything happened quite quickly, and by the end of December 1941, I was on my way to Tiumen.

New Year's Eve

I arrived at the infantry school on New Year's Eve and was immediately assigned to a mortar battalion and sent to a barracks, where my company should soon be gathering.

When I reached the barracks, I found it empty, cold, and poorly lit by a single bare light bulb dangling from the ceiling. Naked metal bunks, bedside stands with open doors—and nothing else. Only the loud ticking of clocks, hanging above the entrance doors, which were wide and strong like gates, filled the empty silence of the space. An ambiguous sensation, as if I had just fallen into a cage, welled up inside me. I wanted to start crying but I controlled myself.

I counted off the bunks. On the right and left were 64 bunks each, arranged in two tiers. That meant there would be 128 students living here: my contemporaries, eighteen- and nineteen-year-old guys. They would be coming from all corners of the country to learn the art of combat. For six months, our commanders would train us; then they would send us off to the front as officers—junior lieutenants.

At the quartermaster's station I was handed a decrepit quilted blanket and a worn-out mattress full of holes. This gave me the somewhat meager comfort of my first barracks bed and was supposed to ward off the cold. I climbed up into one of the upper bunks and wrapped myself a little more tightly in a greatcoat, which I had acquired only a couple of hours before.

Sleep didn't come. So many thoughts were swirling in my mind! How would my first day of army life begin? How would my comrades in the barracks regard me? What would my officers be like, and how would they begin to instruct us? Would I manage to cope with army life? In my musings, I didn't stop to notice that I had already gobbled down my mother's last meat patty, which I loved so much, and I had started in on the shortbread. Mama had provided me with food for the road, warm socks, a sweater, a whole packet of paper and envelopes, a pen, and some pencils; soon all of this would disappear in turn without a trace. Would I make any friends? How would everything go?

The door gave a squeak. On the threshold an unfamiliar tall fellow was standing in a greatcoat like mine, but his hair was still shaggy; on his back was a strange bundle with a strap across his chest. He walked up and adroitly climbed onto the neighboring upper bunk, having first tossed upon it a bedraggled mattress just like mine, an even more ancient quilt, and a pillow without a pillowcase. He removed his strange over-the-shoulder burden and left it on the lower bunk.

"We're going to be acquaintances. Allow me to introduce myself: Aleksandr Ryzhikov, from the city of Gorky. I grew up in a workers' settlement, which was exquisitely described by our great proletarian writer [a reference to the city's namesake, the writer Maxim Gorky]."

I also smiled and introduced myself. There we are, now I was no longer alone!

"Are you lamenting, guy, that your life of freedom has come to an end? Don't rush to grieve. Just be a bit sad, friend, everything lies ahead; they've brought us together for war!"

Then he suddenly remembered, "Jesus, within an hour, it's the New Year! Shall we sing? . . . *A little New Year's tree sprouted in a forest, in a forest it grew* . . ."

I reluctantly took up the song, and we sang it together; then Sasha [the nickname for Aleksandr] said, "Well, then, today you are playing the role of Father Frost, and I'm Snegurochka [the Snowmaiden in a famous Russian fairy tale]. Sound right? Just don't let slip such a memorable event—the first holiday in the barracks!"

He climbed down and set up an improvised table, covering the metallic springs of the lower bunk with his mattress. Then Sasha left, and I began laying out some holiday refreshments. I put down some homemade shortbread, two Astrakhan dried *vobly* [a type of freshwater fish, the Caspian roach], some fruit drops from Gorky, and some Japanese smoked sprats [herring]. Sasha returned with two mugs of water, spotted the spread I had arranged, and exclaimed, "What a table you've set!" He gave the box of sprats a turn in his hands, and then asked, "Where did these come from?"

"A strange story," I replied. "I was sitting in the station at Kyshtym, waiting for a train. Several freight cars had gotten stuck there, filled with these cardboard boxes of Japanese sprats, which were being shipped from Japan to Moscow. But the capital city had no need of sprats at the time, so an order had arrived: within two days, empty and clean the freight cars, and transfer them to the Ural line. So they instantly put all the sprats up for sale on the spot, so that Kyshtym residents were able to stock up with probably enough Japanese smoked sprats to last their whole lives."

"You were lucky!"

We raised our mugs and wished each other all the best for the New Year.

"And now I'll indulge you, friend," Sasha pronounced.

He carefully picked up his strange bag. It turned out to be a case, and inside it was a guitar! Delighted by my astonishment, Sashka [another diminutive form of Aleksandr] announced: "In honor of the New Year! The first arrivals in the barracks! Our acquaintanceship! Give a listen, sir, to songs of our past, our now premilitary lives. Folklore!"

He tuned the guitar, started singing, and sang one song after another without stopping. He played and sang superbly, and the songs—what songs! Before the war, the entire country had been singing them, in peasant households, around the holiday table, in moments of sorrow and joy. At his listener's request, Sasha sang "For the Gal from the Little Tavern" twice.

That is how we greeted the 1942 New Year, falling asleep only just before dawn.

Lessons of the Barracks

Within a week the barracks was full of life and the sound of young men's voices. We quickly got to know each other. Everyone was quickly divided up into platoons, and we were introduced to our platoon leaders. We each received an assigned bunk. Gradually, we were adjusting to army life. And of course we started our training.

Our leaders trained us according to an accelerated schedule. From the first days, we plunged into our studies and worked to the point of exhaustion. Within a half year, I was supposed to become a mortar platoon leader. We did parade drills every day. Twice a week, target practice. Our instructors crammed together lessons in the Field Service Regulations (and you couldn't count them all!), communications, tactics, and infantry weapons, such as the pistol, the rifle, and the carbine; then machine guns, and we would almost be ready for work with mortars. They trained us in hand-to-hand fighting techniques as well. Once a week, we skied up to 20 or 30 kilometers, then rehearsed scouting the location for combat outposts and setting them up. Besides that, several times they woke us up in the middle of the night with alarms, and we would have to conduct nighttime rapid-marches of up to 10 to 15 kilometers, with full combat gear.

It was astonishing! Each leader considered his own business as the most important and tried to impart this personal understanding to his students. For example, the senior sergeant who conducted the parade drills liked to declare, "Without a love for parade order, not a single man can walk properly upon God's green earth!"

The master sergeant, who was obsessed with how we made our bunks and the cleanliness of our boots, constantly harped: "A bed is made with an automatic motion of the hands below the belt." Or: "Tomorrow you'll be heading to the front—and yet you have filthy boots!!"

Our platoon leader, Lieutenant Artur, who could drive any student out of his mind who had not yet learned by heart every paragraph of the regulations, kept drumming into our heads, "Learn the regulations! You'll be healthier for it!"

Our political leader in a most serious manner constantly maintained, "I'll teach you to love your Motherland."

In addition to the basic set of military sciences, we washed dishes, cleaned the soot and scum out of enormous pot-bellied cauldrons, picked up trash, scrubbed the floor of the barracks to a shine, chopped and sawed firewood, and mopped the toilet area and staircase. All of this, both the military training and the domestic chores, were harder for me than for the other cadets, but I eventually adjusted to the strict soldier's life.

At nighttime the barracks experienced their own, different life. My friend Sashka Ryzhikov, for example, gave solo concerts—and what shows they were! Just like in the theater. After several performances, however, his guitar was taken from him. One night the sergeant major suddenly showed up, shouting, "This isn't a bowl of cherries here!" and grabbed the guitar from Sashka. "I'll give it back when you head for the front!"

Sashka suffered without his guitar; he missed it badly and once even started crying over its absence, but he continued to sing in order to spite the sergeant major. He said, "Even without the guitar, I can sing!" Everyone listened to him just as intently without his guitar—they rejoiced and applauded after every song. But he cherished his guitar and was plainly miserable without it.

I will jump ahead and tell you the full story of this guitarist and his guitar.

Within a month, the battalion commander summoned Ryzhikov and promised to return his guitar to him if Sashka would take part in a large concert on 23 February for Red Army Day: Sashka was to recite Maiakovsky's verse about the Red Army to the accompaniment of his guitar. Sashka refused to do it. Another month passed. Sashka didn't train any worse than the other students, and the platoon leader, Lieutenant Artur, even spotted a talent for marksmanship in him; Sashka had a precise eye, and the lieutenant began to train him for exhibition shooting with the promise that if Sashka represented the platoon well at the battalion shooting competition, his guitar would be returned, he would be awarded the "Voroshilov's Marksman" badge, and he would be promoted to sergeant. But Sashka didn't submit to the lieutenant either: he shot badly at the competition. Accordingly, in return he didn't see his guitar.

Ryzhikov was also always one of the fastest men on skis. But at the exhibition ski competitions, he always finished last. This conduct infuriated Lieutenant Artur, who didn't return the guitar but rather slapped extra duty details on Sashka whenever he disappointed the platoon leader.

As it indeed turned out, the sergeant major's threat came true: the obstinate student got his guitar back only as he was leaving for the front.

Soon after the confiscation of the guitar, there was a new nighttime *ChP* [an "extraordinary event or occurrence"—common Russian parlance for an accident or scandal]. The sergeant major burst into the barracks and confiscated two decks of cards from our inveterate card players. The familiar words rang out: "This isn't a bowl of cherries here! You're in army barracks! It is forbidden to play cards here!"

A week passed, and then the sergeant major caught some of the guys shooting craps for money.

The barracks was thrown into a tizzy. How did the sergeant major know everything? Could one of our own be spilling the beans? Suspicions arose. Immediately, relations became tense in the barracks. But this didn't last long. In such situations a "house detective" always emerges in the group, who works to uncover the snitch. After several days of investigation, our own detective established two indisputable facts: "who" and "how." The informer turned out to be the young, plump Feden'ka, who had narrow, shifty eyes. In the after-dinner hour of rest, the most blessed time of the day for the cadets, Feden'ka would run to the sergeant major with a "report." Having once followed Feden'ka when he had set off for the quartermaster's stockroom, our detective crept up to the door and overheard the following approximate dialogue:

The sergeant major: "Here you are, cadet, seven candied fruit jellies."

Feden'ka: "Comrade sergeant major, you promised me ten."

The sergeant major: "Seven's enough for you. Once you find out something more, you'll get some more."

Justice in the barracks was swift. Expressing the general opinion, someone said, "We need to teach this creature not to sell out his comrades!"

For two days, they hauled Feden'ka off the latrine while he was doing his "business," repeating, "Find your candies in your own drawers, snake!" Afterwards, they never caught Feden'ka in that lavatory; apparently, he was running to a different floor of the barracks whenever he had to use the toilet. But this lesson didn't stop his behavior, and he continued to go to the sergeant major with reports. So a new punishment was handed down: he was rolled up in a quilt and beaten black and blue. Tossed down from the bunk, he lay on the floor a long time, moaning and crying.

This all stopped when Feden'ka appeared in the Lenin Room, where almost the entire platoon gathered every evening, and begged: "Forgive me, fellows! After all, we'll all be going to war together. I'm a sinner, forgive me!"

We didn't forgive him. "You sold us out for seven pieces of candy!" For a long time thereafter, the platoon ignored him and avoided him whenever possible.

Such were the first cruel surprises that I encountered at the specialist school. I didn't yet know how to interpret them. Little by little, I got accustomed to and adapted to life in the barracks, and I tried to understand its laws, customs, traditions, and—most important—the character of the officers and students.

The Days of a Cadet

I'll try to tell you how they trained us to become officers, using the example of a single day, which was not different from any other routine day.

Six o'clock in the morning. It is still dark. Just like a blow to the head, the deep voice of the sergeant major rings throughout the barracks: "Get up!"

I leap from my bed. It is easier for me than for Shurka, my neighbor: I'm in a lower berth, he's on an upper. In a flash, I make my bed. We are supposed to have three minutes for this task. If you make a careless error, the sergeant major will force you to do it again and again, perhaps five or ten times over. I wrap my feet and ankles with the binding [Red Army soldiers didn't use socks but rather wrapped their feet and ankles in a cotton binding], stick my feet into my boots; for some reason, they're still damp, and I sense an unpleasant odor.

Aha! Very likely, someone got even for my winning streak in cards last night by pissing in my boots. But I have no time to spare; everything has been calculated down to the minute.

"Get moving! Get moving!"

We rush in formation to the toilet. It is a long, narrow, cold room, with green-painted walls. On one side there are twenty washstands. The water is cold, and the edges of the washbasins have become icy. Along the opposite wall are crude latrines in individual stalls, but the stalls have no doors. The latrines are nothing more than open holes over a raw sewage pit. The line of waiting men usually stretches in both directions.

The day begins with abusive speech and ends with the very same. The latrine is at your disposal for just four minutes. While the fellows are washing, I quickly occupy an empty booth. I change my foot wrappings and rewrap my feet with fresh ones. I have no time for anything else. I'd like at least once to have time to complete my natural functions like defecation. But I'm afraid of making the attempt now, because if you exceed the time limit or the patience of the waiting students, they will unceremoniously drag you off the latrine and toss you out of the stall. In that case, the least evil might be that I soil my underwear. So I leave the rest for later. I brush my teeth, clean myself below the waist with cold water, then rub myself briskly with a towel, until my skin is red. But the senior sergeant is already forming up the platoon: "Get moving! Get moving!"

Everybody is in their undershirts, which have been tucked into their trousers. At a quickstep, we go down the staircase to the parade ground. There, it is Siberia! The temperature is nearly ten degrees below zero. The smoke from the chimneys, like the tail of an angered cat, rises straight up into the air. There is no wind; just pure, frigid air. We are young and strong. We limber up with a short jog, and then already the next command is ringing out: "Exercises! Get moving! Hup! Two! Three! . . ."

We do twenty different exercises for forty minutes total.

Meanwhile, other men pulling duty are sawing and chopping firewood for the kitchen and for heating the barracks. I've already learned, fully and correctly, how to grip a saw with no excess tension in my hands or arms, and fatigue no longer overcomes me when I use one, as it did before. (My neighbor in the barracks, a cadet named Shurka from Leningrad, taught Zhenechka and me how to handle a saw. But I hadn't learned how to master an axe; I didn't have enough strength, flexibility, or sufficiently good vision, so such work for me always ended with blisters and a pile of chips.)

After calisthenics, we run back into the barracks. We put on our field shirts, the buttons on which are gleaming, as they've been scrubbed with a mixture of chalk and tooth powder. In formation, we briskly march to the dining hall.

"Get moving! Get moving!"

It is seven o'clock in the morning, and how much has already been done!

Breakfast. For breakfast, we usually get barley or millet gruel, ten grams of butter, two slices of bread, two little lumps of sugar, and hot tea. On holidays, we get a little more—a tart with jam for each of us.

Meals are a complete science: how to sit at the table, how to use a fork, spoon, and knife—complete books have been written about this. But no one has ever taught us proper table etiquette. Thus, for example, if a cadet licks his plate clean with his tongue, nobody pays the least bit of attention to him. Whether or not you've managed to complete your meal on time is your own personal business. As soon as the time allotted to breakfast or lunch expires, a command rings out; in response, we leap up from our tables and hurry off in formation back to the barracks.

"Get moving! Shake a leg!"

The next three hours are devoted to studying the regulations. There are many, and each must be learned by heart down to the last paragraph. The officer must precisely follow the Field Regulations on the attack and on defense, in winter and in summer, while on guard, and so forth. All of us, both instructors and cadets, know that the field regulations we are learning are outdated, based largely on the experience of the Russian Civil War, with no regard for the experiences and understanding of contemporary warfare. Which means, of course, that they are useless. But our instructors keep quiet about this, and so do we. We memorize the regulations, like the most slow-witted scholars, unable to comprehend, because of our inexperience, the colossal harm they have already brought, and will still bring, to the Red Army, before new ones replace them. For example, according to the then current Field Regulations, an officer must always be located at the front of the attacking line. And that is, indeed, how at first we fought, which meant that the officers unjustifiably sacrificed themselves and we would lose all tactical control on the battlefield.

The class hours spent studying the regulations are some of the vilest. Our platoon commander, Lieutenant Artur, leads the classes. At times it seems he doesn't know anything but the regulations, and doesn't want to know anything else. But in this matter he is a true artist. He begins his classes with the following words: "The Field Regulations must become the first love of the young cadet! The second—his commanding officer."

An Estonian, Lieutenant Artur doesn't speak Russian well. He mangles words and struggles to pronounce certain letter combinations. Whenever he unintentionally makes up a new word, or tortures the pronunciation of another, the cadets laugh—of course, into their sleeves. The only things worse than the classes with Lieutenant Artur are the political classes, where we study Marxism-Leninism and the latest speeches of Stalin.

After the morning classes we have a fifteen-minute break. Then it is off to the parade ground at double time in formation. Before lunch. Every blessed day, parade drills. Though we call it "parading," these drills aren't boxes of chocolates, either. We march along guide ropes: alone, in twos, in threes, as a squad, as a platoon. The commands sound out without interruption: "Left! Right! About face! For-ward!"

Sergeants lead the parading. It seems, perhaps, that they are trying even harder than we are. When you practically leave an impression in the asphalt with your step, it seems you are an angel, especially if you aren't the only one, especially if after the ringing step, dozens of legs rise upward in strict unison. But the sergeant is eternally dissatisfied; again and again come the commands: "Forward step! Forward step!"

We learn how to salute precisely. We know how to stand at attention, like silent statues, our eyes wide open and focused on the commander. We can assume the guard [position], clicking our heels no worse than tap dancers. With bravado we implement turns to the right and left. We stoically endure idiotic carping and loud swearing—both justifiable and unjustifiable. We are always prepared—independently from our own opinion or mood—to carry out any order.

Meanwhile, to stand quietly at attention in the middle of a Siberian winter—without gloves, your naked fingers wrapped around the icy barrel of a rifle—that's no health resort! What kind of dog tolerates such commands? And what's the sense of it?

"Devil take it, who needs this parade drill!" my closest friend in the school, Iurka Davydov, once said with indignation, no longer able to hold back. "What do they want to make of us, little toy soldiers? Who needs these stupidities? I'm sure none of this will do us any good in war."

Iurka asked the very same question at the next meeting with the commissar. The commissar explained to us that parade drill was useful, especially at a military specialist school: it disciplines the cadet, helps each one feel like a soldier, forms a specific skill, strengthens the body, and prepares the cadet to endure the hardships of a soldier's life, especially the long marches.

"That's what your 'parading,' as you call it, will get you at the front," concluded the commissar. "Thus, parade drills are a necessary business."

No one challenged the commissar's words. But Iurka didn't change his opinion. Later he told me about the words of Timoshenko, the new People's Commissar of Defense, who had replaced Voroshilov after the Winter War against Finland: "Every soldier should master parade step, just as he masters his own logic."

"Well, tell me, if that's not idiocy?" Iurka exclaimed indignantly.

However, let us continue. From the parade ground, frozen and hungry, we return to the barracks. A race for the toilet immediately occurs. Then, in formation, we head to the dining hall. Lunch! We get soup, traditionally pea, potato, or barley. The cooks at the school do a fine job, but don't ask for seconds! After the soup, meat patties with macaroni and dried fruit compote follow. Two slices of bread are a fitting accompaniment. We wolf down all the food in seven or eight minutes. We are not allowed to waste any more time than that. And already, the orders are ringing out: "Get moving! Hup, two, three . . . !"

We march in formation back to the barracks. We fling ourselves on our bunks—an hour for rest. The most blessed time!

After this "dead hour," we have classes again until dinner: lessons in combat training, tactics, topography, and communications. We take apart and reassemble rifles and machine guns. Squad leaders time each student to see how long it takes him. We clean our weapons.

Twice a week we have target practice. We shoot at dummies and targets with rifles and machine guns. One day a week, in any weather, we have field exercises: we work with field maps, learn how to make independent decisions in combat and on the march, and so forth.

Dinner. In formation, we quickly march to the dining hall. Plates lined up "in formation" are waiting for us on the tables, with pea, millet, sometimes buckwheat porridge; ten grams of butter; two slices of bread; and two lumps of sugar per mug. If you want more tea, well, add some water to whatever's left in your mug, and drink that. It's also a bad deal, whenever you fill yourself with pea porridge, as you're liable to be up half the night.

After dinner we have tactical classes twice a week, and political instruction every other day.

The very worst thing we had to endure, as it turned out, was not the parade drills or cramming in the Field Regulations, but the political classes. Someone accurately described them as "funerals with honor"—three times a week, we honorably lay to rest the time, which had been "killed" by the classes with the political instructor, the deputy commissar. He was a somewhat strange man: short, with a florid complexion and a considerable paunch, which seemed to us to be impossible in the army. By his entire appearance, he reminded us of a little barrel of beer. He was an educated man, but he was dense and colorless. He always seemed tense, and he often mopped the sweat from his brow with a kerchief. Nothing seemed to come easily to him.

His lectures always mixed truth with lies. It was difficult to determine which was greater. We spent half the lesson time listening to him read extracts from the speeches and orders of the People's Commissar of Defense, Stalin. One of the guys once calculated that on average, there were ten citations from Stalin per class: that meant in a week, thirty; and in a month, 120. That's why the political instructor got the nickname among us of "Stinking Reciter." The single benefit of his classes was when he told us about events at the front, though it must be said that we already knew a lot of this news beforehand. Unfortunately, even at the front I often bumped into a lot of these political instructors: windbags, stupid and distant from a soldier's spirit and from other human feelings.

After the painful oppression of the political classes, at last arrives our most long-awaited and favorite hour of the day—the hour before retreat! "The hour of freedom," as my friend Iurka Davydov called this leisure time. All of sixty minutes, but there is so much to do! Write home, sew up or mend something, listen to the radio, or peruse a fresh newspaper, if you are in the Lenin Room; play at least one game of chess, or discuss the situation at the front—our hearts froze whenever we heard the words, "Today our forces abandoned the city of . . . ." These activities left only a few calculated minutes for personal reading.

Ten o'clock in the evening. The routine training day has come to an end. Everyone in the barracks is in their bunk. The noise gradually subsides. The silence of the night settles over us. But it only seems that way. After the sergeant major and officers leave, a nightlife begins. Card players take up their games of chance; here and there, guys are playing checkers. A regular cascade of anecdotes and storytelling continues beyond midnight. The storytellers among the students try to outdo each other. Many of their stories are as old as Abraham and Sarah, and military personalities occupy a large place in their tales. But most of all, their anecdotes are lewd and obscene.

Once, the Leningrader Zhenechka, no longer able to withstand the lurid talk, rose up from his bunk and peacefully appealed to the storytellers: "Don't you understand that you're talking filth?"

Everyone fell silent. Only one shrill voice rang out, from where Feden'ka and a few of the Cossack cadets were lying: "Shut your trap, faggot!"

But by now appeals are sounding from different corners of the room: "Enough of your neighing, we're nearly bursting our guts laughing, and tomorrow is target practice!"

The night carnival falls silent. The barracks sink into sleep.

But at 6:00 A.M., as always, the voice of the sergeant major loudly growls, "Get up! Get moving!"

Iura Davydov and "Uncle Stiopa"

In our first days of training, the company designated me as a squad leader. I spent one week in that position, but then the students knocked me off my pedestal. Only one person protested this action—Iura Davydov.

The mutiny was organized by "the Magnificent Six." Everyone in the platoon called them "the Cossacks" because they had all arrived from Cossack villages in the Donbass region. Once at the specialist school, they laid claim to a special role among the cadets. They acted like friends of the court, often referred to each other as "the Brotherhood," and bullied everybody else. For some reason I didn't understand, they particularly won the favor of the platoon commander, both on and off duty. By their education and cultural level they weren't very different from our lieutenant. How they wound up at the specialist school isn't clear—the majority of them didn't have a middle-school education. Obviously, some local military bureaucrat had decided that "the war enlists everyone"—in those years a well-known phrase. It was difficult to live together with the Cossacks in the barracks. Cheeky, rude, awful, they were also card sharks and petty thieves (I don't doubt that it was one of them that swiped my first worker's wages, which I had brought from home).

So all the more, I valued my friendship with Iura Davydov. It still pains me to think that we only had our time at the specialist school together, and that our frontline paths quickly separated us. He was killed tragically in January 1945, which I will tell you about further along in the book. He was a superb guy; smart, well read, blessed with intelligence, all of which appealed to me.

He was from Cheliabinsk, where he grew up in a worker's family. His father was a master worker at a steel foundry, and Iura was a robust fellow himself. We both loved to read, which drew us together in the platoon. In conversations, topical discussions of vital questions, and in book debates—in all of these things, Iura stood out in the barracks, which led me to seek his friendship. It was always interesting to be around him. I noticed one peculiarity of Iurka's character: he quickly mastered anything that he liked or that was interesting to him, but just as quickly tore himself away from anything strange to him or that he didn't find useful.

He demonstrated particular talents in cartography; he could quickly and easily figure out the details on any common field map, which might remain inscrutable to the rest of us. The cartography instructor gave him the only "A" in the class and predicted Iurka would have a gleaming officer's career. The envious and stunned Cossacks decided to set up something to knock some of the shine off of Iurka, but thought better of it—Shurka intervened; I have already mentioned him and will tell you more.

Incidentally, a little more about cartography. Three months after the start of our classes, one of the cadets somewhere got hold of a small colored map of the Soviet Union, and, hanging it in the Lenin Room, he began to mark the front lines on it with a pencil. As we saw the lines change, it was clear that the war was not going in our favor. The map increasingly provoked arguments and debates among the students. The "cartographer" was summoned by the school's command to explain himself. Within a week, he was dismissed from the school and sent to the front. The map disappeared as well. We took in all of this quietly, but it forced many of us to stop and think, and gave us a better understanding of "what's right and what's wrong."

In addition to Iurka, there was another Davydov in the battalion—Stepan, or "Uncle Stiopa," as his fellow cadets often called him. I would not be mistaken if I tell you that no one else in the battalion was as fit for the military profession as Stepan was. Quite likely, young men just like him had been selected for the military specialist schools in peacetime, before the rapid expansion of officer training.

Stepan was older than us by all of two years, but his actions and conversation made him seem much more mature. Very likely, none of us were as ready for a self-sufficient adult life as he was. Whatever Uncle Stiopa might undertake, he did easily, quickly, and, most important, with some sense of inner joy, which usually infected others around him as well. It was not hard to catch an expression of satisfaction on his fine, open, manly face. He was a superb shot, knew his weapon inside and out, and knew the Field Regulations—again, superbly well.

Stepan's conscientiousness, his exacting attitude toward himself, and his serious approach to military matters surprised us. One day, we asked him what his secret was. He smiled and answered:

"There's no sort of secret. There are two rules, which I always observe, and I advise you to do the same. One must learn how to fight well and must strive to protect his comrades. The better we learn how to fight, the more successfully we will do this at the front. And if we learn to care for each other here, we will also one day know how to protect a fellow soldier's life."

There's a philosophy of life for you. It was convincing, and many students tried to follow it.

Nobody can remember a case where Stepan Davydov refused someone help. It was particularly difficult for us to learn to disassemble and reassemble a machine gun in a strictly limited time period—here Stepan was irreplaceable. He was also indispensable on marches. And before the march began, he taught us how to prepare for it. He was considered the best student in the battalion, which was an accurate evaluation. Stepan Davydov was the first to be promoted to the rank of senior sergeant (ahead of schedule), and to be entrusted with command of a platoon.

Lieutenant Artur

Our platoon leader, Lieutenant Artur, was an unpleasant person—if you can even call such a man a "person." I never encountered a more evil and vindictive character.

First, a few facts from his biography. When back in 1940 the Red Army had marched into Estonia and "liberated" the people from the bourgeoisie, all officers of the old Estonian Army who had not managed to go into hiding were forced into retirement. Some of these officers were later executed, and the rest were sent to Siberia. The new power in Estonia began to form a new Workers and Peasants Red Army (RKKA). Artur was the son of a farmhand and thus eligible for short-term army courses at a regimental school. He quickly became a lieutenant and was assigned to command Estonian soldiers. Shortly before the outbreak of war, the Estonian units were shipped to Russia and turned into construction battalions. For a long time, they were not released for frontline service; that transpired after the so-called "national units" appeared.

How Artur wound up at the specialist school is a mystery. He was frankly without any understanding of simple human feelings, among them sympathy. Semiliterate, with a low level of culture, he was a man who could not, or more likely did not want, to understand us—that we were also people, moreover young people, and that we could love, be happy, joke around, laugh, and have our own personal interests. To all of this, he was not simply deeply indifferent; it seemed to irritate him maliciously.

On one evening dedicated to Red Army Day, one of the students became acquainted with a young woman in the club and escorted her home. Several times he requested leave, but without result. An incident helped him out. As it turned out, we served guard duty not far from the street where the young woman lived, and one time we let the love-struck guard leave for an hour to visit her. But someone ratted on us, and the vindictive platoon leader sent the fellow to the guardroom. (I also had to spend three days there once, for breaking a ski.)

Just a word about guard duty. How those nighttime guard duties wore us out! Usually we were guarding army warehouses, which had been situated in abandoned churches. Guard service didn't relieve us from our studies, so the whole next day after guard duty, we kept nodding off. Exhausted, one day I couldn't fight off sleep, and I had just dozed off in class when the instructor pounced upon me and snapped me out of my sleep. For my punishment, Artur gave me an extra duty detail.

From the very first meeting, the platoon took a disliking to Artur, and he took a disliking to us. From morning to evening he drilled us, making no exception whatsoever for our youth, our inexperience, or the fact that we had not yet adapted to army life. A commanding officer, as far as we understood, was a mentor; a comrade senior to us in rank; someone we could trust, respect, and be ready to follow into battle. Lieutenant Artur, on the other hand, was firmly convinced that there should be no sort of human relations between the students and their commanding officer beyond those narrowly prescribed by the regulations. That he demeaned his cadets with his boorishness, crude tricks, and rudeness, bordering on mockery, and that he was crushing our spirits, never occurred to him.

Once, failing to notice the lieutenant's approach, I failed to salute him. He immediately ordered me to drop onto the icy ground and forced me to squirm along on my chest and belly for 200 meters. This little tyrant performed similar pranks with other students. But on the day after this punishment, I fell ill. By evening I was feeling terrible, and I requested permission to go to the medical ward. Lieutenant Artur glanced at me with his blank, fishlike eyes and denied me permission, adding a complete lecture to his refusal:

"How do you intend to fight? Are you going to flee the front lines to the *medsanbat* [medical sanitation battalion] every time your little finger is hurting? Drink a glass of cold water with some salt, and your soreness will pass. Are you a soldier or a woman?"

I felt even worse the next morning, so I didn't go to the morning calisthenics and declined breakfast. I simply lay on my bunk and resigned myself to whatever might happen to me for these transgressions. Shurka brought me some hot tea from his dining table. He advised me to go over Artur's head and appeal to the company commander, who gave me permission to visit the medical ward.

Company Commander Koval'chuk

Company commander Senior Lieutenant Koval'chuk, a regular army officer, was a man from a completely different mold and was more gentle and respectful to our circle of cadets. He always found time for us and behaved decently toward each cadet. He often dropped by our barracks to see how we were coming along, and he took an interest in whether we were writing letters to our parents, and what sort of news we were receiving from home. We respectfully called him Iurii Sergeevich. He conducted our tactical classes. Not limiting himself to the dry, outmoded course materials, he filled his lectures with concrete examples from the experience of the [Russian] Civil War and analyzed the successes and failures of the Red Army. He had come to the school from the Far East, where he had fought at Khalkin-Gol and had earned the Order of the Red Star. He always wore this order on the appropriate place of his military tunic, so it was plain to see how proud he was of it.

Today, thinking back on those tactical classes, one can understand how primitive they were. The lectures didn't touch upon the experiences of the ongoing war—there was no analysis of the failures of 1941, no description of the enemy's operations and tactics, no discussion of our successful winter counteroffensive near Moscow. The classes were interesting, but afterwards, our heads were empty—the lectures were simply popular tales about this and that, and nothing more. But I, a future commander of a platoon, or perhaps even a company commander, wanted to know how to act in battle, in the field, on the march, and in the city; how to command men and how to behave in front of them; how infantry should cooperate with tanks and artillery; and how to work with a radio man. I wanted to know details about the enemy and his weapons, and what methods and means were at my disposal in battle with him. After the destruction of the Germans at the gates of Moscow, the high command didn't even consider sending captured enemy equipment to the school for study.

When Koval'chuk dropped by the barracks that day of my illness and caught me lying on my bunk at a time when I shouldn't have been, he immediately took an interest in what was going on. I explained the situation to him and requested permission to visit the medical ward. He granted me permission but advised me not to lie around too long.

I spent almost five days in the ward. When I returned to my barracks and reported to the platoon commander, he chewed me out with obscene insults, accused me of being a "squealer," and deprived me of two free hours, for which he had no authority.

After this endearing little conversation, Iurka walked up to me:

"Learn how to conduct yourself so you don't give that beast an opportunity to pick on you."

"Easier said than done. And just how should I go about doing that?" I replied.

"You know, if the lieutenant orders me to crawl, I crawl. If he orders me to shoot, I'll shoot. But I never have a thought to become like him. And I'm sure that at the front, soldiers won't tolerate a cretin like that for even an hour."

Dimka Okunev—the "Good Soldier Švejk"

Dimka Okunev became the platoon's favorite—he took revenge on Lieutenant Artur for all of us! Some people called Dimka "a bit crazy," others called him "a circus performer." Many people tried to change the style of his behavior, but no one managed to do so: even Artur couldn't break the fellow's character. Even Dimka himself couldn't precisely remember how many demerits he had received.

At first I heard only seemingly fanciful tales about Dimka—the "Good Soldier Švejk" [a reference to the memorable comic Everyman character in Jaroslav Hasek's book *The Fateful Adventures of the Good Soldier Švejk in the World War*]. I witnessed for the first time how artfully he played out a typical scene during a run-in with the company's sergeant major. The sergeant major had forced Dimka to remake his bunk three times. After the third failed attempt, Dimka stood at attention, saluted, and precisely said his lines: "I'll venture to announce, Comrade Sergeant Major, that in České Budějovice we had a similar case . . ."

The sergeant major, understanding nothing, became even angrier, and shouted: "Clown, you're really going to get it (this was his favorite utterance)! You'll learn how to address your superiors properly!"

Dimka, without removing his hand from his temple, again repeated his line: "I'll venture to report, Comrade Sergeant Major . . ."

The barracks burst out laughing. The sergeant major flushed all over; he finally understood that this was a show, that he and Dimka were playing roles in a satire about authority, and he decided to put the brakes on the matter: "You shut your trap, 'Good Soldier.' This isn't a circus show for you, but a barracks! I'm going to report to the lieutenant, and he'll make a 'Good Soldier' out of you so fast your head will spin."

Everyone knew that the sergeant major wasn't going to do anything. He loved to bluster, but in actuality he wasn't a malicious man, and perhaps he himself understood that a little joking and playing around made life more pleasant. He had already seen much in his lifetime and had already sent many young men to the front, including his own son.

The day of the battalion's shooting competition arrived. On the first day of the competition the contestants would use rifles, and on the second day, machine guns. There had been a lot of anticipatory speeches and talks about this contest, and a lot of practice sessions. At first, Lieutenant Artur thought to leave a few of his poor shooters behind in the barracks and report them as sick, but at the last minute the idea frightened him, and he brought the entire platoon to the shooting. Ten men would shoot for each platoon's team, but the battalion's deputy commander would select the shooters from each platoon. When the final results were announced, Lieutenant Artur was ready to do some shooting himself—our platoon had finished in one of the last places. But in the practice sessions, the cadets that had been selected for the contest (I wasn't among them) had proven to be excellent shots. The lieutenant understood what was going on. Everyone braced for what might happen next.

Artur didn't shoot anyone. But soon he received another blow. An episode occurred, the likes of which we had all been eagerly anticipating.

On 23 February, the entire body of cadets was assembled on the parade ground, and the school commandant read out the order of the Supreme Command. It was impossible to forget the final words of this order! "The entire Red Army will make sure that the year 1942 will be the year of the German-fascist forces' final crushing defeat, and the year of liberation from Hitler's swine." "Hurrah! Wonderful!"—resounded in the soul of every man there. We believed in Stalin and didn't think twice about whether or not we would implement his order; there were even a few disappointed voices in the general buzz: "Does this mean we won't get to the front? The war will end without us?"

The war, of course, would last for three and a half more years, and only at the beginning of 1943, at Stalingrad, did the rays of the first dawn of hope appear, which stunned not only Germany but also the entire world.

On that night, as was usual, our platoon's cadets were doing guard duty. Dimka was standing alone at his post. Suddenly, in the darkness through the trees, the silhouette of a man was briefly visible. Dimka spotted it and didn't screw around; he called out according to regulations: "Stop! Who goes there? Give the password!"

The mystery man didn't answer. Then Dimka took his rifle off his shoulder, chambered a round, and fulfilling the duties of a sentry, bellowed: "My first shot will be in the air, the next at you! I'm counting to three!"

The shadowy figure replied: "Don't be a fool, Okunev! It's me, your lieutenant. Put down your gun and fetch the captain of the guard."

The platoon commander advanced directly upon Dimka, who promptly dropped him into the snow with a shot into the air.

"How I've screwed up," the lieutenant moaned. "I never learned the password. You've got to know these swine. . . ."

Time passed slowly. About twenty minutes went by. Dimka was in a long, padded jacket, felted boots, and a fur cap. But for the lieutenant, who was wearing unlined jackboots, every minute on the frozen ground seemed like an hour. The diligent cadet all the while kept his aim on the lieutenant and refused to call for the guard captain.

"Call for the guard captain, Okunev!—Artur shouted—my feet are freezing!"

In response, Dimka said: "Quiet! One must know guard service regulations!— and suddenly added—"I venture to report, Comrade Lieutenant, that in České Budějovice there was a similar case. . . ."

Only after having acted out his favorite scene, the "Good Soldier Švejk" permitted Artur to get up and get the hell out of there.

And that's how the desire to check on his subordinates took a turn for the worse for the zealous platoon commander. The next day, the barracks rejoiced, while Dimka became the general favorite and hero of everyone.

Zhenechka

More than anyone else, Lieutenant Artur picked on Zhenechka. In this case, there were no limits to the vagaries of Artur's evil mind. The cadet, on the other hand, clenching his teeth, unquestioningly carried out whatever order his superior officer gave him.

Why did all the other students call Zhenia Evlev "Zhenechka"? It was a clear sign of their noble ability to sympathize. The company knew Zhenechka's story, that within two months he had lost his entire family—his mother, his father, his dear sister, and his grandfather. Zhenechka was now completely alone.

Zhenechka was in general a special case. He was a seventeen-year-old boy from Leningrad. So tall, it seemed that when he stood on a stool he could reach up and touch the ceiling of the barracks with his long, refined hands. Well-proportioned, with a handsome, kind face that smiled more often than it frowned, this stately young man seemed born to dance ballet, but the times forced him to become a soldier. Whenever Zhenechka walked across the parade ground, not with the crisp soldier's step but smoothly, regally, beautifully—it irritated the sergeants, the almost feminine "citizen" in him showing through in everything, not only in his stride, but also his gestures and conduct, even in uniform dress. We, on the other hand, enjoyed seeing this totally unmilitary, unusual phenomenon.

Sometimes at night Zhenechka would surreptitiously cry into his pillow, something that only the bunk neighbors closest to him knew. The fate of his family, as it was for thousands of other Leningrad families, was tragic. Within two weeks of the outbreak of war, his mother and sister were traveling to the Crimea and disappeared along the way. His father was conscripted into the army and, defending Leningrad, was killed in the vicinity of Kolpino. Zhenia remained with his grandfather, who didn't survive even a month of the blockade.

Zhenia wasn't drafted into the army, as he had just turned sixteen. He did everything in those severe days of the blockade just to obtain a lifesaving piece of bread. He lugged crates to the port, he collected corpses from the streets, he helped carry ammunition to the front, and worked in childcare facilities with orphaned children, the number of which grew daily in the besieged city. The Leningrad Komsomol Committee sent him to work as a nurse in a hospital. He carried out his duties conscientiously, and at his request, they permitted him to live at the hospital.

Random chance helped Zhenechka escape the blockaded city. Stalin ordered the evacuation of about ten academicians who still remained in Leningrad, along with their families, and sent a Douglas cargo plane for them. A few scholars, old, sick, and alone, and under hospital observation, needed escorts. The hospital director, wanting to save Zhenia, arranged for him to be a personal assistant to one of the old men. Zhenia agreed, hoping that he might then be able to search for his missing mother and sister.

Zhenechka's ward turned out to be a famous scientist, now a sick, crippled, half-blind old man, but still possessing a clear mind. He and Zhenia liked each other from their first meeting. After several days' flight they arrived in Kuibyshev, and the first thing Zhenia did was to write letters to wherever he could, to those who might have any connection with the search for missing people, who had disappeared in the chaos and confusion of the first days of the war. He believed that he would find his missing mother and sister.

For about a month the old man and youth lived harmoniously together in Kuibyshev. In the evenings, they would sit at a table, and the scholar would spend hours reciting "The Lay of Igor's Host" to his grateful listener, or telling Zhenia about the great Russian historian Nikolai Karamzin, or narrating the famous writer Pushkin's life and times.

"Entire epochs of Russian history, with all its most famous names, seemed to come alive as he spoke," Zhenechka once told Iurka and me. "It was a wonder! And verse flowed from the mouth of the old man endlessly, as if it was his own direct speech."

Before the war, Zhenia had dreamed of attending Leningrad University, and here his dream came true: his ward, Andrei Pavlovich, the well-known scholar, indeed had the knowledge of a complete university, and he was reading a complete course of private lectures to Zhenia.

Alas, their classes quickly came to an end. In December, Zhenia was called up for the army. The old man tried to do something, to get an exemption for his young assistant, but they quickly sent him a nurse to replace Zhenia, telling Andrei Pavlovich, "Men today are needed more at the front."

"What kind of soldier am I?" Zhenia said one day. "They couldn't even find a greatcoat to fit me because of my height."

Incidentally, Zhenia once saved my life. During one march, I had a sixteen-kilogram base plate for an 82-mm mortar strapped to my back. When we were negotiating a log across a small but rather deep stream, I slipped a little, lost my balance, and fell into the water. It was only a miracle that the steel base plate didn't break my spine. Zhenechka, who was walking immediately behind me in the column, saved me—this tall fellow, with the long arms, grabbed me, and in a flash he managed both to tear the straps from my shoulders and push the base plate off my back. Returning to our positions in the column, we marched farther. My comrades helped me out, and with the permission of the commander, they carried the base plate for me and gave me some dry clothes to wear beneath my wet greatcoat. Someone exchanged caps with me. I returned to the barracks wet and numb with cold. I immediately changed into some dry underwear, rewound my foot bindings, rubbed myself red with a towel—and everything managed to turn out all right.

Zhenia was a good student. He never asked anyone a favor for anything and tried to accomplish everything by himself, but he was also modest, supremely polite, and sympathetic. The only thing he requested was for the orderlies to listen at 10:00 A.M. to the radio show "Search." In those difficult times, the radio had taken upon itself the noble work of searching for the missing. Every week Zhenechka sent a letter to the show, and he always waited for an answer.

In the evenings, he would hurry to the Lenin Room in the hope of catching a performance by the Leningrad poetess Olga Bergol'z by radio. Whenever he heard her somewhat hoarse, low voice, the fellow would tighten up inside, and tears would appear in his eyes. Once, I happened by the Lenin Room while Olga Berghol'z was reciting her poetry over the radio, and I became a witness to Zhenia's inner suffering. On that evening, the poetess was reading some marvelous verse. I can recall only one stanza:

In the filth, in the darkness, in the hunger, in the sadness
Where death, like a shadow, follows upon our heels
So happy we were together
Such stormy freedom we breathed,
That our descendants will envy us.

Zhenechka moved his lips silently, repeating the lines of verse after her. At that moment, the school's commissar entered the room. He walked up to Zhenia and embraced him:

"Son, don't cry. You're a soldier now."

"Yes, yes," Zhenia answered. Then, like a little boy, he whispered, "I won't cry anymore."

In contrast, Lieutenant Artur increasingly sought to belittle Zhenechka. If Artur gave us one punitive duty detail, for the very same transgression he would give Zhenechka two. He would assign Zhenia the most unpleasant work, like cleaning the stables or latrines. Moreover, Zhenia would get these assignments at a time when everyone else was eating, so he was always hungry. We had a talk with the commissar about this mistreatment. Artur sort of laid low for a while but then again took up his humiliating practices. Now, however, he had created a new method of mockery. He would place whomever he thought guilty of some wrong doing at attention, then read him the riot act, which consisted primarily of swearing and insults. His most innocent utterance in our direction was "Don't tremble, cadet!"—this was Artur's favorite expression. Or: "You are a negative element in our platoon!" After such humiliating tongue lashings, you would feel stricken, and it would take some while to regain your composure.

Artur would especially get furious at Zhenechka after some quarrel between them had occurred. Once, Artur asked Zhenia about something, and he began to answer, "I think. . . ." The lieutenant exploded: "Who gave you permission to think!?"

The cadet couldn't refrain himself in the face of such idiocy: "I gave myself permission."

After hearing the cadet's impudent reply, the lieutenant stopped short. Zhenia understood that he had blurted out something improper, but Artur himself didn't seem to want to acknowledge it.

One day, when we had returned from target practice and were just about to go to dinner, Zhenechka collapsed onto the floor and lay unconscious for several minutes. Another time, the company was on a long march, and Zhenechka couldn't even make half the distance; he had to be sent back to the barracks.

Artur took advantage of these incidents and wrote a report to the battalion commander requesting that Zhenechka be dismissed from the school and sent to the front as a private. The battalion commander passed the report up the line of command. The higher command refused the request and issued a different order. First of all, the order sought doctors' medical opinions. The doctors examined Zhenia and his medical record, and explained that Zhenechka's weakness was caused by general emaciation of his body, which had deteriorated during the Leningrad blockade, and by insufficient nutrition at the school. The school commandant ordered a daily food supplement for Zhenechka from the school's reserve, in the form of a glass of milk, 100 grams of bread, thirty grams of butter, and three lumps of sugar.

This food benefit seemed to embarrass Zhenechka. He often turned away from us when he drank the milk or a second mug of sweetened tea. In the barracks, in the soldiers' dining hall, and in the bath—we were all equal, now that we were in the army, and Zhenechka often offered to share his extra rations with us, but I don't recall anyone ever begging even a half-lump of sugar from him. After some time, closer to spring, Zhenia had gained a little weight. But he hadn't recovered fully by the time of our departure for the front. There was a reason for this: he still hadn't received any news about his parents.

As his hopes dwindled, Zhenechka all the more often sought to seclude himself, became more irritable, and became fixed on one thought—of his parents and sister, which didn't leave him day or night. Concerned, Iura had a second talk with the commissar. He, the commissar, advised to leave the fellow alone:

"What do you want from him? He's still quite young, and in such a short period of time, he has been forced to endure so much. You need to give him a chance to strengthen morally and physically. The important thing is he must not go to pieces; look after him; all sorts of things might happen with him."

I tried to figure out why Artur took a disliking to Zhenechka more than to anyone else. I think there was one reason: Zenia was a true intellectual in every respect. I have met many such people among Leningraders, in distinction from Muscovites, among whom, alas, this type of person is rare. I say this by way of self-criticism; I'm also from Moscow.

Shurka

Let me tell you about Shurka. He was from the same region as our Cossacks, but at the school he followed his own line. His bunk was above mine. At our first encounter, he greeted me rather indifferently; in response to my friendly "Hello!" he coldly answered, "That one's mine." I didn't understand, and thought, "Perhaps he's offended, because I've taken the lower bunk?" But this wasn't my fault: the sergeant major determined where each person would sleep. I offered to trade bunks with Shurka, but he declined, or more accurately, made no response whatsoever. Relations with him were difficult and warmed up a little unexpectedly. We were clearing snow off the roof of the barracks one day when Shurka, seemingly a strong and experienced fellow, slipped and fell from the three-story roof. He was lucky, as he plunged into a deep snow bank. Nevertheless, he badly sprained his ankle and spent more than a week in the hospital. I dropped by to see him several times while he was there.

When Shurka returned, still hobbling a bit, and presented to the platoon commander a piece of paper that freed him from parade ground drills and target practice for two weeks, Artur called him a fraud. I rose to Shurka's defense and tried to explain the situation to the lieutenant. He shouted at me: "In the army, don't intercede! The commanding officer knows!" But the platoon supported me.

After this episode, I began to notice that Shurka's opinion of me was gradually changing. He became more kind and sought to help me in those classes where I was struggling. From my first days at the specialist school it became clear that mechanics and I were not, as we say, on familiar terms with each other. Having noticed that my clumsy fingers couldn't even manage with the trigger while assembling a carbine, Shurka spent a lot of time with me, until I could handle it more or less well. Then he forced me to kiss my carbine's stock—as a sign of mutual friendship with the weapon.

Shurka and I often talked together, and in those conversations, he sometimes asked me questions, as if he was testing my political attitudes: "Why are shops in the capital stuffed to the brim with everything you could want, while shopkeepers in the villages only seem to have vodka and cigarettes?" Or: "Have you seen Stalin? They say he is short and that his face is pock-marked, and that he looks not at all like his painted portraits."

Just try to give an honest answer to questions like that in those dangerous times! About Stalin, I would only say, "I never had a chance to see Stalin in person, because we were living in Kharkov. On the other hand, I've seen all the Ukrainian bosses—Kosior, Postyshev, Petrovsky. While we were living there, Kharkov was the capital of the Ukraine, and on one First of May holiday they assembled on the review platform. I was there too, standing on the platform with them."

"And how did this come about?" Shurka asked in surprise.

"We were living in the famous Apartment Building No. 116 on Sumskaia Street, and our neighbor was the old Bolshevik Shleifer. He was invited to stand on the platform with his son, and they took me along."

"How old were you?" Shurka asked.

"Ten. I also saw on that day the famous border guard, Nikolai Karatsupa, Hero of the Soviet Union, together with his German sheepdog Dzhul'bars. As you yourself can understand, at the time they were far more interesting to me than the Party bosses."

"And why did you call your building famous?" Shurka continued his interrogation.

"It is the most beautiful building on Kharkov's main street, designed and constructed by a German architect. This architect, who was also our neighbor, fell in love with a Russian woman during the construction. After he had completed his construction contract, he requested Soviet citizenship, and they got married. But his wife was killed in an accident very soon thereafter. At the time, perhaps a dozen fortunate people had bicycles in the entire city of Kharkov. His wife was one of them, and she loved to ride her bicycle along Sumskaia Street. One day, a truck ran her over. In turn, the architect was arrested in 1936, and we never saw him again."

One day I asked Shurka why he didn't participate in the pranks of his Cossack comrades. In reply, he only gave a dismissive wave of his hand, and said, "Teenagers!" He was often quiet, seemingly brooding and suffering over some secret. He smoked a lot. But the most important thing to me was that he tried to protect me from the intrigues of his Cossack "brothers," for which I remain grateful to him to this day.

The description of my life in these four months at the school will be incomplete if I fail to talk about my meeting with an astonishing young woman by the name of Zina.

Zina

Our instructors were teaching us the art of combat and how to overcome our opponent, but I still didn't understand how they could do that if we never read a single combat manual or even a textbook. Our entire course of study boiled down to "Do as I say!" And if you tried to offer your own opinion, you would hear in response, "Don't be a wise guy! Carry out the order!"

It was difficult, but I managed to obtain the right to visit the library once every two weeks on my own free time, that is, during our "free hour." The school's library primarily served the command staff and their families, so to get the library privileges I had to write an application to the battalion commander and obtain the agreement of the commissar and our company commander. The standard form of the application contained this statement: "I am obliged not to make any sort of notes or excerpts from the books. If I read something I don't understand, I will consult with the commissar."

Once I obtained the permission, filled with joy, I immediately set off for the library. Incidentally, this was going to be my first trip ever to a library, and I was full of curiosity: What would it be like, this library? How did they keep their books there, and how did they find any particular books in their collection, amidst myriad other books?

And now I was crossing the threshold of the library.

A friendly young woman, in the uniform of a senior sergeant, was sitting behind a small table. She looked about twenty-three years of age, no older.

Her hair was cut short, and she had an attractive face. I overheard the person, who had arrived in line before me, address her as "Zina." While they talked, I examined the long rows of bookshelves. Books, like sentries, were arranged in precise order, as if standing watch over their mistress of the house.

At last, the conversation ahead of me ended, and she and I were alone. I formally requested permission to approach her. Zina broke out laughing:

"When visiting the library, I advise you to forget about subordination; I will recognize relationships outside of regulations, as they are simpler."

"Zina, believe it or not, this is the first time in my life that I've ever been in a library! So many books! Such riches, it is simply a wonder!"

"Quite recently, our book collection was much larger," the young woman responded.

"Then where did they all go? Did rats eat them all up?" I joked.

"Worse," she replied. "Rats with human faces."

Such candor! And on the very first meeting! I fell silent, sensing that I had stepped into a minefield. Zina was silent too, intensely gazing at me. I had to change the subject, and quickly!

I began to prattle: "As the war goes on, the press increasingly compares Hitler's invasion of the USSR to the Napoleonic campaign against Russia. After I finish my schooling here, when I wind up at the front, I'm sure that my soldiers will ask me about this. Can you recommend to me a good book about the 1812 Campaign?"

Zina looked at me carefully, as if studying me. "I can see that you are not a typical cadet, that you are a thinker. That's good; librarians value such readers."

She got up from her stool. She disappeared into the depths of the stacks and quickly returned with a book in an exquisite binding. "Here you go, please, take this novel of Vinogradov's, *Three Colors of Time*—it is our best book on the 1812 Campaign. I advise you to read it. You will get acquainted with Stendhal as well, and his personal impressions of Napoleon's campaign in Russia, as Vinogradov cites him frequently."

It was plain that she had read something in my face, and added, "Stendhal was a participant in this campaign."

I blushed.

"Oh, you still haven't learned how not to blush, Cadet," Zina instantly reacted. "Come on, I'll be happy for you."

She understood everything. At that time, I knew only some hearsay about Stendhal, or more precisely, I had heard this name in my parents' house. Myself, I more preferred Wells, Thomas Mann, Cooper, and, of course, Dumas and Jules Verne.

My first encounter with Zina excited me, and within two weeks I was back at the library. When for a short time there was just the two of us, Zina suddenly asked me to tell her about myself. I was surprised: why did she want my life story? I decided not to put on airs and went straight to the point, trying to be brief. I told her about my mother, my father, his arrest in 1937, and how night "visitors" had come to our house with a search.

"They seized two bags full of documents and books, and for some reason, searched for books which had been published before 1933. They seized rare books as well, and it was especially painful to watch them grab a splendid, five-volume collection of Pushkin's works. At the time, like many other reliable workers, Papa received monthly coupons to exchange for free books. He only completed primary school, but he became a highly educated man since he read so much. But they crammed our books into their bag and carried them away. Before leaving, they placed wax seals on the office door to keep the family out. The next day, I carefully removed the wax seals from the door to Papa's office, and took away the best of the remaining books. Then I went to the neighboring apartment building, where one of our uninvited guests lived, and complained about the badly made seals, as though they had fallen apart on their own. This character almost threw me down the staircase, but all the same, someone from his "office" came and placed new seals on the door.

This story seemed to amuse Zina, who was overwhelmed with laughter, "Oh, what a hero, Cadet; how old were you then?"

"About fifteen."

"Stendhal was right: 'Youth is a time of courage.'" She pronounced these words with a special emphasis, and shook a menacing finger at me: "Likely, there was a reason, Cadet, that they gave you library privileges."

Once again, we had found ourselves in a minefield. Probably, she only liked to question the cadets, to find out about our literary tastes, and to try to understand what kind of person was standing before her.

"But now my papa works as the chief of a large construction project in Kyshtym, from where in fact I arrived at this school," I said to complete my story.

"Yes, thank God, rats with human faces didn't gobble up your father," Zina said with sympathy. "I'm happy for you, Cadet."

On this note we parted. But I already knew full well that I absolutely had to return to the library again.

Iulik Gerts and Sasha Pushkarev

How could Iulik Gerts be accepted into the specialist school? He was so nearsighted that he couldn't take a step without his glasses, and only at night did he lay them down to rest on the nightstand next to his bunk. He was thin, with hollow cheeks. He had a nose like a heron's beak. He was clumsy and seemed out of place in formation. Yet it was striking! No matter how much Artur tried, from the very first days, to crush the spirit of the fellow, this cadet didn't yield.

Moreover, Iulik turned out to be the most diligent of all the responsible cadets; he carried out any order from the platoon commander faster than anyone else—and he was always punctual and precise.

Despite his extremely weak vision, Iulik handled all types of weapons superbly, shot as well at targets as anyone else, got on well in parade drills, and was first in knowledge of the Field Regulations. He liked to sooth any complications in relations with the commander and others through a deft joke, instantly finding the right words to ease the tensions. One day, still rather early in our training, Iulik didn't manage to salute the platoon commander in time, and he immediately received a reprimand: "Cadet Gerts," Artur pounced on him, "I order you to salute all the posts in a row."

Iulik smiled and answered with his favorite expression: "A thought, not without sense!"

One time our "Four-Eyes," as the students labeled him, didn't show up at the morning calisthenics. That evening we learned what had happened. It turned out that upon awakening, Iulik couldn't find his glasses on the nightstand. The sergeant major confronted the student, who had missed the morning calisthenics. Gerts told him about the loss, or more likely the theft, of his glasses. Then, right before the eyes of the sergeant major, Gerts walked over to the bunk of Iashka, one of the "Cossacks," whom Iulik had noticed that morning near his bed, and calmly pulled his glasses from beneath Iashka's pillow.

The sergeant major hushed up the matter, and Iulik decided to stand up for himself. That evening, he walked up to the petty thief. "How can you not be ashamed of yourself?" Iulik began in a seemingly calm voice.

"You're a filthy Jew!" Iashka wickedly swore. "Just who do you think you're threatening?"

Right then and there, Iulik punched Iashka in the face and gave him a bloody nose. The Cossacks instantly surrounded the infuriated "Four-Eyes." The situation was becoming ugly, and a brawl was imminent. Just then, the sergeant major appeared and intervened. Two days later, Cadet Gerts was transferred into a different company.

Neither I nor Iurka ever managed to figure out Iulik and, perhaps, become a bit closer to him. In our first conversation with him, he dazzled us with the brilliance of his speech and startled us with his unusually refined manners, which we had begun to lose. I was literally entranced by his manner of conduct and beautiful, intelligent speech. However, Iulik's verbal dexterity left Iurka cold; after the first conversation, Iurka flatly stated, "I'm already sick of this Gerts's phony, manipulating speeches to gain attention to himself. He has a lot of arrogance, hears only himself, and never waits for the opinion of others."

Iurka's words were to the point. Gerts always sought to demonstrate his uniqueness in everything, never missed a chance to outplay or outmaneuver someone, and was a dreamer. It seemed to us that he always had his head in the clouds and that he was full of nonsense. Explaining his own peculiar behavior, Iulik once said, "Life is too short to take it seriously."

One day Iulik called Iurka and me "bookworms," and declared that he was an enemy of books. Yet he once recited from memory Hamlet's famous monologue, "To be or not to be . . . ," to the general silence of the stunned barracks. Iurka and I were also astonished; I, for example, had never even read any Shakespeare.

"I simply can't understand you, Gerts," Iurka once said. "What are you, some sort of genius, or a complete buffoon? Don't be offended; I'm just asking you as a friend."

"I can't even understand myself," Iulik answered.

When Iurka and I met one day to go to the library, Iulik asked caustically: "What, defenders of the Motherland, are you planning to go to the Cathedral of Books? You merrily throw yourselves into books today, but tomorrow you will face the toughest genuine test of your life."

"Go to hell with you and your advice," Iurka said sharply.

Even then, Iulik tried more than once to convince us of the uselessness of reading. "Books will train you to somebody else's thoughts, but that means to opinions that are not your own," Iulik proclaimed. "Reading is only the illusion of thought!"

Iurka and I didn't respond to what we considered to be such primitive views—we walked away, leaving Iulik alone. However, when we parted, Iulik fixed such a long, sorrowful gaze at us that we felt genuinely sorry for him.

The departure of "Four-Eyes" from the platoon didn't upset anyone. It was scarcely noticed, but Lieutenant Artur was plainly pleased.

Soon our platoon was replenished, and Sasha Pushkarev—a strong fellow from the Urals, an athlete, and a first-class student, replaced Gerts. I liked Sasha from the start. He was a strapping, physically mature guy, with prominent facial features, a broad chest, and strong hands. It seemed that such people were born to become leaders. Sasha never became one, but he was successful in sport: he was the captain of the school's volleyball team.

There were few real athletes among the cadets, and the school command didn't show much concern about creating any new ones—it is a long, drawn-out process! But if the school should happen to receive in ready form a volleyball player, a gymnast, a speed skater, or a skier—no problem! Sashka, however, not only excelled in sports but also tried to draw everyone else into them.

Sasha's mental horizons were narrow. In return, his sincerity, kindness and generosity knew no limits. No one ever got tired of him or fed up with him, and he was always open and friendly.

The Commissar

The battalion's commissar visited us in the barracks more often than any other officer. For example, during the period of our studies at the school, we saw our battalion commander all of two times: during our admittance and on the day we took the military oath. We always looked forward to meetings with the commissar, and he didn't let us down. He came to our barracks at times with a happy face, at times with a gloomy face—as we understood, it depended on events at the front. But soon the "soldier's telegraph" brought us the news of the tragic fate of two of his sons, regular army officers, who both were killed in the first days of the war. However, this man always conducted himself in a level temper and sought to be affable and sincere. He had to have a lot of courage and strength of character in order to keep control of himself in that way.

The commissar never avoided sharp questions, he never flip-flopped, and he tried to answer all our questions truthfully, though everyone could tell how difficult this was for him at times. He spoke simply and clearly, explaining things logically and like a geometrical proof. At times his truthfulness bordered on personal bravery:

"On maneuvers once before the war, one of the Reds captured one of the Blues and led him away to his commander for interrogation," the commissar once told us. "The commander was angry: 'Why did you take him prisoner? If war ever breaks out, the enemy's soldiers will immediately start coming over to our side, and we'll have lots of fresh intelligence.' That's how naïve we were. I've never before seen such a terrible enemy, which has been blinded by Hitler's propaganda."

In Tiumen, they opened rear area hospitals for the severely wounded. The commissar made the rounds of the hospitals to visit with the wounded, and he often told us about their dramatic stories and fates. We heard first not from the newspapers, but after the commissar's personal meetings with wounded eye-witnesses, about Red Army soldiers who had miraculously escaped encircle-ment; about cruel mass bombings of civilian trains and steamships; about the senseless death of children and women, who were trying to flee occupation along exposed roads and who were strafed by airplanes; and about German aerial attacks on first-aid stations and hospitals near the front.

With his candid talk, the commissar inspired our trust and confidence in him. Meeting or talking with him, everybody knew that he would not try to belittle them or chew them out, but instead would give them support and help them. The commissar knew how to listen and tried to understand—priceless qualities that, alas, not everyone possesses. His natural simplicity was felt not only in his speech but also in his self-control and his warm, sincere approach to people.

Our meetings with the commissar inspired us and gave us food for thought, and I came to understand that group leadership is a high art form. It seemed that this man was so steeped in goodness, but at the same time he fervently hated the fascists. In every meeting with us he stressed this hatred, and he sought to inspire the same hatred for the enemy in us. He supported his own thoughts with examples from the famous frontline journalists and war correspondents Ehrenburg, Sholokhov, Aleksei Tolstoi, and Konstantin Simonov. We understood that he did this because we were still green, and we still did not know the terrible enemy against whom quite soon we would be fighting.

I should also tell you about a discussion we had on the "Jewish question" one day in a political instruction class. In addition to the *politruk* [political instructor], the deputy commissar who was conducting the class, the commissar himself was present in the room. One of the Cossacks suddenly asked, "Why do the fascists hate the Jews, and why are they killing all of them?"

The *politruk* countered with a question of his own: "Where did you get this information?"

The cadet flushed, began to fidget at his desk, and answered evasively, "Everyone is saying it."

At that we could suddenly hear the menacing voice of the commissar: "You have no right to answer an officer of the Red Army in that way!" Then the commissar, more calmly, told us about Hitler's racist policies and about the role of anti-Semitism in the fascist plans for world conquest.

"The Hitlerites are murdering not only Jews," the commissar concluded. "They are also killing Russians, Belorussians, and Ukrainians. But first of all they are shooting the communists, Komsomol members, commissars, and military prisoners. You must be able to understand politics in order to know how to explain it to your soldiers."

Of all the meetings with the commissar, I recall one in particular. It occurred near the very end of our course of training at the school, and he was sharing with us his own understanding of the role of commanders in war. Everything he said related to us as future platoon leaders, and the entire company literally froze as the cadets listened closely to the commissar's every word:

"For a soldier, his officer is the constant and singular representative of the Motherland. The officer is the person closest to him at the front—in days of success, failures, and perhaps even in the hour of the soldier's death. By his own example, the officer is obliged to teach the soldier love for his Motherland, and this will be the main contribution to our eventual victory. In his own turn, the officer is responsible to the Motherland for the fate of the soldiers entrusted to him, for their upbringing and training, and for taking care of their physical and spiritual needs. To accomplish this is possible only on the basis of soldierly brotherhood—the inner connection between a commander and his subordinates. At the front, the primary concern of the commander is the soldier! Field Marshal Suvorov, who was once walking around his sleeping camp and encountered some sentries, asked them to sing and talk more quietly: 'Let the Russian heroes sleep a bit in peace.' Of course, the songs of the guards could in no way disturb the sleeping troops. But on the next day, the entire camp now knew that the general himself spoke in a whisper, in order not to bother the sleeping soldiers. That is how brotherhood is born. You must strive for this."

Someone asked, "What do you consider to be the most important aspect of a commander's character?"

"Honor," the commissar quickly replied. "Throughout history, in the Russian army, the commander's most sacred thing has been honor!"

Iurka and I gasped! Where was faith in the Party? In communism? Where was fealty to your military oath? For the commissar, it is honor! How the bulldoggish traits of our lieutenant, his attitude toward us, his students—tomorrow's leaders—diverged from what the commissar said! Incidentally, somewhere there was also another thought lurking: perhaps the way Artur treats us is Suvorov's famous dictum, put into practice: "The harder in training, the easier in battle." But no! Not the way Artur was doing it!

But the commissar had more to say on this subject: "An officer's honor—that is his high moral qualities and his loyalty to his oath. Willpower, character, and honor temper courage, and purify bravery—there is no leader without these things."

Later we figured out that these were the commissar's final parting words to us. Evidently, he already knew about our looming departure for the front.

Again, the "Jewish Question"

The conversation with the commissar on the "Jewish question" evidently did no good for the Cossacks in our platoon. A scandal occurred in the bathhouse. No matter how I tried to keep my manly dignity covered with both hands, this primitive ruse didn't work, and it all the more quickly excited the curiosity of Fonia, the most bullying of the Cossacks, who also happened to have the smallest genitals. One day, in the presence of the entire platoon, as we were getting dressed, in a loud voice he said sarcastically in my direction:

"Why are you hiding your cock? Everyone has already seen that you are a circumcised Jew."

I was flabbergasted, as I simply did not expect such vileness. Shurka saved me from the awkward situation.

"Fonia!" he bellowed, and then referred to my circumcision, "for such a historical outrage upon an infant, who now for you is like a bone in your throat, Boris's father was kicked out of the Party. As for you, you can display or hide your own . . . but all the same your filthy soul will forever be nothing but bullshit. Don't pester the cadet any more, you son-of-a-bitch. You got it!?"

Fonia was so shocked that he almost dropped his trousers. He looked sheepishly around at his buddies, seeking support. Not finding any, he lowered his head and let Shurka's insulting warning pass unchallenged. After this unpleasant incident, Zhenechka took to calling the Cossacks a bunch of hooligan robbers. And how else could you call them?

How many dirty tricks did they commit in the barracks! They urinated in other guys' boots, they hauled people off the toilets in the bathroom, they scattered bedding around, they committed petty thefts, they cut others' long johns into ribbons, and they disrupted everyone's sleep. Once every two weeks, a film was shown at the school club; if the Cossacks didn't like something on the screen, they would yell as if they were rabid, and bang their chairs. However strange it may seem, they got away with everything. The other cadets not only could not tolerate them, they despised them, and no one wanted to have anything to do with them. It was not acceptable in the army to complain to the command; this was an old army tradition. The "Cossack brotherhood" also tormented Lieutenant Artur himself, nicknaming him the "Estonian Jew." Everything they did was disgusting, antagonistic, and sad.

In just six months, the specialist school had labored to mold a strong officer from a nineteen-year old romantic dreamer and "intellectual," as the other cadets had characterized me. The school believed it would make me capable not only of handling the fates of other men but also of fulfilling unquestioningly the orders of my superiors. Did it succeed? Was I ready for this? Probably not. I remember an incident that in itself was not so important but that illuminates well my youthful "portrait."

It was a typical day of study. We were memorizing the Field Regulations. I was sitting in the last row, with Turgenev's "Spring Floods" on my lap, rather badly concealed from view by the worn out pages of the manual. Artur, noticing my feeble ruse, pounced upon me like a wild animal in one leap, grabbed my booklet, and, without even a glance at its covers, frenziedly thrust it into the stove, in which, crackling merrily, little pieces of firewood were burning. Stirred up by what I had been reading, detached from reality, and forgetting that an officer was standing in front of me, I blurted out like a little boy: "How dare you! You can punish me, but to burn a great Russian classic . . . !"

The lieutenant, cutting short my angry speech, commanded: "Rise! To attention! Two extra shifts of duty detail! The first for your 'great classic,' the second—for you!"

My classmates were holding their bellies in laughter; only Iurka, as always, remained calm.

When I think back on this story today, it seems amusing to me. But at the time, I didn't find it funny at all. My words were totally sincere; I couldn't understand the lieutenant's action, or the laughter of my comrades.

That evening I scrubbed and peeled potatoes and then washed the bathroom stalls. When I was done, I laid down exhausted on my bunk, with the day's events whirling in my head. Life is so complicated! I'm helpless in everything, and I don't measure up to the school's standards—what horror! Why have I not been able to step across the threshold of adulthood and become an adult? Who can help me? My commanders? No. Who then? We are living in an artificial world—a world of fantasies and illusions. We've learned beautiful phrases but haven't learned yet how to carry out that little bit that we know. Our brains are stuffed with quotations, while at the same time nine out of ten of these dogmas are incomprehensible, murky, or lies. Which are worthwhile, and which are not? Yes, I must stop being false before others and myself. How simple it all seems! But how do I do this? Let just a little time pass, and then we may understand—only the simplest, honorable acts determine the value of a man. Only I myself can and must help myself to become an adult.

How did I regard the lieutenant's action?—Was it really not understandable? The commander—that's authority, the soldier—an unquestioning subordinate. From ancient times to our own days, the military machine adheres to strict subordination.

2

Graduation
April–May 1942

A Mortarman without a Mortar

The oath. We prepared for it enthusiastically. We rehearsed the text of the oath endlessly. On the day of the ceremony, at noon, classes ended. In the dining hall, we were treated to excellent jellyrolls and an extra lump of sugar for our tea. Afterwards I signed the oath of loyalty to the Motherland. Of course, like everyone else, I walked proudly with the awareness of my mission. I understood: soon I would be going to the front.

Time passed, and the stress and pace of our classes intensified. Our free hour was cut each day by half. The number of hours spent on studying the Field Regulations and on parade drills was reduced. Everything was subordinated to combat training. Field exercises became more frequent. Several times a month, the company commander, Senior Lieutenant Koval'chuk, would take us into the field and play out certain combat situations with us. For example: you are waiting to attack, but the artillery preparation has not managed to suppress all the enemy's firing points; should the battalion attack, or should it wait for the enemy's complete destruction? Or: We're on the march, and suddenly German airplanes dive upon the column—what should you do? How should you act at a river crossing if time is short and the sapper unit has not yet come up? Where is it best to choose a position for your mortar platoon? What should you do if the enemy's tanks are advancing on the mortar battery? He presented us with many such unexpected situations and then would lay out alternative possible solutions. We had thirty seconds to ponder the situation and offer a decision. If after thirty seconds the answer he received was silence, he immediately would turn to the next man: "What is your decision?" Once he got the answer, he moved on to a new subject.

It was a useful and fascinating exercise; we had no doubt of that. Nevertheless, in everything we did, whatever scenarios we played out, however we conducted ourselves, taking one or another decision—a certain artificiality was present, far from real combat situations and operations. We were taught many bits of wisdom in field conditions, but these exercises had an abstract character, which became clear to us later when we were far from the training grounds.

Unfortunately, we also wasted a lot of time studying outdated weapons. For example, we thoroughly studied the 1930 model of the Tsarist-era 1896 Mosin-Nagant rifle, when the automatic gun had already begun to appear on the battlefield. At last, we also turned to studying the mortar. We examined the parts of a mortar and its assembly; we practiced setting the sights, and how to determine the range while conducting fire. But we pottered about with the company-level 50-mm M1941 mortar, which had no bipod and was too light to be of any use on the battlefield. We devoted very little time to the 82-mm mortar, not to mention the 120-mm mortar, which we didn't study at all prior to our graduation.

This sounds strange, but during our four months of study at the specialist school, not one of us fired a mortar a single time, even though we had been assigned to a mortar battalion. Our instructors probably planned to give us this chance at some point, but that time never came.

Scandal

One day we were led out for an extra session of target practice. After the practice, a *ChP* occurred. We were returning from target practice exhausted, hungry, and chilled to the bone. We had spent the whole day in frigid temperatures, and the march to the target range stretched four kilometers one way. Lieutenant Artur was moving in front of the platoon, strong, red-cheeked, his chin raised arrogantly. The intense cold was nothing to him! He was dressed in a fluffy fur hat and a beautiful white sheepskin coat, and his hands were in fur gloves. He proudly glanced from side to side as we moved down the street, sometimes bowing to acquaintances—just like a hussar! Women were stopping on the pavement to admire his display. Doubtlessly, he overheard one of the women exclaiming: "What a man! You can't miss with a man like that!"

Artur was literally bursting with pride and vanity. He had always wanted to be first in everything—naturally, at our expense. Now Artur was content—with himself and us, as we had done some excellent shooting on the target range. When we emerged onto the main street, he gave me a sharp order: "Sing!"

I began with his favorite song, and the platoon simultaneously took it up—together, we sang in full voice. Next, as always, followed two more songs—one about the "Wise, Dear, Beloved," the other about the artillerymen, to whom "Stalin Has Given an Order." We grew tired and fell silent; my own throat had become hoarse. But the lieutenant only called out again: "Sing!"

The platoon didn't respond. Artur became furious.

The command rang out, "Gas!" This meant we had to take out our gas masks and put them on. We all complied with the order. Then suddenly: "Double time, march! After me!"

Just try to run in a rubber mask, thickly coated with ice! At this moment, in fact, the scandal occurred. Approximately half the platoon took off running after our commander while the rest—the Cossacks, Iurka, Zhenechka, I, and a few other cadets—didn't budge from our spots. At that moment our spirits had totally collapsed.

We stood for a while and had a smoke. The Cossacks were cursing the "Estonian Jew" for all they were worth. At a slow pace, we headed back for the school, Iurka in the lead.

When we approached the school entrance, we saw Lieutenant Artur waiting for us by the gate, nervously glancing at his watch. We came to attention at his command and, after filling our ears with a stream of foul language, he ordered: "To the parade ground! Three complete circuits! Double time, march!"

We dutifully obeyed. But having completed our second lap around the parade ground, our tongues were hanging out, while the grumbling in our stomachs depressingly announced that at that time, the rest of our platoon was finishing their meals. After the third trip around, none of us were thinking about food any longer—we were all nauseated and upset and wanted only to get back to the barracks and collapse onto our bunks.

The situation in the platoon was strained. Little scraps of conversation were barely audible:

"What shall we do with a snake like that at the front?"

"I'll finish him off in the very first battle!"

We See a Newsreel

Twice a month, with the permission of the battalion commander, after dinner I would go to the school's club for chorus rehearsal. We were preparing a large program for the First of May ceremony. But one Saturday instead of rehearsing, we watched a documentary film at the club entitled, *The Destruction of the Germans at the Gates of Moscow.*

The film was masterful. For the first time, I saw the enemy's face. They were German prisoners. Hordes of prisoners! Sequences of the film lingered on the individual faces and figures of the weakened men. Some of them were wrapped in shawls above their overcoats; they all were without gloves or winter clothing, with their hands stuck deeply into their pockets, and in worn out, torn footgear, even in women's high galoshes. They danced around a little in the hard frost, and from time to time they took their hands out of their pockets to wipe their noses or rub their ears.

New scenes: mountains of abandoned equipment! Ice-coated tanks, trucks and wagons, and artillery pieces, all stuck in the snow or half-buried in snowdrifts. It was clear that the German command had not prepared any winter-formula fuel for the army, or delivered any winter clothing. They had obviously counted upon the blitzkrieg to bring them complete success over the Red Army before winter. But it didn't happen! One of the cadets exclaimed: "If only we could show Hitler this film! Let him see how his valiant Aryans are beating a hasty retreat!"

After the war, it became known that Hitler had seen this newsreel. One can only imagine what feelings the Führer and his generals had as they watched the footage!

That night in the barracks we discussed what we had seen. We started swapping anecdotes about Hitler. I recall one of them:

"Abram, what was it that you wished for Hitler?"

"That Hitler would become an electric light bulb! In the day, he'd be hanging, and at night, he'd still have to burn!

The barracks exploded in laughter.

A Conversation with Iurka

It was possible to visit the school's library only once every two weeks. On my next visit to the library I failed to bring back the book I had borrowed, and I apologized to Zina: I had given the book to my comrades to read. On my third visit to the library, I came with Iurka. I returned Vinogradov's book, *Three Colors of Time,* and asked for Lermontov. Iurka was interested in the plays of Gorky:

"Lucky Muscovites! In the capital, it seems they're always staging a play of Gorky's somewhere. But Cheliabinsk—it's provincial! We like Ostrovsky better."

"I've never seen a Gorky play in my life," I replied, trying to calm Iurka, "and I'm not very interested in seeing one."

Zina burst out laughing: "Oh, guys, I can see that you're just spinning your wheels, and that you have a special relationship with books."

When we left the library, Iurka told me teasingly, "You, brother, have conquered the heart of a senior sergeant! Did you see the way she looks at you? Like she's looking at an icon! Consider yourself lucky that such a lovely nugget got lost in Siberia."

"Hmmm, well . . . it seems that way to you," I interjected.

"Did you like the Vinogradov?" Iurka asked.

"Quite a bit."

"Did you understand why the book is called *Three Colors of Time*?"

"The white color is the color of French kings and aristocrats; we've known this since our childhood from reading *The Three Musketeers.* Red, clearly, is the color of blood, and it symbolizes the bloody revolution. But black . . . ," I trailed off.

"Aha, that means you didn't read the foreword. There is an explanation there," Iurka shot back.

"That was a blow below the belt," I protested.

"Agreed. The black color—that is the color of the clergy. Stendhal didn't have much respect for religion," Iurka explained.

"You've arranged an exam for me and, evidently, slapped me with a 'D,'" I said.

"Go on, we're all novices! Without the war, likely, we'd all remain that way for a long time. Have you ever read the Bible?" Iurka asked unexpectedly.

"I've never read it, and never even seen one," I replied.

"Pity, it's a book on an ecumenical scale. Serious reading. I, honestly, haven't read even half of it, but I still managed to understand a thing or two."

"Tell me about them!" I implored.

I didn't get a response.

"Iurka, are you a believer?" I gently inquired.

"No, that's not for me," Iurka replied. "But still, no one should doubt the biblical commandments: don't kill, don't steal, love your neighbor as you do yourself, and do no evil. But all the same, people obviously kill, steal, and rob. In his *Bygone Days and Thoughts*, Hertzen says that in understanding life, only thinking for oneself will help, " Iurka started to explain.

I interrupted him, "Will the war end this year? Stalin promises."

"Do you believe it?" Iurka replied with his own question.

"I believe it. Iurka, I'm so happy that we met," I finished.

We were approaching the doors to the barracks.

After this conversation, I felt out of sorts for several days. The thought tormented me: Why do I know so little? Why now, when I've almost reached twenty years of age, do I still not know how to think for myself? I recalled the reunion with my father on that day, 19 December 1939, when he returned home from prison. He didn't want to let me go from his embrace, kissed me, and cried and cried, bitterly and for a long time. I struggled free from his embrace and rushed to his tiny bookshelf, on which only a few books remained. I grabbed one book, a little more thick than the others, and happily, joyfully (as much as I could be) extended it to Papa: "Here! I've prepared a gift for you," confident that this book would bring him happiness. He read the title, *A Short Course History of the VKP(b)* [VKP(b) stands for All-Union Communist Party (Bolshevik)], and sighing, set the book to one side. Papa was always delicate; he remained silent, and on account of my gift, only began to cry again.

Before my departure for the army, father never once told me about his experiences in prison. Perhaps he feared for me, or he himself had not fully freed himself from fear. His entire generation had been struck by fear.

Zina's Revelation

On the next authorized day, I headed off for the library alone, without Iurka, as he couldn't come along. At the doors I met an annoyance; a sign was hanging on them: "Health Day." I gave the door a try anyway, and it opened for me. Zina was sitting, as always, behind her little desk, but wearing a black gown over her uniform. We exchanged glances, and I understood that she was happy, that she had been waiting for me. Confused, I began to excuse myself, then to express my gratitude for the reception even though the library was closed, and somehow in the process I dared to touch her arm. I was agitated with emotions. Zina quietly looked me in the eye. Embarrassed, I quickly thought of something to say:

"Zina, what do you think, why don't they let us, the cadets, have books on the history of warfare? Is a platoon commander really not supposed to know how Russian generals have been victorious in the past?

She kept looking at me silently. I plunged on:

"I'm not talking about materials on the current war. Not at all! I just need to know what explains the successes of the German armies in Poland and in France! There is also no literature whatsoever on the destruction of the Germans in front of Moscow. Our superior officers also avoid discussions, they teach us in one voice: 'Do as I do!'"

She at last spoke up, but what she had to say caused my knees to quake, while my heart began pounding from fear:

"You praised the number of books in the library. Well then! They are only pitiful remnants. I began working here in 1938. At that time, the school's head, a brigade commander, began coming to the library three times a day, and he'd lock the door behind him. He would grab book after book off the shelves and order, "This one—into the stove! This one—take it out of general circulation and do not loan it to anyone without my personal permission!"

Her words startled me. Coming slightly to my senses, I interjected and exclaimed, "Did they burn even Frunze?"

"Even Frunze," Zina answered. "And then something happened that was unimaginable: they sent bundles of books, by inventory, to the censors. Next we began regularly to receive whole lists of banned books. That's how, very quickly, our shelves emptied, upon which formerly manuals written by our famous generals and histories, translated from the German and English languages, had stood in all their glory. Before this purge, textbooks and manuals on the art of warfare, strategy, tactics, and history had occupied thirty-six shelves in this library. But by the start of the war, all thirty-six shelves were occupied by *The Short Course History of the VKP(b)*, several books by the Chief of the General Staff Shaposhnikov, and Voroshilov's work, *Stalin and the Red Army*. And then, around the same time, one night they arrested the school's entire command. Overnight, platoon commanders became company commanders, company commanders were promoted in turn, and so on. And you ask about manuals! Where can one find any now? There are not any authors, nor any textbooks. From that world no one has yet returned. Not only people, but books as well. There you have it, Cadet."

"You said something about *Stalin and the Red Army*. We are required to read it."

"Who is requiring it?" Zina asked.

"The *politruk*."

"And have you read it?" Zina inquired.

"Not yet. But there is nowhere I can go where I can read it. The *politruk* promised to check."

I understood that our conversation was quite dangerous, and I wondered how she could be so candid when we were still scarcely acquainted with each other. Of course, what she had said was interesting, as I didn't know about the destruction of the regular army officers, who were all likely communists, and the school's founders. I didn't know about the destroyed books and the censor's prohibitions. And our superiors! Smatterers?

Zina gazed at me, trying to assess my reaction, while I nervously and quietly started backing toward the doors, forgetting even to take the book I had requested from her desk.

"There, what a daredevil you are! What are you afraid of? The truth! And I understood that you didn't know Stendhal." Her sharp, insulting words flew after me, and I swallowed them all with bitterness.

I returned to the barracks in confusion, upset, tormenting myself with her final words: Why, why did I come up with my idiotic questions? And Zina! Obviously, for a long time her courageous heart has been seeking a way out. What a bright young woman! Direct, and intolerant of evil. People don't love women like her, and they strive to get rid of them. Verily, "Youth is a time of courage."

Suddenly I recalled a little episode when I had offended my mother. It had been an awkward moment. When I was little we were living in the Ukraine, in the city of Korosten. My father was working there as a deputy of the chairman of the City Executive Committee. At the time, Korosten was becoming modernized, and my father did a lot for this little Ukrainian city. He oversaw the construction of much new housing, a new power station, several schools, a theater, and a bathhouse, as well as the paving of the city's main streets. During the war the Germans, upon entering the city, not only killed all the Jews but also destroyed the finest buildings.

We were living then in one of the two-story apartment buildings. Our neighbor was a doctor who worked in the local hospital. I became friends with his son, who was my age. We were only about five or six then. This little boy's name was Grisha. On New Year's Day, he invited me to come see his splendid Christmas tree. After the New Year's celebration, I went home in tears and asked Mama: "Why did Grisha get a Christmas tree, and not me?" Mama tried to soothe me and explained everything to me in the following words: "Your father is a communist, and therefore we don't put up Christmas trees. 'Communist' is the loftiest and proudest title a man can have!"

Many years passed. When father was arrested in 1937, I reminded Mama of that childhood Christmas tree and our conversation. "How can it be," I asked, "that communists aren't permitted to have Christmas trees, but they allow them to sit in prison for nothing? There's the 'loftiest and proudest title a man can have' for you." Mama burst into tears. I began to comfort her and deeply regretted what I had just said.

After Zina's revelations, I never returned to the library, not a single time. Not because I resented Zina, or because I was afraid for myself. I was frightened for her. I could not forget my father's terrible sobbing after his return from the gulag. I won't be able to forget them for the rest of my life.

The Order!

At the beginning of May, when the Siberian sun was shining uncommonly brightly and the air smelled of spring, a surprise was waiting for all of us.

On that day, as we usually did, we began to assemble after breakfast to head to target practice. Suddenly, a command rang out: "Dismissed! Fall in on the parade ground!"

The entire school command appeared. The school commandant, a colonel, was walking at the head of the group. He stopped in front of our assembled ranks, and without beating around the bush, he addressed the formation:

"Comrade cadets! I have received an order to send you urgently to the front. We are sending the finest battalion, and we are confident that the Tiumen cadets will not disgrace the honor of the school. After your very first battle, you will all receive your officer's rank."

There were a few more parting words, and then we returned to our barracks. Someone uttered, "There's a nice piece of news for you!" The cadets were quiet. We were waiting for orders, what to do next. What would happen next? When? Where will they send us?

Zina Wants to Save Me

That evening, a man on duty walked up to me: "Some sort of girl in military uniform is calling for you on the staircase."

It was not difficult to guess who it was.

Zina was waiting for me. I recognized her only with difficulty. She was pale, with sad eyes, and her ever-present, somewhat ironical but happy smile had disappeared. I immediately understood that she was very agitated by something.

"We don't have much time," Zina began.—"I need to tell you something important. Allow me to speak with the school commandant. They'll leave you here and transfer you to a different battalion that isn't being sent to the front. You will finish your schooling normally, and you will go to war not as a common soldier but as a junior lieutenant."

So that's what it was!

"Thank you, thank you," I repeated, but I was already shaking my head negatively.

"You understand, Cadet, what will happen to you at the front? You must know it: a soldier in the front lines lives only a week, but on the attack—only a day or two, no matter if he's a hero."

I asked sharply, "Really, should a platoon commander live any longer?"

"I don't know," Zina replied, "but an officer always has at least a minimum choice, while the soldier in the ranks has no choice at all. I beseech you, let me speak on your behalf. I don't think they'll refuse me. You most likely don't know that they've already selected a few cadets from your battalion, pupils with gold medals, to stay and finish the full course of study."

"But I'm a bad student in school," I replied.—"If you don't believe it, check my record. Again, don't do it. We've just given our oath! What will my comrades think of me?"

"Understand me, Cadet," Zina tenderly said, paying no attention to my words, "I don't want you to die. Do you understand? Think of your mother."

"I understand." I turned sour, and my mood changed. I had become precious to this girl somehow, yet we had met so few times. Everything was so unexpected, why was she so concerned about me, who was I to her?

Zina looked at me frighteningly and waited for an answer, but I was silent. Suddenly she gave a sob and burst into tears: "Fool! Fool!"—and then she turned sharply and fled down the staircase.

I lowered my head. Why was everything so absurd? She is so sweet, so good. Perhaps this was our last meeting. We didn't even say good-bye!

Nevertheless, I saw Zina one more time, when the school staff and command was seeing us off.

A Meeting with Mama

Once I found out about our impending assignment to the front, I sent my Mama a telegram, informing her of the news in coded language through a superficially innocent text. She understood everything and immediately came to see me. She took a room not far from the school, made a request to Koval'chuk to see me, and my company commander gave me twenty-four hours leave from the school.

During this short time, which we spent together, a sea of motherly affection enveloped me. However, in response I carried on about some nonsense, like how they were promising us an officer's rank after our very first battle, and how much they would pay us then.

Did I understand my mother that day? She, likely, was thinking about something completely different—whether or not her son would still be alive after this very first battle, about which he was speaking so flippantly. She boiled a full bucket of water and gave me a full bath in a deep washtub, like I was a small child. Then she dressed me in clean, homemade underclothing; kissed my face, my hands, and my feet; and she was crying, probably grieving—was this to be our last meeting?

Mama's arrival brought back memories of Natasha in my mind. Natasha wound up in Kyshtym coincidentally, together with a friend from Kiev. She was teaching mathematics at the railroad school. She was a fairly talented painter. Mama told me that when I left for the army, Natasha painted a large portrait of me from a photograph and gave it to her as a gift.

We both knew Natasha's dramatic story. On the first day of the war, German Junkers in the course of just a few minutes turned the airfield where Natasha's pilot-husband was serving into a graveyard of people and planes. Her husband had been killed, and all the women and children of the flight staff were sent to Kiev.

When we became acquainted, Natasha was pregnant. Mama had extended to her an offer to move from the dormitory where Natasha was living into our house. Natasha expressed her appreciation, but declined. Parting, I told her, "If I survive, I will adopt your child."

"My prince!" Natasha laughed. "Thank you for your kindness and sincerity. If we live, we'll see. The war will not end soon; you still don't know what it is. You don't understand that now you don't belong to yourself—now, Boren'ka, you are a soldier."

Natasha's words were prophetic; I never saw her again.

Mama told me that several acquaintances had already had funerals. She very much wanted to stay and see me off, but I asked her to go home. When she was leaving, they gave us permission to say good-bye.

Farewell, School!

We all have our own lives. But there are events when a fateful moment of your personal life turns out to be the same for many others at the same time. Then not only the time and the place of event unify the people, but a common feeling as well—a single rush, strengthened many times over—and this leaves indelible traces in the mind and soul of a person. Such an event for us cadets was our final evening before our departure for the front.

The entire battalion gathered at the school club. Officers arrived. A broad banner decorated the stage: "Farewell, school! Thank you!" Before the ceremony we had all bathed, put on clean underclothing, and exchanged our worn-out tunics, trousers, and boots for everything new. We had a tasty lunch and dinner. Our skillful cook treated us on our parting with appetizing rolls. We all wrote letters home, then packed our things for the road.

I looked at the happy faces of the other cadets and didn't see any troubling presentiments on any of them. Their faces shined with the ardor of high patriotic feelings. We dreamed of heroic deeds, each man ready to throw himself on the embrasure of an enemy pillbox. We dreamed of becoming officers.

It was a marvelous evening. We read poems, we sang, we played songs on the piano, the guitar, and the mandolin. There was no rejection of anyone who wanted to go up onto the stage and perform. If you will, for the first time there was relaxation in the conduct of the cadets.

I have kept in my memory forever that last evening at the school. Especially its final minutes, when the entire battalion, all 600 cadets, rose from their chairs and started singing to the accompaniment of the band, "Arise, enormous country, arise for the fateful battle. . . ."

I cannot forget the day of our departure either. Everything proceeded ceremonially and with enthusiasm. In a column of fours, we marched shoulder to shoulder across the parade ground, giving salute to the school's banners, as we headed for the school's gates to leave it forever.

For some reason, we had to stand a long time in front of the gates, waiting for them to open. And that is when I saw Zina. She approached the column, spotted me, and not hiding her feelings, came up to me, embraced me, and kissed me firmly. Imperceptibly, she slipped a piece of paper to me with her address, and very quietly said: "May God spare you, Cadet. Forgive my rudeness. I will be praying for you. When you reach the front, write me."

A lump was in my throat—from surprise, emotions, and tenderness, from my recognition of the significance of this minute.

"Thank you . . . for everything! . . . I will read Stendhal without fail. I remembered: 'Youth is a time of courage.' I will try . . . my thanks to you!" I hugged her.

The guys gave a moan but remained quiet, for it wasn't the right time for ribald banter.

I repeat even today: Thank you, dear Zina!

The gates opened wide. Before I left, I turned around once more, looking back through the column of students. Zina was nowhere in sight. When the column had fully entered the street, Fonia nevertheless couldn't restrain himself and mumbled something like, "Even a beast chases after a bitch." The swine. None of the students offered him any support.

The column moved along the streets of Tiumen. Up ahead, a band was playing with drums and horns. Almost all the school's officers came to see us off, and a few went all the way to the train station with us. Each one wished us to become officers as soon as possible and had some unbelievably warm, sincere, and kind words for us.

At the station, we found the train with its coach cars waiting for us, ready for departure. We were hoping that Lieutenant Artur would be coming along with us to the front, that the school would want to get rid of him. But it didn't happen. He accompanied us to our coach car, but there he stopped, shook everyone's hand, and offered the wish that we would all become heroes. When the train started to move, the cadets made some noises: "What a snake! They've left him to ruin more new recruits. A man like him shouldn't be allowed to live among people...."

The first May days of 1942. The train gathered speed. Six hundred 18- and 19-year-old fellows—a battalion of cadets from the Tiumen Infantry Specialist School, were heading west in order to do battle with the enemy.

3

Notes on My Way to the Front
May 1942

On the Train

9 May. The third day en route. We passed through Sverdlovsk. We had a four-hour delay at the station there. While we waited, we ate our fill—whenever someone asked for more, he received it. I sent Mama a telegram. There were many refugees from Moscow at the railway station. I managed to have a chat with a few of them. They had left Moscow in the alarming days of October 1941, and now they weren't allowed to return. People without accommodations, without food, without any knowledge of how they were going to get by, were sending telegrams to the government, still without any effect.

Our *eshelon* [troop train] consisted of twenty-five freight cars, with 25–30 cadets in each. Directly behind the locomotive were the staff car and an open platform car mounting antiaircraft guns. There was another antiaircraft platform car at the end of the train. The commissariat and medical station were in the middle of the train. Most likely, this is how they were now organizing all the military trains, with consideration for the fearful experiences of 1941.

Back at the school, they had given us all dry rations to last for five days. We gobbled it all down in just three days.

The *eshelon* seems to be flying down the track directly toward its destination, stopping only briefly at the smaller stations. Everybody kept asking the same question: what's the rush, why weren't they giving us a chance to finish our full course of training? Evidently the Germans had delivered a strong blow somewhere, and someone now needed our help. Even though we were still green soldiers, for some reason we were regarded as useful for the war.

11 May. Izhevsk. The fifth day on our journey. Where were they taking us? The command remained silent—it was a military secret. I climbed up onto the "pigeon-roost," as we called the upper shelf in the freight car that served as our bunks, and turned myself over to reminiscences. My mind was full of images of the past; they were firmly in place and, obviously, would not soon fade away.

Of course, there was the memory of the most joyful of my recent events—Mama's arrival in Tiumen. But why, why did I persuade her to leave? I mentally thanked the company commander, who gave me leave to say good-bye. . . . Meetings with Zina—sometimes bright and happy, sometimes melancholy. How she could laugh! I had felt like shouting, "How wonderful you are!" but I had held my tongue, trying to find more elevated, noble words, or I had always mumbled something boring and ordinary. What a jerk I am! . . . Was she really right? Is it really true that a soldier on the front lines lives only a week?

From "the pit" [a theatrical reference], voices called out, asking me to sing something from before the war. Everyone knew that I loved the prewar songs more than the others. I decided to joke a little, and in a familiar melody I started singing with inspiration, like in our Young Pioneer days, something no one expected: the Young Pioneer song, "Always forward, shoulder to shoulder, we march in relief of Il'ich [Lenin]. . . ." A few of the guys laughed, while a few others even took up the song. I then sang "Katiusha" and a few other songs, while everyone eagerly joined in. After me, Sasha sang and played on his recently returned guitar. These impromptu concerts became almost a daily tradition, right up to our arrival at the front.

I was not a professional singer, but nonetheless, all the officers at our school recognized me as the best singer at the school. I must have inherited my voice from my grandfather, my mother's father. He worked as a lithographer and sang in his synagogue's choir in Zhitomir'. Later he became the synagogue's cantor; Mama spoke of him often.

12 May. Agryz. The sixth day of our journey west. We had a short delay. The students spent entire days playing cards to pass the time. Half of the conversations, if not more, were about food and the best way to fill one's belly. The rest of the conversations were about women. In six days we have been fed a warm meal only once. Along the way, dry rations are passed to us: sour kissel [a jellylike dish], dried crusts of bread, a little sugar, dried fish, and *makhorki* [crude tobacco]. The lads smoke almost continuously. They curse the command. In the evening, close to night, they start swapping stories again.

"Why does everyone split their guts laughing at these stories? They're just filthy stories," I addressed to Iurka one day, who was lying next to me on the upper berth. "Always after hearing them, you just feel worse."

"Precisely," Iurka agreed, "so much filth that you can't clean it off. 'Do as I do,' that's their motto: don't pay them any attention; let the vulgar people have their laugh."

Then Iurka asked unexpectedly, "Tell me, do you have your own motto, which you always strive to follow?"

"I do," I replied. "It is 'Do the right thing.' And you?"

"Mine is 'Actions speak louder than words.'"

"All the same, Iurka, where do you think they're taking us? After all, you're the smartest guy in the company, everybody thinks so."

"Most likely to the south. You'll see, we'll reach central Russia, and then the freight train will take a turn to the south. Another course is also possible: Stalin—with Zhukov's help!—has swept the Germans away from Moscow, and now he's decided to free Leningrad from its blockade. As soon as we get to Moscow, we'll receive our weapons, climb into planes, and within just a few hours go into battle."

"Hmmm, that just sounds like Jules Verne."

Paying no attention to my comment, Iurka began, as always, to play through the scenarios: "We've left out two *fronts* [troop formations roughly comparable to a British or American army group]: the Kalinin Front and the Western Front. And perhaps anything's possible, Zhukov needs us. He's driven the Germans back from Moscow, and he's thought to drive them back farther—all the way to Berlin, and Stalin supports the idea. The press, it is true, calls these two *fronts* 'the most quiet.' The dubious cliché 'battles of local significance' calls to mind Remarque's situation. Have you read *All Quiet on the Western Front*?"

I nodded: "A terrible affair! Do you really think something similar awaits us as well?"

"I doubt it," Iurka pensively replied.

"Why?" I asked. "War is war, and no one should expect any mercy."

"Here you are right," Iurka agreed. "In the autumn of 1941, back home in the Urals, they began to deliver the severely wounded, who had escaped encirclement by some miracle. They sent those of us who had just finished school to work for a month in a local hospital. While there, I saw and heard so much, I can't for the life of me tell you all of it! But all the same I longed to go to the front, to take revenge for it all. Whoever he is, the common soldier is the hero of our times. What these people experienced in the first days of fighting can't be compared to what Remarque's heroes went through. Back then, in the First World War, the infantry ruled the battlefield, and in attack and counterattack men stuck bayonets into each other's bellies. But not today. It's much more terrible! Bombing raids by airplanes, powerful artillery . . ."

"And your favorite, Zhukov, commands it all!" I interrupted.

"Why my favorite? Stalin thinks highly of him. Zhukov is a powerful general; he's already saved Moscow and Leningrad. Everybody considers him to be a great general; not only we, but the entire world!"

"What about Kutuzov?"

"Well, back then war was different, it's hard to compare. I once counted them up; Napoleon made it all the way to Moscow from the Neman River in just a few days. It's hard to believe! The Frenchmen marched on foot, more than 400,000 strong, while only the cavalry, officers, and generals rode on horseback. But they wound up at the gates of Moscow faster than the German tanks!"

"I know why. It's because Kutuzov was tricking Napoleon, and prior to Borodino he offered no real fight. But we, from the very first day, although we were retreating, fought to the last man; Smolensk alone, for whatever it's worth, held up the Germans for two months."

Night, the clicking of the wheels . . . it seems we are falling asleep. . . . But I am tossing and turning, again these questions, I can't seem in any way to brush them off: why does Iurka know more than me, why can he think more deeply and independently, why is he more educated than me? . . .

I never received any systematic education. But today I understand why. We spent all my school years, Mama and I, following my father around, as we said in the 1930s, "Wherever the Party sends you." This was a time of great changes in the life of the country, and education was changing as well. Educational programs changed endlessly, Russian schools were turned into Ukrainian schools, and vice versa. Moreover, I was a regular loafer—soccer in the summer and skating in the winter took up more of my time than homework and spelling. I studied "whatever and however." Yet Papa had no time for me: he was building communism. My Mama looked after me—my kind angel. She tried to find tutors for me in music and in the German language. At the time it was simple to find one, as remnants of the old Russian intelligentsia still remained. These people were living badly, timidly, often without work or a piece of bread. Only in 1937 did the government graciously authorize to accept them for work again. Do I regret today that I let slip both music and German? Very much! Probably, the excessive indulgence of my parents played its own role, their inability to convince me or even to force me to study, as I should, to sit at the piano, to learn another language. Or perhaps it was my own fault, my inner resistance to any kind of pressure. Did my parents understand this? From my childhood days to the very present, it seems to me that there is someone else living inside me, someone who constantly reproaches me, who doesn't want to understand my actions or me. Perhaps, this inner "pest" is the real reason for the doubts and the lack of confidence that have haunted me from my childhood? To this day, I don't know how to rid myself of them.

14 May. Kazan'. The eighth day of our trip. We have crossed the mighty Volga. We encountered unusual trains more often—transporting entire factories to the east from central Russia; their workers sleep directly on the platform cars next to their machinery and machine tools.

We had stuffed our bellies with pea soup. Get the gas masks ready!

It was my turn to go for water. I draped more than a dozen canteens over my shoulders and quickly make my way to the taps of the pump-house. Suddenly I heard a familiar voice behind my back. Who would think it—Iulik

Gerts! He had also come for water. I waited for him, and we chatted a little. Iulik, as always, mockingly said: "That they've shoved us out prematurely and sent us to the front is also a thought, not without sense. For this they will one day build the grandest monument to us, the Tiumen cadets!"

I was indignant: "I don't understand what you're talking about. You never say what you're really thinking. I believe in victory! I also believe in our eventual return!"

"Optimist. I envy you. You can't even imagine what's waiting for us."

"As if they've given you an announcement," I retorted. "Okay, don't croak about it."

But Iulik wouldn't be Iulik if he didn't have a little joke upon parting: "To our meeting in the next world!"

16 May. We completed our tenth day on our trek. It was night. I couldn't sleep because thoughts were weighing on my mind. Iurka also wasn't sleeping, so we started up a conversation.

"It's only been ten days, and already no one even thinks about the school," I started.

"What's there to think about?" Iurka dryly retorted.

"This and that. The barracks . . ."

"Don't speak about the barracks!" Iurka suddenly exclaimed. "It was nothing but a collection of card players and petty thieves. Yet we're going into battle with them! They're going to rob from their own, even the dead!"

"Iurka, don't be so intolerant. Of course, a barracks is a barracks, and no one will argue with that; at home, understandably, it is more comfortable. But at the school, they uncovered your staff capabilities, which you didn't even suspect you had.

"Let's not argue. The front will judge us. Just know that I am not a military man; I cannot live without freedom of choice, while in the army what choice is there? Left face, right face, forward! Now the war—that is a completely different business. I'll fight honorably. But you must understand that if ability to command depends only on the ability to obey, from such an officer you will get only an executive, never a leader!"

"But, Iurka, not everyone is capable of becoming a leader. And at the front, I only want for the man next to me to be an experienced fellow, someone who knows his stuff—but according to you, he'll be just an executive."

"Here you're right. But someone, after all, must take responsibility upon himself and give the orders upon which the outcome of the battle will depend."

"But Iurka, you're becoming quite the maximalist."

The conversation irritated me, but it also led me to reflect upon my time at the school and suggested several positive thoughts about it. I decided to jot them down then and there, so I wouldn't forget them. Here is what I wrote:

An Ode to the Barracks

Oh, barracks!

The first meeting with you didn't bring me happiness. It took more than a day for me to become accustomed to you and learn to appreciate what you became in my life.

One hundred and thirty two days we spent under your arches!

You united us, urchins, into a migrating flock, and helped us bear, as much as you knew how, the burden of your stern life. You made us stronger! You rid us of many youthful illusions! You helped us more easily complete the sharp turn from our previous, carefree life to the new, far from sweet army service. You introduced us to adult life.

You have made us rougher, more distrustful, and, perhaps—more heartless. This is true. But that's not all!

You gave us new comrades! Your brotherhood, Oh, barracks, extended us a helping hand and helped us survive! You handed us the Field Regulation —our first soldier's primer. You tried with all your might to teach us! With you we learned the rudiments of service and the difficult military science!

Oh, barracks! We often curse you, and not in vain! You were painful and wretched—we counted days down to the minute, when at last we could part from you! When we could forget the stench of male sweat! The unbearable nightly snoring! When we could rid ourselves of the stink of fetid foot-wraps! And the off-color jokes! The nasty anecdotes! The loathsome acts, which went far beyond the limits of decency! They didn't adorn our existence, or make us any more fond of you. Yes, barracks! In one voice, we were ready to say farewell to you! At any price! Even if it meant immediate dispatch to the front! Even if it meant "a hero's death!"

But you, barracks, didn't let go of us, you held onto us tenaciously—you taught us and tempered us.

Now the ORDER has arrived! In response, you ceremonially graduated us. We're going to the front!

"We're from the same barracks!"—these simple words have become our common students' motto. Together we shall go into battle!

I'm confident that if my fellow students had read these lines, the majority of them would have agreed with me. No one could dissuade me from them. I myself, to this very day, despite everything, have kept a pleasant memory of those times.

Not then, or later, did I reread what I had written that night on the train. My ode, as were all my travel notes, which I am reproducing here from memory, were shortly later consumed by fire. How this happened, I must still tell you.

17 May. The eleventh day of travel. Arzamas. We passed through Kanysh and Sergach. In both places we stopped only briefly.

Discussions of the front subsided. No one showed any more interest in where we were being taken. If one of us tried to start up a conversation on this subject, everyone else tried to avoid it. The nearer we drew to the front, the more frequently people were withdrawing into themselves. We stopped giving voice to our thoughts or inner worries. Likely, we didn't want to think about death; it is better to ponder life, as it is easier.

The usual raid on a station market occurred. Such raids had already become a regular practice. Barely does the train reduce its speed when the strongest, most agile, most brazen men hop from the cars and "storm" the women, who are selling goods and food. At first they paid fair prices for the items. When the money ran out, and this happened quite quickly, they switched to bartering: a pair of socks for twenty potatoes; an undershirt for a jar of pickled cucumbers; new, clean foot-wraps and a piece of soap in exchange for a bottle of milk. The closer we came to central Russia, the more wretched the little station bazaars looked. But the raids continued. Gifts from home went for exchange: mittens, tobacco pouches, needles and thread, handkerchiefs, writing paper, pencils, embroidered towels, or salt, which had been squirreled away from the school's dining hall.

When items for trade ran out, the raids took on a brutal character: by deception and force the students took food from the old women and ran away, the women left standing in mute horror, not understanding how such a thing could happen.

On this day, Zhenechka tried to stop the plunderers. The scandal happened before a stop. Four of the cadets, having grabbed some empty bags, were making their way toward the car's doors. Zhenechka blocked their way with his scrawny figure. He stood silently, with his arms crossed over his chest. The group of raiders at first didn't understand what was happening.

"Cadet Evlev, don't make a Christ of yourself, we've seen such before!"

Zhenechka didn't budge. The train began slowing quickly for the stop. The raiders became enraged:

"Get out of the way, Leningrader, don't get yourself into trouble!"

Zhenia didn't react.

Then they decided to move him out of the way by force. One of the four gave Zhenechka an uppercut to the chin, causing his teeth to slam together with an audible clack. Zhenechka didn't react to the blow but simply stepped away from the doors and said: "Men like you, the people of Leningrad have crushed like rats. People are dying there from starvation, but they haven't stooped to robbery."

In response, crude laughter and cruel words rang out: "Don't try and put us down, you little storyteller."

The train came to a stop. Three of the students, throwing open the doors, took off for the station. One—the one who threw the punch—lingered behind.

Zhenechka lay down on the berth and started to sob. The fellow who remained behind walked up to him and tried to soothe him: "I'm sorry, friend, the devil must have gotten into me. We are, after all, from the same barracks."

Usually, it was impossible not to recognize Zhenechka's handsome face, but not now, when it was dissolving into tears. His looks were distorted into an agonizing grimace, his face showing not insult but the deepest bitterness of suffering, and I thought to myself: such people should live forever, for they rise up to defend good from evil. Iurka and I went over and took Zenechka away with us to where we'd been sitting; we sat down closely together, and he stayed with us.

Meanwhile, an ugly event occurred at the little station marketplace. The raiding cadets knocked a frail old woman off her feet. Almost lifelessly, she fell in a swoon to the ground, while two of her jugs of spring water, which she had brought from her village, tipped over and rolled off to the side, spilling out their contents. The plunderers almost trampled the woman. It turned out that she considered this water holy, and she was giving free drinks to the Red Army men who were headed for the front on the passing trains. "The Huns!" Iurka said later on account of what happened.

Looking away from Zhenechka, Iurka and I tried to lighten the scene and joked around a little, recalling funny stories from our childhood and school pranks. Zhenechka, it seemed, was sleeping. Actually, he was lying with his eyes closed and listening to us. Then suddenly he spoke up: "Good heavens, how I envy you, how much you love life! You've probably grown devilishly sick of me. Forgive me. You're bored with my constant preaching and me. I'm not just talking about now, but back in school as well . . ."

"Don't say such things, Zhenechka," I objected.

"No, no, don't speak; I know what I am. Well, you've never once asked me to tell you about the blockade. I'll tell you now. For a month, I worked in a hospital. We fed the wounded crumbs, cooked in boiling water. Nobody grumbled. It was cold, October, and we lacked firewood. Dystrophy and scurvy were rampant. Every morning, we carried the dead out of the ward. Some people couldn't stand it and lost their minds. Everybody dreamed of food. I did too. Every summer, our mother used to take my sister and me to the sea, and I had an unusual dream: it was as if I was in the Crimea, and I'm seeing loads of all kinds of fruit—fragrant peaches and pears, plump grapes . . . Can you imagine? It was a wonder!"

He continued: "The Germans bombed Leningrad every day, and bombarded it with heavy artillery, but all the same, this wasn't the front. The hospital was located in a building of the Gorny Institute on Vasil'evskaia Island. When the patients were falling asleep, I would go into the empty library, and by candle-light I would read. This calmed me, chased away the gloomy thoughts, and filled me with hope. I read only one book, Fraerman's *Wild Dog Dingo* [a popular storybook of that time about comradeship and friendship, intended for older schoolchildren]. How did it wind up in the institute's library? It shook me to the core with its example of pure, good regard of one for another. To this day, when I think of it, my spirits become lighter."

18 May. The twelfth day. The *eshelon* came to a stop in an empty field. Every-one was ordered out of the cars and to fall in beside it. The *eshelon*'s chief and commissar appeared in front of us. Looking over the faces of the cadets with a sullen expression, the chief loudly and precisely pronounced just a few words:

"Who are you—Soviet officers or marauders? Did you think about whom you were robbing? Mothers, whose sons and grandsons are fighting to the death at the front. Remember! Whoever commits one more criminal act will be immediately turned over to a military tribunal."

Having disdainfully spat on the ground, the *eshelon* chief sharply turned and began to walk quickly back to the staff car. Without having said a word, the commissar followed him.

"Back to your places!"

With lowered heads, the cadets dispersed back to their cars.

The *eshelon* didn't stop long, but it was long enough for me to sense a feel-ing of shame. If only because I hadn't done a thing to stop the incident the day before, and I hadn't said a single word against what the impudent cadets had been doing.

Late in the evening, various voices in the car started singing *chastushki*—two-line or four-line folk verses, usually humorous and topical, sung in a lively style. The cadets had gone over to folk tales, which were more decent than the anecdotes.

The command had condemned the marauders, but they hadn't called out any of the cadets, nor had they observed or appreciated Zhenechka's action. Why didn't Shurka force his "fraternity" to stop their raids? I had considered him an honest fellow. Zhenechka disclosed the secret to us. It was painful to find out, but Shurka had yielded to temptation: the marauders were sharing their spoils with him.

On this occasion, Iurka told us a story. His father had started work as an apprentice at the same factory where his grandfather and great-grandfather worked. This was still before the revolution. One day the grandfather discov-ered a piece of material for wiping down machine tools in his son's pocket. "What's this? This isn't yours, and yet you carried it away from the factory?" he sternly asked his son. And then he gave his son a beating.

Did such a watershed event exist for the plundering cadets?

At the various stops, women frequently passed down the line of cars, holding up photographs of their sons and daughters and calling out their family names: "Perhaps somewhere you've seen him (her)?" Time will pass, and then our own mothers will be coming to the trains heading for the front with the same question....

19 May. Murom. The thirteenth day en route. We were given a warm meal today, and it was tasty. At the station, I had a chat with some cadets from the Cheliabinsk Armor Specialist School; their train is apparently following ours along the same route. One cadet-tanker, who I had once coincidentally met in Cheliabinsk, told me that prior to their departure, they had all been awarded the rank of senior sergeant and had received their T-34s directly from the factory. Fine! At the school, the guys had trained on just these machines—terrific! But it all wasn't so simple. It turned out that each tank had its own peculiarities—with the motor, in its working parts, or in its armament. Thus it was impossible to tell in advance how a particular tank would operate in battle. Upon their train's arrival at the designated place, they would immediately move out to the front in their tanks, and each would have to familiarize himself with the specifics of his armored vehicle during this time. Yes, everyone had his own problems.

That night Iurka told me about his first loves. Iura loved Katia, his classmate. Katia was in love with Iura. Then suddenly, the ninth-grade Iura got together with his apartment neighbor Kira, a woman about fifteen years older than him. Iura dropped by to see Kira whenever her husband, Egor, who drove an electric trolley, was away at work.

Kira became the first woman in Iurka's life. Whenever he tried to tell her beautiful words of love, Kira would interrupt him: "We don't talk about love, my young friend, but just simply love." But alas, secrets are hard to keep. The husband unexpectedly arrived home one day, and a scandal erupted. He beat Kira unmercifully, then tossed her in her nightgown into the common hallway, telling her, "Let our neighbors have a look at a slut!" In the morning, the husband sobered up, heeded Kira's entreaties, and forgave her. But with respect to "the gymnast," as he called Iurka, he said, "It will be better if I never lay eyes on him—I'll beat the hell out of him!" Quite soon, Egor and Kira moved to a different apartment building. On this, the story of "Iura + Kira = Love" came to an end.

Leaving for the front, Iurka wrote a letter to Katia and promised, "If I live, we'll be together." But when I asked him, "Will this really happen?" he didn't answer.

Life is a strange thing, that's for sure. We're all crazy. The explanation, obviously, is this: we simply don't understand ourselves. What determines our actions? Desire, judgment, the heart? Most likely, desire. That is the primary motive of human behavior. But am I right?

Listening to the guys' stories about their girlfriends, I got down on myself: where, oh where, was my girlfriend? In the seventh grade, I read Maupassant; in the eighth, Kuprin; in the ninth, Tolstoy; in the tenth, Turgenev; but upon encountering a female, I'd get flustered. I didn't recognize hints, or even open invitations, to become a man. I didn't know how to act in such situations, which is probably why girls didn't find me interesting.

The nearer we drew to the front, the more often thoughts about the future filled our minds. It, the future, once seemed to be like a colorful flying carpet; this was no longer true. Therefore we spoke about it less and less often, though we never stopped pondering it. Again and again I thought back upon Zina's proposal. It was sincere; she wasn't simply trying to hide me in the rear. My turn would have come eventually, and officers are also killed. Perhaps I had really acted like a fool? It is true, in addition to all the "for" and "against" arguments, there was one "but," about which most likely Zina wasn't aware—my Jewish nationality [in the Soviet Union, Jews were officially considered to be a nationality, like Russians, Ukrainians, etc.]. This particular reason said it all.

"Iurka," I asked, "aren't you afraid of the front?"

"What can I say? Yes and no. My father taught me, 'Why fear that which we cannot change?'"

"Haven't you ever been afraid?"

"Perhaps not. I'm not counting small incidents."

"But I have been—twice. Real fear! The first time was at the information office of the prison that was holding my father. They told me there that he had been sentenced to ten years without the right of correspondence. I already knew that this wording meant execution. I returned home in utter despair, but I didn't say anything to my mother. The next day, having stood waiting throughout the night, I again inquired about my father. A new prison guard was at the desk, and he informed me that my father was still being held at the prison, and that they had decided to allow us to communicate with him."

I continued: "The second time, I was terrified by wolves. One winter, late in the evening, I was returning to my village from the district center Shumikh in a horse-drawn sleigh with a driver. It was completely dark, but the road, which ran through a forest, was smooth, and the horse was peacefully trotting along a familiar route. The horse was the first to sense danger. It whinnied and bolted! The sleigh gave such a jerk that I almost tumbled out, and that is when I saw three enormous wolves. They leaped out of the woods directly behind us. They momentarily froze, raised their snouts, gave a terrible howl, and then rushed in pursuit of us.

"The driver didn't panic and lose control; obviously, this had happened to him before. He began to shout at me, 'Hold on to the handrail tighter! If you don't hang on, you'll fall! The horse won't let us down!' I latched on to the handrail. The chase was frantic! The driver was shouting, 'Hang on, hang on more tightly!' I could already see the wolves' huge, dull, yellow eyes—it seemed just four or five more bounds and they would have us. Just then, the driver suddenly turned and hurled a rope at them. The wolves immediately slowed their chase and began to fall behind, their eyes now looking like little distant village lights. Soon we heard the barking of dogs. My fingers were so tightly clenched around the handrail that I couldn't open them and let go of it. But just imagine what it will be like if it is a tank that is coming toward you."

Iurka, as always, decided to deliberate over the matter: "What is fear?"

Unable to hold back the question that seemed to be heavy on all our minds, I asked, "Do you believe that we'll ever get back from the war?"

"I hope so. Only we'll be completely different men by then."

"Then we'll have to meet again after the war. I'd like that very much."

"Me too. We'll hold to it."

21 May. The fifteenth day of our journey. Moscow's Ring Road—that must be it! We'd reached Moscow! If only I could visit it, just for an hour! But we didn't stop long. The train moved on toward the northwest.

That night, just before dawn, they offloaded us at the Toropets station. We were on Tver land now. That was the answer to our puzzle—it's the Kalinin Front for us! Our two-week journey from Siberia had come to an end. The train, having delivered us, immediately left on a return trip.

We were formed up, and the column headed toward some woods at a quick step. I noticed that several cadets kept glancing up at the sky. There it was, the first signs of fear, the apprehension that enemy planes might suddenly appear overhead. We halted near the village of Erofeevo.

The Division's Origin

More and more trains arrived—from Moscow, Central Asia, the Urals, from Siberia and Central Russia. There were many other cadets among the passengers. It turned out that we were the lucky ones after all; cadets from other specialist schools had been delivered to the front after only two months of training.

The last week or so of May became the first days of the forming of a new division, the 215th Rifle Division. It was formed with the remnants of the 48th Rifle Brigade, which had arrived here before us from around Velizh after experiencing terrible, bloody fighting there.

Officers were assigned to us. The majority were also young fellows, like us, in brand new uniforms. Just a couple of weeks before, they had been cadets too, but now they would lead us—they had been most fortunate, since they had managed to graduate from their schools.

The first days at the front! An unbelievable sequence of events had seized us all; a patriotic rush of cadets had blazed up and was burning with new strength. Everything was so new to us: our first division and our first combat officers; the parting of students "from the same barracks"; meetings with frontline veterans; the historic story of the 48th Rifle Brigade's defense of Moscow; and our first nights under the stars!

We were given waterproof capes that could double as pup tents—a useful acquisition in war. On our first night at the front, everyone slept on the grass, wrapped in their capes and covered by their greatcoats, with their kitbags serving as their pillows. We slept soundly, which bespoke of our fatigue, hunger, and the forest air. Everybody had become unaccustomed to oxygen during his two weeks on the train. Although the night was chilly, especially just before dawn, we were prohibited from building campfires. Fires were permitted in the daytime, but only from dry twigs and branches so that they wouldn't produce any smoke to betray our presence.

In the morning, the officers read us our first order! Today, all of us, former cadets, were now soldiers of the 215th Rifle Division of the Kalinin Front's 30th Army. Our army commander was General Dmitrii Danilovich Leliushenko. The *front* commander was Colonel-General Ivan Stepanovich Konev. They didn't forget to tell us that one day of service at the front would be counted as three days of general service. We also were informed that since we were still located in the second echelon of the *front,* we would be fed according to the reduced norms for second-echelon troops—news we received a little less gladly. The soldier's bulletin reported that the division commander himself would organize the division, but he hadn't yet arrived.

Within several days, we were all assigned to our regiments. The division had three regiments: the 707th, the 708th, and the 711th Rifle Regiments. We were happy that we had wound up in a new unit. We were proud of the fact that we cadets were being called the "primary component of the 215th Rifle Division." Iurka and I decided to request assignment to the same regiment, but we were sent to separate ones. I wound up in the 711th Rifle Regiment while Iurka was sent to the 707th Regiment.

Did we, the soldiers who had arrived at the Kalinin Front at the end of May 1942, know what kind of combat situation we had entered, that bloody fighting had been continuing here since January, and that it had already cost tens of thousands of lives? The press had been quiet about the warfare, modestly calling the fighting "battles of local significance."

Part Two

The Rzhev Meat Grinder
June 1942–March 1943

4

Bivouac
June 1942

First Experiences of Life at the Front

I was not even twenty yet, I was still wet behind the ears, but I could march thirty or more kilometers, day or night, with full gear! We were moving up toward the front lines, and for us cadets it was a bit easier than for the others. They jokingly called themselves "puttee-soldiers," and they shot envious glances at our boots. Their soldiers' ankle boots were old and couldn't even take light moisture, but the weather showed no pity, and the feet of many Red Army soldiers were constantly wet.

During the marches, especially the night marches, I and many other young soldiers lent a hand to those who weren't feeling very well and to the "old" soldiers. Don't take the word *old* literally. The ranks of "old soldiers" were simply experienced veterans, and those in their thirties and forties—to us, they were already old men. We always tried to take their guns or knapsacks from them to ease their burden, and at halts we would place a bag under their feet and bring them water to drink or to freshen their faces; we also would take their places for night watch duty. In the war such small gestures of assistance, and others like it, gave rise to frontline brotherhood. One cheerful fellow thought up the slogan, "Soldiers of all ages, unite!"—a play on the Bolshevik slogan, "Workers of the world, unite!" Indeed, we united—and how! We particularly valued these unwritten rules of conduct. They eased our difficult army life, drew the men together, and lifted our combat spirits. Most important, they strengthened our faith in human decency, which a person always needs, particularly during time of war.

Unexpectedly, the command rang out: "Make camp!" We had reached our day's objective, but where were we?

We hadn't even managed to shrug the knapsacks off our shoulders when we heard a new command: "Dig cover!" That is, dig deep slit trenches in case of an aerial attack. Apparently, someone had spotted a German *rama* nearby—a

German FW-189 reconnaissance plane. This was our first reminder that we had reached the front.

The forest where we made camp greeted us affectionately. A light rain had fallen; the air had become cleaner, fresher, and it smelled of pines. Birds were singing. The sun was peeking through the dense crowns of the trees; the low grass underneath our feet was decorated with the first spring flowers—tiny white, blue, and yellow blossoms so small that you could hardly distinguish them. We deeply inhaled the scents of the soft spring earth, admired the kingdom of the birches, and gazed upon the colorful carpets of the forest clearings. At the front, I fully appreciated and came to love nature, especially forests. The forest is the great friend of the frontline soldier. Without it, how can you build a dugout? How can you warm yourself by a campfire in hard frosts? How can you dry out your greatcoat and boots? How can you lay down a corduroy road? At times, it also feeds you better than the cook! Everyone rejoiced over forests, but especially the men from villages:

"In the forest everything feels so right that it seems you are not even at the front."

"What a piece of good fortune. . . . If only I had a dame and a drink right now! Afterwards, I wouldn't even mind passing away!"

The short rain had filled the little forest gullies with water. The cadets rushed to the water and began to slurp it up with their lips. Veteran soldiers forcibly dragged us away: who knows where poison lies in wait for you? I cannot forget one tragic episode, which occurred a little later. Some fresh recruits eagerly yielded to the assurances of an "experienced mushroom hunter," picked some mushrooms, boiled them up—and poisoned themselves when they ate them. It cost seven fellows their lives!

Now the forest was filled with sounds, shouting voices, and commands. The soldiers, as best they knew how, built little huts from logs and pine branches for sleeping and as shelter from the rain. We cleared small areas for the field kitchens. Two platoons were ordered to lay down a road from the camp to the high road we had followed to the forest: with their sapper's shovels they cut branches, laid them down alternatingly lengthwise and crosswise into four layers, and over these layers, in order to compress them, they laid thick logs of identical diameter. Everyone worked in great fervor! Soon after the corduroy road was completed, the long awaited one-and-a-half ton trucks and about three dozen carts appeared on the high road. They were bringing grub!

But the column was unable to travel down the several hundred meters to the forest. The oversaturated ground immediately settled deeply, swallowing the log road. The first to get stuck on the disintegrating road were the trucks, which were loaded to the brim with boxes and heavy sacks. Immediately after them, the carts and horses bogged down. Everyone rushed to help. Some tried to drag the vehicles out of the morass, harnessed in ropes, or put their shoulders to them and tried to push them out, but the truck motors kept dying every now and then; from that day, we christened the one-and-a-half ton trucks "First Five Year Plan trucks" [recalling the difficulties in getting the planned economy going]. Others dragged from the muck the carts and horses, which had sunk up to their bellies in the sticky mud. In order to lighten the load on the carts and trucks, men hoisted heavy sacks and boxes onto their shoulders and in twos and threes, barely able to extract their foot after each step, made their way onto firm soil with their burden. If anyone started to grumble, he was immediately rebuked: "You haven't come to your mother-in-law's for pancakes!" Quite so!

Our first frontline assortment of food consisted of cans of American stew—one can for eight soldiers; a large cold-smoked fish—to serve five; and for each, two sweet biscuits, three tablespoons of millet, two lumps of sugar, and a tiny handful of salt. A packet of *makhorka* [cheap, inferior tobacco] was to be shared among three. The soldiers were especially pleased with the tobacco: "A Tsar's gift!" Newspapers began to rustle, self-rolled cigarettes began to smoke, and someone taught me how to roll a cigarette from a piece of newspaper. The press had been delivered to us before the food arrived.

We eagerly began to prepare our meal. We drew water from the ditches with our mess tins; it had already settled after the rain and had become clear, and little withered roots, pieces of bark, and twigs were visible on the bottom of the ditch. We fervently opened the cans of stew and ground the biscuits for seasoning. Suddenly one of the cadets yelled, "Hush! Stop the noise!"

It had seemed to him that a German pilot high in the skies could catch the sound of the crunch of our biscuits. Loud laughter erupted.

We divided up the stew and biscuit crumbs, then mixed them into the water in our mess tins. I also added a fish head, which was my share of the fish we had divided. Then we turned to the most difficult operation—building a hearth to heat our meal. Many of us had no idea how to do this, or where to begin. That's when the old rule that had been taught us, "Do as I do!" proved useful. Everyone followed the example of the old hands. I scraped the bark off six thick branches and sharpened their ends. Then I took two of the stakes, crossed them, and stuck them firmly into the ground on one side of the fire, then did the same with two more stakes. I laid the remaining two stakes across them over the fire. It was surprising how much experience and skill were needed for such a seemingly simple matter. Everything had to be done with careful thought. The support stakes had to be a certain distance from the fire so they wouldn't catch fire. The cross stake had to be a specific height above the fire for the same reason. It also had to be a little stronger, in order to support the weight of a full mess tin, or else doubled, as it was in my case: I hung both my and Iurka's mess tins over our fire. If you didn't do everything just right, swift retribution would follow: your mess tin would tilt and spill its contents into the fire, or else the entire little structure might collapse.

"Uncle" Kuzia

I took all stages of preparing the meal upon myself. Iurka didn't object, especially after I told him that this wasn't my first experience with cooking and that I knew wilderness skills as well as any forester. In reality this was pure bragging on my part, which became apparent as soon as I tried to start the fire: I couldn't get one going no matter how hard I tried. Iurka was amused but made no effort to intervene in my troubles. Lying on the ground, I tried with all my might to blow tiny embers into a fire, lighting match after match. Then suddenly I heard behind me an unfamiliar, somewhat mocking voice:

"Eh, you're incompetent fellows indeed, cadets."

I straightened up and turned around. The company sergeant major was standing beside me. He was strongly built, had slightly graying hair, an open face, and legs slightly curved like a cavalryman's. He had the "For Courage" medal shining on his field shirt—at that time, not many men had received this soldier's badge of honor. I had already seen this man, who for some reason others addressed not as they should ("Comrade Sergeant Major") but instead in a familiar fashion as "Uncle" Kuzia.

The sergeant major asked me to step aside, checked the stability of my cooking structure, and within a minute conjured a blazing fire. Having explained how he had done this, Uncle Kuzia expressed his surprise:

"How did it happen at your school that you were not taught how to start a fire, even without matches? Where are you from?"

Indicating Iurka, I replied, "Cadet Davydov is from the Urals, while I'm from around Moscow. Perhaps you've heard of this place, Kuskovo?"

"We, brother, are practically neighbors. I lived three stations down the line closer to Moscow from you, near the "Hammer and Sickle"—have you heard of it? Next to it is the Chukhlinka station, then Karacharova, and then it's your Kuskovo. Right, cadet?"

Comfortably settling around the fire, we all sat together for a long while. Kuzia briefly told us his life story. For almost fifteen years he had worked as the deputy head of a children's daycare center at the "Hammer and Sickle" factory:

"My wife and I are childless; therefore I recognized all the children as my own, and they all called me 'Grandpa.' When the Germans approached Moscow, our factory organized a battalion from its workers. We went into battle with training rifles. Almost all of us are now lying beneath the fields of Borodino, but here I am, still alive."

Glancing occasionally at our neighbor, listening to his leisurely speech, I tried to figure out who he reminded me of. For a long time, something about him was nagging me. Then it struck me—he was the living embodiment of Lermontov's Maksim Maksimych. The very same look, the very same conscientiousness and trustworthiness—not an official, but he knew his business perhaps better than any high-ranking officials. We'd only known each other for about an hour, but it was already clear that if all sergeants major were like him, life would be much easier for the soldiers. I pulled my notepad out of my knapsack and began to jot down my impressions.

Suddenly Uncle Kuzia became uneasy, and he cast an alarmed look at me: "What are you writing there, brother, some sort of novel?"

"No, I'm keeping a diary. So many events and interesting people, and I want to write a bit about our meeting as well."

Kuzia spoke softly, but almost in the tone of an order: "Get rid of it, brother! Nothing written is permitted in war, whether you're in the ranks or a general. It can lead you to disaster. There are people who keep a sharp eye for such things." Then he added, in a now louder voice, "Get this idea out of your head right now! Learn how to fight first, and then you can write about it later. Toss the papers into the fire this very minute, and then give the coals a stir!"

I felt very miserable for my notes, but Iurka supported the old soldier:

"Listen to his sound advice; the sergeant major knows what he's talking about."

The next thing I knew, my papers were flying into the fire. Why did I agree to do this? In an instant, my dream of keeping a frontline diary died.

It is well known that human memory is a fragile thing. Later I would regret the sergeant major's "help." But as our ancient saying goes: "Whatever happens, it is all for the best"—and quite soon a new idea struck me to write down the advice of frontline soldiers. I immediately thought of the epigraph to *The Captain's Daughter:* "Preserve the honor of your youth." I decided that this applied to me as well, since we, the young and inexperienced, need good advice most of all. So I began to listen in on the conversations of soldiers more attentively, and I didn't dally to jot down their aphorisms. By the end of the war I had compiled a unique booklet, "A Manual of a Soldier's Rules of Conduct." Later I will talk about it some more.

Lunch was ready, and I invited Uncle Kuzia to sample my first frontline cooking.

"I'll give it a try," he readily agreed. "Thanks for the invitation."

The lunch turned out marvelously, probably because I had added the fish head to the soup; but I must say I had been lucky that it had fallen to my lot! I scooped some soup out of the mess tin, listening to the serene sounds of the forest, and felt, no matter how funny it sounds, a certain affection toward soup. I suddenly recalled how I had been fed in my childhood: "for mother, for father, for grandmother, for grandfather"—while the child obediently albeit reluctantly swallowed the "disgusting" soup.

But today's soup was not just an object of my culinary pride; it was something more significant—a serious step toward independent living. I had to write home about my first frontline lunch!

Uncle Kuzia praised my soup, which raised my already high opinion of my own creation even higher. We all spoke a little more, and then we parted.

I couldn't even begin to imagine how significant the meeting with this amazing man was for my further frontline life. What didn't he teach us, the young—the cadets and new recruits! He showed us to make better use of a bayonet and a sapper's shovel, and how to start a fire in strong winds or rain. He taught us how to use the tiny undulations of terrain in order to reach the enemy lines more quickly and safely. His advice encompassed so much more: from the sensible way to pack your knapsack, to clever and courageous conduct in battle. He also patiently and in detail explained bits of frontline wisdom to us, like, for example, how it was possible even to sleep while on the move, when you're practically falling off your feet during long night marches: two soldiers support a third sleeping soldier under each arm and lead him so he doesn't bump into an obstacle or fall into a ditch.

"Of course, first you must take his gun from him," Kuzia noted, "then trade places. There is nothing wiser: your feet move, while you yourself sleep and your brain gets a rest."

"Nothing wiser"! Then why didn't the infantry specialist school give us such knowledge and experience? In contrast, they taught us how to act according to regulations upon encountering an officer: first you must await recognition, and only then present yourself. It is deathly important—on the parade ground and on the red calico corridor carpet leading to the commandant's office.

Frontline life quickly separated the sergeant major from me, and to the end of the war I didn't learn anything more about him, even whether he had died or was still alive. At the end of 1946, when I had just bid farewell to the army, I one day heard a calm, somewhat muffled voice on the other end of the telephone line. I immediately recognized the voice: Uncle Kuzia! He had looked me up to invite me to a family celebration—his silver wedding anniversary. I attended, where I experienced the joy of reuniting with this astonishingly wise and good man.

Somewhere at the end of the 1950s his wife called me and gave me the sad news: Kuzia had died suddenly of a heart attack. I went to the funeral. I traveled by the electric train up to the "Hammer and Sickle" station platform, just as he had instructed, and along the way I was almost praying. How grateful I was to fate! How often it led me to good people, and they always appeared at a most critical time in my life, as if they had been sent to me by some benevolent spiritual force. Uncle Kuzia was one such gift; how many lives did he save with his wise pieces of advice and his sincere regard for us?

Mavrii

We were all getting ready to sleep—tomorrow was a special day. We were going to meet our commanding officers and be assigned to our units and posts. Suddenly, a very young, short, tow-haired soldier approached us. His field shirt and trousers were hanging loosely on him, as if on a clothes hanger. Asking our permission, he sat down by the dying fire and immediately started to speak:

"You both, it seems, are literate fellows in combat boots, while we are wearing puttees like my dad wore in the First World War, and just chatter a bit among ourselves. I myself am a Mordvinian, I completed fourth grade, repaired wagons at a *kolkhoz* [collective farm], and earned the respect of the people of the village. They call me Mavrii. Now then, tomorrow, you'll see, they're going to split us up and send us wherever they see fit; we'll go our separate ways, and then they're going to lead us to kill our fellow man. So, I'm wondering, what should I do? We are believers; Papa and Mama have both spent time in the North [a reference to the northern camps of the gulag, near the White Sea] for their faith. So, they've brought us here for human slaughter—that's how my aunt has christened this, she says there's no other way to describe what we're doing. Well then, how's it going to be to shoot at another human being? Our faith forbids this."

Here, Iurka broke in and sharply replied: "The German is not human; he is a fascist, a killer. Don't you know this, soldier? Why pity him?"

"That's what they say . . . but is a fascist really not a living being?"

"Well, that's a fine 'How do you do' for you! We're all going to shoot at the enemy, and you're just going to shoot in the air?"

"Maybe . . ."

"Yes, and a tribunal will pass judgment on your living being. You understand that?"

"Well . . ."

"What are you thinking?"

"I'd just as soon do myself in. As I've already said . . . well, . . . you know . . . it's like . . . well, my faith forbids killing."

It seemed that in another minute, Mavrii would start babbling. Had this soldier ever held a real rifle in his hands? Perhaps he had trained with sticks before coming to the front. We had heard about this from some of the other new recruits. Why did he come to us? Did he suddenly want to make a confession? To get some advice, or find some answer to the doubts tearing at his soul?

Plainly, he was too scared to talk about this with an officer or his comrades. For the first time in my life, I had met a religious person. I even began to feel sorry for him, and I wanted to help him—but how? We all, devil take it, were in the same harness; for all of us, this was our first day at the front.

The young soldier was very agitated, searching for the right words, striving to better explain his torments to us. He looked beseechingly at us:

"Well then, what should I do? I've laid all my hopes on you. My aunt instructed me: 'When you reach the front, Mavrii, you'll track down a good man. Trust him, and tell him, tell him everything openly, and seek his advice.'"

"Here, here!" Iurka said, clapping Mavrii on the shoulder. "Hold your tongue, soldier; that is my chief advice. Act as you know best; you're not a child any more, but remember: if you ever fall into the clutches of the fascists, they won't stand on ceremony with you, they'll finish you off quickly, have no doubt."

Unexpectedly, Mavrii reached for Iurka's arm—what's this! It seemed that he wanted to give Iurka a kiss on the cheek, in the Russian way, but Iurka managed to dodge it in time and gave the appearance that he hadn't noticed anything.

Mavrii began to tell us about his family:

"Papa was strict with the family; he used to say, 'Work from early childhood, Mavrii. Don't whine; you're not a woman. Don't be a windbag. Don't wail over hunger cravings or the cold—tough it out. A peasant's life isn't honey, but don't betray it, as in our family it has been passed down through the generations. Stand up for yourself. Live decently. But most importantly, don't forget your faith. Without it, you'll go astray.' That sums it up. But in our platoon, we have few Russians, mostly just Turks (evidently, he meant Uzbeks). They stay quiet, or pray to their God and eat raisins. They brought full bags of raisins with them from home, and eat them amongst themselves—but by their own reckoning, they share just five little raisins with us each day. They're wicked people; back in my village, we have a way of dealing with such people—we dunk their heads under the ice."

I interrupted his monologue. "No, Mavrii, none of that, here you're wrong—it isn't right to dunk people's heads under the ice. Didn't you just notice how your "Turks" didn't cook the food they were given? They ate it raw, which is probably why they treasure the remnants of their raisins. Perhaps our food isn't suitable for them at all. People are different, they have different faiths, but there is no human without some drop of goodness."

Iurka immediately responded: "I'm not so sure. What about the German bandit?"

Mavrii asked, "Why is their God calling these Muslims to battle?"

Iurka burst out laughing: "How should I know, Mavrii, I haven't chatted with them myself—and you're just going to sniff out a good person from among them at a glance?

"I've been kept busy, and to no real purpose—the Turks don't talk in our language, and I don't understand their language."

"Then how will the officers instruct them?"

"They'll have interpreters; they'll be useful."

"This is what I think," said Iurka. "At the front, like in the village, life isn't a bowl of cherries. So we'll be fighting according to your father's rules: 'Don't whine. Tough it out. Don't betray.' In this way, we'll be loyal to our oath."

"That just may be the truth. You guys are all right. Perhaps we'll meet again. Thanks from the bottom of my heart—for the trouble and the company."

Mavrii stood up. Two steps, and he disappeared into the night.

Yes, things weren't easy for the believers, but for the Uzbeks it was many times more difficult. We had all just spent one day at the front, and how many complications there were already! About a half-year later, in the fighting for Rzhev, an amusing incident took place: in the front lines, an Uzbek soldier went missing from his post. He had stood up with his weapon and then just disappeared. Everyone thought he had gone over to the Germans. But the next day, around evening, he came crawling back to our lines, alive and unharmed. In his pocket he was carrying a note from the Germans in Russian: "We don't need such a 'tongue' [Russian parlance for a prisoner willing to talk]. We can't understand him. So we're sending him back to you."

The night turned out to be warm. Iurka and I were always together, but today's conversations with Uncle Kuzia and Mavrii had been a bit prickly. All our thoughts were on the morrow. Understanding that this might be our last "philosophical discussion," as we called our conversations, I asked him, "What do you think, will we be going into the frontline trenches soon? What do we know of the enemy?"

I immediately sensed that Iurka was in a foul mood.

"You've asked two questions. To your first question, that chatterbox Mavrii could probably give a better answer than me, because he's often communicating with God. And you yourself know the answer to the second question. As our "Stinking Reciter" [the *politruk*] instructed us, 'Germans are fascists, killers, marauders, rapists, and Hitlerite executioners.'"

"But, Iurka, not all Germans can be fascists—they have the largest communist party in Europe. Where have all their communists gone?"

"In my opinion, all their communists are snakes, they've defected to Hitler! Some were afraid, some saw personal advantage, others simply believed their 'Führer.' Have no doubt, in our very first battle, we'll be shooting at former communists too."

"We've been trained under the slogan, 'Through hatred—to victory!' But what about the Uzbeks? What do they know about the Germans? Half of them, if not more, are illiterate. What kind of hatred can they have of the Germans? Do they know anything about Germany?"

"You're exaggerating. I think that there are quite a few among them who simply don't want to speak Russian."

Iurka fell silent. Through his words, I frankly couldn't recognize him. On this, our conversation ended, though in fact it had never really taken place.

Upwards–Downwards

The next morning, the soldier's bulletin announced that 300 cadets from the Kamyshlov Combat-Infantry Specialist School and 700 new recruits from Moscow had arrived the previous night. After breakfast, we all were drawn into formation in a large clearing. Before dividing us into separate battalions, the regiment commander made an appeal to the soldiers:

"I want to know if there are any hunters, blacksmiths, mechanics, drivers, tailors, cobblers, medical assistants, or cooks among you. Step forward, but no tricks!"

The commander's query, naturally, caused a general stir in the ranks. Many soldiers stepped forward out of formation, whereupon staff assistants from the regimental headquarters took down their names and skills.

Time passed and noon arrived, but we continued to stand in formation in the field. During this time, as we soon understood, the command was busy making its determinations: who to the infantry, who to the artillery, who to the sappers, to the medical-sanitation battalion, to the armorers, to staff positions, to communications—and all the hunters, to the snipers. From the cadets were formed two separate battalions: a machine-gun battalion, and an assault rifle battalion—though at that time they had no assault rifles. Later I found out that Iurka, who was in a different regiment, received a staff position.

The regiment's commissar appeared. Evidently, we had been waiting for him. He walked along the formation, asking questions of the soldiers; frequently, without awaiting a reply, he hurried on. A tall, thin officer with one stripe on his shoulder strap was walking behind the commissar. His narrow eyes, raven-black short mustache, and dark-complexioned face allowed one to guess his Eastern origins. He turned out to be the regiment's *komsorg* [Komsomol *organizer*; the Komsomol was the youth wing of the Communist Party], Sabit Khalikov. He was addressing, as a rule, only the cadets. Walking up to me, he asked where I was from, whether I was a Komsomol member, what was my education, and whether I had participated in any social work prior to the army. Then he hurried to catch up with the commissar, exchanged a few words with him, then called me out of the formation and took me with him.

Thus, for a short time I became the regiment *komsorg*'s assistant. We quickly became friends, and in off-duty hours we would address each other by name. I filed documents and kept the Komsomol dossiers. If the *komsorg* was busy, I conducted meetings of the Komsomol committee. I helped the battalion *komsorgs* create primary organizations in the companies and batteries. I talked with young soldiers, and if they asked me to do it, I read them articles from the central and army press.

Within two weeks, my Komsomol career came to a sudden end. I accidentally fell under the gaze of the passing regiment Party organizer at an awkward time. He was a gloomy man, who all the political workers in the regiment tried to avoid, aware of his prickly character. It was said that before the war, he had headed a Party commission in one of the district committees, and when investigating individuals, he recognized only one decision: expulsion from the Party. [During the years of Stalin's terror, this was often equivalent to a death sentence.]

My encounter with him occurred under unfavorable conditions for me: I was without my forage cap, wearing an unbuttoned field shirt, without a belt, and, what seemed to irritate him the most, he caught me while I was preparing my lunch. He stopped short when he caught sight of me, and asked with evident irritation, "Who are you? What are you doing in the political office?"

I reported, as I should: "I'm the assistant to the regiment's *komsorg*."

"Why are you busy fixing food in the political office?"

I tried to explain that I had been given dry rations, as they wouldn't let me into the commander's dining room as a private.

My reasons, obviously, weren't convincing to him. Shortly thereafter, Khalikov summoned me, and guiltily lowering his eyes, he asked me where I wanted to go, to which unit. By his expression, I could tell he had suffered a sharp reprimand, so without asking any questions, I requested that he send me to the artillery: "I was trained on mortars."

"OK," he replied, "you'll become a gunner."

5

How I Searched for the Truth, and What Became of It
June–July 1942

In an Artillery Battery

I was assigned to a gun crew as the Number Four man; that is, as the man who carries the shells from the cases to the gun tube. Our gun was a "Forty-five," a 45-mm antitank gun. My duties were not particularly compelling, but one must start somewhere.

Our commander was Senior Sergeant Lenia Loshak. He was twenty-two, a strong man from somewhere near Tambov. He knew his stuff—a high-class professional artilleryman. He related strictly but justly toward his subordinates and treated us all the same. As a result, we all respected him and tried to carry out his every order swiftly and properly.

We had six men in our gun crew. The most important person was the gun layer, since success or failure rested largely on his shoulders. A tank is a moving target; to hit it requires steely nerves, precise calculations, and the ability to evaluate a situation quickly and accurately. I considered our gun layer, Andriusha Paniushkin, to be something of a wizard—he already had two German tank kills to his personal credit.

I immediately took a liking to the "Forty-five." I tried to find out everything I could about it, and to learn the business of the artillery. Veteran artillerymen willingly explained the role of the gun in battle:

"Heavy artillery stands about three to five kilometers behind the front lines. But we duel with enemy tanks and, importantly, unsuppressed enemy firing positions. We are positioned, as a rule, together with the infantry, just 100–150 meters behind them. And in battle, when the infantry advance, we battery men roll our guns after them and try to protect the infantry from tanks. In this situation, the battery falls into an unfavorable situation: the riflemen take cover behind any little mound or wrinkle in the ground, while you are rolling your gun forward in the open. The Germans never fail to spot you, and then they flog you with fire. So we have the expression, 'The barrel is long, but the life is short.'"

Another artilleryman spoke up: "Damn it, the infantry attack, and we're right behind them. The rifle battalion gets to rest at night in new positions, but we get the order: 'Dig in! Camouflage your positions!' The next morning—a preparatory artillery bombardment and battle! When the evening rolls around again, damn it, there is a regrouping: we arrive at a new place at night, and again pick up our spades. You get so worn out that nothing matters any more."

With full knowledge of the shortcomings of the "Forty-five"—it was undergunned in battle with tanks—the soldiers loved it all the same. It was light, just 540 kilograms: if it fell into a shell crater, we could drag it out ourselves. True, it was not easy to carry the shells; a loaded box of shells weighed 50 kilograms, but two could manage it well enough. In battle, each "Forty-five" shell that hit its target saved soldiers' lives. Meanwhile, the gun's maneuverability and broad steel gun shield, which protected men from bullets and shell fragments, turned out to be invaluable to the artillerymen themselves.

In 1943 the Red Army received a new weapon, the 57-mm antitank gun—a superb weapon! It gradually replaced the "Forty-five."

After the war, I read that Stalin once told Grabin, the designer of the 76-mm antitank gun: "Your cannon saved Russia!" Unfortunately, such words were never spoken about the "Forty-five," though it richly deserved them.

Captain Vasilii Ivanych commanded our artillery battery. He was an experienced artilleryman who had been awarded the Order of the Red Star for his actions during the fighting for Moscow. The soldiers all called him "our Chapai" [after the Russian civil war commander Vasilii Ivanovich Chapaev, who was lionized in the 1934 movie *Chapaev*]. Indeed, he himself, though he was ten years younger, tried to resemble his hero: he grew a mustache just like Chapaev's and tended it carefully. But on his young face the whiskers looked unnecessary and didn't give him the desired look of the dashing romantic. I liked the way he talked with us, his young warriors.

"It is important in battle," said the captain, "to select a good position and to dig in your gun in time. Don't do anything else until you complete this task. The German will fall upon you directly, and you won't be able to cope with him. In order to strike a tank more precisely, you must choose the moment when it turns its side armor to you, even if only for a couple of seconds. The side armor is thinner. If you allow a tank to approach too near, it can pick up its speed and rush your firing position—even if you penetrate its armor with your shot, it may not stop. Or else one may burst into flames, but you won't have time to stop another. You must make sure the tank catches fire!"

Combat Training

The battery consisted of three platoons, with three guns in each platoon. It also had twenty-six horses. Our battery was located in two small villages, not far from each other and separated by a beautiful little patch of woods and a small stream. After the Germans had retreated from these villages, in each one only two or three huts and five sheds remained intact. Only the charred foundations and empty doghouses remained of the rest. The inhabitants—only a few were left, primarily old men, old women, and children—were living in dugouts, into which they had dragged everything that they had managed to save. The peasants told us that when the Germans had arrived in the villages, they had first searched out and executed all the commissars, Communist Party members, and Jews, and then they killed all the dogs.

In one of the villages, by some miracle, a decent peasant's hut had been preserved, and the battery command occupied it. On the outskirts of the village, closer to the woods, the battery's soldiers stayed in tents. We concealed our guns on the opposite side of the village, in open trenches, and carefully camouflaged them. A little farther, at the edge of some woods, we built stables for the horses and cleared a space for the field kitchen. Our combat supplies occupied a special position, deeply dug into the earth, and covered by stout beams.

The days passed quickly. We would rise with the sun, spend all day with our arms wrapped around the gun, and then find that it was already night. More than once, the battery commander raised an alarm, checking by his watch to see how long it took us to be ready to move out. "Gun crews, to your weapon!"— the order would ring out; and in a flash each man would take his proper position by his gun. Although the first attempt was a total mess, soon the battery commander was praising the men of the battery.

It seemed that everything was going as it should. I, like everyone else in the battery, received a carbine, a gas mask, two first-aid packets, and a Red Army booklet, in which the sergeant major wrote down my first combat profession: "Artilleryman." How proud I was whenever I glanced at this inscription!

We were fed according to the norms for second-echelon troops, but the food turned out to be tolerable. The cook often added a little something from the forest's bounties, thanks to the efforts of the sergeant major, Osip Osipovich.

From morning to evening our officers kept us busy. Five times a week the battery limbered its guns and moved out for training. We would select suitable positions—a primary position and several reserve positions—deploy our guns, and about 600–700 meters away we would set up plywood tank dummies, after which we would go through the motions of firing on them. Sometimes we were allowed to fire one shell of live ammunition at them. Just try to hit a moving target with one shot! We often did target shooting with our carbines, which proved to be more difficult than shooting rifles—the carbines had a strong recoil action. But we soon got accustomed to this. It was harder to get used to the night sentry duty. Just as back at the school, we were not freed from the next day's exercises after pulling sentry duty the night before.

The constant labor to build firing positions turned out to be even more difficult than night guard duty. How much earth did we dig up and dig up again! For hours, we would not let go of a pickaxe or shovel. We dug until we were wiped out. Then our commander, Lenia Loshak, would tell us, "If you don't manage to dig in your gun or yourselves, it will be your death!" So we would keep digging.

Our gun crew occupied a separate tent. We had among us frontline veterans, new recruits, and two cadets, but we never had any terrible experiences, like the practice of *dedovshchina,* where older soldiers haze or beat new recruits while the officers look the other way. In the evenings, we would sit in front of the tent and settle any disputes, or "have a life talk," as the Ukrainians say. We joked, and smoked hand-rolled cigarettes. We found an accordionist among us who had brought his instrument along with him from his civilian life. Before the war, he had been a horse groomer on a *sovkhoz* [state farm], but in the battery he worked as a team driver.

Whenever we were given a free minute, I liked to question the veteran frontline soldiers. One soldier, who had passed through the terrible year of 1941, told me: "When the German advances on you, he harasses you with cannons and machine guns—he's trying to suppress you and your weapon. And what are you supposed to do? Try to knock him out! You won't take him with a grenade. You must absolutely see to it that he blazes up! Everyone will tell you this."

I ask: "But if it is a combined arms attack?"

"A dreadful business! In this case, the Germans, for the most part, try to play on your psyche; they love to fire on the move—both the tanks and the accompanying infantry. You get little real benefit from such fire, everybody knows this, but it works on the mind, especially on those of new recruits, who haven't been under fire before. I myself more than once gave way. If you haven't managed to knock out or burn an advancing tank, it is better to let it pass over you, taking cover in the bottom of your entrenchment, then fire and fire, as much as you can and however you can—if only to hold up the following infantry and motorized infantry."

The most colorful figure in our battery was the sergeant major, Osip Osipovich, who was called "Both yours and ours." The soldiers perceptively noted the character of every officer, be he a sergeant major, a platoon leader, or even the regiment commander. Everyone knew about Osip Osipovich. He was a resourceful fellow who behaved decently with the rank and file but never forgot about the interests of the command. Osipovich loved to talk, and he often gave us long speeches. He would always say, approximately, the following:

"Who is the sergeant major? The sergeant major is the tail of the army. And what is the army's rear [logistic support]? It is the basis of the army's existence and the main condition for victory. Without the rear, you cannot feed a soldier, nor warm his soul with a little shot of vodka! Nor can you clean him while he's in the bathhouse, which means you can't free him from lice! Without the rear, no tank will move into battle, no airplane can take off, and not a single gun can fire! Not a single general will receive the woman he wants! Have you noted, artillerymen, the significance of the sergeant major? We'll consider that you have. So I will ask you to love and be gracious toward Osip Osipovich, and carry out all my orders precisely."

The Command Dozes Off

Osip Osipovich was my third sergeant major. How many more I would have! It is bad when a sergeant major doesn't have any sense, culture, or education, which often happens. But one can tolerate this. It is three times as bad when a sergeant major doesn't have any trace of ordinary human feelings. The most difficult case, and here you can do nothing about it, is when the sergeant major is an egomaniac, when he is absolutely certain of his superiority over the rank and file.

Osip Osipovich was made of different stuff; he was always ready to help the common soldier. And he cared so much for the horses! Even if you woke him in the middle of the night, he could smoothly reel off the names of all the horses and the color of each one's coat. He took care of the officers. In return, they let him look out for his own interests. But the main thing was that he never forgot about the soldier. Tell me then, how is it possible not to respect such a man, or not to forgive any of his little sins? He was an ideal sergeant major!

However, quite soon the life of the battery sharply changed for the worse, and the soldiers knocked their "ideal sergeant major" off his pedestal.

The first thing to deteriorate was the food. Instead of receiving the cans of American stew, we began to be fed garbage. For those who haven't eaten such stuff, I'll explain: it was merely a little hot water, seasoned with groats, a little bit of herbs, and salt. The stew, just like an apparition, had disappeared from our rations. Were the July downpours of rain bogging down the supply line, or had our allies stopped sending it? All sorts of things come into the head of a person in such a situation: if some sort of absurdity occurs, he tries first of all to find an explanation.

After the disappearance of the stew, it was the bread's turn—the slices became thinner. Then sugar also began to dwindle, and we received our ration of it only every other day. What was going on?

New doubts arose: the officers began to stay away from our drills, handing this duty over to the sergeants. We went out for field training less often. Was it again the fault of the rain? The commissar also forgot about us. They stopped delivering newspapers, so we didn't know what was happening in the country or at the front; moreover, we were deprived of the paper for our hand-rolled cigarettes!

Then something genuinely mean and rotten occurred: our horses' supplies were reduced. Their daily ration of oats was cut to the barest minimum.

Men became noticeably thinner, as did the animals, which we all adored, and which, unlike us, were not capable of finding any supplemental food for themselves. Two weeks passed under the new half-starving regime. Everyone began to tighten up their belts and make accommodations. I, for example, gave up nearly half my rations to those who agreed to take my place for nighttime sentry duty.

Soon, we became totally stunned—instead of putting the horses to harness, they put us there! We had to drag our guns to the training grounds by our own efforts, for there was no other way to get them there because of the heavy rains. We understood that in a combat situation things might be even worse, and we might have to drag the guns ourselves, but what was the point of doing it now? However, there was a reason: the horses were too weak. Artillery horses need no less than six kilograms of oats each day, and they weren't getting that. Things also became rather bad with coarse fodder like hay and straw—where were they to get some? The famished horses, which were not receiving proper care, began to pick at each other's tails and gnaw at manure, and this, God forbid, could lead to great misfortune.

A French cavalryman once spoke about such a situation admirably. To a reproach from Marshal Murat, he replied, "People can go without bread, but horses without oats are not in condition to do anything. Love for the fatherland won't keep them going."

To drag a gun through wet clay soil, particularly when it is raining, is not a pleasant exercise. Moreover, as soon as you reach the training field, worn out and wet, and select a position, without any pause for rest, orders ring out: "Tanks from the front! . . . Tanks from the rear! . . . Tanks from the flank!"

Just try to have time to grasp the order, turn the gun, change the aim, and drag up shells. On an empty stomach, what sort of gunnery practice is that? We collapse, exhausted, one after the other, to the ground. We're all filthy, wet, and, what is more, hungry and angry. Having finished our training, we roll the guns back again. We finally reach our encampment, but the platoon leader or sergeant keeps us in formation for another quarter-hour while he analyzes today's training. Just as he should! Then we fall in and march in formation to the field kitchen. But there we find waiting for us only gruel and watery soup without any meat, and a mug of semisweet tea. It's the same thing every blessed day. It's a good thing that the cook is a decent man, that he asks who wants a little more and never spares another scoop.

New wonders. Normally, many of the men after a meal would go to the stables for a short while, to pet the horses, feed them with grass, and have a talk with the drivers. They, I recall, would often start singing a nonsensical little ditty: "Two for hay, three for the cart, one and a half for the ferry. A lentil with vetch, and I'm not chirping." By this time, however, the singing had stopped. Then suddenly one day everyone was forbidden to drop by the stables, without any explanation.

Such was the situation that had taken shape in our battery. Nobody knew what was going on.

We began to talk about the situation: the horses were becoming emaciated without their oats, yet we were forbidden to take them out for forage, even on fine days—we were told a German reconnaissance plane had been sighted. Matvei, the senior driver, was particularly distressed. He loved his horses like a true artilleryman loves his gun. "We haven't even started fighting, and yet they're harming the horses!"

It was he who finally revealed to us what was going on, and started matters brewing. One evening when we were alone, without any officers present, Matvei turned up and, counting on his fingers, began to lay out his observations to us:

"Fact Number One: friends of the commander with the help of Osip Osipovich are exchanging oats for *samogon* [Russian moonshine]. Fact Number Two: for their own appetizers, they're taking stew and any other sort of grub they want from the soldiers' kettle. Fact Number Three: Just think what they're up to, the bastards! In the neighboring villages, the sergeant major has been finding girls and bringing them back to the commanders. I, an old fool, even gave Osip a horse for this purpose. How can this possibly be! We're almost in a combat situation, yet they're celebrating their masculinity while we get the short end."

A few days later the battery commander suddenly showed up in our platoon area. He ordered us to fall in, and we stood in formation in a steady rain, while he began to scold us like we were little children: "You look like a bunch of slobs! Your field shirts are filthy! And your discipline . . ."

A voice in the ranks suddenly interrupted his speech: "Comrade Captain, they've begun to use us as horses. And we spend all day rolling around in the mud, like pigs."

"Chapai" said nothing in response. Dismissing the platoon, he turned and walked away.

I'm a Delegate

From that very day, the battery began real "military operations" against its own commanders.

First of all, on rainy days we refused to drag our guns to the training field.

The platoon commander, a young lieutenant that we all considered to be an "empty spot," made noises at us and threatened us, but he quickly backed down and agreed to take only one gun to the field.

There we took turns training. Some would mess around with the gun in the swampy muck, while others would have a smoke in the bushes under the constant, damnable drizzling rain. Everyone lost the desire to train. In the evening we would return to the village to dry out, and after dinner, half-dead, we would lie down to sleep a bit.

One evening someone threw a clump of manure from a hardened manure pile at the curtained window of the officers' hut, from behind which you could hear the loud sounds of a gramophone and the officers' merry-making. The sound of shattering glass rang out. The gramophone fell silent. Whatever was going on inside the hut, nobody knew. By the next morning, the window had been repaired through Osip Osipovich's efforts, and now a soldier with a carbine was standing next to the hut—the guardian of the commanders' amusements.

At night in the tents, the soldiers pondered how they should carry on. The same conversation was going on in our tent as in all the others, quite likely, and with each passing night the conversation became sharper.

"How can the commissar tolerate such shameful behavior?"

"But he's with them—dancing, guzzling *samogon*, and banging the ladies."

"The Red Army is the workers' and peasants' army. We're all, officers and soldiers alike, from the same people."

"We may be from the same people, but those who hold power have made saloons for themselves. If Vasilii Ivanych had known about such debauchery back in the Urals, he would have drowned the bastards."

Everyone chuckled, but then the conversation became sharper:

"If only someone would let the division commander know, he'd bring them to their senses!"

"The swine! Tomorrow we'll be going into battle together, and they're sleeping around, and don't even consider us to be human."

"What then, fellows, shall we roll out a gun, and like the *Aurora* back in 1917, take a few pot shots at the counterrevolutionaries? They are real counterrevolutionaries!"

"What are you, crazy? Do you want to lead us all before the firing squad?"

Soon another event occurred. From a laundry line, which stretched between two stakes pounded into the ground near the commanders' hut, someone pulled down our platoon commander's clean shirt and left it lying in the mud. The sentry was punished, which made us all indignant. On that same day, a new commander was appointed over us—our commander "had become ill." Around evening, some of the "old men" in the battery called me out from my tent to have a serious chat:

"You're an educated fellow, and you know the Komsomol command of the regiment. It is impossible to take this any longer; go have a heart-to-heart talk with the commissar—perhaps he'll change his mind? Go have a talk, like one Party member with another. You communists have special relationships, not like the ones we have."

"First of all, " I answered, "what do I have to do with the Komsomol command? Secondly, I'm not a communist."

"For us in the battery, you'll become a communist, if you muster up the courage and tell the commissar the truth!"

The "old men" fell silent, waiting for my answer.

For the first time in my life serious men, much older than me, frontline veterans who had more than once looked death in the eye, were believing in me, relying upon my courage and capability to do a citizen's act in the name of justice. Forgetting the wise saying, "Look before you leap!" I agreed with their request.

I walked up to the commanders' hut and asked the sentry to summon the commissar. The commissar quickly emerged, and he glanced at me with surprise. When I told him that I wanted to speak with him about a serious political matter, he, as always, politely smiled: "Come on, you're talking nonsense, little soldier; what sort of 'serious political business' can you have?"

I wasn't expecting from him an immediate agreement to a discussion. But the commissar suddenly offered to have a little chat in the forest. We took a seat on a fallen tree trunk. The commissar looked, as always, rather dandyish. A young brunette with a well-groomed, full face, he was one of those men, everybody knew, who constantly fussed over his appearance like a woman. I liked him somewhat. Now, plainly, he was ready for an evening party: he was clean-shaven, and his hair glistened with some sort of hair cream, which gave his hair a silvery sheen. The buttons on his shirt, the star on his forage cap, and his boots were all gleaming. He was giving off the scent of some eau-de-cologne, which at that time was beyond a frontline soldier's wildest dreams. How could I measure up against him? I was wearing a faded field shirt and boots that had not been cleaned for a long time, and I had dirty fingernails.

Nevertheless, the conversation took place. I sincerely, frankly, laid out everything as it was. Without resorting to crude words, I began to tell him about the facts and about the mood in the battery. While he listened, he fanned himself with a little branch and didn't ask any questions. I finished my report. Silence reigned. Finally the commissar spoke up, and the conversation didn't go at all in the way I expected. More accurately, no conversation ensued at all. It was a monologue. The commissar spoke rudely, didactically, and scornfully:

"What a hero you are! I didn't imagine! It will be interesting to see how you will be in combat. It turns out, Cadet, that you are also a troublemaker. I hope they didn't teach you this in the specialist school. Remember what I am about to tell you. You are still young and hot-blooded. The calves back in your battery put you up to this, to butt in, while they hide in the bushes. Your entire speech was complete nonsense! What are you getting at? A little more stew meat in your soup? It was all spoiled! Go see the sergeant major, he'll show you the corresponding document. The quantity of oats for the commissaries has been reduced throughout the army—nature doesn't listen to us. Do you think that what is going on these days should be easier for the soldiers? Everything else you said was rubbish. You, soldier, haven't offended just the commissar, but the Party itself! Therefore you deserve punishment. But I'm not a vengeful person, I treat everyone with respect, everybody knows this. Moreover, as you said yourself, we will be going into battle together. Thus think seriously about what I have just told you."

Depressed and stunned, I didn't say a single word. He stood up. Without saluting, we went our separate ways.

Doubts overwhelmed me; perhaps I hadn't found the right words and had failed to engage him in an open, heart-to-heart discussion? No and again no! I was not guilty of anything; it is simply that he was one of those demagogues who cover their vices with high-sounding words. A hypocrite and a blowhard! But there remained a bitter falling-out from my talk with the commissar.

The next day, "Chapai" ordered me to transfer to a platoon in a nearby village. I understood that they were moving me a little farther away from the command's gaze. Clearly, this was at the suggestion of the commissar. Well, if that's what they wanted, I was fine with it.

Gathering up my carbine, my knapsack, and my greatcoat, and saying farewell to the rest of my gun crew, I set off for my new place of service. Before I left, the guys told me that the commissar, in the presence of several people, including the sergeant major Osip Osipovich, had uttered: "Where did he come from, that little Jew?"

"Complaining in the Army Isn't Authorized"
(From the "Manual of a Soldier's Rules of Conduct")

I walked along a narrow forest path, rejoicing over the encounter with the wonders of a green summer forest. A clear sky, the grandest trees, and the clean, fresh air. It was sad to leave my comrades, but at the same time I was feeling happy. Nature literally took me into her comforting embrace, dissolving and dissipating my worries, healing and making me stronger. Suddenly, everything became so easy! To hell with the commissar! To hell with all his contrary words! And what difference did it make in which platoon I served; by the way, they say my new platoon has an excellent commander.

Suddenly someone hailed me and I turned around. Behind me, Sabit

Khalikov was riding up on horseback. Drawing even with me, he stopped his horse: "Why aren't you coming to the Komsomol committee meeting? I called your 'Chapai' twice, and he promised to send you."

I made no effort to explain the situation, nor did I talk about what had occurred. I tried to offer an excuse: "I didn't know about it. Nobody informed me."

Together, we reached the new platoon's encampment. Along the road, Sabit enthusiastically talked about the combat preparations in the division, how it was becoming stronger, and I heard a lot of flattering words about the division commander, Kupriianov.

"I've never met a man like him before," Sabit announced. "He's the best commander one could have!"

Once I reported upon my arrival, the platoon commander assigned me to one of his gun crews, and he didn't ask any questions. I understood that he didn't know about the reasons for my transfer. Sabit asked the platoon commander to release me to attend the regimental Komsomol committee meeting, and he gave his permission on the spot. And suddenly I decided to act: I would have a chance to talk with the regiment commissar. I had to take advantage of such an opportunity!

The Komsomol committee meeting was a special one. The regiment commander was present, as were representatives of all the battalion Komsomol organizations. However, when I arrived for the meeting, I discovered that our regiment commissar was away on other business. I was naturally disappointed, but I remained determined to raise what I believed to be our legitimate complaints before the regiment command.

The meeting's discussion focused on one question: combat readiness. The regiment commander reported that the division commander Kupriianov had visited several battalions and batteries—it was a pity that he hadn't dropped by ours!—and he'd been dissatisfied with the course of training: there was a lot of formal show, cooperation between the different arms of the service was still weak and receiving insufficient attention in training, and the soldiers weren't learning to display initiative in combat.

"The division commander is proposing personally to conduct joint exercises with a tank brigade," the regiment commander concluded in his report. "Our own 711th Rifle Regiment will participate in the exercises. Give me your conclusions!"

After the meeting, I approached the regiment commander and asked, "Could you give me a few minutes for a serious political discussion?"

"Have you spoken with the regiment commissar?"

"I haven't had the chance. Before the committee meeting, I tried to see him, but they told me that he had left for army headquarters for two days."

"Fine, let's talk. I'm listening to you."

The regiment commander politely heard me out, thanked me for my honesty, and promised to look into everything after the commissar's return. Hearing his words about the commissar, I began to have doubts: had I acted properly? Perhaps I actually should have met first with the commissar; he was said to be a decent and principled man. But, after all, he wasn't going to return until two days had passed; would the platoon commander release me again to the regiment? This was probably my only chance. In essence, what difference did it make? Both the commissar and the commander represented Soviet power.

But things turned out not the way I expected.

Four days later, the regiment commissar came to my battery. After conversations with the battery command and a full lunch—Osip Osipovich really outdid himself—the regiment commissar came out onto the steps, sent for me, and, taking a seat in a sunny spot, began to wait for me.

When I arrived, he asked me all of three questions:

"Why have you acted insubordinately?"

I explained how everything had happened.

"Does everyone in the battery think like you do?"

"Everything I set forth to the battery commissar is my own personal opinion as a Komsomol member."

"Did you threaten the commissar?"

"No!" I declared categorically.

While we talked, or more precisely, while I answered the commissar's questions, all three platoons formed up in front of their tents. At the same time, Captain "Chapai" showed up—our commander—and all three platoon commanders. Dismissed by the commissar, I took my place in the formation, forseeing nothing ugly. A command rang out:

"Attention!"

Unexpectedly for all the battery men, not to mention me, the captain called me out of the formation and ordered:

"Hand over your carbine to the platoon commander and report for duty to the commander of the 1st Rifle Company of the 1st Battalion, Senior Lieutenant Sukhomirov. You'll get your Red Army booklet from the sergeant major. You have one hour to gather up your things!"

My blood rushed to my face. My heart was pounding, as if it was suddenly being pressed by something very heavy. What was this? No explanations! What will everyone think, plainly unaware of why they are punishing me? But something else wounded me more deeply. Not one of the cadets, not one of the "old men," who had persuaded me to fight for the truth, not one of my gun crew stepped forward in my defense—not a single person said so much as a half-word! So that's how it was! That's the sort of people we were—"from the same barracks"!

After one hour exactly, I left the battery and headed through the forest to report for duty to some senior lieutenant. I walked fully vexed: however did it happen that the first citizen's deed in my life, completely for the sake of other people, ended in complete failure? While all I personally got from it was an infantryman's petty position, expelled from the artillery?

In Aleksandr Trifonovoch Tvardovsky's immortal poem from the war, "Vasilii Terkin," he writes the following words:

> Along a road to the front
> Walked a soldier in a new greatcoat,
> Snugly belted, as if in formation,
> Catching up with his rifle regiment,
> And his first rifle company.

That's just the way I also was walking then along that road "to my first rifle regiment, my first rifle company."

After some time, it became clear that my efforts had not been in vain. The drinking bouts stopped. The food became better. The commissar resumed his visits to the batteries, bringing newspapers for the men. They began to feed the horses the full ration of oats. Training exercises resumed.

But the repulsive feeling of complete defenselessness wounded me. I had learned that even the highest moral inspirations could ring hollow, if they are not followed by concrete actions. I had received a serious rebuke, and it would not pass without cost. Since that time I have adopted one rule, and I try to hold to it: don't wait for support and approval; if you are confident in the rightness of your cause—act!

6

In a Rifle Company
July–August 1942

The Front Is in a Feverish State

So, now I was an infantryman! We had a whimsical saying, with a kernel of truth: "The wise man—for the artillery; the dandy—for the cavalry; the drunkard—for the navy; and the fool—for the infantry." Well, what of it? A rifleman is a rifleman, and we weren't too proud.

Once I reached the rifle company I was immediately assigned to a squad, which was commanded by none other than our own Shurka! He immediately began to tell me about a situation in the company. The soldiers' discontent had provoked the company sergeant major, and on my very first day I became witness to the squabbles between him and Shurka.

"Why are we still not receiving any mail?" Shurka asked indignantly.

The sergeant major, shrugging his shoulders, answered indifferently: "The mail isn't part of a sergeant major's duties. Our job is to pass along an order on time and to make sure a soldier gets his grub and combat supplies. Meanwhile your business, sergeant, is to fight the Germans."

Shurka got wound up: "What, comrade sergeant major, don't you plan to fight together with us in battle?"

After a moment's silence, the sergeant major answered: "I'll do whatever I'm ordered to do."

During the years of the war, I accumulated a whole "collection" of the most diverse types of sergeant majors. This one was my fourth already. This one was a "dull personality"—such was the opinion of the soldiers, and I shared it.

I hadn't yet managed to find my place in the rifle company, to get used to my new squad and to comprehend my simple duties, when suddenly the regiment raised the alarm, and within a couple of hours the entire division was moving at a quick step toward the nearest railway station. We marched all night, not knowing why or where we were being led. What if the Hitlerite beast had pounced again upon Moscow? Someone recalled the words of the commissar: "A mortal danger is hanging over the country: the Germans are rushing for the Volga!" The "soldiers' telegraph" of the most diverse rumors was coming, as often happened, to the same point: our division was being urgently sent to Stalingrad!

During the night, we marched about thirty kilometers. The next morning I saw the division commander for the first time. He was standing on the shoulder of the road, next to some Soviet-built M11 staff cars, overseeing the passing troops with a calm, attentive gaze. He was tall, well built, and exuded self-confidence. He had a simple peasant's face and lively eyes, which were intensely focused on the passing formation. Probably, one thought was troubling him: would we stand firm, could we cope with the situation at Stalingrad? For he clearly understood—which he had to keep secret!—that there was still much to be done with our division, that we were still not ready, that some soldiers still did not know how to fight. He could not fail to sense the personal responsibility he had for each soldier entrusted to him. Perhaps he was distressed: "Oh, if only for another month or two—then I'd have confidence in the combat strength and spirit of the division."

Then suddenly once again, without any explanation, the column stopped. Next we were directed into a forest for a short halt that slightly revived us after our difficult night march, and then once again we were moving out. But now we had changed direction and were following the rear elements and vehicles, which were disappearing down the road ahead of us. The "soldiers' telegraph" immediately tapped out a new message: Stalin had found out about us and ordered: "Don't take one soldier away from Rzhev!"

So I didn't wind up at Stalingrad.

It is now known that in 1942, fifty divisions were withdrawn from all the *fronts* and sent to Stalingrad, including a few divisions from the Western Front. But for some reason they left our division alone, and we remained in reserve.

A Word about Frontline Division Commanders

I must say that at the front, the regular soldier is more interested in how his division commander presents himself than the commander does himself. Such an assertion may seem incomprehensible or amusing; after all, the division commander is as distant from the division's rank and file as heaven itself. But that's the way new recruits or indifferent people consider the matter. The frontline soldier, however, who finds himself in a new division, will as his first order of business ask not about his platoon commander or the company commander but about the division commander. Why? In the given case, the slightly altered storyteller's introduction is apt: "Tell me who your division commander is, and I'll tell you everything about your company (or platoon) commander."

During the years of war, I happened to see all sorts of division commanders. Some commanded like a Hussar: loudly, at times expressively, whether an order or a word—roaring and thunder! Fail to carry out their order, and a severe punishment awaits you! This is the worst type of division commander, real martinets, who have no interest in the opinion of subordinates, and who recognize only one rule: "Forward! Ura!" In fact, it was for this reason that they acquired the scornful nickname, "Uria!" How much soldiers' blood rests on their conscience?

Other division commanders assumed that the highest sense of the language of command lay in the selection of curses and swear words; in their conception, it was only with the help of abusive language that you could force a man to fight, for war in their understanding is life wrong side out. It is well known that obscene language flourished at all levels of command during the war and became accepted as normal speech. The higher the rank, the more loudly and expressively they swore. According to general opinion, among the marshals of the war years, only Konstantin Konstantinovich Rokossovsky didn't lower himself to such widespread vileness.

The war also firmly attached to some commanders the fitting label "thug" [*mordoboishchik*: literally, snout-puncher]. To them, "a punch on the snout" not only awarded personal satisfaction but also consolidated their personal superiority. Giving free reign to their fists, the "thugs" considered such action even to be a useful lesson for subordinates. And drunkards? It was difficult at that time to name an officer who never touched vodka. However, I have in mind the true drunkards, the alcoholics. The high command excused such "indiscretions" as long as they didn't impinge upon combat success. During the fighting in East Prussia, I knew one division commander who could down at a minimum a whole bottle of French cognac in one day, but who could still, if necessary, drive his battalions forward with a lash.

In my experience, the officers who commanded by the swear word, bottle, or fist were those lieutenants and majors who had risen in the ranks during Stalin's peacetime purges of the military. Literally within an hour's time, they became lieutenant colonels, full colonels, and generals and now commanded regiments, brigades, and divisions. But by 1942 they were all experienced, and they carried on their shoulders the victory over the Japanese, the Finnish campaign, the operation in Poland, the tragic year of 1941, and the battle for Moscow—now, it seemed, they had earned the right to command. This was a new Stalinist generation of practical commanders, who as a rule had little culture and no special education. Such men didn't tire themselves with mental exercise. They didn't flinch before blaming others for their own personal miscalculations. Such blame particularly fell to the lot of those officers who had graduated from military academies.

As the supreme commander, Stalin knew his generals well. The more cruelly and impudently they behaved, the more cheerfully he twisted his mustache. He could not tolerate a disharmonious choir. He often told his assistants, "After the war, we'll quickly put them back in their places, but for now let them jingle as they wish." And that is just what happened.

But no matter how the Stalinist division commanders were as people, for the sake of justice it must be recognized: I didn't notice any cowardly, weak-willed, or apathetic men among them. How many of them were killed on the land of Rzhev! Many!

The Commander of the 215th Rifle Division—Kupriianov

I first heard about our division commander in June of 1942. When it became known that a division commander had arrived to take us under his command and that he had been instructed to organize the 215th Rifle Division and lead it into battle, this news flew around all the regiments, battalions, and companies like lightning. The officers and commissars were interested in whether or not the new division commander could manage such an important assignment, and what his qualifications and combat experience were. We, the men in the ranks, thought and lived by other standards. We were interested in how this man would deal with the fate of thousands of people in soldiers' greatcoats—decently or like a brute?

Soon everyone learned that the division commander was named Andrei Filiminovich Kupriianov, and that he often traveled around the regiments and didn't like to sit behind his desk. He liked to talk with people—and not just officers.

Time passed, and more complete evidence about the division commander began to reach us. It became known that Kupriianov was no fortunate son; rather, he was the son of a poor peasant. He had been serving in the Red Army since the [Russian] Civil War. He had honorably traveled a long military path, rising from the rank of private to that of colonel. He completed the Smolensk Combat-Infantry Specialist School, and then the Frunze Military Academy. His solid service record inspired confidence. When he served as the deputy commandant of the Sverdlovsk Combat-Infantry Specialist School, one of the school's officers once said, "An army without a lockup is not an army." In reply, Kupriianov suggested, "But you must also give some thought to how to do things, so that the jail is empty more often!" In 1941, when the Germans were approaching Moscow, he was urgently ordered to gather 1,000 cadets from his school and organize them into a rifle brigade, then come to the defense of the capital. In the late autumn and early winter of 1941, practically the entire brigade had fallen and now lay under the battlefields near Moscow. They said that Kupriianov wept openly, suffering over the death of his pupils.

The army commander, Leliushenko, an impatient and ardent man, several times demanded that Kupriianov complete the formation of the division more quickly, so as to include it in combat operations sooner. Each time, Kupriianov found justifiable reasons and managed to obtain one more temporary deferment. At that time, understandably, we didn't know about this. Today I can only thank him for this, for we entered battle better prepared, which saved more than a few lives.

A little more time passed, and another bit of news about the division commander reached us. We learned that he didn't shout, didn't swear, and that he addressed the regiment and battalion commanders formally, using their surnames and the formal form of address. He treated everybody the same, regardless of their rank and title, confirming through his own official actions that respect and trust for people can achieve more than yelling, cruelty, or abusive language. He ate the same food we ate and didn't recognize any commander's personal kitchens. This was a most rare occurrence at the front!

I could fully appreciate this division commander only after experiencing other commanders as I passed through the war. Most division and higher commanders had an enormous entourage: personal cooks, adjutants, aides, a commandant's platoon, orderlies, clerks, a fellowship of military political workers, members of the Special Department [an antiespionage office], signalers (usually female), scouts, personal transportation, commissary officers, without fail a harem or a PPZh [field campaign wife], the army bureaucracy—all this combined to form the strongest palisade, which separated and protected the colonel or general from the petty concerns of command. Not to mention the ordinary rank and file—just try to break through such a barricade!

Another month passed, and you could no longer find a person in the division who couldn't recognize Andrei Filimonovich by face. Always cleanly shaven and well-groomed, fully dressed out in army belts, in a new army blouse, above the left pocket of which gleamed a new Order of the Red Banner (which he had received for the fighting near Moscow)—the division commander was always found in the battalions and companies, from morning until late at night, checking on what and how our officers were teaching us. He spent the most time of all among the scouts and in the separate sapper battalion. Later, it became known that the reconnaissance troops of the 215th Rifle Division were considered among the best in the 30th Army.

In their relations with Kupriianov, his subordinate officers appreciated his scrupulous attention to detail and his desire to avoid the slightest miscalculation. He followed the old rule, measure seven times before cutting once. Given this, from the very first day of command he sternly demanded strict fulfillment of his "directions," which is what he called his personal orders. These directions, which were often short and to the point, most often touched upon the training and daily lives of the troops, which instilled confidence and combat spirit in the men.

Upon the arrival of Kupriianov, the entire division turned into a serious combat school. The division commander knew that he didn't have much time, and he hurried to prepare everyone—privates and officers alike—as well as possible for the coming fighting. We understood this, and we tried to do everything he asked of us as well as possible. Whenever we saw a platoon commander, company commander, or often even a battalion commander next to us in the trench, behind a machine gun, or on a tank, we wanted to know how to fight even better.

"To send you to the front untrained means we've deceived and condemned you," our officers often told us. "Thus don't complain about the work and don't be offended—you must learn and learn!"

In his memoirs, the commander of the Kalinin Front, I. S. Konev, expressed his pride that that the infantry units in his *front* were the first to go from digging individual foxholes and dugouts to constructing a continuous trench line and well-built bunkers. For this "frontline experience" Marshal Konev should thank first of all Kupriianov. The division commander taught us to dig trenches and build bunkers as well as the Germans.

The Offensive Draws Near

With each passing day, the combat strength of the division grew. We received new recruits and new equipment from every corner of Russia. The time had passed when men had to use Molotov cocktails to try to destroy a German tank. Soldiers were now equipped with antitank rifles (PTR), which helped defend against the enemy's light tanks, but which were unfortunately also heavy and cumbersome and required two men to carry on their shoulders. Drawing primarily from the cadets, each regiment formed a machine-gun company and a company of submachine gunners, though to be honest, there were not enough submachine guns to go around, and we were all waiting for the pending arrival of more. The division created an artillery regiment, though it was still entirely horse-drawn. We were still waiting for prime movers for the 122-mm guns, which were powerful weapons in battle. Rocket-carrying trucks were deeply dug into trenches and carefully camouflaged—these were the famous "Katiushas." The Germans called these "Stalin's Organs," because of the howling sound of their salvo fire. Prisoners told us that the tremendous firepower of a Katiusha salvo drove some men insane.

We riflemen received semiautomatic rifles with edged bayonets and light machine guns of the Degtiarev type; we called them "Degtiari." Unfortunately, the first battles revealed that the Degtiarev light machine gun's magazine frequently jammed and wouldn't work. Infantrymen received some new dress, such as American boots, and old greatcoats were replaced with new ones sewn from English fabric.

The rifle division is an enormous living organism. Within the first two months, it grew to 14,000 men and women, that is, to its full prewar authorized complement. All these people had to be fed and dressed, and shown concern about sanitation. Heavy and light weapons had to be kept in constant working order. Therefore, such units as the transportation battalion, the field bread factory, the armorer shop, and the laundry appeared—altogether, they formed the division's "rear."

The commanders tried to place experienced men in charge of the regiments and battalions—men who had participated in the battles for Moscow. New orders and medals gleamed on the blouses of many of them. These men, their tales of fighting for Moscow, and their campaign decorations—all inspired our admiration.

Wire communications remained a weakness in the division. A tank would pass over the wires, or an explosion would sever them, and we'd lose the signal. Signalers worked to repair them, but until they were mended commanders would lose control over the fighting. Moreover, without radio communications, the heavy artillery, the tanks, and our airplanes—the primary support for our infantry—were blind and deaf. This state of affairs continued well into 1943 and even 1944, until the Americans equipped half our ground forces and our entire air force with radio communications.

From day to day, we cadets underwent a second university of military training. Now during field exercises, officers paid particular attention to the necessary practical skills in handling the new equipment. We often conducted large-scale combined maneuvers at the level of the regiment and even the division, in which tanks and the artillery participated. We clambered up on the tanks and went "into the attack" with them.

There were several alerts during this period, and battalions would be sent on foot to the threatened sector of the front. Once the emergency passed, we returned to our reserve positions.

In the summertime, nights are short; you lie in your tent and listen to the distant droning, explosions, and rumbles—the ongoing activity at the front lines. You realize that soon you will be joining the show. In short minutes of rest, I liked to go into the forest, select a somewhat drier place wherever I could find one, and turn myself over to memories. I wasn't letting go of my past, though I logically understood I had now long since been living by different standards.

Heavy rains began on the first days of July, and fierce downpours increasingly released torrents of water onto the earth, turning it into one big swamp, but our field exercises never stopped. We often walked around soaked to the skin and exhausted, but understanding the significance of the officers' activity, we didn't grumble, for we knew that a lost day of training here might never be returned at the front! We spent entire days crawling around on the ground as we were taught how to dig in more quickly and deeply. We learned how to fire on the move, from the hip; how to build better machine-gun nests; how to resist feelings of panic on the battlefield; and how to suppress enemy firing positions. In addition we were shown how to move in order to come to grips swiftly with the enemy, how to take cover from enemy fire on the battlefield and in our trenches, how to rise for the attack, and what to do when under hostile aerial attack.

We literally trained to complete exhaustion, and at first we cadets were thoroughly confused—how did it come to be that everything we had been taught at the specialist school was now useless in combat conditions? Someone even said maliciously, "If only we could send those instructors to get the taste of battle, and only then let them teach cadets!"

With time our confusion began to fade, replaced by growing confidence. I liked the words of one officer: "Remember, fellows: risk should always be tempered by common sense!" And that is just what they taught us.

What were the results of all this training? In less than three months in the forests around Tver, a new combat division was created practically under the nose of the enemy. Through the efforts of the division commander, a widely assorted mass of soldiers from every corner of Russia—many of which had no previous combat training whatsoever—formed into a fully trained military unit, well adapted to combat conditions, fully equipped, and with a solidly functioning "tail."

I only managed to see the division commander himself a few fleeting times. But he once spent nearly an entire day with our battalion. He had a high forehead, his hair combed back, and a young face. Now somewhere in his forties, Kupriianov looked ten years younger. His gaze was friendly but focused, as if displaying all the inner strength of this man through his eyes.

Chatting with the soldiers, he was interested in how our training was going, whether or not the men knew their weapons, and whether they could make proper use of the terrain, both on the defense and on the attack. The way he addressed us caught our attention: "lads." In the cruel year of 1942, when things were becoming unbearable both physically and mentally, this odd little word calmed us down and generated a return sense of gratitude inside us. The men in the ranks and the junior officers were struck by Kupriianov's desire to get to know us, and it was impossible not to notice his warm and sincere attitude toward people.

We all noticed that Andrei Filiminovich seemed to treat the cadets with particular warmth and attention. He thoroughly questioned us about our specialist school, our readiness for battle, and our ability to handle our weapons. He showed an interest in our basic needs, and how they were feeding us.

At the end of one day, the full battalion was gathered in a field, and the division commander led a discussion. He analyzed the battalion's condition and explained the importance of training. He didn't say much, but he then spent more time answering our questions. He spoke calmly and without haste; if he thought we didn't understand him, he repeated what he had just said. He was more like a school teacher than a military commander. In his conclusion, Kupriianov said:

"The day for the battalion review has been set. Get ready for it! Combat training is hard work, but it is also a necessary business. In battle, your life and our general success will depend upon our ability to fight."

Order No. 227

It is difficult to forget the day of 30 July 1942. The battalion commander called us to formation and read out an order issued by Stalin. This was Order No. 227 of 28 July 1942, which has since become known as the "Not One Step Back!" order. Listening to the strange lines of the order, everyone froze on the spot, and I could see how the faces of the men in the formation paled.

It was a desperate situation: "Further retreat means ruin for yourself and at the same time ruin for your Motherland." How could we possibly take in these words calmly? This order, it seems to me, is the most revealing and honest document from Stalin during all the years of the war. The battalion commander finished his recitation of the order with the words, "The fate of the Motherland is now being decided in the battles in the south."

In addition to playing on the patriotic feelings of the soldier, the order foresaw punitive measures. For the first time since the Russian Civil War, penal companies for soldiers and penal battalions for officers were reintroduced into the army.

After the war, G. K. Zhukov called Order No. 227 "disgraceful," and he saw in it an attempt by Stalin to shift responsibility for his own miscalculations onto the army. I think instead that the issuance of this order was both a timely and necessary step. The order was not aimed at reprisal against individual officers and soldiers; it threatened only those who permitted themselves and others to retreat without orders—whether he was a top military commander or an ordinary soldier. Stern measures were necessary at the time, so that officers and soldiers understood their personal responsibility for the fate of the nation.

That evening in the tent, everyone talked about Stalin's order. Some men praised it while others cursed it thoroughly. A few men even cried, having learned the truth about the situation on the southern front: their mothers, wives, and children lived on those steppes near Stalingrad, where the German infantry was now marching and German tanks were rapidly approaching the city. What was happening to them now, and what was their fate?

"We've lived out our time," said one old soldier.—"The German's have broken through to the Volga."

Another soldier erupted with crude scorn: "Lived out . . .! Just don't be mistaken—you'll go straight to the penal company for such defeatism!"

"And is that what you wanted? We're scuttling backward like crayfish! Where to next, the Urals? We've made a mess of things, painfully screwed things up!"

"What do you think, old man, should we lie down in front of tanks?" a young voice rang out.

"Hey, Serafim," a neighbor answered, "of course it's more pleasant to lie under a woman, but who else is going to burn the German tanks?"

"The Russian army has never known such a disgrace—to be driven into penal units by machine guns."

At that point, our company commander, Sukhomirov, entered the tent; probably, he had overheard the last remark, and he therefore immediately joined the conversation: "Don't worry, guys. Nobody's going to let them send you into a penal company. But did you know that during the famous battle with the Swedes at Poltava, Petr I propped up his grenadiers with a Kirghiz blocking detachment?"

Everyone immediately fell silent, struck by what they had just heard. But one man spoke up: "But didn't we beat the Swedes without the help of the blocking detachment, wasn't that the way it was?

"Just so! The grenadiers were defending Russian soil from foreign invaders—that's why they won. They are an example to us all. But you've got to understand the directive this way: an extreme situation calls for extreme measures."

"Give us a guarantee, company commander," Shurka invited, joining the conversation—"that we won't lose at Rzhev like the Swedes did at Poltava."

"But we're not Swedes. We're Russians! We didn't come here to lose, because we're defending our soil from foreign invaders."

With that, the discussion of Stalin's order came to a close.

Let me say a few words about the men who wound up in the punitive units. Today we know that about 300,000 men served out their punishment in one of these companies or battalions.[1] I was a witness to how punitive units were the first to break through the "East Wall" in a frenzy on the Minsk axis. How many penal companies and battalions did the commander of the First Belorussian Front, Marshal Rokossovsky, receive for this purpose? Almost all of them fell in the furious fighting. But it was precisely they who were able to break through the powerful, deeply echeloned defenses of the enemy—seven lines of enemy trenches! They opened the way for the tank armies. It must be said, however, that in many cases the Special Departments, which decided the fate of many men accused of desertion or crimes, acted in a completely arbitrary fashion.[2]

Now we know that the Germans also issued analogous directives: they formed punitive companies, blocking detachments, and special tribunals; strengthened the field gendarme units; and expanded the influence of the S.S. on the Wehrmacht. In 1943 alone on the Eastern Front, the German Army formed more than 100 punitive companies.

The Division Commander and the Cadets

Shortly before the division's departure to the front lines, Kupriianov unexpectedly visited the regiment to meet with all the cadets. A lot of people gathered around him. The division commander looked over everyone, then asked: "Does it trouble you, lads, that you weren't given the chance to graduate from your specialist school?"

One of the cadets answered him: "It was upsetting, Comrade Division Commander, that everything turned out so awkwardly."

"Forget the insult, and don't torment yourselves over it. You yourselves now understand how badly you were needed at the front. We are obliged to carry out Comrade Stalin's order, to drive the enemy from the Rzhev-Viaz'ma bridgehead and to take Rzhev! Hitler considers this bridgehead to be an excellent springboard for a new leap upon Moscow. Together, we will not let him do this. I believe in you! You are the foundation of the division! Powerful weapons are in your hands. Our general success and the cost of that success depend upon how well you will handle your weapons in battle. Once we begin to fight, I am confident that many of you will become commanders of platoons, companies, and perhaps even battalions.

"I will stress three points. First, you must suppress the enemy firing points. Secondly, I authorize you to take any initiative. If your commanding officer becomes disabled, don't wait for an order; take command upon yourself. Finally, cooperate with the tanks in battle, just as we taught you to do.

"I also want to say a word about bravery to you. In what does the bravery and perspicaciousness of an officer consist? In Lev Tolstoy's tale "The Raid," an officer judges that a brave man acts on the battlefield "as it should be": 'Brave is he who fears that which he needs to fear, and not that which he needn't fear.' Pay attention, lads, to this simple and very sensible advice. Are there any questions?"

"Do we have enough combat supplies?"

"We have enough. In '41, we had only about ten shells per mortar. Today, we have ten times more."

"What about our equipment?"

"We have powerful artillery of various calibers. We have many tanks. Among them, there is one that is better than any the Germans have—the

T-34. Protect them. Help the tank crews as much as you can, and they will protect you."

"Will we have air cover?"

"Our pilots have given us their word. The Germans have more airplanes. But that state of affairs won't last long, as you will see."

"What about the medical services?"

"They are ready. The division has a strong medical-sanitation battalion. They have sent us highly qualified doctors and nurses. Assist the medics on the battle-field. Take care of your officers and comrades. Don't be afraid of a little blood. But I ask you to consider previous experience. In a few units during the July offensive, many soldiers abandoned the front lines and headed for the rear, under the guise of giving aid to the wounded. Such a thing must not happen!"

"How should we treat prisoners?"

"Don't shoot them! Send them to the rear, they'll sort things out there."

"Will paths to the enemy's defenses be cleared of mines?"

"Certainly! For the infantry, we will clear paths one-and-a-half meters wide. For the tanks, three meters."

"I have a certain question, Comrade Division commander. It is known that in the July offensive, some battalion commanders led their units with unfurled banners, like the 'Whites' in the film *Chapaev*. What about us?"

"I'm not familiar with such cases. I don't permit anyone to do such a stupid thing."

Someone gathered up the courage to ask about blocking detachments.

"I assure you all," responded the division commander, "that I have asked the army commander to spare this division from blocking detachments."

What an unexpected meeting! Soon they knew about it in all the division's units.

Leaping ahead, I will say that the division commander kept his word.

The Company Commander, Senior Lieutenant Sukhomirov

On 22 August, all training was cancelled. The "soldier's telegraph" reported that the division commander was going to review all the regiments before our departure for the front lines.

The review lasted a full day. In the evening, Senior Lieutenant Sukhomirov called the company together. In one of the cozy little forest clearings under a setting sun, the entire company gathered: 129 soldiers and sergeants, and seven officers: the company commander Sukhomirov, the company's commissar, three platoon commanders, the sergeant major, and the company medic.

Sukhomirov spoke with the soldiers calmly, as if nothing particular was hap-pening, but each of us sensed that his words were important and not easy for him to articulate.

"My golden fellows," began our commander, "the day after tomorrow our 215th Rifle Division will go on the attack. For many of us, this will be our first battle. You are immortal! The first battle for a soldier is the most difficult, his baptism of fire. From it begins and by it will be confirmed our sacred soldier's duty—to defend the Motherland! The enemy is strong. But you have also in a short amount of time become more experienced, better prepared to engage the enemy. Remember! If you don't kill the German, he will kill you! Here there can be no hesitations. On the attack, don't panic; strive to keep up your courage. There is nothing more frightening than fear itself. Don't surrender to it! Only a mouse is afraid of everything. We didn't come here to die! We've come to liberate our native land! I will lead you in battle. I will be with you! Those you know well, with whom you have already experienced so much, will be by your side. We will all be in this together!"

The soldiers all listened to their commander, scarcely breathing, and caught his every word, as if it might become their armor and shield in the impending battle. When he stopped talking, silence reigned.

The first to rise and speak was Mikhail, an old soldier from the 2nd Platoon. Everyone respected him for his honesty and sincerity, and for striving to defend his right to observe his religious faith. Everyone knew that he was a religious man, but more people respected him for this than scoffed at him. The commissar once asked Mikhail to remove the little cross that he was wearing when he arrived in the company. Mikhail refused. By his physical characteristics, he was also special—thin as a rail, with a face just as long and thin, for which he was nicknamed "Waste of Food": it seemed that no matter how much he ate, he remained thin by nature. Mikhail often behaved oddly. But on this occasion he made such a strange impression that the entire company groaned:

"Comrade Senior Lieutenant, thank you for your kind, fatherly parting words. We won't let you down. If I live, I won't ever forget such good words. But there is one thing you said, forgive me, with which I must disagree. You, Comrade Senior Lieutenant, called us immortal. Forgive me again, but we all know, only God alone is immortal, while we, simple people, are all mortal. But it doesn't follow that we should fear death. A man's entire life, however it turns out to be, short or long, is just preparation for our meeting with the Supreme Being. Isn't that so? Excuse me, Comrade Commander, Comrade Commissar, and all my comrade soldiers."

Sukhomirov only smiled. "There is an old saying, 'He who fears death is already no longer living.' Isn't that so, Mikhail?"

Sukhomirov then asked if there were any questions. Someone asked right away: "Comrade Senior Lieutenant, and how can we work it out, so that we'll fight a little better, and still remain alive?"

The commissar answered the soldier: "There isn't any reasoning during a battle; in battle, all thoughts are focused on one thing: the destruction of the foe. Drive him back, kill him—that's how you'll remain alive."

In reality, the primitive and pithy advice raised some doubts in us: everybody talked like the company commander. How many times had we heard: "Kill the German!"? But just try to get at the enemy to kill him! For how long had two Red Army *fronts*—a bulky and cumbersome thing!—tried and failed to place a deathgrip on the enemy?

There turned out to be a lot of questions, but they all boiled down to three basic points: whether there would be tank support; whether the artillery would be able to suppress the enemy's firing points; and why, after seven months of trying, had we still not been able to take Rzhev?

"I'm hoping very much for artillery and rockets. There will be tanks; we have more of them now than the Germans. As for Rzhev: the Germans have been lodged in the city for a long time. They're well dug-in, they've strengthened their fortifications, and their defenses are strong. Therefore we still haven't been able to break through them."

Summarizing the meeting, Sukhomirov told us, "Tomorrow evening we'll be moving out, so you won't be able to get any sleep. Get all your sleep tonight. The day after tomorrow, we'll be getting ready to move into our position. That same night, we'll move into the front lines and assume our designated position. The general offensive will begin the following morning. Get ready and support one another, and I'm speaking first of all to those with frontline experience."

The Night before Our Departure for the Front

The officers left—and everyone somehow kept silent and fell into deep thought. For almost 100 days—that is, from the end of May—the division had been located in the army's reserve; for almost 100 days we had been preparing for what was coming and waiting for this event—some with impatience, some with showy patriotism, some with dread . . . and now the time had come.

"Why have we all become so sad, invisible, and quiet, like pebbles on the bottom of a river?" a loud, deliberately cheerful voice inquired, trying to rouse everyone. Nobody responded.

Men were smoking hand-rolled cigarettes and speaking softly, as if trying to preserve their voices; the time was coming when one could shout himself hoarse! As always happens in psychologically complex situations, everyone behaved in their own way. Optimists chatted about all sorts of nonsense, joked, chuckled, and recalled cheerful stories. Others held their tongues, occasionally heaving deep, sad sighs. Many tried to display greater attention to each other even in the pettiest matters. They say, "If you want to cheer yourself up, cheer up your comrade"; perhaps intuitively following this adage, that's how we were behaving. We exchanged addresses: "If something happens, write my family."

We thought about the most important events of our past lives. Simple things, but precious for the soldier, came to our minds. For example, I remembered a self-made aluminum cigarette case; I still keep it to this day.

I saw how some men were burdened by something deeply personal that they didn't want to talk about, but which kept them from sleeping. One fellow suddenly remembered that today was his birthday—he had reached nineteen years of age!—and started reciting aloud things from his past that, perhaps, he was better off forgetting, particularly on this last night in camp, when we didn't know what was lying in wait for us.

"Why are you being so quiet, what are you thinking about?" I asked a young Tatar named Shakura, a light machine gunner in our squad.

He cheerfully replied: "I'm hoping my Degtiarev won't let me down. So I can shoot more Germans."

Perhaps he was lying to me. I had overheard him the day before, as he prayed passionately to his God, asking for His assistance.

One of the veteran frontline soldiers offered some advice to those of us who were still green: "If we go on the attack tomorrow, then you must courageously stride or run ahead. Whatever you do, fellows, don't lie down in any event! You'll find it impossible then to tear yourself away from the earth's embrace and get back up again. My company commander, I remember, warned us: 'I'll shoot everyone who lays down.'"

"Well, what happened, did he shoot anyone?"

"There were a few cases; he shot a few. From then on, nobody else lay down. We'll see tomorrow how our company commander understands the matter, if things don't go smoothly. There's no escaping an order."

I interceded, trying to convince people: "The senior lieutenant would never shoot a soldier!"

That night, I was lying next to Shurka, and he told me his innermost secret, which he had been concealing from everyone for many years. In the 1930s, when Soviet power persecuted the Cossack people, some Chekists [secret police], most likely acting on the tip of an informant, dug up from their kitchen garden his father's old saber, which he had been keeping from the time of the Russian Civil War. His father was arrested and executed, and his mother was exiled to Siberia. His mother's sister, who was living in a neighboring Cossack village, took the eight-year old Shurka under her own care. The deeply hurting Shurka secretly went out into the steppes and howled like a wolf, calling for his father and mother and cursing those who had done this to them. His family's home was looted, and then the village's Party boss moved into it. A month later, the house burned to the ground, burying the Bolshevik Party chief, his wife, and two children under its charred ruins. An investigation stretched on for more than a year, but it was never determined who had started the fire with a Molotov cocktail. When Shurka had been called up for service, he had concealed this entire story.

It was my turn to confess, and I started to say: "I was a poor student. I spent most of my time reading dime novels and playing soccer . . ."

Shurka interrupted me: "But I never read any books. Life was more interesting than books. And I never played soccer. I was more interested in girls. As a boy, I liked to wander around the village: if I happened to come across a window without drawn curtains, I would peer inside at the young women, and I would gaze spellbound at their white breasts. . . . How my heart pounded! How many young ladies I checked out! Our Russian girls are the sweetest, finest on the whole earth; if only I knew how to approach them! Though it is true that I once happened to wind up alone with a mischievous young woman, a real sexy thing, the type about which we Cossacks say, 'A babe who'll knock out your windows!' but she didn't put out for me . . ."

"I couldn't follow you, what was that were you saying?" I softly chuckled.

Shurka clarified his last point, and I resumed speaking about myself: "In '37 they arrested my father, and left my mother and me in a real mess. Mama lost her job. I left school and went to work as an apprentice film projectionist at the "Shock Worker," one of the best movie theaters in Kharkov. Mama and I lived on my wages—one ruble a day. My counterpart and I carried around tins that contained film reels. One and the same film would be showing at two different theaters at the same time, and my counterpart and I would meet halfway, by the Gorbaty Bridge in the center of the city, and exchange reels. He would, let's say, give me the first reel, and I would hand the third reel over to him. We spent all day running back and forth like that, so people called us "the Runners." By some miracle, my father survived. In '39, he came back home. In January of '41 we moved to Moscow. My father forced me to quit work and return to school."

"And when did you join the Komsomol?"

"In '38, when I was still living in Kharkov."

"How could that be? Your father is in prison, and yet you get into the Komsomol!" Shurka was indignant.

"At my interview with the Komsomol district committee, they asked: 'Is your father an enemy of the people?' I answered, 'The investigation has still not been completed.' They didn't seem to want to accept me, and conferred for a long time, but in the end they took me in. Perhaps, therefore, I was joining out of pure spite. Or perhaps, simply like everyone else . . ."

"You always hear Komsomol members saying, 'Like everyone else. . . .' That's rubbish! They tricked me even more cruelly than you. Damn them all! All right, they purged some souls. Now let's talk frankly about tomorrow. What are we fighting for? For the miscreants who killed my father and almost did your own father in? For that Pioneer's red tie of Pavlik Morozov [a darling of Stalinist propaganda, who informed on his own father] or for all your Komsomol members?"

Really, why had I joined the Komsomol? It is amusing that it was only then, on the eve of battle, that I gave serious thought to the matter. What career advantages could we be thinking about at that age? The Komsomol membership card couldn't save anyone from his fate; so many people who carried Party identification cards were executed during the purges. Did I join out of a sense of idealism? What sort of ideals can someone have at that age? But then why did I join? Moreover, Party members and Komsomol members were supposed to be in the front ranks of any attack, in order to give their lives in the name of what? . . . But I didn't share these thoughts with Shurka. Instead, I answered him: "Nevertheless, Shurka, you and I have sworn an oath to defend the Motherland."

"I'm curious, what sort of Motherland are you planning to defend? The one that betrayed our fathers and mothers? For me, it will be the most exquisite, magnificent day when I can strike dead just one commissar or *chekist-osobist* [a secret agent of the Special Department]. They're just dogs that aren't even fit for damnation. No, kind sir, I'm going into battle for different reasons. I'll be fighting against the foreigners who have laid their hands on Russian soil and who rape our women and girls. My Cossack grandfather and Cossack father were always a source of support for the Fatherland and the tsar. So for the Fatherland, I'll never be afraid to lay down my life. But you must never compare yourself to us—you must live on! You are not a Russian, but I know our Russian Fatherland is as dear to you as it is to me."

I'll never forget those animated and painfully sincere words, and those feelings I experienced at that moment, when we were all "on death's door."

The platoon couldn't sleep. "It's going to be quite a show, guys, the high command has grabbed us for a reason," someone said in the darkness.

"Yes, it appears that our turn has come. We've spent such a long time in the rear. But now, likely, they'll be giving us 300 more grams of bread."

"And how much does a German bullet weigh, do you know? Oh, old friend, old friend, is a supplement like that lying in wait for us?

"I don't know who's right here, but tomorrow, I imagine, everything will be different. Why are you chattering like magpies, after hearing about that menacing document? Now they really have us in a bind: in front of us—the German; behind us—the blocking detachment. You advance—you'll get a German bullet, but if you fall back—your own guys will knock you off."

"If you're condemned to die, then let it be worth something," a young voice rang out.

"What's the use of that, old friend?"

"If only we can topple the German . . ."

How different we all were. I dozed off a little, and—it had to be!—I had a short dream. I'm seven years old. I'm walking up to a watchdog. The dog, rising on its rear paws, licks me; he's waiting for something—perhaps I've brought him a little treat? But how can I explain it to him? Mama didn't let me take even the smallest piece of bread: "Whatever people think, it is shameful to feed a dog bread. . . ."

I woke up and remembered the end of this story. The dog was lying quietly, warming himself in the sun. I walked up to him, and when he rose to his feet, I sat down on his back. What was I thinking! The dog became genuinely infuriated, abruptly tossed the uninvited rider off his back, then gave me a strong bite on the leg and ran off. Howling in pain, I rushed home. The wound required thirty-two stitches to close. The dog turned out not to be rabid, just proud. And perhaps the dog considered me to be a miser? A week later, a black van from the city dog pound pulled up, and three dogcatchers grabbed the dog, dragged it forcibly back to the van, threw it inside, and then drove off. Later the kids found out that the dog had been put to sleep. How I cried! Nobody could comfort me.

Before this night, I had never before remembered a dream, and I never believed in them whenever someone would try to tell me about one. I, of course, didn't know anything about Freud and Jung, though I recall one day buying a thin little booklet at a market for a few kopecks, entitled *The Dream-book*, published in Saint Petersburg in 1912. I was curious, so I read it and broke out laughing: it turned out that any sort of dream (and the author introduced approximately 100 subjects) supposedly reflects some sort of real event in your past or future life! Since I didn't have dreams, I couldn't check the accuracy of the author's words. But now on the eve of battle, I had just had the first dream in my life that I could recall. I was curious; did it portend something about the morrow?

Shurka was now snoring, but my neighbor on the other side was whispering to someone, so I asked: "With whom are you whispering?"

I was nonplussed by the response: "With God," he quietly answered. "I'm waiting for a miracle from Him, so I'm praying for one thing: to give me a good omen."

"Do you think he'll hear you?"

"Oh yes, he's heard, he's heard; he sent me a pretty bug. That, friend, is a good omen."

Memories of my grandfather flooded my mind. Soon after my father's arrest, fearing for my fate, Mama sent me from Kharkov to my grandfather in Kiev, where he lived with his daughter, my father's sister. Grandfather once spent an entire night sitting on the balcony, praying to God, asking him for a positive sign about his son, my father. And he received it. The first thing my father did when he was released from prison was to go to Kiev. By that time my grandfather was seriously ill; he had wasted away, worrying about the fate of his son. In 1940, just before his death, he asked me, whatever the life path I chose, not to go into the police, not to engage in commerce, and not to become a fireman. I gave him my word, and I kept my word.

For all of us, these final hours before heading to the front became special. But none of us could imagine that our commanding officer spent the whole night writing letters to our mothers. I don't know how many letters he managed to write, and whether or not every mother received one. My Mama did receive his warm words about her son, and she preserved this letter as something sacred to the end of her life.

Yes, you don't often come across such a company commander. A better one, perhaps, I never knew.

It is worthwhile here to mention another little episode. One evening a soldier fell asleep at his post. Another soldier, a sly fellow, took the sleeping soldier's rifle and brought it back to our company commander: "Look, Comrade Senior Lieutenant, how vigilant I am!" But instead of gratitude, he heard, "I hope next time you'll behave differently: take the post in place of your comrade while he sleeps from exhaustion." Then Sukhomirov added: "I hope you know the name of Suvorov? Once Suvorov told someone about a similar case: 'I advise you to learn to forgive the sins of your neighbor, but not to forgive your own.' Learn to forgive, soldier! And don't tell tales!"

This episode—and soon the entire company knew about it—says everything about our company commander.

We didn't know much about him. Ostensibly, he was a Siberian. He graduated from the Omsk Combat-Infantry Specialist School. He fought in the battle for Moscow. He got into trouble somewhere once, and the army bureaucrats locked him in a deathgrip. Our combat commander never advanced in rank or assignment. Twice wounded, he never received a single decoration.

Sukhomirov ate from the same kettle we did. If the cook prepared a poor meal for us, the company commander didn't hide his displeasure; he would roundly rebuke both the cook and the sergeant major. Before we left for the front he summoned both men, ordering them to remain in the rear and to prepare the tastiest meal for everyone who might return from the battle. He told them not to spare any supplies, so that everyone could have seconds.

A bullet cut him down in the opening minutes of the attack. He was a splendid, courageous man; the very embodiment of the true soldier. That's how I'll always remember him.

7

The First Battle
24 August 1942

Dawn at the Front

They woke us up early, even before dawn. We hastily ate a bite, then gave our rolled-up greatcoats and our knapsacks to the sergeant major for transfer to the transport unit. In return, each of us received a helmet and an "amulet"—that's what we called the little wooden case, suspended on thin but strong twine, in which was stored a small note with our personal information. Because of some sort of mistake in the commissariat, there weren't enough helmets for everyone, and a few guys rejected them, which wound up costing them dearly.

Before surrendering their knapsacks, the old guys in the company first pulled some clean underwear from them and changed into them, observing the old custom to go into battle in clean underwear. Komsomol members turned over to the commissar short notes, in which they had written approximately only the following words: "I'm going into battle. If I die, I ask that you consider me a communist." I also wrote such a note, for I wanted everyone in the company to know—Russians, Ukrainians, Cossacks, and Uzbeks alike—that I was a soldier just like them.

At sunset on 23 August, the units of the division moved out and took to the road, our artillery following us. As we emerged from the woods we saw a lot of tanks. This raised our spirits. We reached the front line when it was already dark. The company immediately occupied its designated sector. The trench assigned to me turned out to be shallow, so I immediately and with great zeal began to deepen it and widen it. One of our "tank hunters," as we called our men who handled the PTR antitank rifles, worked next to me. From time to time, we exchanged opinions on the characteristics of the soil at this location. Once I was satisfied, I nestled down into my shelter and fell silent. The PTR rifleman next to me also was quiet. I knew him well; he was one of our inveterate smokers, and likely he was now suffering from the strict ban on smoking: how can someone go into battle without a last cigarette?

What does the warrior think about at this last hour, minutes before the attack begins? Inside, the soldier is ready to do his duty and to stand fast with his comrades, but he knows well—and nobody can convince him otherwise—that after the battle, not everyone will return alive. But nevertheless, hope never leaves him: he looks around at the other frontline soldiers, considering whether fate will turn away from this one or that one, or lend him a helping hand; well, all right: just let them be wounded. . . . But the thought about wounds raises new concerns: will they carry me off, will they have time to evacuate me from the battlefield, before my lifeblood runs out? . . . Why such doubts? The company has been assigned a medic and a medical orderly, but the wounded will be in the hundreds, perhaps even more. There's also a regimental medical company—but all the same, there are never enough medics. The wounded, particularly the severely wounded, are forced to wait long hours for help to arrive, and losing a lot of blood, they often die before help comes, or on the way to the medical-sanitation battalion. They also often die from shock.

Only medics and medical orderlies have the right to carry the wounded from the battlefield. It is forbidden for other soldiers to accompany the wounded to the rear, and any such attempt to do so is usually considered desertion in the face of the enemy. However, the ultimate decision didn't always follow regulations, for in combat situations one must carefully distinguish between necessary assistance and desertion from the battlefield.

Every veteran has his own notions of war and the battles in which he participated. But whatever the views, the primary event for each soldier in war is the first battle.

With time I came to understand that whether it was the first battle or the tenth, each one was very difficult to experience, both psychologically and physically. It necessarily requires the greatest effort, and it places limitless stress on the body and nerves. The most resolute soldier tries not to think about death. I never saw any completely fearless soldiers. Do such people even exist? Let's assume that I am mistaken and that there are such soldiers. It is not for nothing that we say about such people, "They were born without a sense of fear." As for me personally, on the contrary, I realized that God had endowed me with fear from the very first days of the war. What did I most fear? Two things: to be taken prisoner, and our own *osobisty* [agents of the Special Department]. I didn't know it at the time, but today I would add a third thing: I grew afraid of dive-bombers with their terrible howling sirens. But I was still confident that we would deal with the Germans, for there were more of us, and we were stronger, if only for the reason that we were fighting on our native soil.

Night was now ending, and dawn was imperceptibly starting to emerge from the darkness, when I heard the platoon leader's order passed down the line: "Stay down, don't smoke, and wait for commands. The signal will be a green rocket and a whistle."

Bent over, lightly camouflaged, I leaned quietly against the wall of my trench. Up ahead, on a low rise, the outlines of the German trenches were barely visible. They were girding in a semicircle three villages, which we had been ordered to take at any cost. Before the battle, our commanders had explained to us: with the capture of these villages, a key strong point in the German defenses would be eliminated, and this would open a direct road to Rzhev for the 30th Army. Before us lay a green field with brown patches, small copses of trees, and wooded hollows—all of it blasted and plowed up repeatedly far and wide by shells and craters. To the villages, or more accurately, to what was left of them, it was about 700–800 meters, no more—it seemed like we could reach them without batting an eye.

A soft morning breeze caresses our faces, and the first rays of the morning sun are appearing in a clear, clean sky. The stench of corpses, carried to our trenches with the wind, spoils the scene and the mood of the men. Somewhere nearby, the bodies of those who fell in previous fighting have been dumped— why haven't they been buried? At first, our heads lightly spin from the repulsive odor, and we feel nauseous, but gradually we get used to it.

To our rear, one after the other, we can hear bomb blasts. Junkers? Apparently, they're trying to suppress the reserves, who are moving up to the front lines. How many times have we been warned about concealment! The bombing stops; again it is silent; the enemy still remains quiet. It won't be easy to deal with him, but we have tanks, and not only that, we have "34s", the best tanks in the world! Moreover, our artillery and Katiusha rockets will smash all their defenses into pieces, even before we attack, and our airplanes will give us support—the Germans won't be able to withstand it, so our commanders tell us.... It is quiet. We only hear single shots ringing out, from our lines or their lines, now and then. Everything is deceptively innocent and peaceful, as if a truce has been called; it leads one to think: why must people kill one another? "There is before battle an hour of great quiet, sometimes not an hour, but a minute.... Nowhere else is there such silence, as happens in war," Konstantin Simonov accurately wrote. Only a few calculated minutes remain. Melancholy thoughts of my mother don't leave me. Suddenly a silly rhyme floods my thoughts: "A man swept off his feet from Bassein Street." I have my rifle in my hands, I feel calm, I'm not alone, I have the motionless soldiers of my squad beside me, also holding their breaths; they're here, with me, ready to come to my assistance. I look for signs of movement among the Germans, and I wait for the command. The glow of sunrise on the horizon burns even brighter, which slightly darkens the azure blue of the sky, just like at sunset—is time running backward? No, that cannot be....

Attack!

The first salvoes of artillery shatter the calm air! That means it's 6:00 A.M.: the preparatory artillery barrage! Volleys of Katiusha rockets shriek high overhead as they fly toward the enemy. The roaring and crashing grows—our bombers and ground attack planes have started working over the enemy's trenches. Wonderful! Everything is going just as it should. Everything is according to plan! Above the villages, which we are just about to try to take, enormous columns of black smoke and crimson flames rise into the air—what a pleasant scene! Our tanks emerge from the woods behind us, carrying infantry on their hulls. I give them a quick count—no fewer than thirty! In two lines, they skirt the line of trenches and move resolutely forward. Such power! That's the way!

The company commander gives the signal to get ready. And suddenly I feel as if I am all alone, the only person on earth. A green signal rocket races high into the air. The voice of our commander pierces my brain: "After me! Forward! Cha-a-a-rge!"

Oh, how difficult it is to tear myself from the ground. It seems as if I am sprawled, rooted into the soil, with no arms or legs and no ability to move. Don't I have my arms? "The trench is your last reliable fortress." The final seconds—forget about everything else, soldier: the order has sounded. Get up, friend. Let's go. . . . Forward! Time strangely slows down and moves in fits and starts; at the last moment, I manage to catch sight of the bright sky and the Earth's wonderful field before me—and clenching my teeth, now no longer thinking of anything, as if I've switched off my mind, I rise up slightly in my burrow. The inexorable power of the call of duty instantly forces me out of my trench, shoves me forward, and now I'm running! Together with everyone else, tipping my helmet-covered head forward, just as we were taught to do—bending low, my rifle with its attached bayonet thrust aggressively forward: I hurry quickly, trying not to lag behind those running beside me, and, like everyone, I'm crazily yelling, although I feel a cold trickle of sweat on my forehead under my helmet. But I strain my lungs and shout, "Ura-a! Ura-a!"—and this unifying cry brings with it some new mysterious strength, muffles my hearing, and stifles my fear. We're attacking head on, in echelons, and my company is advancing in the second line. Other men are hurrying in front of us and behind us; whoever is lucky tries to follow the tanks, they're cover all the same; but they are in front of us, as we still haven't caught up with the tanks. Forward, forward, about 300 meters to the heights remains, we've already overcome half the distance! . . . and at that moment, the German trenches speak up. A growing, destructive fire sweeps up and down the attacking lines with a storm of machine-gun fire. The hoarse coughing of mortars follows the machine guns. Artillery starts to roar. Enormous geysers of earth toss the living and the dead high into the air. Thousands of shell splinters, like poisonous hornets, rip into men, tearing bodies and the earth. How can this be?! It appears that our artillerymen didn't reconnoiter the enemy's firing positions; did they just pound vacant space for thirty minutes?

Never mind! The tanks are moving forward with infantry on board. Having successfully navigated the minefields, they are now approaching the enemy's front line, moving with all their mass and firing on enemy positions—they'll fix everything; they're just about to reach the German trenches, where our infantry will toss their hand grenades, while the tanks crush the German positions.

Suddenly Stuka dive-bombers appear above the battlefield from the direction of Rzhev. Confidently and impudently they head straight for the tanks. One tank . . . a second . . . a third explodes from the direct attacks, turning into large black-and-crimson bonfires, but the remaining tanks, quickly dispersing, continue to advance on their objective. The bombers are flying in flights. The lead plane, turning on its siren, gracefully goes into a dive and, having released its bomb on its target, soars skyward again. After it, in single file, dives a second, a third, a fourth . . . a tenth, forming a unique carousel above the hastily scattering tanks. The bloody feast of the vultures, occurring in eyesight of the charging soldiers, causes a commotion: where our are fighters—why haven't they arrived to protect the tanks and infantry? One group of the birds of prey, having dropped its bombs, flies away, but another takes its place, and the whole grim process repeats—having arranged a merciless "funeral procession," they don't let their victims escape the fatal pocket.

From that terrible day I could never bear the wild animal howling of German Stukas. The wailing they emit is head splitting; it freezes your soul, casts you into confusion, paralyzes you like the gaze of a venomous cobra, and lingers in your ears for a long, long time. Even after the war, I never once dared to visit a zoo, because I feared the wail or howl of an animal there might bring me to nervous collapse.

Nonetheless, the German bombers cannot deal completely with our tanks and aren't able to destroy them all; the infantry also, despite the dense curtains of machine-gun fire from the front and the flanks, continues the attack, and our first ranks are approaching the first line of the enemy's trenches. However, they aren't able to reach it in the first rush, and our fighters, lying behind shrubs and little mounds, hiding in little hollows and gullies, open fire on the enemy's firing points from under cover, while the following ranks continue to advance.

A rising rumble and the din of powerful explosions suddenly tear the air! It is the enemy's heavy long-range artillery, trying to separate the infantry from the tanks. Huge gaps appear in the first lines of infantry following the tanks. The air is sucked from our lungs, and it becomes harder and harder to breathe.

My throat is parched and I am tormented by thirst, and I'm suffocating from nausea. Where is the sky, where is the earth, we no longer understood, nor can we feel; our hearts pound as if they are about to burst from our bodies, and hatred rises in a furious wave for those who are so pitilessly destroying us.

"Forward! Forward!" shout the officers who are still alive, many just before dropping dead among their own soldiers. The men are mechanically moving forward, and many are dying—but we now no longer belong to ourselves; we have all been seized by the incomprehensibly savage element of battle. Shell bursts, shell fragments, and bullets are sweeping away the infantry lines, shredding the living and the dead. How can people withstand such a thing? Where can one protect oneself in such a hell? The ranks of the attackers are thinning, but even more new units are filling in the gaps. The remnants of former companies and battalions have turned into a senseless mass of onward-charging, desperate men. The din of battle swallows the cries of the wounded; medics, risking their own lives, rush about, caught between the wall of heavy fire and these terrible cries. Trying to help those they can, the medics drag the maimed and bleeding to the nearest shell craters. In the howl and shriek of shells we stop recognizing one another. Faces have become pale, lips compressed. Many men are trembling from fear. Some men are vomiting. Some are crying as they advance, and the tears, mixed with sweat and filth, stream down their faces and blind their eyes. Some men have involuntarily urinated or defecated from the shock. Wild swearing and cursing fills the air. One man is trying to cross himself on the run, gazing upwards with a prayer. Someone is calling for his beloved Marus'ka.

Suddenly I jerk to a stop; a wounded man has grabbed me, pulling me downward, and is shouting at me directly in the face: "It's me—Zhenia! We're . . . from the same barracks . . ."

Yes, of course, it is Zhen'ka! Our Zhenechka! His gaze is feverish, in his eyes is the black shadow of approaching death. Shaken, I nod my head, and babble something in a whisper: "Yes, Zhenechka, yes . . ."

Heavily straining, he is wheezing in a heart-rending fashion, straining to say something more, but I could barely hear the words: "I don't have . . . much time. . . . Do you understand? . . . Understand? . . . Find . . . my mama . . . I beg you. . . ."

Our company favorite could say nothing more, as blood gushed from his throat and poured down his chest in a wide current. He turned over and fell prostrate to the earth. Everything was over. For a moment, I forgot where I was. . . .

Noise crashed in my ears. I could see Zhenechka's pale face in front of me. It was transformed again—it had become handsome and illuminated, just as before. Frantic cries resounded all around me, from which it was possible to go insane. I got up and started running to catch up with my comrades. Across the battlefield, ceaseless wailing and howling rose above the infernal carnage:

"The damned scoundrels!"

"Where's my foot?"

"Medic! Medic!"

"Pilots, save us!"

"What have you done with us? You're driving us into machine guns like cattle!"

Again, this hoarse voice:

"Marus'ka, where are you?"

Attacking waves of men followed one after another. The conflict flared up, the piles of corpses grew. We drew even nearer to the enemy trenches. This is the most difficult moment of battle. The night before, our sappers had cleared passageways through the minefields, and now remnants of the attackers were rushing through them. I saw the first soldiers as they reached the trenches, broke into them; now frenzied hand-to-hand fighting with bayonets and fists ensued. But I was not able to run up to join it. The last thing that I heard was some sort of senseless cry. With this cry I felt, painfully and sharply, something cold, slippery, and blunt strike me in the back of the neck, stunning me and slamming my head forward against my chest. The strong jolt rocked me sharply, threw me forward, and I crashed face-first to the ground. But I never lost consciousness. I could feel that I was suffocating, that my nose and mouth were filled with earth and dirty grass; I spat it out, and it became easier to breathe. Lifting my head with difficulty, I saw fighters, who were running past a large crater. I had to reach it. I crawled over and slid down into it. For several minutes I understood nothing from the shock of my wound and didn't notice anything around me. Perhaps I was unconscious. Then with shaking hands I felt my head, trying to find out where I'd been hit. My hand bumped into a piece of metal. It had penetrated my field blouse, my undershirt, and somewhat frighteningly become lodged in my neck below the back of my head. What was this? A shell fragment! There was no blood—but this didn't comfort me! Blood and pain will come later, this I knew. Here, probably, I slipped into unconsciousness again.

When I came to a second time, a terrible sight appeared before my eyes. Opposite me, covered in blood and grime, lay a soldier with a split skull and already glazed eyes; it was evident that he had been mortally wounded somewhere close to the crater and had managed somehow to slip down into it. Quite close to me to my right, half-sitting, leaning against the slope of the crater, was another man. He was unconscious. His abdomen had been ripped apart by a shell fragment, and his intestines had spilled out onto the ground. With an arm bloody up to his elbow, he was mechanically striving to stuff them back in again. Looking at the pale, bloodless face, its dull eyes already expressing nothing, I froze in horror: despite the sharply distorted features, I recognized in the severely, perhaps mortally wounded man—Shurka! I began to yell:

"Shurka! Shurka! What can be done for you? What must be done?" The sudden thought of medical assistance seized me with hope. Sliding over to him, I touched his shoulder and tried to rouse him: "Shurka! We're from the same barracks!" There was no response. I burst into tears.

What lofty words! Pronounced just yesterday! About the Fatherland and duty! I had no thought of them now. Only grief! Only pity and grief! I called loudly, appealing to him, and tried to look into his eyes to catch his gaze. "Shurka! Shurka! Wake up, Shurka!"

Suddenly a face appeared above the crater. "Have you been shouting?"

"Yes, it was me."

"Are your arms and legs intact?"

"Yes, they're together."

"Crawl out of there."

I try to explain where I was wounded, and then suddenly remembered: "My squad leader is lying here. How can we help him?"

"Crawl out of there, I've told you!" the medic coarsely bellowed.

I embraced Shurka and kissed him three times on the head.

The medic helped pull me out of the crater, examined my wound, and then indicated a distant patch of woods and a road leading to it: "Get yourself out of here and head that way; perhaps somebody will pick you up along the way."

"But what about Shurka?" I asked.

"Not even God himself can help him now. If your Shurka survives until night, we'll bring him out on a stretcher; I can't do it by myself. As for you, get going, get the hell out of here, we'll do without you."

So I started crawling. I crawled for a long time, automatically, just as they taught us back in the specialist school. I crawled on and on, paying little attention to the bullets and shell fragments that whistled and whined as they passed me, only I winced and covered my head each time one flew by too close. Then I would pull myself together again, and resume creeping and clambering, afraid to move my head or touch my neck, experiencing sharp pain from any piece of rough terrain or too sudden a movement. Whenever the gunfire or artillery fire intensified, I would climb into a shell hole and cover myself with bodies. I strained with all my might for those woods, literally plowing the earth with my nose; likely, I was still in shock.

It took me a long time to reach them . . .

"We're from the same barracks."

Sasha Ryzhikov—a guitarist and singer, and the first person to whom the barracks introduced me.

Iura Davydov—clear-headed, a philosophizer, and a talented young man. I am confident that a bright future awaits him . . .

Stepan Davydov, our "Uncle Stiopa,"—the kindest soul, and a true soldier, he was the first of us to become an officer.

Shurka—an orphan, a wandering soul, and one cannot forget his story about how it was for him on the steppe, having lost his parents. How many evils had befallen him in his short lifetime!

Zhenia Evlev, Zhenechka—his last words were about his mother. I never knew a more fine and handsome fellow. . . .

Dimka Okunev—our avenger, he also died, defending his soldiers; a man of amazing personal bravery.

Sasha Pushkarev, Iulik Gerts, Feden'ka, Serezha Kozhevnikov—they all were killed.

Shurka and Zhenechka fell in the very first battle, and I can say they died in my arms. I don't know the fate of the others.

But I do know that in the hearts of those who remained—we are forever together:

"WE'RE FROM THE SAME BARRACKS!"

The Division Commander and the Cadet

I learned the details of the battle later, when I was already at the medical-sanitation battalion. I recalled much after the war through documents and the recollections of participants in the fighting.

Without regard for the losses—and they were enormous!—the command of the 30th Army continued to commit more and more fresh battalions to the slaughter, which is the only possible way to call what I witnessed on the battlefield. Both the officers and the soldiers ever more clearly understood the senselessness of what was happening: whether the villages were taken or not, for which they were laying down their lives, it wouldn't help in any way solve the problem of taking Rzhev. Increasingly, the soldier was seized by indifference, but the command kept explaining to him that his excessively simple view from the trenches was incorrect. It seems that there was some higher strategy, unknown to the soldier: each captured village was one more step on the path of driving out the enemy.

West of Rzhev, this "driving" proceeded with complications. Here, on the sector of the 30th Army, by the middle of the summer of 1942, the Germans had created a deeply echeloned defensive belt—with more than 500 pillboxes and bunkers, antitank ditches seven meters wide, and three 500-meter-wide belts of fallen trees. Every inhabited point in enemy possession was turned into a self-sufficient strongpoint of defense, with bunkers and pillboxes, fighting trenches, and communication trenches. At 20 to 100 meters in front of the trenches, several bands of continuous barbed wire created barriers to attacking infantry. Every point around had been accurately preregistered by fire. They even foresaw to their soldiers' comfort: almost every squad had its own dugout, with electricity and double-tiered plank beds.[1] By building these deeply echeloned and elaborate defensive lines and positions, the German command intended to make Rzhev inaccessible, and to hold our forces here for a long time. Indeed, in this they were fully successful. For eight months already, the 30th Army had been conducting bloody fighting for Rzhev, but it had not been able to break through the line of enemy defenses.

Concentrating his strength for a new offensive, the commander of the 30th Army, Leliushenko, had made the decision to introduce his primary reserve, the 215th Rifle Division, into the fighting, having reinforced it with a tank brigade and a separate artillery regiment.

On 24 August 1942, the next round of conflict began. In the initial battles of the new offensive, regimental 76-mm guns were rolled up to fire over open sights at enemy positions, thanks to which the division drove the Germans from two villages—Kovorino and Kopytikhi. The third village, Gubino, changed hands several times before we finally took it.

As a result of the August battles, the army managed to penetrate the enemy's frontline defenses in several places, to sweep the left bank of the Volga clear of enemy forces, and to advance to a depth of three kilometers into the enemy's defenses.

Six kilometers remained to reach Rzhev—only six kilometers! However, it took another six months of the cruelest fighting to traverse those six kilometers, to break decisively the enemy's resistance and to force him to abandon Rzhev, the "city-front," as we called it.

Factually speaking, the first combat actions of the division were tremendously costly failures. The 711th Rifle Regiment experienced heavy losses; its training battalion in particular suffered severely, and many of the Tiumen cadets fell in the battle. One fact alone testifies to the division's enormous losses: in the first ten days of fighting, approximately 4,000 wounded soldiers were counted in the division's medical-sanitation battalion.

It was not Kupriianov's fault that when the companies and battalions of his division went on the offensive they ran into strong fortifications and bitter enemy resistance. Besides that, the Germans were better equipped and had complete superiority in the air. Finally, it is well known that one soldier on the defense is equivalent to three attackers.

It was said after the war that while attending planning sessions at army headquarters, Kupriianov didn't like to offer his opinion for general discussion. He had already experienced a lot of grief in front of Moscow and understood the erroneous nature of many of the high command's decisions there, but he could maintain that even more mistakes were made at Rzhev than in front of Moscow. But however Andrei Filimonovich regarded his orders from above, he always tried to keep his self-control, for he realized he wasn't serving a particular place but a greater cause: struggle with the enemy.

In the first days of September, when I was healing in the medical-sanitation battalion, the 215th Rifle Division received an order to force the Volga with one rifle regiment in order to create a bridgehead for further offensive operations west of Rzhev and to cut off the line of retreat for the enemy's Rzhev group of forces. The task was complex, considering the presence of a significant water obstacle and the lack of bridging equipment. The assignment fell upon the 711th Rifle Regiment. It made several attempts to cross to the right bank, but all were unsuccessful: the fighters came under heavy fire as they tried to cross, or drowned, being unable to cope with the current; the remaining men returned to their line of departure. Then the division commander tried to change plans: he decided to shift his effort farther up the left bank of the Volga and force a crossing at a different spot. But this operation too was not crowned with success. The division thus completely failed in its efforts to create a bridgehead on the opposite bank of the Volga.

During a short pause after the initial fighting, a soldier, a former cadet, walked up to the division commander, who was standing amidst some regiment commanders and other soldiers. He asked permission to speak, as everyone knew that Kupriianov always encouraged the initiative of his subordinates.

"It seems to me," said the bold warrior, "that the basic lines of attack for the offensive upon the city were incorrectly chosen. In these places, the Volga River has high and steep banks. If you'll permit me, I'll show you a more suitable place for an offensive on a map."

Kupriianov attentively listened to everything the soldier had to say, then turned to the men standing around him and asked, "But what do you think?"

Everyone nodded approvingly. Then Kupriianov told the cadet-strategist: "Fine fellow! You are thinking correctly and boldly. I am appointing you company commander."

This was unheard of. The news quickly traveled around the division, and the name of the soldier became known to us: Iurii Davydov, our "cartographer" back at the cadet school.

Inquisitively and agonizingly, Kupriianov searched for another way to conduct the offensive. He strove for direct engagement with the enemy while the division still had faith, enthusiasm, and combat spirit. And such a day came! On 21 September the division received an order to attack Rzhev. An assault on the city itself began. It continued for nine days. I should stress that the idea of storming the city came from Kupriianov; the command of the 30th Army didn't support it. The division's regiments, which had created and equipped special assault groups, penetrated the northeast outskirts of Rzhev. The soldiers fought fiercely, frenziedly, led from the front by combat officers who were full of energy and concentration and faith in success. Kupriianov personally appeared at the front, encouraging the attackers and suggesting more effective ways to conduct the battle. Many reminiscences of that city fighting have been preserved.[2]

In October 1942 our division commander was awarded a second Order of the Red Banner.

The Death of Stepan Davydov

During the fighting for Rzhev, Stepan Davydov was killed—our "Uncle Stiopa," who was one of the best of the Tiumen cadets. Many years later, his comrade Pavel Shekhovtsev told me in detail how it happened, and I will cite an extract from his memoir:

> At the end of August 1942, after some long marches our division arrived near Rzhev. The enemy's air force ruled the skies. Those soldiers who could do it tried to think of ways to repulse the vultures. Stepan mounted his Maxim machine gun on a wheel taken from a broken down cart, so it could have a full 360 degrees of motion, thereby creating a device for firing at the enemy airplanes. As a joke, we called his creation "Davydov's antiaircraft unit."
>
> I remember that on 26 August 1942, we suffered a particularly heavy air attack. Junker 87s with their piercing howl were shooting us up with their machine guns and dropping their bombs on us. Davydov, who had set up his antiaircraft device in a camouflaged position in some shrubs, fired burst after burst at the airplanes from his little emplacement. One after the other, two Stukas never pulled out of their dives and crashed into the ground; a third, trailing a black plume of smoke, went down in enemy territory. Within thirty minutes, another air attack came. Ten Ju-88s and twenty Ju-87s dove upon us. It seemed that nothing living remained on the earth below them. However, Davydov's machine gun kept firing at the airplanes. One of the vultures spotted Davydov's position and released its bomb on it. Another plane followed suit, and Davydov's machine gun fell silent.
>
> After the attack we ran over to Stepanov's position. The shattered machine gun was lying on the edge of a crater. A blast wave had thrown Stepanov from his foxhole; he was lying on his back, all covered with dirt. Someone brought a canteen with water, and we began to wash the dirt away from his face and eyes. Soon Stepan regained consciousness, and within three days he was back with the unit. "Davydov's antiaircraft unit"

served as an example for our tank crews. They began to build their own devices for antiaircraft fire. This was near the village of Durakovo. But soon came an order to withdraw.

After a short rest, the 711th Rifle Regiment advanced upon Rzhev. On 21 September 1942, in cooperation with other units, it launched an attack upon the city through an urban forest district. Stepan was firing on the move from his captured German MG, which he had been given to replace his Maxim, until he reached the German trenches. At first the Germans were shaken and fell back, but then they pulled themselves together and went on the counterattack. Bloody fighting erupted for every meter of progress and every building. All the same, the warriors of the 711th and 707th Regiments and also the 2nd Guards Division managed to seize several city districts, where street fighting developed with shifting success.

Days of street fighting stretched on, one day just like the next: either we would seize a building and all the advantageous approaches to it, or the Germans would. At times it wasn't clear where our guys were and where the Germans were. At the height of the fighting, when the Germans, having received reinforcements, launched a counteroffensive with tank support, a terrible misfortune occurred: on 2 October 1942, my comrade and the favorite of the group of cadets, machine gunner of the 711th Rifle Regiment of the 215th Rifle Division Lance Corporal Stepan Iakovlevich Davydov was killed in action. Two days later, when the situation had become somewhat stabilized, we found Stepanov's body by his machine gun."[3]

Stepan considered that a real soldier is distinguished by two necessary characteristics: the ability to fight and the ability to protect his comrade. Stepan demonstrated both one and the other by his own personal example. Only he couldn't manage to save himself.

8

The 359th Medical-Sanitation Battalion
August–September 1942

The Little City of Doctors

On the day I was wounded, while trying to get off the battlefield I reached the road, where I saw a throng of wounded dragging themselves along it. Staggering, I started to drag myself along after them. Trucks loaded with the badly wounded were passing us, often stopping to pick up those who could no longer move under their own power. At last we saw the first aid tents ahead of us, and there were a lot of them. I immediately became concerned: we were about five kilometers from the front line, far too close for comfort; just one shell from a heavy long-range gun, and nothing would remain of all these tents. As if to confirm my fears, I heard a strong explosion nearby. A blast wave shook the nearby woods like the winds of a squall line, and I heared an ominous sound, the crack of falling trees. I moved a little closer to one tent, next to which a nurse was standing.

"Why is the *medsanbat* so close to the front?" I inquired.

The nurse smiled at my alarm: "Don't worry, soldier, during battles we always deploy the medical stations as close as possible to the front. For the wounded, especially the severely wounded, even an extra minute, not to mention an extra hour or day, can be critical to his survival."

I staggered over to the woods. I felt a bit disoriented; it was not easy to step into this different world, where a trampled soul could free itself a little from the terrible sights and sounds of battle, and where hope lived in the magical hands of the doctor, who might bring you back from the edge of death.

The doctors' habitat was a genuine little city in the forest, with broad clearings, expansive green forest glades, and beautiful little forest roads and paths. You felt as if you had stumbled upon a peaceful, quiet little island—a kingdom of tranquility and harmony amidst the whirlwind of bullets and shellfire raging around you.

A post with plywood signs situated at the entrance to the little city served as the basic reference point for all those who arrived on foot or by horse-drawn cart. In a large, double-sized tent immediately opposite this signpost, a triage station was located. Having taken a seat on a little stump, I took a breath and looked around. In the clearing, wounded men were sitting or lying on the grass. A nurse was taking down the names of those who had just arrived, while a doctor would walk up to them, have a conversation with each, give them a quick examination, and often send someone directly to the surgeon's tent, out of turn. Then he would move on, stopping at each patient to make a determination of our future fate.

From one of the tents, a male medical orderly stepped out to have a smoke, and he took a seat beside me. Seeing my downcast look, he didn't ask any questions, but spoke up himself:

"You, soldier, don't worry. Although I'm not a doctor, I can see that you'll soon return to your comrades. Of course, we nurses are medical personnel, but we're also soldiers, just like you, and we have combat experience. Whenever there's an offensive, up to 700–800 men come to us for treatment. Anything can happen even here. Sometimes, a blast wave topples the operating tables with the wounded on them, and the instruments, bandages, and dishes—well, there's no point in even looking for them. By some miracle, a man has been plucked alive from the battlefield and brought here, but here he receives new wounds. Several times after such attacks, we've been forced to start all over again. Such a thing has happened! Once an entire tent, and all the people inside it, were blown higher than the trees. Another time, a shell fragment passed through an operating tent and took off the head of a doctor. That's just what happened! A reliable fellow told me the same thing happened to a nurse once. So shells reach us too. Once a random round struck an ambulance, which had just arrived bringing wounded to the hospital. A real incident, brother! Recently two of our dear female nurses were killed. We were safely situated, it seemed, in a deep ravine. There was a little village not far away, and so they decided to let the female nurses go there to get a little sleep. Just then an air raid occurred! A direct attack! One vile bomb fell directly on the hut, where the nurses were sleeping. Anything can happen here with us! But generally speaking, they don't keep the wounded here long. If they're lightly wounded, they treat the wound and send them right back to their units. If they're hit a little more badly, they send them for a week or two to the convalescent battalion—and then back to the front."

Just then, a doctor and a female nurse stepped out of the tent; the medical orderly joined them, and the three of them quickly headed into the depths of the woods. Yes, there's a hospital for you. . . . Two nurses replaced the orderly, and from them I learned that the doctors were cursing the flow of men who had shot themselves in the foot or hand (especially non-Slavs from the southern republics) and men who were feigning injury. The men who shot themselves were quite creative in their efforts to erase the signs of their crime: they shot themselves through a loaf of bread, a rag, a tin can; they asked other soldiers to help them; or they would raise their left hand above the trench, and a German sniper would help them out. Fakers also annoyed the doctors: a fellow would arrive, holding his stomach, groaning. But often such a "patient" would quietly walk away; having seen the work of the doctors, and seeing that it was not so easy to deceive them. Doctors often saw through all these shams, and then there would follow a confession and a tribunal.

They called for me when it was just before evening. Having heard my story, the doctor cut the clothes away from my wound, carefully examined it, gave it a feel, and then, in a way that I cannot remember, immediately extracted something from my neck. I could feel that my wound immediately started bleeding, but the doctor and nurse quickly staunched the flow of blood.

"A metal fragment, most likely from a German shell" the doctor established. "It was stuck in the soft tissue of your neck. You were lucky, just as lucky, I'd say, as if you had just won a lottery. Now hold still, rascal."

He cleaned the wound, trimming away a little dead skin around the edges, and applied some iodine to it. Then he sewed up my neck and we were done. He laid a piece of metal on my palm about the size of a tsar's five-kopeck coin: "Take it, soldier, a gift from the Germans. As a keepsake."

They bandaged the spot, then handed me a slip of paper with a tent number on it, indicating where I should go next, and instructed me to come back to rewrap my bandages in three days. I was happy, because it seemed that I had gotten off lightly, and in three days I would be back with my regiment.

As I left the tent, I saw more and more wounded arriving. How did the doctors manage with such a mass of wounded? Later, as I watched them work, I realized that our own regiment commanders could learn a thing or two from the doctors' organization and selflessness. I think most of the soldiers who have been in my spot would agree with my opinion.

That first night, I collapsed on my bunk and immediately fell asleep. The tent was loaded to the maximum with wounded—snoring, conversations, the moans and cries of pain, motion; the wounded were constantly getting up, some to relieve themselves, others to have a smoke or get a bit of fresh air. All this was going on around me, but I didn't notice any of it—I slept soundly until they woke me up in the morning and called me to eat.

The next morning I returned to my favorite observation post, the stump from the evening before. I now knew that our 1st Rifle Company of the 1st Battalion of the 711th Rifle Regiment no longer existed. Of the 136 officers and men in the unit before the battle, only about eight privates now remained. The rest were all killed or wounded. Our company commander, Senior Lieutenant Sukhomirov, was killed. The commissar was badly wounded by a shell fragment and sent to a field hospital. Of the three platoon leaders, two had been killed in action.

The fate of the battery of 45s [45-mm antitank guns] in which I had briefly served was also tragic. The artillerymen had rolled their guns forward with the infantry. Junkers had deluged the men and their guns alike with bombs. Many were killed. I learned about this from—who would believe it?—Osip Osipovich, the battery's sergeant major, who told me about it with tears in his eyes. Wounded by a shell splinter in the buttocks, he managed somehow to get off the battlefield and was now lying on his stomach, pitifully groaning, waiting to be sent to a hospital.

Someone told me that our cook had waited a long time for the return of our company, and that he had kept the abundant meal, which our company commander had ordered for the surviving men, warm for hours. A lot of time passed, but nobody returned, and the cook, understanding what had happened, started to cry, and refused to touch any of the meal he had prepared. However, the sergeant major, whom Shurka had so despised, calmly ate two portions of the cooling soup, two portions of the porridge, and collapsed in sleep, filling the forest with his repulsive grunts and snoring.

Seeing a few familiar faces, I tried to find out what was happening at the front, and whether or not we had taken the villages. The majority of the wounded answered my questions indifferently. In response, they typically just turned around and walked away, or moved on without stopping. But one soldier, a little older than the others, told me, "We took just what we were supposed to take. And now you're seeing for yourself, son, how many of us are maimed and mutilated." After that, I didn't press anybody for information, as I understood they simply weren't in the mood for it.

The Operating Tents in a Clearing

Delving further into the forest, I came upon another large, almost rectangular clearing with operating tents. Trucks carrying the badly wounded were driving up, and orderlies were carefully unloading the trucks and tenderly carrying the wounded on stretchers to the edges of the clearing, where they laid the stretchers around the perimeter in a single row. They didn't have enough stretchers, so they used tent canvas to carry some of the wounded. There was a doctor on duty, a nurse, and a few orderlies, and together they examined all the incoming patients. A few wounded men were immediately driven away to the field hospital, which meant they needed a complex operation—a head, chest, or abdominal wound.

Bloody work continued around the clock in the operating tents; the medical team cut off arms and legs, set dislocated jaws and broken bones, and thought up different ways to best reconstruct faces, ears, noses, hands, and feet. But even here men were often dying, primarily from gangrene and tetanus—the soldier is filthy, lice-ridden, and then gets wounded; of course they were given tetanus shots, but often it was too late. When blood supplies ran out, the doctors, nurses, and orderlies themselves became blood donors. The *medsanbat's* pharmacy was meager; wounds, as a rule, were treated with hydrogen peroxide, iodine, rivanol—sometimes Vishnevsky ointment [a natural antifungul medication]—then a bandage was applied. They didn't have enough anesthetics, so then they would use opium, of which the doctors had plenty, to relieve severe pain.

I saw that even here, a hard, not always successful struggle with death went on. I saw bitter tears flowing and torrents of blood, and cruel scenes of human torment being played out. Here there are no false or imaginary sufferings, here everyone is both a hero and a sufferer.

I will tell you about one operation that I witnessed. The doctor had to remove a soldier's leg urgently: gangrene had set in. They tied the poor fellow tightly to the operating table with strips of sheeting, gave him a couple of shots of vodka to drink, then began to saw. In a semidelirium, the man was crying, hollering, thrashing, while the orderly tried to hold him still, but the doctor kept saying: "That's it, dear man, yell, yell, and swear to your heart's content."

Opening his eyes, the soldier began to tremble uncontrollably—having caught sight of his own leg in a basket next to him. "Give me back my leg!" he suddenly implored in desperation. He was in shock from the pain.

I asked permission to help the medical orderlies, and spent all day going around the wounded men on the ground and on the stretchers, giving them sips of water, bathing their faces and hands, and helping them shift to more comfortable positions. I was not allowed to touch any medicines; nurses handled this. Primarily, they gave the wounded the timeless aspirin.

A frontline wonder! Trucks delivered the next party of wounded. Stretchers were placed on the ground. Two severely wounded men wound up side by side; taking a glance at each other, they gave a gasp: two natural brothers had just been reunited. Everyone lying around them had to laugh when they overheard the ensuing conversation between the brothers:

"Is that you, Serega? You're not dead, brother?"

"I'm alive, alive, Ivan."

"Where did you manage to get hit?"

"Some German bastard shot me in the shoulder. I don't know if they're going to be able to save my arm. Where did you get it?"

"I took a shell splinter in the arm. Where did you come from in order to wind up here?"

"From that other world, Vania. I spent all night lying in the field; I had resigned myself to my death. Thank God, some orderlies found me the next morning and dragged me back into this world."

"And I'm back from that other world, too, Serega: blood was flowing from me like from a leaky bucket. God took mercy on this peasant; some medical orderlies dragged me back to the living. But how are things there, brother, in the afterlife? Who did you see, who did you knock around with?"

"It's better on this earth, Vania. I've just met my brother. It had to be! What joy for Mama: we're still alive!"

A genuine show proceeded from that point:

"But did you see our dear cow, that milk cow?"

"Of course, brother Ivan, our cow recognized me—our little milk factory treated me to some fresh milk!"

"Go on with you! And did you notice our dog Zhuchka?"

"Naturally, naturally, Zhuchka as well. Just as he lived without any brains on this earth, he was being just as foolish a dog there."

"Well, and Ryzhy, your cat? What's he doing up there?

"Ehhh, there they explained that chasing mice is forbidden in heaven. The cat was assigned a new job—chief fly-fighter. For every ten thousand swatted flies, a prize. Never mind, he's getting by. On earth he had a reputation as a clever creature, and there they recognize him as a clever creature too. And he recognized me—he licked me all over and purred."

"Yeah, fortune smiled upon you, Serega!"

No matter how much pain they were feeling—aching, piercing, squeezing their chests, or nauseating them—everyone was cheered up by the two brothers.

"What creative fellows! Such jokers!" the wounded all laughed.

Subsequently I took an interest in Serega's fate. They managed to save his arm and sent him to convalesce in a field hospital.

Night after the Battle

The second night in the *medsanbat* was hard for me. At first, I fell fast asleep, but then suddenly dreams came, and what dreams! What was it—nighttime play of the imagination, the echo of terrifying impressions, otherworldly spirits raging? The remainder of the night turned into a nightmare for me; fantastic images held me tightly in their power, forcing me to suffer alongside them, to be happy, to cry, to shudder in horror:

> *Shurka! With his father's sword in a gilded saddle, wearing a tall Cossack sheepskin hat, he is galloping across the battlefield on a majestic gray steed. Not a single bullet touches him! And here they are—the bandits' trenches! Shurka unsheathes his sword*

and is slicing off head after enemy head. Now our troops have already occupied the emptied trenches and are rushing off in pursuit of the cowardly fleeing enemy. "For the Holy Russian land!" the Cossack-swordsman Shurka is shouting, and he spurs his horse after the enemy, continuing to slice off heads! The Germans are falling to their knees and praying, their eyes looking up to heaven, beseeching God to spare them from this human devil.

Victory! Rzhev is ours! Word of the superhero-savior reaches legendary proportions, and reaches even the high command. The supreme leader has demanded that the Russian wonder-bogatyr' [epic Russian hero of yore] be brought before him, so he could see the hero for himself.

Shurka steps out of his tent—in his Cossack sheepskin hat, with his father's sword in its gilded scabbard, he leaps onto his gray-coated horse, and gallops off, chasing the wind, to meet the supreme commander and the high command.

"Where did you get those, hero?" the supreme leader asks Shurka, pointing at the four stars on his shoulder straps. "What sort of highest decoration are you seeking now?"

But Shurka—who is also a brazen fellow!—spits, swears, and declares: "The rivers have implored, the Russian earth itself, soaked with its soldiers' blood, has begged, and the Supreme Being has ordered me to put an end to your disgraceful generalship. The way you are conducting the fight is totally bringing our entire Christian nation to ruin!"

The supreme commander becomes enraged and stamps his box calf boots: "Seize the insubordinate! Tie the recalcitrant up! Shoot him, to teach others never to play the hero like this again!"

But you don't mess around with someone like Shurka. At first, a group of soldiers with submachine guns surrounds him, but then, recognizing their own daring Cossack, they immediately toss down their weapons and cry: "We won't shoot our savior, our holy hero-legend!"

And with that, Shurka, unsheathing his father's sword, immediately cut off the foul heads of the high command.

Scandal! The Red Army had never known such a disgrace in its entire history!

Just then, osobisty from the Special Department appeared, seeking to make short work of Shurka. They seize the hero on the spot and tie him up! They toss him into a frontline prison—a deep, deep pit! But the dishonorable men have forgotten about his loyal steed. Sensing trouble for his master, the horse gallops to the rescue and tramples all the offenders. Shurka the Cossack leaps out of the pit and onto his gray horse, and gallops off into the distance . . . beyond the clouds . . .

I woke up in the middle of the night. It took me a painfully long time to wake up fully. At last I hopped to my feet. I thought I was still lying on my bunk. In reality, I had long before fallen to the floor and I'd been thrashing around there, disheveled, soaked in sweat, with a troubled head. I climbed back into my bunk, where I looked into the darkness and began calling for Shurka, summoning him—if only he was here with me . . .

Instead of Shurka, a neighboring patient stepped over to my bunk, and with a shaking hand he offered me a cup of water: "Here, drink a little water, soldier, it will ease your mind. You were groaning so loudly, calling for some Shurka—remembering your friend, I suppose. Time will pass, and we'll both start remembering together. As for him—a big debt of gratitude. This damned war, those damned Germans . . ."

Waking up again in the morning, it took me a long time to remember where I was and what was happening with me. Breakfast had still not been delivered. Without waiting for it, I left for the forest, to lend more help to the wounded.

And in the operating tents in the clearing that day, a genuine miracle occurred. Two doctors and two military sappers made it happen.

Usually, the trucks arriving with the wounded were loaded with as many as they could carry. Suddenly, however, a truck transporting a single wounded man arrived. He was carefully placed on a stretcher and gently lowered to the ground. Evidently he had been expected; obviously, this was a special case. Personnel gathered: a hospital chief, another doctor, and for some reason military sappers with all their gear. It was becoming clear that something quite extraordinary had happened. Nurses and medical orderlies bustled about.

What only doesn't happen in war! Apparently, a small shell, fired from a company mortar, had struck the man from behind, below the waist, and was lodged there. Having penetrated his uniform, it somehow quickly expended all its energy once it entered his body, and now it was stuck there, with only its stabilizing fins visible protruding from his flesh. Fortunately for him, for some reason the fuse hadn't worked, but you couldn't envy the injured man, who had unexpectedly received such a "gift."

The soldier was lying on his stomach, quietly enduring his fear and pain. His face was covered with perspiration and had darkened from heart troubles. Fearing to move even a tiny bit, he had become as taut as a string, shivering as if a stroke was running down his body. Everyone was worried that the fuse might trigger the explosive charge at any minute, when everyone would be blown to pieces—both the soldier and those working to save him.

All the doctors and nurses were led out of their operating tents. They cordoned off the clearing, letting no one near the scene. The chief of the *medsanbat*, an experienced combat surgeon, who was a graduate of the Leningrad Combat-Medical Academy, himself took on the unique operation to remove the mortar shell, while getting advice from the sappers. A young volunteer doctor assisted him.

The entire *medsanbat* froze in place. The gazes of the doctors and the wounded (the soldiers' telegraph had already spread the news) were fixed upon the operating tent where the procedure was taking place. The operation lasted about an hour. To everyone's great joy, it ended successfully. The sappers in a flash removed the fuse from the mortar round. The doctors also then had to deal with a task no less complicated: they extracted the shell from the body—this was a small miracle—and then stopped the bleeding. Everybody around gave a sigh of relief, a few people even shouted "Ura!" and everyone applauded the doctors and sappers.

The division's newspaper soon had an article about this amazing story, the author of which informed us of the soldier's further fate: he had been sent to a field hospital, since the shell, which didn't damage any internal organs, had brought with it a serious infection.

Sabit Khalikov

When the tension subsided and everyone returned to their normal business, I happened to notice two wounded officers who were lying on stretchers far removed from the others. On one of them I immediately recognized Sabit Khalikov, the regiment's *komsorg*. I rushed over to him:

"Sabit! Fancy finding you here! What's with you?"

"A typical story for a Komsomol organizer," he said softly. "The commissar ordered us to rally the fighting men and lead them forward, but the German machine guns weren't letting us raise our heads. So we didn't reach their lines, and a shell fragment shattered my hip."

Glancing at my bandaged neck, he asked, "How are you, are you badly wounded?"

"Nonsense," I said cheerfully, "just a scratch from a shell fragment. I hope to get back to my regiment soon. How glad I am to see you! How can I help you?"

Sabit closed his eyes, either from the pain or because he had fallen into thought. His face, unshaven, filled with pain, had darkened a little. I constantly sponged his brow and gave him a little drink of water.

Then suddenly he spoke up, speaking very quickly, probably fearing that orderlies would walk up, carry him away, and he wouldn't have time to finish what he wanted to tell me: "You can help me a lot, if you listen carefully to everything I have to say."

I nodded.

"You remember how we parted? Well, so . . . your transfer to the battery was the doing of the regiment's Party organizer. The swine, the anti-Semite! He demanded that you be sent into the ranks, and accused me, he said, of sheltering you in the political section: 'Let your little Jew do some fighting.' I've been wanting a long time to tell you about this, but I never had a chance."

"That's just what he said?" flushing, I asked him again.

Suspicions had crept into my mind as I recalled similar utterances from the battery's commissar. He was just a small-fry. But the regiment's Party organizer! How did he dare? Whenever anybody before had touched upon my ethnicity, this had humiliated me and caused me to blush deeply, though I was not the one who should have been blushing.

"Yes, that's exactly what he said. As you know, I graduated from Kazan' University, where we still adhered to Leninist traditions, and we tried to keep anyone like him away from working with other people. Boris, will we ever meet again? I've done my fighting, and after my operation, they'll probably send me to a hospital far in the rear. So let's speak candidly, like old comrades, or if you want, like father and son, for I'm older than you by ten years, and I've had enough of the front. So here's my advice to you: Don't rush back to the front lines. . . . What, you didn't expect to hear such words? Get used to them!"

My stomach was turning inside. What was he saying? I took his words with some mixed feelings. But he continued to speak:

"I see that my words aren't suiting you. Perhaps I've offended you. You are an honorable fellow, but you are still quite naïve. You can't believe that this regimental Komsomol organizer is in fact advising you not to rush back into battle. So use your brains. How are we fighting? The division commander yells into the phone at the regiment commander: 'If you don't take that village, I'm going to shoot you!'—and then adds a healthy portion of swearing to the threat. The regiment commissar picks up the phone after him and adds his own order plus his own portion of unprintable language. And so everyone, from the army commander down to the company commander, with the help of the commissars at each level, drives the soldiers forward into the chopping machine. And the result! How many killed! You yourself can see—they keep bringing in more and more wounded. And how many men are still lying on the battlefield? We don't have enough paper for all the funeral notices! But they say it's necessary—up to ten separate attacks a day on the same village or piece of terrain, over the same ground. They drive you forward and drive you forward. Just like a woman chases her geese to the river, they chase men toward machine guns! If only there was some sense to it! Oh, I've become ill tempered, Boris, mostly with myself! I've appealed to young men to die for a noble cause. I was ready to lay down my life for it myself! But what sort of nobility is it, tell me, if the commander and commissar issue the order "at any cost!"? That means the soldier must pay. But they haven't prepared him and haven't armed him as they should! It's insanity! This is the second year we've been fighting atop the bones of our own men."

I was silent, shaken by Sabit's unexpectedly harsh words.

"I can see that I've spoiled your mood. Admit it!"

"Yes . . ." I wanted to swallow a little more air.

"I'm right! You should get rid of your illusions as quickly as possible."

My thoughts were jumbled, racing—perhaps I didn't understand or didn't even know all the circumstances. What did he want me to do? Maybe he'd gone too far. That mustn't be! Probably, he was trying to curb my lofty patriotic ardor. But we had to fight the Germans! Even despite the stupidity and ineptitude of our command . . .

The wise Komsomol organizer understood my thoughts without any words spoken: "Eh, how green you still are! I thought more of you. You're hurrying back to the regiment? But stop and think, your regiment no longer exists."

He was right; years later I found out that after two months of the offensive, of the 3,000 personnel in the ranks of the 711th Rifle Regiment, only 200 officers and men remained.

From the first day I had met him, Sabit had always seemed to me to be an honest, direct individual—the finest example of an army political worker. Yet now I couldn't regain my equilibrium. His words had stunned me, and each one had been driven into my brain like a nail, tormenting me. Did this mean that Zhenechka's and Shurka's deaths had been for nothing? And Sukhomirov's? And the suffering of the wounded?! The doctors too—were their efforts for no purpose? Did this mean all of this was in vain?

Pulling myself together, I eventually said:

"Not all of our commanders and commissars are like that. I don't consider my own division commander to be like that. If only you had known Sukhomirov, my company commander, you wouldn't have talked like that. You know, he . . . " —I had to hurry, for orderlies were approaching us—"You've forgotten the most important thing, Sabit! We must drive out the Germans! You know this too! Everything else is secondary to this."

He didn't have time to answer me, as the orderlies had reached us. We quickly exchanged kisses on the cheek, and they carried him off toward an operating tent.

Helping the wounded, I often glanced at the operating tent where they had taken Sabit. The conversation didn't leave me, and I kept turning it over in my mind, trying to understand it—and the motives of the regimental Komsomol organizer. The *komsorg* was supposed to encourage and inspire men to fight, not advise them to duck out of battle. What should I do? Should I follow his advice and try to live a bit longer? Was he trying to protect and save me? Had his severe wound, and everything he had seen and suffered on the battlefield, changed his thinking about the war? I knew Sabit as a good and always life-loving man with a kind disposition, an optimist, and now suddenly he was speaking maliciously! Perhaps his faith in basic human decency and his principles had collided against those he could no longer tolerate, and finding himself in shock, he was unable to restrain himself, and he had spilled everything to me? Had all this been building inside him for a long time? I recalled Iurka Davydov and his criticism of the commanders, but Sabit was no Iurka; he was older, more serious, and deeper. But now the choice was mine to make. Should I agree with him? Just like that, on the fly, change my own convictions and become a different man? But what if I did! Who tolerates criticism of army orders? Especially at the front, in an operational army! I had already been expelled from the ranks of the Komsomol organizers, and then out of the artillery.

Sabit's operation lasted almost four hours. But at last an orderly stepped out of the tent, supporting a pale nurse with difficulty, and he carefully laid her on the grass. Fearing for Sabit, I rushed up to the orderly:

"What's the matter? What happened?"

"With your friend, it seems, everything is fine," he comforted me. "It's just that this young lady inhaled some chloroform, and she passed out."

A week later, Sabit was transferred to a field hospital, and from there, to a hospital in Kazan'.

In the autumn of 1946, I located Sabit and invited him to visit.

Our family was living then in an overcrowded communal apartment with three other families. Altogether, fourteen people were living in this humble abode. My parents, Mama's sister, and I lived together in an 18-square-meter room, but in the first postwar year, our room became a shelter for many of my former frontline comrades. At the front, I had given them my address, and now, returning from the war to various corners of the country, they were traveling through Moscow and stopped at our place. Mama refused no one her hospitality, joyfully received everyone, fed them, and arranged a place for them to sleep on the floor, as there was no other spot to give them. When my father and aunt returned home from work in the evening, everybody—masters and guests of the "house," would seat themselves around our round table under a large, colorful lampshade. There we would wolf down Mama's tasty meals, which she had prepared from the simplest ingredients, and offer toasts to the very best mother in the world. Mama would gaze with loving eyes at the stately fine fellows in their faded field blouses, decorated with combat orders, medals, and the narrow little red and yellow ribbons denoting combat wounds (by the end of the war, I encountered officers and soldiers who had been wounded up to ten times). Mama asked each visitor to talk as much as possible about himself, his combat actions, and, of course, me—and she listened to each man with reverence.

About fifteen frontline veterans spent time with our family in this way. We hosted Sabit as well. After his wounding, for the rest of his life he walked with a cane.

Another Dream

That evening after Sabit's operation I returned to my tent late for dinner. Picking at some cold porridge left for me by the guys, I sat on my bunk and pondered the night ahead, fearing the next unanticipated dream and, no matter how strange it might seem, trying to make sense of my dream about Shurka from the night before and all its haunting images. Had it been an omen? A good one, or a bad one? What was lying in wait for me tonight, and when would it appear? Everyone can ponder dreams that he or she likes, but I had the feeling that this dream had been some sort of prompting. I should change something, or act somehow differently in the future—but how? Recalling what I had seen, I tried to assemble it into one complete picture. But what was its essence?

Without undressing, I collapsed onto my bunk, but just in case, I asked the on-duty nurse for some kind of sedative. She brought me several white tablets; I gulped them down, and peacefully, fell lightly asleep. However, close to morning another vision crept into my sleeping head—even more vividly than the previous night's!

A pair of eyes lit up in the darkness with a phosphorescent glow . . . Zhenechka's eyes! Large, widened, he was gazing directly at me; in them was one question: "Why?" His gaze seemed somehow embarrassed. But the eyes are flashing—disappearing and reappearing.

Zhenechka speaks: "I'm ashamed that I died! People are falling into a bloody river and drowning . . ."

Tormenting memories began to flash through my mind . . . the barracks . . . and Zhenechka . . . the rail car—they are beating Zhenechka. . . . Zhenechka is in my arms—he is saying something. . . . Suddenly an enormous black bird spreads itself above me. Its wings widespread, it has frozen in place. It transfixes me totally with an intent gaze. I try to move, to catch sight of light—and I cannot. I'm a prisoner. I'm tightly clenched and all rigid. It is impossible to free myself, and I'm patiently waiting for something to happen. The bird suddenly takes on a human voice:

"Did you promise Zhenechka to find me and his little sister Sashen'ka?"

"Yes, absolutely. But it's impossible for me now."

"I am releasing you from useless torments and searches. We no longer exist. The Germans killed us in a Crimean quarry."

"Zhenia didn't know about this; he was looking for you to his final day. Are you his mother?"

I'm—your dream . . ."

And everything vanished. The dream disappeared—I woke up. Perhaps the apparitions never even existed? I closed my eyes: would I suddenly see something again? Nothing. I leapt from my bunk and nearly knocked a nurse off her feet. She had been standing beside my bunk, observing me with alarm, as I tossed and turned in my dream.

"What's your problem, soldier? You were shouting so loudly, you weren't giving anyone a chance to sleep. That's forbidden, you must restrain yourself, and calm down!"

"Yes . . . thank you," I agree.

After breakfast, I go to have my dressings changed. They uncover the wound. It is heavily suppurating. They clean it and then apply another dressing with rivanol. The doctor shakes his head and directs me to a convalescent battalion.

All three days I spent at the *medsanbat* were three days among warm-hearted, caring people. The entire staff of the *medsanbat* was totally dedicated to us, the frontline soldiers. Recalling now everything that I experienced and saw during the days and years of the war, I know: I will never forget those people, nor their selflessness and loyalty to duty!

In the Convalescent Battalion

In a combat situation, battalions of convalescents are under the command of the divisional *medsanbat*. Normally, they didn't keep patients long in these battalions. Instead of the typical two weeks here, I had to spend more than a month living according to the special regime for convalescents. My wound continued to suppurate, and the infection was spreading. By the evening of my first day in the convalescent battalion, I was becoming feverish: the thermometer had risen by two or three marks. The doctor kept stating the obvious: "The fragment induced a serious infection; you need more time." Each time after rebandaging of my wound, the nurse would promise, "Well, next time it will get better." But the wound didn't heal—rivanol was a weakling in the struggle with the bacteria.

The convalescent battalion was located in a once-large village three or four kilometers from the *medsanbat*. The village had long been deserted: the men had been conscripted into the Red Army; some had been killed in action back in 1941. The women had been deported to Germany for slave labor. There were also those who followed the retreating German forces, while old people and little children had been evacuated from the combat zone, first by the Germans when they seized the village, then by our forces, once we liberated it. The battalion unit was accommodated in the three huts that had survived intact. A medical station and rebandaging station occupied one of the huts, where the doctor, nurse, and medical orderlies also lived. The wounded were kept in the other two huts. There were approximately twenty patients in our hut. About 300 meters from the village, just in case, deep bomb shelters had been built. After each new battle, about 200 additional men arrived in the battalion, and although approximately just as many would return to active duty at the same time, the battalion was badly overcrowded. Therefore, some of the patients were housed in empty German dugouts, or in tents in the woods. It was fortunate that the weather was still relatively warm, and the patients were of the convalescing type—that is to say, they were still mobile under their own power, which meant they themselves could step off the distance to the mess.

The daily routine was as follows: after breakfast we had a period of so-called light combat training, then lunch, political classes, and three hours of free time. Twice a week we all underwent medical examinations. The command was under pressure to discharge more patients, and they didn't stand on ceremony with the patients, often discharging them before they were fully healed. The doctors considered it most important to stop any infections and to put arms and legs back in working order.

Once there was a scandal. A senior nurse of the battalion happened to overhear a conversation between the division's chief of staff and the chief of the *medsanbat*. The former accused the latter: "Each soldier in your care is authorized to be here, as are all the officers, but you are acting too sentimentally!" The chief of the *medsanbat* made no effort to respond, and he simply sent a commission to the battalion to investigate the situation. The commission of three doctors worked for two days, closely examining everyone. As a result, twenty-one soldiers and three officers were returned to the front.

A senior lieutenant who had an empty sleeve instead of a left arm commanded the battalion for convalescents. His name was Sergei Ivanovich Tokmakov. After his severe wounding and long recovery in a hospital, he had refused an offer of discharge and somehow wrangled another assignment at the front. As a commander he was a brave and decent fellow, who tried as much as he could to support us: he took concern in the timely delivery of our food and looked after the condition of the wounded, the regular redressing of wounds, and the delivery of letters and newspapers. He also conducted our combat training exercises, understandably in a lighter style: he spent most of the time simply discussing frontline experiences, asking each man about shortcomings in their units, and gave advice on how to eliminate them in the future.

The chief of the division's *medsanbat* had under his personal command a sergeant major and a medical assistant, who helped him manage the operations of the battalion. The sergeant major (my fifth by count), Foka Stepanych, had been a medical orderly; he loved order and discipline, so the patients called him "O.D." He paid particular attention to the schedule of our morning reveille and evening retreat. He also looked in on our quarters; if he saw that they were messy, noticed dirty dishes or a dirty floor, or ran into any unshaven soldiers, he always tried to find the key to motivate each man. Then he would deliver his lecture, concluding it with a kindly question: "Do you agree with me?" He was the first sergeant major that I encountered who addressed us in the formal fashion—obviously, following the example of his commanding officer. If the soldier agreed, he firmly believed that the man would immediately take the correcting action. We particularly appreciated the sergeant major when he contrived to build a rudimentary shower for us: he planted four sturdy posts into the ground, wrapped them with tent canvas, and suspended a bucket that had narrow holes drilled into it above the little enclosed space. One man would pour water into the bucket while another man showered. The wounded men could walk around clean and were quite pleased.

In the middle of our hut stood a large solidly built table, made by some village craftsman; obviously, a large family had once lived here. Every morning an important ritual took place around this table. Together with the breakfast, the field kitchen would deliver loaves of bread in large, heavy bags. The loaves were all of the same size, about one kilogram, and each table in the battalion received fifteen loaves. While we all remained outside, one particular soldier with an easy stroke of a sharp knife would slice each loaf into two portions as evenly as possible. Everyone marveled at the faultless eye of the man who did the slicing; it turned out that he was a sniper. Then five men would be invited into the hut at a time; each would stand with his back to the table and call out a number to receive his particular share. I don't recall anyone ever rejecting to divide the bread this way. They say this method of allocating bread among the frontline soldiers was adopted everywhere. I think I will not be mistaken, if I suppose that this system came to the army from the prison camps. Once they found out about this simple method of sharing bread from prisoners, the Germans often shouted to us from their trenches, "Rus, stop dividing up the portions, and let's fight!"

An Unexpected Meeting

On the second or third day of my stay in the convalescent battalion, a young chap of enormous size burst into our hut, his face grizzled like a bear's. But we immediately recognized each other!

"Ryzhii! It's you! Greetings, Cadet Aleksandr Ryzhikov!"

We embraced joyfully at the meeting. We went outside, took a seat on a log by a fence, and Sashka told me about himself. A bullet had caught him in his very first fight, striking him in the arm. It didn't smash the bone, but it had torn out a solid chunk of muscle tissue and had burned his skin.

"I almost lost my arm, but that threat passed, only now it is slowly rotting—Comrade Rivanol isn't helping!"

We chuckled merrily.

"But where's your guitar?" I asked.

"I didn't take it into battle with me; I left it back with the transport unit."

"Perhaps you'll sing a little for us tonight? Everyone will be happy."

"Perhaps," Ryzhii agreed.

We talked some about our families and where different members were located. I told him about the deaths of Zhenechka and Shurka. Ryzhii named off a few more: Sasha Pushkarev, Iulik Gerts, Serezha Kozhevnikov, Feden'ka—they were all dead. I didn't like Feden'ka back in the barracks, and I couldn't forgive his underhanded snitching in return for little jellied candies, but all the same I was sorry for the fellow. He died in a terrible manner. His company was trying to force a crossing of the Volga, and the Germans were resisting desperately, trying to drive our guys back across the river. Fedor died while making the crossing—whether a German bullet caught him or whether he couldn't hang on to the cable stretched across the river, Fedor slipped beneath the currents and never reappeared.

The first battles, and a mournful picture had resulted. Who of us had imagined that it would be this way? We had barely started our combat paths; were they really going to slaughter us all? But nevertheless everyone had successfully passed the test of our characters. I don't know a single incident where one of our cadets cowered or acted badly. But with each passing day, with every new story and new encounter, I was becoming convinced that fate was not ours to determine, that something higher was deciding it.

That evening, Ryzhii came by our hut. I introduced him to everyone. Then he sang three popular songs: "In Our City," "The Song of the Black Raven," and, of course, "The Gal from the Little Tavern"—the crowning jewel of our prewar folksongs. The audience greeted each song with a hurrah. We laid out some refreshments on the table, each man contributing what he could, and without any embarrassment, Ryzhii wolfed it all down in succession. Obviously, he was famished. As he was singing "The Gal from the Little Tavern," battalion commander Tokmakov stepped into the hut. The senior lieutenant liked Ryzhii's singing, but when it was finished, he observed: "Nowadays, lad, they're singing different songs," and he recited the words from a popular front-line song, taken from a poem by Iaroslav Smeliakov:

We must sing some song with sense
For between each line
Both German shell fragments
And bullets from their bunkers fly.

Yes, the time for other songs had arrived; it was impossible not to agree with that. We invited Ryzhii, who had taken his seat among us, to move into our hut.

Soldier "Conversationalists"

Fifty convalescing wounded would have to stuff themselves into one room for the political education classes. They sat on broad windowsills, in doorways, and on the floor. The commissar turned out to be a very irritable man, as temperamental as the devil, and I never met a windbag who was his equal. He conducted the classes in his own unique style: asking a question, he himself would answer it, as a rule using citations from Stalin's speeches. His stupidity was striking. Once someone asked him, "Why have we not been able to take Rzhev for such a long time?" The question was disagreeable to the commissar, but he quickly gathered himself and calmly replied: "The Supreme Commander does not hide the fact that the Germans are stubbornly resisting. But it is necessary to understand that they are defending this way because of their desperation and their fear of retribution for the crimes they have committed."

After this incident, the commissar turned to new tactics in leading his classes. He didn't allow himself to be interrupted, and he tried to fill up the allotted time precisely with his own talking, at which point he would quickly leave.

Meanwhile, I could sense that a dark cloud of bitter and frightening questions was accumulating in every man, and they were lying like a heavy stone on the heart of everyone. Who could we ask about the enormous losses, and how? Why weren't they burying our dead? Why wasn't our air force covering the ground forces? Why were our artillerymen unable to cope with the task of suppressing the enemy's firing positions? What was happening in the rear—why were letters from home filled with a terrible inconsolability? And what of the ferocious conduct of many commanders, commissars, and *osobisty* of the Special Department? Why was the average soldier saying more often: "Don't fear the other side; fear our own"?

These were questions without answers. Some were afraid to ask them—they were aware that they'd be reported; it didn't matter to others, and the third group didn't believe they would get honest answers. One wise soldier said, "What kind of truth are you expecting if that same commander or commissar is certain that 'one of his own' from the Special Department is among his audience?" It turned out that we didn't much trust anyone else or even ourselves. Of course, there were also those who didn't want to argue with anyone, adhering to the old rule "you can't fight a cannon with a peashooter." But nonetheless it was hard for the men to remain silent all the time, and the soldiers did talk among themselves.

Here, in the battalion of convalescents, I received another lesson from the "military university," perhaps the most important—a human one. Among us there were soldiers from various regiments and batteries, but mostly there were new conscripts. It soon became clear why there were so many of them among the wounded in the battalion, as they themselves told us. They had been brought from Penza one night, disembarked from the rail cars, and that same morning—"off the march"—they were driven to assault a hill. Clerks hadn't even had time yet to write their names down on the roster, and the cooks hadn't yet fed them a meal. In military matters they were complete know-nothings, as they had trained for less than a month by this time. An enormous number of them were killed and wounded in the attack. From then on, whenever they delivered a new batch of conscripts, we would say, "They've come from Penza." How many of them fell in their first actions, it is impossible to reckon!

Night approaches. No one can sleep. At first complete silence reigns; each man is absorbed in his own thoughts. Then suddenly, like the first tiny rivulet of spring, somebody speaks up, and then stories fill the air. They often talk of the past, each man remembering something cheerful—how can he not talk about his home, his mistress of the house, his little ones, or his milk cow, who provided the whole village with fresh milk at the same time? Recollecting his past life, whether for the first, the second, or the hundredth time, a man always finds something new, joyous, and heart-warming.

But the frontline impressions! Each man had already accumulated so many, especially when you consider that many of the men who wound up in the battalion had started their combat journey at Moscow in 1941. One recounts when he became regarded as an experienced scout: from his very first mission, when having snuck into a German trench, he managed to snatch a *wachtmeister* [A German noncommissioned officer rank, literally "master sentinel"] who was as plump as a ham—after that, he was no longer "green." Another man can never forget how his division commander kissed him twice on the cheek and awarded him the "For Courage" medal—there was no one better who could knock out a German bunker with just one or two rounds.

And how could a man resist relating the following story? A commander sent a soldier to fetch the mail. There the soldier met not some bullying postal clerk but a sweet young woman—a darling like no other! But no matter how the soldier tried to charm her, no matter what lofty words he spoke, no matter how much he flashed his "For Courage" medal—in general, no matter what frontal or flank assault he tried, he couldn't break through the defenses of the woman's heart. On his way back, he thought up every sort of ruse to convince his commander to return him that evening to the mail service: and the commander sent him, for he himself was badly longing to receive word from his parents in besieged Leningrad. And the soldier—such a persistent fellow—managed to achieve his real aim and win the heart of his beloved.

As is evident, there often comes a time in conversation, a moment of real candor and trust, when a person bares his or her soul, when one wants to speak freely, easily, without worrying about any sharp rebuke or ugly consequence to his words. And really—who knows, we might be living our last days on earth. Four soldiers in the convalescent battalion had already been wounded twice, and one says: "God spared me. But whether the Lord will show me mercy a third time, I don't know." And so an interminable "soldier's talk" starts and flows, and I cannot recall a case when anyone refused to take part. You don't often encounter in life, if you will, such sincerity, truthfulness, self-searching, heartfelt emotions, and striving to understand others. It's such a pity that I've forgotten many of these oral gold mines:

"We were launching direct attacks, you know, upon some village. Which village? Who the hell knows which village! Only a few charred skeletons remained of its former dwellings. Instead of going around the village and hitting the fascists from the rear, our company commander sent us straight up the middle toward the village, right into their machine guns. But the Fritz is no fool! He let us get a little closer—and then started to cut us to pieces. Within a half-hour, you know, he cut down almost an entire battalion, including our company commander. There's no point in feeling sorry for him—he's always been a total fool. But I feel sorry for the guys."

"But that village, did you take it?" a voice rings out in the darkness.

"We took it, we took it. But if we must sacrifice a battalion for every village, how will we ever reach Germany? Here's what I think: a commander must use his brains, and perhaps then he'll be more useful."

At this point, evidently a signaler enters the conversation: "But what's the point of him thinking, when he's planned everything beforehand, and during the battle, there's some foul-up with the communications? Everybody knows that the German reptiles focus their fire on us signalers. They recognize us by our spools of wire and even send snipers to take us out. They kill one signaler and wait for another to crawl out, and then they kill that one too. All the same, when your turn comes next, you must start crawling in search of the break, until you catch the sound of 'Chamomile to Squirrel . . . over.' Sometimes, even worse things happen. Once the regiment commander sent me out to find a battalion, whose signalman wasn't responding. I crawled for a long time under enemy fire, and I was so scared; I didn't dare lift my head, and plowed a path with my nose. Then I happened to bump directly into a machine gunner from the battalion. I felt such a sense of relief, and I asked him: 'Where's the battalion?' This guy says to me, 'What . . . battalion? What . . . can't you see? Here's the battalion for you,' and he gave a little jerk with his head. I lifted my head a little—and all around me are piles of our dead. The machine gunner shouted: 'I'm the only one left! Get going, get back to the regiment, give your report, and tell them to send me some help! The Fritzes want to take me alive! I'll never surrender to them, the swine! Once they get past me, they're going to keep rolling! Do you understand?' So I think the infantryman is right: we don't know how to fight as we should, using our brains; perhaps the German generals will teach us."

Someone rudely snaps at the soldier: "You, Vas'ka, shut your trap. You yourself know what happens to people who talk like that."

A tanker steps into the conversation: "That's exactly right, infantry are nothing without tanks!"

Some infantrymen react to his remark: "What use are you? The tanks do their own thing, while the infantry does its own thing. No, comrade *tankist* [tanker], we don't even know each other yet."

"How should I interpret your words?" the tanker offers in protest.

"Like this," sounds a whole chorus of voices. "While you try to make your way to the German trenches, either you're bogged down up to your drive sprocket in some swamp, or you've thrown a track in some ditch, or the Junkers are scattering you around the field, like matches flung from a matchbox. Your guns quickly fall silent: you've run out of ammunition."

An artilleryman intervenes: "You're worthless, infantry, give some help to our spotters, because without them, what kind of support can you get? What can you guys do without us? It is well known that the artillery is 'the god of battle.' If we only had some more shells, we'd open a path to Berlin."

"There you go! The Germans are rolling in ammunition for their artillery, while we're lucky if you've managed to scrape together ten shells for your gun. What kind of God do you have then? The Germans never spare ammunition— they fire and fire. Our soldiers aren't waiting for death but for the end of the shelling."

"You'd better shut up, infantryman, or you'll go before a tribunal for such opinions!"

"Don't worry, gunner. Here's a little page from your own book. The Fritzes spotted the gleam of your spotter's stereoscope and gave a wallop to our trenches. They put an end to four of your guys, and I was practically buried alive—only one of my legs was sticking above the ground, so they just managed to dig me out."

"There's something I don't understand, "someone asks from the darkness. "The Fritzes like to spout that they are fighting for their Fatherland, but they are on our own Russian soil. Meanwhile we are fighting for our own Motherland, again on our own land, not on their territory. Who are they, the stinking worms, to consider our land as their own Fatherland?"

"Hey, you're talking like a fool," a neighbor laughs. "Ask a commissar to answer your question."

The nighttime free discussion continues. The soldiers, feeling no shyness in the presence of a junior lieutenant, turn to discussing their commanding officers. But they don't mention anyone higher than their company commander, for there are few who even know who commands their regiment or division.

"Our company commander is a brute. It's like he was born in the wild. One soldier couldn't stand it and punched his mug before the battle: I hope he's been taught a lesson on how to treat our guys properly. It seems our company commander thought it over and decided not to retaliate against even that fellow who struck him."

"Our company commander behaves disgracefully in the presence of his commander, just like he's ready to lick his ass."

"Our company commander isn't any better. He's crappy in action and not much better as a person."

"Our guy's a windbag, so we've nicknamed him 'Blah-Blah.'"

"Our company commander gives such awkward orders that you're at a loss what to do: you can't figure out what he wants."

"As we arrived at the front, the commissars were telling us that we were going to drive the Fritzes! But in reality ..."

Unexpectedly, someone rushed up to the table in the darkness and thumped it with his fist so hard that he rattled the dishes on it: "How are we supposed to take your words? You're wagging your tongues! A commander is a commander! You're defeatists! Such people should be put up against a wall and shot!"

A deathly quiet settled over the room. But it didn't last long, as the tanker retorted: "Have you gone clean off your head? How are we defeatists? We've just come out of battle, and tomorrow we'll go right back into battle. We're only speaking in all fairness—that's all! But since you seem to be against this, go squeal to your friends in the Special Department! They love people like you—real idiots!"

"As God is my witness, I won't have anything to do with that! I just became vexed as I listened to you badmouth your commanders."

The neighbor of the angered soldier spoke up: "Hey, Gerasha, Gerasha, those commanders forgive us ..."

The junior lieutenant interrupted him: "Guys, stop! Give a thought, have none of you ever had even a single good commander?"

Everyone spoke up at once:

"Of course, there were, there were ..."

"But where can one find the best?"

"They came and went ..."

"Hey, fellows, fellows"—everyone recognized the hoarse voice of the old soldier—"what are you wagging your tongues about? You're just spreading dirt. Let me try to cheer you up, if don't mind."

"Go ahead, go ahead, Liosha!"

And Liosha told us a story, just like a fairy tale. As has been said more than once: what doesn't happen in war!

"Here's how it was: how the greatest coward, born with a chicken heart, became Hero of the Soviet Union."

"Hmmm, this case, how did it happen?"

"This way. Give a listen. The Germans were attacking Kiev and had us crushed up against the Dnepr River. From the entire regiment there only remained the regimental banner and Private Sidorenko. And it was bound to happen: the rabbit became a lion. This Sidorenko tied the banner around himself beneath his field shirt, found a log on the bank of the Dnepr that was a little longer and a little stronger than the others, and pushed it into the water. He then lay down and tightly strapped himself to the log, then started swimming that log with the current. The Germans were watching through binoculars, but they only saw a dead "Ivan" stuck to a log, floating down the river, and let him go. Sidorenko clung tightly to the log in the water, so he wouldn't drown. He floated down the Dnepr all night, and the next day reached the bank, where one of our other units was defending the river. They dragged the soldier out of the water, asking 'Who is this?'

"And Sidorenko, the son of a bitch, is not a fellow to miss an opportunity—he's a real storyteller! '"Private Sidorenko reporting!'—he says—'From such and such regiment of such and such division! Just before his death, the regiment commander Ivan Ionovich Buchin handed me the regimental banner and said, *I'm entrusting you, soldier, to save the honor of the regiment.* I quickly thought what I should do. In a flash, I clambered down to the river, grabbed a log, and started swimming.'"

"'And where is this banner?'" some officers asked him.

"The soldier shrugged off his wet field blouse and handed the banner over to them. What a hero!

"They sent a report up to the division; the division sent a report up to the army, and from there, to the *Front* command. This headquarters was now not far from Moscow, and they informed the People's Defense Commissariat about the episode. Stalin ordered that the feat of this Russian man should be glorified and written about in all the newspapers. Our Sidorenko became Senior Sergeant Sidorenko, Hero of the Soviet Union. You call it a case? No, brothers. It is fate. God just had a little joke on us with this drama unfolded!"

"And where is your Sidorenko now?"

"Who knows?"

Everything that I saw and heard here, this assembly of human characters, fates and stories, was like a kaleidoscope. My encounters with other frontline soldiers enabled me to present more fully the general picture of the battles for Rzhev in the winter and summer of 1942. Whenever I looked into it later and thought over some of its details, I often felt out of sorts. It is difficult to believe that such things ever happened. These memories troubled me for a long time.

The Death of Sasha Ryzhikov

Another week passed quietly. One evening, as I was strolling with Sasha through the village, we spotted high, open trestles just beyond the far outskirts of the village. The trestles were supporting knocked-out tanks! "Our sepulchral neighbor," Ryzhii gloomily muttered. Who could guess that some idiot would think to place a tank repair shop next to an infirmary?

Ryzhikov's sense of foreboding didn't mislead us.

The day started normally. We got up, washed, and smoked a little while we waited for breakfast. The field kitchen was supposed to arrive at any moment. Suddenly, a quintet of Junkers appeared above the woods. They were flying low, skimming the treetops. Then they climbed high into the sky, and as we watched, they arranged themselves into a chain. That meant that in another minute or two, they would start their sinister round dance. I gave Ryzhii a little push: "Quickly, into the woods!"

He didn't budge. "Don't worry," he replied. "They haven't come for us. Obviously, their reconnaissance spotted the repair facility, our dear neighbors." I didn't stop to hear him out but instead rushed together with the others into the forest.

The attack continued for about fifteen minutes. When we returned to the village, everything around was smoking and in flames, there was a smell of burning, and where our three huts had stood, now deep bomb craters yawned, full of debris and rubble. Everything that had been in the huts—our bags, our everyday items and utensils, our coats—everything had either burned or lay scattered about, tossed by the blast waves.

But where was Ryzhii? Many of the shelters in which wounded men took cover suffered from direct hits. Seven new arrivals and about two dozen convalescing men received fresh wounds, some of which were more severe than those that had brought them here. The battalion commander Tokmakov, a doctor's assistant, and a nurse were all dead. They had dashed out of their hut too late; a pilot in one of the Junkers had spotted the fleeing group and stitched all three with one burst of machine-gun fire. I asked everyone I saw lingering around the crater of our hut, but I didn't find any trace of Ryzhii. He had seemingly vanished.

That evening one of the wounded soldiers, named Kirill, approached me: "Your friend is over there"—and he waved his hand at a nearby ravine.

I rushed over to the ravine. I found Ryzhii lying at the bottom of it. He was dead. A powerful blast wave had flung him onto some large, sharp rocks that lay scattered on the sides and bottom of the ravine. His face all bloody, he was lying on his back with a shattered head.

I had to find his home address. I searched the contents of his pockets but didn't find one. In the pocket of his field shirt I found a worn, folded sheet of paper—it was a poem by Ehrenburg that he had cut out of a paper. It seems Sasha had liked it, and he carefully kept it. It turned out that the lines were about that which was lying now before me on the ground—a dead man, his corpse lying on its back, tossed here by some pitiless force:

What did he die for? He can't answer you.
And if you think you hear something—it's the wind. He died
So that the thick grass here is more vibrant
So that you are crying, which means you are alive
So that there is the rustling of a densely foliaged tree
So that there is the subtle Russian charm
So that to the four corners of the earth
However far you may walk, wherever you may walk
You may meet someone with a better voice, more smartly dressed, or richer,
But there is no one like the one over whom you now cry.

I asked Kirill to help me. We found a shovel and began to dig a grave for Sasha.

The work went slowly; the ground was hard and rocky, and with just one shovel for the both of us, we labored in turns to prepare the grave. Then suddenly, without a word, Kirill began to pull Ryzhii's boots off his feet.

"What are you doing?" I asked in confusion.

"Just what it looks like I'm doing. I want to exchange my stinking puttees for these excellent boots, it seems they're my size."

"Don't you know what they call what you're now doing?"

"So I've been informed. It's just that your friend doesn't really care now, does he?"

Anger boiled up inside me, but I managed to restrain myself, and I tried to appeal to his feelings: "Kirill, I implore you, let's bury the cadet properly; we're not animals."

"What do you want from me? I found him, and I'm giving you help. You, brother, don't know what war is! I've had my fill of it!"—he made a slashing motion across his throat with his hand. "You don't know anything! We're worse than animals. This war will not let go of us before it has finished us off! So let me just walk a little while in normal boots."

"No!" I shouted. "You don't have the right to plunder my comrade! We're from the same barracks!" and swinging my arm, I punched him in the face with all my might.

He grabbed the shovel, but then he stumbled, fell, hopped back to his feet, picked up the shovel again, and his face distorted by anger, came at me with a roar:

"I'm going to kill you!"

"Kill me then! But they sent you to the front to kill fascists!" I managed to shout.

Stopping short, he became flustered. He spat, threw the shovel at my feet, turned around, and stalked off into the forest. Shaking all over, I stood next to Ryzhii's body.

I buried my friend alone. Saying good-bye to him, I audibly offered as a prayer: "We're from the same barracks!"

So one more grave mound had risen. How many of them appeared during the war! Yet then they disappeared without a trace, just like the memory of those people.

On the eve before my return to the front lines, I went to say goodbye again to Ryzhii . . . and couldn't find the gravesite. All the ground around had been freshly turned over by someone's cold, spiteful hands.

To the present day, I keep that poem from the newspaper, which Ryzhii had carefully preserved, as a memento of my uncompromising and talented friend. Perhaps his favorite guitar, which he had left on the transport unit before the battle, still remains and continues to sing in someone's caring hands?

The Special Unit

A short distance from our lodging at the infirmary was located a modest veterinary clinic: a few tents and, beyond a low little fence, a few kennels. We had been warned not to go there, for it was a "closed zone." Sometimes at night we could hear the dogs' barking.

During the air attack, two of the wounded dogs had been killed; their caretaker, a medical orderly, like all of us who were living in the village, had run into the forest to escape the attack and had abandoned his charges. Some of the men rebuked him for this, but the majority justified his decision: "What else could he do? He wouldn't have had enough time to save them."

That evening, the head of the army's special dog unit came galloping up to us. He had found out about had happened, and he brusquely asked, "Where is this swine who abandoned the two wounded dogs?"

The junior lieutenant frustrated his evident intentions: "He's dead." Everyone held his tongue, so as not to blow the cover story.

The "dog chief" was named Kolia. We offered him some tea, gave him something to eat, and calmed him down. He told us that the 30th Army had recently created the first special unit for dogs. They carried out a variety of roles at the front, such as medical assistance, communications, and tank destroyers.

We listened to Kolia all through the night, and he told us about how they trained the demolition dogs. They would tie small packs onto the backs of the dogs and train them to crawl under a tank. Before a German tank attack, they would replace the pack with an explosive charge and a trigger. Of course, it was a bad thing for the dogs, which were blown up together with the German tanks, but the enemy had to be stopped and destroyed at all cost! The Germans feared these dogs even more than our own human tank-hunters; they hunted them, deployed snipers against them, and even created a reward for each dead dog.

Early the next morning, without even stopping for a bite of breakfast, the "dog chief" returned to his special unit. Within a short time, it became known that the special unit had been transformed into a special regiment in the 30th Army.

Soon after the German air raid we were transferred to a different village. At the beginning of October, during the routine rewrapping of my bandages, the nurse joyfully informed me that the infection had subsided: "You're healthy, soldier!"

A few days later I received a new assignment. I left the convalescent battalion sadly, if only because I was parting from many good people. Some came, some left, but each left an imprint of his personality and personal story on my soul. Meeting with them, I came to understand frontline life better and saw, it seemed to me, what was most important in it.

9

A Rainy Autumn
October–November 1942

I Become a Platoon Leader

As it happened, I didn't return to my regiment or even my former division or army. From the convalescent battalion I was sent to the 673rd Rifle Regiment of the 31st Army's 220th Rifle Division. On the paper that I received, it was written that I was to report to the commander of the 673rd Rifle Regiment, Nikolai Ivanovich Glukhov. I served in this regiment until July 1944.

At the headquarters of the 673rd Rifle Regiment, I, still a sergeant but a former cadet, was appointed platoon leader and sent immediately on to the front lines, to the battalion of Senior Lieutenant Malyshev, which was defending a suburban forest on the northeast outskirts of Rzhev. Before I left, my destination was indicated on a map, and I was warned that it was only possible to reach the front lines at night, since during the daylight hours the Germans kept the entire area under fire. Moreover, German airplanes often appeared, looking for targets, and if they noticed something living, they'd try to kill it.

I waited for night and then headed on my way. It was hard to imagine worse weather: cold, tedious autumn rains fell day after day, with a biting wind. I traveled through an area that had seen heavy fighting but was now not being contested. Here, close to the forest, the ancient road to Tver passed through; now bombarded again and again and heavily cratered, the road was all potholed and overgrown by weeds and wildflowers. For the entire distance of my journey, along the sides of the road, in ditches and shell holes, lay piles of corpses in the most diverse poses, both our guys and Germans, all mixed together. They had lain here uncollected since summer. Evidently, the cold clay soil had preserved the dead bodies from complete decomposition. And when I entered the forest, all shattered by shells, I began to perceive the terrible testimony to the current fighting. I could dimly make out in the darkness the fallen trunks of trees, the enormous piles of tangled roots torn from the ground, the shattered skeletons of burned-out tanks and military vehicles, and more corpses upon corpses.

I nevertheless managed to pick my way through the complete darkness to the battalion and reported to Senior Lieutenant Malyshev. The battalion commander was a little bit drunk, but he greeted me affably. As I understood, he had already received notice of my pending arrival from the regiment. Our meeting was brief, and he only asked:

"This means you're the cadet-sergeant?"

"Precisely so."

"This means you've already been in battle and already been wounded?"

"Precisely so."

"OK, we'll have a chat later. Right now, I want you to go into the trenches and take over your platoon. It's not really a platoon, but one of the remnants of my battalion. It's practically the only combat strength I have left! When we broke through to Rzhev, we had practically 300 men, but after that damned night of 2 October, I was left with just sixty-two men. The most important thing, platoon leader, is to maintain communications with your neighbors and me. I can't think of anything else right now. The situation is complicated. If you have to, resist to the last man, and don't count on any help, as there is no one left to fight."

The conversation was over. It was alarming and rather unpleasant. I set off for my platoon.

The platoon occupied about 200 meters of the front. It was just about as far to the enemy lines—in some places a bit closer, in others a bit farther. Once I presented myself to the platoon, I contacted the battalion commander by phone and told him I had taken over the platoon, and then I began to acquaint myself with the men and our situation.

There were about twenty of us. We were a completely international group: ten Russians, three Ukrainians, two Uzbeks, a Belorussian, a Kirghiz, a Tatar, a Mordvinian, and a Jew—me. Curiously, the Mordvinian turned out to be Mavrii! I didn't recognize him at first when he presented himself—he was filthy, with reddened eyes from lack of sleep and a heavy overgrowth of beard. But as always, he was handsome, with a little smile on his face.

"Mavrii! How did you wind up in this place?!"

"Like everyone else, so here we are. In my sleep, the Supreme Being appeared right here in our trench and appealed to me: 'Fight honorably, Mavrii, save Mother Russia, she is dying.' I killed two Germans on that October night!" Pleased with himself, Mavrii gave a laugh.

Again this October battle; everybody kept referring to it! But that would have to wait. Right now, I carefully looked Mavrii over, recalling our first meeting. Not much time had passed since then, but so much had changed, and so much had we experienced! People had changed too, and become completely different! Mavrii was no longer that fledgling who had landed next to Iurka and me on that first day at the front. At that time it had seemed combat would not be easy for him, but war is a quick teacher, and now his faith was even helping him.

"You've changed greatly, Mavrii."

"I'm still what I was—a Christian. I somehow make sense of all this: war is completely godless, neither the Ten Commandments nor the Almighty recognize it. Having witnessed such mass murder, I found my place in it. When I shot the first guy, I was tormented and begged for mercy for the sin I had committed. But now I've gotten used to it, for war doesn't happen without killing."

Again Mavrii had surprised me. He was almost illiterate, yet his mind never seemed to stop working, and he tried to get to the essence of every matter. Even now I agree with Mavrii: war is the greatest evil ever conceived by the human beast against God and against humanity.

"Mavrii, what happened to your platoon?"

"From my platoon, only Kishmek and I remain. The rest . . . the Germans killed them, and now they're all stars in the heavens. That's what I think, and you know it too."

"You've become real sharp, Mavrii. And obviously a sensible soldier."

"We, the men of Viatskaia Oblast [now Kirovskaia Oblast], are loyal patriots!"—and he suddenly raised his rifle above the parapet and took a shot at the enemy across the way.

From the Battalion's History

The platoon received me respectfully. Nobody asked me about anything, probably relying on the cruelest bit of soldier's wisdom: if we live, we'll see. Almost all of my men had already passed, as they say, through fire and water, but among them as well were a few men of my own draft class, who like me had less than a year of service at the front. We all quickly got used to each other.

Before my appointment, Sergeant Pavel Ivanov had been commanding the platoon; now he became my deputy. When we first met each other, I quickly thought that Pavel would have been a better choice for platoon commander than me. He had a lot of combat experience, and he was physically stronger than me. He had been wounded twice and been awarded the medal "For Courage." Unfortunately, when Pasha, as we called him, was worried, he stuttered, which is possibly the reason why higher command didn't want to risk naming him platoon leader.

Pasha told me that the battalion, the remnant of which I was now commanding as a platoon, had been considered a special one in the regiment. Quite recently, Viktor Gastello, the younger brother of the legendary pilot-hero Nikolai Gastello, had commanded it. But alas, he didn't have command for long. Viktor Gastello had arrived near Rzhev at the beginning of August with the rank of lieutenant, and he became the battalion commander. He was a brave and competent commander, and his battalion was one of the first to reach the outskirts of Rzhev. But while storming the city, he was killed by a sniper's bullet. The regiment commander appointed Malyshev in his place. Later I happened to learn that Viktor Gastello had served in the army even before the war—he had been a metal craftsman and instrument maker at a military factory. He loved soccer and played the trumpet in the factory orchestra. He had a combat waiver, but after the death of his older brother he could find no peace and decided to take revenge upon the Germans. And he was killed in action.

I waited for someone to tell me the story of the October battle that was now painfully fixed in everyone's memory. Eventually the time came, and I learned the details of that night from Pasha.

"It caught us all by surprise," Pasha said. "It was night, about 4:00 A.M., when suddenly the air began to tremble, the ground began to quake, and the sky instantly became as light as day from rockets and artillery fire—thousands of gun barrels, simultaneously smashing our front lines. We had never before seen such a show. It was terrible! Soon the German reptiles rose from their trenches, confident that there could be nothing left of us, and they advanced in dense lines. I then came to understand that such close-range fighting can only be called one thing: HELL! Only twenty to twenty-five meters separated us from the Germans, not more, and we repelled them with grenades. Not many in my company survived the battle; of forty-six men, only three remained. It was the same in the entire battalion. . . . Now they've withdrawn the battalion to this quiet sector of the front, supposedly to refit and receive reinforcements. But where can they find them? Occasionally they send us one or two guys. So far it's been quiet here, but our neighboring units at the old position stayed right there and continue to fight for the city. Either our guys are attacking, and the Germans respond with a storm of fire from fortified buildings and basements; or the Germans counterattack, and our guys defend to the death. We now firmly hold nineteen city blocks, while other city sectors change from hand to hand. They say that on the 3rd of October, a composite assault group from the 215th Rifle Division and our 220th Rifle Division repulsed seven counterattacks. Aren't you from the 215th?"[1]

That's how I learned about the men I now commanded.

A Commander's Concerns

My first commander's steps were the most simple. I checked the platoon's weapons, and I was delighted to find that it had two "Degtiari." I divided the platoon into three shifts for standing watch in the trenches. I ordered my men—my first order!—while on night post not to spare any ammunition. We had to let the enemy know that he could not catch us unawares, as happened back on that October night, so we had to give him the impression of our defense's alertness and strength. My soldiers replied: "They don't let us shoot more than five times a night." I trebled this meager norm and immediately contacted battalion commander Malyshev about the matter. He approved my decision.

The next point of business: I decided to work on the trenches, to fix them up and improve them a bit. The trenches, which the remnants of the battalion had entered after the costly September and early October fighting in the city, were in terrible shape. They filled with so much water in the autumn rains that a person could swim along them, and the walls were constantly collapsing. The dugouts, in which we took shelter during German artillery barrages, were no better. They more closely resembled animal burrows. As our first step, we began at night to gather old boards, wood chips, and stouter branches in the forest, and from them we fashioned planking for the bottom of the trench as best we could. Then we gradually strengthened the walls of the trench with beams. We deepened our dugouts and winterized them. To be honest, however, we couldn't handle the construction of a fireplace. It seemed to produce only acrid smoke and soot that filled our dugout when we tried it.

At nights we dug dummy and reserve positions. We shifted to our reserve positions during mortar barrages, in order to protect ourselves from direct hits. At night I also walked around all our positions, checking on the sentries. So it seemed I never managed to get any sleep at night. If I could, I caught some shut-eye during the daylight hours.

After a long night, there rarely seemed to follow any quiet autumn day, when the wan sun might make a brief appearance from behind the clouds. On such rare days when the sun came out, we tried to dry out and make ourselves presentable. As the commander, I had to be an example to my men, so I washed, shaved, and diligently cleaned the sticky mud from my field shirt, trousers, overcoat, and boots. It wasn't easy to do all these things in these conditions, but I never deviated from the normal regimen.

Things were particularly bad for the men still wearing puttees—they were a constant trouble. But suddenly, one day we started receiving a slow but steady supply of jackboots! Off with the puttees! To be honest, we could see that the boots hadn't come straight from the commissariat. When the boots arrived, we could even see old clots of dried blood on them—no matter, water would clean it all off! A few guys only got boot tops—that's just the way it was! At least they protected the puttees from water and mud. I was suspicious: What kind of supply department would give us boots in such poor condition?

It turned out that two of our soldiers were crawling out of the trenches into the woods at night and pulling the boots off of dead Germans. This was an unbelievably difficult and dangerous business, and the guys were just trying to help everyone out. The strong Siberian Volodia Gerasimchuk and the nimble young Kirghiz Tangiz Iumatov were doing this work. The operation required a lot of time. The soldiers, who everyone else started calling "the searchers for God's gifts," worked through the entire night, so that they could return with their booty before first light. They equipped themselves with wire cutters and an extremely sharp garden knife. In order to remove the boot, they often had to cut them off, and sometimes they could only salvage the boot top. Once they returned with the boots and boot tops, they scraped off the mud and other stuff, gave them a good washing and dried them out, then got them back into reasonable shape with the help of thin cords. It was a complete manufacturing process.

The boots helped us out, protecting our feet from the rainwater that always collected in the bottom of the trench, but all the same many of us were feverish, coughing, and had runny noses. But we didn't pay any attention to any of these little life caprices. All the same, several very sick soldiers had to be sent back to the medical-sanitation battalion.

One other "gift of God" really saved us. Beginning on 1 September 1942, frontline soldiers began to receive an "anesthetic" 100 grams of vodka—about a half a small mug, as the soldiers said, "to warm up." To general agreement, our benefactors, who were procuring our boots, always received an extra few drops of vodka (a "double warming") before heading out on a mission, for good luck.

The rains, the damned rains. . . . A rare sun hung low over the forest like a pale apparition. It began to grow colder, but you couldn't start a fire in the constant rain and mud, and also because the Germans were near. In the mornings, if it wasn't raining, there was a dense whitish fog. It hung like a shroud above the trenches and no-man's land; at just a few paces, nothing was visible. In these conditions it was easy for your mind to start playing tricks on you, so we often thought we saw German helmets emerging from the dense wall of fog. Nervously reacting to any slight rustle, we kept all our rifles and grenades at the ready, and we frequently fired at the imagined targets—simply into the fog.

Dreary Trench Life

In general, the trenches came to life only at night. We would dispatch the wounded and sick back to the rear, and in return, we would receive our supplies: ammunition, thermoses with food, vodka, mail, and the occasional reinforcement—usually just one or two guys. The enemy lived according to a different schedule. At night, as a rule, the Germans slept in their strongly built, warm bunkers. They would rise at 5:00 A.M., have a hot breakfast and coffee at 6:00 A.M., and later amuse themselves by issuing us challenges over a loudspeaker: "Rus, let's fight!" And so it would go for the rest of the day.

The days became shorter, and the constant twilight weighed upon people. The soldiers became accustomed to the whistle of a passing bullet, the whine of a shell, the howl of dive-bombers, but I couldn't help but notice that they were all exhausted, and their nerves were stretched to the breaking point. Probably, this was because of the constant expectation of a sudden, strong German attack, against which, everyone understood, we could offer no effective resistance.

It seemed we were in some netherworld. At night the dampness penetrated your entire body to the bones. By dawn your teeth were chattering from the cold. Everything was always wet and stinking, slimy mud was always underfoot, there was nowhere to get away from the muck; it always irritatingly squelched under your feet. The days were constantly gloomy. At times I fell into despair, but I strived not to show it in front of my men. What could we do; how could we overcome these dismal moods? You can't force nature to show its sunny colors, so we just had to endure, to ignore the stench of the corpses, the rain, and the cold. I asked command to send us the divisional newspaper regularly, but most important, I managed to get the platoon withdrawn from the front line for one twenty-four-hour period, so we could get cleaned up in a proper bath-house and get a haircut; I won't mention the lice. From time to time, I read to the men: Sholokhov, Aleksei Tol'stoi, Simonov; and if I happened to get hold of one of his recent columns, Ehrenburg. The men always asked me to read him, "our dear Ilia," over and over again.

In the trenches, we organized and tried to outfit our dugouts with some conveniences. We tried to fashion little stoves from old iron canisters and milk cans. We contrived to make low plank beds and covered them with a dense layer of little twigs to serve as our mattresses. For protection against shell fragments we dug burrows, little rifle-pits into the top of the trench, and equipped them with little shelves to hold grenades and cartridges. We cut steps into the slope of the trench leading up to the firing positions, so if necessary we could reach them more quickly.

Someone had the idea to build a bunker—a real one, with solid cover, a table, benches, and plank beds. Why should we have it any worse than the Germans? We found boards: we took them from busted supply carts we found in the forest. We found some iron clamps. Some guys in the rear sent us an axe and hammer. We even located a carpenter: Nikolai Ivanovich. We set to work and indeed built the bunker.

So the days passed. We conducted fire at the Germans. We were constantly putting broken communication lines back into order. We set up night outposts. We buried ourselves ever more deeply into our dugouts. We tried as much as possible to maintain army regulations: a common reveille, cleaning of weapons, and training: throwing grenades for distance, and target practice with subma-chine guns. Night would soon come, and with it the order for watch duty.

The Warriors of the Platoon

In frontline conditions, if you know how to listen to people about things other than yourself, if you've summoned a fellow warrior to a sincere conversation, he won't duck it. He'll always be eager to respond, and he'll try to pour out his soul to you, striving to relieve himself of troubling thoughts. He'll tell you right away about his prewar life, about his family, his wife or fiancée, his kids, and his mother. I quickly learned the names of many mothers and girlfriends, and whenever I had a chance to talk with soldiers, usually at night, I first of all would ask cordially: "Well, how's Vania (Natasha, Tania, Pelageia Ivanovna) doing; what is he (or she) writing?" Such a conversational style between a commander and his troops seemed sensible to me. I sought to support the warrior, to distract him from the present if only for a short time, and to give his spirits a dose of optimism. But I also needed these talks.

I'm doing my nightly circuit of the posts; a soldier from Kostromo greets me at his post, as if he's been waiting for me for a long time:

"Comrade commander, what a nice surprise! I got a letter from my dear one!"—he carefully pulls two thin sheets of paper of different sizes from an envelope and shows them to me. "Look, here's a photo that my dear wife sent. My son—he looks just like me, doesn't he? Look how my little one has grown, he'll soon catch up to his father."

"Just so!" I agree, sharing the joy with the happy father, although in the darkness I can only guess his expression.

I walk a little farther. Another post, in a rifle pit—it's Trofim Egorych. By age he's one of the young new recruits, or perhaps he was recently in the civil defense; absolutely I must get to know him better. But for now I just ask:

"Have you seen battle yet?"

"And how! I was 'baptised' at Belkovo—I wouldn't wish it for anyone!"

"Why?"

This seems to encourage him to speak: "The thunder of battle was all around—you couldn't hear orders! There was no sort of direction at all! And what can you do in a solitary foxhole?! They seemed to be shooting directly at us from all sides. All our tanks got stuck in the swamp, and we were up to our knees in water. That's the way we fought for more than a week, until we knocked the Germans out of Belkovo. Only two guys remained alive in my company." And then suddenly he asks:

"For that matter, if you don't mind, can I read you a letter home I've just written? I've been eaten up with worries. Do you think they [the censors] will let it through?"

"But it's pitch black now!"

He knows the letter by heart:

"... Don't think, my dove, that I'll return home alive. The state of things here are such that we don't have a chance to careful, and you know I'm no mouse. Look after father; he's already grown feeble. Raise the children well, and try to give them an education. Don't hope that I might come back, but without an arm or legs. Don't read my letters to anyone else. Your Trofim Egorych."

It was a hard letter indeed. How could a wife read such a letter! I stay silent. The soldier is also quiet, breathing heavily.

"Thank you for your trust," I say, interrupting the silence. "Only, why are you, Trofim Egorych, writing yourself off ahead of time? Fate didn't abandon you at Belkovo, and it won't in the future either. As for the censors, you're needlessly worrying." But I think to myself: you can rely on a guy like this, who's both a stubborn fighter and a worthy man.

I make my way to the next post. I see a single figure—something has happened. The fighter is alone, shaking all over, and wiping away tears as he sniffles.

"What are you doing, Kamaev?" I sternly ask. "And where's your buddy?"

Kamaev is one of the new guys, so I'd partnered him for the night watch with one of our experienced men, a former cadet named Vit'ka Basargin, who was a sniper in the platoon.

"My partner . . ."—Kamaev struggles to answer through tears—"We'd dug little shelters in the wall of the trench, I dove into mine, but he . . . he was a bit slow, and didn't manage to reach his. Some German, the reptile, had decided long ago to finish him off. He fired off a round that landed directly on Vitka's position, and they've rubbed him out. I looked for him everywhere, but Vit'ka has just vanished . . . like he's run off to the heavens. The guy was all happy; he had just received a letter from home, and they've had some new suckling pigs born there: 'In my ears,' he said, 'it seems I can hear the squealing of the piglets.'"

What a hard night! But are any of them easy?

Potapych

For some reason, everyone referred to Nikolai Ivanovich as "Potapych." It turned out his last name was Potapov. You were constantly hearing:

"Potapych, mend my boots, they're completely worn out."

"Potapych, fix the gun rest on my breastwork, so it will be easier for me to shoot."

"Potapych, for some reason my machine gun is cutting out when I fire it, perhaps you can check it out?"

For the first time in my life, I saw in Potapych what we call "a master craftsman."

Potapych never refused anyone help. Whatever this stocky, physically powerful man with the masculine wrinkled face did with his strong, muscular hands, it always seemed to go right. Whenever Nikolai Ivanovich made or fixed something, he never asked any questions, for he himself knew precisely how to deal with each job. He never asked anything in return for his work; his "customers" themselves thanked him for all they could. He was constantly busy, but at the same time, he never shirked his own shifts on duty. He was a crack shot. I wanted to appoint him to a sniper team, but up at the battalion they advised me to wait a bit.

One night when the weather was a bit nicer, I had a heart-to-heart conversation with Potapych. He was from somewhere near Voronezh, born into a large but impoverished village with the unusual name "Bobyl'" [in Russian, a *bobyl'* is a lonely, solitary man or old bachelor]. He lived in the home of his deceased wife's sister. He worked as a joiner, though his formal job title at the *kolkhoz* where he worked was stableman. How many huts, sheds, stables, and bathhouses did Nikolai Ivanovich build! He made dog kennels and birdhouses! He "supplied," as he liked to say, fences and wooden crosses for graves, laid down stoves, and repaired leaking roofs! The villagers all loved him and considered him a kind and worthy man. Earning only kopecks at the *kolkhoz,* he still lived comfortably—people young and old highly valued the craftsman's work. But life is life . . . it doesn't always go well.

It happened that Nikolai Ivanovich didn't get along well with the *kolkhoz* director and flatly refused him a request: he didn't want to build a house for the new district Party boss. The *kolkhoz* director, a petty man, became enraged and immediately composed a report about the "private enterprise" activity of Citizen Potapov. He didn't dawdle, and drove to the district procurator—plainly, not with empty hands—and they agreed to lock up the incorrigible private craftsman and tax defaulter for five years.

"Potapych, excuse me. Why did you despise the local Party secretary? He would have rewarded you handsomely, and you would have had a powerful official patron and sponsor."

"Comrade platoon commander, you still must not know me well."

"Well, what of it?"

"Things were this way. One day, this Party secretary came to the *kolkhoz,* summoned us all to the *kolkhoz* office, shut the doors, and for two hours this Party member and parasite rattled on about the happy life of collective farm workers. Once he stopped blabbering, I asked him a question: 'How are we to understand, Comrade Secretary, why cows have paps with round little thing-a-ma-jigs, but goats have teats like little nuts?' It was a silly question, of course, but I just wanted to show up this Party dandy who had no conception about our way of life on the *kolkhoz.* Everyone around me rolled in laughter, but the secretary was stonily silent. How could he possibly answer a question like that?

He excused himself, then tentatively ventured: 'Probably, that's just nature's way.' From that day on, his expression became hard, and he began to pick on me. So why should I build a mansion for him?"

Nikolai Ivanovich figured out that he couldn't cope with the director and the district swindlers around him (at that time, we didn't know the word *mafia*). Potapych immediately went off to see his old fishing friend, who headed the local *voenkomat*, and asked that he be taken straight away into the Red Army. The military commissar didn't get cold feet and leave Nikolai Ivanovich in the lurch: he managed to get Nikolai Ivanovich a military assignment in three days. So Nikolai Ivanovich headed off to serve in a construction battalion. In 1941 he crossed paths with the 220th Rifle Division, which was defending Vitebsk at the time. From then on, Potapov fought in the 673rd Rifle Regiment.

As a construction foreman, Nikolai Ivanovich was excellent. Employing just one assistant, he built our bunker in just four days without using a single nail, working only with the saw and hammer. They made the bunker from half-grown trees that they felled with the axe, and they gave it a planked roof covered by a thick layer of sod. They draped a canvas sheet across the entrance. Potapych made the passage to the bunker at an angle, in order to ward off shell fragments. Inside he built a small table and several stove-couches, one of which he offered to me. Nikolai Ivanovich also turned out to be a creative stove maker. He built an excellent little stove for the bunker from a milk can, attaching a little chimney to it that was almost invisible from above.

Of course, what we had was far from a real bunker, but we all proudly called it that. The completion of its construction was a real holiday for us. The bunker was our common home, where each man could recover his breath from the trench's stench and mud, jot out a letter to a loved one, have a more leisurely bite to eat, read the divisional newspaper, or change his boots. Here I also placed my signalman with the telephone for constant communication with our neighbors and the battalion.

Vasil' Badulia

We were all happy to have another great talent in the platoon. There was a gifted singer among the soldiers, the Ukrainian Vasil' Badulia. The entire platoon knew his story. Vasil' lived in Kanev, where, as is well known, the national Ukrainian poet Tara Shevchenko is buried. As a seventeen-year-old lad, a year before the war started, Vasil' traveled to Kiev, headed straight to the Academic Opera Theater, and presented himself to the chief producer. There, with no ceremony, he announced: "I want to sing on your stage. Will you listen to me?" The producer was dumbstruck, but agreed to hear Vasil' sing.

Vasil' sang an aria from "Rigoletto" and two folk songs. After he finished, the producer embraced him and asked him to come to a rehearsal: "I want to introduce the troupe to 'the Ukrainian Lemeshev'!"

Overjoyed, dancing along the way, the young fellow made his way to a dock on the Dnepr River and took the next steamboat back to Kanev. Standing on the deck, turning his face to the Dnepr breeze, he yielded to dreaming: Kiev was waiting for him, Moscow too; he would be singing in the best theaters of the country and get to meet Lemeshev and Kozlovsky. How happy his dear girlfriend will be—his beloved Olesia! They'd get married . . .

The meeting with Olesia did not turn out as he expected. Olesia didn't express joy at the news—on the contrary, she rudely said, as only a wicked woman can say to a loving man: "It's either me or the theater!" That's how ordinarily and absurdly it all turned out. Vasil' chose his sobbing girlfriend over the theater, for he thought the theater, like his voice, wouldn't be going anywhere.

The war instantly erased all his hopes.

Having heard this story from its protagonist, everyone spontaneously gave Vasil' a scolding, and even more futilely, to his Olesia. Only one soldier, the short, stocky Sasha Pchelkin from near Saratov, refused to join the tongue-lashing: "Thanks to Olesia! Without her intervention, we would never have had a chance to hear the 'frontline Lemeshev'!" Pchelkin's opinion prompted general agreement and laughter.

My memory has preserved Badulia's favorite song:

The night is so moonlit,
Serene and starlit,
That you can even pick up a needle in the grass.
Come out, my beloved, and if
Exhausted by work
Come out if only for a short minute.

To listen to Vasil' Badulia's singing was a great pleasure. His singing brightened our dreary existence in the trenches, for a time transported us back to our normal life, and lifted our spirits. Vasil' loved to perform a song about the Dnepr, but unfortunately, I can only recall a smattering of its lyrics: "Oh Dnepr, Dnepr, you are wide and powerful . . . but your waters are like a stream of tears . . ."

Each day brought a new concert. What didn't we get to hear him sing! Sometimes I even forgot there was shooting going on somewhere nearby, that any minute or second might be your last. Before the war, though we lived in Moscow, I never once attended the Bol'shoi Theater. I wasn't much drawn to vocal music. But the singing of Vasil' in this unusual trench situation was a miracle. And this miracle inspired in me—again for the very first time!—the thirst to hear more and more marvelous melodies. I promised myself that if I survived, I would without fail visit the Bol'shoi. And immediately the thought arose: how wonderful it would be, if I see Vasil' on the stage!

But fate had different plans in store.

Vasil' was generous—he often repeated his repertoire for those who hadn't been able to hear him because they were on watch duty. He became everyone's favorite. Everybody tried to protect him from the dampness, the cold, and German bullets; they dressed him in the best boots, and someone even gave Vasil' his own muffler, then made sure he had covered his throat with it. We sought to make sure he had some warm sweet tea to drink and wrote about him in our letters home, of how lucky we were to have him here with us in the trenches.

Several times I called the battalion, asking them to relay word about the gifted singer to the regiment commander and commissar: they had to save this talented singer and assign him to the army's performing ensemble. Malyshev agreed with me, but for some reason the matter never went any further.

Once the Germans contacted us by radio: "What have you done with your singer?" Actually, for several days our artist had been sick. After receiving the German message, someone recalled that during Vasil' Badulia's performances, firing between the lines on our immediate sector of the front ceased. Within several days, the Germans gave us an even bigger surprise: at night they had crept into no-man's land and tossed a new harmonica toward our position. It lay glittering about ten meters from our trenches. Somebody crawled out of the trenches to retrieve it, then gave it to Vasil'.

At the end of October, a misfortune occurred. A German sniper silenced Vasil's voice forever. This tragic episode became a lesson for me. We often put off things for the morrow. In war, as in life itself, tomorrow may never come.

During the first half of October, the platoon lost three men. They were killed by a random artillery round that landed directly on their position in the trench. Two peasants and a former soccer player, who had played for the city of Minsk's second team. We buried the warriors not far from the trenches, by the road—three little mounds, modest small planks that bore the names of the deceased, and bouquets made of leaves. I couldn't gather myself quickly to write a letter to their mothers.

Each and every day spent in the trenches is a gift of fate. But no matter how strangely, this feeling fades away with time, and soon it seems like everything at the front is as it should be—and you no longer drop to the ground to duck a whistling bullet, and you no longer notice the howl of shells.

My First Officer's Rank and First Letter

Fighting in the city gradually subsided; evidently the summer-autumn offensive had come to an end. Unexpectedly, Malyshev called me:

"You're leaving your platoon command! By order of the army, they're send-ing cadets who didn't complete their training and education to the Tashkent Combat-Infantry School. So turn over your platoon command and march with your things to the regiment. We'll take Rzhev—we'll break through all the way to Berlin, and you, sergeant, will catch up with us somewhere. Don't forget to bring with you a big, juicy melon and a little more wine."

Somehow I didn't believe in the trip to Tashkent—was this some sort of mistake? Nevertheless, I did as I was ordered and turned over the platoon to my deputy, Sergeant Pasha Ivanov, said farewell to everyone, and thanked them for their outstanding service. I gave away my greatcoat and warm socks, as I didn't think I would need them in the south. I put on a padded jacket, and once darkness fell, I got out of the trenches and at a crawl, here and there with short dashes, I made my way to regimental headquarters. From there, having received orders and a pass for army headquarters, I hitched a ride to a village with a funny name, "Kobylkino" [derived from the Russian word for "mare"— *kobyla*], where army headquarters was located. I presented myself and handed over my orders. Then suddenly, the young colonel that had taken my orders chuckled and told me:

"I congratulate you upon your graduation from the Tashkent Combat-Infantry School and upon receiving the rank of junior lieutenant. Excuse me, there's been a mistake, and they haven't had time to prepare documents for you to return to your division. Now we'll drive you back to your division ourselves!"

Indeed, things had turned out amusingly. I didn't know what to be happier about—my officer's rank or the thwarting of the trip to Tashkent? Of course, it wouldn't have been bad to learn a bit more, since I still had only a little, but nonetheless real, combat experience. Speaking honestly, I wasn't longing to return to the filthy, lousy trenches. But thinking of my platoon, I suddenly felt a warm feeling inside, and that night, having returned to the trenches and reported to Malyshev that I had graduated from the military school in just twenty-four hours and now had the rank of junior lieutenant, I was now ex-periencing genuine joy.

The soldiers happily greeted me upon my return, with friendly laughter. From Kobylkino I had brought a fresh issue of the army newspaper with some verses by Surkov, which had been written at Rzhev, and I immediately read them to the warriors gathered around me:

The shell fragments are beginning to howl like a wolf
Across the uncomfortable expanse of this unharvested field.
But when the cannonade falls silent for a minute
You can hear the sad cry of cranes in the sky.

Once again—we didn't have time to say goodbye to summer
Before the chilling autumn suddenly and unexpectedly appeared.
The meadows have become brown, and the summer bird
Above our trenches is drawn to the south.
Horse bones are bleaching in the field,
Through roiling clouds of black smoke, ruins are visible.
You will not find now, our flying guests,
An island of silence anywhere across this wide land.

Everybody liked the poem, but Pasha told me: "I have some news for you"—
and he reached into his pocket, pulled out an envelope, and handed it to me.
"They brought the mail the morning after you left; there's a letter for you from
home. I decided to save it, on the off chance that you might send us your new
address. And here's the miracle—the addressee himself has shown up."

Sheer delight washed over me! Spit on the battalion commander and his
mix-up! It turns out that even at the front, a genuine holiday can occur—and
what a treat! My heart was bursting with joy!

At the time we still didn't know the taste of victory; this was waiting for us
in the future. But meanwhile even such events as receiving a letter from home,
dry weather, the earning of a medal, or a promotion in rank are joyous occasions, and they created holidays!

Mother's first letter! Five months had passed since I had last seen her, when
we had said goodbye in Tiumen. The first letter I had received at the front! I
immediately read it through three times, then reread it again and again for a
long time:

My dear son! After many uneasy days, I finally received your letters. The
first one hadn't yet been delivered when the mail carrier brought two more.
What a fine fellow you are! Having received your letters in this unusual
shape [During the war and at other times in early Soviet history, letter
writers folded their letters into little triangles, called *treugolochki*, and mailed
them like that. This enabled censors to check the contents before sending
the letter on to its address], I recalled how in your childhood you loved
to make little paper ships out of just these sort of paper triangles. You set
them afloat in the largest puddles, creating entire naval battles. One of your
friends, I don't recall who, predicted you would become a sailor.

   If only you knew how many times I read your letters. I wept and
became overjoyed that you were alive. And I laughed. You haven't lost your
sense of humor at the front. You particularly amused me with the story of
your first frontline meal, the tastiest soup in your entire life. And how you
got the fish head, and how everyone who tried the soup called you the
best cook.

I implore you, take care of yourself! Keep your neck covered with the muffler, keep your feet warm, don't drink untreated water, and don't eat anything cold. How you loved it, whenever I fixed meat patties and especially the potato pancakes. Find out from your commanders if it is permissible, and I'll fix potato pancakes for your entire army and send them to the front! Write, my little one, whenever you can. Do you have friends, and is your officer a good one? That's so important, especially at the front. I'm kissing you.

—Your Mama

My dear, sweet, marvelous Mama! It is such a pity that Iurka isn't with me any longer; I would have read him the letter absolutely, and I'm sure he would have shared in my happiness.

A Combat Operation with Regimental Scouts

I hadn't yet had time to slake my thirst for reading Mama's letter when the battalion commander called me and told me to report immediately. I set off for his command post. Malyshev was brief:

"Tomorrow night we'll be sending you some regiment scouts and sappers. Headquarters needs a 'tongue' [a living prisoner-of-war who is willing to talk]. We're supposed to cover them. Pick five soldiers with two machine guns. You'll lead the operation personally. If you happen to need it, we'll support you with mortars and artillery."

Returning to the trenches, I immediately called the platoon together. I explained the given assignment and asked, "Who's going with me?" Everyone was quiet. I calmly waited for a reply. The first to speak up—just think!—was Mavrii. "I'll go,"—his voice rang out confidently.

Seven more men spoke up after him. I chose five: Mavrii, the experienced fighters Volodia Gerasimchuk and Tangiz Iumatov, and two machine gunners. One had been living in an orphanage before the war, a fine fellow; in the platoon everybody called him the "Kazan' orphan." The other was nineteen-year-old Sergei, one of the guys from Riazan', who loved the old story-teller's standard introduction: "In Riazan' we have mushrooms with eyes . . ."; at some point he had told me that he had a fiancée who was waiting for him back home.

At the start of the operation, the scouts showed up; like us, there were six of them, led by a Lieutenant Pavel Chernov.

"Why did you choose this sector of the front?" I immediately asked their commander.

"There are three things in our favor here," said the lieutenant. "The bunker that we've targeted has weak security, practically just a single sentry. Secondly, to the right of the bunker is a pretty large swamp, and to the left of it some hilly terrain. Thirdly, about twenty paces from the bunker, the German trench line takes a sharp turn, which is good for us. At this turn, there is a second sentry. He leaves this turn every eleven minutes and returns after about the same interval of time. Moreover, every thirty minutes a patrol checks this sector of the line: two soldiers and an *unteroffizier* [a German rank equivalent to a sergeant], but we don't have to reckon with them, as we should be able to manage everything in the eleven minutes, before the second sentry returns."

"And our job?"

"Your main job is to give cover as we withdraw with our 'tongue.' I'll describe the plan to you. We'll all leave together. When we're in sight of the German trench, we'll move on ahead, while you separate into two groups, move about seventy meters from each other, set up in your positions and wait for our return. We'll do our job and then start to withdraw. Next is the most difficult part of the mission. After five or six minutes, the second sentry will spot the corpses and recognize that one of his guys is missing. He'll raise the alarm, and the Germans will immediately try to recover their missing guy dead or alive. The important thing is to not let the Fritzes leave their trenches: open fire at the slightest movement. Our group with the prisoner will pass your right-hand position, which should have the commander in it—that's you. As soon as you see us, you'll start giving us cover. Meanwhile I'll be moving over to your left-hand position, and your guys will cover our exit. As soon as I reach them, I'll give you a signal, and we'll all pull back to our trenches. If the Fritzes manage to encircle us, neither our guys nor your guys will get out. They, the swine, know how to punish us whenever we screw up."

"That means that the outcome of the operation depends upon our full cooperation. But how will you grab a 'tongue'?"

The lieutenant smiled. "Our job has been arranged. Our group will make its way up to the first trenches, where it will also split up. Three of us—I and two others, having waited for the patrol and the second sentry to pass, will climb into the trench, take care of the first sentry by the bunker, and then seize a warm and snug Fritz. The other three men will be covering the turn in the trench line and watching for the second sentry. We'll make our way to them with our prisoner, hand him up to them out of the trench, and they'll head to the rear. We'll cover their departure and then also move back. That's all. The most unpredictable part is the return with the prisoner, and this is where in fact you'll help us."

The lieutenant introduced his "hunters" to us, as the scouts liked to call themselves:

"This is our Soldier Petia," and he wrapped his arm around a short, round-faced adolescent. "He's eighteen. He's already tallied two 'tongues.' He has the

Order of the Red Banner. He's always in our snatch group whenever we go on a hunt. The guy has unbelievably sharp eyes, like a lynx, and he knows how to handle the cold steel like an expert—not a single spare motion."

Next to Petia, a broad-shouldered Ukrainian named Mykola, an enormous and powerful fellow, was standing like a cast-iron monolith, looking at me with his pale blue eyes and smiling like a child. He said only one thing: "We'll get it done," as if to comfort us. The third scout, Andrei, was also powerfully built. He was nineteen. Presenting him to us, the lieutenant said:

"He once dragged in two prisoners at the same time: Hans on one shoulder, Otto on the other. Quite the guy! It's just that he's got a lot of arrogance too. And that's Shurik"—Lieutenant Chernov nodded over at a tall, well-built fellow with a lush head of hair. "He can shoot with his eyes closed. He's the favorite of all the regiment's girls!"

The fifth "hunter" was Semen, who had a rough, weathered face. "He ought to be a boxer!" the lieutenant proudly said. "From his looks alone the opponent will crash to the canvas. But at the front this fellow stays busy 'catching babes' as he likes to call it."

I spent some time with the scouts, about two hours, and we looked at them with admiration. We were in the presence of uncommon people. They were all well-groomed and cleanly shaven; their commander, Lieutenant Pavel Chernov, led them by a strict rule: for those in the reconnaissance—only a neat appearance. I didn't notice any posturing in any of them, and they were simply uniformed: quilted trousers, boots, and padded jacket without any shoulder straps. Each man was armed with a pistol, grenades, and a knife. Looking at them, it was hard to believe that they were facing mortal danger. There was no sign of any tension on their faces or in their eyes, much less any fear or indecision, or any fidgeting. They laughed, talked about everything under the sun, and cracked jokes. Only no one said a single word about the upcoming operation. It seemed we were more afraid for them than they were for themselves. Where did they find such energetic, active, and strong men?

The sappers returned and reported that they had cleared a path to the German trenches. At 2:30 in the morning, I contacted the battalion commander and said everything was ready, and received a "Good luck" in return on our departure.

Mavrii's Feat

We jumped across the trenches and then crawled after the scouts. Everything seemed like it was in a dream. At first in the darkness I lost sight of the lead group, but I still managed to make do. Soon we caught up with the scouts at our covering position, and they moved on ahead. My groups split up and moved apart to the predetermined distance. I kept Volodia Gerasimchuk and the "orphan machine gunner" in my group. Mavrii and Tangiz Iumatov were with the second machine gunner, Sergei. The Germans were so confident in their invulnerability that they hadn't set any trip flares or other detection devices out in front of their lines, so for the time being everything was going smoothly. I was worried how the scouts would make their way across the zone directly in front of their trenches, because the Germans were continually sending up illumination flares. But everything was quiet in their direction.

The Germans periodically opened up with short machine-gun bursts and automatic fire, and we could hear the bullets whistling overhead. What sort of nighttime show was this? As someone explained to me later, this area fire was for psychological effect, as if to let you know they've spotted you.

The silvery light of a multitude of flares, penetrating through the damp gloom of the night, was illuminating a fairly broad expanse; the scouts were out there somewhere, but they were moving so skillfully that the Germans didn't detect them.

Afterward, the lieutenant told me how it all went down. Semen "the Boxer" and the soldier Petia took down the sentry by the bunker in the space of fourteen seconds, then the three of them burst into the bunker. After a minute they dragged a half-asleep, frightened German, still in his underwear, with hands bound and mouth gagged, out into the trench. They tossed him like a rag doll up into the hands of the covering group. They quickly wrapped the prisoner in a canvas tent sheet and dragged him away. All this took six minutes.

The second sentry, having discovered the body of his partner and two more dead in the bunker, fired into the air and ran to meet the approaching patrol. We heard all of this, but we couldn't see anything: a few isolated bursts of automatic fire rang out; we could hear loud commands and the trampling of boots. After a minute, alarm signals started sounding and spread along the entire German defensive line. Suddenly the shooting died away. Clearly, I thought to myself, the Germans are getting ready to go after our guys. At that moment, German helmets appeared above the breastworks, and grenades started flying after our scouts. Not waiting for the Germans to leave their trenches, I gave the command to open fire. Both of our Degtiari opened up. The helmets quickly dropped out of sight. Now the entire German frontline began to bristle against us—machine guns began to chatter up and down the line. The scouts passed by us, quickly crawling back to our lines with their booty. A short time later I heard the agreed-upon signal from Lieutenant Chernov and gave the order to withdraw.

It was difficult to foresee what happened next. Evidently, the Germans had spotted my second group and directed aimed mortar fire upon it. Machine gunner Sergei Vdovin was the first to die. Shell fragments struck Andrei in the leg; he himself managed to bind the wound and started crawling farther. The next shell exploded quite close to Lieutenant Chernov, and here an astonishing thing happened: Mavrii, who at that moment was next to Chernov, flung himself upon the lieutenant and covered him with his body. Torn by fragments and covered with blood, Mavrii was dead. Having noticed a small gully nearby, the lieutenant gathered the survivors in it. Here they waited out the mortar barrage, and then bringing the two dead men with them, they started crawling back to our entrenchments.

Our group meanwhile was withdrawing quietly and without interference, for the ground over which we were moving was wrapped in predawn mists. Although the fog covered our withdrawal, it did me a bad turn—to my misfortune, I didn't notice a deep shell hole filled with water, and fell down into it. In the darkness, no one else noticed what had happened, and I remained alone in my icy basin. I began to flounder desperately, trying to clamber up the slippery wall of the hole, but I kept slipping back down into the icy water. Again and again, exhausting my strength, I tried to extricate myself, but my frozen body stopped responding, my legs cramped up, and I realized with despair that I could not get out by myself, but my comrades had moved on. . . . Suddenly I felt a bump, and a pair of strong, extended hands grabbed hold of me—Volodia Gerasimchuk! With his help I finally clambered out. Exhausted, wet, covered by sticky, stinking mud, I laid down on the ground, listening to the explosion of shells, trying to come back to my senses. The trenches were quite nearby, but the guys had stopped, waiting for me. When I had gathered my strength, the soldier asked if we could move on. Shaking, teeth chattering, I could barely crawl. Just then, our own artillery opened return fire! The German fire paused briefly, and we took advantage of this to rush back into our lines. Thus we were all saved.

I phoned the battalion commander, reported the situation, and asked him to send immediately some litter-bearers. I heard only one word in response: "Turd!" After that I considered the battalion commander to be worthless.

The next night, they buried Mavrii and Sergei Vdovin. The day before, Malyshev had called: "You're going to have guests. They're coming to bury your hero."

An esteemed group showed up to say farewell to Mavrii. It included the regiment commander Glukhov and his adjutant, the battalion commander, the scouts with their commander Lieutenant Pavel Chernov, and Vasilii Soshnev, who was a correspondent on the staff of the divisional newspaper *For the Motherland*.

Overnight, Potapych made a coffin from boards that he removed from the roof of our bunker. We laid Mavrii in it, not forgetting his little cross, which he had kept intact.

The stern scout commander started crying when he saw the body of Mavrii, who had given his life to save him. One time Mavrii had said, "The soul of a

man is full of kindness; who can forbid him to give it for another man?" This
man had given everything he could! Deep sorrow possessed us all. The regiment commander, having removed his forage cap, spoke the first words. In the
silence of the night, he spoke very solemnly:

"The saving of a commander by a soldier has always in the history of the
army been considered a heroic deed," he said. "If you will, it is no less in our
time than the ramming of a tank or an airplane, or when a soldier flings himself
upon the firing slit of a pillbox to block the machine-gun fire from within. We
have sent a recommendation to the division to award this soldier the title Hero
of the Soviet Union."

Lieutenant Chernov kissed Mavrii on the cheek and uttered only three
words: "Thank you, friend!"

I spoke last, my eyes brimming with tears, but I gathered myself and said:
"Mavrii's act was not an unreasonable, reckless act. He believed in God, and the
feeling of high duty to other people was fully developed inside this man. He held
his military obligations to be sacred. And for this, God shows his gratitude!"

Malyshev, who was standing next to me, glanced at me spitefully. The
regiment commander shook my hand and thanked me for Mavrii. I warmly
parted with the scout lieutenant and his men. Pavel Chernov embraced me in
farewell:

"Thank you for the support. If you ever need it, give me a call, my guys and
I will always give you help."

The correspondent Vasilii Soshnev approached me: "What a story for the
divisional newspaper! It's a real windfall, an example for many other religious
soldiers; we have a lot of them. Although men like Mavrii—there aren't many,
of course. I'm confident that the Party leadership will welcome this story."

I interrupted him: "I ask only that you don't make an atheist of him; in that
case nobody will believe in the truth of what you've written and you will of-
fend the memory of this man."

We talked for a long time. Vasilii wanted to know more details about Mavrii,
and I wanted to talk about him—our first meeting, his attitude toward war, toward people, and that Mavrii was only nineteen! He fought for all of 150 days!
But neither one thing nor the other prevented him from becoming a real soldier. At critical moments in a man's life, the instincts laid down in him through
his mother's milk emerge, and in Mavrii these instincts were strengthened by
family traditions and faith, about which he liked to say: "It's not important
what a person believes in; just his faith itself is important." We are all connected
with life by many threads, and nobody wants to die. Then suddenly with a
bright flash, this precious life itself poses you a question: "Are you prepared to
sacrifice yourself?" It is difficult to say how a person will behave in this situation. Mavrii's action was truly a heroic feat.

"The true strength of a very religious person consists in the unselfishness of the good work he or she has done. Even if he is not confident that he will be rewarded for this in the next world . . . that's how Mavrii always thought and behaved!"—the article in the divisional newspaper closed with these words. Soshnev kept his promise.

Mavrii's deed made a strong impression on me and stirred me up inside. It raised many complicated thoughts and feelings. No, I didn't become a religious person, but unquestionably, this act had an influence on my soul. I began to study believers more attentively. There were a lot of them among the soldiers, and I tried to understand them better and treat them with respect. If the need arose, I tried to help them.

Vasia Soshnev, the correspondent, was about four years older than me. He turned out to be a surprisingly pleasant and tactful man. I liked him, and we became friends from that night on. We corresponded after the war, when he continued to serve in the army. We met in Moscow on the thirtieth anniversary of Victory Day, by which time Vasilii Stepanovich Soshnev had become a major general. At this meeting, the veterans chose him to be the chairman of the Council of Veterans of the 220th Rifle Division. Together we traveled to Elets in 1981 for the fortieth anniversary of the division's founding. Together we escorted veterans on their final journey. And every year, we marked Victory Day together beneath the combat banner of the division. The Central Museum of the Soviet Army had returned this banner to us one day. My heart has kept a good memory of this postwar period and my lively reunions with my brother-soldiers. I've also kept rare photographs. Where will they go after me, and who will be interested in them?

Pasha Ivanov Is Killed

The Germans missed their *gefreitor* [the German rank equivalent to a corporal]. Anticipating some unpleasantness, after talking things over with the battalion commander I split my platoon into two groups. As a security detail for the first line of trenches I left four soldiers, and with the rest I pulled back into reserve positions.

Actually, two days hadn't even passed when the Germans decided to get even with us in revenge for their helplessness, their dead, and their captured *gefreitor*. They brought down a storm of artillery fire on our front line position—five artillery barrages in the course of one day.

That night we returned to our old entrenchments. Now there were only enormous piles of earth, rocks, and fragments of our thoroughly blasted bunker. And bodies. All four of my men had been killed. We had to dig out Pasha Ivanov's body.

Pasha! Mavrii! Sergei! So many human tragedies at once! How can one endure such a thing? Perhaps this was my fault? But what if the Germans had counterattacked? No, one must not do without a security detail. The damned swine! Why are they here? Why have they come for us? One after the other, the war is devouring the very best—the kindest, the strongest, the youngest! So I wanted to cry out and ask, "Why, God?"

Oh, Pasha, Pasha, so you never became the platoon commander, and it has all led to this. I never asked him about his stuttering, but he once himself told me how it started.

Pavel grew up in a military family. They lived in Kuibyshev, in a military sector of the city. His father was a dashing cavalier who commanded a squadron. He often took his seven-year-old son, placed him on the saddle in front of him, and at a gallop they would ride around the training field with the young boy breathless with delight. Once the squadron commander, flushed after a bottle of the finest port wine, planted the child alone in the saddle on his favorite horse, Zhorka:

"Hang on, son. You, Pashka, must be a cavalryman!"

The horse, sensing that it was not his master on him, didn't budge. Then the father lightly touched the horse on the flank and shouted:

"Giddy-up!"

The horse darted off around the parade ground with the terrified little boy aboard. The father immediately sobered up and rushed to intercept the horse. But it was too late. Pasha didn't howl, didn't scream, didn't fall from the horse—but he was petrified. The psychological effects of this experience lingered for the rest of his life. For the next five years his mother went around and took her son to all the best psychologists and counselors. The doctors told her not to worry, believing that his stuttering would fade away with time. But that didn't happen, and Pavel was never cured of his stuttering.

Pavel didn't dream of a military career. After the war, he wanted to become an architect, to build schools, libraries, and stadiums.

The Frontline Brotherhood

We quickly went to work trying to restore our positions. There were only eight men left in the platoon. But there's no way around the need for a security detail, which meant again I had to send men under enemy fire. During the night we restored communications. I called the battalion commander, reported on the situation, asked him for reinforcements, and asked permission to shift our position. Malyshev called me a coward and refused: "Stay right where you are! Don't move a step! You'll get your reinforcements." The next night we received some new guys—twelve men. It wasn't enough, but thanks for it anyway.

Soon after these hard events that had befallen us, I felt a sharp pain in my legs. Frequent cramps occurred, my feet hurt, my toes became numb, and then my legs almost stopped responding to pain, which was an ominous sign. One of the soldiers set off at night into the forest and brought back some sort of old wet leaves. He dried them out and then began applying them to my legs. This seemed to help a little, but not for long. The cramps and pain in my leg muscles led me to an utter breakdown. My extremities turned into useless logs, and it became ever more difficult to deal with my ailment. But I was responsible for my men; what kind of commander could I be in this condition?

In these sad days and nights I particularly experienced that unique form of human kindness, that frontline brotherhood. The soldiers, as much as they could, tried to ease my difficult situation. They offered me tea and prepared a separate place for me not far from our dugout, to where two guys carried me, supporting me under the shoulders. But I kept having terrible thoughts: what if there's an attack and the Germans break our line? So I never parted from my pistol even for a second. I decided that I would not surrender to the Fritzes, but as the fighting concluded I would kill myself. At night, to stay awake, I tied a cord to my leg and repeatedly gave it a jerk so that the enemy wouldn't catch us off guard.

As much as I didn't want to do it, I finally had to call the battalion commander and report my poor health. The next night, medical orderlies arrived with a litter, laid me down on it, and four dogs hauled the cripple back to the *medsanbat*.

I wound up in the army's hospital and spent about ten days in it. At first I couldn't get around without crutches, but the doctors soon put me back in order, and in a literal sense put me back on my feet.

After my discharge I asked to return to my division. It turned out that only military servicemen in Guards units and shock armies had the right to return to their unit. They decided to assign me to the *front*'s reserve, which would mean good-bye to the 220th! Boldly and with a fair amount of passion, I appealed to the hospital director, "We hold our combat brotherhood dear! For me, a platoon commander, to walk away and leave my soldiers would be wrong." Despite the rules, the director granted my request.

The Brown Boots

At the beginning of November, when the first snows were already covering the ground, I returned to my platoon. A rather delicate episode then occurred. Everyone greeted me warmly in the platoon, but Volodia Gerasimchuk, who I had left in my place, and Potapych even gave me a surprise: new boots, just my size!

But what a wonder! In the course of just one night, my new footwear underwent a miraculous metamorphosis, changing from black boots into brown! I summoned Potapych and asked him to explain these miraculous boots and to tell me where he had found them.

Potapych told me the full story, without hiding anything. He had sewn the boots from the leather of a saddle, which Tangiz Iumatov had in broad daylight dragged off the horse of some cavalry general, who had arrived to visit our division commander Poplavsky. How the soldier managed to make his way to the stable holding the general's horse, how he stole the saddle, and then got back with it to the platoon—well, this Potapych didn't know. (Later I found out that Tangiz had concealed the saddle in a large produce bag on his way back to the front lines.) But now the situation had almost reached the point of a general's tears, for it seemed this saddle had been a personal gift to the visiting cavalry general from Semen Mikhailovich Budenny himself.

As it turned out, even our division commander flew into a rage: he asked for the procurator and ordered a search for the thief, in order to turn him over to a tribunal! Even members of the Special Department, *osobisty*, took part in the searches.

It had become clear that the situation had taken a sharp turn for the worse, and I fell into serious thought. Should I turn in my boots to Malyshev and ask him to forgive the culprits? Of course, they wouldn't give them a reprieve but would condemn them instead. Should I adopt the guise that I didn't know anything, because I'd been in the hospital? That also wasn't the optimal choice, for the *osobisty* might see through my cover story: then the division commander would know everything! So I decided: to hell with them, that is, the boots! I took off my fleeting joys and pulled on my old boots. Having thanked the craftsman that made them, I sternly ordered Potapych to hide them somewhere deep in the woods that very night so that nobody would find them.

The vexed Potapych hadn't even had time to leave my dugout when Malyshev called me and conducted something approaching an interrogation. I promised to look into the matter. But somehow I never managed to get around to it.

Our Lucky Stars: The Aborted Reconnaissance-in-Force

Several days later, an order rang out from the regiment commander Glukhov: a reconnaissance-in-force! The operation fell to our battalion.

I had already heard so many tragic stories about these operations, which in the Russian language were known as "reconnaissance through combat" [*razvedka boem*]. How highly the commanders believed in them and valued them, and with what horror did the soldiers utter this phrase! Rare was the soldier who remained alive after such an assignment, and it was considered a success if you were just wounded and your own guys managed to drag you off the battlefield.

Malyshev summoned his subordinate officers: "At night, two platoons will advance to within fifty or seventy meters of the line of defense. At a signal, we'll create a big racket—machine guns, automatic weapons, grenades, and then the platoons will bound forward and try to break into the enemy's trenches. The operation will start at 5:30. The signal will be a green rocket. Sappers will clear narrow passages through the mine field."

Of course, we were lucky to have the help of the sappers. But everyone knew that in such situations, the first lines would inevitably still suffer great losses from exploding undetected mines, and by this sacrifice they would clear the way for those following.

Even at that time I understood that "reconnaissance through combat" was the brainstorm of the Supreme Commander and his generals. Depending upon the task, they would send a platoon, a company, or a battalion; the size of the force didn't matter. In reality, they were driving people to their slaughter, to their certain death. The point of the operation, as they considered it at head-quarters, was to give the enemy a big scare, so that he might think a large-scale offensive was beginning and cause him to open fire from all his positions, thereby revealing them to our intelligence. Subsequently, we could easily knock them out. In practice, things rarely turned out that way.

In reality, "reconnaissance through combat" was complete hogwash. The most that it might be able to do would be to give us more precise information on the layout of the enemy's forward positions. Given a deeply echeloned de-fense, even this couldn't achieve the permanent elimination of firing positions. Moreover, to count upon the complete suppression of the enemy's weapon emplacements during the attack was complete nonsense. The Germans, inci-dentally as did we, quickly saw through these simple schemes. Meanwhile, a "re-connaissance through combat" primarily just devoured men, just like Moloch [a god of the Ammonites and Phoenicians that demanded human sacrifice], and when the fighting started, the enemy's weapons usually came to life and our infantry, striving for the enemy's positions, poured out their blood.

The war ended, years passed, but this idiotic idea, which cannot be called anything else, continued to live on in the minds of generals. When they were testing the atomic bomb here, they implemented the same type of "reconnais-sance" in its atomic form, and sent thousands of officers and soldiers—infantry, tanks, artillery, and cavalry—to the test site. Yes, the people were dressed in protective suits, but once again they were checking—on people!—the suit's ef-fectiveness against radiation. They used the people just like laboratory mice!

But let's return to our story.

They warmed us up a bit before the operation, dressed us in white smocks for camouflage, and gave us each a shot of vodka, a loaf of bread for two, and some tasty soup with meat and noodles in it.

After midnight we very quietly clambered out of our trenches, slowly crawled up to the designated line and, taking cover behind sparse snow-covered shrubs and folds in the ground, pressed ourselves to the earth. We merged with the cold, frozen ground, but for us on this night, there was nothing more comfortable and reliable.

Above no-man's land, flares burst into light and quickly died out. A pale moon occasionally peeked out from behind the clouds and cast a soft glow across the shallow glittering snow. Soon, as if to aid our concealment, the clouds cloaked the night sky, and it grew darker. The Germans were quiet—they hadn't spotted us. Time passed slowly; from time to time I glanced at my watch and I tried not to think about anything, but my brain worked of its own accord. . . . How would it happen, what would it be like—the last moment of my still young life? Would my soldiers get up to follow me, just to have their lives snuffed out forever a minute later? I had just reached twenty years of age, but on that night I thought about and pitied not so much myself, but my mother—my dear, loving, devotedly waiting mother.

There were sixteen of us in the platoon; the seventeenth had gone the day before to the *medsanbat* with boils. Likely, all sixteen of us were now envying him. A young Tatar was lying next to me, very quietly mumbling something—either praying or, like me, whispering about something to his mother. Beyond him, the barely audible sounds of an Uzbek carried to my ears: ". . . 127, 128 . . ."; apparently he was playing some game unknown to me, or trying to guess at something. Perhaps I should also be trying to predict something? Here: if I catch sight of a star before the attack, it will mean that everything will go all right for my soldiers and me.

Now I was not only watching the hands on my watch but also constantly glancing at the sky, still covered by a thick blanket of clouds. A half hour remained until the signal rocket—a half hour of life for each of us, the sons of mothers. There were also wives and children to consider; one of us, a Belorussian, had five kids already.

Now the minutes roll by at a gallop. I give the hand signal to get ready. I have faith in my men, and they believe in me. A few minutes more. My nerves stretched to the breaking point, I've already laid my submachine gun in front of me. An unpleasant shiver of fear passes down my entire body. For the first time I feel that I'm absolutely frozen. I try to shrink inside myself, straighten my shoulders; tugging at my greatcoat beneath the camouflage smock, I tighten up my belt another notch. That seems to help—already the night seems not as cold and frightening. I try to prepare myself for the difficult minute that lay ahead. I try to forget about the cold, the whistle of bullets, about my possible death, and I force myself to think about the future, about everything pleasant and joyful, about meetings that would still take place somewhere in my future. . . . I glance up at the sky again—and I forget about everything! A star is twinkling above me! My omen—it is solitary and pale, but such a long-awaited and surprisingly precious star! To the present day I try to understand it and I cannot answer the question: did that star really exist, or was it a figment of my imagination? But a fact remains a fact: precisely at 5:30 a command passed down the line in a whisper: "Fall back!"

We quietly crawled back to our entrenchments. Should we believe in fate? I believe.

Within several days we learned that our units were shifting positions, and the movement had already begun. Until the end of 1942, a relative calm fell around the city of Rzhev itself. At the same time, I learned that I was receiving a promotion to company commander, in which position I would immediately have to wrestle with a grave threat facing the Red Army: desertion.

10

Turncoats
November–December 1942

Deserter (Lat.)—turncoat, fugitive, traitor. Desertion—a deliberate, voluntary abandonment of a military unit by military servicemen; one of the gravest crimes against military service.

Military Encyclopedic Dictionary, vol. 1 (Moscow: Ripol Klassik, 2001).

We and They

In the middle of November 1942, the 673rd Rifle Regiment, or more accurately, its remnants, was transferred to the left bank of the Volga River, which had been fully liberated from the Germans in the summer. Here, on defense, the regiment sat until March 1943.

We took position in the Germans' former trenches. They were quite spacious and had been constructed according to all the rules of engineering science. Every bunker had a table, comfortable bunks, and a stove. As became clear later, these stoves had been manufactured in Rzhev in workshops that had been established by the occupiers. The Germans also organized the manufacture of mines and bombs in the city.

The enemy was dug in on the opposite bank of the river. Only the Volga separated our two lines. Right away, incidents of desertion became much more frequent.

The subject of desertion in the Red Army has long awaited special investigation. The conviction is widespread that our people, from the very first days of the war, never lost hope in ultimate victory. That isn't so. In actuality, confidence in victory over the enemy began appearing only in 1943—after the battles of Stalingrad and Kursk. The constant heavy defeats of the Red Army in 1941–1942, the enormous human losses, led a portion of the Soviet people to lose hope of success. In 1942, as in 1941, desertion from the Red Army was still massive. Many deserting soldiers didn't consider their action a betrayal; for them, the prewar reality in the country did not serve as an ideal for which they should die. In fleeing, they saw the single means to escape the Stalinist system of slavery, naïvely believing that the Germans, having defeated the Soviet

Union, would destroy the Soviet regime and make them free and happy. Of course, all these people were also trying to save their own lives.

Along the entire front in 1942, 150–200 men went over to the German side daily, which meant around 6,000 men a month. Looking at it another way, this meant the Red Army was losing almost an entire division on a monthly basis! (At that time, as a result of losses that could not be replaced, as a rule a division in the Red Army was considered to have around 6,000 soldiers.) Desertions swept through the ranks of the Western Front near Rzhev as well. Naturally, they happened in our 220th Rifle Division too.

One of the reasons for this "infectious disease" was the skillful propaganda of the Germans. Indeed, the German propagandists did everything possible to bring Red Army soldiers over to their side, and for the first two years of the war they often succeeded in doing this. But we ourselves were guilty in this because of the lack of readiness of the army and the country for war! *Retreats. Defeats. Losses.* What sort of military art was this? What was the soldier hearing? "Fight to your death! Not a step back! At any cost!"—and, even worse, "Into a penal battalion! Before a tribunal! Shoot him!" Yes, soldiers *defended to their death.* They constantly witnessed with their own eyes the reality of the "losses" being reported in the newspapers. They not only saw it but also experienced it themselves! And they made comparisons between their own existence in the trenches and that of the Germans.

The second winter of the war was coming. The time had passed since the first winter, in 1941, when the German army was dying from the severe Russian winter, surviving only by plundering warm clothing from the local population; when the German soldiers, instead of winter gear and warm clothing, were handed a leaflet, a "Reminder on the Severe Winter Cold Spells," in which they were given pithy advice such as: "The lower part of the abdomen should be especially protected from the cold by the application of newspaper sheets between the sweater and the undershirt. Put some felt, a handkerchief, crumpled newspaper, or a forage cap with underlining beneath your helmet while you wear it. . . . You can make armlets from old socks. . . ."

Now the Germans, in contrast with the first winter, were dressed in warm quilted overalls. The army showed them constant concern and care: they received excellent hot meals daily; they were sent food packages with delicacies from the conquered European countries (our guys, when they found some of these pretty little jars containing unknown victuals, emptied them and found all sorts of other uses for them). The Germans lived in solid, comfortable bunkers with stoves and often with electrical lighting. The frontline soldiers were continually supplied with the newest weapons and equipment in sufficient quantity. Officers and soldiers received furloughs. Officers' and soldiers' brothels enjoyed popularity in the army. The army maintained strict discipline and simultaneously cultivated a spirit of combat comradeship among the officers and men.

But in our army things hadn't changed, and by the end of 1942 our soldiers on the front lines lived in poorer conditions and were dressed significantly worse than the Germans. As a rule, the soldier was dressed in a worn-out uniform: an old field blouse; a faded, shapeless side cap; boots with foot bindings instead of socks; a badly crumpled fur cap; and a worn out greatcoat that let in the wind. In winter, padded jackets with faded bloodstains on them were passed out in the effort to keep us warm. We were fed badly. We couldn't even dream of furloughs. We had forgotten all about a woman's caresses. Our infantry weapons, especially the machine gun, had no comparison to the Germans'. We never seemed to have enough combat supplies, particularly shells and mines. As before, the German air force ruled the skies. Discipline in the units was maintained by the unremitting surveillance of the political staff and the *osobisty* of the Special Department. The command cultivated combat comradeship only through slogans; it arose naturally of its own accord, primarily in the companies and batteries.

The only thing in which we were on par with the adversary by the winter of 1942 was in propaganda lies. But it didn't come from us in the ranks; it was drilled into our heads from above. They pounded it into our brains, and how! From both sides!

Enemy airplanes scattered hundreds of thousands of brightly colored leaflets over the sector of the Western Front—white, green, and blue sheets in which, describing their victories and our defeats, the authors tried to convince the soldier: come over to the Germans, it is the only chance to save yourself. Beneath those lines, cunning text described the life of paradise that former Red Army soldiers enjoyed on the German side: "We treat prisoners well. For those who come over to us voluntarily, by a new order of the Führer, the treatment is even better: they will receive a special certificate entitling them to better food and a number of other benefits. For those who desire to work, we will arrange it so they can work in their own field or profession." Every leaflet without fail contained a pass with an explanation printed in thick lettering: "Tear off and keep this pass. Upon coming over to our side—present it. Legal crossing will save your life."

Investigations by the *osobisty* of the Special Department, pursued in a most painstaking fashion, yielded evidence that many soldiers were collecting and hiding these leaflets, waiting for the suitable moment to present the pass and implement a "legal crossing."

In order to prevent mass escape, the command undertook a number of desperate measures. Possible exits from our forward positions were mined. Commanders and the junior command staff in those units that experienced desertions were harshly punished. They would reorganize not only companies but also entire battalions and send them to new sectors of the front. They went so far as to bring artillery fire down on those trying to escape. The *osobisty* spread secret networks to catch those who might want to desert, and special groups for fighting desertion appeared in all units.

The commander, senior sergeant, and sergeant could be reduced in rank to private for a single episode of desertion in their platoon. For an episode of group escape, the punishment was appearance before a tribunal and a sentence of five to ten years in a prison camp. Prisons were replaced by the creation of a penal battalion for commanders, and a penal company for privates and junior officers (senior sergeants and sergeants).

Enormous attention was paid to the diligent search for and destruction of these German leaflets, a task at which *osobisty* worked successfully. A tribunal threatened anyone who read, kept, or distributed these leaflets with the charge of anti-Soviet propaganda. They judged severely one and all, officers and soldiers.

The political staff increased its work, especially in the front lines. They explained the concepts of loyalty to the oath and duty before the Motherland to the soldiers. The word *Party* disappeared from the lexicon, and commanders and commissars began using a new word, *Fatherland*. They demanded that commanders continuously familiarize their soldiers with publications that exposed the atrocities of the occupiers. If in the first stage of the war our propaganda stigmatized, primarily, Hitler and his comrades-in-arms, it now brought down wrath and scorn upon the "New Order," which was being propagated by the Hitlerites on the occupied territories. At the same time, steps were taken to improve the daily lives of the soldiers; we began to receive better food, bathhouses were constructed, and we were given more opportunities to wash ourselves. But the flights to the German lines continued.

An Aside

Historically, going back to Peter the Great, the Russian army, proceeding precisely from the meaning of the term *desertir* [deserter], always used that word to describe the act of a serviceman going over to the enemy. However, in the Soviet army, especially during the Great Patriotic War [the Russian term for the Soviet struggle on the Eastern Front in World War II] and immediately thereafter, this term was replaced by another, *perebezhchik* [turncoat]. That's why I entitled the present chapter "Turncoats." The words *deserter* and *desertion* frightened the Party and military officials of Soviet Russia—the enormous scale of the mass desertions was indeed painful to behold. The data indicate that starting in 1942, more than a half million individuals deserted from the ranks of the Red Army. It is hardly possible to determine accurately how many fled in

1941. The official data, which I have cited, I think are insufficiently precise, and most likely are too low.[1]

It is well known that more than a million Soviet citizens, dressed in German uniform, served in the German forces on the Eastern Front. They were mostly in the rear, carrying out supply, construction, and security operations behind the operating field armies. What kind of people were they? Some of them were military prisoners, another portion were young people whom the Germans had mobilized in the occupied regions, and finally, there were the true turncoats.

Already by the autumn of 1941 many German commanders on their own initiative began to create auxiliary units from deserters, prisoners, and volunteers from among the local population. At first they called them "our Ivans," and later, now officially, *Hilfswillige* ("those wanting to help"), which was shortened to "Hiwi." They used Hiwis in the role of security personnel, drivers, laborers, loaders, and others. This experiment produced results that surpassed German expectations. No less than 200,000 Hiwis were serving in the rear units of the German army by the spring of 1942, and by the end of the year, around a million. In November 1942 during the Stalingrad battle, Paulus's Sixth Army counted almost 52,000 Hiwis in its ranks: "Russians," as the Germans called all Soviet citizens, composed up to half the personnel in three divisions. In the summer of 1943, "Russians" comprised 5 to 8 percent of the troops in the elite S.S. divisions at Kursk.

Higher German authorities were particularly well disposed to the creation of "Eastern Legions" made up of non-Russian volunteer citizens of the USSR. By an order dating from 30 December 1941, three national legions of volunteers were organized: a Turkestan Legion—from Turkmen, Uzbeks, Kazakhs, Kirghiz, Karakalpaks, and Tadzhiks; a Kavkaz Legion—from Azeris, Dagestanians, Ingushetians, and Chechens; and an Armenian Legion. In January 1942 a Volgo-Tatar Legion was created. There also existed a Kalmyk Corps; several of its units operated in the Soviet rear. The Germans favored the Cossacks most of all: more than 250,000 of them fought on the side of the Nazis.

Hitler easily and quickly approved the formation of forces from non-Aryans—Turks and even Kalmyk Muslims. But he constantly and categorically rejected the creation of Russian allied forces. Several historians consider that this pathological hatred of Hitler toward the Russians, a large number of whom wanted to fight against Soviet rule, even became one of the reasons for his defeat in the war against the USSR.[2]

The total number of deserters from the Red Army during the years of the Great Patriotic War was 588,400 people. During this same period, 994,300 servicemen were convicted of the intention to desert. Of those, 422,700 were sent to penal battalions and companies, 436,300 to concentration camps, and 150,000 officers and soldiers were executed. The numbers are terrible.

Desertions: How It Really Was

Our division stood on defense on the left bank of the Volga, no more than 200 meters from the German positions. Only the ice-bound river channel and the steep banks of the river separated our two lines. The proximity to the adversary gave rise to a new wave of desertions. They ran away in ones, twos, and in entire groups.

To collect the courage to toss aside your weapon and go over to the enemy is already an extremely complicated psychological matter. But the turncoat faced other problems as well. He had to clamber out of his trench up onto the breastwork and then slide down the icy slope to the river; run across the choppy, uneven ice to the opposite shore; climb up the slippery slope, which was something still more difficult; and then face something even more difficult and dangerous: to crawl through the minefield and reach the enemy trenches. And he had to do all this without being noticed by our side, while simultaneously letting his intentions be known to the enemy.

About 5:00 A.M., when the long winter night was still not over, when it was still dark and everyone was still immersed in the deepest, predawn sleep and the sentries' attention has become dull, a fugitive left his rifle, cartridges, grenades, and documents in the trench and set off on his way, trying to reach the opposite shore and climb the opposite bank as quickly as possible. Beyond, he acted strictly according to the instructions of the German leaflets. Even as he was making his way to the German-held bank, and before he had even managed to climb it, he was moving under the cover of German machine guns and snipers, who opened fire on anyone trying to pursue the fugitive, not even letting the would-be pursuers stick their heads above the trenchline. Moreover, in the effort to facilitate the turncoats' safe passage, the Germans cleared several narrow routes through their minefield and marked them with little signs: "Raise your arms and show your pass. Approach the trenches calmly." And, as a rule, the fugitives managed to reach their desired goal.

It began the evening before. Close to nightfall, the crackling of a microphone familiar to everyone usually came over the loudspeaker, and former Red Army soldiers, who had fled to the enemy just the day before, would make an appeal to their former comrades:

"Private Serega Khmel'noi, a soldier of the 1st Company of the 1st Battalion of the 673rd Rifle Regiment, is speaking. Greetings, Vanek! Listen up, dear friend. And pass along my message to the whole company. The Germans received me just as they said they would. I am warm and my belly is full. I've gotten rid of the Jews and the commissars. Within three weeks, they've promised to let me return to my village to see my dear Son'ka."

A second broadcast message immediately followed the first. Now a German was speaking in decent Russian. By his intonation, firm and confident, we could guess that an officer was talking: "Soldiers of the Red Army! Come over to our side! We will hold our fire until 6 o'clock in the morning. We'll be having breakfast at 6:30. If you don't come, you're done for!" The Germans repeated this message daily, two or three times a day.

It's the third loudspeaker broadcast of the day. Again a turncoat speaks:

"Greetings, Vasilek! It's me—Dennis. Come on, friend, leave your crummy life and come over to the Germans. They're decent people, not at all like our foul-mouthed officers. They're giving us French chocolate, Dutch cheese, and Danish ham to eat. We didn't get to eat such things under the Soviets! That's right. I'm serving in a transportation unit. They've promised to let me go home in spring. Come on, gather up your courage and get going! You won't regret it!"

At first during the nightly broadcast appeals and desertion attempts, our regimental artillery would open fire on the fugitives, trying to block the escapes by smashing the ice on the river, but they couldn't maintain the fire for long, as they had to save ammunition. Too, the patches of open water in the ice would soon freeze over again; in the meantime, the Germans would temporarily move their broadcast station to some other place, only to return again later, and again we would hear the names of those who had previously been with us but were now against us: Vasilek, Petukha, Dzhanbai, Grits', Armen . . .

In the front lines there was no way to stifle the hostile loudspeaker propaganda, and every night we all—commanders, commissars, and hundreds of soldiers—were forced to listen to these repugnant speeches. I could hear that their language was not a soldier's natural way of speaking—it was something different, prompted to them by the Germans. But did the soldiers understand this? We had no assurances that they did. Some men scorned both the promises of the Germans and the turncoats; others chuckled, especially at the sweet words about French chocolate; a few wouldn't react at all, as if they had become totally indifferent to it. At the same time, I could see how attentively a few soldiers, old and young, listened to every word from the opposite bank of the river.

We junior officers worried about this. How can we get into another man's mind to figure out what moves him? Perhaps I, as a commander, and others as well, were overlooking something, missing something, and had lost simple human contact with the soldiers?

Meanwhile, a new directive went into effect. Some idiots higher up had recommended periodic inspection of the soldiers' personal effects in the search for the German leaflets, as if this might curtail the number of escapes. Speaking for myself, I brushed aside this advice as ridiculous and immoral, reckoning that this would only lead to more desertions. A search of a man's personal effects would plainly demonstrate to the soldier that I didn't trust him, and this would only engender distrust in return. It seems I had read in a history book somewhere once that after the battle of Austerlitz, the adversaries Napoleon and Alexander I met. The Russian tsar asked the French emperor to show him his Guard. While inspecting the Guard soldiers, Alexander tried to look inside one soldier's knapsack. The Guard soldier pushed the tsar aside and prevented him from even touching his knapsack. Alexander became indignant and complained to Napoleon, who responded: "I don't even have the right to do this. The French soldier is a free man, and the knapsack is his personal property." If only such considerations would inspire every commander! Then there would be no tribunals, and mutual respect would be the rule.

One night there was an alarm in the adjacent company. Three guys had taken off for the German lines at the same time! The company commander almost lost his mind. He ordered that the fugitives be tracked down and wiped out whatever the cost. But just as our guys had managed to crawl out of their trench in pursuit, two German machine guns opened up from two directions. The rash decision of the frantic company commander only resulted in two wounded. Then regiment commander Glukhov, who had received word of the emergency, ordered the artillery to try to smash the river ice to keep the fugitives from reaching the opposite bank. But even that didn't help. The turncoats calmly avoided the explosions, found some cover, waited out the barrage, and then, after darkness fell, successfully made their way over to the Germans. The next night, we heard their voices over the loudspeaker: Vanek, Serega, Dem'ian . . .

The company commander and the lieutenant in charge of the platoon in which the deserters had been serving were relieved of command, sent before a tribunal, and sentenced to ten years each, then sent to the penal battalion. The lieutenant was only nineteen years old and hadn't yet even had a sniff of gunpowder, still waiting for his first battle.

Such was the situation as it developed on our front. It seemed that an enormous black maw had arisen that was going to gulp all us officers down into its hungry belly.

I Devise a "System"

How could we combat the evil of desertion? I trusted my soldiers, and they trusted me. Thus, in my opinion, theoretically speaking we had to build relations between the commander and his subordinates. But in reality this was more complex. There were direct costs for this trusting relationship. Many commanders and sergeants, who forgave attempted deserters and continued to rely upon those, who once might have betrayed their oath, often paid a cruel price for their kindness. But why was it necessary to suspect everyone? To make life on the front lines, where a man already exists in a state of constant stress and danger, even harder?

In my new position as company commander, I had to confront this problem of desertion at the company level. The first thing I did in my new position was to create a "system" to reduce the opportunities for flight.

I decided to divide the forty-eight soldiers in my company into two shifts: a day shift and a night shift. Along our company's sector of the front, which stretched for around 300 meters, I set up twelve posts, with two soldiers at each. There were only around twenty-five meters between each post. No one had the right to abandon his post before the end of his shift. My deputy and I moved up and down the trenches all night long, from flank to flank, checking on the posts and weapons of each man. We would also have short conversations with the men at each post before moving on to the next. All those resting after their turn on watch had to be in their dugouts. I posted an orderly in each dugout, who was not to permit anyone to move more than five steps from it. In the morning, the shifts on our sector rotated.

The important thing in this system was to make careful pairings, so it would be less likely or more difficult for them to make any arrangements. For this purpose I carefully studied the personnel roster of the company, to learn the background of each soldier. We had in our company soldiers from the Urals, from Siberia, from Central Asia, and men who had come from regions now under German occupation. I discovered that there were eight Ukrainians in the company, who arrived at the front from Kazakhstan: why they had been in Kazakhstan when called up for service was a question. I acted in the following fashion: I assigned to one post a man from an occupied territory, and one from an unoccupied region; to the next post, a young Komsomol member and one of the old guys in the company; at the third, a Russian kept watch with an Uzbek; and so on.

At the same time, I sought to make our defense more active—we fired at the least sign of movement. I selected two soldiers as snipers. This had the desired effect; the Germans became more cautious, and it became more difficult to catch one in an optical sight.

Of course, there was no way to guarantee fully against attempts to escape to the Germans. But for the time being, the system worked.

I ran myself sick on those nights—enough for my entire life. But it was not in vain. Almost an entire month passed, and there was not a single attempt to desert in my company. It was a miracle! During the same period of time, four more soldiers ran off in neighboring companies, and their commanders wound up in penal battalions.

Division Commissar Borisov

One evening, battalion commander Malyshev brought the division commissar to my company. That was an uncommon and unexpected event—commissar "rats," as they were sometimes called, didn't often show up in a company's position on the front lines. But this was not true for Leonid Fedorovich Borisov; the entire division knew about him—of course, primarily in absentia. But everyone knew that our division commissar preferred the front lines to his desk in the Political Department, and the men respected him for it. More than that, legends circulated around him. A regular army serviceman (he had been in the army since 1935), back in 1941 he had been one of the first organizers of the underground partisan movements in the areas of Smolensk and Rzhev. They said that near Sychevka in the Smolensk pocket, Borisov and a small group of frontier guards managed in the course of two days, while under constant enemy fire, to rally and organize up to ten battalions from among the disorganized retreating units, thanks to which they managed to delay the German advance by five days.

Having made introductions in my bunker, he immediately requested a cup of strong tea. We brewed it for him. Then we left to tour the trenches. I introduced him to the soldiers, confident that he would make a strong impression on them. Tall, broad-shouldered, and relatively young, Borisov was slightly nearsighted; behind his glasses were lively, experienced eyes. He often removed his glasses and wiped them with a handkerchief, out of habit.

The commissar exchanged friendly greetings with each soldier and asked them questions: How was he being fed? Did he have access to a bathhouse? Was he receiving letters from home? Borisov also spent some time in the dugouts. He was happy when he spotted several recent issues of the divisional newspaper on a table in one of them. In another of the dugouts, the relaxing soldiers were engaged in a card game when the officers and commissar entered. The battalion commander's face twisted into a frightening grimace as he ducked into the dugout behind the commissar. The card players instantly flew into a flurry of action, trying to conceal the cards. Leonid Fedorovich broke into laughter: "It's a pity we don't have more time or else I would join you in your game. I haven't held cards in my hands in a long time. In my old units, where I served before the war, we loved to break out the cards in the evening."

The battalion commander relaxed, and the soldiers started smiling. Borisov asked them not to be timid and to ask any questions that were on their minds.

"Why aren't the Germans dissolving the collective farms?"—the first question rang out. "Does this mean they're also for the collective farm system?"

"Not quite. It is easier for them to plunder the countryside with the help of the collective farm system. In many occupied districts, people have already figured this out."

"Is it true that the Germans are exporting black earth from the Ukraine back to Germany?"

"I don't know, but I admit that the German is capable of something like that."

"Tell me, Comrade Commissar, the People's Commissar of Defense promised that the war would end this year, but we're nowhere near that."

"That just means that so far, we are not fighting well. The better we learn how to strike the enemy, the sooner we'll chase him from our land."

"There are painful delays with the mail."

"I know—we're taking measures."

"If only we could bathe more often—it's a barrier against fleas!"

"We've made a steam bathhouse for each battalion, so get your birch twigs ready!" [It is common practice for Russians to lash themselves with a bundle of twigs while taking a sauna.]

"It seems, Comrade Commissar, that the Germans have reopened the churches in the villages. What are we supposed to make of this?"

"The occupiers are dulling people's senses, so they entice them into churches. They want to make the people more obedient."

Later, we spent more than an hour in my dugout. To the question, how could I explain that there had been no attempts to desert in my company, I told him about my system and highly praised my men.

"What were you doing before the war?" Borisov asked.

"I finished my schooling in 1941, but in 1937 I worked as an assistant in a movie theater. I had to earn the keep for the family after my mother lost her job."

"Was this while your father was in prison?"

"Yes. Fortunately, he returned. Now he's directing a defense facility in the Urals."

"Tell me, what's your nationality?" he asked suddenly.

"A Jew. Excuse me, if it's no secret, does this have some significance to you personally?"

"You've guessed it, Lieutenant: this does have personal significance. By conviction and conduct, I am an internationalist. My grandfather and father raised me to be this way. I myself am from Iaroslavl'; before the revolution, Jews didn't live in our city. But no matter how strangely, our first Red commandant of the city was the former city cobbler—the only Jew in Iaroslavl'. It turned out that he had been a secret member of the Bolshevik Party. He was killed during the Socialist Revolutionary rebellion in 1918. Now let me speak a little more concretely about why I asked you about your nationality. Unfortunately, both in the division and higher up, there are commanders and political workers who don't treat Jews in a very friendly fashion. They consider Jews to be cowardly, crafty, and bad soldiers. I disagree and in my political department, I put an end to such attitudes. You are one of the 'arguments' in my favor. Let's talk about something vital: What do you think, Lieutenant, are the main reasons for desertion?"

"Can I speak openly, Comrade Colonel Commissar?"

"Only openly. What kind of sense would our talk have otherwise?"

"I've thought about this matter more than once. I can name two reasons. First are the continuous failures of the army around Rzhev and the enormous human losses. People want no part of senseless butchery. The second reason is the soldier's hard life. How long can a person labor, when he sees no concrete concern for his well-being from his higher-ups? Especially when the aroma of tasty food wafts over to us from the German lines."

Borisov was silent for a bit, wiping his glasses, then thanked me for the useful conversation and left the company area.

Division Commander Poplavsky and Officers

Soon after Borisov's visit, the division commander summoned all his battalion and company commanders to his headquarters. It was the first time I ever saw General Poplavsky. It had been said in the ranks that the general was a puny guy, but I saw that he was a muscular man. He was pug-nosed. He was wearing a brand-new leather jacket. He spoke sharply, in clipped phrases. His declarations crackled with energy, and it seemed as if every statement produced a new eruption of sparks:

"I will no longer tolerate desertions in my division! We must increase our vigilance! First of all, among ourselves! I will be punishing commanders even more harshly for anyone going over to the Germans!"

One battalion commander leaped to his feet: "They're fleeing like rats from a sinking ship!"

For this incautious outburst, the battalion commander left the meeting as a company commander. He had only been a battalion commander for a month. You had to watch your step around a man like Poplavsky! Later we found out that they slapped a formal Party rebuke on the guilty man "for political immaturity."

Commissar Borisov spoke:

"We, commanders and commissars, are doing a poor job with the ideological education of the soldiers. As a result, people have no confidence in victory over the fascists. Company commanders are not carrying out their basic duties, show little concern for the welfare of their subordinates, and some soldiers, especially from the southern regions of the country, are not enduring the hard life on the front lines. We all need to think about what we can do for them. We also ought to consider that a portion of our men come from recently liberated areas. They want to go home. The farther the army advances to the west, the more this tendency, this longing for home, will grow. You can also find unstable people in the ranks, and possibly even unexposed accomplices of the fascists."

In conclusion, the division commissar mentioned my name and told everyone about the experience of work with subordinates in my company; he evendevised a name for my system: "Not a Step Forward"—by analogy with Order No. 227, "Not a Step Backward!" I will not hide that I was flattered. But a comment, deliberately and loudly tossed out from somewhere among the gathered officers, quickly spoiled my mood: "Of course, the cunning Jew has pulled the wool over all our eyes. We're all just a bunch of idiots, while he's the favorite."

I was highly offended and almost lost my composure, but I held my tongue. What a cheap shot! I wasn't doing this to help myself, but for the good of the army.

The meeting ended and we began to disperse. The chief of the division's Special Department stopped me as I was leaving and introduced himself: "Major Kovalev." He politely asked me to hold up for a bit. Once we were alone, he asked me:

"Do you know about the group of young Ukrainian soldiers? There are eight of them in your company."

"I know," I answered. "But how they wound up in Kazakhstan, I don't know."

"These are kids of parents who had been exiled to Kazakhstan for being unreliable elements during the struggle against the kulaks in the Ukraine in the 1930s. For a long time, they wouldn't take such youth into the army, but now, apparently, they consider them to be OK. But whether or not we can trust them, I'm not sure."

"I believe in them, I've talked with each of them. They're all happy to be fighting against the Germans, and they hope after the war to return to the Ukraine."

"You seem very sure, Lieutenant."

"They're new recruits and they were poorly prepared, but that's not their fault, so I'm bringing them up to speed."

"Just see to it that you're not mistaken; misplaced trust can cost you dearly. I ask you personally to keep me informed about the slightest hint of problems."

On this, the conversation ended, and I headed back to my company.

Back at the company, something rather unpleasant was waiting for me. An agitated Oleg, the company's Komsomol organizer, had been marking time by my dugout, waiting for my return. He was holding a couple of German magazines with lurid color illustrations.

"Look, they fell from the skies right onto our trenches!"—the Komsomol organizer said excitedly. "The bastards, look what they've thought up now: they're tempting our brother with pictures of naked ladies!"

"Oleg," I cut in, "you haven't looked at any of this fascist filth, have you? You've done the right thing by collecting them and bringing them to me. Of course, you've brought them to be burned, haven't you? That's what we're going to do?" I gazed at him intently.

The young soldier answered instantly, his brain working furiously: "Of course! I always counsel my Komsomol members to behave this way."

I tore up both magazines in front of Oleg's eyes, then we both stepped into the dugout and the stove flared as I tossed the material into it. I gave one scrap to my radio operator, who also tossed this trash into the fire.

After Oleg left, I started pondering a different matter: what could I tell my soldiers about the Allies and the "second front." They had been constantly asking me about it.

We never knew what was going on above us, or about the diplomatic struggles that were unfolding between Stalin and the Allies on the subject of opening a second front. We most often learned about all this from the Germans (of course, with a certain amount of outright lying). In 1942 and even in 1943, they had been printing and scattering leaflets over our lines about the disagreements between Stalin and Churchill. At the beginning of 1944 they tried to convince us that the Allies had tricked us, and that there would be no second front in the West. The swine directly wrote: "The Allies have fooled Stalin!" We never received any official announcements about the scale of the Allies' military and material assistance to the Soviet Union.

How did the commanders and we, the soldiers, react to the delays in opening a second front? Gradually, a misunderstanding of what was happening, and even a sense of distrust toward our allies, developed. A simple and understandable thought gathered in all our minds: every delay in opening the second front only protracted the war, which meant more casualties. The Red Army was bleeding, while the Allies only shared new promises, meat stew, and army boots with us. The frontline press and our commissars cultivated this mood among the men, as only they were able. Here is an example from the army's newspaper: Two soldiers are having a conversation. One asks: "How can a second front in the West be opened more quickly?" The other replies: "At least the American boots will be helpful to us in reaching it more quickly."

But then American tanks, airplanes, and the famous Studebaker and Dodge trucks and Willys jeeps began appearing at the front. The day of the Allied landing on the beaches of Normandy—6 June 1944—was celebrated far and wide among the frontline soldiers of the Red Army.

A multitude of jokes and nicknames about the second front circulated among the soldiers. For example, cans of American stew were called "Second Front." Whenever anyone was preparing to open some cans, someone would exclaim without fail: "Open a 'Second Front'!" The English "Matilda" tank, designated to play an infantry support role, was known among the men as the "Crazy Wench." The Studebaker truck (or the *studera*, as the soldiers called it), which fundamentally improved the mobility of Soviet infantry and artillery, was affectionately known as the "Breezy Fellow."

The soldiers gave affectionate diminutive names to other armored vehicles. Thus, the British "Valentine" tank became the *Valentin*, and the Bantam BRC-40 jeep was called the *Bantik* (Little Bow).

Whenever American Lend-Lease Bell Airacobra fighters appeared in the skies overhead, the soldiers would tightly clench their fists, tip back their heads, and joyfully cry: "Come on, guys, give the Germans some stronger venom!"

One of the soldiers, gazing up at the American fighter planes in the sky, said that our best fighter pilots flew in the Airacobra. This was the truth. From the summer of 1942 until the end of the war, the famous Soviet ace Aleksandr Pokryshkin flew the Bell Airacobra. Our pilots appreciated its toughness and armament, and it flew reasonably well at the lower altitudes that prevailed in the dogfighting on the Eastern Front.

A "Bad" Letter

Not quite a week passed, and I learned I had to leave my company and take over a different one. But before this happened, I was unexpectedly summoned to Commissar Borisov. We exchanged greetings, and he invited me to sit down. He immediately pulled a letter from his desk and extended it to me. It was a letter written by one of my men, Seleznev, which had been returned to Borisov by a military censor. The text was short; I can recite it in full:

> Greetings, my esteemed Glafira Petrovna, I bow low before you. Greetings, my dear sister Dunia and Grandfather Efim. First let me say that I am alive and healthy. I hope the very same for all of you. War is a terrible affair. Men could not imagine it. There are no joys. We spend all our days in mud and cold. My boots have rotted long ago. It's such a shame—they don't even feed us well. Only your letters warm us up. The Germans pick us off and cause us constant losses. It's a bad deal, but at least until high command receives the casualty reports, we still get the dead men's rations, so you can eat as much American stew as you like. Don't think that only I see things

this way. All the guys think like I do. The Germans are right next to us. My comrades say: "It would be better if a bullet killed us than to suffer these agonies." Others ask God why He didn't suffocate them in their infancy, if He knew that there was going to be a war like this. It is impossible to get out of the trenches. You'll instantly get a bullet in the forehead. German snipers are hunting us. Nobody wants to die. With that, I'll say goodbye.

"Well, what do you have to say? What a chicken! He's a worthless soldier."

"This 'chicken', Comrade Commissar, is a communist and my closest assistant in the hardest minutes. He has received the medal "For Combat Merit." He's been wounded twice. A true frontline soldier! Forgive me, but this soldier is just writing the truth."

"Do you really think the same way he does?" Borisov asked.

"Yes. But unlike him, I don't write such letters."

"That's it! It means your Seleznev is an immature communist."

"If you'll permit, let's forget about this letter. I'll have a heart-to-heart talk with Petr Vasil'evich. I'm certain the next time we go into battle, he'll be leading the men together with me."

Boris looked at me for a long, long time and wiped his glasses over and over again, but all the same he decided: "OK. I'll try to believe you."

All the way back to my company, I thought of only one thing: what a stroke of good fortune it was that the letter had been returned to the political department and had wound up with Borisov; otherwise . . .

11

A New Assignment
30–31 December 1942

A Letter from Home!

About 60 meters from our company's position, the course of the Volga River had created a slough at a bend in the river channel. The Germans occupied one side of this little slough, and we—the other. Here, our lines were within spitting distance of each other. It probably would have been more expedient if one side or the other had yielded and withdrawn from this narrow projection of water. But neither our command nor the enemy's showed any desire to blink first. However, by some unspoken agreement among the men, the opposing sides here didn't bother each other.

When they informed me of my assignment as the new commander of this nasty sector of the front line, I didn't celebrate: it meant I would have to leave my company, to which I had become accustomed, and the friendships I had formed with the men in it. But an order is an order. On 30 December we warmly said our farewells, and I shook hands with each man.

I had learned about my new assignment that morning. That afternoon, I received the most valuable gift a man can get at the front—and a New Year's gift at that! It was a letter from Mama! She had sent it from Kyshtym on 10 December, probably with the hope that I would receive it by New Year's. Her wish was fulfilled, and now I was reading the letter over and over again:

My dear son: What a fine fellow you are for not forgetting about us! Each one of your letters is a holiday for us. In the morning, I catch sight of Shura, our mail carrier, though the window. A good, kind woman. She walks up with her large mail pouch, which hides so much inside it: both joy and just as much grief. She pulls a familiar triangular shaped letter out of her pouch, and we sit at the table. I fill a bowl of soup for her. I put on my glasses, and read your letter in a loud voice. Shura is somewhat deaf. She listens, eats her soup, and cries. Her husband is at the front. She has received nothing from him since 1941. In the evening, I read your letter to your father over the telephone. He spends weeks at his office without coming home.

The industrial complex is growing. Soon its output, and you know what it is, will be going to its destination. Forgive me for passing along some sad news. You get enough of that there. My sister Fanechka has passed away. We cut off a few locks of her lovely curls as a keepsake. We buried Fanechka in Kyshtym.

I congratulate you on the approaching New Year. May it be happy and victorious for us all. Take care of yourself, my dear son, but understand me correctly. I am not asking you to duck the demands of the army. But remember—you have a weak throat. Don't smoke in the cold. Try not to drink any cold water. In your childhood, you were often sick with angina. Take more steam baths. God forbid that anything leads you down the wrong path . . .

I remember the year 1921. I was serving then in the Red Army's 12th Army. It was advancing on Warsaw. But suddenly in Novograd-Volynsk, I fell ill with typhus, and they left me in a local hospital to die. There were good people there; they nursed me back to health and found some work for me. At the time, we all lived according to the proletarian principle: "Whoever doesn't work, doesn't eat."

In that quaint and green little city, I met your future papa. I was only seventeen then. I had still not completely gotten over my illness. But ever since my childhood, I had loved the theater and took part in local productions. At the city club, we put on some revolutionary play; I don't remember its name. Your future papa came to the show and, like everybody else, loudly applauded our performance. We became acquainted that evening. We began to meet, and fell in love with each other. What your father found so special in me, I don't know. I was still weak, frail, and my hair hadn't grown back in yet. He's a romantic, just like you. We got married. Time passed and you appeared.

Novograd-Volynsk. There we first met, and there you were born. Isn't that fate? Fate is a blue bird, which brought all three of us happiness. I believe that this bird will protect you now.

Yesterday evening I bumped into the director of the plant, where you started work as a lathe operator. He asked to pass along his regards to you. With every passing day, they are increasing their production. . . .

Natasha often spends time with us. She has a new son. She calls him Andrei, in honor of his father. She painted your portrait from your last photograph as a civilian. I've hung it in the dining hall and never get tired of looking at you.

Natasha told me how her pilot husband was killed in the first days of the war. He had just fastened himself into the cockpit of an airplane and was about to take off, but never managed to do it. The German airplanes pounced. They found him dead in his destroyed airplane.

I kiss you, my dear son. Your mother

A Crazy Night

Close to evening on 30 December, I took over my new company. It had thirty-six men and two officers. I first got acquainted with the officers. One of them, Lieutenant Gorbunov, had temporarily been the acting commander of the company. The second, Junior Lieutenant Velen'ky, commanded a platoon. I already knew that Gorbunov had survived a stretch in the penal battalion, had been wounded, and then restored to his former rank—that meant he had fully atoned for his guilt, but what his transgression was, I didn't know. He made a good impression on me—he was a strong guy of short stature. Velen'ky was out of a completely different mold. He was very young, not even nineteen. He had recently graduated from the Omsk Combat-Infantry Specialist School and from there went directly to the front. It was clear that he had not yet been under fire. He was somewhat frail and, it seemed to me, he did not have a very stable personality. He still didn't feel fully in command and he didn't understand people well. He couldn't tell me very much about his men. Understanding his own weaknesses, he was a nervous man prone to breakdowns.

After our conversation, we took a tour of all the positions in the trenches. I cursorily made the acquaintance of the soldiers and managed to have a brief chat with only two or three of them. "Have you ever been in an attack?" I asked one.

"All kinds of attacks," he answered. "It's good when the German buggers off when we attack; then it's everyone forward. If he doesn't, we leap into his trenches and have at him with the bayonet, the snake. Then Fritz comes to his senses and tries to chuck us out. If we don't have artillery support, we retreat, but as long as we have one heavy gun helping us, we kick the shit out of him."

"You've been in an attack—and survived. Good man!"

"It didn't turn out that way for everyone."

Apparently a trustworthy soldier, I thought; you can't go wrong with someone like him. This conversation calmed me down, but all the same I decided that the next morning I had to study the personnel files, change the company's routines, and urgently put my system in place. For the meantime, I asked Gorbunov and Velen'ky to visit all the posts at night.

I returned to my command dugout. Extreme fatigue drew me to my bunk. Tomorrow was the last day of 1942; I'd spent a full year in the army. How naïve and stupid we had been to believe that the war would soon end. Now I knew that with patriotism and a rifle alone you couldn't take the enemy. I thought

back to my arrival at the specialist school a year ago: the empty barracks, Ryzhii, his songs with the guitar. . . . How many of us were still alive? Yet nevertheless, tomorrow without fail I'd greet the New Year with the soldiers, and we'd
organize a fitting salute.

Just then, the junior lieutenant burst into my dugout like a whirlwind. His
face was pale, his coat was unfastened, and he wasn't wearing his fur cap. I immediately understood that something serious had happened.

"Comrade company commander!" he almost shouted. "It's a disaster, a terrible
disaster! A desertion! Two of them—one of the old guys and a new conscript!"

I sprang to my feet. Sleep disappeared in a flash. We rushed into the trench.
Two fully operational and well-maintained rifles and a Komsomol card were
lying neatly on the breastworks, lightly powered with snow. It seems I had met
these (I couldn't bring myself to say the words) now former soldiers; they had
greeted me affably when I had come by their post. Where were they from; how
and where had they fought; what were their names? I knew nothing about
them. The old soldier must have persuaded the new conscript, the Komsomol
member. The latter, I suddenly remembered, had been whining about something, probably as a diversion: it seems he was saying he hadn't been paid in
three months. Yes, my inner voice had misled me. I looked at the abandoned
rifles and suddenly felt queasy. A group flight; that meant the penal battalion for
me, and a penal battalion meant—the end of my life.

I called in the report to battalion commander Malyshev. Then I consulted
with the lieutenants to see if there was something we could do. There turned
out to be nothing.

About an hour later, the battalion commander came tearing in. He had an
osobist with him. By their expressions, I immediately sensed a real roasting in
the atmosphere, and I was to receive it! I reported, as I was supposed to do,
explained the situation, and presented my prepared report. In the report, in
my defense, I had written that I had just arrived at the company the evening
before, and in the course of one night I could hardly have had the time to get
to know everyone or to put my system into place.

The battalion commander didn't even begin to read my report and didn't
seem to hear a word I said; he looked at me wickedly and launched into a
torrent of abusive speech, sprinkled with wild cursing. Suddenly he pulled
his pistol from its holster and struck my head with its butt. "Swine!" he hissed
through his teeth. "All of you bastards are going before a tribunal!"

The junior lieutenant was standing next to me, shaking all over and biting
his lips. It seemed he was going to burst into sobbing any moment. Gorbunov
intervened: "Why are you kicking up a row, battalion commander? The company commander here didn't have anything to do with this. Both runaways
were from my platoon. Put all the blame on me."

"We'll deal with you, too!" the battalion commander responded, growing more infuriated. "And you'll get yours! Don't have any doubts about that!" Fearing for his own neck, Malyshev seemed to have lost all self-control.

Someone urgently summoned a medic, who quickly bandaged my head. The battalion commander left with the words:

"You'd better believe, Company Commander, that this isn't some sort of resort! If you don't set things right, if you let one more desertion happen—you won't get away with it! Then don't expect any mercy!"

The *osobist* was silent, and I gained the impression that all of Malyshev's loud words and his decision to strike me came not just from his character but were also due to his extreme zeal to put on a show for the *osobist*'s benefit. In four months, I had never once seen the battalion commander in a combat situation; he always tried to hide wherever he could. In the army, they called people like him "the dog's tail": he wags to and fro, and just try to catch hold of him!

When everyone finally departed, I suddenly felt quite weak and my head began to hurt badly. I asked Gorbunov to accompany me back to my dugout. Once there, I laid out all my food stash on the table: a few little pieces of fat, a can of stew, an onion, and three lumps of sugar. We poured a little vodka and drank up to the coming New Year. After all that had happened, neither of us knew where we would be meeting it. We tossed down another shot of vodka and started talking:

"Thanks, Volodia, for the support," I said. "I understand how you're feeling; they're going to skin your hide, while the fugitives, the scum, later this very night will wish us all a Happy New Year from the German lines. I know a little about your past; if something serious happens in the future, I'll try to help you as much as I can."

"Wait for it or don't," the lieutenant interrupted, "but either way the *osobisty* won't relax until they've sent me into the penal battalion. For them, we are all just tick marks on a ledger. I've already had to deal with them once; I know what I'm worth to them. Excuse me, but we don't have much time. Mark my word, these scum will soon be coming for me. I want to ask you to send a letter to my mother; here's the address. I'm sure you'll do this for me."

He laid a sheet of paper on the table. I read: "To Alexandra Semenovna Gorbunovaia, Building 16/a Lenin Street, Apartment 16, Sverdlovsk." Gorbunov continued:

> As you see, I'm from the Urals. If you don't object, I'll briefly tell you my story. A year before the war, I graduated from the Poltava Tank School, and I was sent to the Western Military District. I commanded a platoon of the first self-propelled guns. In 1941 they were all torched by German fire, and we became infantry. We were retreating just like everyone else. On

6 November, in honor of the twenty-fourth anniversary of the October Revolution, our battalion commander, the swine, ordered us to take the village Teterino—as a gift to the Motherland and the Supreme Leader. He promised us support—two tanks and some artillery.

At 4:00 A.M. he roused the company awake, explained the assignment, and we moved down to the river, which was not more than a kilometer from the village. We crossed the river and began to envelop Teterino from two sides. The Germans met our company with a storm of fire—we couldn't even raise our heads. The tanks never showed up. We fell back and took up positions along the road leading to the village. I was trying to figure out what to do next, without the tanks. Suddenly a German self-propelled gun came out of the village with some submachine gunners aboard and headed toward us at full speed. Well, I think, now we're done for. Then suddenly I had an idea. I took two submachine gunners with me and bundled some grenades by twos into four "bouquets." Then we started crawling along the ditch by the side of the road toward the self-propelled gun. We were lucky—the vehicle suddenly stopped—and almost directly opposite us, out popped a German officer, who began studying the ground ahead through binoculars.

We approached the vehicle and, leaping out onto the road, we poked the grenade bundles into it. Body parts went flying, and the two who remained we quickly finished off. I hopped into the vehicle and smashed the driver with the butt of my submachine gun. It seemed everything was in working order. I sent one of the men with me back to the company to tell them to move up and follow my vehicle while I began to turn the self-propelled gun around. We moved out together toward the village. But three tanks came crawling out of the village to meet me, and they began firing on the move at my vehicle. They'd noticed, the snakes! I turned my self-propelled gun back toward the river, when suddenly a shell scored a direct hit. The soldiers around the vehicle were killed, and a fragment hit me in my arm.

Returning to the battalion, I congratulated the battalion commander on the great proletarian holiday, then in the heat of the moment I told him everything I thought of him, the bastard, and then added the request to pass along a greetings to the Supreme Commander from the eighteen men who fell trying to take Teterino. This swine dashed off a report on the spot, purporting that I had seized the self-propelled gun with the aim of going over to the Germans, and that I had wiped out my own company for the sake of this attempt to desert. Of course, he also didn't forget about the Supreme Commander; did you notice that I had insulted Comrade Stalin? The *osobisty* and the procurator demanded my execution. The tribunal sentenced me to ten years and then sent me to the penal battalion.

During the summer offensive to take Rzhev, our battalion helped the
30th Army break the enemy's defenses of the city, and almost the entire
battalion perished. I was wounded in the leg, but before that happened I
managed to give a German bunker one of my grenade "bouquets." I atoned
for my "crime" with my blood. They erased my conviction and returned
my rank—everything on the up and up. That's how I wound up in this
damned company. Only now let our comrade *osobisty* ponder this: I won't
go into the penal battalion this time; it's better in the prison camps; at least
there you have a hope of living if, of course, you don't drop dead while
cutting down trees.

I listened to Volodia with bitterness. What a courageous, strong-willed man!
There was so much strength in him, and such conscientiousness. He was also an
experienced frontline soldier, and all this by the age of twenty-five.

Velen'ky interrupted our conversation; behind him, two *osobisty* were standing at the entrance. "You have been ordered, Gorbunov, to come with us to
the Special Department," said one *osobist*. "Grab your things and let's go. The
battalion commander has been notified."

That's how we parted. We never saw each other again. Considering that the
lieutenant had already spent time in the penal battalion, been wounded twice,
and had atoned for his guilt, the tribunal sentenced him to four years and sent
him off to a prison camp.

I went to speak with Borisov and appealed to him on Gorbunov's behalf,
but the commissar shook his head: "The tribunal is an independent institution,
subordinate to no one. Only the *Front* commander can repeal a sentence."

They gave Velen'ky a formal rebuke, and his sergeant was demoted to private. They didn't forget about me either; they postponed any consideration for
my next promotion for six months. Having accompanied Gorbunov back to
the Special Department, Velen'ky returned alone, his eyes reddened from tears.

What a terrible day, or more accurately, night! It seemed that the high command had lost their minds and had made all of us commanders out to be accomplices of the betrayers of the Motherland. What foolishness! If this policy
continued, the army would run out of combat officers. As for the hooligan
attack on me by the battalion commander, in the old army he would have been
shot for it. The public insult from the commander—only the devil knows what
that was about. Incidentally, it is better to answer a misdeed with quiet disdain;
that works better than loud demonstrations. . . . Lord, how terrible I felt! I felt
nauseous, and my head felt just like cast iron, but I had to get up and check
on the company. I had new command arrangements to make, with Gorbunov
gone and Velen'ky without an assistant.

Velen'ky was sitting on a plank bed, his head lowered. Suddenly he exploded:

"Don't you understand that Junior Lieutenant Velen'ky will be the next sacrificial victim of these scoundrels? Can't you see that?"

"Calm down, Serezha," I said, "and buck up. Show a little more toughness and strength."

"What advice! Excuse me, but what's the use of your philosophizing? I'm officially notifying you: if another man deserts from my platoon, I'll kill myself!" With shaking hands, he pulled his pistol from his holster and put the gun barrel to his temple: "That's just what will happen!"

That was simply going too far, I thought apprehensively. Raising my voice, I told him sharply:

"Put down your pistol this very instant, Junior Lieutenant! Calm down and don't forget that we are in a combat situation and we aren't just fighting against the wind. You have been entrusted to lead soldiers! In their eyes, you represent the army!"

The junior lieutenant lowered his gun and holstered it. But he remained standing, pale, and taut as a violin string. How could I calm him down? Losing control of himself, he shouted:

"What kind of officers are we if we fear our own more than the enemy? Such a situation is intolerable!"

I got up from the stove-couch and approached him:

"Stop your whining! I am appointing you, Junior Lieutenant Velen'ky, as my deputy commander. Go check on the men. We have a big job ahead of us."

That seemed to quiet the fellow down. He gave a salute—"Right away!"— and left the dugout.

I lay back down and closed my eyes; perhaps I should go to the *medsanbat* after all to check out my head wound? But factually speaking, I was now all alone. I couldn't leave the company to Velen'ky; he was painfully fragile and extremely naïve. He reminded me of Zhenechka. The war was teaching me ever more how to treat people. The main thing was to free them of their fears, their emotional weaknesses, and their loneliness.

The door of the dugout suddenly burst open, and a sergeant with a stunned face exploded into the room. He ran up to where I was lying, leaned over, and barely opening his lips, muttered: "Comrade Company Commander, the junior lieutenant has shot himself!"

"What?" I shouted, forgetting about my pain, the *medsanbat*, and everything else on earth. I shoved aside the sergeant and, dressed only in my field blouse and trousers, I flew like a bullet out of the dugout.

Within days of Velen'ky's suicide, the word reached us junior officers in the front lines that Stalingrad had been saved. After this great victory, desertions became more rare. German propaganda broadcasts and leaflets, no matter how extravagant or well crafted, no longer had any effect on us. After Stalingrad, there was no force that could shake the Red Army fighter. Faith in ultimate victory became embedded in the minds and hearts of every man and woman. It was literally as if those who had been killed had imparted their strength to those still living.

Thus Velen'ky's suicide, coming as it did just days before the announcement of our victory at Stalingrad, was particularly senseless and hard to take. I especially suffered after it. What a terrible thing to do to oneself at just nineteen years of age! What was it? A manifestation of a weak character, a childish prank, perhaps—stress? Most likely, his spirit could not reconcile itself with all the humiliation and evil, and he no longer wanted to serve under the command of men who only looked out for their own interests. He was probably unable to endure the meanness of some commanders and the cynicism of others. But what about my own Tolstoian philosophy of humility and endurance? What was I serving? Life!

But all the same, the New Year arrived!

It's the front lines near Rzhev, I'm standing with my soldiers in the trenches, and we're congratulating one another. Each man had been counting down the days until the New Year. And now it was here, with all its eternal mystery, hopes, and all its new splendid colors. Clumps of snow are covering the branches of the fir trees, snow lightly squeaks from time to time underfoot, and one can breathe freely in the clean, frosty air. . . . Frontline soldiers always connect New Year's Day with the sanctity of the birth of Christ, with the burning of ceremonial candles. Remembrances of good traditions fill them with hope for the future. So on that night we talk especially about home; read each other letters from mothers, wives, and beloved girlfriends; and share photographs with each other over and over again. Everyone knows about the recent events in the company, and many of the men look at me sympathetically, but nobody asks me about them. Why?

I look at my watch: 12:10 A.M. The New Year is already ten minutes old. I glance out at the quiet, frosty night. The enemy is silent, apparently also tending to the holiday.

For Christmas and the 1943 New Year, each German soldier around Rzhev received a Christmas package: pies, cakes, chocolate, twenty grams of coffee, cigarettes, and alcohol. Those who had distinguished themselves in recent fighting received a special packet from Hitler. Christmas trees glittered in all their units, just as in peaceful times before the war.

We, however, the fighters and commanders on the front lines for the Motherland, received for Christmas and the New Year just our typical "anesthetic" 100 grams of vodka and a piece of herring to be shared between two. We were also given an open-faced sandwich for two to share as a snack. That's how the little song was born that we all happily sang in the trenches:

We're going into battle
For a herring's tail!
And we'll all die as one
For a hundred grams of vodka!

From time to time, illumination flares rose into the night sky, lighting up the enormous field, the solidly frozen Volga, and its steep banks. As they died out, above us the skies of a gloomy frontline night would grow dark again, while stray thoughts played in our minds. Yet I had no notion of the changes soon to enter my life.

My dear, kind mother.

On the day of my departure for the army, at age 19.

Tiumen' cadets, 1942.

*Major General A. F. Kupriianov,
commander of the 215th Rifle
Division, 1942.*

Vice Marshal of Poland S. G. Poplavsky (1946). In 1942, in the fighting for Rzhev, then Colonel Poplavsky had commanded the 220th Rifle Division.

Marshal D. D. Leliushenko (1945). In 1942, as lieutenant general, Leliushenko had commanded the Kalinin Front's 30th Army, in which I started my combat path and received my baptism of fire.

Colonel Leonid Federovich Borisov, Commissar of the 220th Rifle Division, some thirty years after the war.

Colonel Ivan Iakovlevich Gruzdev, Commissar of the 673rd Rifle Regiment, 220th Rifle Division. A 1960s photograph.

General Field Marshal Walther Model (1945). In 1942, then Colonel General Model commanded the German Ninth Army in the Rzhev-Viaz'ma bridgehead.

The author as Komsomol organizer, during a pause in the fighting, 1943.

The summer of 1943, somewhere in the Smolensk forests. None of these officers are older than twenty years of age. From left to right: Kostia (last name forgotten), Anatolii Koziavkin, Ivan Skoropud, and the author, Boris Gorbachevsky.

Destroyed German and Soviet tanks in no-man's land near Rzhev.

The bridge across the Volga into Rzhev, blown up at Hitler's personal order.

German soldier-artist Franz-Joseph Langer at work on a sketch. Langer's sketches depict the events in and around Rzhev during 1942–1943 and were discovered years after the war by Langer's son, Hans-Peter Langer, who accidentally stumbled across them beneath some floorboards while renovating his father's home. Eighty-six of these sketches were put on public display in Rzhev in 1997. I have chosen to include seven here to honor those on both sides who fought in the Rzhev campaign.

German soldiers, Rzhev, 1942.

The first day of liberation for the city of Rzhev, 3 March 1943. The entire city looked like this after almost two years of fighting. Soviet artillery fire was responsible for much of the damage.

The German cemetery near Rzhev. A fragment of a photograph taken by a German soldier, 1942.

The obelisk in Rzhev honors those who fell liberating the city.

The regiment Komsomol organizer, Boris Gorbachevsky, posing beside a knocked-out German tank, 1944.

The team of snipers, the "Untouchables" of the 331st Rifle Division, 1945. Third from the right in the first row of standing men is Major General Berestov. In the same row, on the far right, is the author.

Colonel Shilovich and Captain Gorbachevsky, in the colonel's prized car. Friedeberg, Germany, 1945.

Portrait of Boris Gorbachevsky taken by the German photographer Guntze, Friedeberg, Germany, 1945.

Boris Gorbachevsky, Friedeberg, Germany, 1945.

Reunion of the veterans of the 220th Rifle Division in Moscow on the 30th Anniversary of Victory Day. From left to right: Chetveriakov, Anatolii Koziavakin (both of whom remained in the army and became colonels), Boris Gorbachevsky, who became a civilian in 1946, and the astonishing Vasia Ragulin, who spent eighteen years organizing the reunion. On May 9, 1976, 176 men of the division gathered in Moscow. Ivan Skoropud is missing; he died in 1943.

The author as old soldier, sixty years after the war ended.

12

I Become the Regimental Youth Leader

January 1943

A Twist of Fate

Life in the trenches went on without change. At night I went around the posts and conversed with the men, trying to sense their mood and their attitude toward turncoats. Most of all I just listened to them. New conscripts told me:

"They hurried us on for two months with sticks in our hands instead of rifles: Hup-two-three—and told us that at the front, reality would teach us how to fight and survive. Well, we did learn—to shoot, to bayonet, and to kill the German snake. Many of the guys, before leaving for the front, tricked their girls into marrying them, telling them that if they became widows, they'd get a little something from the government."

By now, the new conscripts had become a little more accustomed to life in the front lines. About the turncoats they'd say: "They've got no cross to bear, they've gone astray, but they'll pay for it. Oh, how they'll pay for it!"

Others judged differently: "Why should I give them the shirt off my back? I just spit on them and forget them, that's all." I also heard things like, "Who knows who this helps—us or the Germans? God isn't saying." It was hard to hear something like that.

In early January, two hastily trained junior lieutenants arrived in the company to replace the dead Velen'ky and the arrested Gorbunov. Now there were three of us to help run the show, so things became easier for me. I had already introduced my system, and the men had seemed to take it in stride.

About a week and a half after New Year's, the battalion commander called me: "Tomorrow at 10:00 A.M. sharp, you are to appear before the regiment commissar Major Gruzdev." In such situations, it wasn't considered acceptable to express any curiosity, but all the same I asked Malyshev what was up, but the battalion commander declined to give me an answer.

The headquarters staff was splendidly situated; I found a whole community of dugouts, not less than twenty, on the reverse slope of a hill some distance behind the front.

I had never met Commissar Gruzdev before, but I knew he became the regiment commissar near Belkovo in July 1942; during the battles for Vitebsk and Rzhev, he had distinguished himself and had earned two Orders—the Order of the Red Banner and the Order of the Red Star. People said different things about him, both good and bad. Some called him a "man of character," while others said he had become too proud, overbearing, and that he liked to lord it over people. I went to the commissar full of conjectures, but I couldn't imagine how sharply it was about to change my life.

The commissar cut a dashing figure. In 1943, Ivan Iakovlevich was twenty-nine. He was well built and had a well-groomed, dimpled face and lively eyes. His uniform was spotless and neatly pressed. There was not a speck of dust on or around him. I must confess that my own appearance at our first meeting was not the best.

He greeted me courteously, offered me a seat, then without any introductory ceremony, as if he already knew everything about me, got straight to the point:

"I've summoned you, Lieutenant, for the following reason. The Komsomol organizer of the regiment, Anatolii Razumov, has been killed. He was a strong political worker, a real smart guy, and the regiment's favorite. We've decided to appoint you in his place. What do you think of our decision?"

Having heard all this, I nearly fell from my perch. What a change! Nevertheless, getting hold of myself, I calmly answered: "Comrade Commissar, I'm a combat officer. They trained me to be a mortarman. If I can speak honestly, I would like to remain where I am."

"But you see, Lieutenant, the question of your assignment has already been decided, so there's nowhere else to put you. The regiment commander Razumovsky supported your candidacy, and battalion commissar Borisov praised you. The battalion commander also didn't object to your candidacy. So it's been settled; you will lead the young people of the regiment. There is no platoon or company for you."

I continued to defend my position. "Excuse me, but I don't have any experience with Komsomol work. Tolia Razumov, as we all knew well, was a professional political worker."

"You're hiding something, Lieutenant. In the 215th Rifle Division, weren't you on a regimental Komsomol committee? I, my dear fellow, was a simple village teacher, but now you see, I'm the deputy commander for political affairs of a rifle regiment. You'll be fine, and you'll quickly gain experience."

I tried to latch on to one more argument: "Comrade Commissar, I'm not a Party member. I filled out an application before my first battle, but I wound up in a *medsanbat*, and then back on the front lines."

"What's the problem, Lieutenant? We'll accept you into the Party tomorrow.

In short, go back to your company, say good-bye to your men like you're supposed to do, and tomorrow come back here with your things and get busy."

"At your command!"

I headed back to my company in a dark mood. Could I handle the new
position? A new life was starting; what would become of it? Moreover, I wasn't
much attracted to commissar work.

Regiment Commissar Gruzdev

I arrived at the regiment command post with my things, as I'd been ordered.
Yes, and what things—just a single soldier's pouch. Having greeted me, Gruzdev immediately said:

"Go wash up and put on something clean, and get your new uniform. Don't
forget to shave; with a grizzled face, you won't look like a Komsomol member.
The deputy regiment commander will help you. I'm giving you two hours.
Put yourself in order, then come back."

I was struck by the commissar's tactlessness about my appearance. Had he
ever been on the front line? Did he know what it meant to sit for days in the
trenches?

But I was mistaken then. The commissar didn't avoid frontline complexities.
And he could serve as an example of courage, as I later learned about his prior
combat experiences.

After two hours, now cleanly dressed in place of a filthy quilted jacket and
a gray Mongolian sheepskin coat, I presented myself in front of Gruzdev. And
there and then I received my first "Party assignment." The regimental doctor,
Lidia Nikolaevna, was coming to visit Ivan Iakovlevich; I was to take a post in
front of the dugout and not let anyone enter.

My sentry duty lasted for almost three hours. "Damn it, what does he think
I am?" I cursed to myself.

What I encountered on my very first day in my new position, seemed
shameless to me, especially after life on the front lines. I decided there and then,
as I stood in the cold outside the door, to contrast everything I would see in
the future among the top brass with life at the front. Did Tolia Razumov also
stand guard over the amorous affairs of the commissar? I told myself next time
I would refuse such an assignment. (But I didn't do it.)

Lidia Nikolaevna finally fluttered out of the dugout just like a bird and hurried off in the direction of the medical unit. Gruzdev immediately called me in,
sat down behind a table, and poured a half-glass of cognac from an unfinished
bottle:

"Drink up, *komsorg*! You did your duty honorably, and I can see you're
frozen."

I tasted cognac for the first time. I could feel the noble drink's warmth spreading through my body. I forgot about my angry tirades and suddenly felt very sleepy; I hadn't slept the previous two nights. But Ivan Iakovlevich detained me; apparently trying to justify his behavior, he began to talk:

"My family has perished; I met Lidia Nikolaevna a long time ago and we fell in love with each other. If we're lucky enough to survive to the end of this war, we're going to get married."

Fate turned out otherwise. In 1943 Gruzdev was sent to the Military-Political Academy in Moscow. He graduated as a lieutenant colonel, acquired a new family (his frontline love was forgotten), and moved to Ivanovo to serve. In the 1970s we met each other in Moscow, when he and his wife came for the Victory Day celebrations.

But back in the dugout, as I prepared to leave, Gruzdev suddenly asked: "You at least know what Lenin said at the Third Komsomol Congress? What the Komsomol's main tasks are as the Party's top assistant? What honors the Komsomol has earned? What the five primary features of the Patriotic War are, as formulated by Comrade Stalin?"

"Are these things really important for a Komsomol member to know as he heads into battle?"

"It is important first of all for you to know! You are now a leader of young men and women! Have I made myself clear?"

Difficult Meetings

My new home was a small, cozy dugout of the political unit. Everyone greeted me in a friendly fashion. We exchanged greetings as we were supposed to do. There were three of us in the dugout: the regiment's Party organizer, the regiment's political agitator, and me. "Make yourself comfortable, here's your refuge now," they said, gesturing at an empty bunk.

I guessed that just two weeks ago, this had been Tolia Razumov's place. As I approached the bunk to drop my stuff onto it, I noticed that there was a small trunk beneath it. I figured it must have been Tolia's, but I didn't ask about it.

Usually for the position of a regiment's *komsorg*, a young communist was selected from among the officer-political workers. But here they had chosen a combat commander who was not even a Party member yet. Power corrupts; I witnessed how some officers, upon receiving a promotion to some higher rank, sharply changed their behavior and started to show arrogance, insolence, even cynicism. Their kindness disappeared, and for the sake of their career they forgot about their comrades, with whom just the day before they had been eating from the same pot of food, or drinking their 100 grams of vodka from the same mug. So I tried to watch myself so as not to break my own inner code of decency. I rubbed shoulders with the men in the ranks and tried to sense their moods, since as a platoon leader and company commander I had become convinced that the combat spirit of people depended largely on their mood and emotional state. To support a person, to listen to his or her every word attentively—these I saw as my primary tasks as *komsorg*.

Before one battle, I was talking with a young soldier, and I asked him, "When will you turn in your application for the Komsomol?" In response, I heard, "You want to make a Komsomol member of me, *komsorg*? You dream of giving me a membership card? I have all of three hours left to live—before we attack. So, Comrade Lieutenant, you'd better find someone else." The soldier's reply rattled me, and I couldn't regain my composure for a long time.

Our regiment commander liked to say: "I would like to kiss every soldier and officer in my command, because they are fighting for our families back home!" But why should anyone want to kiss him back? Every day he was sending hundreds, even thousands of men to their doom. I had serious divergences with him here.

One day an *osobist* called the political unit and asked to meet with me. You couldn't expect anything good from these people. We had a conversation.

"Do you know, Lieutenant, the Komsomol member Abram Rosenfel'd?"

"I've heard of him."

"It seems he deliberately shot himself in the foot. They exposed his crime at the *medsanbat* and he has confessed. There is a report from the company commander. We intended to turn the matter over to a tribunal, but for political reasons we came to a different decision. Commissar Borisov recommended that we speak with you. We want you to have a chat with Rosenfel'd. Try and find out whether this scum intends to fight honorably, and then let us know."

I decided to get Gruzdev's advice on this matter. He, as always, passed the buck: "Borisov has made a recommendation, so now go do it."

I summoned Abram to the political unit. We were alone. First of all, I asked him, "Is it true what your company commander, the doctors, and the *osobists* are saying and writing?" He confirmed everything. He swore never to do such a thing again and explained, "My nerves simply gave out." I asked him to tell me about himself, where he was from, and how he wound up at the front.

Back in his childhood, he had discovered that he had the gift of art. In 1940 he enrolled in the Architectural Institute in Moscow. In the hard days around Moscow in the autumn of 1941, the institute's *komsorg* had proposed that the entire group of students, who had not yet been called into the army, should volunteer for the front. Within a few weeks they were given uniforms and weapons and sent to the distant approaches to Moscow. Almost everyone was killed in the ensuing battle. He and two other students wound up in a hospital and then were sent back to the front:

"I understand that as a Jew, I have a special responsibility. I must fight not only for our Motherland and for myself, but also for my people, who Hitler is destroying."

"You understand correctly," I affirmed. "But you walked away from your responsibility. Do you know, Abram, what awaits those men who intentionally wound themselves?"

"I know. Please, call me Abrash, like everybody calls me. If you permit, I'd like to speak openly. You've summoned me as a Komsomol member, and I trust you."

"Of course."

"I'm from Vinnitsa. There were a lot of Jews in this city before the war, and all the Jewish families observed the religious traditions and spoke Yiddish. Sholom-Aleikhem wrote about it in his stories—it's a classic of Yiddish litera- ture, which is highly regarded in our country and around the world. Perhaps you've heard of him?"

"No, Abrash, unfortunately I haven't read him."

"Read it; you won't regret it. I studied in a Yiddish school and attended the synagogue on Saturdays. In Vinnitsa and in Moscow, nobody ever criticized me for this. At the front, especially in the front lines, I can't observe the Jew- ish traditions. But this company commander, who wrote the report, nastily insulted me in front of my comrades and even promised to send me in front of a tribunal."

"Why?"

"I had asked him to release me from sentry duty on a Saturday. I wanted to pray for Mama and Papa. He shouted at me: 'Does this mean you don't want to fight on Saturdays? Oh, you . . .!' You yourself understand what kind of stuff he then said to me. He beat me unmercifully. I didn't cry; I only said: 'How are you, Soviet officer, any better than the fascists?' He became enraged, and promised to deal with me."

I became angered and indignant after hearing what Abram had told his commanding officer. I said to him: "The company commander treated you impermissibly and insulted your national feelings. But you, you're a fine one! To compare an officer of the Red Army with Hitler's executioners! That's blasphemy!"

At this point I lost all control of myself. Instead of a discussion, I suddenly lashed out at Abrash, knocked him off his feet and threw him out of the dug- out. For the first time in my life, I had raised my hand against another man! How could I have behaved that way? Was that any way to treat a Komsomol member? It was a loathsome act! What kind of leader of youth could I be after that?

For several days I walked around completely out of sorts. Now and then I wanted to seek out Abrash at the front—to seek his forgiveness, for the devil knows what he might be thinking about me now. I thought over what I could do, about how I might defend a Komsomol member from his company commander, who was also an anti-Semite and a dull-witted man. But I never offered a defense for him. There was only one thing left for me to do: I secured Abrash's transfer to a different battalion.

Another difficult conversation. One day an aging soldier with tired, sad eyes approached me, and in a single breath he poured out an entire cascade of short phrases. There was anguish and alarm in his voice, and agonizing tears in his eyes:

"I'm a Leningrader. The docent of the Gertsen Pedagogical Institute. The author of many well-known books and articles about Gorky, our stormy petrel of revolution. I'm forty-four. There's a lot I can do and want to do! I have a wife and two kids. They're right now in the blockaded city. They are dying. Just like all Leningraders. They're starving to death."

I gently responded, "Forgive me, what's your question?" I saw tears welling in his eyes behind his glasses, and he asked, "Please, get me out of the front lines! I'm ready for any duty! Even a transport driver!" What could I say? But he continued:

"Oh God, if I'm killed, who can give a better lecture on Stalin's favorite story 'The Old Woman Izegil' than me? What do you think, perhaps we should write a letter to Comrade Stalin? He'll understand me, better than all of you."

"Do you really think that Comrade Stalin has no other concerns today, while this terrible war is going on?"

He gave an ironic smile and said, "Let me tell you an old parable. One day, for some reason an old woman decided to appeal personally to the Roman emperor with a request. His guards wouldn't let her in, and they told her that His Majesty had no time to meet with her and hear her request. Then the old woman replied: 'If he has no time to meet with his own citizen, that means he can't be the emperor.'"

I thanked the Leningrad docent for his wonderful parable, shook his hand, and said warmly: "Never lose spirit! Don't succumb to any gloomy thoughts. We'll meet again—after the war. I want to enroll in your institute—the best pedagogical institute in the land! I'll most certainly come to hear your lectures."

What wasn't I busy with in my new position! What didn't I do! I tried to inspire the young soldiers by both word and example. After their deaths, I mournfully collected their Komsomol membership cards, now soaked with blood, and gazed intently at the young faces of the warriors in the tiny photographs on the card. I conducted assemblies and meetings. I organized admission into the Komsomol. I greeted newly arriving reinforcements. I talked with journalists, trying to make sure the divisional newspaper told the stories of our Komsomol warriors. I went on reconnaissance missions. On the offensive, I could usually be found among the lead battalions.

I'm especially proud of the fact that I set up a correspondence between frontline soldiers in our regiment and people from many cities and villages. They began to bring the mail to the regiment in large bags. This correspondence brightened up the hard soldier's life. Pen-pal friendships sprang up, and sometimes love blazed up through these letters. Even such messages as the following sometimes arrived at the regiment: "I don't know who will get this letter, but whoever does, let him know that I had three sons. They have all perished. I would like to adopt a frontline soldier and give him all the motherly love still remaining in my heart." There were also shady letters. Their senders, who were most often women, wanted to fish out something from us as a gift. Once even I received one of these melodramatic letters, which had been artfully and exquisitely written. Moved by her letter, I appealed to the authorities and the Komsomol leadership of the city, where this young lady lived, to try to get her help. The reply to my appeal disheartened me. I was informed of a number of things about the writer and advised to get to know people better and not be so naïve.

The most important thing for me became the expansion of my personal horizons. I began to understand better what was going on—now not just at the scale of the company but at that of the regiment and division. I began to ask questions in my mind, which previously I didn't have the time or the insight to answer, since my combat experience was still insufficient. I already understood that war for me, as it was for everyone, was first and foremost a tragedy. War is not only heroic feats and battles, as I had previously imagined. War is also the daily grind of a man trapped in unbearable conditions. It is blood, filth, and sweat. It is life in extreme circumstances. War erases the boundary between good and evil. It makes the unique, sacred gift—human life—worthless.

Yes, I was always dealing with people and I kept eternally busy—but all the while doubts constantly tormented me. My special situation, a certain handpicked position, troubled me. There was no doubt that my new job removed me a bit from death. I thought of Sabit Khalikov and our chance encounter at the *medsanbat*, where he advised me not to rush back to the front lines. At the time, he had been a regimental *komsorg* like I was now. Perhaps I had subconsciously absorbed his lessons and had changed? Was I a different man now? But no place in a combat zone of this war was truly safe. I knew a number of cases when soldiers, from the rank of private up to general, had died not in battle, but accidentally. Just recently, I myself had just missed death by a whisker. I was returning from the front lines with another officer, and a "pleasant" encounter with some Germans took place.

It was evening, in a patch of early growth woods just behind our front lines. About 100 meters from our trenches, we suddenly and distinctly caught sight of three figures wearing field gray overcoats (we called the color "mousy"). How had these scouts penetrated our front line, and what were their intentions? They also spotted us and raised their submachine guns. Had they opened fire, they could have cut us down within seconds. Seemingly, they considered the situation and opted not to reveal their presence by firing at us. Instead, the small group began to withdraw quickly. We raised the alarm and tried to catch them, but somehow they disappeared just as mysteriously as they had appeared.

However it may have been, however you might judge it, it seemed clear to me that as *komsorg* of the regiment, I had a better chance of surviving than as a platoon or company commander. Here in the political unit I was a little farther from a German bullet, and at that time it didn't seem likely that I would have to assault a German trench or sacrifice myself in a "reconnaissance through combat." I had more free time at my disposal and more control over my own actions, and certainly my living conditions had improved. One can only dream about such things in war.

Subsequent events changed these, if you will, naïve conclusions.

Party Organizer Mikhalych and Agitator Stepanych

My neighbors in the dugout were Captain Mikail Mikhailovich Gavrilov, the regiment's Party organizer; and Major Sergei Ivanovich Stepanov, the regiment's Party agitator. Everybody called them "Mikhalych" and "Stepanych." They seemed like nice guys. But it is one thing to judge a man from the outside, and quite another thing to get to know a man from the inside—not by his words but by his deeds. Having served with these two men for nearly a full year, I began to understand them better as people. I'll try to tell you about them.

Gavrilov was from Ivanovo, an ancient Russian city. He grew up in a family from a long line of textile workers. He completed all of four grades of schooling; during his fifth year of education he dropped out and became a factory apprentice. He joined the Komsomol when he was fourteen years old. He soon figured out that being a Komsomol activist had its advantages. After a year, the bright young Komsomol member was chosen as secretary of the factory's Komsomol organization. At this point, life brought him together with the factory's Party chief. In his new role, Gavrilov tried to help that factory Party chief in every possible way: he carted off the Party dues; painted the walls of the Party Room, as well as the walls in the chief's home; drove at the chief's behest to local Party patrons; and organized holidays and ceremonial evenings at the factory. Time passed, and he fell in love with a young Komsomol weaver in the factory. They married. Over the next seven years his wife, Katen'ka, gave birth to four fine boys. The extra mouths made life harder. The factory Party chief helped him out: he made Gavrilov an inspector in the district executive committee, but more precisely, in the Department of People's Nutrition, which controlled and distributed government food rations. A position one could only dream of having!

On the eve of war, Gavrilov was called into the army and assigned to a political staff. He went through a three-month course of training, where he studied *The Short Course on the History of the VKP(b),* Stalin's mandatory and imaginative history of the All-Union Communist Party of Bolsheviks. He was accepted into the Party because of his "working class" origins. In 1941 he was sent to Elets, where the 220th Rifle Division was forming up. Considering his prewar work experience, Gavrilov's superior officers assigned him to work in the commissary as the director of the food storehouse. He punctually supplied the regiments with grub, and so he was chosen to be the Party organizer of the division's rear area. A tsar's position! But he didn't last long in that role, as there were many who were set on obtaining such a lucrative position! At Rzhev, Mikhalych lost a little status—he was removed from his supply post and given the post of Party worker. Then he was appointed to be the Party organizer for the 673rd Rifle Regiment.

Continually rubbing shoulders with Gavrilov at Rzhev, and later at Dubrovno, Orsha, and Smolensk, I came to the conclusion that at the front, this Party organizer was busy with two primary tasks: to stay alive at any cost and to be a reliable commissary for his family back in Ivanovo. Mikhalych was completely indifferent to the misfortunes of others, and he never searched for any motivation or cause by which to lead a soldier into battle other than "For the Motherland! For Stalin!" At the same time, he was kindhearted toward communists and indulgent of their sins, as long as they didn't exceed the boundaries of military law.

The Party organizer himself, it must be said, was far from without sins. He never missed a day when he would toss back not only his own ration of vodka but also that of the tee-totaling agitator, and if the opportunity arose, even more. The man from Ivanovo noticed the well-built village laundress Serafima, who was busty but had a young girl's waistline. He dropped in to see her much more often than he went to the front. One morning, he woke me up right at 5:00 A.M.:

"Come with me, Komsomol member!"

We walked a short way then emerged into a forest clearing, where he planted me on a stump and said:

"See the third dugout in the left row? Once you see the chimney start to smoke, go away. But in the meanwhile, sit and see to it that no Party or non-Party swine disturbs me. Understood?"

What's this, another "Party task," only this time the protagonists have changed? There's the Party organizer for you!

But after some time had passed in our association, I began to notice one strange behavior. As much as he could—and Mikhalych could do a lot!—he tried to shelter me from German bullets. With all his effort, he kept me away from the front lines and out of battles, wherever they occurred, by tying me up with all sorts of busy work. He often dragged me along with him to Party gatherings, meetings, and inspections. I began trying to evade him. Why was he acting this way—was he trying to nurture my Party ideals? Hardly, for I doubt he had ever woken up in the morning with those on his mind. I speculated endlessly about his motives. As it turned out, he was protecting me for his own sake, for the sake of his secret personal interests. But I found out about this only after the war, when, now at home, I read through his letters. Concealing it from me, he wrote letters to my mother during the war, lamenting the situation of his own four sons and claiming that he was "my best friend" and "my father at the front." My "frontline father" so moved my mother to pity that she started sending parcels to Ivanovo, often depriving herself and my father of many things.

Commissar Gruzdev valued Mikhalych; the commissar knew that the clever man from Ivanovo was a very crafty fellow who knew how to get around whomever you'd like and in any situation. So accordingly he entrusted the Party organizer of the regiment with an important sector: the rear. And Gruzdev always felt calm about his decision; the battalions always received their stew, bread, something to smoke, weapons, and ammunition on time.

Once, a crack appeared in my relations with Mikhalych. And what a crack! I thought that after the sharp conversation that occurred between us, Mikhalych would break with me. But he didn't. Here's what happened:

From September 1941 on, the entire country sent entire trainloads of gifts to the front. The father, mothers, and wives of frontline soldiers sent us everything they could, often the very latest things: blankets, undergarments, warm knitted socks and mittens (soldiers often used warm socks as mittens), tobacco pouches, soap, sweets, pastries, cakes, writing paper, envelopes, pencils, dried fruits, wine (from the south), cheap cologne—you couldn't count it all. The gifts came from factories, collective farms, schools, and even kindergartens. These gifts, caringly packed in cardboard boxes and plywood crates, which also contained letters and photographs, brought boundless joy to those at the front.

Unfortunately, the path of the gifts to the front went through dirty hands. Not even half the goods reached the men at the front! Mikhalych abruptly took this "gift business" under the Party's eye, earning the praise of both regiment commander Razumovsky and Commissar Gruzdev for his work.

But, as always, Mikhalych didn't forget about himself. Each time, when gifts arrived at the regiment, he hastily dropped all his other work and headed for the rear in long strides. He always made sure to placate the commissary workers, headquarters personnel, and representatives from the battalions, who had been arguing over every package and who had once even undertaken a discussion of the meaning of the concept "front." One day Mikhalych returned to the political unit with three blankets, and he managed to talk us into taking them.

The gift-sending epic continued—and Mikhalych one day neatly dragged a densely stuffed large pouch full of little things back to the political unit, and then laid the unjustly acquired loot under his bunk.

How easy it is to deceive ourselves! I saw what was happening, but I sought not to get involved. Yet the moment arrived when I could no longer tolerate it, and I decided to consult with Stepanych about what to do. The major brushed me off like I was a fly. Then, relying on my friendship with him, I bluntly told Mikhalych everything I thought about the pouches from the rear.

"Excuse me, Mikhalych," I said, "but what are you doing? You're taking mothers' gifts to their sons at the front, and you're transferring them to Ivanovo. For such behavior you'll get no thanks from the frontline soldiers, for many of them, you know, have wives and children at home just like you do."

They say, "The littlest fly can bite the largest horse." Turning crimson, Gavrilov rudely responded:

"And who's showing any concern for my little ones? The local authority spits on them! What's it to you? Your mother is in Moscow! In warmth and without any concerns!"

"Well, that's really gone too far! Be offended or not, that's your business, but I've now told you my position. You are not only a father; you're also a regiment Party organizer, you talk with people, you proclaim patriotic words! Others are watching you and following your lead! Have you noticed how the guys in the rear area of the division all smell of cologne?"

"You'd better watch your tongue, Komsomol member, you're still wet behind the ears! Now take my advice: don't try and give lessons to your elders."

I said nothing and lay down with my face buried in the pillow. I was sorry for him because of his family, but everything welled up inside me: the soldiers were so anxiously waiting for their gifts, letters, and even that very same cheap cologne, but they were only going to receive a gnawed fin, while the golden fish swam off into different seas!

Stepanych was the complete opposite of Mikhalych; one could say he was a simple creature. To gain an understanding of him was not difficult, so therefore some called him "a kind-hearted simpleton" while others called him "blockhead."

Stepanych looked badly—he had a puffy face with heavy bags under his eyes, as if he was always suffering from some kind of hangover. He drank tea continuously; up to ten or more cups a day. He was ponderous, as if shackled by a heavy armor suit. You couldn't budge him from his spot with a tank. He was often quiet. He had forelocks of hair that fell down over a deeply lined brow. His eyes were concealed behind the thick lenses of his eyeglasses, their temples neatly connected by little strings—Stepanych was always afraid to lose his eyeglasses, always cautious with them, and took good care of them. It was a disaster to lose your eyeglasses at the front; they said that soldiers from burial details and medics often collected eyeglasses from the battlefield and traded them for tobacco and vodka.

Stepanych liked to divide his day into two halves. From morning until lunch, he was immersed in the newspapers, and he liked to neatly underscore interesting notes, facts, and numbers. In the second half of the day, he pored over one particular pillar of science under the title, *V. I. Lenin on Propaganda and Agitation,* daily reading through and summarizing portions of the text. He carried this fat book everywhere with him in a pouch, not entrusting his precious possession to anyone else.

At some point I once asked him, "What's the difference between propaganda and agitation?" He bombarded me with a string of Lenin's quotes, expounding for a long time on that which could have been explained without difficulty within a minute. Plainly, he received enormous satisfaction from the very process of pronouncing words itself. He indeed received the nickname "blockhead" because of the tediousness of his speeches.

Stepanych loved to sing the well-known Red cavalryman's song that went, "We're trampling the enemy under the hooves of our horses. We're meeting the enemy in the Stalinist-style! . . ." While he sang, he would adroitly tap his foot in time to the music under his desk. Once I asked him why he loved this song so much. "Well I was in the cavalry!" Stepanych proudly answered.

Stepanych joined the army in 1938 through a Party directive that called 4,500 communist teachers into the army for political work. Stepanych had lost the martial qualities with which he had entered the army and somehow managed to survive the first year of the war. Thereafter, and until the end of the war, no one ever saw Stepanych with a rifle in his hands again.

Such were Captain Mikhalych and Major Stepanych.

Daily encountering people like this in my position as Komsomol organizer, I could feel how I was becoming ever more dull and apathetic myself, and a spiritual vacuum began to grow inside me. Watching how such people schemed to construct a resort lifestyle just behind the front lines, I thought: "These are precisely the same people who will survive the war. After the war they'll leave the army and start a free life of hunting and fishing; meeting over a bottle of vodka or a cup of tea, they'll start reminiscing with deep pathos over the battles 'where they fought together.' And of course, they'll demand respect from the frontline veterans for the services they rendered."

How different was our life in the political unit from the life of those in the trenches! There they never bothered to lift a hand to salute, and you especially didn't dare order around a soldier, if you yourself had ever screwed up at some dangerous moment, or were never able to display your own personal courage and fearlessness. I was constantly drawn to return to the front lines, back to the people with whom I had started my combat journey. Yes, there it was harder and more dangerous, but there I also felt part of a righteous, genuine life that no matter the paradox, was more joyful than my current life. I saw much around me in the army's rear that disturbed and upset me. But I was troubled most of all by questions about myself. Perhaps something had already changed in me? Would I ever take an independent position? Yes, well, maybe when hell freezes over or a fish learns to sing. To hell with all of them!

Colonel Razumovsky

Another month passed. Increasingly rarely did I visit the front, as I was weighed down by endless verbal and paper bustle: conferences, assemblies, meetings with fresh reinforcements, assignments from the commissar or the Party organizer, or unexpected seminars at the division or army level. My most pleasant event during this month became my acquaintanceship with new comrades, the battalion Komsomol organizers Vania Skoropud and Boris Flegboim. I also befriended a plump, rosy-cheeked little fellow, Sergeant Vasia Ragulin. Within a half year, he would take my place and become the *komsorg* for the 673rd Rifle Regiment.

One day Gruzdev called: "This evening, report to the regiment commander."

"Certainly!" I responded. At the appointed time, I was standing in front of Maksim Petrovich Razumovsky. The colonel invited me to sit down and said:

"It's been a month now that you've been serving as *komsorg* of the regiment. You know the situation at the front, you've spent some time in many of the battalions and batteries, and you've become acquainted with the rear. I would like to hear your opinion of the units which you have visited."

"My impression is a good one," I answered.

"Have you noticed any defects?"

"Yes, I noticed a few."

"I'm listening to you."

"First of all, about the reinforcements. With each new batch, their quality worsens. About half of the most recent arrivals are new conscripts; they're poorly trained, badly dressed and poorly shod, and they're hungry when they arrive. While we're staying on the defense, it would be desirable to hold them a little longer in the training battalion. Political workers and regiment command staff rarely appear at the front, not to mention commissary staff. The work of the mail service is poorly organized. But these aren't the main thing."

"Go on."

"Firstly, we haven't received the promised submachine guns; even the regiment's submachine gun company still carries carbines. Secondly, there is insufficient care for the soldiers in the front lines. The soldiers in the trenches are poorly uniformed, and they're freezing. Their coats are worn out and often torn; many of the coats have flaps that have been scorched by campfires. Their footgear is full of holes, and their foot wrappings are half-rotten. The American low boots have been arriving in ones and twos. There are also defects in nutrition. Hot meals still arrive irregularly, and it would be nice to bring up hot tea in addition. It would be desirable to organize steam baths for groups of soldiers, who could be taken out of the front line at least twice a week."

"What can I say, I agree with you, and I'm glad that a combat officer became the regiment's *komsorg*. We must both ponder all of this and take the appropriate measures. Now let's have a chat about your work. You know about our glittering victory at Stalingrad, and that an enemy army of 300,000 has been crushed there. We must let both our soldiers and the Germans know about this victory, since much is being hidden from the German soldiers. Now your trump card is Stalingrad. Explain to the Red Army soldiers that even here, fighting at Rzhev, we have done our own bit and sacrificed much for the sake of this victory at Stalingrad. This will raise the warriors' spirits and their faith in the success of our efforts. Lieutenant, I'm an old officer, and I'm sure, as you can see, that soon we'll take Rzhev as well."

"Comrade Colonel," I asked, "please give me a few more minutes of your time. Young soldiers and officers want to know more about their regiment commander. If you please, tell me about yourself."

"I understand you. I'll try," said the colonel. "During World War I, I graduated from the Alexander Military School as an ensign. At the end of the war I was a lieutenant, and the acting commander of a battalion. After the October Revolution, I switched my support to the Bolsheviks. I fought in the [Russian] Civil War. After my wounding and convalescence in a hospital, I was sent to Turkestan, where I fought for three years against the Basmachi [the Soviet label given to those who participated in a general uprising against Soviet Russian rule in Central Asia]. Later I served in the North, and I took part in the campaign against Finland. In 1941 I defended Moscow. I served in Rokossovsky's 16th Army, which I now consider a great honor. I was severely wounded. After my spell in the hospital, I was sent to the 220th Rifle Division. For my service in the fighting in front of Moscow, I received the Order of the Red Banner. That, in short, is everything. I don't know if you find what I've said satisfactory."

"Fully satisfactory, Comrade Colonel. Thank you very much."

On this we parted.

Back in the political unit, Mikhalych, having heard my story of my meeting with Razumovsky, added to the regiment commander's biography. After the Civil War, Razumovsky, as a former officer in the Tsarist Russian Army, had been reduced in rank and sent to fight the Basmachi rebels as a test of his loyalty to the Bolsheviks. In 1938 he was "repressed"—targeted by Stalin's purge of the military. After two years in prison, he was released and sent to serve in the North.

The conversation inspired me; this military officer most likely was not just a man of words, and his orders were based on his enormous personal experience in command and in war. I involuntarily compared the regiment commander to his commissar, Gruzdev. Once a modest village teacher, Gruzdev had entered a new role and had changed so quickly. Party work didn't interest him, and he seemed to care less about what the officers thought of him, much less the soldiers. He knew he was the highest political authority in the regiment and believed he was the conscience of the regiment. It was useless to try to convince him of something, and I would never think to speak with him openly as I did with Razumovsky.

13

Operation "Hunt"
February 1943

"All Hopes Are on You!"

At the end of February, an event occurred that agitated not only the regiment but the entire division as well. Colonel Razumovsky received an urgent order to capture a German officer within a week at any cost. Precise information was wanted on the enemy on the opposite bank—his combat capabilities and immediate plans.

Regiment reconnaissance scouts left our lines each night for this purpose, but no matter how hard they tried, they failed to reach the German trenches. The same thing was happening in other regiments of the division. The division commander, General Poplavsky, believed that something lay behind the Germans' tight security: apparently, the enemy was doing everything possible to keep his pending retreat concealed, so as to break contact with the "Soviets" completely and to dig in successfully in new positions. The division commander had the idea to broaden the net to capture a German officer by including officers in all the regiments, in order to attract more volunteers for this "hunt." He himself went around all the regiments to meet with volunteers and to select the "hunters." A team of volunteer scouts was organized in each regiment. In our regiment, eight officers were selected by Colonel Razumovsky and Commissar Gruzdev and presented to the division commander. I was included in this "Magnificent Eight," most likely because of my position as the regiment's *komsorg*. The general didn't waste time on any fiery speeches, but simply laid out a concrete proposal to us:

"Boys," he said, "I need a 'tongue.' Help me out! We must haul in a German officer. Whoever accomplishes this will be written up for a decoration. Moreover, if you want a woman—you'll get one. If you want leave to see your mother—we'll give it to you. You'll get all the vodka you want. All our hopes are on you! A 'tongue' is needed without fail and urgently so. Pick yourself some volunteers and get going. The regiment headquarters and political unit will help you. Any questions?"

There were no questions. We already knew the practice: if you managed to capture a "tongue," an honor awaited you—as a rule, medals. If you returned without a prisoner but some useful documents, you'd get nothing.

Who at twenty years of age doesn't dream of carrying out some important mission for his homeland? To become famous! Looking at the Orders decorating the service jacket of a general, even we dreamed of glory. In those days, Orders and medals were very highly valued—people made much of you if you had them.

After the war, we proudly wore our combat decorations on our military field blouses or our civilian jackets without any prompting. Thanks to them, we enjoyed well-known benefits, which had been created back in the prewar period. For example, we received small sums of money for tobacco; had the right for free round-trip travel, once a year, to any point in the country, by railway or water transportation; received subsidized housing in apartments; and so forth. For us frontline soldiers, all of this was important.

Then suddenly after the war the government, supposedly at our request, deprived us of all those benefits. We knew: the country was in difficult circumstances, and we had to accelerate the rebuilding of cities, factories, hospitals, schools, and libraries—all had been demolished, torched, and befouled, and the government's means were not large. But here two moral factors arose. In the first place, we honored veterans never asked anyone about anything! If the government had come to us honestly, if its leadership had said, if you will, "we owe you frontline soldiers a lot (at that time they still didn't call us "veterans"), but excuse us, we don't have the means to repay you, therefore support the government and voluntarily refuse all your benefits for some time," I'm sure everyone would have agreed. But to treat us the way the government did was dishonorable!

Secondly, there must be honest mutual relations, on the basis of law, between a government and its citizens. What a simple truth! In the postwar years we still didn't understand these "fine points," but we sensed them. During the war, we were called to perform a great deed in the name of the Motherland, of Stalin. We stepped forward in response, not sparing our lives; we stepped forward for the sake of saving the Fatherland. In the name of the Fatherland, we were awarded decorations—some posthumously, others still living. But once the war came to an end, we became superfluous to our Fatherland. That is why—as a mark of protest!—each year on May 9, for Victory Day, I put on only one soldier's medal that is precious to me: "For Courage," which I earned at Rzhev.

One other point, which was unexpected and psychologically difficult for many of the frontline soldiers: returning from war, we expected to see a renewed society, more free and democratic. We were the victors! That which waited for us in the cities and especially in the villages plunged many of us into shock.

Then thirty years passed, and now people were shouting at us frontline soldiers: "Lord, when finally will you die?" I never confused a crowd with the people as a whole, but I strove not to use the benefits due to me. [As time passed, younger Soviet citizens began to resent the fact that Red Army veterans were allowed to cut in front of lines, though many veterans refused to take advantage of this.] I knew that it was harder for those shouting from the crowd, normally old women, to live than it was for us veterans.

We Hunger for the "Hunt"

The general's address suited all of us to a "T." The officers joked:

"An Order is a fine thing! But a good-looking woman is no worse!"

"But think how much better—both a medal and a woman!"

I watched General Poplavsky and listened to him, and he impressed me all the more as a person. Not only his calm, friendly manner of speaking but also his general appearance. He was solidly built, with a prominent nose adorning an open face, and he had arms and hands like those of a blacksmith. His words sounded sincere, and each of us understood the significance of what he was saying for the future successful operations of the division—and even of the army.

It is impossible not to mention one other circumstance. We were not professional reconnaissance scouts; therefore the general's request generated a special excitement in our hearts. We were young, strong, and at that time in life when it seemed we could bear the weight of the world on our shoulders. Finally, we all had frontline experience, which meant we would not disgrace ourselves—no one doubted this.

To a man, we wanted to test our strength against the adversary, to outduel him. Did any one of us understand the danger of this duel, did anyone think about death? Both yes and no. Everyone knew that the Germans were not a laughing matter. And in the present situation, joking about them was simply impermissible. Actually, in recent weeks the adversary had locked and sealed his front against us—it was impossible even to approach it! Not even the regimental and divisional scouts had been able to deal with this cordon. But there was a strong incentive, and we believed we could do it!

I immediately suggested an idea to Poplavsky: under the guise of being fugitives, we together with a few handpicked men would steal up to their front lines with knives, pistols, and grenades—and once there, we'd see how things would turn out. He rejected my plan. The "Hunt," as the operation was called, started that very night. I selected a group of five young volunteer soldiers and managed to stoke each with my confidence and desire for success. I also told them about the division commander's promises. The men in turn revealed their innermost desire: to spend even a short time back home is always the constant dream of the soldier! It, this dream, indeed became my main trump card in recruiting volunteers.

For a half-day we discussed, consulted, and searched for the best plan. Everyone understood that the slightest mistake would mean a bullet in the forehead. That night, we stealthily made our way to the opposite bank. But once there, we could find no way to reach the enemy's lines undetected. The Germans were constantly sending up illumination flares, sometimes suspended from parachutes. These would hang in the air and linger for a long time, but in the short intervals between launches, when the darkness would briefly conceal us, we managed to creep forward all of a few meters. Then a new flare would light up no-man's land, we would freeze in place, blending with the snow in our white camouflage smocks, and we waited and waited. Hours passed; our sortie dragged on and continued for an impermissibly long time. At such a pace, we would never reach the German lines before dawn, so I gave the signal to withdraw. I understood that this was useless, and we had to think up something different.

The next day, just as we gathered to consult with the scouts and headquarters staff, the operation was cancelled. It turned out that the night before, when our venture met with failure, some regimental scouts had nabbed a "tongue," an *Oberfeldwebel* [a German rank equivalent to sergeant major] named Willi Brandt from Cologne. Success! Word of this exploit instantly flew around the entire regiment.

The scouts provided details of the prisoner snatch, which actually proved to be only a partial success: they hadn't been able to return with the prisoner himself. The German, a strong and stout man, put up a desperate struggle, and they had to finish him off. But the scout platoon leader, Lieutenant Shevchenko, together with two sergeants brought in the man's identification tag, pistol, and soldier's book [*soldbuch*, the identity document booklet carried by all active-duty German soldiers]. From these, we managed to identify the German unit in front of us. Of course, this wasn't everything that the general was expecting, but nonetheless, it was the first successful step. Good fellows! Both the sergeants in the successful mission were Komsomol members. I decided to meet with them, for I wanted to know in more detail how everything happened.

For several days, the triumphant scouts walked around as heroes. Even though the scouts had not returned with a living prisoner, General Poplavsky decided to reward them. Lieutenant Shevchenko left for his wife and children somewhere in Riazan' Oblast.

A Banal Situation for the Komsorg

For several weeks, rumors had been circulating around the headquarters about the withdrawal of the adversary's forces from his present positions. The "soldier's telegraph" was reporting the same thing. Gradually, we all became convinced that only skeletal forces remained in the German lines to cover the withdrawal, and the command came to the conclusion that a "reconnaissance through combat" was necessary.

Just before dawn, the regiment commander Poplavsky, Commissar Gruzdev, two artillery spotters, some headquarters staff members, and I all gathered at an observation post to watch the attack. Why did the commissar bring me along? It wasn't like him. We didn't see any of the company that had received the assignment to probe the German lines, but we knew the company was already prepared for the attack.

Then suddenly the order rang out: "Attack!"

A signal flare arced into the sky! In the twilight just before sunrise, without any artillery preparation, the company bounded across the frozen river, forced a crossing of the Volga, clambered up the opposite bank, and surged toward the enemy trenches. At first the Germans were confused by the unexpected appearance of Russians right under their noses, but they quickly regained their senses and opened a furious fire from all types of weapons. Our regimental artillery immediately replied, at first striving to cover the attackers, then shifting fire onto the enemy positions. But by now the entire company had dropped to the ground under the heavy enemy fire. History seemed to be repeating itself: we would seize a foothold on the opposite bank of the river, but then the Germans would drive the attackers back into the river. Less than 100 meters remained to reach the German trenches, but our soldiers in their camouflage smocks, with their carbines and submachine guns, were lying on the snow, the air above their heads pierced by the howling of shells and the whistling of bullets. What power on earth could get them back up off the ground? Colonel Razumovsky didn't tear his eyes away from his binoculars; he was plainly nervous, and I understood why: if the company didn't get up and get moving forward again into the wall of enemy fire, it would soon be cut to pieces by enemy mortar fire, which would probably start up at any moment. The situation couldn't continue like this for long; someone or something had to get our people up and moving again, no matter what the cost. I hadn't even had time to finish this thought when Gruzdev suddenly turned to Razumovsky and said:

"Maksim Petrovich, the regiment *komsorg* can rally the men and get them moving. He's a combat officer, and I have no doubt he can handle it."

Colonel Razumovsky slightly hesitated, then gave the order:

"Get moving, Lieutenant. You must get that company back up on its feet and attack! The artillery will give you support. If you consider it necessary, I will send up more men. Get it done!"

"At once!"

I rushed for the dugout's exit. I thought Gruzdev would say something to me in passing and wish me good luck. Nothing! Not a word!

I quickly hurried through the trenches toward a spot where I could get down to the ice on the river more easily and safely—if only I could reach it. In such minutes, when your life is hanging by a thread, it begins to seem as if in your entire previous life, you—Fool! Fool!—had never paid enough attention to your instructors. Your thoughts rush by at a gallop. Khalikov had once said, "A banal situation for the *komsorg*. . . ." Now it applied to me! There was something absurd about what I now had to do. While I was making my way to the pinned-down company, the Fritzes could pick me off a thousand times over! I would be the only upright, moving target, and the point of what I was trying to do would be obvious to the enemy. Put a cork in it! You don't discuss an order—you carry out an order! But my heart wanted to believe in something—that my assignment was a good one, that I might save people—but it was also a bad order; I would hardly be able to reach the company. But I had to act!

I rushed along. The place where I could slip and slide down onto the river ice was just ahead. What's this? An unexpected obstacle! Two soldiers' greatcoats loom in front of me, blocking my way; the pair is afraid to cross a little piece of ground, exposed to the fire of a sniper in a factory smokestack across the river. What should I do? Well, here's to it! Grabbing hold of a solid lump of ice, I hurl myself forward into the lower back of the fighter in front of me. He leaps up, as if stung by a spur, and rushes forward, forcing the comrade in front of him to do the same. They safely gallop across the dangerous interval. I fling myself after them, and at that instant the sniper manages to hit me in the left arm with an explosive bullet. Part of the sleeve of my leather jacket flies away like a bit of fluff. I am wearing a quilted jacket beneath my leather jacket; bullet fragments become stuck in the wadding and set it on fire while other fragments bury into my arm. Blood is pouring from the wound. I run into the nearest dugout and bandage the wound. It turns out that I have darted into the bunker of a company commander. I call the command post and report on my injury:

"If the regiment commander believes it essential, I will try to reach the opposite shore."

Razumovsky slightly hesitates with his answer and, obviously, decides to send a different officer. I can plainly overhear him tell Gruzdev:

"One dead *komsorg* from a 'reconnaissance through combat' is enough."

The thought flashes through my mind: there's the honest explanation for Tolia's death!

They sent a member of the headquarters staff in my place. The German sniper dropped him dead into the snow. Somehow, the company commander himself managed to rally his men, and they burst into the adversary's trenches. Hand-to-hand fighting erupted there, which is always a cruel fight to the finish.

Captured prisoners confirmed that their units would soon be retreating to new positions. The reconnaissance was successful. But there was a fallout from the action. As often happens in war, there is some sort of annoying lack of coordination, an unexpected additional expense—and the losses turned out to be disproportionate to the achievement. Yes, the artillerymen piled up many Germans—but our own soldiers as well! Several shells had fallen on our own men. The question raises itself, what were the artillery spotters in the observation post looking at?

The next morning I went to the *medsanbat.* They repaired my damaged arm. Now my arm was in a sling—they said, for two weeks. I decided to return to my regiment.

An Extraordinary Event

The regiment persistently prepared for a final attack on Rzhev. Artillerymen took care of the factory smokestack on the hostile bank, so we were finally freed from the German sniper who had caused us so much trouble.

A scandal erupted the day after Shevchenko's return from the leave that had been awarded to him after his partially successful prisoner snatch. The enraged division commander Poplavsky drove up to the regiment command post with some officers from the Special Department. Nobody understood what had happened. The regiment commander summoned his staff and political unit to his command dugout. Once inside, General Poplavsky ordered that the regiment's chief scout be brought before him immediately. Shevchenko was quickly brought in without any explanation. He, sensing a roasting, nevertheless maintained his composure—until he ran into the general's infuriated gaze.

A wild scene then ensued. Poplavsky asked the scout platoon commander just one question:

"What are you—a Soviet officer or a piece of shit?"

Shevchenko went deathly pale and quailed in his place. He wanted to say something, apparently, in his own defense, but the division commander had already advanced upon him. The heavy hand of the general tore the straps off Shevchenko's shoulders with a jerk, then came smashing down on the upper jaw of the now former officer. Spitting out some teeth with blood, Shevchenko flew to the floor and howled like a badly wounded beast. But this wasn't a howl of pain or a cry of protest—it was more like a cry for mercy.

"Get up, swine!" the general commanded.

Shevchenko staggered to his feet and immediately received a blow to his lower jaw. Dumbfounded, we stood along the wall of the dugout, not understanding what had happened or what the scout was accused of doing. He was now crawling along the floor of the dugout around the general, mechanically repeating one thing:

"Forgive me, forgive me . . ."

From despair, pain, and terror, Shevchenko decided not to rise to his feet again, fearing another blow from the general. Like a worm, he squirmed up to the general's boots and tried to embrace them. Poplavsky twisted his face in disgust. A new blow followed, then a boot to the face. Shevchenko flew into a corner of the dugout and huddled into a ball. Dazed, confused, he now understood little of what was going on; his whole body was trembling, and he could only whimper. Oh God, how much longer would this bloody reprisal continue? For whose benefit has this demonstration been intended? I'm not a quaking maiden, I don't need any sedatives, but I was totally appalled. At this moment, the general's voice loudly, like a judge handing down a sentence, broke the deathly silence:

"A man without character is not a man, but a nobody. This scoundrel has committed a crime. He will stand trial. He has soiled the officer's honor. Excuse me, but I am in a hurry. The regiment commander will accompany me to my car. The commander of divisional reconnaissance will make an announcement to all of you."

The officers from the Special Department lifted Shevchenko by his arms, dragged him bloodied and barely alive out of the dugout, and led him away.

Captain Mishchenko was brief in his statement to us:

"The general for some reason checked up on your scouts. He turned in their report to the army, and the report passed up to the *front* command. There they are always checking and rechecking the intelligence; the *front* has agents behind enemy lines. As a result, it was discovered that this German unit, which Shevchenko's intelligence indicated we were facing, is currently located in France. Your Shevchenko never even laid eyes upon any *Oberfeldwebel*. All these supposedly captured 'items' had been pulled out of the regimental supply train by his scouts, where they had been secretly keeping them since the summer offensive. By order of the division commander, your regimental scout platoon now has a new commander. Are there any questions?"

Everyone was silent.

Two days later, the regiment's officers were summoned to the regiment command post. They drew us up in a line facing the execution spot. *Osobisty* brought in Shevchenko and placed him twenty paces in front of our line. A representative from the division's military tribunal, a lieutenant colonel, read out the sentence. The regiment commander called an officer from out of our line, a major from the headquarters staff, and, having handed him a submachine gun, ordered:

"Carry out the sentence!"

The condemned man collapsed onto his knees in the snow, swollen all over, almost toothless, mumbling something, then with tears in his eyes he cried out some disconnected words, hoping for mercy to the very end:

"Don't kill me. . . . I'll atone with my own blood. . . . For the sake of my children . . . don't kill me!"

I suddenly recalled that Shevchenko had been wearing a wedding ring. I remembered it precisely; I saw it on him that evening, when the general was severely dealing with the rogue. It was not on his finger now.

We heard a burst of submachine-gun fire. Had the hands of the staff member been shaking, or did he do it intentionally? The condemned man was still alive. He no longer could see anything, and didn't understand what was happening with him. He couldn't rise, but he crawled, mumbling something with his toothless mouth, covered with blood, trying to reach the standing line of officers; if they spared him, he would lick all their boots. But they never spared anyone like him. With a few quick steps, the regiment commander approached and fired several rounds from his pistol into him. The twisted, lifeless body lay frozen on the bloody snow.

It was the first time I had witnessed a public execution—moreover, a man from my regiment and a comrade combat officer, but I felt no pity for Shevchenko, nor probably did anyone else. One question occupied us all: why had the platoon leader done this; did he really not believe that sooner or later they would expose his crime? He had drawn two other young men into a shady enterprise and ruined them. He had considered himself cleverer, smarter than the rest. The madman!

Immediately after the episode, Gruzdev summoned me to appear before him. He didn't invite me to sit and tried not to look in my direction. We both remained silent, as if we had just returned from a funeral. Finally, Gruzdev spoke up:

"Your first serious black mark. You also share some blame in what happened; both sergeant scoundrels were Komsomol members. You at least knew them?"

"Yes. I took away their Komsomol cards."

"Their fate has already been decided. Both have been judged and sent to the penal company. You don't have enough acumen, Senior Lieutenant, this is important in political work, and you must . . ."

I was quiet and listened to the commissar. He was speaking to me in the language of the Special Department, actually demanding that I turn every Komsomol member into an informant. In these minutes I despised the commissar. But what could I do? Turn around and walk out of the dugout? Taking a deep breath and clenching my fists, I replied, "I will take heed of your observations."

Back at the political unit, neither Stepanych nor Mikhalych questioned me about my conversation with Gruzdev. The former, as always, was sipping tea, lost in his reading; the latter, sitting on the edge of his bunk, was cleaning his cigarette holder. Well, never mind. I threw off my boots and belt and lay down. So much had piled up over just the past several days! The brutal treatment of Shevchenko at the hands of division commander, the terrible act of execution—God forbid that I ever see or experience such things again! Now the commissar, too. My thoughts would not let me go. Why had my age peer—an officer with two decorations, a scout, the elite of the army—acted this way? Was it because of stupidity, or an indiscretion of youth? Perhaps, as I knew, everything had come too easily to him in life? He had confronted no obstacles, neither in his childhood nor in his school years. He had graduated from military specialist school with a scouting orientation—and had been immediately entrusted with the command of a regimental scout platoon. A free Cossack! He had twice before been lucky and had nabbed a "tongue." Stop! I strive to recollect: apparently, each time he had not returned with any "booty" from enemy territory. That's how he did it! Did really no one pay any attention to this? That meant the deception had already been going on for some time, and he thought this time, too, he could cheat the command.

As a consequence, a sergeant from the scout platoon had testified at the tribunal that on one of the operations they had strayed into a swamp, where they had laid up for more than a day: "We had a badly wounded man among us. By order of the platoon leader, we abandoned him, promising to send back medics. But we didn't send anyone back to the man." This was strange: Shevchenko didn't take care of his soldiers. Such a thing was totally out of character for a real scout. For anyone in the scouts this was something sacred, but even more so for an officer! Even their dead, not to mention their wounded—scouts are obligated to bring back their own.

In the reconnaissance troops, a man could quickly distinguish himself. This particularly attracted people with prior convictions, and we had a lot of them. If you distinguished yourself in the scouts, you would immediately be given a paper that erased a prior conviction. Shevchenko didn't want to accept any "marked men," as they said of soldiers with a tarnished past. Why?

How could they have placed such a man in command of the scout platoon, knowing that the scout platoon is the eyes and ears of the regiment? They had chosen a man with a cool demeanor and cunning eyes, who acted with great aplomb, but who was actually stupid and unreliable. How could such a poisonous mushroom become a scout? Scouting needs a strong man, with strong hands, who can run faster than a hare, who has sharp teeth and an iron fortitude, who can cut his way through any wire, and who everyone respects as a brave, fearless man. Perhaps Shevchenko had possessed a few of these merits, and they outweighed his main demerits? Perhaps those who made the decision had a momentary lapse of judgment; they were always in a hurry and didn't bother to ponder the essence of the man. But I must ask again: how could such a person become a scout platoon commander? It was a shame that they had promoted the reliable Chernov and his scouts to the army-level reconnaissance, and had replaced him with Shevchenko.

From the Notes of Tolia Razumov

That evening, sitting in the political unit's dugout, we drank tea and discussed the recent events. For a long time, I had refrained from asking any questions about the details of Tolia's death, expecting that Mikhalych or Stepanych would tell me about it one day. But they had held their tongues. I thought they were probably just trying to protect my nerves.

Suddenly I sensed an urge to inspect the contents of Tolia's little suitcase, which had been lying beneath my bunk ever since my arrival in the unit. I thought to myself, "So much time has passed, but I haven't yet touched Tolia's suitcase or found out what's inside it. Perhaps there's something important there?"

I reached under my bunk and pulled out the old little suitcase. Examining its contents, I found several small bundles of papers bound with tape. One bundle contained letters from home (with the passage of time, I later returned them to Tolia's mother). Another bundle contained sheets of notepaper filled with small handwriting in pencil—sketches of thoughts, reflections, impressions, and short notes about meetings with people. I immersed myself in reading them.

It seemed that Tolia had been collecting material about the Red Army's commissars for a planned book after the war. Considering these notes interesting, I've decided to share them here. Here is what Tolia had written:

About myself: at seventeen years of age, having just finished my schooling, they told me: "Go—defend your Motherland"; so I went. When I was nineteen, I graduated from a military-political specialist school. I already knew full well that communists led the way into battle, so I became a communist. They ordered me: "Go straight for the machine guns!" Soldiers followed me to their own deaths. They said to me: "If you don't kill the German, he will kill you"—so I killed them. They told me: "You have no right to surrender." I always kept the last bullet for myself. At twenty-one years of age, I became a regiment Komsomol organizer. They told me: "Now, you're the guide for the regiment's youth!" . . .

"Commissar"—this word has resounded proudly for many years, and even today it has not faded. I hope after the war that many wonderful books, plays, and films about the heroic destiny of the commissars will appear.

In the specialist school, I read that during the American Revolutionary War of 1775–1783, in George Washington's army, as well as during the French Revolution of 1789, "commissars" played a major role. I don't know much about this. Once I get back from the war, I must read Anatoly Frantz's book, *The Gods Are Thirsty*.

Is it interesting to study how commissars first appeared in the Red Army? Legends surround the achievements of the commissars in the Civil War. I should research this subject.

We have highly regarded the image of the commissar from early childhood. Especially military commissars. Our families, our teachers, our Young Pioneer detachments, movies, and literature have all raised us to think this way. The character of Levinson—the commissar of a partisan unit from Alexander Fadeev's tale *Razgrom* (The Rout)—became my first childhood idol. How many times did we, as kids, run to see the film *Chapaev*, with its unforgettable character Dmitrii Furmanov, the commissar of the famous 25th "Chapaev" Division?

Once in school, sometime during the seventh grade, a military commissar came to visit us. When he unbuttoned his leather jacket, we caught sight of the Order of the Red Banner on his uniform. One of the lads asked our visitor the number of his Order. He told us, "Sixty-eighth." Aha! Suddenly the image of Commissar Voikov, who was glorified by the revolutionary poet Vladimir Maiakovsky, filled my thoughts. The White Guards killed Voikov.

The authority of the commissar in the Red Army has always been great! This tradition has been carried down since the Civil War. But at the same time, one must admit that had this tradition not existed, many tragedies in the first days of the war would not have occurred. It was precisely the commissars who had assured everyone in the army—from the general down to the soldier—that there would be no war with the Germans. Comrade Stalin had said so himself! Germany would not attack us.

Commanders couldn't reach a single decision without agreement of the commissar. After the principle of unity of command was introduced in October 1942, all the same, some commanders continued to take counsel from the commissar. Now commissars have become deputy commanders for political affairs. How did commanders greet the liquidation of the institution of military commissar? Calmly. The majority considered it a correct measure to take, but a few lost all confidence in themselves and began to consult with their deputy political commander even more frequently. It is more accurate to say in these cases that they relied upon their former commissar.

What was the reaction of the commissars to the introduction of unity of command? They bit their tongues and made no protest, but a few were ready to kill themselves. It seemed to them that the complete collapse of the Red Army had arrived, which meant revolution would soon follow. Sometimes, commanders who were not accustomed to independence in command came to the rescue of these former commissars. In general, it seems to me, in each case it depended on the respective intelligence of the commander and the deputy political commander, on their tact and ability to handle themselves in any situation. Many former commissars were sent for retraining, so that they could become commanders, if only in the infantry.

Why did soldiers call the political workers in the regiment "commissars" after the introduction of unity of command in the army? Probably because the basic aim of their activity at the front didn't change much. The political worker, just as was true for the commissar before, was the political supervisor over the adherence to Party demands within the unit, in a way a sort of unique personal blocking detachment to prevent a retreat from Party dictates.

I am the third Komsomol organizer for the 673rd Rifle Regiment in the past two years. The first was killed back in 1941 around Vitebsk, the second was severely wounded. . . . What will be my fate? I don't know.

At first I didn't think I had enough frontline experience. Then I mastered my position and understood that my primary task, like that of all political workers, boils down to forcing the soldier to fight at any cost (few can be persuaded). That's what they taught us at the military-political specialist school. So that's how I behave. My heart is heavy whenever my eyes meet the gaze of a soldier.

I have begun to notice that I have become like all the other political workers. As soon as I try to waver from banal speeches and empty gestures, they immediately try to bring me back into the common "herd." Well, it is far too much!

You can't overcome the Germans with a simple "Hurrah!" They know how to fight stubbornly and have better weapons than we do. They have a strong army. Many commanders ignore these obvious facts. We stay silent. For praising the Germans, one can wind up in front of a tribunal . . .

With contempt, I found out that some soldiers, among them a Komsomol member, were raising a hand above the parapet of the trench in the hope that a stray bullet would strike it. From military prisoners it became known that the Germans at first laughed at these "Ivans," but then began to help them. The number of self-inflicted wounds is growing. The command is furious. But the matter extends beyond the self-inflicted wounds. Such cases have a serious influence on morale, and inspire the German soldier. There is no avoiding this fact.

Somewhere I once read the following saying: "No one can become someone or achieve anything, not having first learned to be oneself." Am I often being myself? Moreover, what does "to be yourself" mean? I ought to think seriously about this. They say that human feelings disappear in war. Animal instincts replace them. That is true. But I have noticed that in suitable conditions, human feelings are resurrected. Apparently, this is how we differ from animals.

I have participated in several battles with the Germans. I have seen how comrades die and enemies perish. At first I found it totally gut wrenching when I saw a bloodied body. But now I am used to it. I am now accustomed to all the horrors of war.

Why do soldiers often distrust us officers? Their distrust is painful. They don't like us very much, but they submit to our directions. Unfortunately, this situation suits many political workers. What I've written above should be pondered.

We are "Stalin's generation." This says everything about us. Am I proud of this? Why do they respect a man at the front, be he a soldier or a general? For his honesty and steadfastness. Among us officers, both these qualities are often lacking. Why is this so? We all grew up in the Soviet era.

Thinking about the acts of the army's bureaucracy, I see nothing new in them. In my school years, I loved to read books about wars. Many authors did not speak kindly about those in the rear. Even Suvorov took personal aim at them. Often, they do not even do what they are supposed to do. Oh, if only a writer like Anton Pavlovich Chekhov would let loose on this "fraternity." But where could such a writer be found today, and who would permit him to touch upon such a topic?

I heard a story. In the difficult year of 1941, they reported to Stalin that approximately two million military servicemen were lounging around in the rear areas of the Red Army. The Supreme Commander immediately ordered the rear area to be swept, and all the personnel sent to the front. It never happened. Probably, even Stalin had forgotten something. . . . Who then was the main "provider" of supplies and ammunition in the Red Army? Military horse-drawn carts! There were not enough vehicles in the army. Apparently the Supreme Commander had forgotten as well about the Russian roads. Finally, "who, where, when" has anyone in history been able to handle the bureaucracy? No one!

We've been lucky with Commissar Borisov. You rarely find such a man in an army environment. Several times, when the situation permitted it, he gathered us together and told us certain details from the division's history. It was especially interesting to listen to him when he explained why the Germans campaigned against and executed commissars, communists, and Soviet intellectuals. The Germans saw in these people the main ideological support for the Soviet regime.

After reading through Tolia's notebooks, I set them aside and discovered a thin green envelope lying on the bottom of the suitcase. Inside the envelope were seven sheets of paper containing tiny, neat handwriting. It was clearly a story that Tolia Razumov had written. I thought that at some time I might try to publish the story in honor of the fallen *komsorg* Tolia Razumov. I am doing this now:

7,000 Steps to Immortality

This story occurred around New Year's Day 1942 in besieged Leningrad. Few know about it. Nevertheless through separate kernels of the story, which later became known, I will try to reconstruct it, without losing touch with the truth of the time. . . .

It was a frigid day; the gloomy sky of early morning promised nothing good. A group of five men, far from young, dressed in whatever they could find that might help keep them warm, gathered on Sennaia Square; the majority of them lived nearby. The trolley had long ago stopped running.

One of the men, a little younger and a little stronger than the others, had dragged along a string of sledges behind him. He had carefully lain little canvas bags on them, each one containing only the daily ration of bread—125 grams [a little more than 4 ounces]; cottonseed flat cakes; and a few short, narrow strips of leather cut from a belt strap [Leningraders had long before started holding up their trousers with string or cord]—if you sucked a bit on the leather, your acute sense of hunger would deaden for a short while.

The oldest fellow gave a sign. Then they headed on their way. Where were they going? Why? Nobody asked, and they didn't say a word. They moved slowly, carefully supporting each other. The eldest walked in front, leaning on a cane—the only one for all five. A woolen stocking covered his face, like all the others.

Now here's the Sennaia Market. Not so long ago, human voices and the cooing of pigeons sounded all around, streetcars clattered, and the air was intoxicating with the scents of flowers, honey, warm bread, and pickled cucumbers. All had vanished. The human voices and birdcalls had fallen silent; the market stalls had become buried under dirty piles of snow; and the doors to the pavilions yawned wide open.

The buildings, emptied, covered by ash, greeted them with semidarkened windows, behind which had disappeared even the shadow of human life. In this building Sonechka Marmeladova once lived; at one time a tavern had been next door, where Sonechka met Raskol'nikov. Not far away was the dwelling of the old lenders. . . . [These are all literary references to Dostoevsky's *Crime and Punishment*, which was set in St. Petersburg.]

The enormous shop windows of the Apraksin and Gostiny department stores appeared. The windows of both buildings were now without glass; only a few dirty scraps of the window sashes remain; everything wooden had been taken away for heating fuel. All around is dirty snow, mixed with trash. Seemingly, these were the same familiar streets, crossings, and buildings, but without people everything seemed strange and unnatural. They had all been born in this city—"magnificent, proud," with its "beauty and splendor."

After every thousand paces, they stopped to rest. After 2,000 steps, the man towing the sledge pulled the cottonseed cakes and some little lumps of bread out of the bags. They chewed slowly, then made their way farther down the road. On the half-empty streets, no one paid them any attention, as if they were apparitions moving along, not living human beings. Those few people they encountered were busy with their own affairs. Some people were carrying a bucket or cans of water, drawn from the Neva or one of the canals, on their own little sleds; the water supply had long ago frozen and stopped working. Other people were dragging along boards, handmade funeral wagons for the dead. Up to 4,000 citizens were dying each day. They had started dying back in November, when they had lowered the food norms for the fourth time. But after the fifth reduction in daily rations, closer to winter, a catastrophe ensued.

The group of five moved ever farther from Sennaia Square. They crossed Nevsky Prospect. Somewhere at its far end, the needle of the Admiralty spire gleamed. They reached the Passage Women's Store and saw again the broken, empty shop windows. Now the confectioner's shop The North, which not long ago had been famous for its tortes that were acclaimed across the country. Now the shop was closed, but people gathered and stood by its doors. Now there was a grocery store here, where on rare and fortunate days they managed to get a scrap of food with their ration cards.

They walked along the icy streets between mounds of snow. There was no one to remove the ice. They stepped carefully and tried to avoid the most dangerous spots. They walked, paying no attention to the deafening sound of nearby explosions. They walked, guided by one thought: WE'LL REACH IT! and having mustered glimmers of strength, WE'LL SEE IT!— PUSHKIN'S HOME AT 12 MOIKA, where THE POET lived his final years, and where he passed away.

The biting cold kept slipping inside their clothing, and it became increasingly difficult to preserve the remaining traces of warmth around their bodies. The first, most harsh winter of the blockade was happening; those who were lucky enough to survive it would never forget this terrible time until the ends of their days on earth.

It seemed they had passed the halfway mark of their journey. The wan sun showed itself only rarely. "How fine it is on this Earth," thought one man. "Yet why is there so much evil, pain, and suffering?" He very much wanted to share this thought with his friends, but he remained silent. They mustn't speak, they had decided. They had also agreed *a priori* that if one of them didn't have the strength for the trip and fell down, the others would go on. It was cruel to even contemplate something like that. But such was the reality, and they all understood it. They knew, perhaps, that they were walking along the road toward the same conclusion—death—and that they might not come back. But they had even reconciled themselves with this possibility after careful reflection.

The third and fourth thousand steps were the hardest. Their legs were growing stiff and numb, they weren't responding to signals well, and it seemed as if just a bit more, and they would hopelessly cease to obey the command to move.

The fifth thousand paces went more easily, although the hunger was causing terrible cramps, their brains were becoming cloudy, and tears filled their eyes. But they continued to move on. It wasn't far now . . .

They passed the closed House of Books, with its striking blue globe on its roof. This sight inspired so many memories. And what memories! After all, it had been their second home. Each time they had visited this bookstore, a feast awaited them—large or small. One man recalled how he had miraculously acquired the thin little tome *Evgenii Onegin* here, the famous Suvorinsky edition of 1911. What a find for a book lover—a diamond for his entire life! Another man found by chance the single-volume Pushkin—a jubilee edition of limited printing! A third thought about *The Book of Tasty and Healthy Food,* which had been published before the war. The fourth, an inveterate hunter and fisherman, had purchased a complete library about his passion, and was so proud of it! The fifth had compiled a unique collection of books about waterfalls, which had become world famous.

At last, the corner of Moika. They turned toward the embankment. Only an extremely short distance remained to the place, where they had come each year on the anniversary of the famous poet's death. Today they had arrived early, but was this really so important?

Here is the proper place to say the following. They were thinking least of all about heroism. It is more fitting to call their journey madness. But now, having thought it over a little, I value their act differently. They went to the last resting place of the poet not to say goodbye to life—but to find in their unusual adventure a new fortress for the heart. Also, perhaps, whether they desired it or not, they were demonstrating to their fellow citizens that a person has unique reservoirs of strength.

At last they reached their destination.

Seemingly suddenly before their eyes loomed the familiar and dear white, three-story building, the main entrance, and the doors through which HE had once passed. Everything had been boarded up and was covered by snow. There was also complete silence. Nobody was expecting them. Nobody greeted them. No one saw these exhausted faces and eyes. No one sensed the weak but joyful beating of their hearts.

They stopped and formed a semicircle. They removed their caps for several seconds, as a sign of respect and gratitude. They bowed low before their idol. Then suddenly—Oh, a miracle! The subdued rays of the sun penetrated the tired, pale clouds with a warm glow and lit up all thirteen windows of Pushkin's home! Suddenly, an expansive window flickering with light opened in the gray, leaden skies, and in reality or the imagination of these barely living, starving, frozen people, a stunning vision arose: there, from that blazing height, the frenzied Bronze Horseman was galloping toward them like an impetuous whirlwind on his proud, powerful steed.

The wanderers froze. And then the one pulling the sledge, perhaps this had also been agreed upon previously, stepped slightly forward of the group, and his quiet, slightly quivering voice said:

Stand in splendor, City of Peter, stand
Unshakeable, like Russia . . .

Just a half a stanza—but what a couplet! For such days! They sounded like a hymn and prophecy!

A different voice and a new stanza:

What power resides within it!
And what fire inside this horse!
To where do you gallop, proud steed.
And where will your upraised hoof strike?

And again the voice fell silent; he had no more strength to say more. [These are lines from Pushkin's immortal and imaginative tribute "The Bronze Horseman," dedicated to the famous Statue of Peter, which stands next to the Admiralty in St. Petersburg.]

Irreversibly, the unbearable evening twilight gathered around the group. It was time. The senior of the group gave a sign. But no one moved from his spot. One more final look. Then they set out on their return path. Back into the cold and emptiness.

Who were they? What do we know about their fates? Our story—is it truth or legend? The war has already given rise to so many such tales, and continues to create more. Ostensibly, two of the five men had worked in the Pushkin's Apartment Museum back in the 1930s. . . . Beyond is silence.

Part Three

From Rzhev to the National Border

March 1943–July 1944

14

On the Heels of
the Enemy
March 1943

The Liberation of Rzhev, 2–3 March 1943

For almost fifteen months, the 30th Army under the command of General Le-liushenko had been conducting cruel, bloody battles in the Rzhev bridgehead, trying to take the city. The month of February 1943 became decisive in the struggle for the city.

All through the second half of February, the army command had been receiving intelligence that the adversary was preparing to abandon Rzhev. The commander of the 215th Rifle Division, General Kupriianov (he became division commander at the beginning of February 1943), had the same evidence. The situation became highly charged. By that time I was serving in the 31st Army's 220th Rifle Division, so I will cite the recollections of a veteran of the 215th Rifle Division, radiotelephone operator Kh. Kh. Iakin:

> The Germans were being relatively quiet. They let loose bursts of fire
> from machine guns and submachine guns from time to time, and launched
> illumination flares without end. We often sent scout parties from our side
> and skirmishes erupted; that is to say, we were conducting "reconnaissance
> through combat" operations. The evening of 2 March 1943 was no different.
> We sent a group of twenty-two men headed by a sergeant major to test the
> German front line. After a short while, the sergeant major returned alone
> and reported that his platoon had fallen into an ambush, and that the entire
> group had perished.
>
> Sitting by the telephone apparatus, I paid attention to the voice of the
> general [division commander Kupriianov] as he spoke with the commander
> of the 711th Rifle Regiment, Major Gutarga. The voice of the division
> commander pricked up my ears, since he was talking in an agitated tone
> not typical for him. He was saying that other reconnaissance scouts had
> not found any Germans not only in Rzhev, but also along the approaches
> to Olenino. Immediately over the battalion net, orders went down to the

company commanders, and soon we were getting reports from them that there was nobody in the German trenches.[1]

Kupriianov became lost in thought. The entire *front* was at the ready, waiting for orders to go over onto the attack. What should be done, if just two or three hours previously an entire platoon of reconnaissance troops had been wiped out, if fire had still been coming in a continuous stream from the enemy side of the lines? What if it turned out that the enemy's trenches were not empty? "At any cost"—Kupriianov rejected this tactic. He also knew the opinion of the new army commander, Lieutenant General Kolpakchi: use extreme caution, and don't yield to temptation caused by unconfirmed intelligence reports. What should be done in this complicated situation?

Kupriianov made his decision independently, without asking the opinion of the army commander. With a commander's feel for the situation, he understood clearly that the moment of truth had arrived, that any day now, perhaps even the next day, the Germans were going to leave the city. If you delayed, and missed the moment—the enemy would manage to break contact from the pursuers, then take firm position in a previously prepared line of defense, and then again, there would be blood and losses. So he gave the order: "Let's extend our communications wire into Rzhev!"

On 2 March 1943, having received the order to advance, the 215th Rifle Division entered the city. The next day, forward elements of the division were occupying the city center, Soviet Square.

At the height of the fighting for Rzhev, Andrei Filimonovich Kupriianov had been offered a higher post, which had he accepted it, meant he would have had to travel to the Soviet Far East. The division commander refused categorically: "Until I take Rzhev, I'm not going anywhere." Indeed he kept his word; his 215th Rifle Division was one of the first divisions to enter the city that had been abandoned by the Germans. The army newspaper proudly reported the news on 4 March 1943, under the banner headline "In the Last Hour."

Andrei Filimonovich stood on the high bank of the Volga and gazed upon the destroyed city. There it was, Rzhev, for which thousands of his comrades in arms had given up their lives. But one must not stop, not even for an hour. The army commander gave the order to pursue the quickly retreating enemy, so as to not give him a chance to break contact with us. They left a wasteland in their wake.

Unfortunately, after the liberation of Rzhev, Andrei Filimonovich lived only seventeen more days. On 20 March 1943, near the village of Novo-Lytkino, he was severely wounded by a shell fragment. Eyewitnesses told me what happened:

The division headquarters stopped in the village of Novo-Lytkino. On the morning of 20 March, Kupriianov held a meeting with his subordinate officers at his headquarters, then spent some time at the front. By evening, elements of two divisions, General Kupriianov's 215th Rifle Division and Colonel Khazov's 369th Rifle Division, met on the same road and became a bit entangled. The road traveled through the little village of Bol'shoi Monastyrek, which was situated atop a high hill. The enemy was quiet. Indeed nobody knew that one of his rear guard elements had dug into a forest, just two or three kilometers from the village—they were watching and waiting for the moment when the maximum number of our troops would be concentrated on the hilltop.

Just as the sun was setting, twenty enemy artillery batteries unexpectedly struck at the little village. At that moment, Kupriianov was located in a little home, where the operational group of his division's headquarters had set up. As the first rounds began falling on the village, he ran out onto the porch and was immediately wounded by a fragment from a shell that exploded nearby. Just a few moments later, another shell blew apart two walls of the house and smashed the large stove. The woman of the house, and four officers of the headquarters staff who had been sitting around a table near the stove, were killed.

The artillery barrage lasted fifteen minutes. The wounded general was transported to the *medsanbat*, but he died en route. By instruction of the army commander, the body of General Kupriianov was taken back to Rzhev and buried there—in the city that he had helped to liberate.

On 22 March in a letter to Kupriianov's wife and children, the army commander, Kolpakchi, wrote: "Today we will be escorting our combat friend to his final rest. The ancient Russian city Rzhev, which units of Comrade Kupriianov's division were the first to clean from the fascist scum, has become the final landmark in his life. The city will eternally honor the memory of the Bolshevik General Andrei Filimonovich Kupriianov. The entire combat collective of the army expresses to you our deepest condolences."[2]

An obelisk now stands on a high hill in the center of Rzhev—a monument to the fallen general, Andrei Filimonovich Kupriianov.

I can still remember how quickly the news of his death reached us. If you will, the 30th Army never knew another division commander like him: highly professional, wise, strong-willed, and thrifty with respect to each soldier's life.

How happy Andrei Filimonovich would have been had he survived to the end of the war and known that his 215th Rifle Division had become the 215th Red Banner Smolensk Rifle Division, awarded the Orders of Suvorov and Kutuzov! How delighted the general would have been knowing that this combat honorific of the 215th Rifle Division had been bestowed upon it for its role in liberating his native Smolensk.

The Pursuit

After the liberation of Rzhev, our forces kept moving forward, pursuing the Germans as they withdrew from the Rzhev salient. We didn't have time to stop and rest, for it was important not to let the enemy withdraw without hindrance and consolidate in new positions. With constant skirmishing against enemy rear guard units, we advanced, winning back a mutilated and emptied native land. But we also confronted another familiar antagonist. The first warm breath of spring had melted almost all the snow, turning it into slush, and soon the roads turned into a swampy sludge—we marched, barely able to move our feet. Overcoming with unbelievable labors the onset of the spring *rasputitsa* [literally, the dissolution of roads, when the spring thaw turned Russian dirt roads into morasses], the division moved westward, approaching Smolensk.

The land around had been disfigured by the blasts of bombs and shells and had been filled with mines. There was a lot of trouble with the mines, which also slowed our movement. At the same time, we had to lug everything for ourselves—our rifle, cartridges, kit bag, gas mask, sapper's shovel, canteen, and grenades. As we labored to move forward, some men were most surreptitiously ridding themselves of one or another of these items. It was especially hard for the machine gunners, the antitank riflemen, and the mortar crews. Even horses could barely pull their cannons along, which kept getting stuck in the muck. We started off at dawn each morning and slogged along all day. At a short halt we would collapse, hardly finding a place even a bit drier, and our eyes would close of their own accord. But it seemed that no sooner as that happened, someone would be nudging you in the side: "Get up, brother!" and we would march wearily on. We encountered buildings or huts rarely. Forest after forest, road after road—or more precisely, lack of roads.

At first we battled only against rear guard elements. The Germans were retreating quickly, and whenever leaving an area, they left behind a barren wasteland. Whenever they had time to manage it, they blew up, destroyed, torched, or mined everything: "Here you go, Ivan, take your prizes!" The detours— and you couldn't avoid them—were all mined; the roads were also mined, and people occasionally triggered them. Between Gzhatsk and Viaz'ma alone, the Germans blew up fourteen bridges.

Whatever official Russian historians might say, this was one of the best-planned and skillfully conducted withdrawal operations of the entire war. We were unable to trap the German Ninth Army and elements of the Fourth Panzer Army in the Rzhev salient, as had long been our ambition. General Model's forces suffered relatively small losses. Once could not say the same thing about the Soviet forces. Every attempt to fix the German Ninth Army in place during its withdrawal led to fresh casualties in our ranks.

We moved through a scarred, scorched land, which smelled of the smoke of torched structures and the stench of corpses. The Germans still didn't understand anything—neither what they had done nor the approaching retribution! Hearts became filled with hatred for the enemy, and raised voices more frequently declared:"Once we reach your land, you sons of bitches, we're going to pay you back in full!" It was terrible to look at the old men and women, but especially at the children, who were wandering among the piles of ashes that had once been their village. Encountering the victims of this scorched earth policy, our soldiers would give them their last piece of bread, their last biscuit or lump of sugar, their last undershirt or towel; army cooks fed them from the field kitchens. The division would move on, leaving the poor victims behind and carrying away a hatred for the enemy in their hearts.

The division entered Kupriianov's home region, the land around Smolensk. There were frequent engagements against German rear guard units. Then there it was—the village of Golenishchevo, where his grandfather, mother and father lived, and where Andrei Filimonovich was born. As a young boy, from the age of eleven, he had grazed cattle.

By now, in pursuit of the rear guard elements of the retreating adversary, the 31st Army had advanced to the west some 150–160 kilometers in twenty-one days since the liberation of Rzhev, Viaz'ma, and Gzhatsk. But on 24 March, in the area of the villages of Sergeikovo and Pantiukhi, it was forced to stop when it bumped into enemy fortifications. Worn out and weakened by the frequent skirmishes, our units didn't have sufficient strength to go into battle from the march. In anticipation of a counterattack, without even a day's rest, we set to fortifying new positions for ourselves.

We learned on 31 March that the offensive had ground to a halt everywhere along the Western Front's entire line. Smolensk still lay ahead, where according to reconnaissance reports the adversary had already created a firm defense, intending to halt our offensive. The command understood that it was not possible to take Smolensk from the march. We had to let our rear services catch up, but the spring thaw was already here, which badly delayed the movement of supplies. We had to replenish the ranks of the weakened battalions and satisfy the troops' needs for new equipment and ammunition.

It became apparent that by the beginning of summer, a lull had fallen over both sides. We understood this as well as the Germans. However, the difference in the plans of the two sides was great. Our forces fortified their positions as a respite while preparing for a new offensive, and out of concern for a possible enemy counterattack. The German army constructed its defense, knowing for certain that another Russian offensive was unavoidable, and was preparing to defend stubbornly.

The 220th Rifle Division was one of the first to be withdrawn from the front lines into the second echelon. The remnants of its regiments were located in one of the extensive tracts of forest that are numerous in the area around Smolensk. We built dugouts—this we had learned to do quickly, put up our tents, dug slit trenches to serve as bomb shelters, and hid and camouflaged our artillery. I was instructed to build a social club. Due to inexperience, we made the roof too flat, and the next day it collapsed from the rain; we were lucky no one was hurt. In the future, I didn't tackle any more construction work.

When we repaired the building and restored the club to working order, the new division commander, Colonel Vasilii Alekseevich Polevik, visited the regiment. He briefly summarized the results of the March battles: "The division coped with its assigned task. But the losses were significant."

The Telegram

On one of these typical days, the next batch of mail arrived, carrying with it a telegram from my father. The chief doctor of a Moscow hospital had added a concluding note. Father was notifying me that my mama was in the hospital in serious condition. The telegram's text was ominous. What had happened?! Possibly, she was at death's door, or maybe she had already died? I was alarmed. What should I do? How could I help her? There was little chance they'd let me go to Moscow. A leave of absence! No, there was no point even to dream about one; the frontline soldiers had forgotten these words. I showed the telegram to Mikhalych and Stepanych. The Party organizer and agitator saw the matter differently. Mikhalych firmly said:

"You're panicking needlessly; the regiment is in the second echelon. We'll hardly be moving anywhere before summer, so we can get by without you for a week. If necessary, I'll go to Commissar Gruzdev myself. If the regiment commissar won't get involved, go see Commissar Borisov up at the division, he'll help you."

I arranged matters with Gruzdev unexpectedly quickly. Ivan Iakovlevich was for some reason in a fine mood; having heard me out and quickly skimmed the telegram in his hands, he gave approval for a leave. A successful start! Razumovsky, having read the request, also didn't draw out the matter, but he warned me that a regiment commander only had the right to give a leave for no more than three days.

The next hurdle—the division's political department. I had no doubt of Borisov's support. However, Leonid Fedorovich wasn't there when I arrived: he had gone to army headquarters. His deputy, Lieutenant Colonel Kudriavtsev, was filling in for him. Kudriavtsev was a dry, prickly, expert demagogue. This situation complicated matters, but I had no time to wait for Borisov's return, so I went in to see Kudriavtsev. After a few cynical expressions about "precious little son and dear little mama," he completely and to my great surprise made his decision: "On the occasion of his mother's fatal illness . . . nine days of leave in the city of Moscow." I expressed my gratitude to the lieutenant colonel. Parting, he casually uttered, "Bring back from Moscow three bottles of the best vodka—I'm sick of this frontline swill."

Now the final hurdle—deputy division commander for rear services Lieutenant Colonel Khitrov. I knew him—a warm, expansive fellow. Having read the telegram and my request, he summoned his adjutant on the spot and instructed him to fill out all the required documents urgently at division headquarters. Then, having spotted my worn-out boots, he categorically declared, "You want to show up in the capital looking like that?! What will Muscovites think about the army?"

He called his department and ordered them to issue me a pair of boxcalf boots from his personal reserve. Americans had sewn them at the special request of Stalin for senior officers of the Red Army. Leaving, the lieutenant colonel wished me a safe and happy reunion with my mother, then without any modesty added, "Bring me a couple of bottles of 'Khvanchkara' Georgian wine, I've always really wanted to try it. They say it is Stalin's favorite wine."

About two hours later, the adjutant handed me my leave papers, a travel warrant for the train, and a pass, and promised me a ride to Viaz'ma to catch the train. "They'll take you straight to the train," he said, then cheerfully added, "If it's possible, grab a bottle of something for me, too."

15

Moscow
April 1943

On the Way

Next I found myself in Viaz'ma. The city was all torched and demolished. Not a single clear street remained. There was also no train station—only ruins. The platforms were also smashed. We, a small group of officers, were standing in a cleared island amidst the sea of rubble, waiting for a train. All around, the major railroad junction of the Western Front was in noisy operation: steam trains were whistling, trains were coming and going. There was heavy security. The long barrels of antiaircraft guns were poking out everywhere from their emplacements. It was amazing: the Germans had left Viaz'ma on 12 March—it had taken less than a month for our railroad workers to establish the regular operation of supply trains, and they had even laid down a passenger route to Moscow. It is true, however, that the trains still required antiaircraft protection.

At 9:00 P.M., a wonderful little steam engine quietly pulled up in front of us, pulling four passenger cars and a flat car mounting antiaircraft guns. Literally out of thin air, *osobisty* materialized by each car, checking documents. Seemingly everything was in order, and I was permitted to go. Joyfully, greeted by a conductor, I boarded the car. It was a wonder! I was going to Moscow! Right away!

Everything seemed marvelous and new to me, as if this was my first time on a train. It was warm in the car: the windows were thickly curtained. Along the length of the corridor between the seats, pairs of tiny, violet-blue lights softly glowed in the ceiling. I hadn't slept the previous night, so having tossed my kit-bag into the overhead compartment, I took a seat and immediately settled back in it, looking forward at last to catching up on my sleep for the next two days. Then just as quickly, I was hopping to my feet! An enormous military man with colonel's straps on his broad shoulders was standing in front of me, and his deep baritone voice filled the entire cabin:

"Glory be, I've found at least one living being! Huh, I thought they never let a brother leave the front!"

I shot out of my seat in front of the colonel and saluted.

"There, there, now young man, don't be embarrassed," the colonel said in a friendly way. "Allow me to introduce myself: Ivan'kin Semen Zakharovich."

My neighbor seemed fully at ease—plainly, he was used to traveling. He took off his coat, neatly hung it up on a solitary coat hook somewhere above our seats, adroitly placed his forage cap on the same hook, then having combed a few hairs on his head, he hoisted a little suitcase. Responding to his question, I explained the reason for my leave as he pulled a bottle of vodka, two little glasses, and several open-faced sandwiches wrapped in paper out of his travel bag.

"Well, Senior Lieutenant, let's drink up to our acquaintanceship!" Semen Zakharovich cheerfully announced; he already seemed to have been drinking. "Your story characterizes you as an excellent son and testifies to your commanders' high regard for you. It must mean you've earned it! But do you know, Senior Lieutenant, who Andrei Vasil'evich Khrulev is?"

"Of course. He's the chief of the Red Army's food supply service."

"Let's assume that's the case. You see, Colonel Ivan'kin Zakharovich is one of Khrulev's men. Just so you know whose company you are keeping!" [Lieutenant General Andrei Vasil'evich Khrulev was a deputy of the People's Commissariat of Defense and chief of the Main Quartermaster Directorate of the Red Army.]

From our further conversation I understood that the colonel was an important person. It turned out that he was returning from an assignment—for more than a month, he had been traveling around the headquarters and rear areas of the Western and Kalinin Fronts. General Khrulev had sent Ivan'kin on this mission in response to an order from Comrade Stalin, who wanted to look into a complaint.

"Have you heard about Operation Mars?" Ivan'kin asked.

"I've heard of it, but I don't know much about it. Our division didn't take part in it, so we weren't supposed to take any interest in it."

"Really?" Semen Zakharovich was surprised. "Well, then, have a listen. In June 1942, the Novosibirsk Oblast Party Committee appealed to Comrade Stalin with a request for permission to form a volunteer Siberian Corps. Stalin gave his go-ahead. They formed a division in Novosibirsk, while in Krasnoiarsk, Omsk, Tiumen, and Barnaul, they formed four separate rifle brigades. That's how the Sixth Volunteer Stalin Siberian Corps arose, formed around a core of Party and Komsomol members.

"Let's move on. As it happened, from the very first day after their departure from Selizharovo, the volunteers experienced a disaster: the army had forgotten to place the 40,000 troops on rations. For seven days they journeyed toward the front, not receiving any sort of regular food. The command of the 41st

Army passed out up to 400–500 grams [about a pound] of bread a day from its
reserve stocks—that was all! The consequences were catastrophic. Hundreds of
sick men, many of whom could not endure the deprivations, died even before
they reached the front. When the corps finally reached its destination, it was
urgently necessary, with the help of medics, to bring the weakened people back
to health."

Shaken, I quietly listened to Semen Zakharovich.

"Let's go on," the colonel continued. "On 25 November of '42 the corps
was thrown into battle in that same Operation Mars. Marshal Zhukov, first
deputy of the People's Commissariat of Defense, conducted the operation.
Their assignment was to break the enemy's resistance. No way! The soldiers
had been poorly trained, and the corps was full of emaciated, haggardly men. It
ended in disaster: in several days of fighting the corps lost almost 70 percent of
its strength. The Stavka is looking into the losses, and the Supreme Commander
is personally interested in the main thing: to find out just who neglected to
put the Siberians on rations. Commissary chiefs are blaming the commanders, while the commanders in turn are blaming the commissary chiefs: they
say they've been calling about the matter and filing oral reports. But I didn't
uncover any written claims. Even though as you know, you can't do anything
at the front without a piece of paper. Right?"

"That seems to be the case."

"Of course, you're probably interested in why I'm telling you all this. You
see, Senior Lieutenant, it is important for me to know not only what the high
command thinks about this case—I've heard enough of their speeches—but
also what they think of it down in the regiments."

I spoke cautiously, fearing this may be some sort of provocation: "I agree
that a written claim is necessary. But it also happens that a claim does exist,
and it has been filed properly and in time, but still it's no easier for the soldier
because of it, because a response never comes."

Semen Zakharovich pricked up his ears: "Perhaps you are indeed correct,
but to discuss these things in public, as you've seemed to note correctly, 'isn't
proper.'" As you can see, even my Young Pioneer's sincere reply had put him
on guard.

Today I would have answered the colonel differently: don't try to make a
naïve man out of Stalin! The Supreme Commander knew everything—the
horrifying casualties, the soldier's hard life at the front, and even about where a
claim had been filed, and where it had not, and who was the guilty one in this. It
is well known that Stalin received detailed information from the *fronts* through
three channels. *Front* commanders and army commanders told lies: embroider-
ing some things, painting over others. The political organs were gossipers. Iosif
Vissarionovich fully trusted only one agency, and Lavrentii Pavlovich Beria ran

this agency [a reference to the NKVD, the People's Commissariat of Internal Affairs—a predecessor to the KGB].

We tossed down another glass of vodka, having first offered a toast to the Siberians at Semen Zakharovich's suggestion, which seemed to honor him. Then he changed the conversation:

"Come on, Senior Lieutenant, let's talk about peaceful matters. I'm a straightforward fellow and I respect honesty in others. So answer everything truthfully. Are you married?"

"No."

"Do you have any children?"

"No."

"Do you have a girlfriend at the front?"

"No."

"Are you attached to the bottle?"

"Only so far as the 'anesthetic' 100 grams."

"It seems then that you are as clear as glass. The conclusion: a promising future groom! You see, Senior Lieutenant, I have a grown daughter. She has a romantic nature—'Little Blossom,' I call her. She studies in an art academy. She's no plain Jane. She has plenty of admirers, but so far she hasn't found anyone she likes. We live without her mother, Praskov'ia Ivanovna, bless her, who died a year ago. I worry for my daughter. Let's get to the point, we're both adults; let's make sure we understand each other. If you become my son-in-law—I'll pull you out of the front and bring you back to Moscow. You'll make, my man, a fine career, and I'll see that you get into a military academy. Within about ten years, you'll be donning a general's stripes. Little Blossom will be meeting us at the station, so you can see my dear Liudochka and decide for yourself what to do next."

I was in a difficult situation. What a mess! I decided to show restraint for the time being and wait for events to unfold:

"Thank you, Semen Zakharovich. This is somehow most unexpected, excuse me. . . . Perhaps we can sleep on it, since I got no sleep at all last night."

"Were you counting stars?"

"No, I was worried about my mother."

The train pulled into Moscow early in the morning. The "Belorussian" train station was gleaming in the rays of the morning sun. Our documents were checked, and we headed for the exit. Liuda appeared, a likeable, snub-nosed young woman. Her hair fell around her shoulders from beneath a kepi, and she was wearing some unthinkably colorful jacket—the very image of a Futurist of twenty years' age. [Futurism was a major trend in Russian poetry in the early 20th century that pursued a defiantly antitraditional program. Members of the Russian Futurist movement, like Maiakovsky, were often noted for their colorful garb in addition to their radical new poetry.] Suddenly a voice in my head said: "Eh, what kind of nurse would she make on the battlefield?"

The colonel introduced me:

"A man from the front. He's traveled to Moscow for several days to see his sick mother. Take a look, he's a promising fellow."

"Papa, you're always too direct," turning up her little nose, Liuda interrupted.

"By the way," Ivan'kin turned to me, "where is your mother being treated?"

"In the hospital on Durov Street."

"No, really!"—the colonel burst out laughing. "That's right next to the maternity center where Liudushka first appeared on this earth. We'll rush you there in my car."

Within fifteen minutes I was walking into the hospital.

The Meeting

What joy—she was alive! I found out about this right away at the information bureau. As I approached Mama's ward, a young woman in a white medical gown stepped out of it. After gazing intently at me, she smiled:

"Are you the son of Evgeniia Borisovna?"

"Yes, and you are . . ."

"Yes, I'm the doctor in charge of Evgeniia Borisovna. My name is Roza Iakovlevna."

"How's Mama?"

"She's sleeping now. Come with me for a few minutes."

We reached a quadrangular office, which had been built in the center of the second floor at the junction of two corridors. Frosted glass served as its walls. As I understood, this was the post for the doctor on duty. The room had only a small table with a desk lamp and two chairs. I sat down opposite Roza Iakovlevna and began to listen.

"Evgeniia Borisovna came to us in critical condition. For almost a week, she lay on life support. We couldn't establish a diagnosis right away—most likely, it was a serious infection she acquired from a blood transfusion. We considered it necessary to summon you. Now the crisis has passed, but your mother is still very weak. If nothing happens, we'll discharge her in about ten days, so you can take her home."

"Forgive me, doctor," I politely stopped her, "they've only given me a few days' leave from the front. I'm very touched by your concern over Mama. Will you permit me to see her?"

"Of course. When your mother arrived here, she immediately started talking about you, told us a lot about your life, showed us photographs, and read us your letters. She's very proud of you."

I very quietly entered the ward, sat down on a stool next to my mother, and started to wait patiently. Seven pairs of eyes of the other women lying in the ward looked at me. Likely, Mama sensed my presence; she opened her eyes but couldn't recognize me immediately, and she wiped her eyes with her hand a few times.

"My son, my dear" she reached out for me—"how did you wind up here?"

"Mamochka! First tell me what you were dreaming, then I'll unveil my secret."

Mama broke into tears and began kissing my hands; they were the tears of unbridled joy.

"I was dreaming of the golden fish, and I asked it to help me see my son before I died" [a reference to a famous Russian fairy tale about a golden fish that can grant wishes].

"Now you see, I'm together with you! Why die? Live on, Mamochka!"

"My brave officer! It seems now they're praising you so highly? What happiness to see you alive, healthy, and strong!"

We spoke for more than an hour. I told her about myself and my comrades and joked a little. Roza Iakovlevna interrupted our meeting when she entered the room.

"And here's our angel, Roza Iakovlevna, my young savior! She takes good care of all of us."

"Evgeniia Borisovna, it is time to rest," the doctor said.

I submitted to the doctor's instruction. Parting, Mama asked:

"Does Papa know about your arrival?"

"Not yet. I came from the train station directly to see you. I'll come back tomorrow. Shall I bring you something? What would you like?"

"Thank you, dear son, I don't need anything."

As I walked out, all seven women suddenly started applauding me. It was quite unexpected and touching. I bowed to the entire ward. What amazing neighbors Mama had: not one of them asked me a single question about their own dear ones, though likely many of them had husbands and sons at the front. With such thoughts I went outside.

Moscow of 1943

Before me lay the city of Moscow. What joy! Mama is alive! Soon I will see my father! I'll meet my friends! My head was spinning with happiness. I hadn't seen the city in almost two years. Moscow had gone through so much in that time! It had withstood the hell of bombers. A heroic city! For the first time in the entire war—it was precisely Moscow that had stopped the fascist hordes. Not a single capital in mainland Europe had managed to do that! With stupid stubbornness Hitler had promised daily: "Tomorrow Moscow will become

German!" But it desired to remain Russian! Muscovites had stood up for themselves. More accurately, the entire country had fought and stood up for Moscow!

The sun was shining; I walked through the streets of Moscow, filling my chest with the spring Moscow air. I went down Durov Street to the boulevard. I went past Durov's Corner, the joy of Moscow's children, and headed for Samotechnaia Square.

The Theater of the Red Army—I couldn't recognize it! For purposes of camouflaging this tall, monumental building in the shape of a five-pointed star, architects and artists had turned it into either a forest or some sort of garden. How did they manage to do this? Unbelievable!

Now here's Central Market, full of people and food. What didn't they have here! Milk, potatoes, meat and lard, vegetables. . . . They also sold watches, firewood, books, clothing, needles and thread, and soap here. But at what prices!

"Have you no shame?"—the words burst out from me.

Glancing at my officer's shoulder straps, the collective farm women in their white peasant shawls lowered their prices a little.

I purchased a scrawny chicken, three tomatoes, five cucumbers, and half a kilogram of cottage cheese—and I had to pay 1,000 rubles! Three kilograms of potatoes cost 300 rubles; a liter of milk, 80 rubles. For a pair of second-hand boots, you had to pay 2,000 rubles. Not so great watches could be acquired for 1,500 rubles each. Most of the customers crowded around enormous bags of potatoes, which had plainly been brought from some place far away.

Now for home! I heard the touchingly familiar ring of a tram not far away—"Annushka"! Muscovites swore mightily at trams, saying that they ran without timetables, or that people were forced to wait too long for one, but I loved to travel on them, especially when I took "Annushka" home from Samotek Street to Sretenka Street, one of my favorite streets. But this time I decided to go on foot. I threw my kitbag, now holding the food I had purchased, over my shoulder and set off on my way, humming my favorite little tune, "On the Tom-cat and the Cow." Proud of the provisions I had acquired, I emerged onto Sadovoe Kol'tso, looking around as I walked, not wanting to miss a single sign, shop window, or street poster. Everything became cause for reflection; everything was important and interesting to see and remember.

Back at the front I had imagined that I would find a city without people—so many people had died for it, so many had been evacuated, and the hunger, the bombing raids! (Later I found out that in 1941 alone, more than two million residents had been evacuated; that is, half the city's population.) But the city was full of people; I attentively peered at the passers-by: how they had all changed—their expressions, their gait, their clothing, even their footwear. The civilians were dressed in identical fashion and badly: many men and women were wearing padded trousers, jackets, and work overalls; on their feet, almost all of them were wearing rubber footwear: boots, overshoes, and galoshes.

There were an unusually large number of servicemen out on the streets. Many of them, most likely, were staffers: their faces showed self-confidence, and they looked well fed. Their uniforms were spotless and crisply pressed, and they all seemed to be rushing somewhere; in the capital, you could compile a whole book from their service addresses: the Stavka, the General Staff, the Ministry of Defense, the Main Political Administration, the People's Kommissariat of Internal Affairs, the colossal commissary apparatus, the Main Aviation Administration, and antiaircraft defense. Another category of officers on the street was people who had been discharged from hospitals. There were dozens of hospitals in Moscow, and it was noticeable how the discharged former patients leisurely strolled around the capital, soaking up the spring air and sunshine, happy to be back on their feet and to find themselves unexpectedly in the capital—another day or week, and they'd again be heading back to the front.

I dropped into several stores. All the conversations in them revolved around food. Presently they were distributing food according to ration coupons, but it often happened that there was nothing you could get for your coupons, often for several weeks in a row. Dependants were receiving practically nothing— only bread and salt. Vodka was sold only to those with special coupons they had received for good work. However, in the stores you could freely quench your thirst with as much hot water as you wanted.

Around the newsstands—there were now more of them on the streets— people continuously gathered, reading over each other's shoulders, discussing the latest news, and lambasting the Allies for dragging their feet in opening a second front; someone even hurled the vile accusation "Saboteurs!" at them. Everywhere around the city were mounted and foot patrols; they were especially frequent in the city center and around the train stations. As I made my way home, I was stopped twice. Moscow was still a closed city, and it would likely remain that way for a long time to come.

New Impressions

Father opened the door. He had been expecting me, because Roza Iakovlevna had notified him of my arrival in Moscow. We spoke until evening. He told me that while he was in Kyshtym, temporary residents who had settled into our apartment in Kuskov had burned his entire library, down to the last book.

"What can you do? A cartload of firewood costs 400–500 rubles; people were burning whatever they could find in order somehow to survive the hard times. Many buildings still have no heat, and in many apartments and establishments, homemade stoves have appeared. A strict limit on electricity has been established, and with the onset of spring the power outages have become more frequent. The capital still keeps a strong, albeit somewhat lighter, ring of antiair-craft defenses around it—the Americans have helped."

In the evening I began to call my friends. I was able to reach only Mark Podobedov, and I invited him to meet me at a famous and popular restaurant the next day.

Mark and I feasted at the commercial restaurant Aragvi. We each ordered a Jewish salad—a few green lettuce leaves plus three or four olives—a tasty Russian porridge with cracklings, and a bottle of Borzhom mineral water. We each drank 50 grams of vodka. For this meal, I had to pay 1,000 rubles.

Mark told me that in 1942 things had become easier in the city, chiefly because the fear of Moscow's capture had subsided. But the cold, hungry winters became a test for all the citizens. In the hardest times, famished people had boiled potato peelings and the soft inner layer of bark; they steeped pine needles and additional ingredients to make a vitamin drink. They slept in sweaters and socks, even in outer garments, under two or three blankets. Not everyone managed to survive this terrible time. People who had been exempted from military service underwent constant inspection of their status. They were beginning to recruit previously exempted categories: "We'll find a place even for you in the army," the local military commissars were saying in persuasion.

"They've twice tried to get me to enlist," Mark said. "But with my heavy asthma, where could I go?"

Exiting the restaurant, we walked down to Gorky Street just as we used to do, and there we parted: Mark had to hurry to report for a chemical defense exercise. At the time, all of Moscow was preparing in case of a chemical attack from the enemy; young and old alike were studying the brochure "Be Prepared for Chemical Defense!" It was all nonsense; the Germans would never use chemical weapons. In response, the Allies in just one day would have reduced Germany into an utter graveyard. Even Hitler understood this.

I stopped for a short time on Pushkin Square. Here children were playing war around the statue to the poet, just as they used to do. But how had the character of their games changed! They were now not splitting into "Reds" and "Blues," now it was all different: there was "Ours"—their favorites, and "Fascists"—the opposing, evil, despised killers of their grandfathers, fathers, and older brothers. Just think, how even the little children's perception of life had changed! They no longer wanted to learn childhood songs, to make little animals or figures out of plasticine, to play the piano, to skip and jump. While playing in the sand or drawing on paper, children were shooting down hostile airplanes, knocking out fascist tanks, sinking their ships, or taking prisoners. In these games, the terrible excesses of war had permeated the still-developing mind of the child and become a major theme in his or her daily life.

I walked along Gorky Street to the Belorussian Station, took the No. 12 trolley bus, and rode it to the Central Station. Along the way, passengers told me that in 1941, trolley buses had transported wounded soldiers from the front lines by this route.

The entrance to Red Square was closed, but I managed to spot the imitation of a three-story private residence that had been built to conceal Lenin's Tomb. Only quite recently had I learned that a sarcophagus carrying Lenin's body had been transported to Tiumen back in 1941. How many times had we students, training in the Tiumen special school, marched past the building in which Lenin's sarcophagus was resting, singing our march songs, but none of us even guessed it at the time.

Large models of city buildings were arranged along the Kremlin's walls. The same sort of wooden or plywood structures filled Red and Manezhnaia Squares. I hoped to enjoy the sight of the gleaming golden cupolas of the Kremlin's main cathedrals, but I didn't see them—for camouflage, all the cupolas had been painted over with black paint, while the red stars on the towers of the Kremlin and the all the crosses on the cathedrals were tightly wrapped in canvas. The Kremlin's buildings were disguised by paint to look like apartment blocks from overhead. From the Borovitsky to the Spassky Gates, a sandy artificial road had been laid down—from high above, it looked like a highway. This "camouflage smock" did much to save Russia's sacred place from bombing raids. According to rumors, only a few bombs still managed to fall on the Kremlin's grounds. During the first raid, a 250-kg bomb fell on the Great Kremlin Palace, penetrated the roof and the ceiling of Georgievsky Hall, but didn't explode: it crashed into the floor and broke into pieces, having created a large crater in the parquet. Other bombs left no particular damage to the buildings, but they did kill people.

What a great blessing that the Germans didn't take Moscow! By order of Hitler, according to military prisoners, a special sapper team had been organized with the order to demolish the Kremlin down to its foundations. Napoleon also didn't manage to ruin the Kremlin, although he had issued a similar order.

I went down into the metro and took the subway around all the stations from Revolution Square to the Pokrovsky Gates. It was an unusual feeling—literally as if I had fallen into some enchanted underground kingdom. But the passengers seemed to pay no notice to the marvel—gloomy, stern-faced, many with knapsacks on their backs or brief cases and bags under their shoulders. Some were standing with loaded little carriages.

Nelia

How quickly time passes—almost half of my leave was over! At the front, it always felt like time passed at a snail's pace. On the fourth day of my leave, my mother received her discharge from the hospital, and father and I took her home. That evening, Mama organized a small tea party, to which she had invited Nelia, the daughter of my father's friend Vladimir L'vov.

Nelia was Mama's surprise for me; she had already mentioned her back at the hospital and had told me about her family. Nelia's father had separated from his wife and had brought back his two little girls together with a Moscow beauty; having met L'vov, this woman had left her husband, an important general, in the rear. Mama had said:

"You'll see Nelia. She's a medical institute student. A charming, modest, respectable young woman. Father and I were terribly concerned that you would fall in love with some frontline slut and bring her home with you."

"Oh, Mamochka," I retorted, "such affairs don't turn into marriages right away."

"Oh, yes, they can! Aren't your father and I a contrary example to what you're saying?"

Now the designated evening had arrived. Mama drew a bottle of tasty fruit liqueur from her untouchable reserves. Nelia arrived on time and immediately commanded general attention, adorning our evening with her presence. She made us laugh with amusing medical stories and anecdotes, displaying her turbulent energy, cheerful disposition, direct rapport, and inexhaustible wit—with no trace of vulgarity. In general, we shared a lot of laughs and spent a pleasant evening together.

There was a lot to like about Nelia, but for some reason she just didn't "grab" me. I accompanied her home. Walking slowly, Nelia told me about her institute and Moscow life:

"They're enlisting more and more doctors for the front, so many of the senior students are being drawn into the hospitals to work. So far, even though the siege situation has been removed, the curfew that was introduced in 1941 remains in effect. From midnight until 6:00 in the morning, the city stands still: people hide in their apartments, the squares and streets become empty, and the lights are turned off—such a darkness falls over the city that the floors of buildings are indistinguishable from the pavement; people are falling and crippling themselves and getting lost on the way home. They had to paint the lampposts and pavement curbs white so people wouldn't stumble into them and trip over them."

I could see traces of this white paint on the streets.

Like all Muscovites with whom I spoke, Nelia particularly remembered one night—New Year's Eve, 1943—when the curfew had been lifted:

"On that night many people, off their rockers with joy, celebrated the holiday right on the streets, in the squares, and on the boulevards. And now rumors are circulating that they're going to lift the curfew for Passover too, and every-body's waiting impatiently for it."

Signs of the war were evident at every step. The windows of buildings still bore large "Xs" of paper tape. We often passed signs indicating bomb shelters or blood collection stations. Above the building numbers and in the entrances, the normal light bulbs had been replaced by dark-blue light bulbs, but even they, as Nelia explained, were lit only until midnight. In the evening hours, just as before, strict light controls were still in effect. Volunteer teams took turns at night, standing watch in case of fires. All vehicular headlights were still equipped with masking nets: if the headlights were on, the nets had to be lowered. The net muffled the headlight beam, so it projected only a barely visible, narrow strip of light on the road ahead. By now it seemed the need for all this had passed.

Along the way, Nelia stopped me several times next to buildings and told me curious stories about the places, which previously I had passed repeatedly, not paying any attention to them. I had not thought earlier about any of the things Nelia told me; walking with her, within just an hour I had learned quite a bit new.

We were walking down toward Samotek when Nelia pointed at a dark, three-story building situated on a small hillock:

"Here's where the famous Anatomical Theater has been standing now for more than a hundred years. Who hasn't visited this theater, how many specta-tors hasn't this 'Anatomic' known! . . . Now, it's true, it is called the Institute of Legal Medicine."

"You also visit it?" I asked.

"Of course, for students it is compulsory."

We stopped by a building on Kaliaevskaia Street.

"I live here," said Nelia. "This building was constructed in the 1930s for the Soviet and Party elite according to a design by American architects. In 1937, all its residents were shot. Out of two hundred apartments, they left only five alone." Suddenly she remembered: "Oh, it's almost curfew!"

The time had flown by imperceptibly, and, of course, we had lost track of the curfew. I became worried: I didn't want to take any chances—people were saying that they dragged the detained people away and held them in custody all night, together with prostitutes, and that they'd only start looking into each case the next morning.

"Don't worry," Nelia calmed me, as we entered her home, "call home and spend the night here. We're used to it; now every family keeps a camp bed. But we'll let you have my bed, so let's go to my room."

A beautiful, majestic woman entered the room after us.

"Galusha," Nelia introduced her stepmother.

We greeted each other.

"I'll make your bed up on the divan in the dining room," the lady of the house proposed.

"No, no," Nelia began to protest, "I myself will sleep on the divan, and we'll let the guest sleep in my room. He'll be more comfortable there, and in the morning he won't trouble anyone and can sleep as long as he'd like."

The general's lady nodded once in approval and left us alone in Nelia's room.

"Remember, my friend!" Nelia suddenly pronounced pathetically, "When you become a general, the most beautiful woman will run away from you, if you display any rudeness to her and don't rid yourself of your rough soldierly habits. Especially if she meets a man like my father—the highest sort of intellectual and such a wise man."

The further events unfolded like a bad joke. Nelia left and returned with a full bottle of liquor, two glasses, and a box of crackers from the dining room.

"Well, frontline soldier, let's drink to the occasion!"

I hadn't managed to deal with the first glass, which was setting my insides on fire, when she poured up a second. I thought, "What's her hurry? And why is she only pretending to drink, and diluting her own hard liquor with water?" The liquor kicked like a mule! But I, devil take it, wanted to show off!

After the second glass, I could feel I was becoming tipsy and my brain was becoming foggy. I pronounced some incongruous, utterly nonsensical words, and Nelia laughed boisterously. Glancing over my decorations, she twirled the medal "For Courage" in her hands and said seductively:

"Such a brave officer, so many combat honors, but with a woman—a frightened little bunny."

After these taunting words, I went on the attack, and began to unbutton her blouse—and then I promptly passed out on the spot. I couldn't remember a thing afterward.

They took off my boots, undressed me, and tucked me into bed. But I only understood this the next morning. Oh God, what had I done! Humiliation and shame!

That's how my first night with a presumed fiancée turned out.

When I finally woke up, Nelia wasn't home. A note was lying on the nightstand: "Farewell! Consider everything that happened as a joke. Call me after three days. We have been invited to a birthday party for my best friend Elena. You'll find it interesting. We'll meet at 5:00 P.M. Buy some flowers for Lenka [a diminutive form of Elena] at the market."

Not a single warm word. Incidentally, did I really deserve any?

The Party

Nelia and I were a little late. Along the way, Nelia had time to tell me about where we were going and the woman of the house.

"Lenka's father is a diplomat, some bigshot. Whenever Olga and I are feeling famished, we call and rush over to Lenka's house; she always feeds us. We call her Princess."

The guests were already sitting around the table, impatiently waiting for us. The hostess introduced me, seated me next to herself, and introduced her friends. Olia and Igor' were Lena's [another diminutive form of Elena] classmates; they were young and made a great couple. Filipp was a gifted journalist who was being published in all the central newspapers.

Toasts followed one after the other. We drank to Lena, to her parents, and to student friendship. As I quickly understood, these were people who had known each other for a long time, and who valued their old friendships; they talked about each other in enthusiastic tones. But of course, Lena, the hostess, ruled the room. Literally—a "princess"! Nature had bestowed her with many gifts. She was lively, fascinating, and behaved simply, without any affectations or coquettishness. The company around the table wholeheartedly admired her, and it was noticeable that this universal admiration gave her a sense of personal satisfaction and pride. I also raised my glass to her:

"Let's drink to a charming woman! To Elena, who everyone admires! Consider me one of them!"

Lena clinked glasses with me and immediately began to address me with the intimate "*ty.*" [The Russian language still adheres to the distinction long ago abandoned in the English language between the intimate "thou" (*ty*) and the formal "you" (*vy*).]

The evening was a success. Everyone felt unfettered and danced and joked. When I was dancing with Nelia, she asked: "Do you like Lena?"

I didn't hide my feelings: "Very much!"

"Today a surprise is waiting for us," Nelia added. "Lenka's mother is coming; she just returned from evacuation."

I had already learned from my father that the top executives of the factories and the State Committees had been permitted to bring their wives back to Moscow.

Filipp held everyone's attention when conversation turned to our allies and the long awaited second front.

"When at last will our allies decide they want to get moving?" Lena exclaimed with anger.

"I think most likely it will only be next year," Filipp said. "It is sad to say, but Churchill announced that they would not succeed in opening a second front on the European continent this year." Here, Filipp stopped and told an anecdote: "Two Muscovites are standing before a post, which has been totally pasted over with theater posters. On all of them, in large, bold lettering, it was printed: 'A. Korneichuk. The Front.' One man says: 'That's an absolute must; simultaneously in the four best theaters!' The second replies: 'The Allies can't even find a way to open a second front, while we Muscovites have opened four at the same time!'"

"Who has seen Leonov's 'The Invasion'? They say it has been nominated for a Stalin prize."

No one had seen it, but Olia said, apparently, what everybody was thinking: "I've heard 'The Invasion' is a weak play, worse than Korneichuk's masterpiece, 'The Front.'"

Nelia resolutely started to protest: "I got two tickets to the Moscow Art Theater; tomorrow I'm going with Boris to see Leonov's production."

At this point, the topic of conversation changed to one that I realized was very important to the citizens of Moscow. Igor asked me:

"What do you think, will the Germans bomb Moscow again?"

"I don't think so," I replied. "The Germans have been quite busy with other matters since Stalingrad, and I don't believe they're even thinking about Moscow now."

Filipp interceded. He said that according to rumors, in the last month Stalin had sent for the generals of the Moscow air defenses four times, demanding that not a single enemy airplane appear over Moscow. He was angered back in March when fascist aviation had twice tried to break through to Moscow. Our antiaircraft gunners shot down fifteen of the 100 airplanes that were flying toward Moscow.

Rumors, rumors. I came to the conclusion that the Germans must have bombed Moscow heavily. As I now understood, Moscow was living according to rumors, which reminded me of the "soldier's telegraph" back at the front. In both cases, the cause was probably the same: the absence of timely and reliable information.

Sitting next to me, Nelia quietly said, "Filipp is a colorful figure, a well-known ballet lover. But in general, he's a braggart and a poser."

That was precisely my opinion too. Why had he grown a mustache? It didn't help his appearance at all. But the general fashion everywhere now, not just in Moscow, was a mustache "a la Stalin."

Filipp, likely just to distract the gathering, idly asked:

"What's new at the front?"

"Oh you, vermin," I thought to myself. I grew angry; the front was not just some post papered over with theater notices! I answered in the same tone:

"Since the New Year, they started distributing field blouses without pockets to the soldiers."

Everyone understood my response, but it didn't seem to embarrass Filipp.

Lena treated us to some real British tea; I had never had such a tasty cup of tea before. We all got ready to leave, and Filipp regaled the guests, apparently, with a previously prepared plum:

"I've heard that *Pravda* will soon be printing Sholokhov's 'They Fought for the Motherland.' It's a promising title . . ."

In the corridor, we spent a long time saying our goodbyes, kissing each other, and thanking the hostess. Then suddenly she approached me, and showing no embarrassment in front of the other guests, she began to unbutton my coat and declared in a commanding voice:

"But you, Senior Lieutenant, will stay here to wash the dishes."

Confused by her action, I glanced at Nelia. She imperturbably supported her friend:

"It's the hostess's birthday; you should do what she wants."

The guests broke out laughing, and Olia joked:

"Lenka's in her repertoire."

"But how will you get home alone?" I turned to Nelia.

"Filipp will escort me."

I remained alone with Lena.

Elena the Beautiful

The lady of the house led me into the kitchen, then left, as it turned out, to change clothes. Meanwhile I neatly washed and dried every dish—Saxon porcelain! Suddenly Lena was standing next to me in a carefully contemplated short gown. She threw on a beautiful apron in front of me, then carefully started washing the no less precious stemware and glasses: old monogrammed wine glasses and drinking glasses.

"Why are you trembling? You're not at the front, you know."

"I don't shake at the front."

She laughed, and then—what clumsiness!—a dinner plate slipped from my hands and fell to the floor. Only shattered fragments remained of the Saxon porcelain. I blushed and began to apologize, anticipating a stern scolding, but she started laughing again:

"For the broken plate—two extra shifts on duty! It seems that's the accepted punishment for the guilty in the army? Now go and take a bath, you're just from the lice-ridden trenches. You'll find some pajamas there. In the morning you'll clean up the apartment and take out the trash."

When I entered the bedroom after my bath and turned on the light, the first thing that caught my eye was a small book with a wine-red cover, which was lying on a nightstand next to the bed. I opened it: a Bible! In English! Published in London! She's a religious woman? She knows English?

Lena came into the room. She had let her hair down, everything was somehow special, and the scent of her marvelous perfume enveloped me—she seemed like a goddess to me!

"Come on, Officer, Sir, straight to bed!"

I obeyed. Lena herself spread out a little rug on the floor, got down on her knees, and started to pray before an icon. How had I failed to notice it? Then she read aloud in English from the Bible, and the light was turned off. A "Niagara waterfall" of sensations poured over me—I forgot about everything else on earth and took pleasure in our togetherness; I never wanted this special night to end, when for the first time in my life I came to know a woman.

At dawn the next day, I was still dozing, but suddenly woke up with a start. Lena, tired, was still sleeping. I looked at her luxuriant red hair, which lay scattered across the pillow, her sleek, beautiful arms—and admired this natural wonder. How strange—this woman had just coincidentally and suddenly entered my life, and in just one night she had managed to make a man from a boy!

Shurka had been right when he placed a woman's beauty and woman's love above all else—above books, soccer, anything! Yet together with this, a vague thought wandered into my mind. Likely, my torrid night with Lena had not been love at all, but passion. An overwhelming passion! But who will judge me and cast the first stone? In my worship of it I had experienced heightened feelings, an almost sacred service to beauty. That night I was Suvorov himself!

Lena, who by now had opened her eyes, stretched out to me:

"God save you; this disgusting war, how many lives has it warped and ruined? Who can explain why people have been killing each other for thousands of years? Even Homer in front of Athens raised criticism toward Aries, the God of War, calling him 'an infernal madman.'"

"You know Homer?"

"No, my dear, I like his verse. Homer was a sage poet of ancient Greece. I advise you to read his poems, if only once in your life—they are the work of a philosopher."

"Great," I managed to say. "Lenochka, last night I heard that you were praying for some Fedia. Who is this man?"

"I'll satisfy your curiosity. I have a husband. We met two years ago, before the war. At the time, Fedia was finishing his studies at the Institute of Military Translators. Now he's at the front, and every blessed day I pray for his safety. But with you, dear, I'm in sin. I adore sex. Especially with such young men like you. But you can't understand this. A person is a being, born for faith, but you, my dear, are an atheistic communist, and therefore you're not capable of understanding my honest repentance before the Almighty."

"You're not fully correct, I also have faith. At the front, just like here, those people live easily who live according to the principle 'war hurries everything.' But I adhere to a different principle: war doesn't forgive."

When I left, we touchingly said our good-byes. Lena made the sign of the cross over me. I gave her the beautifully carved little wooden cross that Mavrii had given me.

The next day, as I accompanied Nelia to the show, we had a conversation.

"My friend, I won't force you to marry me," Nelia said. "Just think of me as your 'might have been wife.' Poor Evgeniia Borisovna, she is distressed."

"Can you forgive me for staying with Lena? You yourself placed me in an ambiguous position."

"Go on with you! On the contrary, I'm happy for you. Soon you will be returning to the front, and how your fate will turn out is unknown. If Lena bestowed some joy upon you—splendid! I think you'll understand me if I cite a few lines of Simonov to you:

And those, whose time has come in battle
And who will have little chance to live until dawn,
It will still be easier for him if he can recall that yesterday
Someone's hands were caressing him.

Nelia continued:

"You are honest and decent, but still green—both in spirit and in mind. Don't get angry about what I've said, it's the truth. Shoulder straps and medals decorate you, but you still have a lot to learn. You don't know how to appreciate and love a woman. Think of Pushkin—he placed a woman on the highest pedestal. But you . . . within a month, you'll forget about both Lena and me (unfortunately, it seems I forgot about both of them sooner than that). Don't be upset, you're still quite young. If things become tough for you, write!"

I quite uneasily heard out Nelia's monologue. I was unsettled; was this really my portrait? Many years would pass before I understood the true sense of what Nelia had said, and the kindness of her words.

A Manly Talk

On the seventh day of my leave, Father's friends invited us to the restaurant in the House of Architects. Close friends gathered around the table, all of them experiencing the delight of the friendly meeting. An unusual event was waiting for us: the famous artist Aleksandr Vertinsky and his beautiful wife were sitting at the table next to us. They had just recently returned from living abroad. Their two little girls were playing on the carpet around their table. Both later became actresses.

Someone of those sitting around our table said: "Moscow is full of rumors about Vertinsky. They're enticing emigrants to come back one by one, promising them God knows what, and they're presenting Count Aleksei Tolstoy as an example. But so far, only Vertinsky among the 'big birds' has decided to return. Rumors are circulating that Kuprin is also planning to return. But Bunin has been inflexible. The return of the emigrants to Russia is big politics and a delicate matter."

After the meeting, Father suggested we take a little walk, and while we walked, we talked.

"You've grown up, matured," Papa said. "You're a fine fellow for writing Mama frequently. Your letters for her are like the air itself she needs to live. We congratulate you as well on your money voucher. (After the war, when I returned home in 1946, the news simply stunned me that since 1942—the year I received the voucher—my parents hadn't touched a kopeck of it.)

"In turn, Papa, I'm proud of your Kyshtym feat."

"Don't exaggerate. In my opinion, you're the star. Just think, you volunteered for the army. I approved of your decision, even though I understood that you'd soon wind up at the front. You passed your first test as a cadet at the Tiumen military school. Your second test—at the front: you became an officer. Is it hard for you there?"

"Sometimes. But I've already gotten used to it. I've been wounded twice."

"You didn't write about that."

"I was protecting Mama."

"What's been the hardest thing?"

"Probably the first battle. From the company, only eight of us remained to answer the next roll call. It is thought that as the regiment's *komsorg*, I'm a little farther from the front lines, but in reality, not always so. The regiment's two prior *komsorg* officers and four battalion-level *komsorg* have perished. But, Papa, the front is not only fighting."

What could I say to my father? Could I really explain that worst of all was the condition of uninterrupted stress and the endless heavy physical labor? There were also the fear of death, the death of comrades, the mutilated people—when the pain and suffering exceeds all possible limits, and when a man, no longer capable of enduring the torment, prays about one thing: "It would be better if I died." There were also the hunger, the cold, the unbearable heat, and the sleeping in snow, in filth, in standing water. The complex relationships between subordinates and the command. But the front is also the priceless soldiers' comradeship, and the faith in the weapon in your hands. There were, of course, two more circumstances; they were both outside the general list. One was the high feeling of military duty to the Motherland. But on the other hand, there was treachery.

Now I think: how can a man endure all of this? Probably, our youth helped us. In his or her youth a person is stronger and more adaptable; it is easier for him or her to adjust to circumstances. Yes, only youth permitted us to withstand and to cope with this hell.

"I want to speak with you about one vital question." Papa lit up his next cigarette. "Your Mama asked me about this. You are now at the age when any young woman can seem special. I ask that you understand us correctly: don't hurry with your choice and with marriage. You must finish your education, acquire a profession, and find your place in life. As long as I'm healthy, I will try to help you. There are so many shattered fates—young people hurry and then repent. Don't be offended; children more often than adults wind up in difficult situations, seek a way out—and easily yield to suggestions."

"I'm no longer a child, Papa."

"Not for Mama and me. Well, fine, let's not speak more about this. What do you think of Moscow?"

"Honestly speaking, not very much. Everywhere, people introduce me as a man from the front, but not once has anyone seriously taken interest in our frontline matters: how we fight, what we think about, how we live. It seems to me that Moscow is endlessly remote from the front; it is a completely different world, a military bureaucracy."

"You're incorrect," my father interrupted. "If everything was as you maintain, the front wouldn't hold out even one day. According to your logic, even I'm a bureaucrat."

"I understand that life is hard for everybody, even for those in the rear. But these endless conversations about firewood, ration cards, limits, searches for a piece of soap, and the street lighting irritate me. There is a war going on!"

"Again you're wrong. Yes, there is the war. But it is precisely the rear that frees the front from many concerns. And a man can't live without sustenance. It is very hard for people to have no light, no heating. Have you noticed that all the fences have disappeared in Moscow?"

We had reached our house, and Father said:

"Nonetheless, I'm happy that I've encountered not that youth whom I escorted to the station back in December 1941, but rather an almost grown man. How much your mother and I want to wait it out and to see you return from war. Of course, as a victor."

"You forgot to add: as a bachelor too!"

Father burst out laughing.

The Farewell Evening

The eighth day of my leave was ending. The next morning, I would leave for the train station and . . .

My parents prepared a farewell dinner. L'vov and Nelia, and Khannan Zatuchny, an old friend of my father's, came; an old family friend, Lev Korostyshevsky, arrived from Tula—as always, unexpectedly. Mama invited Roza. The evening before, I had traveled to the commissary store and obtained dry rations for nine days, including some American products; they made an excellent supplement for the table.

The evening, thanks to L'vov, turned out to be special and very cordial, although it was also sad. I found out that Korostyshevsky's son Senia, my childhood friend, had been killed in the first days of the war, on the western border. I also didn't rejoice over the rapidly approaching parting from my parents.

Zatuchny, seizing the initiative from L'vov, plunged into a discussion of the second front:

"Everyone wants for the Allies to land forces on the European continent as soon as possible. But the Allies aren't ready for this operation. It is well known how the raid on Dieppe in 1942 ended—with enormous losses. But what, are the Allies sitting idly by and waiting while the Germans and we mow each other down, as the majority believes?

"Here is my answer. Gradually increasing its strength in England, the Americans and British have invaded North Africa and at El-Alamein, they have destroyed a 300,000-man army of Italians and Germans. Practically speaking, this victory meant the collapse of the German blitzkrieg on the Suez Canal. More than 270,000 men have been taken prisoner, and Field Marshal Rommel himself barely managed to steal away on an airplane. [Of course, this is how Zatuchny understood the events in North Africa at the time.] The significance of this victory is being hushed up in our press."

Zatuchny continued:

"The plans of the Allies? I'll give you an answer. Their next move from Africa? Most likely to Sicily. From there, plainly, to Italy and then to France. I think that is the approximate strategic plan of the Allies. Do the Germans know this? They know, but they cannot handle the air and naval might of the Allies. Armadas of American and British planes are daily bombing Germany, turning German cities into ruins and disrupting their communications. Tell me, really, is this not war with our common enemy—fascism?"

Having finished what was in practical terms an entire lecture, which compelled the guests to push away from their food and listen attentively, Zatuchny turned to me:

"What does a man from the front think about my conception of the situation?"

"I'm not offering a reproach, but while they work out their strategic plans, every year, day, and hour of the war's continuation mean more and more sacrifices. Primarily ours! Is this just? The opening of a second front is a concern for everyone—in the rear and at the front. But the matter is being dragged out."

But the talkative Zatuchny had already moved on to a different topic.

"Where are we headed?" he asked profoundly, raising his right hand. "From socialist ideals to pan-Slavism. From the Soviet model of life—to service of the Fatherland. From Red commanders—to officers and soldiers with Tsarist shoulder straps. The bells in newly reopened churches in Russia are pealing ever more loudly."

I hadn't thought deeply about the details of Stalinist policy; I only knew that Moscow had recently held a World Assembly of Slavic Peoples.

Nelia and I went out to have a smoke on the staircase landing. For all the days of my stay in Moscow, I hadn't smoked a single cigarette; but today, worrying and hoping for a meeting with Roza, I lit one up. Nelia and I again argued.

"Your father told me that you are rebuking Muscovites as if they're not interested in life at the front, and called this narrow-mindedness. Is this true?" Nelia asked.

"It's true!" I stubbornly confirmed.

"That's a shame! You really don't understand how tired people have become. Look at these drawn, sallow faces, these hunched figures, the sagging women's breasts, and I'm not speaking about their clothing. The people are giving everything they can to the front: husbands, sons, daughters, spiritual and physical strength—but the end of the war is still not in sight. Don't judge the life of the average Muscovite by Lena's example; Lena is washing cucumbers daily, though one cucumber costs twenty rubles at the market.

"But the young people! They are in a terrible situation! They work twelve-hour shifts at the factory—with no days off, without normal sleep and a normal diet. Horrible housing conditions; millions of people are living in barracks. Yet every night all these children stand watch on the rooftops . . . but their youth is passing! And what of the girls! They want love, a personal life, to wear nice lingerie, and not the same poorly washed bra she must keep wearing over and over again, and to have just one pair of undarned stockings. I'm not even talking about a bar of soap or perfumes—those are beyond the wildest dreams! But it is worst of all for old people; they are dying like flies! But everyone keeps making patriotic appeals to us."

Stricken, I listened to Nelia silently, like a man without a tongue, and thought: who of us is right? Of course, it was hard for a frontline soldier to understand how the home front was living. But it was also hard for people in the rear to understand us, the frontline soldiers. What was going on with all of us? I suddenly wanted to change the subject, to end this unpleasant conversation, so I asked:

"Why did you take me to see Leonov's play?"

"In the press, they are calling the play the most serious comment on the war; I thought it would be interesting to hear the opinion of a man from the front."

"The actors performed their roles strongly. But for the spectator it was boring, far-fetched, and far from real life. So it seemed to me. A real play about the war, probably, still lies in our future."

But on this evening, speaking honestly, Roza was occupying my mind and commanding my attention. She was dressed modestly, without any adornments, but quite tastefully; I liked the fine features of her face; her beautiful black hair, which had been neatly pulled back into a bun; her large gray eyes, which calmly and attentively took in all the guests. But for some reason, she didn't look in my direction; probably because she was feeling too shy. She blushed when Mama said some kind words about her. I also liked her simple but sincere toast: "To a good Mama and her valiant soldier."

After such a toast, I decided to act: if I was lucky, things might go at a good clip.

Roza

Mama asked me to escort Roza home; it turned out that she lived in Mar'inaia Roshcha, which was a dangerous district of the city even before the war. For the first time in Moscow, I took my pistol with me.

Roza was silent almost the whole way. I couldn't endure it:

"Did you enjoy the evening?"

"Very much. Lovely, sweet people surround your family."

"Then why are you being quiet, doctor?"

"I don't know, all kinds of thoughts . . ."

"For example?"

"I'm tormented, should I invite you into my house or not?"

"Invite me!" slipped out of my mouth: I was becoming more and more drawn to her.

Roza burst out laughing: "Great, only don't then become angry: the conditions at my place are terrible, even shameful."

At last we reached Roza's home. Deep darkness in the courtyard and entrance, then a narrow, creaking staircase with a rotted, sticky railing. We cautiously climbed to the second floor—until we reached it, I probably lit a half-box of matches one match at a time to light our way. Roza opened the door. Again, darkness, but this time a long, gloomy corridor—its right side was cluttered up with ramshackle furniture, stinking with mold and rot. Along its left side were twelve doors. It was an enormous communal residence.

The second door led into my lady's little room. Roza approached a table in the center of the room and lit the wick of a kerosene lamp. The modest furniture of her residence appeared before me. Roza had found space for an old worn-out sofa, three little shelves with books, and a sideboard along three of the walls. In front of the far wall stood a low screen, which appeared to be concealing the "bedroom." A rack with a few nails was hanging on the door, upon which the hostess hung the greatcoat that she had taken from me, and her own overcoat. It was chilly in the room.

I stood quietly.

"Once again excuse me for my god-forsaken hole of a residence." Roza said with embarrassment. "You are the first person that I've invited to my room. Take it as a sign of respect, because you are from the front, after all. As you can see, we have no electricity, no baths either; the kitchen and the toilet are at the end of the hallway. But I'm grateful to fate even for this. My parents and I were living on the outskirts of Moscow; my parents are still there. But by some miracle I managed to obtain a Moscow residence permit and this room, and they've even put me on the list for improvements."

"Does everybody have rooms like this here?" I asked.

"Pretty much the same. We have a resident, an alcoholic, they call him Fedot; he managed to build himself a homemade heater and sells places around it to the other residents. On cold days, people purchase a spot around the heater and occupy it from morning on; they take turns warming themselves up. However, my pride is my telephone, which they gave me because I am a doctor. Incidentally, make a call, so they won't be worried at your house."

I dialed the number . . . and told a lie that I again had let slip the start of curfew, so I would be spending the night with the L'vov family.

"Deceiver," Roza laughed out loud, shaking her head. "But, so be it; I'll let you stay the night here, and you can have the sofa. Now I'm going down to the kitchen, where I'll brew some tea for us. We'll drink the tea with some tasty jam."

I stayed behind to examine her small library. Books about medicine were standing on one shelf; another was full of published Russian classics, while the third contained some poetry books. Then we comfortably arranged ourselves around the little table, and we drank tea while Roza told me about her family and her life:

"I practically don't live in this dump; this winter I'm trying more often to take watch duties, and I often spend the night at a friend's place. When they provided me with a telephone, life here became simply hellish. Residents threw themselves at my telephone, but I permitted them to use it only if they had an emergency. That's when it all started! Anonymous letters, threats—they tossed empty vodka bottles into my room, calling me a drunk and a prostitute. These claims prompted inspections and I had to appear before investigative commissions . . . but why complain? This is typical for life in a communal residence."

"Roza, dear, tomorrow my train leaves at 11:00 A.M. sharp, I'm returning to the front," I beseechingly looked at her. "We have only one night. Just one night! (It seems I had lost my mind! What was I doing?) Do you understand my words?"

Roza fell silent and looked at me with widely opened eyes in surprise. I sensed their tender, warm light. Our gaze met, and in our eyes wild flames began to flicker, and it suddenly became impossible to extinguish them. What was this, fantasy or some amazing reality? We hesitated for a few moments, then in a fit of passion rushed to embrace each other and then fell into an endless sea of delight.

Later she caressed my hair and whispered: "My dear, from the first minute that I caught sight of you at the hospital, I understood: my hour had come! All these days I have been waiting for your call."

"How hard it will be to part from you, my poetic beauty!"

"Why did you say that?"

"While you were preparing our tea, I looked over your library."

"Would you like for me to read you my favorite poet?"

"Konstantin Simonov?"

"Good Lord!"

"Nikolai Tikhonov?"

"What are you saying!"

"Who then?"

"Just listen. The poem is called 'The Lovers' Litany'"

I quietly listened. She read it twice.

"Do you like it?"

"Very much. Who wrote it?"

"Kipling, an English writer and poet. He hasn't been very welcomed here; they say he's 'an orator of Britain, masters of the seas.' But today Britain is our ally, so they finally published a small volume of his poetry. I'm sure that in your childhood, you read his wonderful tales—*The Jungle Book* and *The Second Jungle Book*. But his verses are uncommonly lyrical."

"You sing them?"

"Rarely. I accompany myself on the guitar."

"You're a delight! Now I've come to understand that love is always unexpected; the main thing is not to let it pass."

"Perhaps you're right. But for a long time I've been wary; before you came along, I've experienced deep disappointment, which shook me. When we first met, I was terribly worried whether or not we would understand each other. War is horrible; it turns people into beasts. How good it is that you haven't become one yourself, and that you've managed to preserve your human feel-ings. Now I'm not so frightened; you're here, you came into my home and became part of my soul."

I listened to her, kissed her, but I was troubled by one thought: how unbear-ably quickly time flies, even a beloved woman can't stop it, and how stupid the saying was: "Happy hours don't count against you." She was my ideal! Would fate allow us to meet again?

But she kept talking, and she was saying things that could sweep any man off his feet: "Before you, I didn't know that I could be so happy, and I didn't believe in the sincerity and purity of relationships; now I know that I was fool-ing myself, and you helped me understand this."

Then we froze—we simply looked at each other in silence, and this silence told us more than even the loftiest words. It wasn't a dream—I had one desire.

"I love you, Roza."

"All men, when they're right next to a woman, fall in love—that's what my patients tell me, they share a lot with me."

"You don't believe me?"

"I believe."

"Then I'll be brief. The Wedding Registry Office, I think, opens at 10:00 A.M. We'll go to the nearest one, and I'll persuade them to register us. From there, we'll go directly to the train station—you'll accompany me."

"Are you sure? Why are you rushing so, why have you made this decision?"

"I'm afraid I'll lose you."

"Have you thought about your parents? How will they react to your scheme? And what of my parents! I don't have the right to deceive them. No, it's better if you write me. But I'll wait for you, longingly wait for you."

"Perhaps you're indeed right," I agreed, to my own surprise. "I will write to you."

Why had my ardor suddenly chilled?

Beyond the window, dawn was breaking. I caressed her hair and thought about her—the woman with whom I was intending to spend my entire life. Her love was pure and boundless—a gift, sent to me by fate.

They say that youth is like a lark; it is full of its own morning songs—in honor of itself and in honor of love.

I never wrote her a single letter.

The Belorussian Station

Father accompanied me. Nelia also came along. Together, the three of us stood on the platform. The train was due to arrive at any time, and already by evening it would be delivering me to the front.

We joked and laughed, but there was anxiety in all our hearts, which didn't leave us for a moment. Would we ever see each other again? That morning, as I prepared to leave, Mama cried; I told her that I would write her, and I kissed her and tried to calm her down, but what could I say to comfort her? Papa tried to keep up his spirits and just smoked more than usual.

A train with six passenger cars pulled up. There were even more passengers this time, heading back to the front—primarily officers recently discharged from hospitals. They checked our documents and tickets, and then started loading passengers. Papa gave a sigh, nodded at my travel bag, and said sadly, "I'm seeing off a son who has a suitcase full of vodka, but without a single book."

We burst out laughing. Actually, my travel bag was fully stuffed with bottles of vodka, strands of garlic, and bags of onions.

Nelia asked permission to speak a minute alone with me. We stepped off to one side. She thrust into my hands a cute little toy bear.

"Here's a talisman for you, it will protect you: I had a well-known Moscow gypsy woman cast a spell on it. What will you call it?"

"Vasia"—I gave it the first name that popped into my head.

Dear Vasia accompanied me through the entire war. It is protecting me even now. I regard it not only as a relic but also as a soldier regards an old friend.

"Hold on, son," Papa said on parting as he clapped me on the shoulders.

Nelia and I parted tenderly. She even kissed my little bear Vasia.

The train started moving.

Gathering speed, the train carried us to the west. I stood by the window, watching the passing landscape flash past me. But my thoughts were far away. Two wonderful women had given me their love, and one more had become my friend; such things rarely fall to one of our brothers. But I would very quickly forget all three of them. Was it because of the frivolity of youth, or that "thick soldier's hide," as Nelia had said, or simple heartlessness? The answer was, if you will, something else. The front cruelly, just like tongs, gripped all of us; there was no escaping it, and the front didn't let anyone escape the lasting, overwhelming feelings that it generated, and it left many bitter traces.

Meanwhile, the horses of war kept galloping and galloping. Meanwhile, villages kept burning and burning . . . and while all this goes on, you, the soldier, don't belong to yourself. After Moscow I saw many things in a new way. For the remaining two years of war, each of us—at the front and in the rear—lived through so much that it would be enough for three lifetimes.

How the landscape had changed beyond the train's windows! In the immediate environs of Moscow, wherever you glanced, you saw people busily tending to the earth: on every free piece of land in courtyards, around buildings, even by the side of the road, people were cultivating the soil and preparing kitchen gardens. But now I saw a mutilated land, literally as if some giant hellish steamroller had been working here. Villages had been reduced to ashes. Empty fields, overgrown with weeds. Entrenchments and antitank ditches scarred the land. Thoroughly devastated forests cut down and mangled by bombs and shell fragments. Sickly glades; highways and roads that had been battered unmercifully. Settlements that had been demolished down to the last brick. Grain elevators and railroad stations had been wiped from the face of the Earth. And dugouts, dugouts among the smoldering ruins. Only rarely did the solitary figure of a person loom. That's the way it was all the way to Viaz'ma.

Moscow already seemed to me like a distant planet—we, the frontline soldiers, and the Muscovites whom I had met, were strangers to each other: I didn't sense any pride in them for our army and our combat efforts. Was it because we were still fighting badly? Meanwhile, people in the rear were waiting for victories, waiting for a quick end to the war.

Toward evening, the train pulled into Viaz'ma.

16

The Liberation
of Smolensk
April–September 1943

Attack Preparations

The withdrawal of Model's Ninth Army from the Rzhev salient had opened a path to the west for the Red Army. Pursuing rear guard elements of the adversary, the forces of the Western and Kalinin Fronts earnestly approached the Smolensk land bridge—an enormous Central Russian stretch of elevated terrain lying between the Dnepr River and the Western Dvina River. The idea of quickly liberating the ancient Russian city of Smolensk from the German occupiers gripped the soldiers' hearts. Issue after issue of the divisional newspaper published essays about the historic past of the city and its residents, in particular reminding us of the popular struggle against Napoleon's army. Each soldier understood that any particular settlement on our path had at some time been bound to the fate of the Motherland.

In 1941, Hitler had announced to the entire world that the German army, upon having opened the "Smolensk gates," would soon conquer Moscow. But life overturned the plans of the aggressors. In heavy fighting for Smolensk, the Red Army had delayed the Wehrmacht for two months—months that had saved the city of Moscow. Without those bloody battles in the September days of 1941, it is hard to say how the battle for Moscow would have turned out. It seems to me that historians have not fully appreciated the battle for Smolensk—the Red Army's first major blow against the adversary in the initial period of the war.

The task of opening these very same "Smolensk gates," which Napoleon had opened almost 130 years before Hitler, lay before us. Only now we were going in the opposite direction. Beyond the gates lay the tormented lands of Belorussia and Poland, and farther on—Germany.

The German command clearly understood the full seriousness of the situation that was taking shape on Army Group Center's front, so it had concentrated enormous strength in the Smolensk bridgehead—more than forty divisions. Defensive lines stretched to a depth of 120–130 kilometers, presenting six primary fortified belts of defense.

However, Hitler and his strategists didn't take into consideration several essential new facts in their planning. First, the Red Army was gathering strength and wrath. In 1943 it had become a different army, having passed through the harsh school of battles, in particular around Rzhev. Second, each warrior, marching westward, had painfully witnessed the German occupiers' "New Order," and this was not propaganda footage but living tragic images of what the enemy had done to Russian land.

And now, standing on the defensive, we were preparing for a new offensive.

The division received a major influx of new troops. Over the four months from April to the start of August, the soldiers, moving mountains of earth, had fortified strong centers of resistance and had built strong points at the company and platoon level equipped with machine guns. In sectors vulnerable to tank attack, they had dug antitank ditches and placed antitank obstacles and built hedgehog positions—and mined everything they could. Dozens of kilometers of entrenchments, shielded by coils of barbed wire, had been dug, together with communication trenches. From morning until late into the night, Vasilii Alekseevich Polevik, the new commander of the 220th Rifle Division, went around the regiments and battalions, inspecting their work. A few officers looked skeptically at the daily exhausting labor undertaken by the division commander: "Why are we doing this? At any time now we'll be back on the offensive; defense is a temporary matter."

The colonel patiently explained: "The essence of the defenses we have created, possibly for not long, is the prevention of a sudden spoiling attack. Do you want to bleed the division white before our offensive even begins?"

It is curious, but the soldiers didn't grumble. One Ukrainian soldier explained their mood better than anyone else: "Let's hope it tempts the enemy to strike!"

Together with the construction of fortifications, the division commander organized combat training for the rifle battalions and companies. Not far behind the front lines, a concealed place had been selected to serve as a training ground. Here the soldiers, particularly the new soldiers, rehearsed attacks, learned how to repel counterattacks, and practiced tank-infantry cooperation.

An amusing incident occurred while we were in reserve. One day we learned that a theatrical troupe with three actresses was going to visit the regiment. Commissar Gruzdev ordered me to receive the troupe, greet them warmly, and escort them while they were in the regiment area. Mikhalych, Stepanych, and I decided to organize a small reception for the actresses. We scrounged for food to serve (as I recall, we were able to find 20 grams of butter and five potatoes) and began saving our daily 100 grams of vodka for the special occasion. We even decorated the walls of our dugout as best we were able. The eagerly awaited day soon arrived, and the actresses put on a show for the soldiers. They sang, played guitar, and recited poetry to the warm applause of the officers and soldiers. When the show ended, I asked the young women, who were no more than twenty-five or twenty-six years of age, to visit our dugout. They agreed, and soon we were toasting each other and talking about our lives at the front and in Moscow. But suddenly I heard the harsh words of our regiment commander: "Bring them to my bunker!" The ladies didn't seem too interested in leaving, and they promised to return. They never did. We waited for them in vain, continuing to down shots of vodka. Quite intoxicated, I cursed the regiment commander and resolved to bring back the actresses at gunpoint, if necessary. Mikhalych, equally drunk, staggered over and handed me his pistol. I grabbed it, got up, went outside, and decided to head to the commander's bunker. Lord knows what might have happened if just then a vehicle hadn't stopped in front of me. An officer stepped out. He asked me: "Where are the actresses? I've come for them at the request of the division commander." The general took the three actresses from the colonel. For all I know, the young women wound up traveling up the ranks of command all the way to the army level!

On 5 July, the regiment was suddenly warned: a "surprise" from the other side was anticipated. Everyone—from the division commander down to the last soldier—spent three or four days (I don't remember exactly) in the trenches on combat alert. Behind us, a well-equipped artillery regiment, complete with rocket launchers, took position. More machine pistols and submachine guns had appeared in the companies. A tank brigade arrived. The adversary now and then bombarded our front lines—likely they too were on the alert.

Soon the order to pull back arrived, and, like lightning, word traveled around the regiments about the grandiose battle at the Kursk-Orel bulge. It had started on 5 July and continued for several days. Now we knew why the warning of a "surprise" had been issued.

The success at Kursk prompted general joy.

"Now at last," the soldiers said, "it's kaput for them!"

"Exactly so, it is time to prepare the hearses . . ."

Alas, there were still almost two long, bloody years of war before the final victory and the final burial of the German army.

The Division Goes into Battle

7 August, morning. An artillery cannonade announces the beginning of the offensive on the Smolensk bridgehead for three *fronts*—the Kalinin, the Western, and the Baltic.

After a ninety-minute preparatory artillery barrage, the battle for Smolensk begins to unfold. Company after company rises and goes into the attack. From the very first battle, the fighting is vicious and bitter. Despite the adversary's counterattacks and his superiority in the air, and overcoming the wall of heavy machine-gun fire thrown up by the enemy, our units break into the hostile trenches and begin chewing their way through the enemy's defenses.

7 August, night. Division commander Polevik introduces fresh forces into the breakthrough sector, supported by artillery fire.

8 August, morning. The 1st Battalion of the 673rd Rifle Regiment reaches Shishlovskaia Roshcha and the village of Rybki. Artillery and mortar batteries shift their fire onto the adversary's second and third lines of defense.

8 August, afternoon and evening. After a massive artillery barrage, the battalions surge into the enemy's second line of trenches. The Germans strengthen their resistance. Heavy fighting erupts, and battles go on for every clump of ground.

9 August, morning and afternoon. The adversary brings up reserves to the breakthrough sector and with several energetic counterattacks throws the regiment back to the first line of trenches. The number of dead and wounded swells on both sides.

The 673rd and 653rd Rifle Regiments cling to the ground they've gained with difficulty. The advance grinds to a halt. German assault groups, actively supported from the air, manage to drive wedges into the division's lines. The situation becomes critical. At that moment, as the battalions of the 673rd Rifle Regiment begin to waver, Sergeant Vasilii Ragulin deploys a self-made banner, and with a shout: "For the Motherland! Ura-a!" he gets prone soldiers to rise to their feet and leads them into a counterattack. The Germans are stunned for several moments. The retreat of the battalions has been stopped.

Here is how this turning point in the battle was described in the divisional newspaper: "He (V. Ragulin) was the first to hurl himself at the enemy. The battalion *komsorg* Boris Flegboim and many soldiers rushed after him. They managed to restore the situation. A grenade exploded near Ragulin. His face inundated with blood, he, paying no attention to the wound, immediately cut down a German officer with a burst from his submachine gun."

However, the command comes to a conclusion: the danger of the operation's collapse has not disappeared, and there is a need for the reallocation of forces. The command for a general withdrawal is issued. The active measures of the German air force are particularly worrisome.

9 August, evening. After a reshuffling of forces, the 673rd Regiment goes back onto the attack and again seizes Shishlovskaia Roshcha and the village of Kudinovo, as well as Rybki. Without slackening the pace of attack, we force a crossing of the Vidosa River.

10 August. With the support of tanks and airplanes, the adversary counter-

attacks again and again. The fighting grows even hotter. Both sides are suffering heavy losses. Soldiers are showing unparalleled stubbornness and courage; in some battalions, only twenty or thirty men remain. The entire regimental artillery moves up to fire over open sights. Many tanks are knocked out and left burning. Finally, unable to withstand the pressure, the adversary gives way.

11, 12, and 13 August. The 673rd Rifle Regiment continues its pursuit, although the men remaining in the ranks continue to dwindle.

By the end of 14 August, Spas-Demansk and hundreds of villages have been liberated. The division is pulled back into reserve. The 251st Rifle Division takes its place at the front.

During the course of this offensive, our division was pulled back into the second echelon for replenishment four times, which testifies to the severity of the fighting and the serious losses.

Division commander Polevik arrived at our regiment headquarters. Normally a stern, taciturn man, this time he openly displayed his admiration for the courage of the men and thanked the soldiers for their stubbornness and bravery.

"Where's your hero," the division commander asked of Gruzdev, "the one who inspired the soldiers into the counterattack?"

Gruzdev presented Ragulin to the division commander. The commander walked up to Vasilii and said, "Thank you, Sergeant, you fight well!" Polevik embraced him, kissed him on each cheek, and attached the Order of the Red Star to his field blouse. This was the sergeant's first decoration.

Within a week, the division was again deployed on the front lines. We continued to press the enemy. The Germans retreated, yielding one defensive line after another.

In the middle of September, after a short pause and regrouping, the offensive resumed. Our forces rushed to exploit the enemy bridgehead's ruptured defenses; Dukhovshchina and Iartsevo were taken. We were now only a stone's throw from Smolensk.

Approximately 20 kilometers from Smolensk, the *Front* command detached the 220th Rifle Division from the 31st Army and temporarily assigned it to the 68th Army, which was to bypass Smolensk to the south. We entered the city of Krasny. Soon, another city fell to the blows of the 68th Army—Dorogobuzh. At one time, Kutuzov had given battle here to the retreating French.

In the city square at the center of Dorogobuzh, the Germans had created a cemetery of their dead. We saw many soldiers' graves, marked by birch crosses with German helmets hanging on them. As they marched past, our soldiers gleefully threw off the helmets and knocked the crosses to the ground.

On 25 September 1943, the city of Smolensk was liberated. On that same day, another ancient Russian city, Roslavl', fell to the advancing Red Army.

Boris Flegboim and Ivan Skoropud

During the breakthrough of the defenses of the Smolensk land bridge, two lieutenants who were battalion *komsorg* in our regiment were killed: Boris Flegboim and Ivan Skoropud.

Boris Flegboim arrived in the division at Rzhev. Short, with kind gray eyes beneath brows thoroughly bleached by the sun, his face was still covered by soft, golden fuzz. At first he seemed to me like a boy who had accidentally wound up at the front. Like me, he had been graduated prematurely from a military-political school. But my first impression was quickly dispelled. The things I liked most about Boris were his friendliness and his uncommon courage.

By some miracle emerging intact from the Rzhev battles, he fell near Seli-zharovo, not far from Iartsevo. It occurred, as they later told me, at the moment when the *komsorg*, urging on some soldiers by his personal example, leaped from a parapet into the adversary's trench, where he was cut down by a German submachine gunner.

He was from Sverdlovsk, and he grew up in a family from a long line of pharmacists. His grandfather, father, and mother worked long years from day to day, mixing healing powders and practicing their curative magic over bottles of medicines. The authorities paid them kopecks, but the dynasty of Flegboim pharmacists was well known to many city citizens, who valued their work and knew that in a difficult hour, they would help you.

From his father, Boris inherited a pedantic character: precise and stern. In a very short period, he altered his official status as *komsorg*, turned it into a vital job, and became an essential man not only for his Komsomol members but for all the soldiers of the battalion as well. The complexity of a situation never frightened Boris; he rose to the defense of the weak and knew how to get the strong to follow him. The soldiers considered him as one of their own and highly respected him as a person. You could talk about life with him and get some advice, if you couldn't get it from home, or in frontline situations.

I remember one incident. The regiment was moving toward Viaz'ma, pursuing the retreating enemy, and sometimes we managed to step on the Germans' heels. One day they counterattacked us. The Germans put up a screen, trying to stop us, or else even hurl us back a little farther from their rear guard. Flegboim's battalion commander was severely wounded. Boris didn't lose his head; he dropped down behind a machine gun, and when it ran out of ammunition he crawled over to another machine gun. For this battle he was awarded the medal "For Courage."

Unexpectedly Boris turned in a request: he was asking to be transferred into the reconnaissance unit. They refused his request. Then for some reason he decided to become a sniper. Again they refused him. I thought a lot about his desire to switch his position. No, he wasn't searching for death—more likely a constant craving for risk possessed him.

Once, during a short lull near Rzhev, he invited me to a game of chess. I was surprised: chess at the front? Boris burst out laughing. He pulled a small cardboard box out of his kitbag, upon which a chessboard had been drawn, and a little canvas bag with chess pieces, which had been carved out of clay and then somehow processed for strength. We played two games. I lost both of them. It turned out that even as a young boy, he had been the chess champion in his home city's Palace of Pioneers, and later, playing in a local chess club, he had received the "Master" title. It is hard to believe, but whenever we had a few free minutes, the *komsorg* taught the young soldiers how to play the game. It was not coincidental that they nicknamed him "The King."

Boris couldn't tolerate empty rhetoric and long-winded speeches, which unfortunately were widespread among the officers. One time a company commander tried to scold the battalion *komsorg* for being overly familiar with the men in ranks. The *komsorg* pulled a little notepad from his kitbag and read to the extremely surprised officer the advice of Peter I: "Don't stick to the manual like a stubborn mule, for while regulations have been written into the manual, the times and occurrences have not."

I was always struck by his bravery, his ability to keep his cool under fire, and I once asked him, "Where did you get such a fearlessness?"

Boris was a bit confused, tried to find some good reply, then muttered, "If he is afraid, then the officer has no business being at the front."

"Not everyone is capable of this."

"I agree. But you yourself know how it was for us at Rzhev. Up to ten attacks a day, and all of them without a lick of sense. The soldiers kept asking, 'Why are you treating us this way?' Tell me, what should I have said to them in reply? So I learned how to fight too. I wasn't the only one to pluck up courage and fury in front of Rzhev. There'll be enough for Smolensk, for Orsha, and all the way to Berlin as well."

It is hard to lose a frontline comrade; each time it is a blow to the heart. If people die beside you every day, it may seem that you'll get tired of feeling the sharp pain of the loss and that you'll become indifferent and callous. I can testify—this isn't true!

I also don't accept the notion of the "battle intoxication," which attests that a soldier going into the attack is seized by some general frenzy and forgets about himself. I'm sure, in an extreme situation, even in the attack, a person remains himself.

Yet another cruel blow—the loss of Ivan Skoropud. Ivan was called the "Quiet Guy" [*molchun*], and it was true that he wasn't very talkative. But we became friends. I still keep a photograph from 1943, taken somewhere in the forests around Smolensk, that shows a few regimental and battalion *komsorg* together, including Ivan and me.

Ivan Skoropud was born in Poltava, to the family of a teacher. They were neighbors of the writer Korolenko. Vania's father sometimes did the odd job for his neighbor, so the writer often invited him to his literary readings. Under the influence of his father, Vania was drawn to Ukrainian literature and developed a taste for the rich Ukrainian folklore. He also loved the melodious Ukrainian folk songs, which were often sung in his family. He read a lot, and memorized the poem "The Eneida" by the classic Ukrainian poet Kotliarevsky. He loved the poems of Lesa Ukrainka. When I discovered this, at that moment we became close—I also knew "The Eneida" and loved the verse of Lesa Ukrainka: at the Kharkov school where I studied, Ukrainian literature was taught by an intellectual of the highest order, Vasilii Ivanovich Sokol—a superb pedagogue, an expert in Ukrainian literature, and a playwright. Some of his plays were staged in Kharkov's theaters.

When the war started, many people fled Poltava. The Skoropud family was evacuated to Novosibirsk. But the father Ivan remained behind under German occupation—for the sake of his pupils. Soon thereafter, the German commandant received a report from an informer, which accused Ivan Skoropud during the Revolution of maintaining contact with the writer Korolenko— "a defender of the Jews." As way of proof, Korolenko's connections with the "Beilis Affair" were introduced. [Vladimir Korolenko had written letters and spoken out against the false accusation of Jews during the time running up to the Beilis Trial. Menahem Mendel Beilis had been accused of murdering and mutilating the body of a thirteen-year old Ukrainian boy in 1911. The case sparked a vicious anti-Semitic campaign in the Russian press, which accused Jews of blood libel and performing ritual murders.] Not pondering the matter long, the *Obersleutnant* [lieutenant colonel] made his decision: "For exhorting others: Hang him." I learned this information after the war, in the 1970s, when my wife made a business trip to Poltava.

The younger Ivan Skoropud became a medical instructor in the army. During the battle for Moscow he demonstrated his courage: he carried eighty-six wounded men from the battlefield while under fire. On 5 March 1942, the medical instructor was awarded the Order of Lenin. He was the only one in the entire division to hold such a high honor. Dubovsky, the division's commissar, while presenting the hero with the Order, advised Ivan to join the Party and recommended him for Komsomol work. That's how Ivan Skoropud became a battalion *komsorg*.

The tragedy occurred in the first days of the offensive on Smolensk. Ivan stepped on a mine that blew him to pieces; they managed to identify his remains through a birthmark on a detached leg.

Learning of the death of Ivan, I asked Koshman, a battalion commissar of the 653rd Rifle Regiment, to permit me to bury the *komsorg* with the highest honors. We laid his remains and a photograph of the lieutenant in the coffin. During the funeral someone casually remarked, "In this life, we are all just specks of dust." This seemed offensive to me, and I gave him a sharp rebuke.

Whenever times were tough and someone was on the verge of panic, Vania liked to say: "Heaven isn't a place on earth." A wise Ukrainian saying.

The Dead Battalion

An enormous forest began about two kilometers from our position, leading to an elevation covered by a birch grove. The height was in German possession—probably, it was one of the security outposts in front of the main line of defense. Regiment commander Razumovsky ordered battalion commander Major Podchezertsev to take the hill.

At dawn, after a brief preparatory artillery barrage, the battalion commander led his soldiers toward the grove of birches. We were flanking the German position from two sides. The battle was short; the adversary understood that he couldn't hold the height and retreated. As was evident, the task of the outpost had been to observe our movements. As we climbed the hill, we could still hear the receding sound of engines as the Germans fell back.

Empty German dugouts greeted us, with signs of an interrupted breakfast spread out on the tables. Podchezertsev reported the situation to Razumovsky and set up posts for an all-round defense. The troops, after a cheerful announcement by a sergeant major about the fitness of the abandoned German food for consumption, eagerly took to the coffee and biscuits with sausage. I, however, decided to check the posts and have a chat with the sentries: that the adversary might try to return to a readily abandoned position could not be excluded. It turned out that this possibility worried not only me. Coming back into a dugout, I overheard a scrap of conversation:

"I don't like the sudden flight of the Germans, Ivan," the deputy commander for political affairs was saying. "It's the first time I've seen such a thing."

"I agree with you, Osia. Is this a trap?"

Podchezertsev and his deputy commander for political affairs, Osip Iudin, were talking; privately, they addressed each other by their first names.

"What will we do if they return?" Iudin asked.

"Fight," the battalion commander answered. "By evening the regiment commander promised to send up two 45-mm antitank guns and some reinforcements, and a mortar platoon is on its way."

The radio squawked, and I was handed an order from Gruzdev: "The *komsorg* will return to the command post immediately."

"Again I'm being extricated! But what does he need?" I was surprised.

"Let's forget about it, guys, I don't want to go back, and the situation here is complicated."

"An order is an order," the battalion commander objected. "Get moving, *komsorg;* we'll manage without you."

We quickly embraced, and I left the birch grove. I never saw them alive again.

While I was making my way back to the command post, a battle had already erupted on the height. It turned out that several self-propelled guns accompanied by submachine gunners had emerged from the forest, heading in the direction of the grove. Razumovsky ordered the artillery to cut them off from Podchezertsev's battalion by fire. The battle on the hilltop flared. After two hours, we lost communications with the battalion. Razumovsky, alarmed by the prolonged silence, sent scouts and some radiomen forward to investigate the height, but they didn't manage to reach it—they were met by heavy machine-gun fire. It had become clear: the adversary held the height again. But where was our battalion?

Closer to evening, Razumovsky summoned me: "We need to find out what happened to the battalion. If we detach a company, can you lead it to the summit by the same route Podchezertsev took?"

I confirmed that I could. A company was quickly gathered, with a scout platoon attached to it. Twilight was already falling, and the regiment commander handed me his American-made flashlight. The unit and I set out into the gathering darkness.

The situation repeated itself. After a quick skirmish, the Germans abandoned their positions again.

We found a tragic scene on the hilltop. The ground was piled with the corpses of our guys and Germans. At the place where the commander's dugout had been, a deep crater was yawning. Razumovsky contacted me for a situation report. It was clear that the German attack had been sudden; judging from the position of the bodies and the wounds, savage hand-to-hand fighting had occurred. None of our men survived. There was no one who could tell us how everything happened, and no one to advise us whether something similarly cruel and unexpected was lying in wait for us.

The wind slightly rustled the branches of the delicate birch trees, and it was quiet in the pretty birch grove. But this silence was oppressive. Both the living and the dead were silent. I picked a bouquet of flowers and laid it on the ground among the dead. The ground accepted everyone—soldiers and commanders. They were together in battle and were now resting in the same common grave.

The frontline press said not a word about the incident. Soon, a new regiment commander came to replace Razumovsky. Everyone began to forget what had happened. But I didn't. I had lost two comrades. I was attached to them; on marches, I always sought to be with their battalion, and together we had traveled the path from Rzhev to their final resting place on this nameless height. Had this operation been so necessary? I kept asking the question and never found an answer.

In my memory, Ivan Podchezertsev and Osip Iudin have been preserved as an inseparable team: one, a real commander; the other, a real commissar.

Iudin was serving with the battalion even before Podchezertsev; he was somewhat younger than the battalion commander, but they had liked each other from the first meeting. Osip had graduated from a pedagogical institute, and before the war he was teaching literature in school. In contrast with Pod-chezertsev, he wasn't a professional soldier. He wound up as a political worker by chance.

Podchezertsev was compact and thickset, with an almost round face and closely cropped hair. Iudin was tall and thin, with a head of luxurious black hair and a fine face with an inquisitive look. One was a major, the other, a senior lieutenant. Both had traveled the path from Moscow to just beyond Smolensk. Each man had been wounded twice. Neither man reached the age of thirty.

"A strong fellow"—that's what his subordinates had to say about Pod-chezertsev, having in mind not only his external appearance. Strapping, broad-shouldered, with powerful arms, what did Ivan not do prior to the war! He worked as a combine driver, then from the combine transferred to the tractor. One time he drove his tractor out onto a highway when the motor suddenly died, and a car struck his tractor. He was sentenced to three years in prison. He served one year, but there they reviewed his case and released him. In 1936 he was drafted into the army. He finished military school, then served a year near Ternopol. Somehow, Podchezertsev wound up under the eye of Khristo-forovich—that's what they called Colonel Bagramian then, who at the time was chief of the Kiev Military District's operations staff. One day Bagramian's vehicle got stuck along the road to Ternopol after its engine had started sput-tering. Ivan fixed the problem in one minute. The colonel thanked him and wanted to bring him along with him, to take him as an assistant, but for some reason it didn't happen.

Podchezertsev didn't like fancy talking; he appreciated the simple Russian word. He didn't drink or smoke. God forbid, if he ever laid eyes on some intoxicated company commander—a reduction in rank surely followed. He was the first of the commanders to abandon the faulty prewar manuals that proved useless in this war, and he began to learn how to fight from the Ger-mans. He was one of the first men in the division to master radio communi-cations. He actively responded to the call by the *Front* commander to apply principles of military engineering to the construction of trench defenses, in place of haphazardly arranged foxholes and entrenchments. The battalion commander wasn't very fond of the tanks and their crews, but he became tight with the artillerymen and mortarmen. He sought to select experienced fighters for his battalion. On the attack, he always searched for the weakest points in the adversary's defenses and then led his battalion to break through at one of these spots. He tried to take care of his men and was a good soul—everyone knew this, and many soldiers tried to get into his battalion. Razumovsky considered Podchezertsev's battalion to be his special assault force, and he always gave it the hardest tasks, confident that Podchezertsev could handle them.

Once, as I was leaving to visit another battalion, Ivan gave me a German Solingen razor, a valuable present. He gave a sad smile and said, "Now whenever you shave, you'll remember Osip and me." Only now as I write this do I recall that he often seemed sad when I saw him, as if something was troubling him. Perhaps this was a presentiment?

17

The Fighting for Orsha
October 1943–May 1944

Liady

The Stavka was planning for the liberation of Belorussia to occur in 1944. However, our 673rd Rifle Regiment, having forced a crossing of the Mereia River on 7 October 1943 with a resolute push, forced its way into Liady—the first liberated point on Belorussian soil.

Overcoming enemy resistance, we carefully avoided the famous steep slopes of the riverbank on the outskirts of Liady, which, according to the testimony of Caulaincourt, had brought terror to the ignominiously retreating French army: "At Liady," Caulaincourt wrote, "we had to descend such a steep slope, but its icy surface was so crowded with the bodies of many thousands of men and horses, which were simply tumbling downward, that we were forced to do what everyone else was doing; that is, slide down on our own posteriors. The Emperor had to descend in the same fashion."[1]

Liady was a large village situated on the high banks of the Dnepr River. But instead of the region's fruiting apple trees—the pride of Belorussians—we found piles of ashes and cut-down gardens, and streets overgrown with nettles and tall weeds. People were jumping out of dugouts to meet us, disbelieving their own eyes. In pitiful rags and barefooted, they came running up from all sides, shouting something hoarsely and loudly—and then they all hurried toward the river. Not understanding what had happened, we ran after them.

On the riverbank, by the side of a ditch, we found many bodies—women, old men, children. More accurately, we were looking at their badly decomposed remains.

In the district, a partisan unit had been operating. One day, a German security unit comprised of disloyal Russians surrounded the partisan unit. After a stubborn battle, the entire partisan unit was wiped out. The Germans learned of the partisan unit's connections with the people of Liady. On 2 April 1942, Gestapo personnel burned the village and, having lined up its citizens on the ashes, shot every tenth person. For over a year and a half, the residents had not been permitted to bury their family members—the Germans wanted the dead to remain as a frightening warning.

Together with the residents, we held a mournful assembly at the place of execution: we vowed to take revenge upon the fascists.

What was the purpose of the Germans' atrocities? Obviously, they were meant to frighten the people. But the atrocities generated a reciprocal reaction: hatred for the occupiers. The people's rumor mill spread word of atrocities far and wide, refuting the propaganda about "The New Order." People themselves could sense that it was incomparably worse to live under German rule than in the *kolkhozes*. So the Hitlerites were fighting against the Bolsheviks, while at the same time pushing the people toward the enemy they were fighting. At the entrance to Liady, the Germans had erected an enormous wooden panel. On it, they had hung an artfully produced sign with the inscription: "Greetings from Joseph Goebbels to the Belorussian people on the occasion of their liberation from the Bolsheviks." Now, taken down and tossed onto the ground, the sign was being trampled underfoot by our marching soldiers.

It was precisely here, in Liady, where the soldier's saying was born: "Don't go into battle like a polite guest; gather your fury."

Reinforcements

The Red Army had broken open the gates to the west. But the victory was not decisive. Trying to liberate Mogilev and Orsha, the troops of the Belorussian Front [formerly the Central Front] encountered stubborn enemy resistance and could not break that resistance from the march. This meant that we had not succeeded in taking full possession of the Smolensk axis of advance. Key positions at Vitebsk, Mogilev, and Orsha remained in enemy hands. New bloody battles lay in store for us.

In the middle of October 1943, the division was withdrawn into reserve. Soon a new batch of reinforcements arrived. I, together with other staff members, was instructed to receive the "freshly baked" soldiers.

My meetings with the new recruits left me dissatisfied and unhappy. Many of them were from the southern republics, which meant we would have to teach them some Russian quickly. Many had never held a rifle in their hands before arriving here and didn't even know what it was called. You ask one Uzbek fellow:

"Do you understand what a rifle is, and what it's for?"

"I've never thought it over, Comrade Officer."

"Well, give it some thought now. When you go into battle, shoot at the fascists. And if they come after you, you simply can't get by without it. The rifle is your protection. Do you know what a fascist is?"

Silence.

I had to carry on such conversations. Many of the new soldiers were uneducated and illiterate. A few, for example, thought islands floated on the sea. But I sought from the very first minutes of their arrival to help the new conscripts feel as equals among equals. I asked the company commanders to place their new soldiers under the wings of experienced soldiers. We had to teach the new arrivals how to overcome the fear of tanks and how to handle their fear during bombing attacks, particularly from Ju-87 Stukas. We had to teach them how to handle themselves on the battlefield and on the defense, how to rise from the ground at the start of an attack, and how to understand and always remember their responsibility to the oath they had taken. Finally, they had to learn the elementary things—an understanding of which flank was the right flank, and which the left.

Bombing attacks were the most difficult thing for them both physically and psychologically.

"Remember, friend," experienced frontline soldiers told them, "if an airplane is flying at a high altitude, it is harmless for you—screw him, and let him fly on. But when he comes at you in a dive, strafing you, or he's already released a bomb—then take cover: the bomb, damn it, will undoubtedly fall nearby."

The Germans bombed us for entire days. Where was our air force? We never saw it. Up to thirty or forty German airplanes would wheel above us, releasing their deadly loads in turn. Whenever the Junkers appeared, the howling of the new recruits was terrifying.

It was hard to teach these people to adapt to frontline conditions. But no matter how strangely, it was easier to deal with this category of new recruits than with a different segment of the reinforcements. In step with the liberation of occupied regions, the ranks of battalions and companies would be fleshed out with local residents as well. Of course, they were only those who had not collaborated with the Germans. Most often these were just opportunists: why bother with them? They had been hunted down and rounded up, and many of them, not all, were sent to fight. For some reason these sorts of recruits were nicknamed "fiancés." There was no noticeable sign of a willingness to fight with fervor among them. Many of these recruits looked at their new position as a cancer, which, naturally, only raised hatred in their hearts for military authority. The mobilization of people of draft age in the newly liberated regions was a complex issue, but their appearance in the acting army was not very welcome among the commanders.[2]

It was around this time that I encountered one conscript that I will never forget. One day, a truck rolled into our bivouac area, carrying a strange cargo: four young women, a large samovar, and bags of tea leaves and sugar. The truck was on its way toward the front lines. The regiment commander pulled me to one side and quickly explained that this was a mobile brothel. Two of the women were to service the company and platoon commanders; the other two women were to brew tea for groups of ten soldiers selected from the rifle companies by the sergeant majors. He ordered me to follow the truck and to see what was going on.

The truck stopped shortly before it reached the front lines. Two men helped the women unload the samovar and the bags of tea and sugar. Groups of soldiers, mostly Central Asians who drink green tea like Russians drink vodka, gathered around the samovar, plainly satisfied to receive the freshly brewed tea and be out of the trenches. Off to one side, however, I noticed a short line of officers outside a dugout, mostly junior and senior lieutenants, sitting and smoking. I approached the men and asked what was going on. One replied, "Take a seat, Senior Lieutenant, grab a spot. A free ticket to paradise waits." I declined the invitation. Later, I had a chance to speak briefly with one of the young women. She told me that her name was Inna. She had recently escaped the Germans, reached our lines, and had been conscripted into the Red Army. There they informed Inna that her role was to indulge the officers, and promised her decorations and a leave of absence in return. Inna sadly told me, "I just hope they don't write down in my soldier's booklet that I was a frontline prostitute." Once the day ended, they loaded up the truck and moved on without any ceremony.

Rumors later swirled that this was an idea of Stalin himself, adopted from the Germans. It was widely known that the Germans operated brothels for their officers and soldiers behind the front lines. If so, this must have been a brief experiment that failed. I never witnessed or heard about another such mobile brothel for the rest of the war.

7 November 1943

After regrouping and a short rest, the division again entered the front lines east of Orsha. Here the Germans were resisting fanatically, trying at whatever the cost to stop the Red Army's offensive.

On 7 November, in honor of the national holiday, the adversary decided to surprise us with a gift of his own: he undertook a counterattack on the regiment's position. The situation at the front became fluid, and enemy self-propelled guns with submachine gunners managed to penetrate the lines and advance into the depth of the regiment's defenses. A handful of soldiers under the leadership of battalion chief of staff Senior Lieutenant Kuznetsov tried to stop the enemy, but failed. The attackers quickly advanced in the direction of the regiment command post.

The recently assigned regiment commander Colonel Semen Vladimirovich was shaken, and lost control over his battalions. He turned to Commissar Gruzdev and asked:

"What shall we do?"

"What do you mean?" Ivan Iakovlevich was surprised. "We fight!"

"But we only have our personal sidearms!"

"But we also still have communications! The "God of War" [the artillery] will help us!"

No longer paying any attention to the despondent face of Epifanov, Gruzdev turned to the artillery spotters who were with us in the bunker: "Radio your commander: we need URGENT support!"

Within a few minutes, the guns began to thunder.

I unholstered my pistol and laid several grenades down next to it. The self-propelled guns were rapidly approaching; only about 250–300 meters remained to our position. But suddenly one erupted in flames—a direct hit. The remainder divided and began to encircle us. The spotters kept passing target co-ordinates back to the artillerymen over the radio. A storm of fire blanketed the Germans, but the self-propelled guns reacted calmly, only firing occasional rounds in our direction. However, having drawn up to the command post, they poured shell after shell into it. We hid in the bunker, relying upon its strong cover. However, "The Hut," as Gruzdev had named the bunker with some irony, couldn't take the punishment and collapsed. The fatal blow tossed us in every direction and crushed us under the ruins—a few men fatally, a few more were badly hurt, and others received a concussion. Both of the artillery spotters who had been assigned to us perished. But the artillerymen didn't need any further corrections—they had called down an impenetrable wall of fire that blocked the way forward for the Germans and eventually forced them to withdraw.

We excavated the dead out of the rubble and buried them, while the wounded were sent back to the *medsanbat*. I received a concussion in this unexpected tussle, and for more than a week I had trouble hearing.

Gruzdev reported to the division commander Polevik about our unhappy experiences. Epifanov was relieved of his command and returned to his previous place of service in the NKVD forces. Thus ended the career of "the careerist in colonel's straps," as the staff officers had christened Semen Vladimirovich.

The Fighting for Orsha

We didn't succeed in liberating Orsha in 1943. Having crossed the Dnepr River on anything available that floated, our first attempt to take the city from the march resulted in failure and heavy casualties.

The regiment greeted the start of 1944 in new savage fighting along the Orsha axis. On 21 February, our units again tried to break the German defenses. The Germans withstood the assaults. It is my belief that these attacks failed because of insufficient preparation of the offensive.

In the 1970s and 1980s many military commanders published their memoirs, informing us of how their armies, corps, and divisions fought under their leadership. In these memoirs, one frequently encounters a remark similar to this one: "Unfortunately, before the start of the offensive, not all of the adversary's weapons emplacements had been suppressed." Yet we would add: "resulting in unjustifiably many failures and enormous losses." That's the way it was at Rzhev and Orsha, Kharkov and Voronezh, in the Crimea, at Warsaw, and in Königsberg and Berlin.

Orsha is a major rail hub. Hitler had once flown into Orsha and held a well-known conference here, where the plans for Operation Typhoon were worked out. Here was also where the Chief of the General Staff Frantz Halder met with the German Army Group commanders during the battle for Moscow. And Orsha was where the headquarters for Army Group Center, under the command of General von Kluge, was located. The German command decided to hold Orsha at whatever the cost, in order to turn it into a second Rzhev for the Russians.

The liberation of Orsha turned out to be a difficult business. An intense month-long period of preparation and training preceded the offensive. During these days I visited the companies that had been assigned to lead the attack. What struck me during my meetings with the soldiers, especially the young ones, was the conquering spirit that had appeared in them.

In one of the companies I unexpectedly met Mikhail, a soldier from the company in which I had started my own frontline journey. "Mikhail!" I exclaimed joyfully. How many memories did our reunion stir up! Our first battle! Company commander Sukhomirov! His call to action: "The Immortals!" But then Mikhail suddenly spoke up: "Only the Almighty is immortal."

He hadn't changed a bit: still gaunt and withered, with a unique, triangular face with a tuft of beard like a billy goat's on his chin. In response to my exclamation at his comment, he calmly said:

"He's supreme, while I simply am."

"That means you're alive!"

"So it would seem. The vermin only maimed me, but I'm still in the ranks."

"Our medics don't leave people behind, and our doctors heal them!"

"If only it was so, dear fellow. From your lips straight to God's ears. Eh, our company that was—and now no one's left! Just you and me, and we're together."

"Well, a few more."

"It gnaws at me, kind fellow, why in front of the Almighty I deserved such benevolence, and remained alive after the Rzhev slaughter."

"Don't think about it, Mikhail."

"Says you! After all, God is breathing through us. Could it be that He's assigned us to the reserve? Either strategically speaking or tactically so?"

"Mikhail, will we take Orsha?"

"Of course! Orsha isn't Rzhev, and we've become a bit wiser since then. The platoon leaders today are not the same shabby works (*khalabuda*) as they were then. Moreover, today I will tell you that platoon leaders have become even stronger than our former battalion commanders."

"It appears they now have more confidence?"

"Definitely."

"Others think so too?"

"Definitely."

"That means, Mikhail, that we'll take Orsha!"

The conversation with Mikhail gladdened me. Time passes quickly: I had already been fighting for two years, and these years had changed much. "What has taught the warrior the experience of war?"—that's what an article printed in 1942 in the newspaper *Krasnaia zvezda* [*Red Star*], written by division commissar Kolonin, asked in its title. Here is how he answered it:

Firing over open sights has become an ordinary matter. This requires, understandably, seasoning, steadfastness, and great skill. The infantry has also overcome "tank fear." Today they no longer rush about or moreover run away at the sight of approaching enemy tanks, but meet them with all types of infantry antitank weapons: grenades, Molotov cocktails, and antitank rifle fire.

Nor do airborne landings frighten the Red Army men today: often, even before the parachutists land, they are being shot while in the air.

These are the changes we've seen. Over the ten months of war, not only fighters in the front lines have managed to become tempered, but the entire staff as well, including service personnel in the rear. Who can forget how much trouble they caused for us at one time, the attacks of the enemy air force on our supply columns and motorized columns? And now? Now, having caught sight of a German airplane, the supply train stops, and the wagon drivers and vehicle drivers pick up rifles, and at the command, they fire upon the aerial adversary. German pilots have felt the danger of our small arms ground fire and have begun to stay at a respectful altitude, which significantly reduces the accuracy of their bombing runs and strafing attacks. Our fighter has seen the German foe in all his forms: the arrogant German of summer, the beaten German of winter, and the German who has lost all human decency. Our fighter has seen and understood that the most reliable means to achieve victory in battle is to close with the foe as quickly as possible.

The commissar was right. The spirit of our army itself had changed, especially by 1944!

The Oath

From military prisoners we learned that the notorious German 197th Infantry Division was opposing us. There was a special reckoning for this division—its soldiers in 1941 had hung the partisan Zoia Kosmodem'ianskaia in Petrish-chevo. I had the idea to write an oath, "We'll take revenge for Partisan Zoia!" and take it to the soldiers for their signatures. The commissar approved my initiative.

After the death of Boris Flegboim, Lieutenant Anatolii Krashennikov replaced him as battalion *komsorg*.

On one of the days, when it had become a bit quieter along the front, I took Anatolii with me and crawled up to the frontline trenches. Here is how the episode was later described in the divisional newspaper:

> Taking advantage of a short lull, two men descended into the frontline trenches of the 673rd Rifle Regiment—a regimental *komsorg* and a battalion *komsorg*. Both of them were exhausted, eyes reddened by lack of sleep. But they were in a cheerful mood.
>
> "How did you manage to slip through?" the frontline soldiers asked. "German snipers are everywhere."
>
> Having caught his breath, the regimental *komsorg* answered:
>
> "You can't get used to it, but I've seen worse. Remember Shishlovskaia Roscha?"
>
> "Who could forget it? Here's a memento," Vasilii Ragulin pointed at his Order.
>
> "But now this is what we have going on," the regimental *komsorg* said quietly, as if summoning the comrades to gather around him. "We have three members of the Regiment's Komsomol Bureau here at the front. The fighting is hard, and we need to keep up the men's spirits. . . . At present, we're fighting against the 197th Infantry Division. Its bloody footprints on our land are well known. We're finding photographs on prisoners and the bodies of their dead that display many of their atrocities. The soldiers of this division executed Zoia Kosmodem'ianskaia."[3]
>
> Further, the commissar read a few lines from the oath:
>
> *Our hatred knows no bounds! We swear to take revenge upon the fascists for all their evil acts. And that day is not far off, when we will liberate the Soviet land from the fascist vermin, who wormed their way into our country . . .*
>
> There is a proposal to discuss the text of the oath to the Motherland with the soldiers and officers: "Not a step backward, only forward, to destroy the enemy!"

"What's there to discuss? We believe you and support you," Ragulin smiled.

"Err, no," the regimental *komsorg* started to protest. "The letter with the oath is a collective one, thus everyone must know about it and support it by their own signature."

"But we don't have a pencil," someone objected.

The regimental *komsorg* read out the full text of the oath and proposed:

"Now let's act accordingly. It is dangerous to walk around to all the positions together. So pass the text down the trench line. Each man should familiarize himself with it, then sign it and pass it along to the next comrade."

That's indeed what they did: they attached the sheet of paper with the oath to a pencil stub and gave it to the soldiers.

"When this procedure had nearly reached the end," the newspaper sketch said later, "up to fifty fascists suddenly hurled themselves upon our positions in a counterattack. The soldiers picked up their weapons. . . . The regiment *komsorg* himself dropped two of the Hitlerites in their tracks. Many soldiers distinguished themselves. A few of our fighters perished, leaving behind their signature on the text of "The Oath" as their last will and testament."

The article is correct; just as I was preparing to leave the trenches, gunfire erupted and machine guns began to chatter. I was gazing at a nearby soldier and recognized him as a new recruit, Andrei from the town of Sezran. Totally inexperienced, he incautiously raised his head above the parapet before I could stop him and almost immediately received a bullet to the forehead. He had been unaware that every German company had a couple of snipers on its roster. He wasn't wearing a steel helmet, but an older helmet made of simple iron, and the sniper's bullet pierced right through it. As Andrei's dead body slumped to the bottom of the trench, I took up a suitable position and opened fire on the advancing Germans with my submachine gun. I laid several grenades next to me, just in case. That difficult minute had arrived when the law of war determines who will kill whom. In these moments, it seems we are no longer Russian or German soldiers, nor even humans. We have become animals.

The German sally quickly faltered. Did I kill two fascists, or perhaps even more? Who knows? Germans were falling, as were several of our own guys, but maybe I didn't hit anyone. I can't be judged. All I know is that in the brief action, I fired two complete magazines of ammunition from my submachine gun.

A few days later I sent the text of "The Oath" with 120 signatures to Moscow, to the Radio Committee. Approximately a week later, the radio broadcast it to the entire nation, and mentioned my name as well. After the war I learned that my mother's sister had heard the broadcast at work and immediately rushed to my home to tell my parents about it.

Hard fighting ensued on the approaches to the Berezina River. Bonaparte in the battle at the Berezina managed to save the bones of his army, but the actions of Marshal Kutuzov to this day raise heated controversy: there is the opinion that Kutuzov, an experienced politician, simply gave Napoleon a chance for salvation, understanding that the complete destruction of the French Army would disrupt the current balance of power in Europe disadvantageously for Russia. But now Rokossovsky at the Berezina gave the Germans no chance to save "the skeleton" of their army—he demolished the enemy and continued further pursuit of the broken fragments. The liberation of the capital of Belorussia lay ahead.

18

Forward—to the West!
June–July 1944

Operation Bagration: He Who Laughs Last, Laughs Best

According to a series of 31 May 1944 Stavka directives, the Red Army began final preparations for its largest offensive of the war to that date—a combined offensive of four *fronts* designed to crush the German Army Group Center in Belorussia and clear the path to Poland and East Prussia on the Minsk–Warsaw–Berlin axis.

At this time, Army Group Center was holding a large salient jutting into our lines, known as the Belorussian Balcony, based upon the "fortress cities" of Vitebsk, Orsha, Mogilev, and Bobruisk. Their defensive fortifications were strong and deeply echeloned, and they took advantage of the difficult terrain in the area. But misled by our masking and deception measures and their own erroneous assumptions, Hitler and the German high command made a profound strategic error. Believing that our main 1944 summer offensive would fall south of the Pripiat' marshes, Hitler had concentrated nearly all the main panzer and motorized formations on the Eastern Front to the south, in the Ukraine. Thus, Army Group Center lacked the mobile forces necessary to counter any of our tank breakthroughs.

For Operation Bagration, the Stavka arrayed the reinforced forces of the First Baltic Front, First Belorussian Front, Second Belorussian Front, and Third Belorussian Front around the German salient. Led by General I. Kh. Bagramian, General K. K. Rokossovsky, General G. F. Zakharov, and General I. D. Cherniakovsky respectively, each *front* was commanded by a highly capable, experienced general who had passed through the harsh academy of the initial war years.

The Red Army had its typical quantitative superiority over the defending German forces, and in the designated breakthrough places, the *fronts* held an enormous superiority over the enemy in men, tanks, and artillery. But the Red Army of 1944 was a qualitatively different one from its previous versions. The new Red Army had been tempered in battle and was now equipped with the latest military equipment. Command and control were greatly improved, and thanks to Allied military assistance through lend-lease, the full effects of which were now beginning to tell, the Red Army had far greater mobility. For the first time, the complete superiority of the Soviet air force was evident.

The Stavka also prepared thoroughly and in great detail for the offensive, including such aspects as training, reconnaissance, and the coordination of forces. Under strict secrecy and rigorous measures to conceal our movements, formations were shifted and redeployed to concentrate strength at the selected points of attack.

As part of the massive preparations for the offensive, in early June 1944 our division was transferred to the 36th Rifle Corps, 31st Army, of the Third Belorussian Front. Our army's mission was to attack along both banks of the Dnepr River in the direction of Dubrovno and Orsha and, together with the 11th Guards Army, liquidate the German Orsha grouping.

Before the start of Operation Bagration, on several occasions the Germans had broadcast to us:

"Don't let our hedgehog bite you in the ass, Ivan! Hee-hee . . ."

After these transmissions, our annoyed division commander, General Polevik, would tell us, "OK, we'll show them 'hee-hee.'"

On 23 June at 6:40 A.M., the first salvoes of Katiusha rockets soared into the sky, which announced the onset of Operation Bagration. The artillery, mortar, and aerial attacks struck the adversary simultaneously with unbelievable force. "Just try, German, to hold out!" our frontline soldiers joyfully kept repeating.

Inspired by the previously heretofore unseen support on the ground and from the air, our soldiers rushed into the attack. It was the job of our division to take Buroe Selo—one of the enemy's main strong points on our army's line of advance toward Dubrovno.

Skovorodkin's 653rd Rifle Regiment was the first to go into battle. But the attackers ran into heavy walls of fire from "not fully suppressed" enemy weapon emplacements. Polevik threw the 376th Rifle Regiment at the designated breakthrough spot in support. But this regiment too was stopped: the wall of fire forced the soldiers to dig in up to their ears. The first two days passed without any visible result other than heavy casualties.

"Hee-hee!" again rang out over the airwaves.

General Polevik flew into a rage. But then a situation arose that allowed the division commander to undertake a successful maneuver. Our division's right-flank 673rd Rifle Regiment, attacking relentlessly along the Moscow-Minsk highway, penetrated the enemy's defenses here and forced the Germans to retreat. The left flank of the enemy around Buroe Selo became exposed. The division commander ordered the 673rd Regiment to withdraw back across the Dnepr River, redeploy, and then force a new crossing of the river at a different location. The regiment smoothly carried out the assignment. After this maneuver, all three regiments struck the adversary simultaneously and from different directions. At 2:30 A.M. on 26 June, enemy resistance at Buroe Selo collapsed and the Germans abandoned the town to prevent their encirclement.

In this battle, as I was dashing across the Minsk highway, I had a very close call with death. Some German fool tried to plug me with a bullet. Like a razor, the bullet neatly clipped the watch off my left wrist and blew it to pieces.

On this day, I also encountered a German Ferdinand heavy tank destroyer for the first time. These German marvels, which mounted their powerful 88-mm PAK gun on the chassis of a Porsche Tiger, had been deployed on the Minsk highway as a tank barrier. Some T-34s calmly maneuvered around the barrier, approached it from both flanks to extremely close range, and then shot up the armored monsters from their 85-mm cannons without any fuss.

Minsk

Time was pressing; it was necessary to reach Minsk as soon as possible and continue the pursuit of the retreating enemy. Tanks led the way, followed by the leading units of our division—mechanized infantry on Studebaker trucks. The rest of the division advanced on horse-drawn carts. Having reached the city's outskirts successfully, we disembarked and entered the city as scattered fighting was still going on.

The city was burning. After three years of German occupation, it represented a terrible spectacle with its emptiness, lifelessness, and destitute streets. A multitude of corpses, both German and ours, lay scattered about everywhere. Grenade explosions and gunfire were still erupting, and from time to time tanks rushed past, leaving plumes of dust in their wake. The smell of burning lingered in the air. Groups of frightened residents were reluctant to emerge from building basements, ditches, and dugouts, still not believing what was happening and that their liberation was at hand.

Our mechanized infantry had followed the tanks into the city. Leaping from the trucks, our soldiers started rooting Germans out of buildings, basements, and sheds. By the middle of the day, a battalion had reached the House of Government and the House of the Red Army, the tallest buildings in the city. The Germans had mined both buildings and prepared them for demolition. People from the underground resistance helped the sappers make their way to the subfloors of the building so they could cut the wires leading to the demolition charges. On the top floors of the buildings, which had recently been liberated from the Germans, red flags began to flutter in the wind—I had passed them out to soldiers before the start of the offensive.

People then rushed to embrace us, and there were tears of joy! Moonshine appeared, and the people brought us modest treats, kissed us repeatedly, and thanked us. From all directions, partisans were leading captured Germans, some of whom had changed into civilian clothing, which seemed to amuse the partisans: "We almost let the vermin get away! We didn't recognize them at first glance!" By the end of the day, handmade flags also began to fly over many buildings; surviving citizens had raised them.

We didn't stop in Minsk, but passed through it to a designated assembly point and stopped in the nearest village. Having washed and eaten a bite, the exhausted soldiers dropped onto the grass. General Polevik strictly ordered: "Don't touch anyone before morning!"

The Mobile Battalion

Within the framework of the continuing operation, the 31st Army's commander ordered the formation of a mobile battalion of around 200 men, to equip it properly, and send it without delay toward the Neman River. The battalion was ordered to reach the Neman, avoiding all battles, and seize a bridgehead across it, in order to secure a crossing place for the entire division. The battalion was ordered to be ready to move out at 5:00 A.M. on 5 July.

Colonel Kudriavtsev was placed in command of the mobile unit, which was mounted on Studebaker trucks. Kudriavtsev already had considerable experience for a task like this, as he had previously commanded a forward detachment [*peredovoy otriad*].

The commander of the 673rd Rifle Regiment, to which the division commander had entrusted such an important job, created the unit from experienced frontline soldiers—they came primarily from the 2nd Battalion and formed the core of the unit. The commander of the 2nd Battalion, Senior Lieutenant Zakhar Diudin, and his deputy commander for political affairs, Lieutenant Georgii Myshinsky, also became part of the new unit, as did the battalion *komsorg* Lieutenant Pasha Bernikov, who was an experienced, intelligent officer. The regiment's political department included me in the unit as well.

The mobile unit was well armed: fifteen light machine guns, one heavy machine gun, and three 45-mm antitank guns, as well as snipers and antitank riflemen. All the soldiers received PPSh-41 submachine guns. We were equipped with two radio sets—and even medics—and we received dry rations for five days. The vehicles were loaded to the maximum with ammunition, fuel, and food.

On 5 July at 5:30 A.M., the unit set off on its way. The vehicle with battalion commander Diudin led the column, acting as both the scout and combat security. Colonel Kudriavtsev followed Diudin's truck in his Willys jeep, which also had a radio set and a guard. The rest of the column followed Kudriavstev's jeep.

I rode in the tail vehicle, so I could observe the entire column and advise the colonel of anything happening behind him.

The trucks followed a strictly defined route on a map. We moved along forested roads, trying to avoid main thoroughfares, heavily populated areas, even small villages. Every three hours the column stopped for twenty or thirty minutes to communicate by radio with the division and allow the men a rest. The July day was long, the evening was bright; the trucks didn't stop until midnight, and by 5:00 A.M. with the first streaks of dawn, we loaded up again and moved out.

Following my rule to remain among the rank and file, I refused a spot in the truck's cabin and sat together with the soldiers in the back. Next to me on my right was Il'ia Selekhov. Il'ia was from a family of peasants and had been serving since 1941. He was a former border guard—the only surviving man from his border unit. Wounded three times, he had been decorated with the Order of the Red Star. Now he was telling me about his early war experiences:

"About a day or two before the start of the war, a middle-aged woman tending a flock of geese appeared on the enemy side—the western bank of the Western Bug River—and she was shouting to us: 'The German is coming for you.' As soon as a German patrol approached her, she turned to her flock as if she was shouting at the geese. But she kept shouting her warning to us, several times, with all her might, so that we would catch her words. Returning to our border outpost, we told the chief and the commissar about the woman's warnings. The commissar only started laughing: 'It's some sort of crazy woman or provocateuress. Comrade Stalin has assured the army and the Soviet people that there will not be any war with Germany, so provokers are spreading gossip. The Germans are our best friends!' That very night, our border outpost ceased to exist, and it was 'our best friends' that did this to us!"

"Did the commissar perish?" I asked.

"Both the commissar and his wife—'Machine Gun Anka.' Having watched the film *Chapaev,* his wife was quite taken by the character of Machine Gun Anka, so that is what we called her. This woman learned how to operate a Maksim machine gun even better than her husband. She took her place behind one in the first minutes of the battle, yet was killed in the same first minutes. It goes without saying that in 1941 we were, as they say, just hoping things would work out all right."

Fedia Levkov spoke up; he had been fighting since 1942, had been twice wounded, and was decorated with the medal "For Courage"—he had saved a truck loaded with explosives and some people from an explosion. Fedia said:

"I'm from the Orel region, from the village of Starukha—that's what it's called [*starukha* in Russian means "old woman"]. Corn and grain are our business. We worked from dawn to dusk, and they paid us 30 kopecks for a day's work. Enough for a little kitchen-garden and a couple of goats."

A Word about the Soldier

Before the war I had never once spent time in a village, and I could only imagine what they were like from the books of Tolstoy, Turgenev, Leskov, and Chekhov—they were in the school curriculum, but they offered only depictions of the old, prerevolutionary village. I learned about the Soviet village for the first time from our servant, seventeen-year-old Tania. In the beginning of the 1930s, during the period of collectivization and the notorious famine in the Ukraine, Tania's parents had been sent to Siberia, but she had managed to escape to her native village. At the time, we were living in the Ukraine, in Krivoi Rog, where my father was managing a mine. Tania came to my father, honestly told him everything that had happened to her, and asked for a job with the mine. Papa brought her home. I didn't really understand what she was saying, and didn't try to parse the new words I was hearing: "*kolkhoz*," "kulak," "middle class," "poor peasant," "militia," "exile," "resettlement," and "work norm." I was then only eight years old. Sholokhov's *The Virgin Soil Upturned: Part 1*, which I had studied in my final year of school, also told me little about life in the Soviet village. It seems I must have read it with closed eyes, or the assignment came at the most difficult time of my youth, when my father was sent away to prison for twenty-eight months.

The first time I saw a village was in November 1941, when I had been sent as an agent to that village for a month. The impression I gained then was a painful one.

Having wound up at the front from the Tiumen specialist school, and during the years of the war, I served in five *fronts* with four different divisions, and I met many peasants in soldiers' greatcoats—Russians, Ukrainians, Belorussians, Tatars, Kazakhs, and Uzbeks. These people had an enormous influence on me—on my attitude and character. In fact, their influence on me was even greater than that of all my commanders and commissars. From the Russian peasant I gained a sense of reason—it was the school of schools, a font of life wisdom and nobility.

The peasants helped me understand better why our villages turned out to be so empty and impoverished, and how today's *kolkhoz* peasant differed from Tolstoy's heroes. Passing through Russian and Belorussian villages, I saw much sorrow; listening to the stories of the *kolkhoz* men and women, I sought an explanation or understanding for why they forgave Soviet power for all the outrageous and terrible things it had done to them. They seemed to shrug it all off. Moreover, in the difficult hour, when the Motherland was on the threshold of death, they came to her aid so readily. Why? For what cause?

The explanation probably lies in their way of life. These people lived on the land, and it had filled them with simple wisdom, faith in humanity, and a belief in the sanctity of labor—which indeed formed the basis of all human life, handed down to us from God. Some days I heard them say, "Children and the infirm will be made noble. And how can one live without nobility?" There is often something almost childlike in the Russian peasant—sincerity, a desire for truth, and a faith in seniors. Talking with these people, I learned that human intelligence and culture are not at all defined by one's education or erudition, as encyclopedias maintain, but rather by the inner molding of the heart and soul. It is not for nothing that people have long been using the expression, "a warmhearted friend," to describe a peasant—and this is the highest praise.

The whole community would gather to see the peasants off to war with a simple expression: "Go with God!" Winding up at the front, the peasant understood that he wouldn't likely live long in the war. But I never noticed any bitterness or spiritual cracks in any one of them, or any hostility toward military discipline. Tvardovsky, like no one else, caught these special strands in the peasant spirit, and through this insight so successfully composed his poem about Vasilii Tiorkin. I read this poem several times to the soldiers, and they would ask to hear it over and over again. The average soldier accepted the character of Tiorkin as his own comrade and brother.

I was often present at soldiers' conversations, and I myself took part in many of these "manly little talks," as I affectionately called them. I noticed that most often in these tales of home, the light of hope was present in all their dear ones and families: the hope that the war would soon end, and that things would change for the better.

"I have a son—he's literate, the first one in the village," a conversation started. "After serving in the army, he remained in the city, studied to become an engineer, and now we're putting our trust in him . . ."

In all these conversational beginnings, a latent question was detectable: "What will our life be like in the future?" Probably, it is precisely this hope, and this humility before the elements, wherein lies the secret of the peasants' forgiveness and impassive attitude toward authority, toward the war, and toward all the other adversities and sudden turns of life—in the hope that even these would pass and somehow everything would change for the better, and some eventual gain would emerge from all the current pain and suffering.

The Soldiers' Aphorisms

Any sort of social intercourse can be instructive. But to what end? I've already told you about my first day at the front and my encounter with "Uncle" Kuzia, when I developed the idea of jotting down the advice of experienced soldiers after I burned my diary. Day after day in the dugouts, directly in the trenches, in the field, in the woods, often around a campfire, I collected bits and pieces of a soldier's wisdom. I can't remember a single case when someone declined a friendly conversation. That's how an entire manuscript arose, which I entitled, "A Compilation of the Soldiers' Rules of Conduct." I didn't try to hide my undertaking, and I often read my notes to young commanders and new recruits. Nonetheless, in order to protect myself and to derail any hostile critics, I started my "Compilation" with a bunch of Red Army slogans about proper obedience and behavior in battle.

Despite my precautionary measure, one day, having heard about this eccentric officer who was collecting aphorisms, a high-ranking commissar summoned me. After flipping through a dozen pages, he gave a smirk: "People will learn how to fight even without your scribblings, so I advise you to occupy yourself with something more useful. Your direct responsibilities are to spend more time at the front, to inspire the warriors, and get them to rise into the attack. So go do it! And no more conceits!"

What stupidity! In the German army any soldier, not to mention officer or general, could keep a diary. I found out about this, understandably, much later. But at the time I kept quiet. However, there were a lot of unflattering things said about this Party grandee. This son of a bitch had reached the point where he forced new Party members among the soldiers in the frontline trenches to make their way from the frontline to the rear in order to obtain their Party card, sometimes under direct fire.

I finally calmed down when the divisional newspaper printed a dozen rules from my "Compilation" under the heading: "Words of Advice from Experienced Frontline Soldiers (from the frontline notes of Captain Ch.)." The division command read the article; some praised it, others held their tongues, and someone, as was usually the case, had a laugh.

Unfortunately, my labor of many years burned up during a fire in the Count's Castle, where the division staff was located. This occurred in Hungary on 12 November 1945, on my birthday.

I've since forgotten much of what I had written then, but all the same I was able to recreate some of it by memory as an example of that which helped me and other soldiers survive:

A COMPILATION OF THE SOLDIERS' RULES OF CONDUCT
Take care of your honor from youth.
Never forget about the oath you've taken.
Guard your unit's combat banner [guidon or colors] with your life.
An order from the command is the law.
Don't discuss an order; carry it out.
Don't argue with the command—it is like spitting into the wind.
Don't be caught by a commander who is in an angry mood.
Don't take a step on enemy territory without permission from command.

There's no complaining in the army.

Strive to put one past the commanders, but you'd better not get caught!

Guard your commanding officer.

Die if you must in doing so, but rescue a comrade.

Help out old soldiers and new recruits as much as you can.

Preserve frontline comradeliness.

Remember the feeling of fellowship.

Forget the bad, but always remember the good.

Don't do anything thoughtless.

Don't ignore the advice of experienced soldiers.

Don't eat anything salty or sweet before a march.

Don't stuff your belly before a battle. Try to limit your intake.

Always keep a couple of bread morsels and a flask of water in reserve.

He who has a little tobacco is the man who has a holiday waiting for him.

To eat to your fill is just as important as having reliable cover.

Learn to eat and sleep on the move and in any weather.

If you're wounded, don't be afraid of the blood.

Don't catch your own bullet in battle.

Remember, a bullet flies more quickly than you can react.

In a combat situation, forget about shame! Nobody will judge you.

Don't ever yield to panic in battle, and suppress your fears.

Don't rely upon your eyes and ears: they can trick you.

Kill the adversary; otherwise the adversary will finish you off.

Learn to hate the enemy: without hatred, you won't overcome him.

Don't shoot prisoners.

Don't read enemy leaflets.

Don't praise the adversary and don't believe his cunning speeches.

Don't pass along rumors and gossip. Cut them off!

Don't hope that the adversary will forgive your inexperience.

Don't keep personal notes at the front.

Learn to hold your tongue.

Don't confide anything to an unknown person.

Search for, find, and use your own ingenuity in battle.

Get used to difficulties—don't walk away from them, but overcome them.

Any success requires endurance and patience.

Become friends with the earth—it's your best friend in combat.

Find some cover from enemy fire even on flat ground.

Strive, as much as possible and wherever possible, to deceive the enemy.

Don't miss an opportunity!

The lazy soldier is a burden to all.

Remember Suvorov's principle: each soldier must know and understand
   how to behave in combat situations.

Bullets see no differences between ranks.

There is nothing more pleasing than when someone fires at you and misses.

Always treat everyone else the same and be prepared to come to their
   assistance.

Carry out an order responsibly, never relying on the off chance that it may
   be rescinded or become unnecessary.

Remember, it is not WHAT you are doing that is important, but HOW you
   do it.

If you've given your word, keep it no matter what it might cost you.

If you meet a woman—don't let the chance slip to celebrate life; another
   chance may not come along.

After the war I learned that analogous rules, suggested by military practice
and soldiers' wit, exist in many armies. They traditionally curse the commissary,
in jest or even seriously; they don't have much regard for generals; and they
don't believe in the commanders' capabilities.

On Reconnaissance

On the evening of 9 July, the column of Studebakers reached the highway
leading to the Neman. It is approximately 230 kilometers [143 miles] from
Minsk to the Neman River; if you took the highway directly and without halts,
it was two days of travel. It took us nearly five days of driving to reach the river.
On the map it appeared that we were a little north of Grodno, in the district
of Shembolets. Our goal lay just a bit farther ahead; only a large forested tract,
split by a ribbon of highway, separated us from it. Upon reaching the highway,
Colonel Kudriavtsev stopped the vehicles, ordered the unit to form up, and
gave us a short speech:

"I congratulate you, officers and soldiers! We have reached the Neman
River, which Napoleon crossed in 1812, and 129 years later—Hitler's army.
Within an hour, we'll reach the banks of the Neman and make our crossing to
the opposite bank. The entire division is supposed to cross behind us. I'm confident that this unit will not let down its comrades. The situation is still unclear;
therefore I ask all of you to prepare for possible combat."

Actually, at this time the forward zone of the advancing armies had become
crowded and confused: the area was swarming with people, equipment, various
auxiliary and special units—including our mobile units, which were pursuing
the enemy—and remnants of German units, which were hurrying after their
own retreating armies.

The first truck of our column had just pulled out onto the highway when the men aboard it spotted a parked string of vehicles about 300 meters ahead down the road. Who were they—ours, or theirs? Our column stopped. Colonel Kudriavtsev sent forward some scouts.

"Germans!" they reported, having returned. "A few tanks and five or six vehicles with infantry."

"Reverse! Into the forest!" the command followed.

The trucks turned around, and soon we came upon an alternate forest road leading to the river. Our scouts told us that the Germans on the highway had paid no attention to our departure, plainly supposing that we were Germans trying to catch up with our own unit, just like they were.

At the approach to the river we spotted a forester's lodge.

"Are there Germans around?" Kudriavtsev asked an old man who emerged. "When was the last time you saw them?"

"The German was here; it was yesterday," the old man said. "They blew up the bridge and left. Over that way, toward Grodno." Then he added: "But if someone wants to get across, there's a way. There's a large, strong raft nearby. The Germans left it behind in 1941. It will support both vehicles and guns."

What luck! As it turned out, it was the only way to get across.

That night, the entire battalion crossed the river using the raft. As a covering force, the colonel left one gun and a squad of soldiers behind by the forest road where it exited down to the river. Once on the opposite shore, we rolled the trucks and remaining 45-mm guns a little farther from the bank and camouflaged them.

The first order of business was to determine the strength of the adversary confronting us and what his plans were: whether he was intending to continue his retreat or was trying to dig in and turn the Neman into a new defensive barrier.[1] At dawn the colonel decided to send some scouts in the direction of Grodno. I was designated to lead the group.

Taking a Studebaker and three scouts, as well as a light machine gun and an abundant number of grenades, we set off on our way. I sat in the truck's cabin next to the driver. After several minutes of driving, we exited onto a country road and found ourselves in a small village. We stopped by the first homes and questioned the peasants who emerged from them: "Where are the Germans? When did you see them last?"

The answer was pretty much the same one that the forester had given us the day before: there were no Germans here or in the next village; they had rolled away in tanks and vehicles toward Grodno.

We moved on, taking with us a volunteer Polish guide, who offered to help us make our way out of the forest and onto the macadam road leading to Grodno. I had just fallen asleep when we pulled out onto the highway.

I woke up from a sharp jab in the side. "Look, Comrade Senior Lieutenant, Germans!" the driver shouted and immediately slammed on his brakes.

We had bumped into a German outpost! An artillery battery was deployed like a barrier across the road leading into Grodno. Nearby, likely a whole company of Germans was drawn up in formation, listening to something their commanding officer was telling them.

Without any order from me, the driver turned the Studebaker back around—and by this action saved us all! He drove the truck at high speed while I shouted back to the junior lieutenant through the open door: "Get ready for battle!" By now the Germans had spotted our truck and opened fire. The first shells began to catch up with us. At that moment the driver, spotting a road into the forest, sharply swerved onto it and accelerated. The Germans also shifted their fire, but now they had to fire blindly in the direction of the forest road.

At last everything fell silent. We stopped. Only now did I notice that our Polish guide had disappeared. Had he gotten frightened and slipped away from us in the chaos, or had he been instructed to lead us into a trap?

We had to gather information about the enemy's dispositions and movements, so in every village we passed through, I sent the scouts to have a talk with the villagers. On our return route, I carefully examined all the near and distant hills around us for signs of the enemy. One of the scouts, apparently misinterpreting my activity, sighed dreamily, glancing at the chain of hills: "There must be some nice dames beyond those hills ..."

Having returned to the battalion's position, I reported to the battalion commander about everything I had seen and heard, and I had a remarkable conversation with Colonel Kudriavtsev, which I consider to be the most important of all the conversations I had with any command throughout the war.

"Grodno is occupied by the Germans," I said. "Local citizens have seen a lot of tanks positioned in the villages along the Neman. But the most important thing is the fact that we have three heights in our area. If the Germans occupy them, they'll be able to throw us back into the river. If we hold them, then we'll block their way out of Grodno."

I asked for a map and showed them the location of all three heights. The colonel attentively heard me out without interruption, thanked me, and then said:

"We're not supposed to do what you're proposing. I have been ordered to cross the Neman, seize a bridgehead, and secure a crossing for the division. It should be arriving on the tenth day of our mission. The army will immediately send up pontoon and sapper battalions to erect a crossing. I can't take any chances. We're just a small handful of men in comparison with the adversary, and they have tanks and artillery."

Senior Lieutenant Zakhar Diudin supported me:

"I agree with the *komsorg*'s opinion: if the Germans occupy the heights, the division won't in any way be able to cross here."

"Comrade Colonel," I tried again, "we won't be able to drive them from those hills. There will be a lot of blood spilled!"

"Senior Lieutenant, this isn't 1942," the battalion commander confidently objected. "If it becomes necessary, we'll call for the air force." And with that he ended the discussion.

To be honest, just in case, he ordered the battalion to occupy the nearest hill, and all night long the soldiers dug entrenchments.

Unfortunately, my fears were realized.

By the very next day, the situation was changing radically: the division seemed to have forgotten about us. Two regiments and the divisional artillery turned away from our little bridgehead and moved toward Grodno, drawn into the fighting for the city that the 3rd Guards Cavalry Corps had already initiated. Denied support, we experienced repeated attacks by heavy forces, and in the very first battle Kudriavtsev himself was mortally wounded. He was a good man, regular army, but he was also a stubborn and exceedingly cautious man of little initiative.

Fighting for the Neman Bridgehead

Late in the evening after my return to the battalion, I settled down on the riverbank, beneath the spreading branches of a tree that overhung the river, and decided to grab a little sleep. The next day promised to be difficult. Twilight was gradually shrouding the riverbank and covering the swiftly flowing river. A strong, cold wind was sweeping down from the hills flanking the river, flinging spray from the water surface and sometimes covering me with a chilling mist. In the village next to us, there were the ruins of bread ovens, which had been built at the time when the Emperor's Grand Army was crossing the Neman. At one time, Napoleon's army was hiding beyond these high hills, and somewhere nearby, on the river bank, Napoleon's own tent had been pitched so he could observe the crossing. But Napoleon was gone, just as Hitler himself would disappear one day, while the indifferent river all the same still flowed and would continue its endless, playful motion. Napoleon and Hitler were conquerors, villainous geniuses over whom God would judge, as Mavrii would have said. It seems that I nevertheless managed to doze off . . .

The rumble of an exploding shell, which had plonked down into the river, snatched me from my slumber. Immediately I heard the loud voice of Colonel Kudriavtsev:

"Everybody up!"

Quickly clambering back up the slope to the crest of the hill, we took position in the entrenchments we had dug during the night. At dawn, the battalion accepted the first battle.[2]

Enemy aviation and artillery began working over the entire location of the battalion. The previously silent hills erupted with lethal volleys of fire. I involuntarily recalled the words of the scout, "There must be some lovely dames beyond those hills." Meanwhile, a little distant from us, a pontoon battalion had reached the river and was quickly throwing up a crossing. The enemy airplanes left us alone and rushed to attack the pontoon. Under constant shellfire and bombing attacks from the enemy, the sappers completed a new bridge, but toward evening it was demolished by bombs.

After the initial bombing and the preparatory artillery fire, enemy submachine gunners launched an attack upon us, supported by machine-gun fire from self-propelled guns positioned at the bottom of the hill. The attack shook us, and Colonel Kudriavtsev was mortally wounded early in the fight; but Zakhar Diudin, who replaced the fallen Kudriavtsev, rallied us to counterattack. Tossing grenades at the attackers, we managed to hurl them back off the hill. Battalion *komsorg* Pavel Bernikov received a concussion. Fragments from a nearby exploding shell severely wounded Diudin, and the deputy commander for political affairs, Grigorii Myshinsky, replaced him. The opening bombardment had knocked out our 45-mm guns, and all of our machine guns were gradually put out of action. The situation grew precarious. The adversary was trying to hurl us back into the Neman, whatever the cost.

One day remained until the division's arrival. One day! We had to hold out until at least the forward regiment arrived. We had to endure, to hold on! Just then, the enemy again made a rush at us. None of us was thinking about heroism, just as we gave no thought to death; the remnants of our battalion strove at whatever price to resist the enemy's onslaught.

As the sun began to set, the deputy commander for political affairs sent me a note: I was urgently to ferry the severely wounded across to the opposite bank, locate the approaching 376th Rifle Regiment, and inform them of our serious situation, so that through our combined efforts we might force the Germans to abandon the heights they had occupied.

I clambered down the hill to the riverbank, found the raft that had been concealed in the lee of a sharp bend in the river, and hauled it to where the wounded were located. There were twelve of them, including Zakhar Diudin and Pasha Bernikov. Together with a surgeon's assistant and two medics, we neatly loaded all the wounded onto the raft, then carried aboard the body of Colonel Kudriavtsev and floated across to the opposite shore. Scouts from the 376th Rifle Regiment met us there! The wounded men were immediately transferred into the care of doctors from the *medsanbat*.

The regiment prepared to cross. There was not a single boat or log to be found, so men from the regiment dismantled empty huts and quickly built rafts from the material. The regiment's Party organizer, Captain Kirill Koshman, was the first to cross aboard our raft, together with about twenty men. We were old acquaintances and rejoiced at our meeting. As we crossed the river, I tried to explain the mobile battalion's situation precisely and quickly.

"Understood!" Koshman said as he drew his pistol from his holster. "We won't waste any time; they're waiting for us. You stay here and report on every-thing to the regiment commander. We must urgently prepare to receive more wounded—we'll have to ferry them across during the night. You must find the commander of the antitank battalion and advise him where best to deploy his guns, and mark the location of the enemy-held heights on their maps. At dawn we'll set about the process of taking them. If necessary, we'll need the support of rocket launchers. Until we've established radio communications, I ask you to stay with the regiment commander."

Koshman was a fearless man, full of initiative. Leading his detachment of men, he immediately headed for the hilltop positions.

During the night, I saw to the evacuation of sixteen more wounded men. The main body of the 376th Rifle Regiment began crossing the Neman. I spent the entire day with the regiment. Everything that Koshman requested was carried out.

On that day, for the first time I saw how human hatred and combat rage were stronger than the fear of death. The warriors leaped from their rafts, and without pausing even a minute, they rushed forward, streaming around the flanks of the enemy-held heights. These were soldiers who had passed through long-suffering Belorussia, and what they had seen there was even more terrible than what they had seen at Viaz'ma, Rzhev, or around Smolensk. They came under enemy fire, but there was no force on Earth that could have stopped them.

By the end of the day, the situation had sharply changed. On the night of 16 July, Grodno had fallen, and the rest of the 220th Rifle Division was moving to our assistance; Guguev, the commander of the 376th Rifle Regiment, informed me of this development. Having given up Grodno, the Germans began to re-treat hastily, abandoning equipment along their way. They also abandoned the heights that loomed over our bridgehead. Our Il-2 Shturmovik ground-attack planes appeared above the Neman, and they hunted down and attacked the panicked, fleeing enemy forces.

Exactly a day after the liberation of Grodno, on 17 July 1944, tens of thou-sands of Germans at last managed to complete their march to Moscow, toward which they had set out so eagerly in 1941. But now they were arriving not as conquerors but under escort as prisoners. More than 52,000 of them were captured in the early days of Operation Bagration and were marched along the Sadovoi Ring road under the gazes of the gathered passersby. My parents soon wrote me about the impressions that Moscow's citizens had as they watched the prisoners march past.

For the liberation of Grodno, the 220th Rifle Division was awarded the Order of the Red Banner. Battalion commander Zakhar Diudin and battalion *komsorg* Pavel Bernikov received the same honor. The Party organizer of the 376th Rifle Regiment, Kirill Koshman, was awarded the title "Hero of the Soviet Union" for his role in the forcing of the Neman River. They decorated me with the Order of the Patriotic War, first degree.

After the war, finding myself in Minsk, I visited the Belorussian Museum of the Great Patriotic War. There I saw documents about our mobile battalion, which had defended the Neman bridgehead.

The National Border

As soon as the battle for our bridgehead ended, our mobile battalion was disbanded. Though strictly speaking, there was hardly anyone left to disband.

But our 220th Rifle Division was already moving farther to the west. Brushing aside several covering forces along our way, at 8:00 P.M. on 17 July 1944, our division was gazing upon the national border! It was a special day and hour for each person who was lucky enough to experience this tremendous moment! Yet this literally historic event was occurring on the evening of the very same day when the captured Germans had been marched in disgrace through Moscow. Coincidences are astonishing, and there seems to be something enigmatic about them.

Reconnaissance troops scouting ahead of our main force were the first to reach the national border. Out of breath, one of them ran back to meet the marching column of our division, shouting: "The border! The border! Ura-a!"

The column sped ahead, and then we all came to an abrupt halt. That strip of land that is called "the border" lay before our common gaze. At first all of us, soldiers and officers, quietly took in that which had always seemed so menacing and unattainable, and which people always sensed to be strongly and permanently defended. Literally like crazy men, we looked all around, asking the same questions: where were those traditional attributes that in our imagination we always associated with the Soviet border? Where was the barbed wire? Where were the long, deep ditches that separate two countries? Where, finally, were the border markers and guard towers? What of the barriers? There was none of this. It had all disappeared somewhere.

Later we learned that the residents of the nearest village had wanted to carry off the dismantled border markers for firewood, but the local authority had refused them permission, possibly foreseeing that they might be needed again one day. We even saw them, these symbols of the border: they were lying next to a patch of woods, arranged in neat stacks, in anticipation of their renewed life.

The border! How many times had artists painted it! How many songs and verses had poets and composers created about it! As school kids, we had tried to forget the song that had been drilled into our heads at lessons:

> The borders of the Soviet Union
> He has closed to the black ravens,
> He has garbed them in concrete and stone
> And forged them in cast-iron.
> So let us sing the song, comrades,
> About the greatest sentry,
> Who sees and hears all—
> Let us sing the song about Stalin.

We wanted to forget these lyrics as quickly as possible.

But now each of us sensed with our entire being the greatness of that which we were experiencing! We knew it was a special moment in our lives. Then, without any command, men began firing into the air to celebrate and salute our accomplishment. They fired from submachine guns and rifles, carbines and pistols.

Then the unbelievable started! Everybody rushed to embrace each other. Some fell to their knees, raising their arms toward the sky. Others rushed to the solitary border marker that had been raised and emplaced for this ceremonial occasion, and were hugging and kissing it, and tearing off chips as keepsakes. A few men were gathering soil and wrapping it in handkerchiefs. And everybody was dancing! And how! What dance didn't they do—Russian, the *lezginka,* and the Ukrainian *hopak*! They were doing the *chechetka* [a tap dance] so adroitly and creatively that everyone was delighted, applauded, stamped their feet, and started dancing themselves. Accordionists and guitarists were by now playing, and men started singing ditties. Everybody strained to catch the clever words and clapped along. Men would step into the ring of clapping men from their place in the circle and perform a newly improvised ditty.

> Soon the war will end,
> Soon Hitler will be kaput, we vow.
> Soon our temporary wives
> Will be bellowing like a cow.
> Oh you, pigeon-toed Hitler,
> You'll surely pay for your sin.

In that world the girls will be asking:
Who made off with all our men?

For just a few minutes, people became completely different—unfettered, they straightened their backs and stood taller; pride appeared on their faces, and their eyes sparkled. If only for a short while, the terrible memories of the days of retreat and death slipped away, the years we endured together, the tears over those who passed away—all vanished in this moment of common triumph and joy! How splendid that we had lived to see this hour! That we were among the first of the first to cross this fixed geographical boundary, which was so precious to us all, and toward which we had all been striving so long! It seemed to all of us that the end of the war was now just a stone's throw away.

It was a truly unforgettable day. It was as if orchestras were playing and drums were banging in our souls! Our hearts, intoxicated with victory, were bursting with pride at the duty we had fulfilled.

A documentary film crew arrived. After some brief words of greeting from the commander of the 653rd Rifle Regiment, Skovorodkin, the dancing and singing came to an end, everybody formed back up in column, and the film crew started filming the triumphant moment as the regiment marched in ceremonial step past the border post and across the border.

The heroes of the crushing defeat of the Germans at Moscow, Rzhev, Smolensk, Vitebsk, Minsk, Orsha, Grodno, and on the Neman were marching. And each soldier, as he passed this solitary border marker, gave it a salute, taking it as a symbol of the liberation of our native land from the fascist filth.[3]

Part Four

In Poland and
East Prussia

July 1944–April 1945

19

"The Untouchables"
July–December 1944

The Caprices of Command

The road rolled on farther to the west. On 18 July 1944, the division entered Polish territory.

Approximately a week later, the new chief of the Political Department, Colonel Kovyrin (Borisov had been promoted to a new position), summoned me and congratulated me on my own new promotion. I was now the assistant chief for Komsomol affairs of a division's Political Department. By army order, I was transferred to our neighbor, the 31st Army's 352nd Rifle Division. Saying farewell to my comrades and turning over my post as regimental *komsorg* to Vasia Ragulin, I hurried to my new place of duty.

When I arrived, it turned out that my post was already occupied. The 352nd Rifle Division's chief of the Political Department, Colonel Efimov, informed me that my predecessor, Captain Kuzin, had only been lightly wounded and was just about to return from the hospital, so the army was hurrying to return him to his post. Efimov asked me, however, to linger in the division's rear for a couple of weeks.

I hung around the division's rear for nearly a month with practically nothing to do. Over this period, the division advanced more than 100 kilometers [around 62 miles] and had experienced several fights. I sensed a certain scornful attitude in Efimov's attitude toward me. I hadn't liked this fat colonel from our first meeting: I find people who won't look me in the eye unpleasant. Captain Kuzin never did return. At last I figured out that they were messing around with me.

Getting no satisfaction from the command, I wound up calling the Political Department of the 31st Army; the deputy division commander for rear services, a fine fellow, helped me reach the number. The army's office asked me to call back after two or three days. I called back and was invited to meet with them. Upon my arrival, I was immediately handed a new assignment: I was ordered to report to the 331st Rifle Division—"the best in the 31st Army," as I was told at our parting. I would remain with the 331st Rifle Division until the last days of the war.

Division Commander Berestov and Chief of the Political Department Shilovich

I traveled to my new posting with some trepidation: the bad experience with Colonel Efimov had deeply discouraged me, and moreover, a division's Political Department is a complete institution with twelve to fifteen political workers. How would they receive me? My new position also troubled me: a higher army rank naturally brings about different relationships with soldiers and officers: would I be able to cope?

Two meetings occurred on the day of my arrival in the 331st Rifle Division. I met first with the division's chief of the Political Department, Colonel Shilovich. Aleksei Adamovich invited me to sit and in front of me opened the solidly sealed packet that I had brought with me from headquarters. Having looked over the files, he asked:

"Tell me, Senior Lieutenant, does what the army's clerks have written here correspond to the truth?"

I shrugged my shoulders.

"You see, in my time I have seen many references and I know that there is often a lot of phony stuff in them. It seems—on paper—that you have a capable man in front of you, but in actual fact they write this drivel to get rid of him as quickly as possible, so they paper over the blemishes and send him off. They've hit upon the idea of scattering political workers to the various units! But who'll take an unknown officer without great references?"

"The chief of the Political Department of the 352nd Rifle Division received this same file, and for some unknown reasons he didn't want to take me on board."

"Well, I understand these sorts. Efimov doesn't have much respect for your type. But I'm a Belorussian, and we've been living together with Jews like brothers for ages. My own wife was a Jew, and we lived happily together for almost a quarter century."

"Forgive me, why did you say 'was'?"

"We lived in Moscow, but her mother lived in Minsk. A week before the war started, my wife went to visit her mother. They both perished. They couldn't get out of the city in time."

I expressed my condolences.

"Well, fine, let's talk about the important thing. The division is preparing for new fighting; we're going to be attacking East Prussia. Why am I telling you this? You must remember, Senior Lieutenant, how we'll be entering enemy territory—without any sentimentalities for the Germans! They're going to get exactly what they deserve for their villainous crimes! That is the firm instruction from the Main Political Directorate of the Red Army and Navy."

He paused for a moment to let that admonition sink in, and then continued:

"Now about current business. Get acquainted with the division and its Komsomol members, with the officers, and with the political workers. I'll be brief about my expectations. I love people with initiative. In any situation, act in the way you think best and understand, that is to say, the decision is yours. It is important only for me to know one thing: where you are at all times. If you're needed, I'll call you myself. You'll be living together with the other members of the Political Department. That is all, it seems. But now you must see the general." Shilovich picked up the phone, called the division commander, and asked him to see me.

I was now the assistant chief for Komsomol affairs of the 331st Rifle Division's Political Department. Even more important, I felt like a free bird: now I was subordinate only to the chief of the Political Department.

Within several minutes I found myself standing before the 331st Rifle Division's commander, Pavel Fedorovich Berestov. I presented myself according to regulations. The general stretched out his hand and gave me a firm handshake:

"I love the Komsomol; I was a member myself. In 1929, as young man, the Party mobilized me and sent me to a village to organize the collectivization work there. The very first day, after I finished my gallant speeches, the peasant men gave me such a thrashing that to this day, I'm a little deaf in my right ear."

Two more officers were sitting in the room at a table, upon which was spread a map. The general introduced us:

"Colonel Lobachev Kirill Afanas'evich, the division chief of staff; we've been fighting together since the Moscow battles. And this young major is Levushka Rappoport—he's our assistant to the division chief of operations. He's my 'Shafirov' [a reference to Petr Pavlovich Shafirov, 1670–1739, famous Russian statesman under Peter the Great and chief translator in the Russian Foreign Office for many years, renowned for his knowledge of foreign languages]. I hope you know your Russian history?"

As the general talked, I began liking him more and more—his openness, simplicity, and sincerity. The star of the "Hero of the Soviet Union" medal, which he had received for the Belorussian operation, was gleaming on his field blouse, along with three Orders of the Red Banner and the Order of Suvorov. But in addition to his chest, his entire mouth was shining with gold. I thought to myself, "How strange, he doesn't seem to be an old man." The general burst out laughing:

"I see, Senior Lieutenant, that my gold teeth have surprised you more than my medals. Isn't that so?"

"That's true," embarrassed, I confirmed.

"It's a memento of those years, when in 1937, Komsomol members at the prison knocked out all my teeth, just like they did to Rokossovsky, but at the same time they also broke one of my ribs and all my toes. In 1940 I was lucky, and they released me; it seems Timoshenko had put in a word for me. Now we serve under the command of Ivan Danilovich Cherniakhovsky. The youngest general in the army, he's just thirty-nine years old. He's as wise as Solomon! A military professional of the highest order, he graduated from the military academy; there aren't many of those today." The general shot a glance at the table: "Do you know how to read a map?"

"Yes, we had an excellent instructor at the specialist school."

"What specialist school did you attend?"

"The Tiumen Combat-Infantry School, to be a mortar platoon leader. But we never managed to complete our training; we only studied for four months, and then we were sent to the front."

"If necessary, do you know how to handle a machine gun or mortar?"

"Absolutely."

"That's splendid! The three of us were just now trying to figure out where we might best strike the Germans. They've deployed select units on the border, and they're defending stubbornly. Our guys seized a few border settlements and villages near Gumbinnen but couldn't hold on to them. Such a thing hasn't happened to us before. The maps are terrible. As soon as we find officers among the prisoners, we send them immediately to Levushka so they can help him figure out where we are. And you, Komsomol member, for some reason have been stuck at the rank of senior lieutenant for quite a while. Your new post is that of a major; we'll ask Aleksei Adamovich to do a little something for you. (I was awarded the captain's rank in March 1945.) Now we've gotten to know a bit about each other," the general concluded the conversation. "If you need something, come see me. And you yourself let me know if we're neglecting something among the soldiers."

A Special Attachment

The news was stunning. Already by the next day, many knew about it through the grapevine. The division commander officially announced the news. Calling together the regiment and battalion commanders, the general revealed:

"Twenty-three female snipers are coming to join us. They're recent graduates from the Higher Sniper's School in Moscow. Army headquarters and the chief Komsomol leader have called me and asked that I receive the team personally and ensure normal frontline conditions for them. You only have a few days before they arrive, so get ready." Then he added sternly, "Remember, comrade officers, all these young women are untouchable! Whoever lays a finger on one—I'll rip off both his officer's straps and his head!"

"Untouchable"—it was necessary, but what a word to come up with!

The officers took the news differently. Some ridiculed it—calling it a typical Komsomol show. Others expressed themselves tersely: "We'll take a look at these 'warriors': not even a month will pass, and they'll be blown away by the wind."

But everyone took the preparations for their arrival seriously. We found decent quarters for them and made the proper adjustments, taking into account the nature of the contingent. We enclosed their quarters with a high fence and installed strong locks. "We don't have enough wire for the nest," some officers joked. The autumn was cold, so we delivered warm undergarments, boots, padded jackets, padded trousers, and hats with earflaps to their quarters. We even chose a warden for their residence—we entrusted this role to the chief of the division's bath and laundry unit, primarily because he was a teetotaler. One of the 31st Army's best snipers, Lieutenant Zhora Kasimov, was appointed to command the new sniper team. The experienced sniper Nikodim Ivanovich became the team's sergeant major.

On the day of arrival, the entire command turned out to greet the young women. Having left their kitbags in their quarters, and having slightly freshened themselves up from their long trip, the women formed up in the courtyard. The first woman stepped smartly out of the line and precisely reported:

"Katerina from Zatsepa. Senior Sergeant. Reporting for duty in the active army."

"Natal'ia from Krasnaia Presnia," announced the next in line.

That's how they all presented themselves—by their place of residence. All of them, with the exception of one, were from the Moscow area.

"Antonina from Smolensk Boulevard . . ."

Inspired, tender young faces, eyes full of enthusiasm; light, shapely figures and clean boots still carrying a Moscow gleam; neat overcoats; and hair gathered up beneath their forage caps. We looked at them and were awestruck—not a single plain-looking little thing among them! It was like a selection of fiancées! Likeable and attractive! "Yet why did the general think up this 'untouchable'? Just say any enchanting word and one of these ladies will come after you, because both they and we are nineteen or twenty years old"—that's what many of us dreamed aloud on that day.

The young women were given two days to rest after their trip, during which time Lieutenant Kasimov had a conversation with each and checked her ability to handle her weapon, and led several group discussions. Sharing his own experience, he compared a sniper with a minesweeper, saying:

"In both one case and the other, there is a fatal risk; therefore the sniper, like the minesweeper, must act with certainty, or else there will be trouble. When you go to meet the adversary, you must respect the sniper's two basic principles. First: the sniper must have confidence in his or her every shot. Second: shoot sparingly, but accurately!"

Legends circulated around Lieutenant Kasimov; therefore the women listened to him attentively. Often he was saying something well known, but to them it seemed as if they were hearing it for the first time. It was plain that the commander's words inspired the women but also caused them to reflect: would they be able to act correctly in a real situation?

Kasimov himself, on the other hand, was troubled by the fact that all the women could recite precisely, like a memorized verse, those things that constituted the sniper's craft—endurance, accurate shooting, and keen observation. "If you show patience, skill will come," the women confirmed. But at the same time, not once did any of them reveal her attitude toward the opponent with whom she would have to fight. Therefore, their commander concluded his final discussion with them with these words:

"You will be shooting at a real person, but this person is our enemy, the fascist scum! Never show him any pity! As soon as you begin your combat service, the most important thing for you will be to overcome this psychological barrier as quickly as possible. This is not easy. But you must always remember: the fascist must never be allowed to walk around freely, even behind his own heavily defended lines. We must force him to sense his own unavoidable death!"

After these classes, Kasimov reported to General Berestov:

"All the snipers are ready. I checked their knowledge of their weapon, their ability to use an optic sight, and their understanding of camouflage. They are familiar with the tactics of a sniper duel. Excuse me, Comrade General, but they are still quite young, and they haven't yet seen the enemy face-to-face— they don't yet understand what sort of beast he is. It is still premature to talk about their professionalism, but the women have enough patriotism, which means their ability will show up on the battlefield."

"Precisely, Lieutenant! Instruct them, share your experience with them, and take care of them. You are responsible for the life of each sniper."

"I promise, Comrade General."

"Fine. If you need something, come see me. I hereby authorize the sniper team to begin operations at the front."

"At once! We'll start tomorrow. We'll make the Germans hide like cockroaches."

On the next day, Lieutenant Kasimov, "Katerina from Zatsepa," and two other women moved into the front lines.

First Losses

The soldiers in the forward trenches were guarded in response to the arrival of the women, all asking the same question: would the young ladies be able to cope with the Fritzes? Meanwhile, the Germans across the way had dropped their guard: they didn't know that we now had a sniper team, and not anticipating any trouble, they were freely moving about in their trenches.

Kasimov divided his command of twenty-three snipers into three groups, with seven women in each. The groups rotated turns of every other day at the front line. Two women remained behind on duty each day. A day's operations started at 4:00 A.M. and lasted until evening twilight. Usually the snipers went out in pairs, stealthily creeping out into no-man's land, closer to the enemy, where they would select suitable primary, reserve, and decoy positions.

Kasimov was often at the front, monitoring the snipers' activities, trying to evaluate their performance. Twice a week he held training classes, where he analyzed each group's shift at the front.

The first days passed uneventfully. The following days were even calmer. Yet a problem arose on our side. The men often began to pester the women, some calling them "clever rascals." They tried to coax the young women out of doing their duty, telling them things like, "Don't busy yourself with such work, we'll deal with the Fritzes ourselves. It's better that you look after the campfires, and warm our bones."

It turned out not to be a simple matter to overcome this new psychological barrier of masculine chauvinism. "Tonia from Smolensk Boulevard," the most spirited of the women, found a way:

"Airplanes are the first matter of business, and the boys, the boys are a secondary concern!" she proclaimed. Then she added seriously: "Guys, just like you, we've come to fight, not to mess around with love affairs. A common duty has fallen to both our lots: let's set aside the frolicking until victory."

Soon the first tragedy occurred. "Natasha from Krasnaia Presnia," who was generally considered the best-looking of all the female snipers, slipped as she was descending a slope down into the trenches and tumbled downward. Just before she reached the trench, a burst of automatic fire caught her. A bullet penetrated her right shoulder and buried itself in her chest.

Everyone turned out for her funeral. Her friends sobbed without embarrassment. We all tried our best to comfort them. I can recall no other occasion at the front when anyone offered someone else so much consolation. They loved Natasha in the team, praised her beauty, and thought she had a promising future in the movies or the theater. The young woman herself was thinking about something completely different; she dreamed of getting married and quickly having three children.

This was yet another serious psychological challenge for the sniper team. Would the young women be able to overcome it?

After the funeral, the next shift, "Tania from Zemliany Val" and "Tania from Meshchanskaia," went out without any hesitation. Toward morning, two Germans started out for an artesian spring in no-man's land. Two bullets caught them before they could reach it. Another bullet dropped their comrade, who had hopped out of the bunker to find out what had happened.

So the two Tanias had opened the scoring for the team.

"Not bad!" the division commander said approvingly. "Three for one!" Then he decorated the two young women with medals.

The next week passed without result. The Germans were starting to be more cautious: they now understood that they were being observed through a sniper's scope.

Meanwhile, the young women's situation at the front became intolerable—whenever Kasimov wasn't present, the men at the front were badly pestering them, simply not letting them do their work. One officer, a strapping fellow, grabbed the slim little "Zosia from Samoteka" and tried to drag her into his dugout. Some nearby soldiers who witnessed this unpleasant scene tore the young woman from the paws of their commander and gave him a few solid punches, without concern for the possible consequences. There were no consequences: the lieutenant thought better than to report the incident. But the women filed a protest with Kasimov and refused to go into the frontline trenches without his presence.

Several days later, "Klava from Chukhlinka" was killed. She was a sweet, modest young woman. A skilled knitter, she made wool mittens for everyone. She dreamed of becoming a first-grade teacher after the war.

The women lost their nerve and became frightened. As we said in the trenches, "There is nothing more frightening than fear itself." But the team was experiencing this situation for the first time. Kasimov encouraged them and tried to help them overcome their fear. This was hard for his pupils to do. Someone even recalled that Klava had been killed on "an unlucky day"—she had experienced premonitions of her own death and was talking about it the night before.

Then unexpectedly a scandal occurred. Taking advantage of the departure of Kasimov and his sergeant major for an all-army gathering of snipers, three artillery officers cut a hole through the fence surrounding the women's residence, got the "bath-house" commandant drunk, tied him up, tossed him like a doll under a plank bed—and presented themselves to the young women like hussars. They had brought with them a guitar, some liquor, and some snacks, as if to show their respects to the fallen team members by arranging a funeral meal. The ladies drank and cried, cried and drank.

The next morning, the sniper shift reported late for duty. The battalion commander on the sector of the line where they finally showed up prohibited them from going out, fearing it was becoming too light for safe movement into their positions. "Vera from Taganka," who was considered by her friends to be the bravest of the team, disobeyed the order and tried to work her way into position. As a result, a German sniper shot her in the arm, smashing the bone. She had to be sent immediately to a hospital. The battalion commander, infuriated, called the sniper's behavior nothing but a cheap stunt, not bravery. A sign appeared on the gates in front of the snipers' quarters: "Now here live the 'Touchables.'"

Kasimov soon returned, called the team to order, and sharply told everyone off, calling what had happened "a disgrace." The team's warden, trying to justify himself and cursing the impudent artillery officers up and down, declared that they had forced him to drink a glass of vodka: "Just try not to drink up to Comrade Stalin!" was his excuse.

Kasimov refused to listen to him and removed him from his position. Then he asked "Katia from Zatsepa": "Did you know, Senior Sergeant, how swinishly the officers were treating the commandant because of you? Were you aware of their plans?"

She answered for herself and all the other women: "No, we didn't suspect a thing."

Kasimov didn't believe her and relieved the senior sniper of her duties.

The snipers' sergeant major, Nikodim Ivanovich, heard everything and didn't say a single abusive word. But his stony silence was a bitterer pill for the young women to swallow than all the stormy scolding from their commander.

Sergeant Major Nikodim Ivanovich

I have to say a few words about Nikodim Ivanovich—the next personality in my army collection of sergeant majors. One of the young women said about him, "He's nothing less than an angel from heaven."

This man was getting on in age, a father of two daughters. He had a strong character. In a candid outburst he had said one day: "I've experienced everything in life; I've been on the steed and I've been trampled under its hooves." From the very first meeting with the sniper team, he adopted a wise position and never wavered from it: he loved all the women equally and never showed any preference for any one of them. He considered all their requests and wishes attentively, and at times he indulged in a bit of whimsy with them. In every possible way, he tried to make the women's daily existence more tolerable. He redecorated the interior of their quarters so that it wouldn't look like a barracks. He reached an agreement with a neighboring wealthy Polish family to allow the young women to bathe in their home in exchange for a bit of stew. He requested from higher command the permanent use of a solidly built army cart with a driver and two horses. When the division moved forward, the snipers loaded their rifles and all their belongings on the cart, and that's how they reached the German border. Every day, Nikodim Ivanovich would check their guns and jot down his observations about each rifle, knowing precisely who the owner was.

The women respected Kasimov, appreciated him as an experienced commander and sniper, and accepted his leadership. Nikodim Ivanovich was a different matter—they loved him like a father and friend. The sergeant major's word was more precious for the young women than gold. They turned to him for advice and help and confided their closest secrets to Nikodim Ivanovich. The most appealing aspects of this man, I believe, were his pure conscience and sense of kindness, which he never lost in the war. Evidently, the team saw these same qualities in him and valued them highly.

For his part, Nikodim Ivanovich became deeply attached to the young women, seeing his own daughters in each one of them, and he felt great joy whenever he managed to do something nice for them. He experienced the death of each woman as the loss of a family member, and he grieved bitterly over each one. At his request, they wove wreaths of artificial flowers in the village for every funeral. Nikodim Ivanovich himself, consoling the weeping members of the team, kept telling them: "One day we won't be grieving, one day . . ."

That's how the sergeant major stood out in my frontline collection of sergeant majors.

Nikodim Ivanovich did a lot to change the attitude of the men in the trenches toward the female snipers. The time did indeed come when their attitudes changed. Once that happened, the warriors in the trenches called the women "sacred" and felt sorry for them, especially the older soldiers; one man even offered prayers for their safety each time one of the teams went out on assignment. Upon the appearance of the snipers in the trenches, the men began to greet them, offering them their support:

"That's the way, sniper girls!"

"Shoot them, the vermin, and make it easier for us!"

Relations with the officers were more complex. Just a step beyond the gates, and hungry male eyes followed their every move. The regiment commander, in whose area the snipers' quarters were located, behaved worst of all toward the women.

He served notice of his passion even at their first meeting. Eventually, "Tamara from Tsvetny Boulevard" could no longer resist his charms. Receiving a note from the lieutenant colonel—a stately, handsome, relatively young man—with an invitation to visit the regiment headquarters, the young woman agreed, without first seeking permission for the visit from her commanding officer.

The regiment commander's adjutant arrived for her that evening and secretly led her away.

Someone alerted the general: "A sniper has run off!" Grabbing me to come along with him, Berestov rushed off in his car for the regiment.

Once we arrived, Berestov flew at the regiment commander: "Just who are you trying to ravish? Don't you have enough of your own whores in the regiment?"

"No, no!" exclaimed Tamara. "I love Sasha!"

The general was surprised and stopped his scolding of the regiment commander.

Amusingly, the furious lieutenant colonel ordered that the snitch that had informed on his tryst be shot if he ever showed his face around the regiment. By the way, I was that "snitch."

"Hang on, German!"

I repeatedly happened to observe how complicated and unpredictable sniper work was. First of all, the opponent is no fool and is in no hurry to wind up in someone's sights. For the sniper himself or herself, however, any blunder or the slightest mistake can result in his or her own death. Second, without endurance, self-confidence, even "a hunter's passion"—a sniper is not yet a real sniper. Third, there were a lot of ace snipers in the German army, and their optical sights were far superior to ours. Entering the war with Russia, the Germans already had a sufficient number of well-trained marksmen in their units, while in the Red Army, the sniper movement developed, as far as I can recall, only after 1941.

We had no notion of how women would conduct themselves in the sniper role—it seemed to us that in critical situations they might lose their heads. Moreover, we assumed that women were not inclined to take risks, and that they probably didn't have enough endurance. But the "sniper gals" refuted many of our initial doubts. Time passed, more new notches began to appear on the butts of the snipers' rifles, the Germans began to whine, and the scornful attitude and conduct toward the women finally vanished completely. "Try to figure out which is stronger—the whale or the elephant?" the officers of the Political Department joked. They began to respect and love the young snipers in the division. They introduced a special atmosphere into our lives and forced many of us to wake up and see that the front was still far from the end of life. But even the young women themselves, I noticed, were changing, and they had become more serious.

Soon, there were seven Fritzes on the tally sheets of our young women. There were perhaps even more, but it is not always possible to determine the results of a shot precisely. Returning from an assignment, the snipers would report: "I don't know whether I hit him or not, but the Fritz dropped."

The most difficult episode was "Liuba from Sretenka's" multihour encounter with a German sniper.

Try to picture yourself one-on-one with an opponent, to turn yourself into an invisible person, to become a totally immobile object. Eyes quickly tire, the muscles of the arms and legs grow numb, and the body either becomes soaked in sweat from the heat or tries not to shiver from the cold; sometimes fear appears.

In Liuba's case, one day while on an operation she committed some small blunder; she grew certain that a German sniper had spotted her and was waiting for her next mistake. Liuba froze, convinced that the slightest motion would mean a bullet to her head. She remained frozen like that until late evening, sometimes crying, but not daring to sob, feeling that she was growing so deeply rooted into the earth that she would not be able to free herself from it.

Once darkness fell, Kasimov, who had stealthily approached the young woman's position, attached a rope to her ankle and dragged her back to safety. He carried her almost breathless body into a dugout, wiped her down with vodka, then gave her a couple of gulps from a flask. When she finally recovered, he led her by the arm back to the snipers' quarters.

But there were also situations when neither Kasimov nor anyone else could help a sniper. A German sniper ace shot "Dina from Oruzheiny Pereulok" through the head while she was moving. The pain of this tragedy was particularly acute. The team loved the blue-eyed young woman with the sweet, cheerful disposition and the melodious voice; she dreamed of becoming a pediatrician and wanted to cure all the children of the world from the diseases that were tormenting them.

Kasimov was the first to sense that after Dina's death, something very important had happened in the team, and he understood: at last, hatred and a desire for revenge had been born. "Hang on, German!" Kasimov said. "Now you're going to see a real hunt!"

One day "Galia from Elekhovskaia" told me about her first shot:

"I had been watching for a long, long time. Then suddenly I saw him, a young German. He was sitting on a little stump, and he had kind eyes. . . . What should I do? But of course one must not hesitate. I fired. Then I immediately regretted what I had done, and I started to cry."

From that point on, Kasimov and I knew exactly that the question "What should I do?" would not be a problem among the snipers.

The New Year: 1945

By order of the army, for a short period half the sniper team was transferred to a neighboring division. During this time I had an idea. We all understood that the young women needed a short breather, that at their age a girl's youthful heart is open wide to love while these young women had to kill and kill again, which, you can imagine, is a far from simple burden. So I decided to arrange a surprise for them—to organize dance evenings.

Of course, first I had to clear it with their commander. I went to chat with Kasimov. Sergeant Major Nikodim Ivanovich, hearing about my plans, smiled broadly and praised the idea. Kasimov reacted differently and frowned:

"I'm categorically against the idea! The dances will distract them from their business, and the men will hanker over such blossoms, however hard that may be for you to believe. We might lose the team."

I tried to persuade him, and referred to the general—only to try to get Kasimov's consent. The lieutenant held his ground. Then I proposed a compromise version: "Let's start it! And if we find out we've made a mistake, we'll stop it." With that, the commander finally agreed.

When the entire team had reassembled again, I held a Komsomol meeting among them. We tallied their results: the snipers now had fifteen fascists to their credit.

"It seems there is a point to feeding us!" one of the women shouted out.

"I agree," I confirmed, "and I intend to send a report about your combat efforts back to your sniper school from which you graduated."

I kept my surprise until the end of the meeting:

"Starting next Saturday, we will be holding dance evenings. Officers will be coming as guests, and we have enough cavaliers for all of you. There will be music. If you invite me, I'll also come."

My announcement was greeted with rejoicing.

Three of the young ladies invited me. I chose Rita, the single non-Muscovite on the team. Short and shapely, she attracted me with her soft, velvety speech and her radiant smile. It seemed to warm me all over.

We really only became acquainted at the first dance evening. Rita was from Odessa. She had traveled to visit her aunt in Moscow on holiday when the war broke out. She was initially accepted into the sniper school on a conditional basis, but she turned out to one of the best shots in the school, so they soon dropped her conditional status.

We met rarely, but with every encounter I liked Rita more and more. In sum, we had a typical frontline romance. We greeted the 1945 New Year together. This holiday always inspires hopes for the future! It seemed that the war might end at any time, we were young, and a happy future was waiting for us—but Rita was killed in Germany. I will tell you about this later.

In the beginning of January, the division started advancing again. The snipers were withdrawn into reserve. Now there were seventeen of them. Three of the young women had been killed, one was in the hospital, and two of the "Untouchables" had been sent home because of pregnancies.

20

In Poland

January 1945

An Encounter with Journalists

The fate of Germany was no longer in doubt, and the question now was, How long it would be before the end arrived? Our leadership, the Allies, and the Germans all understood this. But the latter continued to resist fanatically. The German command, disregarding losses, ordered its commanders to defend every line on the path to Germany's borders. The Soviet command, for its part also not reckoning its losses, demanded its commanders to attack!

On one of the first days in January, a heavy enemy artillery barrage suddenly started falling on the division's positions, and then German self-propelled guns and submachine gunners quickly advanced upon the junction between two of our regiments. The foggy weather prohibited the operation of our air force—something the enemy had obviously taken into account. The Germans crushed one regiment almost immediately, but the second regiment offered stiff resistance, including an antitank battalion in its counterattacks. The fighting intensified. It continued until late in the evening. By this time it became known that the enemy had carried out simultaneous attacks on several sectors of the 31st Army's front—it was either a reconnaissance-in-force or an effort to disrupt our pending offensive.

An article was published in the divisional newspaper about the heroic feat of two members of a 76-mm gun crew, Ivan Skudnov and Sergei Pantiukhov: with their gun, they had inflicted heavy losses on the attacking submachine gunners and held up the German attack, but the Germans were eventually able to seize the two wounded fighters. The article said the Germans had then savagely carved five-pointed stars into the Russians' bodies before finishing them off with their knives. "Meetings of revenge" were conducted in all the battalions: soldiers and officers spoke, vowing to avenge the death of the two heroes. The division's chief of the Political Department, Colonel Shilovich, summoned me: "Drive the bodies of the two Komsomol heroes to Suwalki. They must be buried with honors." I took a junior lieutenant and three soldiers with me. We loaded two coffins onto our truck and set off on our way.

Suwalki is a small, beautiful Polish city, situated 80 kilometers [almost 50 miles] from Krakow. When we arrived, I left the coffins in a local hospital with the junior lieutenant and three soldiers for the night, while I went to meet with the local commandant and secured his promise to help us with the funerals.

I had some free time at that point, so I decided to get acquainted with Major Lebedev, the editor of the army newspaper *Na Vraga!* [At the Enemy!], who was in Suwalki at that time.

Lebedev greeted me warmly, and once he learned about the purpose of my trip to the city, he immediately requested permission to write about the two fallen artillerymen for his newspaper. My conversation with him made a strong impression on me—this was an intelligent, educated man, a historian by profession, who had graduated from the Moscow Pedagogical Institute. When the war started, he was taking special classes for combat journalists. He was interested in finding out whether people read his newspaper, and how officers and soldiers regarded it. I tried to answer all his questions. After some tea, Lebedev invited me to a meeting with his editorial board: he had recently returned from an army conference of political workers and was intending to report about it to his journalists.

"For tomorrow's edition, I want to tell you an interesting story that I heard at the conference" that's how the major started his speech to his coworkers. "You know that at the initiative of the Supreme Commander, after we cross the German border, we will be permitted to send packages home—once a month, up to ten kilograms for officers, and up to five kilograms for soldiers. In connection with this, a member of the *Front*'s Military Council, Lev Mekhlis, said that Comrade Stalin had been interested in the question of how the soldiers would be able to gather odds and ends, not having any transport? Mekhlis brought to Stalin's attention his recent conversation on this subject with soldiers. Here was how one soldier reasoned: 'The knapsack on my back is my transport. I'll always have two kilograms in it. As for the other three, I'll get that in the next conquered town.' 'The Supreme Commander,' said comrade Mekhlis, 'was satisfied by the soldier's answer.'

"But now the essential matter," continued Lebedev. "Soon we will enter East Prussia. The command is concerned by the question of how our soldiers will behave toward the civilian population. An army is a mass of living people, and each one has his or her own personal score to settle with the Germans. For the last four years of the war, we have motivated the army under the slogan, 'Death to the German Occupiers!' But the German people and the military criminals are not one and the same. Doctor Freud said, 'The restriction of one's aggression, possibly, is the most serious sacrifice that society demands from an individual.' In war, as we all know, it is particularly difficult to subdue human aggression."

The major added:

"There are enough alarming signals even today, in Poland: robberies, rapes, outrages upon religious symbols and things like that. They are even stealing from their own. The Germans brought tens of thousands of books, including many rare editions, which they had plundered in our country, to Plissa. There they had stored them in warehouses converted from former barracks. But then, having found out about this, Red Army units that entered the city committed outrages at the warehouses, and many valuable books were stolen. To a demand to stop their scandalous behavior, the plunderers replied: 'We are conquerors, we're allowed to do it.' The *Front*'s Military Council demanded an immediate end to the thefts. In this instance, it seems to have succeeded. But what might happen tomorrow, when we arrive in Germany? Will the soldiers obey their officers? From everything that has been said, it is clear what is required of us," Lebedev concluded. "We must urgently take up the matter of correcting our propaganda."

The journalists who stepped forward to speak after Lebedev started complaining: "They've thought of this too late!"

"It's hardly possible to change something in motion . . ."

The editor turned to me: "Let's listen to the assistant chief for Komsomol affairs of the 331st Rifle Division's Political Department. He came to Suwalki to bury two heroes who were killed in the most recent battle. By the way, I ask everyone who will not be busy to come to the park tomorrow at 10:00 A.M. for the funerals."

I stood and told them approximately the following:

"They say that in Stalingrad, when the capitulating Germans crawled out of their burrows and formed into the prisoner columns, one of our officers, pointing at the surrounding ruins, told them loudly in the German tongue, so that everyone could hear: 'Remember! When we come for you, on your soil, to your cities, we will turn them into just these sorts of ruins!' The soldier is waiting impatiently for the hour of retribution, almost unable to bear the anticipation. He is determined to get to Germany and settle old scores—despite whatever lofty appeals we might make and, even, orders. Thus the task before all of us is large and difficult."

On the Day of Warsaw's Liberation

Having spent the night at Lebedev's place, early the next morning I headed back to the hospital. A hospital attendant escorted me to the recreational hall. On a table, draped with black velvet, were two elevated coffins; at the head of each stood a tall silver candelabrum with brightly burning candles. A Polish Roman Catholic priest behind the table was quietly reading a prayer. I politely greeted the priest, and then summoned the junior lieutenant. We went out into the corridor. Having explained the schedule of the funeral ceremony, I asked if anything had happened during their watch overnight. Somewhat troubled, he told me:

"After midnight the chief doctor of the hospital arrived and asked the soldier on guard duty to open a coffin. He explained his request by saying that he wanted to see the fascists' brutality with his own eyes."

"And did the guard let him?" I interrupted the junior lieutenant.

"Yes," he answered. "Grigor'ev was on duty, a sensible fellow, and the doctor's request seemed like a natural one. Soon I arrived to check the sentry, and in the doorway I collided with a stranger. He told me something that was impossible to believe."

"And what did he say?"

"He told me that he didn't find any star cut into the body of the deceased. Then for some reason he started smiling."

I summoned Grigor'ev and asked him. "Why did you open the coffin without the permission of the junior lieutenant?"

"I didn't notice anything odd; it was the chief doctor after all. Forgive me."

The junior lieutenant and I burst into the chief doctor's office. Catching sight of the chief doctor, the officer was shocked and dismayed:

"This isn't the same man who came by last night."

I didn't stop for elaborations; it seemed the doctor was in a hurry to leave as well.

"A festive demonstration is just about to begin," he explained excitedly. "Today the Red Army liberated Warsaw! Six years of occupation and suffering! Our Warsaw is free again! Thank you!" Joyfully, he seized our hands and firmly shook them.

Everything had become so jumbled: the funerals, the liberation celebration, and the strange night visitor. Just who was it who had come by last night and why? Had he really spoken the truth about the absence of any signs of mutilation? But now I had no time to ponder those questions—I had to rush to the funerals.

Everything was ready upon our arrival. A common grave had been dug, wreaths and flowers had been delivered, citizens had gathered, and a ceremonial guard of Polish soldiers stood in formation. A photojournalist from the army newspaper had also arrived.

There were a few speeches. The head of the city council promised that the Polish people would never forget the liberators of Warsaw and the two young heroes. The priest offered a prayer. A farewell gunshot salute rang out.

Having thanked the local authorities and the attending citizens, I drove a little post into the ground above the grave and attached a small plywood board to it, which carried the inscription of the heroes' names: "Ivan Skudnov. Sergei Pantiukhov."

Today, I wonder what has happened to that grave and that little marker with the names of the fallen. How did the Polish people regard the liberation of Warsaw? As I recall, it seems to me that at the time they were of two minds about it. As I understood from ensuing conversations with them, they were unquestionably happy that their capital had become free. But at the same time, they didn't want Russians to become the masters of their country. History offered prior examples.

Exiting the park, I observed placards in the Polish tongue pasted everywhere—on lampposts, the walls of buildings, and on fences. In thick, hand-drawn lettering were the words: *Za vil'nost' i ne podleglost* [For Freedom and Independence!]. Who had made these signs, and what did these words mean? As I looked around my surroundings in bewilderment, a procession of the city's residents and peasants who had plainly come from nearby villages appeared on the main street. The people were carrying national flags, icons, and bouquets of flowers. In front of the procession, I spotted the same Polish priest who had been offering prayers over the coffins the day before. He beckoned to me, inviting me to join the celebratory procession. I considered it improper to decline the request on such a great, joyous day for the Polish people. The procession wound up at a Roman Catholic church, which greeted the marchers with pealing bells.

The priest turned and addressed the crowd. I stood near the priest and, listening to his sermon, thought a bit about it: "What a bore! Isn't it simpler just to tell everyone: 'Live by the truth, mankind!' That's the simplest and best sermon. No, God's cloister isn't for me." Later, when I had become more acquainted with the Polish people and had studied their lives, I understood how primitive and trite my judgments on the church had been.

When I said goodbye to the priest, he said: "It seems to me, my friend, that you are searching for life outside yourself, not realizing that life is always within you. Think over what I've told you, and you'll see that I'm right."

In the years of the war, during the period of immeasurable suffering for the Polish people, the Catholic Church never betrayed its flock. It became a spiritual support for the people, which permitted them to endure the terrible German violence against them. At Auschwitz, which I visited after the war as part of a tour group, they showed us the cell that had held a Polish priest (I can't remember his name now). He voluntarily went to the gas chamber in place of a Polish Jew who was the father of three children. Similar examples from that time are not isolated.

I often asked Poles the same question: "You are a religious people. Almost all of you are Catholics. The Church is your second home. Your faith in God is unshakeable. But, tell me, have any of you ever seen God?" One Polish woman replied once, only half-joking: "God exists—we believe in this truth. But why should we see Him? The important thing is that He sees us."

After the service ended, I decided that I had to meet with the city commandant to thank him for his help. As we were parting, I told him: "We're leaving now. I believe the Polish people will not forget their liberators."

"I'm not so sure," the commandant replied.

"How so?"

"Here's why. There was an episode today, which apparently you still don't know about. Today, on the day of Warsaw's liberation, apparently on orders from above, units of the *Armia Krajowa* [AK—the Polish Home Army, the largest Polish underground resistance movement to German occupation, loyal to the Polish government in exile] have emerged from underground. Did you notice the slogan "Freedom and Independence!" on the streets? That was their doing. We've already taken down a bunch of these signs, and by evening we'll free the city from this filth. But these degenerates have wounded the priest! They just called me, he's in the hospital; thank God, his life is not in danger."

"Polish people themselves shot their own priest?" I couldn't believe what I was hearing.

"The previous priest fled, and this one was brought in by our army; he's from Leningrad. It may be surprising, but the congregation accepted him and believes in him. A junior officer in the Cossack cavalry is officially helping me, he's also a former fellow countryman, and he's placed two squadrons of cavalry at my disposal. We've blocked all the exits and entrances to the city. Be careful, Senior Lieutenant, the *Armia Krajowa* is a serious and insidious opponent; we're still going to have a lot of trouble with them."

"Thank you, Major, for all your help and advice!"

We said our good-byes.

The Death of Iura Davydov

When I returned to the division, all the officers were talking about one thing: some terrible news from a neighboring army had arrived. A large unit of retreating S.S. men had attacked a regimental school for new recruits the night before and had cut down seventy-nine soldiers. One radio operator managed to survive the attack, and he reported the tragedy to army command. An assistant to the regiment chief of staff, a Major Davydov, had also been killed.

The news stunned me. It couldn't be! Major Davydov! It had to be my Iurka—Iurka Davydov! "We're from the same barracks"—we would never again have the chance to say these words to each other. What a career! And what an absurd, cruel fate. They said he had just arrived the day before to inspect the soldiers' training and had lingered to spend the night there.

A Heavy Conversation

I reported to Commissar Shilovich about the completion of my assignment. I didn't say anything about the occurrence that night in the hospital, as I had decided to have a talk first with the editor of the divisional newspaper.

I knew Captain Egor Tishin, the editor of the divisional newspaper, well and respected him as an experienced journalist and man of brave convictions and deeds. We had become friends from the first days of my arrival in the division. We fully trusted each other, so I asked him directly: "Why did you arrange a scene?" He instantly understood me and replied sharply: "It had to be done!"

After the war I often heard this phrase. Egor's answer didn't satisfy me, so I decided to press for an explanation.

"Do you think that the editorial board made an improper decision?" the captain asked me.

"Do you really not understand what the Germans will do when they find out about your forgery? They'll make duplicates of the newspaper article and circulate them among their soldiers: 'Look at what the Soviet propaganda is doing!' Why did you do this? Especially when our soldiers have marched across their native land and seen with their own eyes what the fascists have done. Moreover, each soldier has his own score to settle with the Germans. We didn't need another atrocity to motivate them."

"I agree. But you must understand me! A critical moment has come; we've reached the beast's own lair—now any and all methods of propaganda are acceptable, as long as they help finish him off!"

"But you and I both know that propaganda is a sharp, double-edged weapon!"

"I agree. I understand your fervent desire for the truth. But haven't you encountered similar examples from the side of the adversary?"

"I've seen them, and more than once."

"Let me give you an example of what their own propagandists are writing. As we were liberating Latvia, this was what they were writing for their own soldiers: 'The Bolsheviks drove away all the Latvians, whom they had caught on the streets before our arrival. They took all their valuables from them first, then doused their homes with gasoline and burned them to the ground. Those Latvians who refused to go with the Bolsheviks had their arms and legs chopped off, their tongues cut out, and were left lying in the streets. They nailed people to walls, even children. We saw this with our own eyes. If the bandits ever reach our cities, they'll tear us into pieces.' What do you have to say to that?"

"I'm not convinced by what you are saying."

"You want to purge the Soviet soldier of hatred toward the fascists, which also means you want to free the Germans of feelings of guilt. This is a dangerous logic."

"You didn't understand me correctly. Can you imagine what awaits the civilian population when the army enters East Prussia?"

"I don't see any great danger in your concerns. So what if the army does some plundering? So what if the men give a few hundred thousand German women a try? This is just as natural as it is understandable. It is something common to all the soldiers. The frontline soldiers will take some old clothes from the Germans and they'll send the items back to their women in their devastated villages, which were destroyed by the Germans. It's just! A time will come when we'll put everything back in order! Incidentally, you should know that I published that article at the direction of your boss."

I was speechless. The final comment uttered by Egor struck me to the quick. Shilovich! The division commissar! A colonel! What then can we expect from junior officers and the soldiers? Well, the future would reveal to us which one of us was right. I remembered this conversation, my naïve trust in the truthfulness of the divisional newspaper, and what had happened in Suwalki with a sick feeling for a long time.

Shilovich—the Division Commissar

My entire life in the 331st Rifle Division was spent under the sign of the Political Department. I was directly subordinate to Shilovich until the division was disbanded in June 1945 in the German town of Friedeberg. During the time of our joint service, I closely observed my commanding officer, and I can offer a sketch of him.

Aleksei Adamovich Shilovich loved the old aphorism, "What matters is not what happens, but how we perceive it." The colonel himself looked at any event optimistically, an attitude that he passed on to us, his subordinates. I think this aphorism explains a lot about the character of my superior.

Sometimes he seemed to me like an absent-minded man who is looking for a cap that is still resting on his head. He easily forgot important decisions, even his own personal orders, which often made him look funny, more like a parody of a military-political chief. Having graduated from a two-year pedagogical institute, he, just like Gruzdev, had been a modest rural schoolteacher before the war, teaching mathematics and physics. It was hard to understand how a person who had so little military bearing could rise so quickly in the ranks.

His relations with the division commander always surprised me. Superficially everything appeared normal: they respected each other and didn't argue about anything large or small. But Berestov, as it seemed to me, appeared to value Shilovich not as a person but as a formal token: he kept the commissar next to him, just as he was supposed to do, but Berestov rarely troubled to consult with Shilovich before making a decision, which incidentally seemed to suit Shilovich just fine.

The staff of the Political Department regarded Shilovich critically and condemned the negative aspects of his character: haughtiness, constant self-absorption, and a well-known pomposity. As for me, I caught myself not always being sincere with Aleksei Adamovich, and the unpleasant question kept asking itself: was this prudence or hypocrisy?

I was struck by his seeming total indifference to losses. Not everyone is capable, especially in wartime, of acutely feeling someone else's grief. This is understandable; for this you have to have a heart and to possess an ability to commiserate, if only with simple sympathy. Shilovich behaved strangely. Whenever he received a casualty report, he would heave a sigh and respond in the same fashion: "That's war. War, as you know, doesn't occur without sacrifices." How did he become such a lord and master, so egocentric and indifferent to human sorrow? In my opinion, this wasn't even a manifestation of arrogance as much as it was simply indifference and a personal coldness.

As a man, Aleksei Adamovich loved to eat tasty food, to arrange better living quarters for himself, and to fuss over his clothing. He often drove to the *medsanbat* for health checkups. Through these things, both on occasion and without occasion he tried to convince us, his subordinates, that he was an uncommon man of great merit. But the two Orders of the Red Banner that decorated his dress coat always surprised me. What had he done to deserve them?

Did the schoolteacher from Poles'e dream of becoming a colonel, an important political boss, of meeting personally with Comrade Stalin? That he might do great deeds, marked by the highest government honors?

They say the gods smile rarely. But fate with God's blessing had long been shining on Shilovich. The wheel of his fortune took a sharp turn in the notorious year of 1937, when people were being led from their prison cell to be shot on a daily basis, while others were being promoted at a dizzying pace. Aleksei Adamovich figured out in time that membership in the VKP(b) was an indispensable condition for life success. Then he, a teacher, the sole Party member in his district, was suddenly summoned to Minsk to appear before the First Secretary of the Central Committee of the Communist Party of Belorussia, Panteleimon Kondrat'evich Ponomarenko. Soon thereafter, at the personal request of Comrade Ponomarenko, he was enrolled as a student at the V. I. Lenin Military-Political Academy. At that time, after Stalin's purge of the general-officer corps of the Red Army, they were taking almost anyone into the military academies and specialist schools, violating both admission standards and many years of tradition. Shilovich was accepted as a "national cadre" and as a representative of a new, totally unsullied generation.

He had time to complete three years of study at the academy. In 1941, his class at the academy was turned out ahead of schedule with the rank of battalion commissars. All thirty graduates, at the personal request of the First Secretary of the Moscow City Committee of the Party, Comrade Shcherbakov, were placed at the disposal of the City Committee. Comrade Shcherbakov personally received them all, and after some fiery ideological parting words, he sent them out to take positions in the people's volunteer divisions that were forming at that time.

Within two months the division in which Shilovich was serving, along with many others, had been destroyed at Viaz'ma. There were few who survived those tragic days intact, and the wounded battalion commissar wound up by chance in a Moscow hospital. When he was discharged, fate again smiled upon him. Ponomarenko, who at that time was starting to organize the Central Staff of the partisan movement, took Shilovich under his wing.

For an entire month the battalion commissar trained in a special detachment: he learned how to make parachute jumps and to shoot accurately, to go without food and water for extended periods, to start a fire without any matches, to orient himself in a forest at night, and to run faster than a beast. After the special training, which not everyone could endure, Shilovich assumed the identity of a "Pras'ko Shumkovich," and together with a group of *chekists* [members of the Soviet secret police], he was dropped in the woods near Volyn'. The battalion commissar was to activate a partisan movement in the Ukraine, which at the time was lagging behind the partisan activity in Belorussia. "Pras'ko Shumkovich" spent six months in the Ukrainian forests, during which time he met such legendary partisan leaders as Kovpak and Rudnev and helped to organize several partisan units.

In 1942 Shilovich returned to Moscow. He reported to Ponomarenko on the condition of the partisan movement in the Ukraine and its prospects; but most important, he proposed the idea—of course, claiming it was his own—of a raid by Kovpak through eighteen oblasts in Belorussia and the Ukraine, in order to recruit large numbers of people to the partisan movement. Kovpak had already given his approval for a first, though much smaller, raid, claiming he already had enough people but not enough weapons. Ponomarenko was delighted by the battalion commissar's idea.

After careful deliberation and discussion, Ponomarenko sent a short note to Comrade Stalin, informing him of the idea for a major raid. Three days later, Ponomarenko and Shilovich (who now had the rank of regiment commissar) were summoned to the Kremlin. The conversation lasted for twelve minutes. Regiment commissar Shilovich gave a five-minute report on partisan activities in the Ukraine. Stalin praised him and instructed Ponomarenko to recommend the bold commissar for the Order of the Red Banner. Then he gave the go-ahead for the organization of a deep raid and instructed that Kovpak's partisans should immediately receive supplies of weapons, ammunition, explosives, kerosene, food, and medical materials by airplane.

For a year, Shilovich worked in the Central Staff of the partisan movement. He flew into Belorussia several times. He secretly spent time in Minsk, where with the help of some underground operatives he learned of the death of his family.

In 1943 Shilovich was honored with his second Order of the Red Banner, promoted to the rank of colonel, and, at his own request, placed at the disposal of the Main Political Directorate of the Red Army and Navy. From there, fate sent him to the 331st Rifle Division.

I learned all these facts of the biography of Aleksei Adamovich from an instructor in the Political Department, Kolia Shevchuk, who handled personnel files. How much of it is true and how much of it a fabrication, I don't know.

They say that the strength of a man lies in how well he knows how to conceal his own weaknesses. Shilovich didn't bother to hide his weaknesses, confident that he had earned everyone's pardon.

General Berestov

A few words about the general, with whom I became friends and under whose command I continued to serve until my departure from the army. He was an uncommon man. I rarely met men like him at the front.

When on the attack, for example, the general loved to keep his command post moving forward. He liked to rush to his new position in his Willys, and from there he would prod his subordinate commanders by radio: "Why are you stuck? Get moving!" He never cursed, but he gave every order in a strict tone of voice, not brooking any objections. All the regiment, battalion, and battery commanders knew about these "games" he played—and always tried to conform!

At the same time, I must also pay him his due: whenever higher command demanded a result "at any price," the general agonized. In such situations he always would get together with Rappoport, spread out a map, and meticulously look for a way to accomplish the order with minimal losses.

Another thing about him was amazing! Even if the division commander had been directing a battle all day, at night Pavel Fedorovich would inevitably invite the next scheduled "lay" [*nalezhnitsa*] from among his personal "harem" to come see him. There were so many members of his harem from among the division headquarters staff—radio operators, clerks, typists—sometimes we wondered if the man ever slept!

At the same time, he was intolerant of weaknesses in others. Frontline veterans know: there are days when you want to forget everything, to be left alone, and even to cry a little. Alas, Pavel Fedorovich didn't brook such "nuances." But who among us officers and commanders could permit simple human feelings in others or ourselves in those harsh years? Probably, there were not many of us.

We loved and respected the general in the division but were a little afraid of him. Not without reason! While Berestov could overlook some foibles in his officers and soldiers, he never forgave cowardice. But as we know, not everyone can be brave in every situation. It sometimes happened that the general's wrath was unjust.

21

In East Prussia
January–February 1945

The First German City

Through the binoculars we could plainly see the tall, pointed steeple of a church; the clean, level streets; the neat, red-roofed two-story buildings, surrounded by gardens; and in the center—a small rectangular square with a fountain and a lot of greenery. The town of Treuburg [the present-day Polish city of Olesko] lay before us. The division was preparing to take its first German city.

Then the order was issued to attack. Intense fighting for Treuburg continued for four days; several times the city changed hands, until at last the German units became exhausted and retreated. We couldn't understand why the adversary had defended Treuburg so stubbornly. The city didn't have any strategic significance, and yet the Germans paid such a high price for their recklessness—several hundred killed and wounded, many burned out tanks, and a devastated city. We thought perhaps it was because not far away, in the Romintensky Forest, lay Hermann Göring's hunting lodge and castle.

The solution to this riddle quickly emerged. It turned out that the Germans had "prepared" for the city's surrender. Almost immediately after the fighting ended, a few officers in the Political Department and I entered the city and walked along its streets. At almost every intersection, large posts bore signs that read: "Pay close attention to what the Bolsheviks have done to the first city taken by them in East Prussia. This is how they will treat all the cities and villages of your beloved Homeland, and all of us Germans. Defend your Great Reich from the Red barbarians!"

In reality, as we later learned from the testimony of prisoners, on one of the first days of the fighting, when we were still struggling with the enemy on the approaches to the city, the Germans themselves, by order of Joseph Goebbels [Nazi Germany's minister of Public Enlightenment and Propaganda], forcibly expelled the citizens and then blew up and burned the finest buildings in the city: the church, the water works, the movie theater and bank, the sports halls, and the main street, where stores and a high school were located. Over the next several hours, they trucked in people from nearby districts, and brought in film crews and journalists to record on film and print the city ruins, and the fear and grief of the sham residents. Even the park and its beautiful swans were destroyed: almost all the trees were burned, the swans were shot, and it was announced that the "Asiatic hordes" had killed them and eaten them.

The city was empty as our regimental column marched along its main boulevard. Not a single soul was visible. Cows were bellowing in a heartrending fashion, and we could hear the barking of dogs. Then unexpectedly a tall, hale old man hopped out of a partially destroyed building, holding some sort of booklet in his outstretched hand, and with joyful exclamations, he rushed to meet our column. One of the Red Army soldiers, who didn't understand German words, without pausing to try to figure out what the German was saying, stepped out of the column and with all his might, smashed the German's head with his rifle butt. Bleeding heavily, the old man fell to the cobblestone pavement. As the column marched past the prostrate man, more soldiers joined to taunt him as much as possible and to finish him off—they kicked him with their boots, stabbed him with their bayonets, and then spat upon the corpse. A *politruk* stopped by the dead man's mutilated body. He lifted the blood-soaked booklet of a member of the Communist Party of Germany, wiped off the cover, and hid it in his map case. Saying not a word, he set off to catch up to his place in the column.

I witnessed this scene. It was the first death of a German civilian that I saw in Germany. Catching up to the man who had crushed the German's skull with his rifle butt, I asked him:

"Why did you kill him? He plainly was not a soldier, and there was no way he could have harmed us. An old man, a communist, it is possible he spent time in prison for his political allegiance to the German Communist Party. Just think, for many years he kept his Party card at the risk of his life."

The soldier gruffly answered:

"To me, Comrade Senior Lieutenant, they are all the same—just scum. I won't find any peace until I kill a hundred of them. You'd better ask yourself how you wound up so alone in your opinion."

It was not difficult to understand either his hatred or that of the soldiers who had spat on the German. But how many more Germans would they have to kill, humiliate, and tear to pieces in order to sooth their grief, dull their hatred, thaw their icy souls, and find inner peace?

But in the meantime—the hour of retribution had arrived!

Soldiers, literally rabid with fury, burst into badly damaged homes and shattered or destroyed everything they could find. The inhabitants, fleeing the city, had departed in such haste that they had left everything untouched; they hadn't even had time to make their beds, and now the mirrors, the dishes, the service sets, the rarest porcelain, the glass goblets, the cut-glass pitchers—all were flying to the floor. Germans had lived here! They took axes to armchairs, sofas, tables, and stools, even baby carriages. That is the way the first wave of national hatred boiled to the surface. No one—not a single commander or *politruk*—tried to stay the soldier's hand, understanding that this would be a senseless, useless gesture, as the frenzy was uncontrollable.

We had all of one day to rest. Someone milked the cows and treated his comrades to fresh milk. For the first time in the entire war, we ate tasty food to our fill—foreign products, in pursuit of which we cleaned out the homes' pantries and cellars; at the same time, we stuffed our knapsacks with cans of chicken meat and pork, with jars of jellies and jams. The soldiers jokingly wondered if we would have time to eat it all before the war's end. I found a German shepherd puppy, gave it something to eat, and then took it along with me.

In the morning, just as we received the order for moving out, cannons began to roar from the nearest hills, where the retreating Germans had dug in; several Stukas appeared in the sky, and from the forested tract around the city, on three sides, tanks emerged with lines of attacking infantry behind them. Our artillery opened up in reply. So it all started once again! The terrible thunder of exploding shells, and fighting for every street, block, and building. Suffering casualties, we nevertheless managed to consolidate our grip on the city once and for all.

The Commissar's Lessons

Several days later, I myself became an involuntary participant in an incident. It hit me so hard that for several days afterwards I felt like I didn't know who I was.

One frosty, sunny day Shilovich summoned me, sat me down beside himself in a sleigh, and we slowly traveled down the empty streets of a captured city. We stopped in front of a hotel by the name of the Edelweiss. The driver stayed on the street with the sleigh while we climbed up a handsome, broad, carpeted staircase to the second floor of the building. Here, hotel rooms stretched along both sides of the corridor. Why had we come here; why had the colonel brought me along?

Next something happened that I could never forget. We entered a room and Shilovich walked up to some enormous windows, which filled the entire room with sunlight. Suddenly he began to tear down the velvet curtains. Grabbing a spare bag that he had brought along, he stuffed toiletries into it right down to the rolls of toilet paper—it was the first time I had ever seen toilet paper; for my entire life, we had gotten by with sheets of newspaper. By now Aleksei Adamovich had pulled a knife from his bag and had set to work on a leather couch and two large leather armchairs—it was the first time I had ever seen such beautiful and elegant things in a private residence. Within several minutes, the leather had been stripped from the couch and the chairs, and then it was the turn of the paintings. Working swiftly and deftly, he cut the canvases and pulled the paintings from the frames, leaving them to hang empty on the wall. He did everything efficiently and, it seemed, with real enthusiasm. Next, plainly basking in a sense of delight, he neatly stacked the paintings and rolled them up into tubes, and then tied them up with some cord he had brought along.

I quietly observed the activities of the chief, not understanding what I should do or how I should behave. But he suddenly pounced on me:

"Why are you standing there like a puppet? In another day or two, soldiers will find this place—and from all this luxury only bits and pieces will remain. Why did you think I brought you along with me? So you could take a few things for yourself. Send them to your Mama!"

I suddenly figured out that this wasn't his first time and, plainly, that he had done some scouting—how did he know where to go? Then, still finding myself in something of a trap, I also took a few things: a colorful, wooden children's inkstand; two dressing gowns, a man's and a woman's; a portable typewriter; and two rolls of toilet paper.

We went around ten of the rooms, and the colonel barbarically emptied each one; I helped him pile his loot by the hallway doors. The driver, who had come upstairs to help, hauled everything downstairs, stuffed everything into bags, and then loaded it all onto the sleigh.

I slept badly that night: although I had taken some trifling things, in reality I had been no different than the colonel. How easily—in just an hour!—did all my lofty principles come crashing down. I vowed that such a thing would never happen again with me.

A few days later Shilovich, leaving his deputy in his place, rolled off to Poland for three days in his personal Willys with a driver. Such absences were frequent with him. He typically described them in the paperwork as trips for medical consultation with some urologist. In actual fact, his current flame, a captain of the medical services, was located in the second echelon. The Political Department staff knew about everything, but everyone kept silent.

On the Ideological Front

An anti-Russian hysteria arose from the first days of our army's march into Germany. The colossal storm that it unleashed on the eastern districts of Germany filled the hearts of millions of Germans with terror. Everywhere we saw German leaflets entitled *Rotmord* [The Red Death], calling upon their soldiers to show no mercy to the Russians: "These aren't humans, but creatures, beasts, Asiatic hordes."

In return, Il'ia Ehrenburg directed his famous leaflet at the Soviet soldier, which thundered, "Kill the German! Kill the German!—That is your mother's request; kill the German!—Your child prays . . . nothing will bring you so much joy as a German corpse."

The *Front* drove ever farther into the heart of East Prussia. We moved forward with constant fighting, marching past the hunting lodges of aristocrats, prosperous farming villages and estates, and ancient Prussian castles. We fought our way across water barriers. The Germans, forced to yield cities, towns, and villages to our forces, fell back toward the Baltic Sea.

The commanding general of Army Group Center, Colonel General Hans-Georg Reinhardt, had asked Hitler to evacuate the German civilians in the threatened areas to a safe place well before the crisis erupted. Hitler had refused.

The snowy winter and the cold spring with their sharp, cutting winds, and the constant heavy fighting left civilians nowhere to go. The legend of an "impenetrable" East Wall had collapsed. The rapid advance of the Soviet forces; the complete lack of preparation of the civilian population for war on their own territory; the wild, at times fantastic rumors, which circulated around the darkest events—all this led to a massive, panicked flight of the civilian population. Thousands of women, old men, and children, abandoning their homes, struggled westward like migrating herds. Those who hadn't had time to evacuate fled into the forests and swamps, hiding wherever possible from their inevitable punishment. All this led to the deaths of many thousands of refugees, primarily old people and children.

Terrible excesses occurred in East Prussia in the initial frenzy of Goebbel's propaganda: a series of mass suicides. In the Danzig region, soldiers from the 23rd Artillery Division stumbled upon a shed containing eleven children from the ages of two to fifteen years, and four women about forty years old—some of their throats had been slashed, while others had slit wrists. Those who were still barely alive refused all medical help: better to die than to wind up in Russian hands. A single male, named Erwin Schwartz—as it turned out, the initiator of this horror—indicated that he had been influenced by instructions from the Nazi Party: "Fight, with whatever you can and however you can, against the Russian troops." Moreover, he had been certain that no one would find out about his role in the slaughter, since rumors would immediately fly around that Russian soldiers had done this to the women and children.

On 19 January 1945, the People's Commissariat of Defense of the Soviet Union issued an order demanding the cessation of mistreatment of the German population, a halt to the outrages, and to take the strictest measures against those who were perpetrating them. This Stalin order is evidence that such excesses had been occurring from the very first days of fighting on German soil. The military leadership, following Stalin's instructions, issued their own orders, taking into consideration the realities of the situation.

The Soviet Army entered East Prussia with a sacred feeling of righteous retribution. But often this feeling turned into blind hatred, and it became almost impossible to stop this massive upwelling of malice—at least in the initial stage of our presence in Germany. Moreover, many officers and political workers were convinced that after all the evils that the Nazis had perpetrated on our soil, against our people, the Soviet soldier now in conquered Germany could behave however he wished.

Through the entire war, from day to day we heard the direct and clear-cut slogan: "Kill the German!" Reality itself, the inhuman cruelty of the enemy, called us to this act. Propaganda called us to this, nurturing a sense of vengeance in our soldier. The works of the best poets, writers, and journalists called us to this: Sholokhov's "The Science of Hatred"; Konstantin Simonov's famous verse "Kill Him!"—frontline soldiers knew it well and highly regarded it;[1] Aleksei Surkov's "I Hate"; and the incendiary essays of Ehrenburg. "Kill the German; Kill One—Then Kill Another," Ehrenburg had written. There was an enormous supply of vengeance toward the enemy in his article "On Hatred"!

The elements of hatred and revenge had by the end of January 1945 become a raging, inundating river. If we are to be honest, all sorts of things took place: brutality, sadism, cynical crude acts, unbridled lust, and at times even murders. In this raging storm of retribution the primary instigators of the violence became the commanders and political workers, the commissary staff, and the SMERSH [Soviet counterintelligence department] agents, as well as the military commandants. An insignificant portion of the officers sought not to have anything to do with the general madness of violence against people. For example, in Poznan and Heiligenbeil, my comrades saved women from rapes. Individual commanders and political workers who openly protested over the outrages against the civilian population suffered for it; among those who did was the later well-known dissident Lev Kopelev.

Unfortunately, the Russian press has been concealing the truth about the Red Army's conduct in Germany now for more than sixty years. Here's what the twelve-volume official history has to say on this subject: "Not all Soviet soldiers correctly understood how they should behave in Germany. In the very first days of combat in East Prussia, there were a few incidents of improper conduct." Here is another striking example: in his memoirs, K. K. Rokossovsky wrote, "It must be said that our people demonstrated real humanity and nobility on German soil."[2] Other former Soviet military commanders have written similar things in the same spirit in their memoirs.

In 2005, a videoconference of Russian and German historians on topical questions of the Second World War took place in Moscow and Berlin. A Russian historian from the State Humanitarian University, Elena Siniavskaia, who participated in this videoconference, declared that the Red Army had never made a formal study of the outrages inflicted on the civilian population in Germany. She acknowledged only isolated cases of inhumane treatment on the part of Soviet servicemen toward the local population and maintained that they had been fully prosecuted all the way up to military tribunals.

I won't argue with Elena Siniavskaia or make accusations against her. It's a pointless venture. I'll assume she simply doesn't know the real facts. Fortunately, such declarations receive a sharp rebuke from Western historians. German, American, and English historians, relying upon documentary sources (including Soviet ones) and the testimony of eyewitnesses, have a different understanding of the catastrophe that befell the German population in East Prussia. For example, see the recent books by Antony Beevor (*The Fall of Berlin, 1945*) and Max Hastings (*Armageddon: The Battle for Germany 1944–1945*).[3] I can also recommend publications in the Russian language that discuss this topic, such as L. Kovaleva's *Khranit' vechno* (Keep Eternally), Otto Lasch's *Tak pal Kenigsberg* (The Fall of Königberg), and Sergei Gol'chikov's *Pole boia—Prussiia* (The Battlefield—Prussia), electronic versions of which can all be found on the Internet.

22

To the Shores of the Baltic
March–April 1945

The Fighting for Landsberg

East Prussia, Landsberg [present-day Gorzów Wielkopolski]. This city played a dramatic role in the history of our division.

By an impetuous drive toward the shores of the Baltic, the forces of Marshal Rokossovsky's 2nd Belorussian Front were trying to cut East Prussia off from the rest of Germany. After fourteen days of the campaign, the 2nd Belorussian Front had split the German forces in East Prussia, and by 26 January 1945, it had reached the coastal belt of the Baltic Sea. This glittering operation became the shining hour in the life of Konstantin Konstantinovich Rokossovsky—it was his confirmation as a man of firm will and strong mind, and the pinnacle of his ascent as a great military leader, a virtuoso of the art of war.

The officers of our division, roused by Rokossovsky's masterful operation, constantly discussed the details of his unfolding campaign. Some considered it to be the finest operation of the entire war. Division commander Berestov admired the marshal above all others, and with laughter he liked to relate about his conversations with captured German officers: "They tried to find out Rokossovsky's age from me, and the academy from which he graduated, but when I told them that the marshal was forty-nine and had only a fourth-grade education, that he was the son of a machine operator and had worked as a stonemason, they nearly fainted."

As we were completing the operation to cut off the East Prussian group of enemy forces, we approached the town of Landsberg. A railroad, which had major significance for the adversary, passed through the outskirts of Landsberg—it was his only means of escape from the tightening noose of the Red Army around Königsberg. Only a few days, or perhaps, hours, remained for Germans to escape the closing pocket.

Without regard for losses and introducing elite elements into the fighting, the Germans had managed to break through and seize the railroad junction that lay just outside Landsberg, but they were unable to go any farther. Trains that were trying to evacuate infantry and armor from the pocket began increasingly to jam the station's right-of-way. To try to clear a passage, they were forced to unload the self-propelled guns, tanks, and artillery from the open platforms of the trains and put them on the move to fight a way out, while lines of submachine gunners rushed to follow them.

But these were different times—it was now 1945—and the adversary's vehicles, men, and trains became easy prey for our air force. On fine weather days, our air force seemed to hover almost continuously above the German positions—more than 500 airplanes flew repeated sorties during this day. Katiusha rockets set fire to German tanks and self-propelled guns, and scattered and destroyed their infantry. Instantly along the entire extent of the front, tall columns of fire and smoke rose. Explosions, leaping from place to place, ran up and down along the horizon and soon covered everything around with smoke and dust. The reverberations of enormous explosions echoed back to us; the railway junction turned into a conflagration, and clouds of black smoke billowed high into the sky. Powerful bomb strikes and artillery fire swept away everything and began turning the city into a mass of ruins. As a result, all the railroads leading from the city were knocked out, and the fields around were piled with enemy corpses. Pushed together into a solid mass by the circumstances, a dense body of enemy troops, abandoning the railway junction, started rolling back toward the city.

Meanwhile, General Berestov had been driving our division forward with his customary energy. We took Landsberg from the march, entering it on the opposite side of the city from the rail junction, and found an empty city. Thousands of panicked citizens had fled at the sudden and unexpected approach of Soviet troops. Streetlights were still burning, and residents had not bothered to turn off their house lights or porch lights. The hands on the enormous clock tower in the city center still showed the correct time.

Without stopping, Berestov pushed us through Landsberg and out the opposite side, driving toward the rail junction beyond, not realizing that our division was now inadvertently a bone in the throat on the path of the enemy's retreating army. Before we could react, the onrushing enemy mass was already upon us, and the two "fists" collided. On several sectors of our front, the Germans immediately managed to push our units back. The division fell back to the city's outskirts, where the fighting intensified and became a massive struggle.

It became increasingly difficult to withstand the uninterrupted, furious pressure of the attackers, who were literally fighting for their lives. An artillery regiment assigned to the division tried to salvage the situation, sparing no ammunition. A tank brigade was thrown into the battle. But we could not stop the enemy's advance. Night fell, but the struggle continued. Unable to endure the pressure, our units began to waver, and some began to abandon their positions.

The situation had become critical, and General Berestov understood: just a bit more, and enemy armor would break into the city, overrun our positions, and simply by their mass destroy the entire division. So the general gave the order to fire upon the fleeing men. Within a few minutes, a blocking detachment of machine gunners was organized. The Germans failed to break into the city.

Having failed in its original effort, and having lost many men, later that night the German command sent two armored S.S. columns in a flanking movement around both sides of the city, and soon the ring around our division had been slammed shut.[1] We were encircled for two days. During this time, all the roads leading to Landsberg were jammed with Soviet troops and tanks coming to our rescue. Guard units arrived with rocket launchers, and the relief force soon broke the German grip on the city and forced the Germans to retreat. Shturmoviki [the famous Il-2 ground attack planes] appeared in the skies, turning the retreating columns of Germans into mass graveyards of people and twisted metal.

So, in our case the help came in time, and our brief encirclement didn't cause us serious difficulties. The true disaster befell our divisional rear area, which had inadvertently found itself in the direct path of the enemy armor columns.

The Tragedy in the Division's Rear

A complete lack of concern held sway over the division's rear. It had received no communications from the division headquarters in the city, and no one was expecting such a turn of events, especially since it occurred at night.

The German armor materialized suddenly out of the darkness. They surrounded the village where the division's rear services were located. Illumination flares streaked into the night sky, and a storm of artillery, machine gun, and automatic weapon fire fell upon the division's rear units. Attacking German infantry swept through the village, tossing grenades through the windows of homes. Deafened, frantic people dashed out of homes in only their underclothing, or jumped from the windows of upper floors, all trying to reach the presumed shelter of some nearby woods. But even there, they ran into German submachine gunners. In a frenzy—at point-blank range—the German soldiers shot down everyone in turn—men, women, wounded, and every living thing that they laid their eyes upon, even the horses and cows that we had acquired. The *medsanbat*, the gunshops, the headquarters' motor pool, the bakery, the laundry—were all turned into piles of debris within several minutes. Flamethrowers torched the storehouses, tents, and supply carts, which were loaded with food and ammunition for the front.

Almost the entire sapper company perished instantly. They had been withdrawn from the front just the day before for a rest.

A small group of officers and soldiers, caught in a home on the outskirts of the village, put up desperate resistance. For more than an hour, they defended themselves with machine-gun fire and repelled the Hitlerites. But then a self-propelled gun pulled up and methodically reduced their cover down to the foundations.

Doctors, nurses, some of the wounded and soldiers, and a few officers had time to take cover in homes that were situated farther from the woods, and were trapped in deep, strong bunkers beneath the homes. The Germans delivered an ultimatum for surrender and gave them fifteen minutes to think about it. Everyone refused. When the Germans attempted to enter one of the bunkers, they were met by a burst of automatic fire. So the Germans dealt with them by turning their bunkers into gas chambers: they brought up self-propelled guns to the buildings, knocked out the windows, inserted hoses attached to the vehicles' exhaust pipes, and ran the engines at full power. The trapped men and women inside were in torment, gasping for air, and died from suffocation.

In another one of the bunkers, seven of the female snipers were taking cover. The Germans tossed grenades into their shelter and then torched the women, some still alive, with flamethrowers. Nikodim Ivanovich perished as well. His body and one of the young women's bodies were found locked in a tight embrace—likely, in the last minutes of her life, seeking protection, she had rushed to the sergeant major, and he had offered her the shelter of his own body.

Only a few survived this bloody slaughter. As was evident, even in the most difficult circumstances, if a person doesn't lose his or her cool, he or she can try to find some way to stay alive. A captain who was assigned to the Political Department's motor pool managed to hide himself in a cellar among the dead. He lay among the corpses for almost two days, feigning death. Several times, fascists appeared on the staircase leading down to the cellar, shined a flashlight over the bodies, fired a burst or two into them just in case, and then relieved themselves and left. The captain was lucky, for a bullet never touched him, and he remained unharmed. However, the ordeal caused his hair to turn completely gray, and afterward he always stuttered. Unfortunately, he died later in Vienna in a motorcycle accident.

So many tragedies occurred that night when our rear service area was overrun! A doctor in the *medsanbat* was killed, but his wife, also a doctor, was in the city at a field medical station and avoided her husband's fate.

The savage, frenzied marauding continued for a long time. When we were finally able to return to the village, as we drew near we saw enormous puddles of blood and dead animals—they had even killed my German shepherd. Windows were shattered, and empty, broken, scorched window frames gaped in the damaged buildings. Then we found bodies and more bodies, many with knife wounds—they had finished off the wounded with knives and bayonets.

Looking at the dead—those suffocated by gas; those shredded by mortar and automatic fire, and grenades; those half-cremated by the squirts of flamethrowers—I became numb, and almost out of my head with hatred for the killers. My hands were shaking in impotent rage. The newspaper editor had been right: "If the entire world goes mad, you can't put it in chains; but the insane, fanatical killers must be suppressed, finished off, and destroyed!"

The nightmare that I witnessed seared itself forever into my memory and soul. Even today, it is so difficult to think back upon those dreadful images, and I'm constantly pulling myself back from the paper even as I am writing about it. I saw so many dead people at the front, people who had often died after unbelievable suffering, but such a cruel, bloody mass spectacle, filled simultaneously with such great tragedy and sorrow, I never saw before or since.

Then there were the funerals. We laid more than 300 bodies of the dead into a common grave. It was especially difficult to reconcile ourselves to the death of the young female snipers. My girlfriend Rita was among them. Everyone was crying, and human tears soaked the grave. We all felt orphaned; we had not only lost lovers but also friends and assistants, men and women who had come to give us a helping hand, together with whom we shared so many bonds, and had passed through and survived so much. They perished just two months before the great Victory Day for which we had all been so eagerly waiting.

General Berestov arrived to pay his respects. He removed his forage cap from his head and took in what was happening with a glance. Then he deeply bowed before the dead, and straightened back up without saying a word. He went down the line of weeping mourners, trying to comfort them with a quiet word or two.

The German Hospital

In their haste to flee, the retreating Germans had failed to evacuate a major army hospital in Landsberg and had left it abandoned. When we entered the building, we found it was packed and overflowing with badly wounded, primarily bedridden patients. We looked at them—pitiful, defenseless; and not one of our officers or soldiers lifted a hand against them in vengeance. The division commander gave instructions to the chief of the *medsanbat* to take the hospital under control and to try to stock up its supplies of medicines and bandaging materials. But there were also SMERSH officers present who outranked the doctor, which later led the general to make a fatal decision.

We had an urgent need to reconstitute our division's *medsanbat* after its destruction in the night massacre outside the city. We asked higher command for assistance. The army helped us by sending medical personnel, and through the efforts of the division and the German doctors and nurses who were recruited to assist, we were able to resume the treatment of wounded in the city. All the regiments shared their medical assistants, medical orderlies, and vehicles to transport the wounded in order to assist the hospital's work. Shilovich instructed the major in charge of the reorganized *medsanbat* and me to visit the German hospital and familiarize ourselves with the situation there—perhaps the German doctors and nurses would be able to hunt up some medical supplies for our *medsanbat*.

Already on the threshold of the hospital, the stench of rotting and disinfection filled our nostrils. Along the walls of the corridor stood buckets holding rotting, bloody bandages and gauze, full of maggots. There were hardly any medical orderlies to be seen, and there were few nurses, for almost all of them had run off. To get a full view of the situation, we had to enter the patient wards. When we appeared in the doorways, the rooms fell into tense silence. Dozens of patients, using overcoats as blankets, sat or lay on the beds. Almost all of them had crutches or canes leaning against their beds next to them, or wheelchairs sitting beside them. An unbearable stench hung over all of them; the heavy, stuffy air in the room was nauseating. The rooms were full of unwashed human bodies, probably full of parasites. Most of the men's faces were dark and gloomy, expressing only apathy or melancholy—they didn't even look in our direction; but more than a few looked at us with undisguised malice in their eyes; a few were so frightened and alarmed that they seemed on the verge of nervous collapse. But all without exception clearly realized their precarious situation—they had been abandoned and left at the mercy of the Russians, so they were gripped by a sense of utter despair and hopelessness. They also, without exception, were expecting nothing good from us. When I tried to have a chat with one or another, they all, as if they were wind-up dolls, said the same thing: "I took the oath to the Führer, and I was only carrying out orders."

In one of the wards I noticed a man wearing a plumed cap. Someone explained that it was the local pastor. Almost alone among Landsberg's residents, he hadn't fled but had remained in the city to help the wounded with God's word, offering them comfort and salvation, which had become the last refuge for the religious patients. We got acquainted. The pastor politely thanked us for our help with the wounded and told me that General Berestov had given him a bodyguard, one of our soldiers, for safe movement around the city.

I chatted with the German doctors. There were only three of them left in the entire hospital. The major who was accompanying me reached an agreement with the senior doctor: in exchange for medical supplies we would feed their wounded and help with their treatment. The major also informed the German doctors of the S.S.'s nighttime destruction of our *medsanbat* and its reprisal against our own wounded, and he asked them to tell their patients about what had happened. After examining the hospital, which was accommodated in a former gymnasium, we decided that our *medsanbat* should be housed in a similar large, empty building somewhere on the outskirts of the city, a little more removed from combat operations.

Exiting the hospital, we stumbled upon the naked, mutilated body of a German woman. We later learned that it was the corpse of the hospital's senior nurse. I think the body had been specially placed there in our path, telling us: "Look, Soviet officers, sirs, what your army is doing to us."

We tried to find out what had happened. It immediately became clear that some soldiers in a unit stationed next to the hospital had learned from their comrade medical orderly, who was working in the hospital, that the senior nurse had sharply protested against the transfer of medicines and bandages to the Russians and had become furious. This was just that sort of case where it only takes a spark to start a conflagration. The nurse paid a terrible price for her protest. The soldiers dragged the woman into a neighboring building, beat her savagely, and, having ripped off her clothes, an entire platoon took turns raping her. Then, as she was still barely living, they had spread her legs apart and shoved a liquor bottle between them, ripping her perineum. The sight of the senior nurse was utterly horrifying. I instructed her corpse to be removed immediately and apologized to the German doctors.

We made our report to the general. He ordered sentries to be placed around the hospital and decreed that no one should be permitted to enter it without his permission.

Soon long-range German artillery began dropping shells accurately onto targets in the city, inflicting heavy losses on our units. The casualties multiplied. The SMERSH officers at the hospital reported to the division commander that someone in the hospital was secretly working to pass targeting information to the German artillery. Scouts twice searched the entire premises and failed to find anything. They didn't believe there was some German spotter in the hospital. In the meantime, the accurate barrage on the city continued to fall, and the SMERSH men continued to insist they were right and pressed Berestov to take some action to stop it. Finally the general yielded and ordered: "Get rid of the hospital!" Nobody expected something like that from Berestov. Only my boss, Colonel Shilovich, supported Berestov's decision.

Just the evening before, the hospital had been alive with its normal routines and the sounds of plaintive German singing; by morning the building was empty. All its inhabitants had disappeared. My comrade, who dropped by the hospital that morning, found only empty beds; blood-, sweat-, and urine-soaked mattresses; and piles of artificial limbs, splints, and crutches. What had happened to all the wounded, doctors, and nurses, God only knows.

None of the officers asked any questions, and no one made any inquiries about what had become of the wounded German soldiers and the hospital staff. Even the pastor and his bodyguard disappeared. I was troubled by heavy thoughts: perhaps what had occurred to the German hospital was only just punishment for the tormented deaths of our wounded and the killing of our female snipers?

A Special Assignment

The next day, Berestov summoned me to his command post:

"We need to sweep the city of marauders. I'm giving you five submachine gunners—your Komsomol members. Here's your weapon"—and he extended to me a short, gnarled walking stick. "Beat their mangy butts with this little club, regardless of their rank."

"Understood!"

I heard the order all right, but what was I supposed to do? I had never received such an unbelievable order before. Of course, I wouldn't have to shoot anybody, but I couldn't understand why I was to beat them with a walking stick. But I despised pillagers, and here was my chance to punish the swine!

Passing through several city blocks, I bumped into some soldiers who were plundering a store. Four of them were standing in front of me with bundles on their backs. I lined up my five submachine gunners in front of them and ordered:

"Drop your stuff on the ground immediately! Go get rifles and head immediately to the front!"

At that moment, a scene occurred worthy of the pen of Gogol' or Chekhov. A black "Emka" [an M-1 four-seater staff car] slowly wheeled around the corner of the street, piled with "goods." Accordions and paintings rolled into tubes had been tightly strapped to the roof, and in back, three or four bicycles had been attached to the spare tire.

I flagged it down and thought: "Now you'll do a little dance for me; I'm going to knock the stuffing out of these plunderers! No matter who they are! Who else would be sitting in an Emka but a ranking officer?" The car came to a stop. Out climbed an unfamiliar general, who took to giving me a real tongue-lashing. He held nothing back and paid no attention to my team of submachine gunners, who were unable to conceal their laughter at my predicament. I became disconcerted, then angry, and I thought, "Well, to hell with all of them!" The angry general hopped back into his staff car and drove away.

After what had just happened, it seemed ludicrous to give the guilty soldiers I had just caught a dressing down, so I dismissed them, gathered my submachine gunners, and we moved on. There were no further incidents.

Having reached the front lines, I passed along the division commander's order against pillaging to the regiment commander, and then told him about my episode by the store. He burst out laughing and calmed me down: "Those were my guys! It's a good thing you didn't touch them."

Of course, the rank and file thought primarily of taking petty things. But not the general officers! They plundered on a massive scale, sending back their loot in train cars or even in airplanes. Naturally, the general officers didn't pillage themselves; their aides obtained and delivered their loot to them. I knew one division commander who during his relocation from Germany contrived to secure an entire freight car for himself and loaded five bedroom sets and six dining room sets in it; when they asked him for what purposes he was shipping so much furniture back to Russia, he calmly replied, "They're for an officers' club."

Around a Campfire

I always loved to spend time at campfires during the years of war. Soldiers normally gathered around them if they had the chance. There they could warm their worn-out and exhausted bones, dry out or change their soggy boots, and drink some hot tea. They used these opportunities to talk a bit about life, discuss the most recent fighting, or—most important—recall old comrades, pass some jokes around about commanders, or share some news from home.

The particular campfire I want to tell you about, which was located in the courtyard of a large farm manor, seemed unusual to me for many reasons. Bookshelves, paintings, books, family albums, piano sheet music, wooden trinkets, and busted chairs were flying into the fire to keep it fueled. All of this was burning splendidly and brightly, illuminating those who were sitting around the fire. I stopped short at some distance from the fire. Five privates were sitting around the fire: Kondrat, Pas'ko, Pavel, Ivan, and Nil—that's how they introduced themselves when I joined them a bit later.

The soldiers were pouring tea from a smoke-smudged teapot, munching on slices of bread that had been smeared with jam. Chuckling, they were sharing their opinions about German women. Each man told the others, as if giving a report, about the victories he had scored on the sexual front. Kondrat had experienced six women. Pas'ko had taken advantage of four. "An old buzzard" had fallen to Pavel's lot, but another had been "quite painfully young." Ivan complained about bad luck: "one stinking old lady." Nil, as he put it, had "made fully a dozen women happy." Comparing German women to Polish women, everyone came to a general conclusion: the Polish women were more sexually dexterous, lively, and passionate.

"The German women are so painfully cold and dry. They lie there beneath you totally without moving, only "Oh!" and gasps—they're so quiet, it's as if God himself has taken their speech away. Don't bother waiting for a good word from any of them. You have to work at it, like you're going into battle. We know this one German babe. You give her something to eat, and let her have a drink—she says just one thing, "*Gut*." Then when you give her a good tumble, again, just "*Gut*."

"I think," said Kondrat, "that our women both know more endearing words and are better in bed than either German women or Polish women."

"I agree with you so far as German ladies go, Kondrat," Nil joined the conversation, "but as for Polish women, I've never seen such a circus in my life—they're not just women, but female acrobats or circus riders!"

"You're lucky," Ivan sighed heavily. "I tramped across all of Poland and still remained a virgin."

Everybody burst out laughing. At that moment, I stepped up to the fire, and having greeted everyone, I asked if I could join their little circle. The soldiers willingly made a space for me around the fire, and when I told them I was a captain, they immediately responded with a few words of approval and welcome. Someone uttered with a slight sigh of resignation:

"Help yourself to whatever we have, Captain."

"What are you saying?" Ivan offered in mock offense. "Don't go giving away the bank. We were only whispering about our spoils of war, and that's been permitted beyond our own borders. We're just making a lot of noise, brothers, as if we've all become rich men!" Jokingly, he added, "Don't be squeamish about the schnapps and roast chicken."

They poured out a little more tea for everyone, in equal measure: tomorrow would be another long march. Only when conditions permitted would they break out the liquor and drink hard. They treated me to some bread and jam, and we all had a nice bite to eat and drank a cup of tea.

"Now tell us, Captain," Pavel finally said, "why did the stinking German come crawling into Russia with war, especially when his pigs live better than our peasants? It makes a man furious to see the wealthy way they live!"

"The German people aren't guilty," I objected. "It was Hitler who outfoxed and outwitted the people, and forced them to fight and to kill."

"Er, no, Comrade Captain, I disagree—you yourself have seen that the Germans have been fighting willingly," Kondrat entered the discussion. "They pillaged and raped as they pleased, and covered all of Russia with gallows."

"Just wait a bit, friend, just wait a bit!" Pavel became aroused. "Hitler got the better of Poland in seventeen days and took care of France in six weeks. He grabbed half of all Europe, the son of a bitch. So then the Fritz men and women became tempted, thinking that their Führer would tie us up with a couple of turns, and they'd have access to all our grain, chickens, and geese."

"You speak the truth," Nil joined in. "They wrote off Russia prematurely!"

Ivan opened his knapsack and pulled out something that looked like a brightly colored cigar box. I was surprised as he drew himself up in a pose of exaggerated dignity and importance:

"Shall we have a smoke, Comrade Captain? We can just forget about cigarette butts now! I rounded up some cigars—five identical boxes of them! I'm going to send a package back home to Man'ka. Then when I get home, I'm going to sit on the bench in front of my house and smoke them slowly, just like a general. The guys are salivating over these boxes: they've never seen a label like this one."

"What kind of cigars do you have there, Ivan? Havana, American, Dutch, or perhaps German?" I took an interest. "Take a look, what's printed on the box?"

"It seems to be German, but I don't know much about that language."

"If you don't mind, hand me that box," I asked.

"Of course," Ivan agreed.

I turned the box around and grinned:

"You've made a mistake, friend."

Ivan furrowed his brow. He didn't understand what I was talking about, but nevertheless he grew concerned:

"You're joking, Comrade Captain? That looks like some smoke printed there on the box. Though to be honest, a tobacco worker senses there's something a bit strange about them."

"I'm not joking. They hang these little things—I don't know what the Germans call them—on their Christmas trees. So it would be better just to toss your 'cigars' into the fire. As for Mania, get some other package ready for her."

Ivan was embarrassed by the general laughter.

We started talking about the packages for home. Each of these five men had already sent three packages back home. They had all wrapped German boots into the first package; the soldiers treasured them: they were a bit thinner and shorter than our boots, but they were made from leather, not from canvas. They also placed three bedsheets in the package, because you couldn't find them high or low in the villages; and those who managed to get hold of any lay wristwatches on the bottom of the package.

The second package home was full of items for the women and girls. The third, for the little boys: exquisite little toy automobiles—who had ever seen such things in Russia? But they also included little shirts, vests, boots, and trousers. In every package from the front they added needles, thread, buttons, twine, and more watches, which were the most prized items among our rank and file.

They intended to fill the fourth and fifth packages with tools and hardware: chisels and planes, augurs, boxes of nails and screws, files and axe handles, and whatever else they wanted. But they wouldn't forget to include more bedsheets, wristwatches, and brightly colored tablecloths. Of course, for their fathers and mothers: a dress here, a shawl there, a properly fitted suit, and shoes.

"They say that Comrade Stalin has issued a directive to create a stock of abandoned German items for our packages home. The project will get started …"

"Eh, if only the authorities would give us freedom, spare us from *kolkhoz* troubles, and think up something like the NEP! [the New Economic Policy—a limited relaxation of the strict, centralized controls over the economy introduced by Lenin after the Russian Civil War] If they'd only set us free, we could rebuild and feed all of Russia within five years."

That's how the men reasoned among themselves. Like everybody, they fervently longed to return home as soon as possible and to rebuild their lives in a better way—to restore the farm, their homes, and the yard; to resume their bee-keeping; to plant a garden, and to restore the apple trees. Of course, our peasants had no chance to catch up with the economic development of their German peers, even by their old age—unless, as Stalin was promising, we managed to build communism by then. But in the meantime, the Red Army's peasants were mentally grasping a foreign experience and starting to gain an understanding of how things might be different back home.

It never happened. The hopes of Ivan, Kondrat, Pas'ko, Pavel, and Nil were never realized after the war. But that evening, spent around a soldier's campfire in East Prussia, lingered in my mind. It turned out to be my last meeting at the front with these "delegates," as I named these peasants in soldier's coats, whom the war had gathered together from all over Russia.

Early the next morning the artillery began to thunder. The army moved on for the shores of the Baltic.

23

The Final Steps
to Victory
April 1945

Königsberg

12 March 1945. It is only 18 kilometers [11 miles] to the shores of the Baltic. The German Army Group Vistula, commanded by Heinrich Himmler, has been split into pieces and pressed back into a narrow belt along the sea. It is now in its death throes. Despite the pending doom, the enemy resists stubbornly. Just like at Stalingrad, Hitler has given a personal order and made an appeal to the troops, forbidding them to abandon their positions or to surrender. The German command tries for as long as possible to keep major forces of the Red Army tied up around Königsberg, to prevent their transfer to the Berlin axis of advance. Königsberg is encircled by land but is still receiving ammunition and reinforcements from the central regions of Germany by sea. By the same means, civilians, wounded soldiers, and army rear services are being evacuated by ship.

Three armies of the 3rd Belorussian Front were taking aim at the bastions of Königsberg, trying to carry out the assignment given to them by the Stavka: to take the city and to liquidate the remnants of Army Group Vistula on the Samland Peninsula.

6 April, 12:00 P.M. After a powerful artillery preparation, the assault on the city's fortifications begins. The enemy is putting up stubborn resistance, and furious counterattacks follow one after the other. By the end of the day, by joint efforts of the three armies, we manage to penetrate the outer circle of the fortress's line of fortifications, fight our way into the outlying districts, and sweep 102 city blocks free of the enemy.

West of Königsberg, the rail link has been severed to its port of Pillau—a naval base of warships and transports and its sole remaining lifeline. The threat of isolation hangs over the Königsberg garrison. Once before, back at the end of January, Soviet forces had cut the rail line between Pillau and Königsberg. In response the German commander had launched a sally from the west side of Königsberg with a panzer division and some infantry and antitank support units. The weather had prohibited the operation of our air force, and we had been unable to hinder the adversary's operation to reopen the lifeline and introduce fresh reserves into the fighting for the city. This time, however, there will be no breakout to save the city.

7 April. With the dawn, taking advantage of the clearing skies, our air force launches three heavy raids on the fortress: 516 long-range bombers, under the cover of 232 fighters, set upon the city, destroying enemy forces and smashing fortifications and artillery positions. The base at Pillau is also subjected to multiple mass air attacks and naval artillery bombardment.

Meanwhile the infantry, strengthened by tank and antitank units, wheels large-caliber guns into position to fire over open sights at enemy-held buildings, and under the cover of air support and artillery fire, they break into the city's center, with special assault detachments leading the way. In the course of the attack, 130 city blocks are taken, as well as three forts, the marshaling yards of the railway station, and factory complexes. The savage fighting doesn't fade even with the onset of darkness.

8 April. The storming of the city with all types of forces, with the support of artillery and the air force, continues. The Königsberg garrison has been surrounded and split into pieces. In the northwest and southern districts of the fortress, the enemy's resistance has been broken. On this day alone, 15,000 soldiers and officers are taken prisoner. Attempts by the Hitlerite command to organize breakouts from both within the city and from outside it are unsuccessful.

9–11 April. The fighting intensifies. Under constant aerial bombardment and heavy artillery fire, the adversary loses unified direction of his forces. The garrison is doomed.

12 April 1945. Overcoming the pressure from Nazi loyalists, and to avoid further casualties in the army and among the civilian population, the commanding German general Otto Lasch issues the order to surrender.

Thus, one more enemy grouping in East Prussia ended its existence. More than 30,000 officers and soldiers marched into captivity. The adversary suffered more than 40,000 dead. As for our losses, to this very day—more than sixty years later!—we still don't know them.

General Lasch, who had decided upon surrender, was given a death sentence in absentia by Hitler. His family suffered cruel reprisals: his wife and eldest daughter were imprisoned in Denmark, his brother-in-law in Berlin was arrested and placed in one of the Gestapo's torture chambers, and his youngest daughter was tossed into a prison in Potsdam. Lasch himself suffered eleven years of Soviet captivity.

Königsberg was dead. Streets and buildings had been turned into rubble, and more than 90 percent of the city's structures were damaged or destroyed.[1] Among the ruins, soot, and filth, some survivors wandered like ghosts in search of food. In the center of the city, only one place remained untouched—the old church, which holds the remains of the great German philosopher and scholar Immanuel Kant. Not a single bomb fell on it, not a single shell struck it. Was it a coincidence, or fate? Rumors circulated, saying that Stalin himself had ordered that Kant's grave be preserved, having read somewhere in Karl Marx's writings that Marx had thought highly of the philosopher.

The Death of Battalion Commander Okunev

The taking of Königsberg is considered one of the most shining operations in the chronicle of the Great Patriotic War. But was it really? Let's suppose: had General Lasch not capitulated, fighting for the fortress would have become prolonged, as it was, for example, in Breslau. In that case, historians could hardly have reveled in the "great victory." We'll note that not one city in East Prussia, other than Königsberg—not Heiligenbeil, not Danzig, not Gdynsk—capitulated, despite the calls for surrender from our commanders.

During our storming of the fortress, our "Good Soldier Švejk," Dimka Okunev, died. A former cadet, a favorite of our training platoon, by 1945 he was a battalion commander. He refused to lead his men into certain death—he had received an order to lead his men under fire on a direct assault upon enemy bastions, protected only by their metal helmets. When they threateningly asked him, "Do you know, Captain, what awaits you for refusing to carry out an order?" the battalion commander Dimka replied, "I'm quite aware; are we really still studying in the preparatory class around Rzhev? But now you answer me! Why storm the fortress? Why give me an order to kill myself, and wipe out my remaining fighters, if we're going to force the adversary to surrender in just a few more days, after our bombs and shells do their work?"

No one, not even the "Good Soldier Švejk," had the right to refuse an order. Especially if it came from the Supreme Commander Stalin himself![2]

Battalion commander Dmitrii Okunev did not change his mind. What was there left for him to do? He emptied a glass of vodka and shot himself. That's how one of the "Last Mohicans" of our Tiumen cadet class perished—"we were from the same barracks."

Moscow joyfully saluted the victors who had stormed the ancient fortress, which the Germans had considered impenetrable. But no one—not the generals in their memoirs, or the official historians—remembered either Captain Okunev or any others among the fallen. How many were there? Who were they?

In 2005, Sergei Gol'chikov's book *Pole boia—Prussiia* (The Battlefield—Prussia) was published in Kaliningrad, the former Königsberg.[3] The book had a very limited printing—only 350 copies. In Gol'chikov's opinion, after the liquidation of the main German group of forces in East Prussia, there was no military need for the storming of Königsberg. It was sufficient just to hold the city in blockade, and thereby spare the lives of thousands of soldiers in the street fighting. The author is convinced that ideological considerations dictated the decision to storm the city.

A New Directive

The fighting for Königsberg was still going on when in the 11 April issue of the *Krasnaia zvezda* newspaper appeared the antifascist and at the same time anti-German article by Il'ia Ehrenburg entitled "Enough!"—in which the furious publicist condemned all Germans without exception as a single criminal band. Moreover, he revealed a negative attitude toward the Allies, accusing them of having sympathies for the Wehrmacht. He suggested that the German army in the final stage of the war was fighting only on the Eastern Front, while on the Western Front "they were surrendering their cities to the Allied armies by telephone."

Three days later, on 14 April, the *Pravda* newspaper published an article under the title, "Comrade Ehrenburg Is Simplifying Matters," in which Ehrenburg was subjected to heavy criticism: "It is amusing to identify the Hitler clique with the German people!" The chief editor of the *Krasnaia zvezda,* David Ortenberg, was removed from his post and sent to the front as the chief of an army's Political Directorate.

They announced to us, the political workers in the ranks, that the international environment had changed, and now it was necessary to bring the German people around to our side. The entire political staff was mobilized to explain the fundamentally new approach of the Soviet government to the officers and soldiers. The soldiers greeted the news ambivalently and didn't even bother to hide their negative attitude toward the arguments of the political workers. I often heard the question: "How can it be that for so many years we were called upon to kill the German, but now the high command is singing a different tune?" A few of the more courageous fellows declared even more scathingly: "We trust Il'ia [Ehrenburg] more!"

We, the officers, knew little about what was going on at the top, far from the front, and relied primarily on news reports, conjectures, and speeches from the top brass that visited the army. But the 14 April *Pravda* article criticizing Ehrenburg factually did not change the situation with the excesses in East Prussia.

Only on 20 April 1945 did the Stavka—or more accurately, Stalin—issue Directive 11072 to the *front* commanders: "You are required to change the attitude toward the Germans, both toward military prisoners and toward civilians. Cruel treatment of the Germans only forces them to resist stubbornly and to refuse to surrender. The civilian population, fearing bloody reprisals, is organizing into bands (a SMERSH fiction!). Such a situation is unfavorable for us. A more humane treatment of the Germans will ease the implementation of our combat operations on their territory. It will also doubtlessly reduce the stubbornness of the Germans on defense."

Genuine changes occurred only after the appearance of this directive. The arbitrary treatment of the population began to diminish sharply. *Front* commanders, military councils, the army's Political Directorate, and the divisions' Political Departments all worked to implement the Stavka directive.

"Hitler Is Kaput!"

During the time of all the fighting in East Prussia our division never received any replacements, so it was forced constantly to consolidate regiments and battalions. Before the decisive advance to the shores of the Baltic, the division command had created special assault detachments out of the former regiments and battalions, which were supported by regimental artillery—76-mm and 45-mm guns.

The detachment, with which I operated, consisted of 100 riflemen divided into four groups, with each group having two machine guns. A tank brigade moved along the highway ahead of us. Behind our detachment, mortar units with 82-mm and 120-mm mortars followed. Il-2 Shturmovik ground attack planes covered our detachment from the air. Where had the German aces gone, who just a couple of years before had felt themselves masters of the skies? They were nowhere to be seen.

Captured officers confirmed the difficult discussions going on in the enemy camp: who was in condition to oppose the colossal power of the Russians, and to organize the basic direction of the forces? How could they close up the ranks of the soldiers if all the officers and soldiers understood that the war was lost? But a dedication to Hitler and their military oath remained in the German army to the very end. Nobody wanted to surrender, to become a Russian prisoner, and nobody believed the promises of our command, that we would spare their lives. Tanks crushed them, Katiusha rockets destroyed them, but again and again they rose in our path. Everywhere—on the walls of buildings, on posters, on knife handles—we saw one and the same call: "Loyalty and fortitude."

But what kind of "fortitude" was there? It was only the howl of despair! In order to stop the resolute advance of the Red Army, by special order of Hitler, young adolescents and old men were summoned into the army and formed into the so-called *Volkshturm*. Now adolescents who still had no facial hair were sitting behind machine guns or holding panzerfausts [antitank weapons]. Most of them had not even reached sixteen years of age, but the weapon in their hands still sprayed deadly fire everywhere.

These scamps, as we called these ninnies, had already burned a lot of our tanks. Our artillerymen would roll up their 76-mm guns to fire at point-blank range and smash the embrasures from which they had been firing, but the scamps with their panzerfausts would just scuttle into the cellars and continue to send out their flaming warheads. We would get to them even there—first with artillery, and then grenades would go flying into their hideouts. Only then would they begin to surrender: gradually, timidly, they would emerge from the cellars with upraised hands. They would look around watchfully or frightenedly, but the adolescent *Volkshturm* soldiers, down to the last boy, would shout out in Russian a memorized expression: "Hitler kaput!" We had long become accustomed to such scenes and would laugh.

Once I walked up to a surrendering lad of around fifteen years of age. The soldier's eyes were red and tearing from lack of sleep, his nose was running, there was a familiar stench, and lice were crawling around his collar. But the boy didn't notice any of these things; he was trembling, and he was afraid to lower his hands without permission. I searched him, found a knife, and then pulled a sheet of paper from the pocket of his coat—it was "The Oath." I translated it on the spot and read it out to the Red Army men around me:

"I swear by God to fulfill this sacred oath! I will unquestioningly obey the Führer of the German Reich and the German people Adolf Hitler, the Supreme Commander of the Armed Forces, and am ready at any moment like a brave soldier to sacrifice my life for this vow."

What should we do with such a vile little creature? The detachment commander walked up, grabbed the *Volkshturm* private, sharply spun him around, and gave him a good kick in the rump with his boot. The lad, without turning around, took off running for the nearby woods like a frightened rabbit.

Only Seagulls Are Crying over the Sea

Ahead lay the Baltic Sea. A little more pressure, and the Germans would be trapped with their backs to the sea. They'd have nowhere else to go, and it would become the final situation. *Then at last!* . . . Everyone could now see the looming victory, the end of the war! Wound up with unaccustomed energy, looking death in the face, our assault unit chased the enemy, taking position after position—always pressing forward! In a fury, the soldier fired burst after burst, shell after shell—from machine guns, submachine guns, and heavy guns. Yet the thoughts were hammering in each soul: it's still going so slowly, just a few kilometers a day! And the commanders would rage: "Faster! Forward, forward!" But bullets and shells know no mercy, and the land around was densely mined—the slightest misstep to the left or right, and you'd be blown sky-high. Only by evening would the thunder of battle pause for a short while: both sides were spent and needed a rest. Wherever the darkness found them, soldiers would collapse to the ground like mown grass. But with the dawn, the cacophony of battle would resume. Again the unpleasant screech of shells, the hoarse sizzle of *fausty* [panzerfausts], and the heavy return bursts of machine-gun and submachine-gun fire. But it is impossible to stop the men. Hope is leading us forward! Just a few more hard days! A few more local breakthroughs! A few more desperate efforts—then we'll have them! We'll drive the damned scoundrels into the sea! And then . . .

But how many men were fated to see that day? Heavy casualties by now had reduced our four groups of assault detachments into just two.

Those people somewhere in front of us might break contact with us and take to their heels; we have to keep pressing them. The air is heavy. There is no wind, and it is hard to breathe. My throat is parched and my teeth feel gritty. Sleep no longer comes to us, and we also don't feel like eating. We feel nauseous and unsteady on our feet. We are unwashed, unshaven, in worn-out greatcoats. But the sea lies just ahead! We'll reach it soon—we're just about there! It still isn't visible, but the scent of the sea is in the air. Like an oasis in the desert, each man is dreaming of it and thinking about it every minute, and longs to see it. You begin to believe there is a God, and you ask him fervently: "God, help me! Help me make it, God."

When we finally emerged from a dense fog, a strong sea breeze instantly, like a knife, parted the veil that had been shrouding the earth, and a mesmerizing image materialized in front of us. The waters of a harbor were shining in the sunlight like an endless golden paradise. Along a narrow beach that stretched for many kilometers around the harbor, thousands of German soldiers were standing with upraised hands, without weapons—these had been placed neatly on the ground in front of them. Around them, along the entire shore, lay piles of corpses in countless numbers, and smashed and abandoned vehicles and equipment—tanks, artillery pieces, field kitchens, and wagons. Beyond lay an even more surreal sight: bobbing on the surface of the sea were the bodies of humans and horses, the skeleton remains of boats and launches, the wreckage of combat vehicles, mutilated trees, torn sheets of newspaper, and dead fish—and the entire macabre graveyard was swaying and rocking in the water like some apocalyptic vision.

There were thousands of Germans, just dozens of us. Sheer terror and complete confusion were in the eyes of the Germans. Our eyes were shining with joy and a sense of great pride!

How much had we sacrificed, how long had we been waiting with growing impatience and fervor for this hour! At last it had arrived! Each of us who reached the sea had been dreaming of this moment and wanted to say something momentous and special to mark the occasion. It was a significant historic event! But we all felt deathly tired. The tank crews were silent. The artillerymen were silent. The infantry was silent. Only seagulls were crying above the sea. Their cries gladdened our souls—and tore at our hearts.

Without making any arrangements, we all headed down to the shore. One of the officers loudly shouted at the Germans, who were waiting for an order:

"Get the hell out of here!"

The Germans immediately began to form up into columns—it seemed there was no end to them—and moved out for the rear. No one was guarding them; no one was even thinking about them anymore.

We walked down to the shoreline and dropped at the water's edge, some to their knees, some squatting, some simply bending over and grabbing their knees—and each man touched the foaming gray water with a trembling hand, filled their palms, and washed their face, hands, and head with the breathtakingly cold water.

Later we found out that in the Baltic Front, soldiers who had broken through to the coast had filled a whole cask with sea water—for the Great Stalin. They sent three more bottles of Baltic seawater to their *front* commander. Film crews recorded these stirring moments. Rokossovsky's soldiers also dispatched a courier to their commander, who was carrying a valuable load: three bottles of Baltic water. In his memoirs, Marshal Rokossovsky describes how he tasted the salty water and even drank a bit of it.

Nobody filmed us, and nobody bothered to interview us, but we weren't even expecting any gratitude. "We honorably did our duty"—that's what each of us was thinking. But our lips were sensing an intoxicating, bitter, and salty mixture of tears, sweat, and the long-awaited moisture of the Baltic surf.

The sea was breathing in the rays of the setting sun and crashing on the shore in foamy waves. Then the sun sank fluidly into the sea, disappearing from the horizon, and the rays of the sunset began quickly to dim. But the growing darkness didn't affect our mood at all. Something was slowly rising inside us, filling us, overflowing us—we were bursting with happiness. Division commander Berestov drove up to us on the shore. He stepped out of his vehicle and strolled a bit along the water's edge. Then he stopped and stood for a moment, gazing out into the gathering darkness. Finally, he headed toward our assault group. Out of force of habit we had already formed up and were waiting for orders. Captain Sirota was just about to salute and present what was left of our detachment, from which you could no longer form even a platoon. The general smiled and gave a dismissive wave of his hand: "Come on, guys . . ."

Neither Pavel Fedorovich Berestov nor the soldiers were ashamed of their tears and didn't bother to try to hide them. We stood that way for a long time, everyone together, gazing into the distance, where the elements of the sea and sky were flowing together in the sacrament of the horizon. It was one of the most amazing, unrepeatable, unforgettable moments in my life! Likely, all who had managed to reach this far and who were then standing on the beach were feeling the same way—the sensations of Victory gathered around us and filled our hearts.

One of the Ukrainian soldiers abruptly broke the silence: "Hey, fellows!" he said loudly to everyone around. "Look up! Look at all those birds flying westward toward the setting sun."

Everybody raised their heads. It was a most magnificent sight! Straining against the wind, seagulls were soaring above the sea. There was a multitude of them, beyond counting.

"Fellows! We're just like those birds!"

We stood on the shore and wept—from the indescribable beauty of what we had seen, and from the joy of finally reaching our long-sought goal. We cried too for those who did not make it, and for everything we had experienced. Who knows what each of these hundreds of people was silently thinking on that beach as they became gradually chilled by the night sea air? I suddenly thought of my Mother. If only she could be here now, together with me!! How happy she had been when at ten months of age I had taken my first steps around the room, how much she later suffered whenever I came home late, and how she had cried as she saw me off to the front. It's a sacred word—Mama!

24

The Last Days of the War
May 1945

Two weeks later our division was hastily loaded into a troop train and sent off to the Czech Sudetenland to deal the final blow to the forces of General Schörner. En route, we learned that the Stavka had transferred the 31st Army, including our 331st Rifle Division, from the 3rd Belorussian Front to the 1st Ukrainian Front. Thus once again I was to find myself under the high command of I. S. Konev. I had started my combat service under him at Rzhev back in 1942, when he was then commanding the Kalinin Front. The general had lost that battle since he had been unable to take Rzhev. Now as a marshal in May 1945, he was famous as a great commander, having learned well how to fight "on soldiers' bones." In his memoirs, he gave a little praise to the 220th Rifle Division, in which I was serving at the time, which was a pleasant surprise for me to read.

The railroads from Königsberg to Saxony were jammed to the limit; Stalin was moving forces from the Baltic and central Germany to southern Germany, and as a fatalist, he was doing so urgently. German planes made a frequent appearance in the skies above us, but our fighters constantly and courageously dueled with them and held them off. We took turns guessing about our ultimate destination: were we going to finish off the Germans in Dresden, or head straight for Prague?

Our division disembarked from its trains in Saxony on the night of 6 May 1945. Berlin had already fallen, but the impression began to form among many of my fellow officers that the division was once again at the epicenter of major events, no less difficult than the ones we had faced in East Prussia. I was struck by the concentration of force that the Red Army had gathered here. There were many tanks and towed artillery pieces on all the roads in the region, ready to move out at any time. It looked like an enormous steel armada.

For all we knew, our adversary, the German Army Group Center, still remained a dangerous opponent. It was the largest German grouping still in the field, with more than 700,000 men, and still had lots of tanks, artillery, and airplanes. Field Marshal Ferdinand Schörner was now commanding the enemy grouping. He had received an instruction from the new German government, headed by Admiral Dörnitz, to continue combat operations against the Red Army, so as to allow as many German troops as possible to flee to the west and to surrender to the Americans.[1]

On 2 May, after the fall of Berlin, the Stavka had demanded that the 1st and 2nd Ukrainian Fronts prepare as soon as possible for an offensive operation into Czechoslovakia. The plan was to strike two blows in the general direction of Prague, from the north by the 1st Ukrainian Front and from the southeast by the 2nd Ukrainian Front. The Prague operation anticipated the encirclement of the enemy and the dispersal of all his forces in Czechoslovakia. But, of course, the ultimate prize was Prague itself. Stalin strongly intended to seize the capital of Czechoslovakia prior to the total cessation of hostilities.

This operation also included the participation of the 4th Ukrainian Front. It would operate from the east in cooperation with the right wing of the 2nd Ukrainian Front, but it was not supposed to be directly involved in the attack on Prague itself.

Polish, Romanian, and Czechoslovak forces also took part in the operation. Altogether, more than 2 million men and women, 30,450 artillery tubes and mortars, 1,960 tanks and self-propelled guns, and more than 3,000 airplanes were involved in the operation. The Red Army could permit itself such a concentration of combat forces on one axis only in 1945!

The 31st Army's role in the Prague operation was going to be secondary. Operating on the far left flank of the 1st Ukrainian Front, its task was to provide flank protection to the northern prong of the attack on Prague, making sure that any German groupings to the east of Prague would not be able to interfere with the advance on the capital.

On 7 May 1945, the 1st Ukrainian Front (the left wing and center) went on the offensive with five combined-arms armies, including our 31st Army. That same day, our 331st Rifle Division received the order to advance its regiments into the Sudeten Mountains. Its task was to cover the roads leading to Prague from the east at all costs. Some of the more imaginative officers anticipated all sorts of dire scenarios, and they commented upon the mission in all seriousness: "Now we're in for it, lads! Hold on! We're going to be like Panfilov's men in front of Moscow. We'll make our stand to the death!"[2]

For this operation the 331st Rifle Division organized the advance into multiple mobile battalions. We rolled southward, meeting little organized resistance. In fact, the day before, on 6 May, Army Group Center had initiated a general retreat from Czechoslovakia. The Germans were trying to reach the relative sanctuary of the American lines, and they largely avoided major contact with our units. Most of the German formations were scurrying out of the pocket we were trying to establish, and the 331st Rifle Division only encountered small straggling groups. But we continued to advance through the Sudeten Mountains, setting up screening outposts and blocking detachments on the roads leading toward Prague from the east.

At this time, much of the fighting was already occurring to our west and in the city of Prague itself. As in the case of Warsaw, in early May the citizens of Prague launched an uprising against the occupying German forces. They were anticipating the near arrival of either American or Red Army forces and were trying to save the city from major destruction in the final days of the war. Residents blockaded the city streets, and thousands of civilians took part in the rebellion.

The Germans reacted swiftly to the uprising because it threatened to block the route of retreat for their units south and east of the capital city. Schörner ordered, "The uprising in Prague must be crushed!" German forces began to move on the city from various directions: from the north, the S.S. Panzer Division Das Reich; from the east, the S.S. Panzer Division Wiking; and from the south, a regiment of Das Reich that had become separated from its parent formation. The German garrison inside Prague, initially taken by surprise, began to organize a ruthless response to the uprising; hundreds of citizens were rounded up and executed.

Although both American and Red Army forces seemed within easy striking distance of Prague, neither side made any attempt to come to the relief of the uprising.[3] The Americans seemed not to realize the political ramifications if Stalin took Prague, while Stalin seemed to be repeating the policy he had shown in front of Warsaw in 1944: allowing the uprising to be crushed prior to entering the city. Help for the rebellion came from an unexpected source: General Vlasov's Russian Liberation Army (ROA).

Realizing that Nazi Germany was now doomed, Vlasov made a desperate calculation to side with the Czech uprising, perhaps hoping that a successful uprising might bring political sanctuary for the ROA soldiers from a new nationalist Czech government before the Red Army reached the city. Major General Sergei Kuz'mich Buniachenko's 1st ROA Division turned against the Germans, routed some German units guarding the airfield, and took control of it, destroying some fifty airplanes and 100 tanks in the process.[4] The Czech populace greeted Vlasov's men joyfully, as liberators.

Events were now moving quite quickly. On the evening of 7 May, German troops in Prague abandoned the city in order to join the general retreat toward American lines, leaving behind all their tanks and heavy weapons. Realizing that the Red Army would now inevitably seize Prague, at 3:00 A.M. on 8 May, General Buniachenko gave the order for the ROA 1st Division to pull out of the city and join the flight to the west. When units of the Red Army entered

Prague on 9 May, they immediately began rounding up and executing Vlasov's soldiers who had remained in the city after the departure of Buniachenko's division.[5]

My division took no part in direct fighting for the city of Prague. But all of us, officers and soldiers alike, received the medal "For the Liberation of Prague" from our government. What were we doing at this time? We were still in the Sudeten Mountains, watching the roads leading through them to the west. I was with the command of one of the mobile battalions, and we regularly went around the blocking positions we had set up to check on them.

The Day of the Great Victory

At 8:00 A.M. on the morning of 8 May 1945, our mobile battalion was moving into the suburbs of the town of Schlewitz in the Sudeten Mountains. It had been ordered to seize the railway station there and then to advance farther. Though at the time we didn't know it, the world was now celebrating: the enemy had been vanquished! We found the streets of Schlewitz full of animated people in their festive national costumes. They were waving little flags in greeting that they had plainly sewn the night before, and tossing flowers and souvenirs at our vehicles. Everybody was rushing toward the town center for a celebratory meeting on the occasion of their long-awaited liberation from the occupiers.

The Germans had abandoned the town only that dawn. An elderly Czech woman told us that three officers, who had been living in their home, in their hasty departure had not had time to gather their overcoats. A second woman was asking us what she should do with a dog that the Germans had abandoned.

Someone needed medical assistance. One fellow was joyfully reporting that he had uncovered a food storehouse on a neighboring street.

I jumped off the truck and checked the time on my watch: I had only ten minutes. I crossed the street, stopped at the nearest home, and knocked on the door. A young, attractive woman opened the door. I asked in German for a glass of cold water. Unexpectedly, smiling pleasantly, she answered me in flawless Russian: "Come on in, Captain, I'm a Russian."

I entered and immediately found myself in a luxuriously furnished parlor. Paintings in expensive frames decorated the walls. It seemed I had seen them somewhere before, but I couldn't recall where.

The lady of the house brought in a bottle of wine on an elegant tray. "I think," she said coquettishly, "you've earned a bottle of French champagne today." Taking my leave a few minutes later, I thanked her, and then mustered up the courage to ask her: "What's your name? How did you wind up here?"

"I'm from the Crimea. My name is Vera, and how I wound up here, I'll probably have to tell you at some other time," she replied.

As we took leave from each other, Vera tossed some stunning news at me: "London Radio has just reported that this evening, in Potsdam, German generals will sign an act of unconditional surrender."

I gave her some friendly advice to gather up her things as quickly as possible and to head home. A few minutes later, our column of vehicles, with a battery of 57-mm guns in tow, moved on down the road. That evening we celebrated Victory Day.

All of us frontline soldiers could write complete novels about these happy hours in the lives of millions of people on the planet. Three days later, things became more peaceful even on our sector of the front.

Very quickly, our battalion reached an outpost that we were instructed to reinforce. In general, all of our operations in the Sudeten seemed like children's games. If only one of the fifteen divisions that the enemy had positioned in Czechoslovakia had fallen upon our position, little would have remained of us. But, according to the latest intelligence, the German units had begun their retreat to the west even before our arrival in the Sudeten.

The division took up defensive positions and placed so-called combat outposts on the roads leading to Prague. It had no fight with the enemy. Other divisions were still busy with that. After the hard fighting in East Prussia, our division wasn't even up to a game of tag with the enemy.

Meeting with one of our forward posts during a routine tour of our positions, we were all shocked by what we found. During the war, none of us had ever seen such a show like the one we encountered there.

The soldiers were all drunk. They had formed up such dancing circles that it seemed the ground was shaking. In a garden in front of a three-story house around an enormous bonfire, the flames of which almost seemed to leap to the sky, soldiers—some in their undershirts, some barefooted, not wearing service caps or belts, were doing folk dances and whooping as if they were mad. Crowds of similar wild men were gathered around the dancers, furiously clapping their hands to the music. Gunshots into the air were ringing out. A harmonica was playing in accompaniment with a piano. Brother-Slavs had dragged an enormous table out of the premises and onto the lawn, and were feasting at it. Emptied bottles of wine were rolling around everywhere. Interspersed among the soldiers, Czech men and women were dancing, local peasants in their stylish national dress. That, roughly, is the scene that appeared before us.

The lieutenant colonel, an assistant to the division's chief of staff, immediately flew into a rage at the sight of this carnival scene, which seemed to him to be totally inappropriate for a military environment. He grabbed the post commander by the shirt and began to shake him.

"What's going on here?" the lieutenant colonel began to thunder. "Instead of an alert combat outpost—drunken feasting and revelry. Senior Lieutenant, you have big troubles waiting for you. But in the meantime, I am relieving you of duty, and I request that you immediately hand me your gun!"

Everybody around fell silent immediately. The soldiers and the local citizens were waiting for what would happen next! And this is what happened next:

"Scram, you!" the senior lieutenant spat out with surprising disdain. He was literally shouting in the senior officer's face: "The war is finally over! The enemy has been defeated! Victory! But nitwits like you don't know a damn thing, and even if you do know something, you hide it from your subordinates and wait for instructions from above! The Allies accepted the unconditional surrender of the Germans yesterday [7 May 1945] in Rheims, and tonight before midnight the Fritzes are going to sign another final capitulation in Berlin."

The lieutenant colonel was confused, fell silent, and then mumbled—"O Lord! How did I miss such an historic event—victory?" But then he likely thought to himself, "How did this fresh-faced little officer find out about it? Did the Czechs announce it, or did he learn it through the 'soldiers' telegraph'?"

Without any orders, in a single bound we officers and soldiers, who had been standing by our vehicles, spontaneously rushed to meet our comrades and exchanged celebratory hugs and kisses with them. How many days and nights had all of us, participants in the war, waited for this day! We took off our caps, unfastened our belts, and joyfully plunged into the common rejoicing. Soldiers grabbed the embarrassed lieutenant colonel and tossed him into the air, then carefully lowered him back to the ground. But now he was shouting at the top of his lungs, "Dance, fellows! You've earned this bright holiday!"

Suddenly I seemed to hear a familiar voice—"Comrade Captain! Comrade Captain!" I turned around and immediately recognized among the soldiers standing in front of me the small group of men who had celebrated my promotion to captain together with me back in Prussia around that campfire. I responded:

"Hey, back then, it seems there were five of you, but now I see only three."

"You're right, Captain! The war has been mowing down our brothers to the final day. Vas'ko, you remember, that dark-haired boy from the Ukraine, has been left behind forever in Prussian soil. Nil wound up in a hospital bed in Königsberg. He got hit in the last battle."

Now we were reunited again on that first or second night of victory (I confess my memory has become a bit blurred about these multiple capitulations): Pavel, Ivan, Kondrat, and I. We sat together next to the bonfire; we didn't say anything for a long time but just gazed into the fire. It seemed to me in these minutes that each of us was making our own reckonings with the war, remembering both the living and the dead. Yet each of us understood that it was precisely him, the common soldier, and no one else who had achieved this miracle. Victory!

What was I thinking about that night? The reader may find what I'm about to say to be paradoxical. Despite the bloody ordeals, the human tragedies, and the inconceivable hardships that continued for the 1,418 days of the war, I was thinking that we, its participants, would always remember the war years as the most significant, shining, and honorable episode in our lives. That is indeed what happened.

The silence was broken. The first to confess was Kondrat:

"Back in Prussia, I shared a conviction with my Marus'ka. Somehow, I believed that I would survive this war. The Almighty helped me! Yet how do you think my woman answered me? 'Don't come back to the village, my dear. You're the only soldier out of 220 homes still alive. The widows will persecute you and me.' But I was born in that village and lived there for almost 40 years!"

Pavel chipped in with his own topic:

"My little brother, Iashka, returned from the war without either hand back in '43. His Dun'ka approached him, as if to caress her invalid hero, as if to kiss the stumps of his arms. But instead, the bitch blurted out into his face, 'Damn your nurses for writing me on your behalf for more than a year. I waited for my man, and instead a worthless cucumber has shown up at my door.' My little brother didn't give in to that bitch. He started to practice some sort of Hindu yoga exercises, to try to be able to do things with his feet instead of his hands, so he could function independently and start a new life. But she, that wicked woman, kept pushing Iashka farther and farther into a corner. (O, woe unto disabled people in the Soviet Union—both during the war and after it!)

"'We invalids have become superfluous,' Iashka wrote me in his last letter, before he killed himself.

"I had my own score to settle with the fascists," Pavel continued. "After the liberation of Kiev I learned that the Germans and their Ukrainian accomplices had executed thirteen of my relatives at Baba Yar, including my three-year-old kid, Vovochka. A week before the start of the war, I received the last letter from my twin brother, Mark. The regiment in which he was serving was positioned just eight kilometers from the border. On the very first day of the war, 22 June 1941, his regiment was completely annihilated, and Mark went missing in action. But I hid my emotions that day."

Unexpectedly, Pavel roused himself and asked me a question:

"Do you want us to celebrate, Captain?"

"Definitely! The whole world is rejoicing!" I replied.

"We need to still think it over," Pavel said. "After all, the cost of this war was terribly high, and we've all been damaged by it."

"But we're the victors, damn it!" I almost shouted.

"You never can tell, my grandma used to say . . ."

That's how my first night of victory came to an end.

But what was gnawing at the spirits of the soldiers and officers that day and night? We had fought with the enemy with a clear purpose, not sparing our lives, so as to save our Motherland. And we had saved her! Now how would our Motherland greet us? That was the chief question on all our minds. But the trumpeters and drummers were already raising quite unseemly praise, from the very first day of Victory, to the pockmarked devil [Stalin], as if he was the one who had gained the Great Victory, and not the Russian soldier.

Everything was jumbled together back then in people's minds—both great joy and great sorrow, exultation and sadness, and even fear.

Reversing our march, our mobile battalion again stopped in the suburb of Schlewitz. We were to pick up a truck that had been left at the railway station. While the battalion rested, I walked over to the familiar house. A young man opened the door. I asked him about Vera. The new proprietor shrugged his shoulders. The authorities had given him, a commander of a partisan detachment, this house as a token of gratitude for saving the town from destruction. He courteously invited me in to have a drink in honor of the victory. We drank a toast in that same parlor, with the same paintings on the wall in their expensive frames. Had anything changed? Suddenly, I caught sight of two portraits on one wall: the president of the country, Eduard Benes, and the Communist Party leader Kliment Gottwald.

The partisan, noticing my gaze, categorically declared: "There will come a day when we communists will remove one of those portraits!" At the time, I didn't catch the significance of his words, although I gave a thought to how quickly events were occurring. Just three years passed when the Czechs really did remove the portrait of Benes, after the Czech communists and their leader Gottwald had seized power in the country, with the help of the Soviet Union.

Three Blissful Days, 11 May 1945

It was 8:00 A.M., 11 May 1945. Peace had arrived. The battalion had been placed in the reserve and was awaiting an order. Our powerful Studebaker trucks were safely hidden away in factory garages.

The command had taken up a luxurious villa in which the owner of three textile factories had once lived. An enormous, magnificent park with a handsome hotel surrounded the villa. A gardener told us that the owner was a German who had run off with his wife, children, and servants two weeks earlier. During the war, the hotel had served as a hospital. Now our infantry and artillery filled the park.

At 6:00 A.M. that morning, the German Army Group Center had formally capitulated. Thousands of prisoners, officers and soldiers, were now moving along the highway through Schlewitz. The railway station was a prisoner collection point. The villa where we were staying was on a hill, and I had an excellent view of what was happening down on the highway.

Toward lunchtime the situation was changing. Civilians began appearing on the road—first in ones and twos, then in small groups, which soon turned into a throng of people. An uninterrupted living current of refugees filled the highway. Carts crawled along with entire families aboard; some were pulling along little carts loaded with their belongings while a few others were trying to pick their way on bicycles through the dense mass of people. The majority of refugees were on foot. People were plodding along, barely shuffling their feet. Many of them were wearing wooden shoes. The sound of these shoes tapping on the pavement grew, turning into a rumble. The people were poorly dressed. Former camp prisoners were among them, growing in number on the road, still wearing their prison garb. On many of them, there was still a distinguishing symbol that let the Nazis know how they should treat their slaves. No one had evidently bothered yet to tear off the symbol.

By evening, the picture on the highway was changing once again. Armed Czechs in civilian clothing, with white bandages on their sleeves, were setting up roadblocks on the highway close to the city. They were stopping all people leaving the city and taking everything away from them. It looked just like a scene from Russia back in 1917.

The next day, representatives of the local authority arrived at the villa and invited us to a meal. A sumptuous table had been set right in the middle of the town square. We drank, embraced, and swore to eternal friendship. After the fete, they invited us to an evening performance by a troupe of French cabaret singers who had gotten stuck in the town. We wanted to go, but alas, we were expecting orders.

Returning to the battalion, I noticed another new appearance on the highway. SMERSH officers, all carrying brand-new submachine guns, had seemingly descended en masse from the heavens. They had set up a swinging gate on the highway, taking the unceasing human traffic under control. As we later learned, several regiments of these men had been flown in on airplanes directly from Russia. They set up controlled checkpoints (KPP) on all the roads in the Soviet zone.

As I observed, they were first of all interested in any of the returnees wearing an "Ost" [East] symbol. Out of formality, they checked the people's documents. Where had they been? They checked to make sure none of them was carrying a gun. But they didn't confiscate anything from them. They were politely inviting the Ost returnees to continue their journey aboard trucks, which were standing on the side of the road. A few officers, my comrades, and I descended the hill and approached the KPP.

"Where are you taking these people?" one of our guys asked a senior SMERSH officer.

"We aren't hiding anything from anyone," he calmly replied. "The Americans and British have set up camps for displaced people in their zones. We're doing the same thing. We want to help Soviet citizens who were driven into captivity return home to their Motherland."

That was true, as far as it went. But it wasn't the full truth, as I will narrate later. Very soon it became known that in just a few weeks after the end of the war, Soviet troops established more than 100 so-called filtration camps in the Soviet-occupied zone of Germany.[6] Thousands of men and women who had been driven by the Nazis from the occupied cities and villages into forced labor in Germany were brought together in these camps. An underlying task was in operation, which wasn't mentioned at the time, but its idea became clear later—to prevent the massed flight of former Soviet citizens to the West.

As we prepared to leave the highway, suddenly a scene took place in front of our eyes, about which I must relate. The SMERSH officers had stopped a man and woman. I had noticed them walking together, hand in hand. The man turned out to be French, about thirty years of age, thin and short. His traveling companion was about a head shorter than him; she was heavily worn out, but her face still bore traces of her former beauty. In their eyes, which just a few minutes before had been glowing with the love they had found together, there now appeared wild fear.

Neither the man nor the woman, who wore the patch "Ost" on her clothing, understood why they had been stopped, or what was happening. For the first few minutes, the Frenchman was so confused that he couldn't gather the few words of Russian that he knew on his tongue. Then he began to resist desperately, refusing to let go of the woman. He fell to his knees, pleading to God: "Why is the Almighty being so miserly with His divine grace?" He had given them just three days of bliss together. The Frenchman spoke in French, then German; he cried and implored. But the SMERSH officers didn't understand him. More correctly, they were chuckling, not wanting to understand the Frenchman.

They quickly and expertly separated the two, and then loaded the Russian woman onto one of the trucks. Then, unexpectedly for everyone, the Frenchman headed for the truck after the Russian woman. But they stopped him and explained: "You are 'West' but she is 'East,' so you have to go in different directions." Literally crazed, the Frenchman stood for a few minutes until the truck carrying his beloved disappeared around a bend. Then, staggering, he set off alone in the direction of Schlewitz. He couldn't understand why they had been separated, or how he was supposed to live on. Would he ever be able to find another woman to love? In our youth we unfortunately often only see that which is right next to us, and we rarely ponder that which is hidden from us.

We were all agitated by what we had seen. Someone suggested we catch up with the Frenchman. Once we met Francois, as he was called, this is what he told us: he and his love had become acquainted by chance. Together with a group of other French military prisoners, he had been working in a German auto repair shop while Tania was working as a farm laborer on a nearby German farm. Once, she had caught the Frenchman in the farm owner's field when he was trying to pull a couple of withered carrots from the soil. She could have turned him in, but she didn't. From then on, she would leave some vegetables for him at a prearranged place. How this charitable work could have ended for her is difficult to imagine. In an ideal case, the owner would "only" have beaten her up.

Freedom came unexpectedly for them. They spent three days together in the proprietor's now empty home—the three most blissful days of their lives. They dreamed about the future together. Francois told her about Paris and about his delightful mother, whom he adored but hadn't seen for many years now.

Tania didn't know any French, and he hadn't mastered her native tongue. They primarily resorted to German to make themselves understood. The main thing was that they were now free, and their hearts and souls henceforth belonged only to each other. Love, in such situation, has no need for any rules of grammar.

Now Francois was crying helplessly, like a child. He wouldn't calm down until he had found Tania, and he absolutely was going to write a letter to Marshal Stalin. Very soon, however, Marshal Stalin would take an interest in the morality of his subjects and would publish a law that banned marriage to foreigners.

I couldn't forget that story of "Romeo and Juliet" in the Sudeten. I recalled it thirty years later, when in Kiev I happened to see Valentin Zorin's play, *Warsaw Melody*—or at least, that is what I think it was called. In the play, a Soviet combat officer and a Polish woman (played by the outstanding actress Ada Rogovtseva) fell in love with each other but couldn't go against The Law.

In those first postwar days in May of 1945, my thoughts were approximately the following: "The war is over. Peace has arrived. With it, for all of us frontline soldiers who by some miracle remained alive, has come the end of sufferings, the fear of death, and our fear for our near and dear ones. All of us who escaped from that bloody hell should become as brothers. Why now should a small symbol, devised by some social malefactors, separate those who have gone through enormous physical and emotional suffering and drive them apart? Why deprive the normal rights of free men to choose their own lives and turn them back into slaves?" Naïve reasoning, but I didn't take it any further at the time.

Soon we were back in Germany, where new thoughts, feelings, and interests engulfed my comrades and me. I forgot all about Schlewitz and Vera.

25

Subjugated Germany— *"Guten Tag, Lower Silesia!"*
May–August 1945

In the Hills of Silesia

On 16 May 1945 we received an order to move to Lower Silesia in the south-eastern part of Germany. Our division was to be based in the town of Friedeberg [presently the Polish town of Mirsk].

We slowly rolled along winding, hilly roads in our Studebaker trucks. Czech civilians stood along both sides of the road, waving and cheering as we passed. Peasants had come out to greet us, and they gave us a warm welcome.

Back in February 1945, forces of the 1st Ukrainian Front, smashing through all German resistance, had advanced from the Sandomir bridgehead on the Vistula River deep into Silesia, driving over 500 kilometers in the process. In comparison, from our starting point in the Sudeten Mountains, our destination of Friedeberg seemed just a stone's throw away.

We drove through Saxony and entered Lower Silesia. The first city we approached there was Bunzlau [Boleslawiec].[1] Our march was halted on its outskirts. There, on a small rise directly by the side of the same road over which Russian soldiers had passed in 1813, stood a monument to Marshal Mikhail Illarionovich Kutuzov, the conqueror of Napoleon. He had passed away in this city on 16 April 1813.

Demonstrating his deep respect to Marshal Kutuzov and the Russian army of the Fatherland War of 1812, in February 1945 Marshal I. S. Konev, commander of the 1st Ukrainian Front, had established an honor guard in front of the monument. Ever since, all combat units passing by the monument gave it a salute in tribute.

That same day, other staff officers and I took a quick side trip and visited the apartment where the famous commander had lived his final days and had died. It had been carefully preserved as it had been during Kutuzov's time. We all signed the visitors' book.

A legend had grown up around Kutuzov and this area: supposedly, the dying commander had ordered that his heart be buried here, "so that it could remain with the Russian soldiers." Everyone in Russia and Germany believed in this legend.

At the order of Tsar Alexander I, and with the permission of Kutuzov's widow, the body of Mikhail Illarionovich was brought to St. Petersburg. It took a whole month and a half for the coffin with the embalmed body inside to make its way to the Russian capital. Everywhere, people gave their respect to the great commander. About five kilometers from the city on the Neva, they removed the coffin from the cart that had been carrying it, and carried it on their shoulders to the Kazan' Cathedral.[2]

For more than 150 years, people believed in the legend that Kutuzov's heart had been buried in Germany. One example: in 1913, on the one-hundredth anniversary of Kutuzov's death, the Moscow Military-Historical Society at one of its meetings examined the question of returning the marshal's heart to the Motherland. This tale seemed so real that it was supported by solid publications and sources, right up to the *Great Soviet Encyclopedia*.

At the end of the 1950s, when I was working on my book *Kresty, kostry i knigi* [Crosses, Bones, and Books], I spent a lot of time in Leningrad at the Kazan' Cathedral, where the crypt with Kutuzov's coffin had already been located for so many years. Even then I heard from museum staff about this legend. But no matter how convincing this legend seemed, the facts eventually refuted it.

In the words of B. Sokratilin, who in the 1930s had been an inspector for the supervision of the historical monuments of Leningrad, Sergei Mironovich Kirov, the Party boss of Leningrad at that time, had in 1932 formed a scientific commission and had instructed it to investigate "Kutuzov's heart." The commission, opening the tomb, established that the heart was still with the remains of Kutuzov's body in the coffin. The conclusion of the researchers was kept secret for a long time. The members of the commission held their tongues, knowing that to let the secret slip might be the end of them.

The division remained in the suburb of Bunzlau for the night. The commanding general decided to send a team of combat engineers and headquarters' staff ahead to Friedeberg, in order to find places to house the division's headquarters. I was included on this team, and we left immediately. Having arrived in Friedeberg, we knew that the first order of business was to select a sector of the city for locating the division headquarters.

We chose a contiguous stretch of ten buildings on the town's outskirts. Some of the homes were empty, but Germans were still living in the others. We had to evict them and suggested that they move into any of the other many empty residences in any other part of the town. We offered all the evacuees help in moving their things into their new places, but they all refused our assistance. Having loaded all their belongings, but primarily jars of canned vegetables, onto small carts, they quickly abandoned our district. None of them, I noticed from the loads on the carts, had been interested in the fate of their service sets, wardrobes, paintings, or elegant carpet runners. Suddenly somewhere nearby, the playing of a grand piano was audible. Obviously, one of the new refugees had decided to play a beloved musical miniature on it for one last time. Meanwhile, the combat engineers swept all the designated homes to house the headquarters staff for the presence of mines and explosives.

Friedeberg

That same day, the deputy division commander in charge of our team instructed me to meet with the city's burgomeister. Before the meeting, I decided to take a brief nap. The loud pealing of a bell woke me up. "So," I naïvely thought, "someone has deliberately dared to make such a racket and to disturb my sleep." Leaping out of the bed, I washed up and set off to see the burgomeister.

In no hurry, I ambled along the streets, and my curiosity about my surroundings seemed to grow with every step: everything around me seemed unique, beautiful, and well tended. During the fighting in East Prussia, I hadn't paid any attention to all the German cities and villages through which we passed; they were all left in ruins after the fighting. But now everything seemed to catch my eye, especially the architecture and detailing on the similar three-story buildings, all of which had been painted a shade of yellow and which stood in perfect alignment.

I quickly gained the impression that the war had bypassed this town, and the residents hadn't tasted any sorrows or sufferings. The streets had all been scrubbed clean, paving stone by paving stone, and everything was bathed in a greenish light, most likely by the sunlight filtering through the verdant trees, the branches of which arched over the sidewalk from both sides. Wherever you looked, blossoms decorated the windows of the homes. A small lawn, surrounded by flowers, stretched up to each front door. There were none of the fences that seemed customary in Russia. Decorative streetlamps were arranged along every street. Many little bridges, with slender fanciful railings, connected the opposite banks of a swiftly flowing, narrow river, which split the town into two parts. Not a corner of the town had been marred by a single uncaring human hand—that's how it seemed to me on the first day of my arrival in Friedeberg, and I immediately fell in love with the place. It was a quiet and cozy little city.

Friedeberg was also conveniently located. It was not far from Dresden—70 kilometers—and an even shorter distance, about fifty kilometers, to the Czech border. It was not more than 100 kilometers from its capital city of Breslau [Wroclow]. Fine highways connected all of them with Friedeberg. These roads were kept clean, and highway markers were everywhere.

One thing that quickly caught the eye was the number of closed businesses in the town. The shuttered beer halls; the bakery; the watch repair shop; the small, two-story hotel; the café; and the porcelain china shop—they were all dark and silent, and only the advertising signs belied their presence.

The sight of women in floral print aprons, who were busily preparing for their first encounter with the Russians, also struck me. The news of our division's impending arrival had already reached them, and now they were fussing about in front of their residences, meticulously tidying their gardens and lawns. The first conclusion formed inevitably in my mind: the Germans knew how to look after and protect their personal lives and property. Here it was in front of me, that thing I had read about more than once: "classic German tidiness!"

I was reminded of this later, approximately twenty years after the war. Being in Poland, I paid a visit to Auschwitz. Before this visit, I had read a lot about this terrible concentration camp and had seen films about it. But one must see Auschwitz with his or her own eyes! As confirmation of what I've just said, let me offer a few examples.

"With classic German neatness," little children's shoes had been precisely arranged by their sizes on long shelves of one of the warehouses (they hadn't yet had time to package them up). In another warehouse, I saw packets of pressed women's hair arranged on shelves "with classic German tidiness" (they hadn't yet had time to send them off). Women's hair had been used for preparing helmet linings for soldiers of the Wehrmacht, as well as for making warm socks for their feet. In a "special" storehouse, metal cylinders containing the lethal gas Zyklon were arranged "with classic German order" (they hadn't had time yet to use them for their intended purpose).

At the Nuremberg trials, the commandant of Auschwitz had testified in detail how he had managed to do his "creative work" with "classic German accuracy" in order to murder four million men, women, and children in a little more than two years. What can one say about this "classic German tidiness" after what I've written? Is it absolutely bereft of morality? I don't know.

First Meeting with the Burgomeister

Willy—that's how everyone addressed the burgomeister. He greeted me affably and listened attentively to everything I had to say to him. The conversation was of an official nature, so I spoke German slowly, often pausing to choose my words carefully or to correct a word here and there; nonetheless, a dialogue ensued:

"I have been instructed to make contact with you. Tomorrow, a Russian military unit will be entering your city. We'll implement all measures in consultation with you. Do you agree?"

"Of course."

"Starting tomorrow, the city will be under occupation, and we will establish the regime. You will receive instructions in the German language. Tomorrow at 12:00 noon you must appear at the commandant's office with full information about the population."

"I will do all you say."

"Day after tomorrow, all residents will be placed on rations. I don't recall them exactly, but approximately the daily ration for each person will consist of the following: 200–300 grams of bread, 25 grams of meat, 50 grams of lard, 50 grams of cheese, and 100 grams of herring. Each child will receive 1.5 liters of milk a day."

"Thank you!"

"I'll ask you to explain to all your citizens that the Red Army has entered a subjugated Germany in order to liberate the German people from Nazi tyranny. As soon as you place your life on democratic foundations, we will leave your country."

"Thank you for the explanation."

"Allow me to ask you several personal questions. Were you appointed to your position by the former regime?"

"I am a Social-Democrat. I lingered in a concentration camp for four years. I have just returned to my native town. The previous burgomeister ran off. At the request of the pastor, the people gathered and elected me as their new burgomeister. I have a question for you, by the way, which is troubling many citizens. Your generals, when they took German soldiers into captivity, promised to release them immediately after the war's end. Can people have hope that this will soon happen?"

"The war ended twenty days ago, Willy. We still don't know anything about when they will free your officers and soldiers."

At the end of the discussion, this is what Willy told me about Lower Silesia:

"Gauleiter Karl Hanke, the Nazi fanatic, ruled here with an iron hand. Goebbels considered him to be the best gauleiter in Germany. He was the organizer of the fortress city of Breslau, where so many Germans and Russians died. When Hitler replaced Himmler, he appointed Hanke in his place. This scoundrel tried to escape from Silesia. According to rumors, Czech partisans caught him and executed him. Whether this is true or not, I don't know."

"Tell me, Willy, do you have a family?"

"My son was killed in the desert. He was serving in Rommel's Afrika Korps. When they arrested me, my wife moved to Dresden, to her cousin's. She died during the horrible, unexpected bombing of the city; I am now living at my sister Klara's home."

"Willy, I have two requests: as soon as possible, re-open all the private establishments that the people need. And invite your citizens at 12:00 tomorrow to a meeting with Russian soldiers and officers."

Unfortunately, not a single resident of this town came to the meeting.

The Photographer's Daughter

After my meeting with Willy, I spent a long time strolling around the town, taking in its clever architecture and its mass of greenery, which covered the entire area. I was surprised by many of the street names. Some of them carried the names of German composers, other the names of German commanders. Suddenly, a marvel—Ivan Turgenev Street. I wondered what link this famous Russian author had with Lower Silesia?

Near the city center, on Friedrichstrasse, I noticed a signboard—"Photography"—on the first floor of a three-story building. I decided to drop in to give it a try. At my ringing, a middle-aged, tall, thin German opened the door. For several moments, the German looked me over with uncommon curiosity—likely trying to figure out what need I had of him. I introduced myself and asked if I could enter. We sat down at a round table, apparently in a parlor, and began to talk. Soon a woman appeared and set down two cups and a miniature samovar in front of us.

"Allow me to introduce you," the photographer said, turning to me. "This is the woman of the house, my wife Emma."

As we sipped our tea, the photographer and I conversed:

"Tell me," I asked. "Have you been living in Friedeberg long?"

"We arrived here from East Prussia even before the war. I inherited this house from my deceased older brother. Indeed, we had been intending for a long time to get away from the cold, eternally raw and damp climes of East Prussia. Emma has asthma, and her doctor told her to find a dry climate. Silesia is a paradise for her. Clean mountain air. The largest forest preserve in Europe is located here. Did you know that in Friedeberg, greenery covers more than 80 percent of the area? Where else in the world can you find such a city-garden? There are many curative springs in Lower Silesia. Eva Braun came here often for treatment. I hope her name is familiar to you? Russian tsars, diplomats, and writers have also traveled here."

"Did you ever serve in the Wehrmacht?"

"No. I'm not a Party member, and I'm long past fifty. But more importantly, I had polio when I was a child, which left me lame. My right leg is more than four centimeters shorter than my left. I had to use crutches whenever I walked, because of the imbalance between my legs. Now I get around with a cane."

"Herr Friedrich, I have a proposal for you. Can you help our soldiers and officers? Many of them will soon be returning home without a single wartime photograph of themselves. We will compensate you!"

"I'll do as you ask, Captain. Free of charge. But we have one serious problem."

"What sort of problem?"

"Do you have any camera film?"

"But where do you usually get yours?"

"In Breslau, but now this is impossible. I'll try—in memory of my son Kurt's name. He was killed in action at Leningrad. There will come a time when I will travel to Russia and find my son's grave."

"Excuse me. I didn't know of your loss. So, we're in agreement. I'll report to my commander."

"Let's start with you," Friedrich jokingly said to me.

That's how these photographs came about. I have preserved them to this day.

As we were preparing to say our farewells, a tall, shapely young woman entered the parlor. She had a dark complexion and an unusually expressive face for a German, with large, widely spaced gray eyes.

"This is my daughter, Lotta," Friedrich announced as he introduced me to the young woman.

I sprang from my chair. I could feel my heart start to pound. Somewhere, I don't know where, the angels began to trumpet! I interpreted their unexpected call as a good omen from the heavens.

Lotta asked permission from her father to make a trip to the milk bottling plant. Perhaps they'd give her a little milk. I accompanied her out onto the street, where I asked her permission to escort her to her destination. I received an unexpected reply:

"Tell me, Captain, if there, back in Russia, a German officer was seen escorting a young Russian woman, what would the people have said about her? Take a look at the windows in the surrounding buildings and you'll notice that we're being watched. Of course, if you order me or compel me, I'll comply. But I'm certain you won't do this."

"You're right," I answered with disappointment. "Well, we'll meet again. But I would like for you to let your father know that in the future, I'll try to arrange it so that they'll deliver milk directly to your home. I sense that milk is very necessary to you, since you, a single German woman, openly went out into the street today and are fearlessly walking alone to the bottling plant."

"You understand correctly. Emma, my mother, needs the milk. She is a very sick woman. Won't you drop by our place tomorrow at 6:00 in the evening? It is Emma's birthday."

"Thank you. However, I can hardly come tomorrow. But I'll soon take you up on your invitation."

I was twenty-two years old; Lotta was nineteen. I paid a visit to the Guntze family five days later. Their residence was located in some woods on the edge of town. Lotta and I began to see each other. Lotta showed me around the most beautiful sections of the town, and we liked to climb the high and steep hills surrounding the town, from the top of which opened distant vistas over the fields, valleys, and rivers. Once, we traveled to the Sudeten. We visited a cemetery where her father's older brother, his family, and Emma's grandfather and grandmother were buried. I never again saw anywhere such a clean, well-tended cemetery, where the gravestones were inundated with blossoms and the foliage of the trees, which inclined over the gravesites.

Lotta also showed me another of Silesia's interesting sights—its oldest, legendary oak tree, which had a massive trunk ten meters wide. People liked to say that King Frederick the Great had planted it himself. Many popular legends and tales had grown up around the tree. It was genuinely difficult to tear myself away from the sight of this magnificent tree, but Lotta pulled me away and we began to talk:

"What were you doing before the war?" I asked Lotta.

"I was a student. Like all young German men and women, I was a member of the Hitler Youth, carrying out my labor obligation. I worked in a textile factory. I'm curious, what do they call your version of our Hitler Youth in Russia?" Lotta suddenly asked me.

I didn't decline to answer. I tried to give her a summary account of Russia's Komsomol. I explained to her the goals and tasks of our youth organization. She gasped when I told her that more than 100 million young men and women had passed through its ranks since the moment of its founding by Lenin in 1918.

"Did you, too?"

"Yes, even I."

"Are you a communist?"

"Yes. I joined the Party during the war."

"Then who's your God?"

"I'm an atheist. Membership in the Party is incompatible with religious faith. But I very much believe in fate; there are many times when I should have been killed! During the war, I had my own Captain Nemo. You've evidently read Jules Verne? In the most critical situations, Captain Nemo appeared and deflected the touch of death away from me."

I could see how attentively Lotta was listening to me. What I was saying must have interested her. She spoke up:

"It seems to me that what you've just described are also acts of God. I'm a Christian. I belong to the Protestant Church. I've believed in God since my early childhood. Our pastor is a kind and educated man. I advise you to get acquainted with him."

"Is it true that two thousand German Protestant men of the cloth sent a greeting to Hitler in the 1930s?" I asked.

"I've never heard about that. But I read in the newspapers that Stalin congratulated Hitler on his fiftieth birthday and for his victory over France."

"Do you have a fiancé? I can tell by the ring on your hand."

"Yes. We're betrothed. Fred is seven years older than I am. He's from Breslau. He worked in a company with which Papa had some business. They called him up into the army in 1942. He spent one year training as a cartographer. Afterwards, as I learned from his letters, he analyzed enemy maps that fell into the hands of the Wehrmacht. After the American landings in Normandy in 1944, Fred went missing in action. I don't know anything more about him."

"Did you love him?"

"Both yes and no. We didn't see each other very often, and I didn't know him well. I understood even less what love is."

It was now getting pretty late, so I reluctantly said my good-byes.

"Unfortunately, it will be a week before we can see each other again," I said ruefully. In response, Lotta tightly hugged me and gave me a kiss.

I spent nearly the next ten days with some units that were situated in some woods four to five kilometers from the city. Setting out for the units, I first of all wanted to get to know the mood of the soldiers and officers, to find out what they were thinking about in these first postwar days spent in Germany, and to understand how they were perceiving this new, peaceful situation. Together with the regimental Komsomol organizers I tried to get a sense of the new conditions for our work with the young soldiers. Had their weapons become rusty? Had their combat spirit dried up? How was their discipline? This was the circle of questions that concerned us, and for which I wanted to get answers.

The older soldiers were uniformly waiting for word about their demobilization. They had no desire to serve any longer. They spent their time striving to obtain discharge papers, wandering around the largely deserted villages that had been emptied that spring, and rummaging for odds and ends. Discussions with them always normally ended with the same words: "I want home!"

The young soldiers behaved differently, more cunningly: they were living for the moment. There is an old Russian proverb: "Live for the day; tomorrow isn't yet here, and yesterday has already gone." But they also weren't showing any further zeal for their duties.

The junior officers were often closing their eyes to this or that transgression or indiscretion. Many of them were trying to get back to the Motherland as soon as possible, so they could begin their studies in regular military schools.

I remember in particular one intriguing conversation with a company commander. The senior lieutenant, gazing at some tanks and artillery pieces that were dug-in and camouflaged, told me:

"Now there is no more need for these 'playthings.' They'll soon be going to scrap metal."

"Why do you think so?" I was surprised.

"Why then is a United Nations being created?"

"But there will always be an army in every state, don't you think?"

"No, Captain," the senior lieutenant replied. "I don't intend to do any more fighting. I'm twenty-six. I don't have any skills as a civilian. I'll probably become a groundskeeper, don't you think? It's a bit too late for me to learn any trade."

There was truth in what the officer said. But less than a month passed after our conversation when suddenly one ordinary evening, a verbal command traveled around the entire division within a half-hour: Sleep in your uniforms, no leaves of absence, everyone to be on the alert. They rolled the guns out of their shelters, fully refueled the tanks, and distributed fifty shells to each T-34.

The division was held for seventy-two hours in such a state of combat alert. Then, the all-clear was sounded. I still don't know what was happening then, and what caused the alarm. But there's the United Nations for you.

Two episodes happened while I was with the units, which disturbed me and not only me. In one battalion, located not far from a railroad station, a few drunkards had found the opportunity for a drinking spree: an abandoned cistern full of methyl alcohol that was for some reason standing by itself on the tracks. They managed to get hold of it, punched a hole through the metal, and filled their canteens with this dangerous liquid. Thank God, people didn't succumb to the temptation and follow their example! Experienced soldiers knew the risks of this "spirit": blindness, paralysis, sometimes even death. The regiment commander, informed of the men's discovery, immediately formed the battalion up in a field and thoroughly irrigated the stomachs of our brother-Slavs whose names appeared on his list.

While this "water procedure" was going on in the field, to roaring laughter of the spectators, officers went around the empty tents, and if they discovered any drop of alcohol, they unceremoniously poured it out onto the ground. "It's a must," I thought, "to come out of the war alive, only to die from your own idiocy!"

The second event went worse. A regiment commander and five of his subordinate officers organized a wild drinking party one night. They drove to the Czech region, returned with three young single women, and spent the whole night together with them. The next morning, having presented them with gifts of rations, the officers sent the girls back home, but only after making an agreement to meet again. Three days later, all six of the "brave warriors" were being treated at the medical sanitation battalion for a venereal disease. In July 1945, up to 30 percent of the officers of the division were in the hospital with this disease.

As I understood it, for the soldiers and the officers alike, the so-called sexual question had become the most important thing. The men were finding their way to German women by every possible means, and there were many places where their paths might cross—the milk bottling plant, local dairy farms, the textile factory, the post office, transportation, army communication posts, the cemetery, and the road to the commandant's office. "We can't go on this way," I concluded. "We need to do something so that people don't feel as if they're locked in cages and won't go looking for trouble at every opportunity, wherever they might find it." I conducted a gathering of the division's youth. But the time for meetings, for orders, to force soldiers to go into battle, to make them march through mud and in the pouring rain—always forward, forward!— had passed.

I understood that the soldier no longer had any need for the commissar's word, for propagandistic rhetoric, for loud words about the Great Victory, for the Party, or for Stalin himself, thanks to whom this war was won. He, the soldier, knew better than anyone what Victory meant, and what it had cost him, his family, and his children. The soldier was reading and rereading all his letters from home, and he now had little interest in what would happen with Germany; he was longing for his village, for his own native home, though he already knew that ruin, hunger, and hopelessness were waiting for him. I realized that the officers and the soldiers had become estranged from one another. Yet it had been only yesterday, in war, with the perpetual fear of death, with its blood and shit, when all of us—privates and commanders alike—had been united as one, and had valued military comradeship above all else.

What were my own thoughts like at that time? I was still flush with the emotions of Victory Day. It seemed to me that it would always be an eternal, special holiday above all other national, religious, and family holidays.

I was experiencing a feeling that I had done my duty, and this thought warmed me and lifted me. My entire life seemed now in front of me, but I couldn't see it outside the army. I had come to love the army, and I viewed it as an uncommon unity of wills, as a powerful collective assembly of people, and as the country's most reliable support. These were naïve, romantic opinions, and remote from the genuine, cruel, terrible future reality of what my beloved army would become after the return to Russia.[3] But all this was ahead of me.

The Germans

One day soon after our arrival in Friedeberg, we received an army directive to begin the reeducation process among the Germans. Colonel Shilovich laid the responsibility for carrying out these instructions on me. It was plain that my small knowledge of the German language had played a major role in his decision, as well as my previous initial contacts with the burgomeister and other Germans.

Prior to this, I had only encountered Germans with guns in their hands, implacable in their martial spirit and their hatred for Russians. Now I had to meet with different Germans, but where was the guarantee that they would not be just like those whom we had previously encountered on battlefields? I carefully looked over the directive, then appealed to Shilovich:

"Comrade Colonel, this is some sort of absurd notion. How can we reeducate adults who have grown up in the conditions of a different society? Friedeberg is a small city; it had only around 3,000 citizens before the war. There are in the town today eight widows, six invalids, and four families that have lost fathers or sons who are missing in action. For the most part, these losses occurred on the Eastern Front. Propaganda and reality are different concepts; I hope you'll agree with me.

Apparently Shilovich was sick of my "theorizing," and he sharply cut me off.

"Orders and directives from above in the army are not discussed, but carried out. It seems lately, Captain, that you've been dabbling in politics."

I fell silent, and then with his permission I left Shilovich.

"Where to begin?" I thought to myself. "I'll give films a try." I put in a request for the army to send me several films. The reactions of the people to these films, I supposed, would determine my further moves.

Willy helped me open the long-closed movie theater in town and track down a projector. We cleaned the theater and scrubbed the floors. I set a date for the grand opening. About fifteen people came to see the first film, *From Il'ich's Lamp to Dneproges*: eleven women and four invalid men. Soon after I started the film, I could hear people loudly laughing and obscenely swearing, evidently trusting that I wouldn't understand their words. Perplexed, I turned and asked Willy: "This isn't a comedy; why are the spectators laughing?"

Willy tried to calm me down. "You're still so naïve, Captain. Even our cows were living with electricity long before Il'ich's lamp. Did you know, Captain, that Americans built Dneproges? But the film speaks as if this construction project was the highest accomplishment of socialism. The Germans didn't blow up the dam; your own guys did it."

So the film was less than a success. As the old Russian saying goes, "The first pancake is always lumpy." I decided to wait and see what would happen with the next film. About 100 people came to the second film, *Raduga* [The Rainbow].

This was the first time I'd seen Wanda Wasilewska's film.[4] It was a low-budget piece of propaganda, giving an account of the evil occupiers and their atrocities in Russia. As the film played, I sat in the front row and tried to translate scenes from the film into German. As the lights came back on in the theater, I counted no more than six people who had stayed for the end of the film.

"Why so?" I once again asked Willy.

Here's how he answered me:

"People don't believe in what the film is showing. For them, the Wehrmacht is as clean as a new pane of glass. Your people and the S.S. created the evil, especially in the Ukraine and in the Baltic countries."

"And the Germans weren't killing Jews?"

"The newspapers have written that even before the war with Russia, Hitler made a proposal to Stalin to relocate 2.5 million Jews from Germany and Poland to Russia, but your leader refused to accept them."

At the time I didn't believe Willy. But here's what history has to say about all this. More than fifty years passed from the end of the war before the myth about the Wehrmacht's noble nature was dispelled in front of the Germans' eyes. In 1995 an exhibition about the crimes of the Wehrmacht took place in Hamburg for the first time. It was entitled "The Wehrmacht, 1941–1944" and organized by the Institute of Social History. It created something of a sensation. Viewers at the exhibition saw that the generals, officers, and soldiers of the Wehrmacht were the same sort of ruthless bandits as the S.S. All of Germany was shocked.

In the first days after the division's arrival in Friedeberg, the remaining population all seemed to vanish. The streets were largely empty. The Germans recognized only three routes: to the town commandant for rations; to the church for prayers; and to the cemetery to visit the graves of their ancestors. In Silesia, the Red Army churned out troubles no less than it had in East Prussia. Tensions in the city eventually declined, but not immediately. I have photographs from Friedeberg in the summer of 1945 in which people are visible on the streets. But the time for this didn't come quickly.

One Sunday, Willy invited me to the fiftieth birthday celebration for his sister. I arrived with two other officers, my comrades. I saw Klara for the first time. She was a tall, lean woman with large, wide eyes, with some sort of fantastic turban of hair on her head. This woman had an authoritative air about her, if only by the expression on her face. She spoke loudly, probably due to her many years of experience as a teacher. Willy once told me about his sister: "When I returned to my native city from the concentration camp, Klara was the only person unafraid to greet me."

Thanks to Klara, the evening was a real success. The guests all congratulated her and wished her every happiness. Willy procured a keg of beer from somewhere, which we quickly emptied. The time had come for the Germans' favorite form of amusement—a game called Candywrapper. According to the rules of the game, those who lost a round had to carry out some suggestion of the proprietress—for example, sing some familiar song, give a little dance, kiss a woman, crow like a rooster, and so forth. All of this, understandably, was accompanied by laughter and was supposed to be in the spirit of good fun.

One of my comrades, a captain, lost, and Klara's pronouncement was such that I wanted to spit in her face. She announced that she wanted the captain to drop to the floor, crawl under the table, and shout, "I'm a Jew!" The captain, naturally, refused to carry out Klara's command. To demonstrate our protest against Klara's insulting request, we all stalked out of the birthday woman's house.

"There's a real fascist viper for you!" the captain said, expressing the general opinion as we left the house.

The next day, I ran into Willy and asked him what he thought of his sister's disgusting conduct.

"Klara, like many other Germans, as you will see, still lives in the past. A lot of time must pass before Germans rid themselves of their Nazi influences. Incidentally, many Germans were infected with anti-Semitism even before Hitler's rise to power. Therefore they showed indifference to the National Socialist Party's program to deprive Jews of their German citizenship."

"Not all Germans are like Klara," I replied.

A few days later, a real scandal occurred in the division. The men continued to talk about it for a long time afterward. General Berestov summoned the chief of the medical-sanitation battalion and gave him instructions: in special situations, the medical-sanitation battalion was to render medical assistance to the residents of Friedeberg and to treat invalids with needed medicines.

Having heard the general out, Lieutenant Colonel Svirsky leaped out of his chair, and nearly shouted at the general:

"You can discharge me, punish me, send me in front of a tribunal, but I refuse to carry out your command."

"Why?"

"Germans are all rats! At Landsberg they wiped out the *medsanbat*, shot all of the wounded, and murdered my wife! You know all of this. I can't even look at them, Comrade General!"

Pavel Fedorovich grimaced. The general was not fond of such scenes of insubordination, but restrained himself and responded calmly:

"You're a reasonable fellow, Lieutenant Colonel Svirsky. War is one thing. Now it is peacetime, and that is a different matter. How can we not help the sick, the invalids, and the aged? It is Zhukov's directive that I have passed on to you, and we are obliged to carry it out."

"I see no difference between the German and the fascist. To me, they are all killers." The chief of the medical sanitation battalion dug in his heels. "Some did the killing while others supported them. Isn't that so?"

As everybody in the division knew, the general never altered his decisions once he had taken them.

"Get out of here, Svirsky! Go think about these instructions, and once you see the wisdom in them, get busy with them."

Among the other officers, naturally, this incident provoked arguments. Some supported Svirsky; others, the general. But soon, a small receiving room for the local population opened in the medical-sanitation battalion.

After my failures with the movies and Klara's shocking performance, understanding my wounded feelings, Willy once told me, "Don't think that all of us Germans are like those 'civilized' beasts that tortured and murdered your women and children, like the film *Raduga* accurately depicted."

Here's what he told me next: "In Silesia, not far from Friedeberg, lived one of the ancestors of the famous commander Helmut Möltke—James von Möltke, his nephew. On the inherited farmstead where Möltke lived, in 1942–1943 secret meetings of Germans took place. They were discussing the future Germany, after its downfall, which they all believed would happen. They called their group "the Circle." The Gestapo arrested the entire group, and in 1945 they were all executed."

On some evenings, I still managed to visit the Guntzes and to meet with Lotta. One evening, pointing at the piano that decorated the sitting room, I asked Lotta:

"Who plays the piano?"

"Emma and I. Emma gave me music lessons when I was a child. At the age of ten, I gave public concerts. Life without music is unthinkable to me. As soon as everything settles down, I dream of entering a music conservatory. Do you believe such a time will ever come?"

"I do."

"And what do you think of music? Who is your favorite composer?"

I was silent. My life was such that I had grown without much connection to classical music. Generally, I liked songs from popular films. I finally threw out the first name that came to mind—Tchaikovsky. I tried to hide my ignorance of the music that Emma and Lotta performed. But Lotta seemed to sense my predicament and refrained from further questions on the subject on that occasion.

The next time I visited the Guntzes, Frau Emma and Lotta sat down to the piano and began to play a four-hand version of Tchaikovsky's famous *1812 Overture*. It was the first time I'd heard this piece, and the performance was a generous gift, made for me by two sweet women.

Lotta and I often talked about music. More accurately, she would talk about music and I would listen to her. Lotta proudly declared that Germany had given mankind the gift of five great composers: Beethoven, Haydn, Richard Wagner, Bach, and Mendelssohn. She honestly added that Mendelssohn was never performed during Hitler's reign.

Back in her earlier school years, Lotta had visited the home where Beethoven was born, had lived, and worked. It was now a museum. Lotta had also traveled to Bayreuth, where there were annual musical festivals dedicated to Richard Wagner.

"Richard Wagner," Lotta said, "was Hitler's favorite composer. He thought of Wagner as his own spiritual leader. The Führer knew the libretto of many of Wagner's operas by heart. 'Everything started with him,' he often liked to say."

"Do you consider it proper that Mendelssohn was never performed under Hitler?" I asked Lotta.

"Of course not. And I wasn't alone in my thinking. But it wasn't considered proper for me to express my opinion."

I suddenly recall my meetings in Friedeberg with a most uncommon man. Allow me to say a few words about him.

Back in my first days in Friedeberg, several times I dropped by an auto repair shop, where I always found this man at work there. Either he was repairing bicycles, or wrestling with a sewing machine, or turning out some piece on his miniature machine lathe, or resurfacing some cracked saucepan or pot.

Hillard was over sixty years of age. He was heavily wrinkled, with a rough face and hands, and he was always dressed in black trousers, a black shirt, and a black smock, all of which, no matter how strange it seemed, were neatly pressed and ironed. Hillard didn't like either the "Reds" or the "Brownshirts," as Willy liked to characterize them, and he had learned to keep his silence. It was for this reason, perhaps, that the bigwigs respected him. If something wasn't quite right with their vehicles, they brought them to Hillard for repair.

Continuing to puff on his pipe, the mechanic would question the client about what had to be done. Nobody could remember a case when Hillard had declined to help. Honoring Hillard's high professional qualities, his wisdom, and his discipline, the citizens of the city had declared him to be a master. That is how everyone treated him: the rich and poor, the young and old. He was a genuine hard-working, professional German master, and was widely regarded as such.

Hillard lost his wife and two sons in the war. The mother could not endure the loss of her sons: one in the West, the other on the Eastern Front. Possibly, that is why the master never hurried home and spent almost the entire day in his repair shop. He was deeply aggrieved by an Almighty who had treated his family so coldly and indifferently.

The pastor called upon Hillard at the repair shop several times and tried to soothe his aching heart, but without success. Hillard constantly asked the question, "In the name of what did my children have to die?" Yet he could not find a reasonable answer. The master lived comfortably, but clearly felt that the day was coming when his eyes and hands would give out, and then all hopes would be on his sole remaining daughter, who had not abandoned him but constantly warmed him with her kindness and caring.

The young woman had decided not to get married as long as her father still lived, and she dedicated her entire life to him. It came as a great shock to me one day when the master planted me on a green chair and suddenly poured out his thoughts and feelings in a torrent of words. Plainly, the moment had come when he could no longer endure his pain in silence; he spoke resolutely, and told me angrily about what he had been pondering and carrying inside himself for so long.

"In 1933," the master said, "I voted for Hitler. To be sure, his promises were so fine. But all that came of them is failure, the collapse of Germany, and the collapse of the German psyche. Will we ever be able to make our way out of this scum into which Hitler drove the entire nation? All of mankind hates us Germans. We know this."

I listened to Hillard's revelations and tried to cheer him up.

"The main thing has already been done," I said. "The German people have been liberated from this abominable and terrible fascist regime. Now everything depends upon you yourselves, the German people!"

A common project bound us together. I had noticed a car and motorcycle, partly concealed by canvas, parked in the corner of the garage. Of course, their former owners had brought them in for repairs, but now the owners had run away. I asked the master if he could repair the Fiat car and BMW motorcycle, and give them to me. He replied:

"Sure I can! I'll have it done within a week."

I understood that the car was far above my rank. I offered it to Shilovich. He eagerly accepted it, hired a chauffeur, and began to drive around in it. Meanwhile, I rode the BMW—the best German motorcycle, a real animal, a monster. I was confident that I'd be able to "tame" it. I promised the master that I'd pay him well. He declined the money and only addressed kind words to the Red Army: "You've earned it!"

Our acquaintanceship almost ended in tragedy for both him and me. But I'll talk about this in a moment.

For so many days, I saw only frightened, beseeching expressions on the faces of the people in the city, and heard only one and the same question escape their lips: "Lord, what will become of us?" But I lost patience in the hope of trying to convince the Germans to have confidence in a normal future and, at last, to stop fearing the Russians.

I resolved to pay a visit to all the invalids. The former Wehrmacht soldiers greeted me cautiously, and a few of them unkindly. It seemed to me that not one of them believed in what I was saying, but I later learned this wasn't so. Willy confided to me that the Russian captain's round of the invalids had made a strong impression on the population. Perhaps, a time of reconciliation was approaching.

Unexpectedly, an incident surprising in itself came to my assistance. One morning a drunken Red Army soldier appeared in the town square, not far from the doors of the church. Where he had come from, God only knows.

At first, swaying unsteadily on his feet, he swore mightily at the "vile Germans." Thank God they didn't know the Russian language! The pastor came out of the church and implored the intoxicated Russian to leave the square. Each didn't understand a word the other was saying. After a short time, the soldier tugged at the fly of his trousers, fussed about a bit with his business, and then at last when he was ready, released a strong stream of urine in the direction of the pastor, just like a fountain. The pastor covered his face with his hands and exclaimed, "Oh, my God!" He was troubled most of all by the fact that the faces of his congregation had appeared in the church's windows.

At this moment, the general, who was passing through the square in his Willys jeep, caught sight of the scene. He stopped the jeep, got out, and approaching the soldier, he asked: "You, brother, what's going on here?"

The soldier seemed momentarily dumbstruck; wasn't it obvious what he was doing? Then, noticing the general's shoulder straps, he immediately tightened his belt, straightened out his field blouse, and clearly reported, just as he was supposed to do:

"Private of the 214th Rifle Regiment, 2nd Battalion, 1st Company Ivan Chechik—I'm pissing on the damned Germany!"

"Did you finish your business?" the general asked, after bursting out in laughter.

"Not at all, Comrade General!"

"Come on, brother, finish up, and get back to your camp."

The soldier once again pulled his member out through the opened zipper, and let loose another stream in the direction of the pastor. The pastor quickly ducked inside his church. The windows immediately emptied of the maidenly faces, which had been staring at the soldier. Having bellowed another couple of choice expressions, accompanied by a stream of juicy Russian profanities, the soldier finally fell silent. The general's adjutant immediately grabbed him, and in a flash hustled him into the back seat of the jeep. The next day, the entire town was laughing about the episode, whether tittering over the pastor's hasty retreat or guffawing at the spectacle of the plump Russian being unceremoniously trundled into the back seat of the jeep.

The next day, General Berestov forced the now sober Ivan Chechik to return to the church with a translator and his own platoon commander. The soldier confessed his wrongdoing and apologized in front of the pastor.

Before they left, a telling conversation took place in the church between Private Ivan Chechik and his platoon commander. The lieutenant told me about it later:

"Well, that's enough gaping at the ladies," the lieutenant had said to Chechik. "Let's go."

"Don't rush me, Commander, there's all the 'ma'amzelles' one could want around here. I had five such women one day back in East Prussia. Two of them asked me to do it again, once I'd finished with them. Imagine that . . . and I was seeking vengeance! I didn't honor their requests."

"All right, let's go, joker! You'll see enough such mademoiselles in your lifetime."

And so that's the way it had gone. In East Prussia, in Berlin, and in Silesia. Returning to his unit, Private Ivan Chechik spent the next five days in the guardhouse.

After this entire episode, perhaps because General Berestov had taken swift action against the drunken soldier, citizens began appearing on the streets again, for which I was indescribably happy. The clock repair shop, the bowling alley, the café, and the beer hall all quickly reopened. Naturally, the German beer hall proprietor bought his Pilsner from the Czechs.

News

I returned to the headquarters after my next tour of the units. There was a heap of news and events waiting for me. First, I found a real "parcel fever" going on upon my return—the officers were totally preoccupied with getting their hands on things and sending them back home. "This isn't a good sign," I thought to myself. "It presages something bad, but we have no way of knowing what it might be." What eventually happened resembled rats fleeing a sinking ship.

The staff officers, political department workers, SMERSH agents, and quartermaster service had all stopped worrying about their direct responsibilities. In general, all human energy around the headquarters was devoted to the acquisition of goods and the dispatching of parcels. Now, instead of the two packages that officers had been allowed to send home each month, people were sending five to ten. How they managed to work this, I don't know. The deputy chief of the division's Political Department, Lieutenant Colonel P. I. Izzhak, set the record. In one and a half months (May–June), he sent sixty packages back to his native city of Odessa.

Before the war, Petr Ivanovich had been the second secretary of the Party's

Odessa Regional Committee. The lieutenant colonel had previously shown no particular zeal in his military duties. Now, however, he had turned into an "invisible being" in the direct sense of the term and had lost all semblance of a normal human being. He no longer met with anyone, and nobody ever saw him anywhere. He forgot the way to the officers' dining hall. How he still nourished himself was a riddle.

From the window of my room, which was located on the second floor, it was easy to spot the tousled, grizzled, half-crazed officer, working in his undershirt with rolled up sleeves, totally focused on his obsession. He sorted through his booty by hand like an automaton, indifferently stuffing items into parcel boxes.

One of those June days, Lieutenant Colonel Izzhak set off to the army headquarters and there met with a General Russkikh, a member of the Military Council and a kind, intelligent, and sympathetic man. Izzhak somehow managed to receive a seventy-day furlough. Returning to the division, he bartered at the commissariat for a military cart, loaded it with boxes of American canned food, bags of sugar, dried bread crumbs, and oats, and then tracked down a private, a former Odessan, who was due to receive his demobilization papers soon. The next morning, at dawn, in secret, saying good-bye to no one, Izzhak left the Political Department and the town.

The chief of the Political Department didn't happen to mourn his loss. He had long been bearing the deputy's own workload. He was more likely happy to have rid himself of this loafer.

Did Petr Ivanovich ever reach Odessa? I don't know.

The second episode turned out a little worse. An order arrived from the army bearing the stamp, "Top Secret." The division was required to seize a lot of things from the local population in accordance with an attached list, and then send the loot to the *Front*'s Captured Items Administration. We had ten days to carry out the order.

I will recite from memory what Russia acquired from this one small German town, because the reader will probably find it interesting to know:

Motorcycles—3
Bicycles—161
Pianos—16
Radios—49
Sewing machines—more than 100
Gramophones—84
Gramophone albums—more than 3,000
Wall clocks—90
Mantle clocks—130

Telephone sets—around 150

Enameled kitchen pails—around 200

Cast-iron cookware—more than 30 sets

Tools—around 300

Leica cameras—over 40

Rugs and floor runners—more than 400

Copper doorknobs—hundreds

Roofing iron, bricks, tiles, lime, and sand—much

Dairy cans—more than 100

Antique service sets—more than 50

Ruberoid™ roofing rolls—many

And so on, for example:

Baby carriages

Wall paintings

String, thread, and sewing needles

Joiner's glue and emery paper

Kitchen meat grinders

Dental instruments

Window glass of various sizes

New footgear, especially high boots

Typographical equipment

Boards, logs, and plywood

Copper wire

Magnifying glasses

Steel, cast-iron, and ceramic pipes

In 1917, when seizing belongings from the people, the Bolsheviks called such an act "expropriation." As the expropriations from the German people were going on in 1945, Hillard asked me to spare his radio receiver. After conferring with Colonel Shilovich on the matter and gaining his consent, I went back to Hillard and told him that he could keep his radio for the month remaining until our division was scheduled to leave the area. When the ten-day limit had passed and the soldiers had taken away all the seized items to the divisional depots, the town commandant sent for Hillard.

Hillard confessed to having the radio set and, unaware of my arrangement with Colonel Shilovich, told the commandant that I had given him permission to keep it. The commandant didn't bother to investigate the matter but immediately typed up a report and sent it to the SMERSH office. There they processed the processed the document quickly.

In the 331st Rifle Division, in distinction from many other divisions, the division commander didn't allow the SMERSH agents to arrest officers without his personal authorization. The chief of the SMERSH department, Major Rybtsov, could refuse to submit to General Berestov's arrangement and do whatever he thought necessary. He was not subordinated to the general. But Rybtsov didn't argue with Berestov, for he understood that the division commander could always have an influence on his career either positively or negatively. Maybe it could even mean an extra medal on Rybtsov's chest.

In the given case with me, the major, saying not a word, laid the commandant's report on Berestov's desk. The general, taking in the contents of the paper in a glance, almost snarled, "What a swine!" Then he immediately ripped the paper into tiny pieces, and added, "Don't be angry, Major; just pretend that you've made no report about anything, and the radio receiver will be turned into the depot this very day."

I reported to the division commander at his first summons, and spotting Rybtsov sitting next to him, I turned pale. One could expect nothing good from this man. The clever general dispelled the tensions:

"You're lucky, Captain, that our division has such an excellent chief of SMERSH. This very day, that radio set will be turned over to the depot!"

"Yes, sir," I answered. "Consider it done."

But what about Shilovich? He had conveniently forgotten about his part in the agreement, and now he was sitting next to the general and holding his tongue. You can bet that I didn't say a thing about him!

That very day, I turned Hillard's Telefunken radio receiver over to the depot, having first obtained it from Hillard. The master only shook his head in sadness and felt sorry for me. I never learned what was in the commandant's report about me, but it couldn't have been anything good.

Fortunately, they didn't take my motorcycle away from me. I rode around on my beast of a motorcycle for about three weeks. I could reach any battalion on it in just a few minutes. I drove the bike like the wind, and it was responsive to my touch. Sometimes I liked to speed across the Oder River and zip down to the Czech border, which was no more than 60 kilometers [36 miles] away. The Czechs would treat me to a mug of beer and a few kind words, and then I'd already be speeding back to Friedeberg.

One day, I had an accident. On one of the sharp turns in the road, apparently, I lost control over my iron "monster" for several seconds. The bike headed toward a light fence in a field, beyond which lay a steep rocky precipice with a boulder-strewn brook far below. I barely managed to turn off the motor and went into a skid. I fell heavily, and the motorcycle flipped over and over and became a tangled mass of metal on the highway. I blacked out.

I awoke in unfamiliar surroundings: in some German home, lying on a bed.

Two elderly Germans were sitting beside me and were sighing and lamenting, offering prayers to God. How did they, the poor things, manage to drag me from the highway to their home? I thanked them endlessly.

I asked them to bring me a mirror. I took a glance in it, and my heart sank: my face was lightly scraped all over, my eyes were black, and my trousers and military blouse were torn in many places. My arms were badly bruised and bleeding. I asked the old man to run to the medical-sanitation battalion in order to send an ambulance for me. I do recall one curious detail. As soon as I regained consciousness, I immediately reached for the right pocket of my tunic, where I usually kept my Party card. And of course, I checked whether or not I still had my pistol.

An ambulance arrived for me. The medical orderlies, laying me on a stretcher, stuffed me into the ambulance, dragged my wrecked motorcycle to the ambulance and threw it in after me, and took us both back to the medical-sanitation battalion.

Three days later I retuned to the Political Department. Colonel Shilovich, giving me a proper scolding, ordered me immediately to present myself to the division commander. Berestov received me out of turn, and as he always did, spoke tersely:

"Well, hero, your riding around has gotten you into trouble! Turn over your motorcycle to the divisional depot this very day. You need to have a long life. You still have a lot of work ahead of you."

There was one more piece of news, a most unpleasant one. Lower Silesia was to be turned over to Poland. This was one of the repartitions of Europe after the war, as I later found out, thought up by Stalin. And the Allies gave his suggestion their blessing. After Stalin's death, in the Russian State Archives in Moscow, historians found a geographical map of Europe dated to the summer of 1944. Back then, the tip of Stalin's red pencil had drawn a circle around Lower Silesia, which indicated it could remain part of Germany. Later, the "Father of Nations" changed his mind: he gave Lower Silesia to Poland as compensation for taking away from it two of its best cities: L'vov and Vil'nius.[5]

I was still not fully recovered from my motorcycle accident: my left arm and right leg ached. One day I was sitting in my room, reading the divisional gazette, which was still coming out. They had sent one of this gazette's best journalists, Semen Rakovshchik, to Podol'sk, where the Central Military Archive of the USSR Ministry of Defense was located. They sent him on an official three-month mission to gather materials on the history of the 331st Rifle Division. It became known that other divisions had sent their own journalists to the same place. I never saw Semen Rakovshchik again, just as I never saw a history of my own division.

The soldier on duty dropped by and announced that they were calling me from the nearby controlled checkpoint. Some young German lady was there, muttering in her own language, and seemingly asking for me.

"It's Lotta! She wouldn't have come without a real reason," I immediately decided. "Has something happened?" I put on my service cap and, limping, hobbled to the checkpoint, where I found her waiting. It was impossible to recognize Lotta: she was pale, like a very sick person, and trembling with fear. She announced that an hour ago, her father had been arrested. Friedrich was at the commandant's office. What news! I asked Lotta to go back home and comfort Frau Emma. "I'll try to find out what's going on!" I promised her upon our parting.

A meeting with the commandant never promised anything good. We all tried to avoid him as much as possible. But I immediately fell upon him: "What, have you gone crazy? You've arrested a photographer. He's made 120 portraits of officers and soldiers for us. Guntze was never a member of the National Socialist Party, and never took up arms against us. What's the deal? Fill me in. Otherwise, I'll call General Berestov."

"Go ahead and call, Captain. This swinish German failed to turn in his camera."

I burst out bitterly laughing: "If he turns in his camera, he won't be able to photograph our heroes! The General has authorized him to turn over his camera a month from now," I explained to the senior lieutenant.

The commandant began to fidget in his chair: "It's a bad thing, Captain, that you stand up for them. I'll have to write you up. You're a suspicious character!"

"Go ahead, Senior Lieutenant, write me up!"

The commandant may have written me up; I don't know. But nothing came of this incident, and Friedrich was released. Perhaps the commandant feared the wrath of General Berestov if he questioned the general's arrangement with the photographer.

After the incident with the motorcycle, the chief of the Political Department had given me two days leave. I sought Willy's advice; how would it be best to spend these two days? Willy arranged a tsar's holiday for me. With the permission of Frau Emma, Lotta and I went to the nearest spa.

While the war was going on, the Germans had continued to travel to spas, and what spas they were! They placed us in a miniature coach, painted red. A toy steam engine pulled the coach along. An hour later I found myself in an enchanted world, likely from the tale of *1,001 Arabian Nights*. Low wooded hills encircled the entire space of the resort. An unusual vale lay between them, covered by a velvet blanket of grass, strewn with flowers. The blue waters of a lake glittered nearby. The masts of handsome yachts were rocking on the waves. Lotta and I descended one of the hills in a cable car and made our way along a narrow path to an enchanted home. There was more glass in it than wood. A plump, ruddy German immediately came out to meet us. He introduced himself to us:

"I'm the proprietor's assistant. I take care of his property. Herr Deitrich hopes, as always happens after a war, that everything will settle down eventually so he can return."

"Indeed it must happen, but there are still so many narrow-minded and evil people," I chuckled.

Several minutes later, Lotta and I were jumping from joy like children! We would have two full days alone together!

Here for the first time, Lotta confessed her love for me. She wanted to spend the rest of her life with her Captain. She told me:

"I'm ready to go back to Russia with you. There is one curious book in our home library. It says that during the Russian Army's 1813 campaign beyond its borders, many Russian officers were quartered in Saxony and Silesia. They liked to organize evening dances, and fell in love with young German ladies. Our women willingly married them, and the officers took them back to Russia with them. The Germans understood that many difficulties awaited them. They weren't accustomed to difficulties, but that didn't intimidate them. They were even ready to adopt a new faith."

I was silent for a moment, trying to think of the best way to express what I was about to say to Lotta. She wasn't going to be happy with my reply.

"We officers don't have the right to marry foreigners." That, approximately, was my answer to Lotta.

"Why, why?" Lotta almost shouted, and her painful cry remained in my ears for a very long time.

She then told me about her friend: "We graduated high school together; her name is Doris. One of your artillerymen has fallen in love with her. He is older than her by fifteen years. But they have fallen in love with each other. This officer, who has more decorations than you, got down on his knees before her, kissed her hand, and sobbing, told her the same thing you just told me."

Once again she pleaded, "Why, why? Why do they treat your combat officers so cruelly? In the German army, Hitler gave his permission even to common soldiers to get married in whatever country they were stationed."

While we belonged to one another with the time we had remaining, we tried not to think about the future. But again and again, we tormented ourselves and could not find a way out of this idiotic circle.

Two days later we returned to Friedeberg. We walked together through the entire town, firmly holding onto each other's hands. That evening, when I arrived at the Guntzes', I found all three of them in the drawing room, sitting at a table. They were waiting for me.

Where the piano had been standing, adorning the parlor with its presence, there was now a gaping void. The tall, antique wall clocks had also disappeared. One could no longer hear their precise ticking. There was now only blank wall in their former places. I suddenly remembered how Friedrich had once told me their history. His elder brother had acquired these clocks in Switzerland even before the First World War.

Friedrich, Emma, and Lotta were all desperately gazing at me when I entered the room. As I realized, they were all waiting for me to explain to them why their piano and wall clocks had been taken from them.

I began to ponder what I should say to them. Here, approximately, is what I came up with to tell them:

Let me give you an example. In 1942, I was fighting as a soldier at Rzhev. It is exactly 100 kilometers [60 miles] from this city to Moscow. Colonel General Walter Model was defending this important strategic center, which had been converted into a fortress. Hitler called Model his "Lion of Defense," and that was the truth. It was a genuine bloody slaughterhouse there, which daily ground up both Russian and German soldiers. Hundreds of thousands of Russian soldiers, I believe, and tens of thousands of Germans soldiers fell in the fighting, and their corpses lay in heaps across the battlefields. The burial teams couldn't cope with the task of burying all the dead in at timely fashion. We suffocated on the stench of the dead.

But the time arrived when even this lion, licking his wounds, began to retreat. Then this swine ordered his soldiers to leave a wasteland behind them. This was very likely even more terrible than the bombing of Dresden. The German soldiers blew up everything that could be blown up, with people still inside, and burned everything that could burn, with people still inside. I saw this horrifying wasteland myself: many towns with just one street left intact by some miracle, and piles of ashes marking the former places of homes and dugouts, where old men, women, and children had been living. Marching past those smoldering ruins, where homes and those gloomy dugouts had once stood, we gave the homeless victims of the fire everything that we could: we took off our undershirts, pulled a reserve pair of underwear, or a towel, or a puttee from our knapsacks; we shared our mess tins and spoons and didn't spare our last lump of sugar or dried bread. Our cooks fed them out of our own kettles, leaving less for us.

But our troops always marched on, while the citizens remained behind in their miserable dugouts. Why did this cannibal, this German general, behave this way? He received the Knight's Cross with Oak Leaves, and Hitler awarded him the title of field marshal. What did all these trinkets cost in comparison with the destroyed human lives? Did he really not understand that with these actions, he was embittering the Russian soldier and giving rise to an ineradicable hatred for the Germans?

The fact that they've taken things from you is both bitter and offensive, but Model is first of all guilty in this. Believe me, everything they've seized from you are trifles in comparison with that wasteland into which an enormous expanse of Russia was turned, wherever the Wehrmacht passed.

But I am confident, friends, that Germany has not been struck down once and for all, that it will be reborn, and you'll get back everything that you've lost.

All three of them had begun crying. Their tears flowed for a long time. Meanwhile, I sat opposite them, with my hands tightly clenched, and sincerely suffered for these simple German people. Meanwhile that criminal, Field Marshal Walter Model, having suffered defeat in the Ruhr against the Americans, had shot himself. He understood perfectly well how the Allies would treat him, a war criminal. But at the time I couldn't know about this, and I couldn't inform the Guntze family about it.

Farewell, Division!

On 10 July 1945, our division was disbanded. At 11:00 A.M. they gathered the division's entire command staff at the headquarters. Along the wall of windows on one side of the room, tables were standing, set with enormous platters of bread slices with ham, cheese, and even red caviar: to be sure, the quartermasters had outdone themselves. Next to the platters were tumblers of vodka—the "frontline 100 grams." Everybody gathered at the tables, and having tossed down their tumbler of the national spirit, everyone turned to having a bite of everything offered. We all laughed, joked, swapped anecdotes, and discussed the upcoming courses of study for officers, which were due to start in August. Nobody had the least inkling of what was waiting for us all.

At noon, the general, his deputy, the chief of staff, and Colonel Shilovich entered the hall. The general, having looked over everyone standing in front of him, immediately began to deliver his speech, or more accurately, his farewell address to his subordinate commanders:

"Dear combat friends! As sad as this duty is to me, I am obliged to inform you that today is the final day of our division's existence. The war is over, and the Ministry of Defense has initiated force reductions. The country needs the skilled hands of workers.[6]

"This doesn't mean that we've become superfluous. Those who have served at the front are priceless. We are obliged to pass along the enormous combat experience that we've acquired to a new, young generation that must serve in the army."

Pavel Fedorovich ended his speech with the following words:

"I thank you all for your honorable service, for your loyalty to the Motherland

and your duty. Together, we celebrated the great Victory Day. May all of you mark this wonderful, historic occasion for many years to come!"

Silence fell upon the hall, and it seemed that no one wanted to be the first to break it. The silence continued for a long time. Likely, each man present was saying his own farewell to the division.

The general went around to all of us, giving each of us an embrace and three kisses on the cheeks. Then he excused himself, because he had to leave us: he and Shilovich had to report immediately to the army. He turned over the speaking role to his deputy. The colonel then addressed us, sharing more information about what was to follow:

All the same, the division has been given five days, until 15 July. From 16 July, the railroad will be closed to the army's units. New engineering and construction units, fitters, electricians, and mechanics are already arriving in Silesia; we are to turn over all our transportation to them. In accordance with a resolution of the Soviet government, the dismantling of German industry as reparations to our country is starting.

The day after tomorrow, that is, on 12 July at 0600 hours, all our heavy weapons will be sent to the Central Group of Forces in Vienna. At 1200 hours that same day, four troop trains will be at the railroad station, ready for the departure of those officers and soldiers due to be demobilized, as well as all female personnel.

In addition, the division will send twenty-eight officers to Moscow for assignment to military academies and to higher military courses. A day later, army personnel clerks will come to those remaining and determine your further status as officers. Each one of you will be given the question about where you want to go: to Vienna, to the Central Group of Forces; into the reserve; or to serve in Hungary.

Civilian employees will continue working until 25 July, and then, together with the medical-sanitation battalion, they will be sent to Vienna. The medical-sanitation battalion will leave behind a small emergency aid station in Friedeberg. Only the commandant's office will remain until 15 August, in order to maintain order and to supply the local population with produce. After turning over the town of Friedeberg to the Poles, it also will be sent to Vienna.

All of you in the headquarters are immediately to receive a copy of the order 'On the Schedule of Disbanding the 331st Rifle Division.' If you have any questions today, I ask you to direct them either to me or to the chief of staff.

Again there was silence, enough to drive one crazy. Then suddenly something close to a shout rang out, like a blow to the head: "There's news for you!" Someone couldn't restrain himself and began crying heavily. Another man sincerely burst out sobbing, holding his head in both hands. A third man unexpectedly cried out: "What will I do with my woman; what will I tell my *frau*?" There were also soft shouts: "What an absurdity—they won't let us go home, and they won't let us serve either. They've put us down as reservists!"

Like everyone else, I was saddened by the news. I sensed the loss of something very important in my life. But to speak honestly, my present division had never become for me as close and dear as the 220th Rifle Division had been. I had found no comrades in the 331st Rifle Division, except for Egor Panin, the editor of the division's newspaper, and, possibly, the general. He had always treated me warmly, frankly even solicitously, from my very first day with the division.

After the meeting, I dropped by to see Egor and asked him to step outside to have a smoke, which meant "we need to talk." We went outside together, and I immediately began to pester him:

"I have a girlfriend here, a German. Give me some advice about what I should do. I've decided to go to Hungary and to take her along with me. But our relationship will be apparent there."

"What, are you nuts? I've always thought you were a sensible fellow. You know, they'll immediately sell you out. Then they'll send you to Kolyma [a notorious site in the Soviet gulag], just like they're supposed to do. It will be the ruin not only of you but also of your beloved woman."

I decided to press the matter, paying no attention to Egor's critical remarks: "I've already asked the chief of the medical-sanitation battalion to hire Lotta as a nurse, a dishwasher, or as a lab assistant. Whatever he wants; one can always think of something. But you know what Colonel Svirsky told me in reply? 'You've what, gone mad? Your woman doesn't know a single word of Russian. She'll immediately fail in whatever task she's given.' I suggested that he just put Lotta to sleep for the trip to Vienna, and told him that when we get there, I'd take responsibility for her. His only response was, 'Well, aren't you the joker! But you'd better stop and think about what you're proposing to do.' The swine! How much have Colonel Svirsky and I endured together in this war. Together we suffered the tragedy of the *medsanbat* at Lansberg, and together we buried Tema Svirsky. Who helped him rebuild the medical-sanitation battalion from scratch?"

Egor cut in: "All right, all right! Calm down. Don't get carried away with your fantasy! Explain the situation frankly to your girl. If she loves you, she'll understand. Finally, just roll the dice; give her your Moscow address and telephone number. Perhaps she'll wait for you. Agree with her to meet again after five years, no sooner. No one can help you now in such a hopeless situation."

I fell asleep and woke up with the thought of our fate. I had wild dreams that night. For example, Lotta and I are tearing along in a carriage to Paris.

The Musketeers of the Guard meet us, and D'Artagnan presents us to the King . . .

The next night, I had a completely silly dream. Willy had given me a refugee's certificate. Changing out of my uniform into civilian clothes, I became a naturalized Fritz. Together with all the other refugees, I was heading for Germany. We passed five controlled checkpoints without any problems. Only about 20 kilometers remained to the German border. But wouldn't you know it, a final checkpoint before the border. By some law of the jungle, a reptilian SMERSH officer was there, intently checking everyone's papers, and then suddenly, fixing his gaze upon me, he declared: "Until you tell me who you really are, I'm not going to let the column pass."

At that point, oh horror, the anti-Semite Klara crawls out of the column, and adjusting the pile of hair on her head, she shouts: "That one's a Soviet officer—a Jew!" The SMERSH officer seizes me by the scruff of the neck and flings me down onto the asphalt.

I woke up and suddenly recalled that I had decided to go to Hungary. There were altogether six of us officers that had made this decision. They had assigned us to a certain artillery brigade. It was presently located about 19 kilometers from Friedeberg but had become stuck there, as was happening with many other army units that were on the move. The brigade was only going to continue on to Hungary after 15 August. Lotta and I would still have a whole month together, and surely we'd think up something in that time.

The other officers and I reported to the artillery brigade and moved into a splendid German home. We lead a carefree life there without any superior officers hovering over us. Naturally, the only thing that connected us with the artillery brigade was the officers' mess. Several times we journeyed down to Bratislava, and several times we visited a women's processing camp: we were trying to figure out what it was. This wasn't life but a fairy tale. Such was the gift we received in the initial peaceful days after the war.

Early one morning I hopped on a bicycle, having grabbed dry rations for two days, and I pedaled with all my might. Three hours later I was entering the Guntzes' home. I was going to spend two days with Lotta. I didn't dare be away for longer than that.

That evening, when I lay down to sleep in the room that had been offered to me, Lotta entered the room, bringing pajamas, a large pitcher of hot water, a towel, and a deep basin. She had me lower my feet into the basin and then washed my feet. At first I protested, but nothing came of that. Lotta stayed with me throughout the night. The two days flew by. I rode off back to the brigade, but then on the next day—back to the Guntzes. On one of my visits, I suddenly noticed as Lotta tossed the Russian-German dictionary, which I had given to her for studying the Russian language, under the bed.

The Second Advent

After 16 July 1945, I watched as a gigantic operation unfolded in Silesia, one with which I agreed at the time: by order of Stalin, Silesia was to be stripped bare before the Poles arrived to take it over. The Captured Items Administration from Moscow oversaw the entire operation. Its representatives didn't have to search for where the "hidden treasures" were buried. Moscow had already known for a long time and had precisely determined what was to be taken from the Germans and sent back to Russia.

Later, I learned that even before the war had ended, the Soviet Council of People's Commissars had already issued decree after decree on the removal of industrial enterprises, the rarest books, works of art of the highest technique and technology, and the best scientists and specialists from the Soviet zone of Germany for shipping back to the Soviet Union. I have collected more than 100 such edicts of the Soviet government in my personal archives, starting from 4 May 1945.

In each of them, the objects for seizing and dismantling are precisely indicated, including in Silesia. For example, the dismantling of a specific German Krupps ammunition plant that produced artillery shells and fuses was specified in one of the decrees.

The author Gavriil Popov talks in detail about this reparations operation in his book *Voina i pravda: Tsena pobedy* [War and Truth: The Price of Victory] (New York: Liberty Publishing House, 2005). I will try to describe only that which I saw myself, how they removed everything that they could from Friedeberg.

The textile factory was completely dismantled. All the fabric storehouses were emptied, which meant thousands of meters of cloth were taken. Our division got the spoils: each officer received up to fifty meters of fabric, while they distributed twenty meters to every soldier. Only the walls and roof of the milk bottling plant remained. Five mechanical workshops and automobile garages were loaded onto Studebaker trucks and delivered to the rail cars waiting at the station. From the local farms they took cows, which were also sent back to Russia. Most curiously, workers demolished the spa resort where Lotta and I had spent the two best days of our youth.

All the buildings, the swans, the steel cables, the rails, the cross ties, the pretty little coach cars, the miniature steam engines, the cable cars, and the kitchen equipment were loaded onto rail cars. Who benefited from all this in the future?

"That's the German sons-of-bitches for you"—the laborers and soldiers were all swearing. "The war is going on, while they drive around to spas. That only got them into trouble!" Trucks rushed along the streets one after the other.

They were carrying turbo generators, rusty pipes, and boilers that had gone to scrap, along with sand, tiling, bricks, and lumber.

On one of these days, I accidentally overheard the conversation of two German women who were standing next to me on the sidewalk: "Let them take it all away, let them! As soon as possible! We will build new factories and mills—more modern ones!"

From my reading of Gavriil Popov's book, I learned that in 1945 alone, 74,000 train cars traveled from Germany to Russia, and altogether prior to the formation of the German Democratic Republic—400,000 train cars. The Soviets took away everything from the Germans that they could lay their hands on and sent it all back to Russia.

My Last Meeting with Willy

On 14 August I rode my bike into the town of Friedeberg as usual, but at first I went to the commandant's office. The commandant announced that the Poles would be arriving in two days. I rode on to see Willy. I explained the situation to him and asked him to prepare the local population for this somber procedure. They were all going to become refugees, or "displaced people." I thanked Willy for all his help and support and for his constant effort to bring me closer to the local citizens. Then I gave him some words of advice:

"Don't be afraid of the path ahead. They're going to give you rations for four days. Everyone must pick them up today. If you ever get to Czechoslovakia, there you can exchange your Reichsmarks for the Czech koruna. In the Soviet zone, and in any other zone of Germany for that matter, the Czech currency will help you. They are establishing camps for displaced persons everywhere. Social and religious organizations have begun to help refugees. The most important thing it to make sure all the refugees get documentation of their status.

"Stay out of the sun and heat. Try to move in the cooler morning and evening hours. Everywhere you can find it, stock up on clean water. Ration it carefully. All elderly people absolutely must bring along walking sticks. On halts, leave somebody to keep watch over the walking sticks: you never know what might happen.

"Everybody must bring along spare changes of underwear, light clothing, and jackets or cloaks against the rain. Try to check to see as well if you can find some carriages in your former homes. Hillard has built four small carts. That's all I can do for you, and all I wanted to say. I'm sure that we will live to see a better day for Germany, and a time when Russians and Germans will no longer be enemies!"

Willy burst into tears. "Thank you! May it be so," he said.

When we left two days later, I found out that the commandant had only given the refugees rations for three days. "The commandant's a dirty thief!"— what else could I say about him?

The Parting: "We Want God!"

It was 16 August 1945, almost three months to the day since our division had left the Sudetenland and had arrived in Friedeberg. I went to where the units of our division had been based during our time here. I climbed a high hill, from which one could see far and wide—the whole area. Not long ago, the regiments had been stationed here, the traditional loud army commands had rang out, and twice a day a trumpet call had signaled reveille and retreat. Now all around me was peace and quiet. It seemed even the birds had flown off somewhere in pursuit of the soldiers.

How much effort it took to form up a combat division! I thought back upon how the 215th Rifle Division had been born, and recalled my first division commander—Filimon Andrianovich Kupriianov. Perhaps I'd been lucky with my commanders.

Just two days ago, the church had been full of people. They were praying and appealing to God. And in their appeals to God they were summoning ever more faith, which would help them endure the trial that had fallen to their lot.

I returned to the town and went immediately to the Guntze home. They were all bewildered and pathetic as they packed up their things.

Lotta cried through the entire last night. She kept pitifully exclaiming: "Emma won't be able to bear this!" As much as I could, I tried to comfort Lotta and the other Guntzes.

The day of parting had arrived—17 August 1945. I suffered through it from the beginning to the end. I stood on the sidewalk across from the church, together with soldiers from the commandant's office. The first Poles arrived in a vehicle: a lieutenant, a noncommissioned officer, and some Polish junior commissioned cavalry officer. The commandant and burgomeister welcomed them amicably. They spent several minutes all signing some previously prepared documents. Then the Polish lieutenant, having tucked the papers away into a portfolio, addressed the burgomeister:

"Henceforth the town of Friedeberg, as does all of Silesia, belongs to Poland. I'm giving all of you three hours to gather up your things and leave, and one minute later there'd better not be a single German in this town!"

Willy sent messengers to all the homes. Very quickly the square began to fill with people. The people walked with lowered faces, many with tears in their eyes. They were dragging tightly stuffed rucksacks behind them, or pushing carriages with infants in front of them, or leading children by the hand. The Polish lieutenant attentively watched the human whirlpool and frequently smoked.

The pastor appeared in the doors of the church in full sacramental dress, with a black band around his right sleeve. He climbed a rostrum that had been erected for him and looked at the crowd of gatherers. The Polish lieutenant boiled up in anger: "Is this some sort of German devilry in a Polish town, without my permission?"

I couldn't tolerate the insolent behavior of this dimwit and calmly asked him, "What, are you going to order someone to shoot the pastor, Lieutenant, sir?"

The lieutenant bit his lips and started to smoke another cigarette. The pastor stretched out his hands to the crowd and addressed the believers: "My dear ones! A most difficult hour has arrived for all of us. They are forcing us to leave our native places, our homes, and the graves of our ancestors. We are submitting to them, but this doesn't mean that we have humbled ourselves. Be strong, disciplined, and help one another. Don't lose the spirit of the Lord in your hearts. Remember, God is with us! We will all unite in one prayer! Amen!"

Suddenly, all the gatherers in the square, about 2,000 people, began to chant in one voice: "We want God! We want God!" This cry, like a strong clap of thunder, rang above the entire neighborhood.

Willy began to line the people up into a column. At this moment, a young woman ran up to the Polish lieutenant and asked permission to run to the cemetery and back, to say goodbye to her mother. She swore that she would catch up with the column. The lieutenant merely gave her a dismissive gesture of his hand and told her to get back into the column. Then he addressed me:

"Captain, properly speaking, what are you doing here?"

"I'm carrying out the order of my general to monitor the evacuation."

At this moment, my comrades rode into the square on motorcycles. The lieutenant grinned insidiously, telling me:

"Your assault team, Captain, has arrived."

"Listen, Lieutenant, why are you being so obnoxious? You should be grateful to the Red Army, which conquered such a splendid part of Germany, but our Supreme Leader has given it to Poland."

"What do you mean, 'thank you'! Your Supreme Leader has taken the two best cities of my country!"

I stood there a bit longer and took a last look at the town hall, the abandoned homes, and down the highway. In the distance, the silhouettes of the departing refugees were now barely visible. The Polish lieutenant, obviously quite satisfied with his decisive actions, glanced in my direction: "They're saying that I have nothing left to do here, and that I need to get out of this now Polish town."

Almost as soon as the column of refugees had begun to move, my comrades had begun imploring me to return to the brigade. Two Studebaker trucks loaded with five cows were going to be leaving at 6:00 A.M. the next morning—our ride to Hungary. As we left Friedeberg, this is what I was thinking about:

In those first postwar days, millions of Germans were making their way along the roads of Europe back to the vanquished Germany, chased off their own lands by Russians, Poles, Czechs, and Lithuanians. They were driven like lepers from all the territory, wherever the conqueror's foot had trod. The displaced Germans toiled along the roads frightened, half-starved, with broken spirits, not knowing what their future held for them. In total, Germany took in around 15 million refugees from the lands it had been forced to abandon, including 2.5 million Russian Germans. Almost 2 million Germans died during this forced migration.

Years have since passed. The Poles have turned Lower Silesia into one of Europe's finest spa areas, and into a recreational mecca for Europeans. Three times after the war, I traveled to Poland to see friends. They showed me a map of postwar Poland. The previous names of German cities had been changed on it, as if they had never existed.

The Russians have a saying: "Never go back to smoldering ruins." We often use it when someone is thinking about trying to rekindle an old romance. I never once returned to Friedeberg, a place connected to one of the best experiences of my military youth, and which I always fondly remember.

Today, Lower Silesia is again full of Germans. They generously compensate the Poles for keeping their former towns just as they had looked, and for taking care of the cemeteries where their ancestors lie.

But all this lay in the future. Back on the morning of 18 August 1945, we were just six Red Army officers climbing aboard two Studebaker trucks for the trip to Hungary. Apparently, the brigade command was afraid that zealous Soviet authorities might confiscate both their trucks and the cows, so we had been asked to make sure that they all arrived safely. Three days later, after spending a day in Vienna, five cows and six Red Army officers in two American Studebaker trucks arrived in Hungary.

Afterword:
Reflections on the
Fighting for Rzhev

The fighting for Rzhev in the years 1942–1943 became one of the most inglorious pages of the long-suffering Red Army in the history of the Great Patriotic War. Just one venturesome Rzhev-Sychevka operation alone in January 1942 led to the destruction of three Soviet armies and the death of more than 100,000 men in the forests around Rzhev and Viaz'ma.

Fighting along the Rzhev-Viaz'ma line continued for 502 days. In the span of this time, the Red Army launched four major operations to try to take Rzhev. To the present day, military historians still debate the number of dead at Rzhev and Viaz'ma from these four operations. According to official data, these operations alone generated staggering losses—1,324,823 Red Army officers and soldiers. This figure is greater than those that occurred separately in the battles for Moscow, Leningrad, Kursk, and Berlin. The casualties in the battles for Rzhev were twice as great as they were at Stalingrad.[1] The 1999 All-Union Scientific-Practical Conference, which was dedicated to the Battle of Rzhev, disclosed even more terrible losses in dead, wounded, and captured—around 2 million. On 3 March 2006, on the sixty-first anniversary of the liberation of Rzhev, local media offered a new figure for the casualties suffered by the Red Army around Rzhev: more than 1 million soldiers and officers killed in action.

In my own experience, my 215th Rifle Division, which entered the battle in August 1942 with 14,000 soldiers and officers, lost 7,000–8,000 mostly young lives in the subsequent fighting for Rzhev around the villages of Galachovo, Polunino, and Timofeevo. Many among the dead were my fellow cadets back in Tiumen.[2]

German losses were also heavy. Forten Esmeyer, a former staff officer in the German Ninth Army's 26th Infantry Division, which served in the Rzhev-Viaz'ma bridgehead, estimates that the German army lost between 300,000 and 450,000 men in the battles for Rzhev.[3]

Our soldiers christened the battles for Rzhev the "Rzhev meat grinder," into which Stalin, Zhukov, and Konev fed division after division. Forty-two mass graves in the Rzhev soil contain the remains of servicemen and women from more than 140 rifle divisions, 50 separate rifle brigades, and 50 tank brigades.[4] The tragedy of this battle consisted not only of the unparalleled sacrifices but also of the lack of success of these operations. The heavy losses and unimaginable human suffering were not offset by any compensatory reward of combat success, a fact that generated bitterness and despair among the survivors.

Any analysis of the enormous casualties and lack of success experienced by the Red Army around Rzhev must begin with adversary we faced. The Germans at Rzhev had qualitatively better equipment, more experienced officers, much superior command and control over their forces, extensive combat experience, and professional soldiers. Colonel-General Walther Model, a talented and experienced commander, commanded the German Ninth Army at Rzhev. Moreover, after the winter retreats from Moscow, the Germans had been in position for several months and were occupying strong fortifications in the Rzhev salient, which they defended with firm resolve. Their bitter resistance for every clump of earth, as if it was their own native soil, often led our front-line soldiers to wonder what was making the Germans fight so courageously and stubbornly.

To offset these German advantages, the Red Army had only numbers. Over the course of the fifteen months of fighting for the Rzhev–Viaz'ma bridgehead, we held a significant quantitative superiority in men and equipment. At the designated breakthrough sectors for our attacks, the Red Army's superiority in numbers grew to six or eight times the strength of the German defenders, sometimes much more. According to data provided by N. Belov and T. Mikhailovaia, the superiority of the 30th Army over its opponents, for example, in the summer of 1942, was 10–20 times in men, and 20–30 times in armor.[5]

In August 1942, Kalinin Front commander I. S. Konev used D. D. Leliushenko's 30th Army to hammer repeatedly at the German defenses around Rzhev, trying to exploit the Red Army's quantitative superiority in men and equipment. Without regard for losses—and they were enormous, as we've seen—the 30th Army command continued to hurl more and more fresh battalions into the slaughter, which is the only way to describe what I witnessed on the battlefield. Subordinate commanders and soldiers began to see the senselessness of what was happening, and as the slaughter continued seemingly without end, the soldiers were increasingly gripped by a sense of apathy and indifference.

If anything, even more intense fighting was going on just north of Rzhev, on a different sector of our Front. Farther south, toward Viaz'ma, Western Front commander G. K. Zhukov was launching his own series of costly frontal assaults, which gained only a few kilometers and drove the Germans from Zubtsov, but nothing more. By autumn of 1942, our forces were just 6 kilometers from Rzhev, as our forces had ground slowly forward at a terrible cost against the German defenses. Just 6 kilometers! In November 1942, Konev and Zhukov would repeat these bloody assaults on the Rzhev salient during Operation Mars. But it would require another six months of intense and bloody fighting before the Red Army managed to overcome these 6 kilometers and finally force the enemy to abandon the long-suffering city of Rzhev.

Dmitrii Volkogonov, in his book *I. V. Stalin: A Political Portrait— Triumph and Tragedy,* cites a remarkable retrospective conversation between Stalin and A. I. Antonov, chief of the General Staff's Operational Directorate, about the failed 1942 offensives against Rzhev.[6] Here is a fragment of that discussion:

> "Comrade Antonov," asked the Supreme Commander, "Have you ever stopped to think about why many of our offensive operations in 1942 were not completed? Take a look, for example, at the Rzhev-Viaz'ma operation of two *fronts*. . . . How do you explain these failures?
>
> "We operated in a stereotypical fashion," Antonov answered, "without inventiveness. We hadn't yet learned how to break though a defensive line simultaneously on several sectors, and we made a poor use of tank units to exploit our initial successes. . . ."
>
> Stalin interrupted Antonov, and offered his own conclusion:
>
> "The main thing is that having learned how to defend, we didn't yet know, and even now, we don't know much better, how to attack. . . . In brief, we still don't know how to fight well."

The historian V. V. Beshanov notes that in later years, Soviet marshals echoed Stalin's explanation, justifying their initial failures in 1941 and 1942 by claiming that "they were only still learning how to command, familiarizing themselves with the enemy, and gaining experience."[7] Beshanov and other historians consider such claims to be self-serving and childishly naïve, as do I. However, the explanation that the Red Army and its commanders were still only learning how to fight in 1942 contains a kernel of truth.

We cannot forget the mass repressions and purges organized by Stalin in the prewar period, when almost the entire high command cadre of the Red Army was destroyed. The bloody executions continued in 1941. In addition, many more commanders and officers were lost in the terrible disasters of the first six months of the war, so that by 1942 almost the entire leadership cadre of the Red Army had to be replaced. By 1942, the Kremlin could no longer select the best of the best to command, but quite often the best among the worst. These men were entrusted with the command of million-man armies, thousands of guns, and hundreds of tanks and airplanes. They were still learning how to lead and direct large masses of troops that had to be trained, armed, and coordinated, and the commanders were still struggling to organize cooperation between the different types of forces.

Furthermore, the Red Army in 1942 was still a clumsy instrument. It lacked modern means of communication and professionally trained regiment, battalion, and company commanders, while its soldiers were often conscripts with only the most limited basic training, or no training at all. Thus, the commanders were not being deceptive when they asserted that they were still learning how to fight. But they turned out to be not very capable students, which led to the seemingly endless defeats at Rzhev, the enormous losses, and a constant fear of the supreme command with each failure. All this was in spite of our vast superiority in the quantity of troops and equipment.

Though Stalin's statement to Antonov was essentially correct, it was typical of him to evade his own complicity in the state of affairs. After all, Stalin was the Supreme Commander, and he intently followed the operations of his generals and constantly demanded of his generals that they engage the enemy "at any price." Even timid attempts by the *front* commanders to prevail upon Stalin to stop the "self-destruction" of the armies, if only temporarily, never found any response. With the iron discipline—even fear—that Stalin had imposed on his subordinates, the commanders continued to fling battalion after battalion, brigade after brigade, and division after division into the meat grinder at Rzhev. Stalin and his subordinate commanders all fought not with skill but with numbers. Even worse, they all became so accustomed to simple methods of fighting with the enemy that many of them didn't even bother to learn new combat methods or tactics before the war's end.

It has been painful, however, for the fortunate survivors of the hellish Rzhev meat grinder to see the way official Soviet and Russian history has treated the Rzhev battles. The distortion and concealment of what was happening around Rzhev began even while events were unfolding there. On 26 August 1942 in its daily news summary, the Sovinformburo of Moscow radio made the following announcement: "On the Western and Kalinin Fronts, our forces have gone over to the offensive, broken the enemy's line of defense, and driven the strong adversary back 40 to 50 kilometers. As a result of this successful offensive, our forces have liberated 610 villages and towns, including the towns of Zubtsov, Karmanovo, and Pogoreloe Gorodishche. The Germans have lost 45,000 soldiers and officers. Fighting continues on the outskirts of Rzhev." From beginning to end this announcement was misleading. It concealed word of two previous operations: the Rzhev-Viaz'ma offensive of January–February 1942, and the Rzhev-Syvechka offensive from 30 July to 25 August 1942. Both of them, as is known, ended in failure, and there is only silence about our terrible losses.

When the German Ninth Army finally abandoned Rzhev on 2 March 1943 and slipped away from contact with our forces, the combat situation report of Western Front of 3 March said, "On 3 March, the Western and Kalinin Fronts went on the offensive, seized Rzhev, and began to pursue the enemy." The

German withdrawal was orderly; when we went in pursuit, we entered the cities of Ghzatsk (5 March), Sychevka (8 March), and Viaz'ma (12 March) after brief skirmishes with small German rear guard elements. But in the Sovinformburo announcement, we didn't "enter" these cities; rather, we "seized" them, or "drove the Germans from," and so on.

Neither of the *Front* commanders, G. K. Zhukov or I. S. Konev, ever revealed the full truth about the bloody fighting for the Rzhev-Viaz'ma bridgehead. They shared only a few cursory observations, even though they bore direct responsibility for this costly campaign. D. D. Leliushenko, the commander of the 30th Army in which I fought, devoted only nine lines to the fighting for Rzhev in his memoirs. Each of these aforementioned generals fought for more than a year near and around Rzhev, but they all evaded responsibility for what happened there.

Yet history is always full of paradoxes. After the liberation of Rzhev, G. K. Zhukov and I. S. Konev became marshals, while D. D. Leliushenko was promoted to major general. Stalin decorated all three with Orders. Meanwhile, the bodies of those common soldiers who had demonstrated amazing heroism and steadfastness before making the ultimate sacrifice for their motherland were thrown into mass graves and largely forgotten.

Not one division of the Red Army that fought in the Rzhev-Viaz'ma bridgehead was ever awarded the combat honorific title of "Rzhev." Why not? Didn't any one of them deserve it? The essence of the matter, likely, consists in the official desire to avoid any reason to remind people of the battles for Rzhev.

The inattention of researchers to the study of the battle of Rzhev is a serious oversight in Russian historiography. Only David M. Glantz, the important American scholar, has shed light on one of the operations to liberate Rzhev— Operation Mars—in his book *Zhukov's Greatest Defeat*.[8] But the other operations and battles designed to take the city remain unexplored and have yet to be deeply researched, examined from all angles, and summarized. Their role in the general history of the Great Patriotic War and the development of the Red Army into a formidable weapon has yet to be established. But the Rzhev "meat grinder" is still such an explosive subject that even to this day, official Russian historians are afraid to speak the whole truth about it.

We have in our hands primarily individual, scattered publications by writers and journalists, as well as by local authors and regional authorities, and some invaluable veteran reminiscences and memoirs. From these materials, it is possible to learn much of the bitter truth about the battles for Rzhev.[9]

I thought long and painfully about how to communicate the full horror that I saw and experienced at Rzhev. Then suddenly I spotted a modest collection of poems by the Moscow frontline poet Nikolai Maiorov, *Blizko k serdtsu!*

[Close to the Heart!][10] The following sincere, heartfelt poetic lines touched me deeply and seemed a fitting way to honor my fallen comrades at Rzhev:

> We knew all the regulations by heart.
> What's death to us? We are above even death.
> We have been laid out in ranks in our graves
> And we are waiting for a new order.
> Let them not think that the dead cannot hear
> When their descendants speak of them.

Time never stops. It inexorably moves forward, replacing one generation with the next. More than sixty years have passed since the events discussed in this book. In November 2007, I reached eighty-five years of age. For my birthday, a young, talented American woman named Marsha Szymanski wrote a poem and dedicated it to me. I want to leave the reader with the words of this poem.

> *The Old Soldier*
> The old soldier is cooking—
> Borscht. Smells of the old country
> envelope the oversized tin can
> that is his summer home,
> here in the Berkshires.
> There's a sparkle in his eyes,
> his laugh, large and inviting,
> laces his broken English,
> *"Eat, eat. Maybe Cappuccino?"*
> he asks, blending East and West
> like the melting pot
> of his adopted land.
> He's a Zen master now,
> words his daily practice.
> He pushes paper mounds
> from the pressed-board table,
> His sacred space. Lined sheets
> with cryptic letters, words
> that hold the secrets
> of his heart, long ago stories
> only ready to be told.
> He leans over the pot of red broth
> growing pale with time. His hands,
> stained red with beet juice,
> grip the ladle, spoons out memories,

in small mouthfuls, the metal gun
that never quite fit the writer's hand.
Life is life he reminds me over dinner.
later tonight his pen will move
with an urgency, like birds
preparing to fly South,
feeling winter's breath at their back.

Notes

Chapter 6. In a Rifle Company

1. There are other official data that indicate throughout the war, 428,000 people served time in the penal units. Incidentally, even these numbers are low. Specialists at the Institute of Military History estimate the total number of men who served in a penal company or battalion at 1.5 million (including former imprisoned criminals). To this day, unfortunately, there are no precise data on the fate of these people. The calculation of losses in the penal companies and battalions at the front was, to say the least, imprecise.

2. The 2004 film *Shtrafbat* [The Penal Battalion] speaks honestly about this. See the review written by Boris Sokolov, "*Shtrafbat glazami istorika*" ["The Penal Battalion" through the Eyes of a Historian], *Novy meridian* [The New Meridian] no. 576, 2004.

Chapter 7. The First Battle

1. This is according to materials in the collection of the Rzhev Museum of Local History.

2. See, for example, the story of one participant in the storming of Rzhev, G. S. Medvedev, who was a section commander in a 76-mm gun battery of the 707th Rifle Regiment: "Na 'Rzhevskom platsdarme'" [At the Rzhev Bridgehead], in O. A. Kondrat'ev and L. D. Mel'nikov, eds., *Rzhevskimi dorogami voiny* [Along Rzhev Roads of the War] (Rzhev: Rzhevskaia tipografiia, 1992), pp. 9–12.

3. P. P. Shekhovtsev, "Pamyati tovarishcha" [Memories of a Comrade], in *Rzhevskimi dorogami voiny*, pp. 50–53.

Chapter 9. A Rainy Autumn

1. Editor's Note: According to Horst Grossman, who was commanding general of the German 6th Infantry Division at the time of this battle, the Germans attacked the 30th Army's positions in Rzhev with the 5th Panzer Division's 14th Panzergrenadier Regiment and a battalion from the 31st Panzer Regiment, supported by a company of tanks from the Grossdeutschland Motorized Division and batteries from the 189th Assault Gun Battalion. By the time of this fighting, Grossman writes that the city of Rzhev had become a cratered landscape with no recognizable buildings or streets. The German surprise attack struck a carefully prepared, deeply echeloned defensive position, buttressed by dug-in and carefully masked tanks, which the 30th Army had thrown up with lightning speed. See Horst Grossman, *Rzhev: Kraeugol'ny kamen' Vostochnogo fronta* [Rzhev: Cornerstone of the Eastern Front] (Rzhev: Rzhevskaia Pravda, 1996).

Chapter 10. Turncoats

1. G. F. Krivosheev, ed., *Sbornik Grif sekrenosti snyat: Poteri vooruzhennykh sil SSSR v voin-akh, boevykh destviiakh i voennykh konfliktakh. Statisticheskoe issledovanie* [The Seal of Secrecy Has Been Removed: Losses of the Armed Forces of the USSR in Wars, Combat Actions, and Military Conflicts. A Statistical Investigation] (Moscow:Voenizdat, 1993).

2. B. Muller-Gillebrand, "*Sukhoputnaia armiia Germanii: 1933–1945*" [Germany's Land Army: 1933–1945] (Moscow: Izografus [Eksmo], 2002).

Chapter 14. On the Heels of the Enemy

1. Kh. Kh. Iakhin, "V pamiati ostalis' navsegda" [They Have Remained in My Memory Forever], in *Rzhevskimi dorogami voiny*, pp. 88–90.

2. I.Z. Ladygin and, N.I. Smirnov, "V bessmertiye otdaet prikaz" [In Immortality He Gives the Order], in *Rzhevskimi dorogami voiny*, pp. 238–241.

Chapter 17. The Fighting for Orsha

1. Armand Caulaincourt, *Pokhod Napoleona v Rossiyu* [Napoleon's Campaign in Russia] (Moscow: Gospoltizdat, 1943), p. 345.

2. On this topic, see Nikita Khrushchev, *Vospominaniya: Izbrannye fragmenty* [Memoirs: Selected Excerpts] (Moscow:Vagrius, 1997), pp. 142–143.

3. Editor's Note: One of the photographs depicting Zoia Kosmodem'ianskaia being led to her execution, found on the body of a German soldier, can be seen on page 11 of photographic Insert 2 in Rodric Braithwaite, *Moscow 1941: A City and Its People at War* (New York: Vintage Books, 2006).

Chapter 18. Forward—to the West!

1. Editor's Note: From Gorbachevsky's account and the eyewitness testimony of the civilians, it is clear that the 220th Rifle Division's forward detachment had bumped into retreating elements of the XXXIX Panzer Corp's 5th Panzer Division, which crossed the Neman River in this area on 13–14 July 1944, then immediately moved south toward Grodno. The 5th Panzer Division was a familiar antagonist, as it had delivered the 2 October 1942 counterattack in the city of Rzhev that had hammered the 220th Rifle Division and other divisions of the 30th Army. See Rolf Hinze, *East Front Drama—1944: The Withdrawal Battle of Army Group Center* (Winnipeg: J. J. Fedorowicz, 1996), pp. 96–97.

2. Editor's Note: These German counterattacks were launched initially by the 5th Panzer Division, which later received support from the 3rd S.S. Panzer Division Totenkopf. Hitler had directed the latter division to the Fourth Army near Grodno to reinforce the effort to eliminate the Soviet bridgeheads across the Neman River north of Grodno. Rolf Hinze, in his detailed study from the German perspective of Model's efforts to establish a new line of defense in Army Group Center's sector after the shattering effect of "Bagration," observes: "The advance of the 5th Panzer Division north of Grodno against enemy forces which had crossed the Niemen in this area was successful up to a dominant height west of the river." This was probably the hill being held by Kudriavstev's mobile battalion and the 220th Rifle Division's 376th Rifle Regiment, as described by the author. See Hinze, *East Front Drama*, pp. 97–102.

3. In the 1970s and 1980s, a copy of this film was being kept at the Zoia and Aleksandr Kosmodem'iansky School in Moscow.

Chapter 21. In East Prussia

1. After the war, this poem found its way into all the poet's collected works under a different title, "If Your Home Is Dear to You!" When Simonov was asked why he had changed the title, the poet answered: "Then, in the war, whoever read the title immediately understood that it referred to the fascist aggressors. But today, such a title would raise doubts in the readers' minds: who should be killed?" Incidentally, Simonov considered that "hatred could not be long sustained" ("Notes on the War"). The writer was mistaken. One example that refutes his belief: anti-Semitism.

2. Rokossovsky, *Soldatskii Dolg* (Moscow: Golos, 2000), p. 381.

3. Anthony Beevor, *The Fall of Berlin, 1945* (New York: Penguin Books, 2002); Max Hastings, *Armageddon: The Battle for Germany 1944–1945* (New York: Alfred A. Knopf, 2005).

Chapter 22. To the Shores of the Baltic

1. Editor's Note: There were no S.S. armored formations in the Heiligenbeil-Königsberg pocket. Possibly, this was a unit from the Hermann Göring Parachute Panzer Division, which made several attempts to escape the pocket. The men of this division had been issued S.S. camouflage uniforms earlier in the war, and their tank crew uniforms were black, which naturally led the Red Army soldiers to believe they were S.S.

Chapter 23. The Final Steps to Victory

1. Königsberg was destroyed initially in 1944 by a heavy raid of Royal Air Force bombers.

2. In his memoirs, Bagramian spoke of Stalin's repeated demands to storm the fortress.

3. Sergei Gol'chikov, *Pole boia—Prussiia* [The Battlefield—Prussia] (Kaliningrad: self-published, 2005).

Chapter 24. The Last Days of the War

1. General Schörner deserted his forces on 8 May 1945 and flew off in a Ju-88 bomber, heading for southern Germany. The airplane had to make a forced landing in the Austrian town of St. Johannis. Having changed out of his uniform into civilian clothes, Schörner tried to disappear among the local population. Local residents caught him and turned him over to the Americans. He didn't surrender to the Americans, as some historians maintain. There is a photograph of Schörner in American custody, and he is wearing a light summer jacket and a pair of shorts. I think the reader will agree with me that a general doesn't surrender in a pair of shorts! The Americans turned Schörner over to the Soviet Union as a war criminal. A Soviet tribunal sentenced him to twenty-five years in prison. After serving ten years in the Vladimirsky central prison, Schörner was released in 1955, together with more than 5,000 other German prisoners, following a state visit to Moscow by Konrad Adenauer, the Federal Republic of Germany's first chancellor. Once in West Germany, Schörner was sentenced to serve an additional four and a half years in prison for his brutality against his own soldiers. See K. A. Zalessky, *Kto byl kto v Tret'em Reikhe: biograficheskii entsiklopedicheskii slovar'* [Who Was Who in the Third Reich: A Biographical Encyclopedic Reference] (Moscow: AST, Astel', 2002).

2. The comparison with Panfilov's men was an exaggeration. The legend of Panfilov and his men was formed in the first year of the war and painted a dramatic and heroic episode of resistance to the German invaders. According to 1941 press reports, twenty-eight men of Major General Ivan Vasil'evich Panfilov's 316th Rifle Division were dug-in on a hilltop on the Volokolamsk highway on the approaches to Moscow. On 16 November, their positions

were repeatedly attacked by the 2nd Panzer Division, which they fought off with self-sacrificial infantry close assaults using Molotov cocktails and hastily rigged antitank demolition charges. According to the legend, Commissar V. K. Klochkov exhorted the soldiers with the declaration, "Russia is huge, but there is nowhere to retreat. Moscow is behind us!" He then wrapped a string of grenades around his waist and threw himself under one of the tanks. By the end of the day, the wreckages of more than thirty German panzers littered the slopes and hilltop, and there were only five survivors. Two days later, the 316th Rifle Division became the 8th Guards Rifle Division in honor of its men's achievement and self-sacrifice. In the late years of glasnost, when many Soviet myths were being unmasked and discredited, questions arose about the story of Panfilov's men and their heroic stand. The journalist who wrote the initial story back in November 1941 even acknowledged exaggerations in the original story, under pressure from *Pravda*'s editor-in-chief. Since then, debate over aspects of the story has swirled among journalists, historians, and a handful of surviving witnesses.

3. Editor's Note: On 5 May, Twelfth Army Group Commander General Omar Bradley had met with Marshal Konev, commander of the 1st Ukrainian Front, where he received a warning that the Americans should not interfere in Czechoslovakia. Yet Eisenhower had already been told by U.S. Army Chief of Staff George Marshall to stay clear of Prague; both men said that Prague was not part of their military plans, and Marshall was "loath to hazard American lives for purely political purposes." See Anthony Beevor, *The Fall of Berlin, 1945* (New York: Penguin Books, 2002), p. 401; for Marshall's quote, see Max Hastings, *Armageddon: The Battle for Germany, 1944–1945* (New York: Alfred A. Knopf, 2005), p. 486.

4. S. K. Buniachenko (1902–1946) was a former member of the Communist Party and had served in the Red Army. He was a graduate of the distinguished Frunze Military Academy. As brigade commander in the 59th Rifle Division, in November 1942 Buniachenko was captured by the Germans and placed in a prisoner-of-war camp in Kherson. There, he learned about Vlasov's appeal for volunteers for his Russian Liberation Army and announced his desire to join the renegade command. He initially taught in schools for training student officers, then fought in France against the Western Allies. For his meritorious service, the Germans decorated him with three medals and one Order. After the decision to organize the ROA 1st Division was made, Buniachenko was placed in command and quickly brought its strength up to 20,000 men, primarily Ukrainians. General Buniachenko was captured by American troops near Prague, then forcibly repatriated to the Soviet Union, where he was convicted of treason and executed.

5. According to incomplete evidence, the Red Army summarily executed more than 500 men of the ROA 1st Division once it entered Prague, including some who were discovered and shot in their hospital beds.

6. Stavka VKG directive, "O poriadke priema i soderzhanii sovetskikh i inostrannykh voennoplennykh i grazhdanskogo naseleniia—osvobozhdennykh ot nemetskoi nevoli" [On Organizing the Reception and Holding of Soviet and Foreign Prisoners of War and the Civilian Population—Liberated from German Captivity] no. 11086, 11 May 1945. See S. Ia. Lavrenev and I. M. Popov, *Krakh III Reikha* [Collapse of the Third Reich] (Moscow: AST, 2000), 572–574.

Chapter 25. Subjugated Germany

1. Today located in western Poland, the city of Bunzlau has been renamed Boleslawiec. Despite its German coloring, Silesia has historically been a Slavic province. Situated on the upper and middle course of the Oder River, Silesia was Polish territory starting in the tenth century. In the course of the War of Austrian Succession (1740–1748), Prussia seized much

of Silesia. In 1922, only one part of Upper Silesia was returned to Poland. In 1938–1939, the entire region came under German authority. In 1945, by a decision of the Potsdam Conference, Lower Silesia was transferred to Poland.

2. After 1917, the Kazan' Cathedral became the Museum of the History of Religion and Atheism.

3. Editor's Note: This is probably a reference to the rise of the terrible practice of *dedovshchina* in the Soviet Armed Forces, an extreme form of hazing of new recruits by more senior soldiers, which leads annually to numerous deaths or lasting physical and psychological damage among the new conscripts.

4. Wanda Wasilewskaia (1905–1964]) was a left-wing Polish author who later served as a war correspondent and a colonel in the Red Army's Political Directorate. She also became head of the Soviet-created Society of Polish Patriots.

5. Viktor Baranets, "Kak Stalin perekraival Evropu" [How Stalin Redrew Europe], *Ob'ektivnaia gazeta,* April 16, 2007.

6. The Red Army ended the war with more than 10 million men and women on its rosters.

Afterword

1. This is according to data in G. F. Krivosheev, ed., *Sbornik Grif sekrenosti snyat* [The Seal of Secrecy Has Been Removed] (Moscow: Voenizdat, 1993).

2. See "Rzhev," *Entsiklopedicheskii spravochnik* [Encyclopedic Reference Book], part 6, "*Rzhevskaia bitva (1942–1943)*" [The Battle of Rzhev (1942–1943)] (Tver, 1990).

3. See E. Fedorov, *Pravda o voennom Rzheve: Dokumenyt i fakty* [The Truth about Wartime Rzhev: Documents and Facts] (Rzhev: Rzhevskaia tipografiia, 1995), p. 217.

4. "Rzhev," *Entsiklopedicheskii spravochnik*, part 6, "*Rzhevskaia bitva (1942–1943).*"

5. N. Belov and T. Mikhailovaia, *Rzhev 1942: Bitva za vysotu 200* [Rzhev 1942: The Battle for Height 200] (Tver: Tver izdatel'stvo, 2000), p. 41.

6. Dmitrii Volkogonov, *I. V. Stalin: Politicheskii portret. Tom II. Triumf i tragediia* [I.V. Stalin: A Political Portrait, vol. 2: Triumph and Tragedy] (Moscow: Izdatel'stvo Agenstva Pechati Novosti, 1989), p. 299.

7. V. V. Beshanov, *God 1942—uchebnyi* [1942—The Year of Training] (Minsk: Kharvest, 2002), p. 8.

8. David M. Glantz, *Zhukov's Greatest Defeat: The Red Army's Epic Disaster in Operation Mars, 1942* (Lawrence: University Press of Kansas, 1999).

9. In addition to those previously cited by me in my endnotes, I call your attention to a few more of these materials: *Eto bylo na Rzhevsko-Viazemskom platsdarme* [It Was at the Rzhev-Viaz'ma Bridgehead], vols. 1 and 2 (Rzhev: Izdatel'stvo Kimrskaia tipografiia, 2000), and vol. 3 (Rzhev: Izdatel'stvo Kimrskaia tipografiia, 2003); B. Ershov and O. Kondrat'ev, *Rzhevskaia bitva: Srazheniye za Polunino. Sbornik materialov* [The battle of Rzhev: The Struggle for Polunino. A Collection of Materials] (Tver: Russkaia provintsiia, 2001).

10. Nikolai Maiorov, *Blizko k serdtsu!* [Close to the Heart!] (Moscow: Politizdat, 1989).

Selected Bibliography

Beevor, Antony. *The Fall of Berlin 1945*. New York: Penguin Books, 2002.

Belov, N., and Mikhailovaia, T. *Rzhev 1942: Bitva za vysotu 200* [Rzhev 1942: The Fight for Hill 200]. Tver': Tver' izdatel'stvo, 2000.

Beshanov, V. V. *God 1942—uchebnyi* [1942: The Year of Training]. Minsk: Kharvest, 2002.

Caulaincourt, Armand. *Pokhod Napoleona v Rossiyu* [Napoleon's Campaign in Russia]. Moscow: Gospolitizdat, 1943.

Ershov, B., and Kondrat'ev, O. *Rzhevskaia bitva: Srazheniye za Polunino. Sbornik materialov* [The Battle of Rzhev: The Struggle for Polunino. Collected Materials]. Tver': Russkaia provintsiia, 2001.

Eto bylo na Rzhevsko-Viazemskom platsdarme [It Was at the Rzhev-Viaz'ma Bridgehead], vols. 1–3. Rzhev: Izdatel'stvo Kimrskaia tipografiia, 2000, 2003.

Fedorov, E. *Pravda o voennom Rzheve: Dokumenty i fakty* [The Truth about War-Time: Rzhev, Documents and Facts]. Rzhev: Rzhevskoe proizvodstvenno-poligrafidieskoe predpriiatie, 1995.

Glantz, David M. *Zhukov's Greatest Defeat: The Red Army's Epic Disaster in Operation Mars, 1942*. Lawrence: University Press of Kansas, 1999.

Gol'chikov, Sergei. *Pole boia—Prussiia* [The Battlefield—Prussia]. Kaliningrad: self-published, 2005.

Grossman, Horst. *Rzhev: Kraeugol'ny kamen' Vostochnogo fronta* [Rzhev: The Cornerstone of the Eastern Front]. Rzhev: Rzhevskaia Pravda, 1996. This is a Russian translation from the German, *Rshew: Eckpfeiler der Ostfront (unterveranderter Nachdruck)*. Wolfersheim: Podzun-Pallas-Verlag, 1980.

Hastings, Max. *Armageddon: The Battle for Germany, 1944–1945*. New York: Alfred A. Knopf, 2005.

Haupt, Werner. *Army Group Center: The Wehrmacht in Russia, 1941–1945*. Atglen, PA: Schiffer Publishing, 1997.

Hinze, Rolf. *East Front Drama—1944: The Withdrawal Battle of Army Group Center*. Winnipeg: J. J. Fedorowicz, 1996.

Khrushchev, Nikita. *Vospominaniya: Izbrannye fragmenty* [Memoirs: Selected Excerpts]. Moscow: Vagrius, 1997.

Kondrat'ev, O. A., and Mel'nikov, L. D., eds. *Rzhevskimi dorogami voiny* [Along the Rzhev Roads of the War]. Rzhev: Rzhevskaia tipografiia, 1992.

Krivosheev, G. F., ed. *Sbornik Grif sekrenosti snyat: Poteri vooruzhennykh sil SSSR v voinakh, boevykh destviiakh i voennykh konfliktakh. Statisticheskoe issledovanie* [The Seal of Secrecy

Has Been Removed: Losses of the USSR Armed Forces in Wars, Combat Operations, and Military Conflicts: A Statistical Investigation]. Moscow: Voenizdat, 1993.

Lavrenev, S. Ia., and I.M. Popov. *Krakh III Reikha* [Collapse of the Third Reich]. Moscow: AST, 2000.

Maior, Nikolai. *Blizko k serdtsu!* [Close to the Heart!] Moscow: Politizdat, 1989.

Muller-Gillebrand, B. *Sukhoputnaia armiia Germanii: 1933–1945* [Germany's Ground Army: 1933–1945]. Moscow: Izografus [Exmo], 2002.

Popov, Gavriil. *Voina I Pravda: Tsena pobedy* [War and Truth: The Price of Victory}. New York: Liberty Publishing House, 2005.

Rokossovsky, K. K. *Soldatskii dolg* [The Soldier's Duty]. Moscow: Golos, 2000.

Shefov, Nikolai. *Bitvy Rossii* [Battles of Russia]. Moscow: Voenno-Istoricheskaia biblioteka, 2002.

Sokolov, Boris. "Shtrafbat glazami istorika" [Penal Battalion through the Eyes of a Historian]. *Novy meridian* no. 576, 2004.

Volkogonov, Dmitrii. *I. V. Stalin: Politicheskii portret. Tom II. Triumf i tradediia* [I.V. Stalin: A Political Portrait. Vol. 2: Triumph and Tragedy]. Moscow: Izdatel'stvo Agenstva Pechati Novosti, 1989.

Zalessky, K.A. *Kto byl kto v Tret'em Reikhe: biografichekii entsiklopediicheskii slovar'* [Who Was Who in the Third Reich: A Biographical Encyclopedic Reference]. Moscow: AST/ Astal', 2002.

Index